How to Avoid Probate—Updated!

Books by Norman F. Dacey

HOW TO AVOID PROBATE—UPDATED!

HOW TO AVOID PROBATE!

WHAT'S WRONG WITH YOUR LIFE INSURANCE

DACEY ON MUTUAL FUNDS

Norman F. Dacey

How to Avoid Probate—Updated!

A Herbert Michelman Book

Crown Publishers, Inc.   New York

Printed in the United States of America
Published simultaneously in Canada
by General Publishing Company Limited
Library of Congress Cataloging in Publication Data
Dacey, Norman F

How to avoid probate—updated!

1. Estate planning—United States. 2. Probate law
and practice—United States. 3. Estate planning—United
States—Forms. 4. Probate law and practice—United
States—Forms. I. Title.
KF750.Z9D33   346'.73'05   79-24868
ISBN: 0-517-539349 (*paper*)
ISBN: 0-517-539330 (*cloth*)
10 9 8 7 6 5 4

Contents

Please note that all forms are on pages
which are perforated for easy removal from the book

How to Avoid Probate—Updated!

Prologue

It began on an evening in 1964.

During thirty-five years of professional estate planning, I had become acutely aware of the abuses of the probate system—and of a little-known method of avoiding them—and I had begun telling people how to use that method.

On the evening in question, I arrived home, picked up the newspaper, and was confronted by a headline that read: "Dacey Enjoined from Practice of Law." Without giving me any notice or opportunity to be heard, the Connecticut Bar Association had arranged for a judge who was one of its members to issue an injunction requiring me to stop telling people how to avoid probate. My lengthy subsequent efforts to have the injunction lifted proved fruitless, and I puzzled over how the court's gag order might be circumvented. Finally I concluded that if I could not *tell* people the formula for probate avoidance, the answer was simply to write a book that they could read and thus gain the knowledge that the legal establishment was so determined to keep from them.

The result, in 1966, was *How to Avoid Probate!*, a large paperback book that not only explained what probate was and spelled out the ways in which it was victimizing the country's widows and orphans, but provided a do-it-yourself guide to probate avoidance. Within thirteen weeks the book had become the Number 1 best seller. The Masters and Johnson book, *Human Sexual Response,* was Number 2 on the list. I don't claim, of course, that I made probate more interesting than sex—it was just that millions of American families had had painful contact with the probate system at one time or another. They knew that they had been "taken," but they did not understand the mechanics of how it had been accomplished. All they knew was that family money, which should have come to them, had gone instead to strangers. *How to Avoid Probate!* told them exactly how it had been done. It explained how greedy lawyers and politicians had preyed upon rich and poor alike for generations.

One and a half million copies of the book were sold—and the cries of public outrage rattled the windows in the Chicago headquarters of the American Bar Association.

In its review of the book, the association reported glumly to its members that:

> The burden of Mr. Dacey's writings is devoted to detailed criticisms of some antiquated, unnecessary and perhaps questionable procedures which are a part of the probate systems presently in force in some states, and which there contribute in a major way to the present expense, delay, publicity and lack of security in the probate of decedents' estates. . . . Mr. Dacey and his book can be of substantial benefit to the Bar in helping to bring into focus for its own members some of the weaknesses that do in fact exist in many of the ancient probate procedures which have long since outlived their usefulness and which now need revision or refurbishing, if not elimination.

But an article in *Time* magazine disclosed that the ABA had asked its members on the staff of the Federal Trade Commission to initiate an investigation of the book and its claims. Commission investigators asked me to supply them with the names, locations, dates, and texts of each of the hundreds of radio and television appearances and lectures I had given during the previous months. I told them that they were welcome to investigate, but that they had better do their own work.

When Boston University Law School invited me a second time to address the faculty and student body, FTC investigators requested permission to sit in the front row and tape my talk, but the dean turned them down flatly, characterizing it as a petty effort at entrapment unworthy of a federal agency.

The next reaction came from the New York County Lawyers Association, a trade association against whose members tens of thousands of complaints of unprofessional conduct had been filed by consumers of legal services. Incensed by the book's disclosures of wholesale abuses of heirs by New York lawyers and the city's probate court system, the association filed a complaint in the New York Supreme Court (curiously, in New York, "supreme" doesn't mean what it means everywhere else—there, the "Supreme Court" is actually the lowest statewide court), charging me with criminal contempt of court for having written the book. In their frenzy to protect their exposed flanks, the lawyers carried their attempted book-burning to the extreme of naming the book's publishers and two leading book-selling chains, Brentano's and Doubleday, as fellow conspirators in the alleged contempt of court and demanding the issuance of an injunction prohibiting further printing or sale of the book.

How, you may ask, does the writing, publishing, and selling of a book get to be "contempt of court"? Their argument ran like this: Books give information. My book gave legal information. Giving legal information constitutes the practice of law. Anyone who practices law without having been formally admitted to the bar shows contempt for the courts. Those who aid and abet such a course of action are equally "contemptible." Thus, in writing, publishing, and selling *How to Avoid Probate!,* Crown, Brentano's, Doubleday, and I had all been guilty of criminal contempt of court.

I thought that the association's action would be promptly dismissed as simply a self-serving effort by a group of rapacious lawyers to deal with what they regarded as a threat to their pocketbooks. But then, as had the Connecticut Bar Association in the injunction matter, the New York group arranged for the charge to be tried before a judge who was one of its own members—and it is hard to lose when you are both complainant and judge! When I asked Judge Charles Marks if he was a member of the complaining association, he said that he "couldn't remember"—although he had been paying dues in it for twenty-three years! Then I asked him to set a date for the jury trial to which the criminal charge entitled me, at which time I would present the testimony of authorities that the writing of a book was not the practice of law.

At that point the New York Civil Liberties Union intervened to warn Judge Marks that the proposed injunction would be a gross violation of constitutional rights and of the public's right to know. In its brief, the NYCLU said:

We argue here not only for Dacey's right to speak but for the public's right to read, so that the truth will be more likely to evolve. It is not the function of the State to suppress what it considers offensive or incorrect. In fact, it is a major function of the First Amendment to disable the State from undertaking such activity. Under our system, the free interplay of ideas rather than the paternalistic hand of the State must be depended upon to ensure that the incorrect and the offensive will not prevail.

The major purpose of Dacey's book is the exposure and correction of an alleged evil which afflicts the public at large. Since it is a crucial function of the First Amendment to assure unfettered exchange of ideas for the bringing about of social and political change, it is clear that Dacey's book, which has as one of its major functions criticism of an existing institution, occupies a particularly privileged position in our

society. There is no justification for the State to suppress it.

Dacey's book has played a major role in crystallizing public opinion against the probate system and bringing pressure for reform to bear on the system itself. It is no coincidence that only after publication of the book did the legislature of this State enact a reform bill calculated to remedy certain probate abuses. It is clear, therefore, that Dacey's book has been far more than a voice crying in the wilderness in the field of probate reform.

It is the public policy of the State to encourage free and open discussion of our institutions. The effect of suppressing the book would be to immunize professional activity from lay criticism. If this book can be suppressed, any book which vigorously criticizes professional practices and points the way to reform or avoidance of those practices by a specific alternate mode of conduct may also be suppressed.

Judge Marks listened and then announced that he would take the matter under advisement. The next thing I knew, he had issued a finding of "guilty" and ordered me to pay a fine of $250 or spend thirty days in jail.

That was it—no trial, no hearing, no testimony by authorities, nothing. It was justice New York County Lawyers Association-style.

The association's charge that the book's disclosures of a means of avoiding probate had constituted the "unauthorized practice of law" prompted the *New York Times* to observe that:

The "unauthorized practice" committees too often seem more interested in protecting the lawyers, and since they are usually more zealous than the committees which are supposed to discipline unethical lawyers, their activities frequently leave a bad taste in the public's mouth. Last week, the New York County Lawyers Association topped them all when it obtained an injunction against the book's sale and distribution and succeeded in having Mr. Dacey convicted of criminal contempt.

However, even the bar association's lawyers could not cite a precedent for convicting a person for criminal contempt for writing a book. . . . Officials of the bar association insisted that they only objected to the forms, but many observers feel that the bar was showing poor form itself.

I appealed Judge Marks's decision to the Appellate Division of the New York State courts where it was reviewed by five judges. Four were loyal, dues-paying members of the association. The fifth, presiding Judge Harold Stevens, was not. Not surprisingly, the vote was four to one against me, Judge Stevens writing a vigorous dissenting opinion upholding my constitutional right of free speech and declaring that the mere fact that *How to Avoid Probate!* was regarded by lawyers as a threat to their trade was no excuse for banning the book. But the

4–1 decision stood, of course, and I turned to my last recourse, the New York Court of Appeals in Albany—the state's highest court.

Of the seven judges sitting on that court, only one was a member of the New York County Lawyers Association, and he dutifully voted to find me guilty. But all six nonmember judges voted to reverse the lower courts' findings, adopting as their own Judge Stevens's dissent, which had said:

> There is no showing in the record that this book has exploited the public or led its members astray improperly or incorrectly.

Not only had New York City's clubhouse lawyers and judges suffered an ignominious defeat, but the state's highest court had certified that there was nothing "improper" or "incorrect" in the book's charges that the probate system was nothing but a legal racket.

Curiously, two weeks after the high court's decision was announced, the *New York State Law Digest,* the official publication of the New York State Bar Association, reported that the court had found in favor of the lawyers association and that I had lost the appeal.

Understandably resentful of the bar's efforts to deprive me of my constitutional right of free speech and the public of its right to know the facts about probate, I filed an action for damages against the association in the federal court in New York. But United States District Judge Inzer Wyatt, cheerfully acknowledging that he was a member of the association and therefore one of the defendants in the action, promptly ruled that he and his fellow members were immune from suit on the grounds that they had been acting as self-appointed prosecutors. When I appealed his ruling, a panel of three judges of the United States Court of Appeals for the Second Circuit in New York did everything but descend from the bench and publicly embrace former Associate United States Supreme Court Justice Arthur Goldberg, whom the nervous lawyers had hired to defend them on the appeal. They ruled that:

> It is clear that the objective of the association . . . was to suppress [the] book and to prevent the views expressed therein from being available to the general public. [This indicated a] desire to have "bookburning" judicially approved [rather than a desire to protect the public from unqualified practitioners of the law.]

But, said the court, the fact that Judge Marks, sitting in the lowest court, had found me guilty was evidence that the association had "probable cause," and on the strength of that they upheld Judge Wyatt's dismissal of my action for damages, ignoring the fact that there had been no trial before Judge Marks and that he had been a member of the complaining association. The United States Supreme Court declined to hear my appeal.

Meanwhile, the lawyer-son of the Fort Lauderdale, Florida, probate judge wrote—and the *Florida Bar Journal* published—a libelous article stating that I had been convicted of a crime in Connecticut, a statement that was the subject of a later retraction and public apology by the article's author and the journal's editors. When I sued for libel, four Florida judges sitting in the federal court there ruled that the Florida bar was an arm of the state government and therefore immune from suit. The libeling lawyer was let off the hook on the grounds that I was a "public figure," and according to a court ruling in a celebrated case involving the *New York Times,* you may libel or slander a public figure to your heart's content and he can do nothing about it.

Next, the Connecticut Bar Association distributed a booklet nationally, in which it accused me of counseling people to violate the law by evading the payment of taxes. In *How to Avoid Probate!,* I had warned that in many areas safe deposit boxes were blocked on the death of an owner, and I recommended that husband and wife have separate boxes in which each keeps the spouse's will, insurance policies, and other important papers that need to be readily available in case of death. Most tax evasion schemes originate with lawyers, and the Connecticut lawyers thought that they perceived one in the advice I had given. The booklet was launched with a televised and broadcast press conference, the association's president speaking feelingly of his organization's desire to save people from the jail term to which they would surely be sentenced if they followed my advice. A blizzard of news releases carried the story across the country, and when my request for the withdrawal of the booklet was rejected, I had no recourse except to sue the association.

For seven long years the lawyers' group wriggled and squirmed and resorted to every legal strategem known to the trade to avoid being brought into court. Finally, on June 13, 1974, a jury in the Superior Court of Connecticut found the association guilty of malicious libel and ordered it to pay me damages of $60,000. An astonished judge told the press that it was the first time in the history of the republic that a bar association had ever been found guilty of breaking the law.

The association appealed the verdict to five of its own members acting, as they like to put it, "under color of law" as the justices of the Supreme Court of Connecticut. The state has a law that specifically prohibits a judge from presiding on any action in which he has a pecuniary interest or in connection with which his impartiality may reasonably be questioned. Drawing the justices' attention to the fact that they had each been ordered by the jury to contribute to the libel damage award, I cited their disqualification and asked them to observe the law and withdraw from the case. They flatly refused and, instead, heard the appeal, reversed the jury's findings, and ordered the case retried.

One of the inalienable rights secured to all citizens by the Constitution is due process, the right to a fair trial before an impartial tribunal. Aside from the Connecticut statute debarring them from sitting, then, the justices were restrained by the Constitution from presiding on their own case. That they had some misgivings about their bold violation of state and federal law was indicated by the fact that seven weeks after they had heard the appeal—but before they announced their decision—they negotiated with the Board of Governors of the Connecticut Bar Association the passage of a special resolution purporting to grant to the justices a remission of their association dues equal to the amount of any contribution they might be called upon to make to the libel damages awarded me. This was intended to eliminate the "pecuniary interest" in the case which the law had specified as one of the grounds for their disqualification.

Nothing could be more illustrative of the sorry level to which bench and bar has fallen than this transparent attempt to evade both the letter and the spirit of a law that had been enacted to guarantee all Connecticut citizens a fair trial.

Any claim that the individual citizen involved in a confrontation with the legal establishment is assured of justice by his right to a trial before a jury is illusory when the legal establishment is in a position to contravene the findings of that jury by the simple expedient of appealing the decision to a juryless higher court where its members sit as judges.

On the strength of this impropriety, I instituted suit against the five justices in the federal court in Connecticut, charging that aside from violating state law in denying me a fair trial before an impartial tribunal, they had deprived me of my constitutional rights. There, United States District Judge Robert C. Zampano—like the justices, a member of the Connecticut Bar Association—promptly dismissed the action on the grounds that where Title 42, Section 1983 of the U.S. Code states that "every person" who denies a citizen his constitutional rights may be held liable in damages, it does not mean judges. Declining even to consider the merits of the complaint, he simply ruled that judges are immune from being called to account for wrongdoing.

The United States Court of Appeals for the Second Circuit, the same panel that had earlier sustained the New York County Lawyers Association's self-serving effort to have me held in contempt, upheld Judge Zampano's ruling that judges are above the law.

In May 1978, I asked the United States Supreme Court to condemn the Connecticut high court's denial of due process and to order a rehearing of the bar association's appeal from the libel award before justices who were not themselves a party to the libel action. The nine justices in Washington voted unanimously not to intervene.

The action of this "old boy" network in proclaiming that its members are above the law outrages democracy and the Constitution, and disturbs a citizenry already revolted by the plethora of legal improprieties in recent years. There is nothing in the Constitution or laws of the United States to support this doctrine of "judicial immunity." The only ones who say that judges are immune from suit are other judges. From the highest court in Washington down to the lowliest rural justice of the peace, judicial independence has become a cloak for judicial absolutism.

In A.D. 1215, the Magna Carta ended the claims to "judicial immunity" asserted by King John's judges. In the American Revolution, the people again protested judicial deprivation of their rights. The king's judges were hung in effigy and forced to flee. With the colonies in arms, the only "judicial immunity" was that provided by a fast horse.

In time, the bench and bar resumed their corruption of the civil process until the Congress, determined to stamp it out for all time, passed the Civil Rights Act of 1871, which specifically outlawed the doctrine of "judicial immunity." Now, like a noxious weed, it has reappeared and, as we have seen, is to be found at all levels of the state and federal courts.

Those who administer the law have seldom been sympathetic to the rights of people, as witness the fact that it took almost a century after the Civil War and the passage of the Civil Rights Act of 1871 to get the black man out of the back of the bus. This probably accounts for the fact that in every revolution, it was always the lawyers and judges who were the first ones led to the guillotine.

Meanwhile, noting that the Connecticut justices' deprivation of due process had also been a violation of the U.S. Criminal Code, I filed a formal criminal complaint with Peter H. Dorsey, the United States Attorney for Connecticut. Acknowledging that he, too, was a member of the Connecticut Bar Association, Mr. Dorsey indicated that he was not about to file a complaint against five of his fellow members. I then filed a suit against him under a federal law that provides that officials who are in a position to intervene to prevent a deprivation of civil rights and who refuse to do so are liable for damages. District Judge Zampano obligingly dismissed that action against his fellow association member on the ground that prosecutors, like judges, are immune from suit. A grateful Connecticut Bar Association shortly thereafter rewarded Dorsey with its highest office. The United States Court of Appeals again affirmed Judge Zampano's disregard for the civil rights laws, and the United States Supreme Court again declined to review the case.

Dozens of law journals have carried articles bitterly assailing *How to Avoid Probate!* A curious aspect of this wave of negative opinion has been the youth—and consequent lack of practical experience and understanding of the problems the book highlighted—of the authors, who invariably were recent law school graduates still imbued with the idealism of students and not yet educated to the cynicism of probate practitioners. An assistant professor at Boston University Law School, who had written a slashing attack on the book, admitted sheepishly that he was scarcely twenty-eight months out of law school, had never set foot in a courtroom, and had no understanding of the probate process. When I cited some of the things that were going on in the outside world, he nearly went into shock. The *Illinois Bar Journal* presented the "expert" criticism of a young lady, the ink on whose law school diploma was not yet dry. Not all the critics were youths, however; the *Kansas Bar Journal* contained an article written by a law school dean of that state. A letter I wrote to him in an effort to straighten out some of his misconceptions was returned, marked "Moved, left no address." The law school of which he allegedly was dean reported that he had gone and it had no idea where he could be found.

All in all, not a very responsible lot of commentators.

With few exceptions, most of the critics of the book predicted that disaster lay ahead for those who acted upon its advice and used the tear-out trust instruments it provided. A decade has passed since those dire predictions were made, and literally millions of trusts have been established using the forms. In many hundreds of letters I have been told that the reader had followed the instructions given in the book, that a spouse or parent had since died, and that everything had worked out exactly as the book said it would.

So far as I know, there has been only one case in which a trust form from the book has even been contested. In Houston, Texas, Virginia B. Miller placed two pieces of real estate in trust, using a form which the book provided for naming one beneficiary to receive property upon the death of the owner. When she died fifteen months later, an aggrieved relative to whom she had chosen to leave nothing petitioned the local probate court to declare the trusts invalid. The probate judge cheerfully obliged, appointing a local lawyer (who else?) as administrator of Ms. Miller's estate with instructions to file suit in the civil court to obtain possession of the real estate. After losing in both the lower court and the court of civil appeals, the administrator—goaded by the probate judge—took an appeal to the Supreme Court of Texas, which not only upheld the trusts but offered the opinion that:

> [Ms. Miller's] plan was a good one. Living trusts often afford greater protection, more privacy and considerable economy.... If the owner of property can find a means of disposing of it *inter vivos* [during his lifetime] that will render a will unnecessary for the accomplishment of his practical purposes, he has a right to employ it. The fact that the motive of a transfer is to obtain the practical advantages of a will without making one is immaterial.

Much has happened since that 1964 newspaper headline put me on notice that the legal establishment would tolerate no interference with the profits it was deriving from estates being put through the probate wringer.

One widely syndicated newspaper editorial recalled this delightful quote from Kurt Vonnegut, Jr.'s, *God Bless You, Mr. Rosewater:*

> In every big transaction there is a magic moment during which a man has surrendered a treasure, and during which the man who is due to receive it has not yet done so. An alert lawyer will make that moment his own, possessing the treasure for a magic microsecond, taking a little of it, passing it on. If the man who is to receive the treasure is unused to wealth, has an inferiority complex and shapeless feelings of guilt as most people do, the lawyer can often take as much as half the bundle, and still receive the recipient's blubbering thanks.

The editorial added this comment:

> Instead of blubbering thanks, a probate lawyer today is more likely to get a cold stare from relatives of the deceased. This is in large measure due to the crusade of one Norman F. Dacey, the non-lawyer author of *How to Avoid Probate!* Dacey's basic advice is that the property be placed in trust before the death of the owner to avoid having a will probated and paying heavy legal fees. But his real offense, in the eyes of many lawyers, was putting dozens of detachable forms in his book that the reader can use to follow this advice—without consulting a lawyer. No magic moment there!

The one and a half million copies of *How to Avoid Probate!* which have found their way across the land have helped countless families escape what the late Senator Robert F. Kennedy called "a political tollbooth exacting tribute from widows and orphans."

The legal establishment, promising much, has delivered only token probate reform. It is useless to hope that the abuses of probate will be corrected in our time. In such circumstances, it is important that every individual American who has labored to build financial security for his family—and who prefers not to name the legal establishment as one of his heirs—take advantage of the means provided to avoid the abuses.

This book provides those means, expanding upon the message of *How to Avoid Probate!* and extending its benefits to many new asset areas not even dreamed of when the first book was published.

The American Bar Association-sponsored American Assembly on Death, Taxes and Family Property reported in 1977 that:

> There is a need for *more public education* about estate planning.... In particular, it is desirable that readily available options in statutory and other form be developed to permit the *simplified* and *inexpensive creation of ... trusts....* The bar should encourage the trend toward various devices permitting settlement of estates with little or *no court involvement ...* and with *only minimally necessary involvement of lawyers.* The development of procedures for transferring property without administration should be encouraged, as should *"do-it-yourself techniques"* [emphasis added].

No clearer endorsement of this book and its "do-it-yourself" plan for estate administration could be found. The text provides the "public education" which the Assembly speaks of, and the forms provide the "simplified and inexpensive" means by which trusts may be created without any necessity for the "involvement of lawyers" and without any "court involvement" in the administration of such trusts. The Assembly provided everything except the name of the book and its price—an inadvertent omission, no doubt.

Having thus confirmed that *we* are on the side of the angels, let us next look at those who are on the other side. Let's look at the lawyers.

CHAPTER 1

The Lawyers

Why is there always a secret singing
When a lawyer cashes in?
Why does a hearse horse snicker
Hauling a lawyer away?
CARL SANDBURG

In a world where learning is quite generally respected, what is there about lawyers that makes them so universally looked down upon? The antipathy dates back to the earliest times; in Luke 11:52, we read: *"Woe unto you, lawyers! for ye have taken away the key of knowledge: Ye entered not in yourselves, and them that were entering in ye hindered."* Is it because "the lawyer's soul is small and unrighteous," as Plato wrote so long ago? Or is it that there is a consensus that Jonathan Swift was correct in the observation he made in *Gulliver's Travels* in 1735 that:

There is a society of men among us bred up from their youth in the art of proving by words multiplied for the purpose that black is white and white is black, according as they are paid. To this society, all the rest of the people are slaves.

Speaking of a contemporary, Samuel Johnson—himself a lawyer—quipped: "I do not wish to speak ill of any man behind his back, but the fact is that he is an attorney."

Students of history will recall on page 536 of Volume 1 of *The Decline and Fall of the Roman Empire*, the distinguished British historian Edward Gibbon recorded that:

In the decline of Roman jurisprudence the ordinary promotion of lawyers was pregnant with mischief and disgrace. The noble art which had once been preserved as the sacred inheritance of the patricians, was fallen into the hands of freedmen and plebeians, who with cunning rather than with skill, exercised a sordid and pernicious trade. Some of them procured admittance into families for the purpose of fomenting differences, of encouraging suits and of preparing a harvest of gain for themselves or their brethren. Others, recluse in their chambers, maintained the gravity of legal professors, by furnishing a rich client with subtleties to confound the plainest truth, and with arguments to colour the most unjustifiable pretensions. The splendid and popular class was composed of the advocates, who filled the Forum with the sound of their turgid and loquacious rhetoric. Careless of fame and justice, they are described for the most part as ignorant and rapacious guides who conducted their clients through a maze of expense, of delay, and of disappointment; from whence, after a tedious series of years, they were at length dismissed when their patience and fortune were almost exhausted.

Half a century later, Alexis de Tocqueville, in his classic *Democracy in America*, remarked that American lawyers seemed "hostile to the unreflecting passions of the multitude, anti-democratic and responsive to the lure of private interest and advantage." In his day, Associate Supreme Court Justice Louis D. Brandeis echoed the charge. Lawyers, he wrote, consistently opposed constructive legislative proposals in the public interest, while failing to oppose legislation in behalf of "selfish interests."

In our own time, President Jimmy Carter, in a 1978 speech to the American Bar Association, accused its members of devoting their time to protecting the "comfortable insulations of privilege." The bar, he said, is "a hierarchy of privilege, with 90 percent of our lawyers serving 10 percent of our people. We are overlawyered and underrepresented. . . . During most of the struggles for equal justice in our time . . . much of the bar sat on the sidelines or opposed those efforts."

The Frenchman Jean de Crèvecoeur, after his immigration to the United States, described the early American lawyers as "weeds that will grow in any soil that is cultivated by the hands of others; and once they have taken root, they will extinguish every other vegetable that grows around them." His thinking regarding lawyers was generally representative of his time; the *Fundamental Constitutions* of Carolina declared it "a base and vile thing to plead for money or reward," while in Massachusetts, the *Body of Liberties* permitted anyone who could not plead his own cause to retain someone else for assistance "provided he give him noe fee or reward for his paines."

The popular detestation of lawyers may have been enhanced by the view of them offered by the distinguished Yale Law School professor, Fred Rodell, in his book, *Woe Unto You, Lawyers!*:

In tribal times, there were the medicine men. In the Middle Ages, there were the priests. Today, there are the lawyers. For every age, a group of bright boys, learned in their trade and jealous of their learning, who blend technical competence with plain and fancy hocus-pocus to make themselves masters of their fellow men. For every age, a pseudo-intellectual autocracy, guarding the tricks of its trade from the uninitiated, and running, after its own pattern, the civilization of its day. It is the lawyers who run our civilization for us—our governments, our business, our private lives.

Concluded Professor Rodell: "The legal trade is nothing but a high-class racket."

With financing from the Pren-Hall Foundation, the Missouri Bar initiated a comprehensive and probing study of the legal profession's public image, with the intention of incorporating the findings into a book which would gratify the vanity of its members. Alas, the book project had to be abandoned when returns from the first 5,000 people questioned turned up the curious sociological fact that only 35 percent of them believed that lawyers were honest—which meant that 65 percent thought that they were dishonest or at least entertained serious doubts on that score.

A 1973 Harris poll found that only 18 percent of the public had confidence in law firms, a somewhat lower approval rating than that of garbage collectors. As *New York Times* writer Linda Greenhouse put it: "Nobody seems to like lawyers these days," while Professor of Law Stephen Gillers of New York University Law School, author of *The Rights of Lawyers and Clients*, recorded sadly in the *Times* that: "Lawyers are not popular these days. Nearly everyone seems to have a lawyer horror story to tell. There seem to be more lawyer horror stories than there are lawyers."

It would appear that many who may not be poetry lovers nevertheless agree with Keats, who wrote, "I think we may class the lawyer in the natural history of monsters." United States Army Brigadier General Walter Ulmer, Jr., was quoted in *Time* magazine as saying, "The Goddam lawyers are ruining the Army." It was Mr. Dooley who boiled it all down into the fewest words: "They'd be no gr-reat har-rm if they was all hanged."

Yet, despite all this, lawyers graciously accept Tocqueville's early classification of them as "the American aristocracy." Even today they see themselves as a sort of master race, deserving of all the best things in life. The Illinois Bar Association expressed the view that "the respect for the legal profession and its influence in the local community will be raised when the individual lawyer occupies his proper place at the top of the economic structure," while the American Bar Association has circulated a film to its constituent local associations which features a lecture by Texas attorney J. Harris Morgan in which he explains that "it is in the

public policy of this country that you be prosperous." Prosperity, he explained, meant earning at least $55,000 a year.

There need not necessarily be an equitable relationship between the work they do and the compensation they receive for doing it. In one Truth-in-Lending case, a settlement was reached in which the plaintiff received $400 while his attorney received $12,000 in fees. In another Truth-in-Lending action, the plaintiff was paid $2,000; the attorney claimed, and was paid for, 350 hours of work.

Former ABA President Chesterfield Smith told an interviewer: "I have to represent only wealthy people." Why? "This is capitalism. Our standard of living is high. We're selling time just like a store sells a shirt. If you don't like this shirt, you buy some other shirt."

The story is told of an austere British judge who opened his court one morning by saying: "Gentlemen, I have in my possession two bribes—a draft from the plaintiff for five thousand pounds and a draft from the defendant for three thousand pounds. I propose to return two thousand pounds to the plaintiff and decide this case strictly on its merits."

The story is not all that farfetched—the chief justice of a midwestern state's supreme court was removed from office when it was disclosed that he had accepted a $50,000 bribe from one of the parties in an action before his court.

In A.D. 1215, the barons exacted from King John in the Magna Carta the promise that "to none . . . will we sell justice." Aside from the blatant sale of justice as illustrated above, there is another, more prevalent trafficking in law—today, we live in a society in which justice is, to all intents and purposes, for sale.

Jerry Paul, the attorney who defended Joan Little, put it this way: "Given enough money, I can buy justice. I can win any case in this country, given enough money. A jury is twelve people deciding who has the best lawyer." In a column titled "Lawyers, Lawyers Everywhere," newsmen Jack Anderson and Les Whitten complained that "the legal processes have become encumbered with procedural rigmarole—unnecessary routines designed more to enrich lawyers than to serve the public—[and] all too often, the legal decision goes to the client with the most money."

In the contest for justice, money buys better odds. Have we really progressed much from the days of the Old West when cattle barons had hired guns to deal with their problems?

When justice is bought and sold, though, isn't it time for us to do something? The law may be the business of lawyers—but it is the concern of everyone who cares about the kind of society in which he lives. When Chief Justice Warren Burger can warn, as he did, that "the harsh truth is that . . . we may well be on our way to a society overrun by hordes of lawyers, hungry as locusts, and brigades of judges in numbers never before contemplated," should we not pause and consider that the cost to us of a society dominated by these money-hungry lawyers is not merely economic? Justice itself suffers.

In the past fifteen years, the number of U.S. lawyers has climbed from 296,000 to 462,000. The nation's 168 law schools will unload nearly 35,000 new lawyers upon us this year, and the number of such graduates increases each year. The American people already support two-thirds of all the lawyers in the world. (Lawyers are almost unknown in China, so perhaps Communism *is* a more advanced society.) In the city of San Francisco, one out of every one hundred adult males is a lawyer. At the present proliferating rate, the effects a decade or two hence of having such a substantial proportion of our population imbued with what Tocqueville noted was a conviction that it constituted an "American aristocracy" must give us pause.

Lawrence Silberman, a former deputy U.S. Attorney General, warned recently that: "The legal process, because of its unbridled growth, has become a cancer which threatens the vitality of our forms of capitalism and democracy." Some ask naively, "But what would we do if we didn't have lawyers to get us out of our messes?" What such people don't understand is that all too often it is the lawyers who got us into the messes in the first place. There are 45,000 lawyers employed by the U.S. government. Lawyers *in* government, for instance, produce complex legislation and regulations, creating endless business for lawyers *out of* government. And, as top Washington lawyer Fred Dutton has explained, "Lawyers are paid to complicate, to keep a dispute alive, to make everything technical." Sir Thomas More, in his classic *Utopia,* explained that in that ideal society *"they have no lawyers among them, for they consider them as a sort of people whose profession it is to disguise matters."*

There is an old maxim: The more lawyers there are, the less justice there is. The story is told of a small town that didn't have enough legal work to support its one lawyer, but then a second lawyer moved to town—and from that time on, there was plenty of work for both!

Perhaps we have enough lawyers. Perhaps we should limit the new entries each year to a number sufficient only to balance the normal attrition of those who retire, die, or are disbarred.

There is no need to limit the number of, say, paperhangers—we are not at their mercy because, in a pinch, most of us could hang paper. But as the Yale Law School's Professor Fred Rodell has pointed out, the lawyers have seen to it that the law is carried on in a foreign language. Not that it deals, as do medicine and engineering, with physical phenomena and instruments which require special words to describe them simply because there are no other words. On the contrary, the law deals almost exclusively with the ordinary facts and occurrences of everyday business and government and living. But it deals with them in a mysterious mumbo jumbo which completely baffles the ordinary literate

man. As Professor Rodell explained: "The lawyer's trade is a trade built entirely on words . . . and as long as lawyers keep carefully to themselves the key to what those words mean, the only way for the average man to find out what is going on is to become a lawyer."

Heaven forbid! What is needed is not more but fewer and better lawyers. America needs a radical "de-lawyering." Perhaps we should mount some sort of aerial crop-dusting operation directed at law schools and other breeding places.

(In fairness, I should acknowledge that a contrary opinion is held by Thomas Ehrlich, former dean of the Stanford Law School, who holds that the basic cause of the legal pollution is not too many lawyers but too much law. But that brings us back to square one, for those laws are largely the product of the make-work efforts of lawyers.)

We could probably bear the burden of the hungry horde of lawyers of which the Chief Justice has spoken were it not for the fact that so many of them are incompetent or dishonest, or both. As he told the American College of Trial Lawyers, "ours is a sick profession" marked by "incompetence, lack of training, misconduct and bad manners. Ineptness, bungling, malpractice, and bad ethics can be observed in court houses all over this country every day."

Among the factors in the worsening image of the bar cited by Burger were "title lawyers and real estate lawyers who engage in miscellaneous chicaneries to bilk home owners, and the family lawyer or probate lawyer who 'borrows' from trust funds or gouges his clients."

The Chief Justice reported that his own extensive checking with judges all over the country had produced the astonishing consensus that somewhere between 75 and 90 percent of the lawyers appearing in their courts were grossly incompetent! Moreover, he reported, these incompetents had "a seeming unawareness of the fundamental ethics of the profession." In a more recent address to the British bar in London, Burger condemned "the low state of American trial advocacy" and charged that the U.S. legal process is "one of the slowest in the world." Joseph W. Bishop, Jr., Richard Ely Professor of Law at the Yale University Law School, confirmed what the Chief Justice had said, decrying what he termed "the stupefying incompetence of many practicing lawyers."

From the foregoing expert testimony it is clear that the legal establishment is imposing upon the American public an unconscionably low standard of professional service that would not be tolerated for one moment in, say, the practice of medicine. What that establishment is engaged in is, in fact, the *malpractice* of law.

This fact of bumbling legal representation takes on added significance in the light of the Supreme Court's ruling in *Link* v. *Wabash Railroad Company* that:

There is certainly no merit to the contention that the dismissal of the petitioner's claim because of his counsel's unexcused conduct imposes an unjust penalty on the client. Petitioner voluntarily chose this attorney as his representative in the action, and he cannot now avoid the consequences of the acts or omissions of this freely selected agent.

Persons needing to employ legal procedures have no way of knowing whether a particular lawyer is an expert or a bungler—if he's the latter, his fellow lawyers will remain silent and let him go on preying on the public. If he works true to form and bungles the case, the highest court in the land will give the frustrated citizen a cold stare and a curt "You picked him!"

The Constitution purports to guarantee to every American a full measure of justice under our laws. But if the legal establishment permits him no alternative to hiring its members—and then provides him with only one chance in ten that his cause will be adequately represented, it is denying him due process. It is depriving him of a right secured to him by the Constitution—and it is doing so with complete impunity, for *it* is the agency with whom he must file any complaint of such violation.

Chief Justice Burger told the American Bar Association assembled for its annual meeting in St. Louis: "The American public is aware of the moral and professional deficiencies of lawyers, is hurting and doesn't know what to do about it, but wants to do something."

But it *is* doing something. As the realization of the extent to which it has been victimized by this monstrous fraud has begun to dawn upon the public, the first cries of outrage are being heard—and the premiums for legal malpractice insurance are beginning to soar.

In Washington, an organization named HALT (an acronym for "Help Abolish Legal Tyranny") has begun recruiting members nationally. Its burgeoning ranks testify to the public's disenchantment with lawyers. In Maine a regional group has created LAW, Inc., to challenge the organized bar. These are manifestations of growing public resentment of legal tyranny.

Lawyers reacted nervously when courts twice recently appointed Massachusetts constitutional law authority Nathaniel Denman, a descendant of Lord Chief Justice Denman of England but himself a nonlawyer, to represent litigants.

An American Bar Association Special Committee on Evaluation of Disciplinary Enforcement, under the chairmanship of retired Justice of the Supreme Court Tom C. Clark, reported that:

After three years of studying lawyer discipline throughout the country, the Committee must report the existence of a scandalous situation that requires the immediate attention of the profession. With few exceptions the prevailing attitude of lawyers toward disciplinary enforcement ranges from apathy to outright hostility. Disciplinary action is practically nonexistent in many jurisdictions; practices and procedures are antiquated; many disciplinary agencies have little power to effect steps against malefactors.

Cyrus Vance, when he was president of the City Bar Association of New York, appointed a committee to investigate the effectiveness of disciplinary procedures in the city's legal establishment. The committee's report three years ago concluded: "A disciplinary system that moves slowly, and in secret, then ends up disciplining [only] a miniscule percent of those whose conduct is complained about can be neither effective nor credible." The study found that many complaints against lawyers were not investigated, seemingly out of a "desire to avoid difficult cases." In other cases the committee found a tendency to accept the attorney's word as against the complainants and to close the case without further investigation. It noted that the majority of cases investigated involved misconduct by small practitioners and proposed that more investigations be directed at complaints against Wall Street lawyers and other more prominent members of the profession against whom it found many complaints have been filed, only to be ignored by the grievance committee.

The bar members paid little attention to the report. Between April 1, 1977 and December 31, 1977, more than 1,900 complaints were filed against New York City lawyers. Of these, only 13—less than 1 percent—were disciplined.

All lawyers are supposedly required to adhere to a Code of Professional Responsibility, departures from which are regarded as wrongdoing.

Monroe Freedman, Professor of Law at Hofstra Law School, wrote in the *National Law Journal:* "A substantial majority of the Bar lacks even a passing familiarity with the Code of Professional Responsibility." In one such recent action, Federal Judge Lawrence W. Pierce in New York dismissed the claims on the ground that "the Code is aspirational in character" and violations of it may be dealt with only through the bar's own ineffective grievance procedures.

In its coverage of the February 1977 meeting of the American Bar Association in Seattle, the *Wall Street Journal* reported that "leaders of the legal profession acknowledge that a person who hires a lawyer can't be sure that the one he picks is either competent or ethical," while in another article titled "Shyster at the Bar," the *New York Times* noted:

For years, concern has mounted among leaders of the legal profession that the machinery for disciplining unscrupulous lawyers is not doing its job in many communities. The result . . . unethical lawyers are going unpunished because the legal profession has showed too little stomach for cleansing its own house. . . . There is a tendency for many local bar association grievance committees to resolve complaints in favor of the lawyers and discount the clients' claims. Moreover, few grievance committees are self-starting; the entire bar of a community may know that

John Lawyer is a thief and a scoundrel, but typically nobody expects the grievance committee to proceed against him, unless a victim files a complaint or a public scandal occurs.

The system of grievance procedures allows unscrupulous lawyers to continue to practice when they should be disbarred, the newspaper charged. Citing that only 2 percent of the transgressors were hauled before grievance committees, and only .02 percent of them were disciplined, lawyer-sociologist Dr. Jerome E. Carlin laid the low number of disbarments to "lax enforcement."

Being a resident of Connecticut, it is understandable that I would be more aware of legal abuses there than of those in other states. Still, Connecticut is no better or worse than the rest of the country, and what happens there is typical of what happens elsewhere. Where there is the practice of law, there is corruption.

Curiously, their own corruption is seldom apparent to lawyers. Not far from where I live, the president of a tri-city bar association was tried and found guilty of embezzling $40,000 from an estate. His lawyer made an impassioned, almost tearful, plea to the court asking that the thief be given only a suspended sentence because "for a lawyer, the disgrace is punishment enough." A sympathetic court provided the relief sought and the lawyer was turned loose, free as a bird. A friend reported that he saw him living the high life in an expensive New York restaurant a month later—while other men were serving time for stealing a loaf of bread.

In Derby, Connecticut, an ex-probate judge stole $18,000 from an estate and he, too, received a suspended sentence.

In the course of a single year, five Iowa attorneys embezzled $972,000. In Baltimore, Attorney Morris Levine converted to his own use $150,000 of the $180,000 insurance and profit-sharing plan proceeds in the estate of a local businesswoman, telling the family that he had collected only $30,000. He was tried, convicted—and sentenced to three weeks in jail!

A New York lawyer "converted" $42,500 of his client's money for his personal use over a three and a half year period. Found out, he returned the money, was censured by the state's bar association—and left free to continue practicing law. Another New York lawyer took $2,500 of a client's money for his own use. He "gave misleading testimony during an official investigation," according to a bar association report—and still escaped with nothing more than censure. "The lawyer made restitution," explained Daniel Goldstein, public relations director of the New York State Bar Association. "He stole nothing. They [the judges] felt justice would be adequately served by a censure, rather than a disbarment."

Chesterfield Smith once said that he wouldn't trust 20 to 25 percent of American lawyers. It was an "insider's" view—he's a former president of the American Bar Association.

Two old friends of Jimmy Carter, one a former president of the Georgia Bar Association and judge of the state's Court of Appeals, the other a former bankruptcy court judge, were charged in 1978 with improperly intervening at the Justice Department on behalf of two Georgia labor leaders who had been indicted for embezzling a third of a million dollars in union funds. The amoral hoodlums who run many of our most powerful unions are kept in office through the legal shenanigans of lawyers who know full well that they are representing crooks.

The *New York Times* reported the results of a professional survey which disclosed that during the course of a typical year, 22 percent of all the lawyers in New York engaged in one unethical practice or another.

Watergate disclosed an administration layered with lawyers—one critic called it "a government *of* lawyers, *by* lawyers and *for* lawyers"—which provided the most humiliating example of governmental corruption in the nation's history. The slap-on-the-wrist punishment meted out to the wrongdoers, mostly suspended or short sentences providing a few months of seclusion in which to write their memoirs, left many Americans shaking their heads at the brand of "justice" dispensed by the legal establishment when its own members were involved.

One Watergate figure served four months in prison for his part in the break-in of the office of Daniel Ellsberg's psychiatrist. Evidencing the legal establishment's sense of humor, upon his release he was given a job teaching ethics at the Golden Gate Law School in San Francisco. Disbarred in 1975, he was quietly reinstated in 1979 by the Washington State Bar Association.

It's all very well to inveigh against the bar's wholesale deviation from rectitude, but the Chief Justice might make a greater imprint upon the history of his time if he frankly acknowledged that his periodic exhortations to his brothers-in-law to mend their ways were falling upon deaf ears, and instead applied his energies and the vast prestige of his office to a vigorous plan to clean out the Augean stables of the profession of law.

Not long ago, a law professor who represented a private client was so incensed over the conduct of the federal trial judge handling the case that he planned to lodge a formal complaint. Only then did he discover that there was no appropriate body to file a complaint with. Legislation before Congress would create such machinery, but such proposals have been strenuously resisted by most judges.

The disgraceful 1979 televised spectacle of the justices of the California Supreme Court snarling and snapping at each other like so many pit bulldogs did nothing to enhance the bench's image.

It would be wrong, of course, to suggest that there are no honest lawyers, for there are—just as there are four-leaf clovers. Finding either is widely regarded as a stroke of rare good luck.

The trouble with honest lawyers is that they stand

silently by, watching the crooks and the incompetents in their profession victimize the public—and they never raise their voices. Their silence makes them accomplices to the crime.

There are faint stirrings of a challenge to the bar's stranglehold on the administration of justice in this country. In Washington, Barbara A. Reeves, special assistant Attorney General in charge of the antitrust division, disclosed that "our initial research indicates that bar associations may be engaged in conduct that constitutes monopolization, attempts to monopolize and boycotts in its efforts to quash any competing alternative methods of handling legal services.

"The lawyers' monopoly is often the result of friendly interaction between legislation drafted and passed by lawyers in state legislatures, coupled with restrictive bar association rules and codes."

The *New York Times,* noting that there are many routine legal procedures which could be done more cheaply by nonlawyers, has observed that "lawyers have erected a monopoly of sorts, by promulgating rules on what constitutes 'unauthorized practice' of law. The profession, by and large, dislikes books that tell potential clients how to avoid probate. . . . Such do-it-yourself books give misleading advice, lawyers say."

It is not concern for the public's welfare that motivates the bar's opposition to these efforts to achieve probate avoidance; it is simple greed. When *How to Avoid Probate!* became a best seller, the Institute for Business Planning, a legal reference service that publishes books of assorted forms that are to be found in all law libraries (and which for years reprinted my trust instruments with high praise), sent the following letter to every attorney in America:

Emergency Bulletin from the Institute for Business Planning to its friends in the legal and estate planning professions.

HOW TO LICK THE DANGEROUS DO-IT-YOURSELF CRAZE FOR AVOIDING PROBATE. . . .

Dear Sir:
We have just prepared a special report that will knock the "do-it-yourself" wills and estate planning craze into a cocked hat. Enabling you to cope with today's serious threat from amateurs who get "avoid probate" notions out of books, this urgent report can turn a nightmare for the professional into a windfall of new wills and estate planning instead.

Due to the popularity of these "do-it-yourself" methods, laymen . . . are denying you the fees you

rightfully deserve. The situation calls for immediate action. . . . So much is at stake that we can say without exaggeration that failure to get hold of these reports now could cost you a fortune in fees.

That's what the shouting is all about, then—the "nightmare" loss of a "fortune in fees" wrung from the widows and orphans of America, fees that the lawyers "rightfully deserve" but that they are being "denied."

It was this clearly evident attitude which led the chairman of a Senate subcommittee investigating the bar to ask if the American Bar Association "is more interested in protecting the pocketbooks of its members than in delivering services to those who need them most."

New York State's Chief Justice Charles D. Breitel probably had the same thought in mind when he warned that if lawyers "just go grab, grab, grab, they may be killing the goose that lays the golden egg."

The legal establishment's reasoning defies understanding. In Austin, Texas, an attorney named Merrit F. Hines was appointed by the court to defend a man accused of the brutal murder of an eight-month-old baby girl. The evidence was irrefutable and the man was convicted and sentenced to death. Then it was discovered that Hines had neglected to pay his state bar dues, and the bar invoked its rule that anyone delinquent in his dues could not practice law. That Hines was an experienced and competent lawyer was irrelevant. The death sentence conviction was reversed, Hines paid his dues, the man was retried, convicted, and executed. At great expense to the taxpayers, the bar's right to collect a few dollars in dues was upheld.

Nearly everything we buy is made more expensive by lawyers; there are very few areas of human endeavor from which they do not profit. But there is no area from which they derive a more outrageous profit than that of probate.

There is continual grumbling about the confiscatory nature of death taxes in this country. But legal fees charged in connection with estate tax returns filed in 1973 totaled an incredible $1,218,450,000. That amount was equal to 30 percent of the total estate tax revenue collected by the federal government in 1973 and *three times* the amount collected in state death taxes for that year. Thus we see that our complicated estate tax laws, fashioned by lawyers, are a major contributor to the prosperity of the legal profession.

What is this probate system which is so profitable for lawyers?

CHAPTER 2

What Is "Probate"?

In every legal jurisdiction in America there exists a special court which concerns itself with the administration of estates. Sometimes called the "orphans," "surrogate," or "chancery" court, its most common name is "probate court."

A properly drawn will should state your wishes as to the disposition of your property and name an "executor" whose duty it will be to see to it that your instructions are carried out. The executor will present your will to the probate court with an inventory of the assets and liabilities of your estate. The court will determine that the document is legal in both form and execution and will "accept" it for probate. Through the medium of a court-ordered legal notice inserted in a local newspaper, your creditors will be notified of your death and given an opportunity to present their claims. The notice will also serve to alert interested parties who may wish to enter a legal objection to the disposition of your estate in accordance with the terms of your will. The court will hear the claims of all such parties and rule upon their validity. If the terms of your will are unclear, the court will "construe" them, deciding officially what you meant.

If you have died intestate—that is, without leaving a valid will—the state will write your will for you. By this is meant that, in the absence of a legal and valid will, your estate will be distributed in accordance with the law of the state in which you live. That distribution may bear no resemblance to the one you would have specified had you elected to spell out your wishes in a will. The probate court will appoint an "administrator" whose duties will approximate those of an executor who would have attended to the details of probating your estate if you had left a proper will.

If through illness or senility an individual becomes incompetent to handle his own affairs, relatives or other persons responsible for him may appeal to the probate court to appoint a "conservator" over his assets to protect them against loss. In the case of a minor legally disqualified by reason of his age from acting on his own behalf, the court may appoint a "guardian" to act for him if he owns, or is to receive, property in his own right.

If under the terms of your will, you establish a trust for the benefit of your heirs naming as trustee an individual or a bank, the probate court might be called upon to appoint a successor trustee if the individual trustee dies or the corporate trustee resigns or goes out of business.

If there is no surviving parent, the probate court will act to appoint a guardian of the person and property of minor children.

While there may be many variations of the above, as well as additional peripheral duties, these are the principal concerns of the probate court. Your legal residence determines the jurisdiction of the probate court. Perhaps you reside in two or more places—you have a home in the country in Connecticut, a town house in New York, and a winter home in Florida. The legal profession will bless your memory and the probate judges in all three jurisdictions will lick their chops. Each will make as good a case as he can that you were a legal resident of his bailiwick and will seek to enfold your estate into the jurisdiction of his court.

A wealthy New Yorker died leaving a valid will in which he declared himself to be a legal resident of New York City and specifically directed that his will be probated there. Not so, said the probate judge in the small Connecticut town where he'd had a country home. Ruling that the deceased had spent enough time at his country home to be considered a resident of Connecticut, the judge assumed jurisdiction—and that's where the will was probated.

Perhaps the place of your legal residence can be established beyond question. But that property you own in another state—the house in Florida, the retirement site in sunny Arizona, the farm you bought in Vermont—these can be a real nuisance. They will require an "ancillary administration," which simply means that they'll have to be probated where they are. The lawyer who handles the probating of your estate at the place of your legal residence will hire another lawyer at the place where the out-of-state property is physically located. By the time your estate gets through paying for this legal daisy chain, your shade, gloomily peering down from some heavenly point, will be wishing you'd simply rented.

The probate procedure is time consuming. In a survey to determine the time involved in probating an estate, a questionnaire was sent to knowledgeable attorneys in all fifty states inquiring as to the time required to clear the average estate through probate in their jurisdictions. They were asked to indicate the most appropriate description from among a wide choice ("less than six months," "six months to a year," "one to two years," etc.) Overwhelmingly, the time indicated was "two to five years." If there is any complication or any contest by the heirs, it can drag on interminably.

It is the general practice to permit a widow to draw a modest allowance from the estate during the course of probate. Other heirs, including children, do not ordinarily have this privilege, however, and none of the heirs—the widow included—has access to the principal until probate is completed.

The probate procedure attracts publicity. Every newspaper has a reporter assigned to cover the probate court. If the decedent is at all known in the community, or if there is anything unusual about the size of the estate, the nature of the assets, or the identity of the heirs, these private matters become newspaper headlines. This not only provides grist for the gossip mongers but also attracts the attention of unscrupulous persons who regularly prey upon beneficiaries to separate them from their financial security. On the basis of probate court records, lists of widows are compiled and sold to such persons.

The probate procedure is costly. In an article in a national magazine, a well-known estate attorney answered questions about probate. Asked to estimate the costs of estate administration, he replied:

> On small estates of $10,000 to $20,000 they are likely to be, on average, 20%. On medium sized estates of, say $100,000, they probably would be around 10%. On larger estates they would be a smaller percentage.

Avoiding probate does not mean avoiding taxes. Taxes are something else again. What we are talking about avoiding here is the expense, the delay, and the publicity of probating. So far as the expense is concerned, a leading legal reference service gives the following estimated costs of estate administration (the figures include lawyers', executors', appraisers', and probate court costs but do not include taxes):

GROSS ESTATE LESS DEBTS, ETC.		PROBATE AND ADMINISTRATION EXPENSES	
From	*To*	*Amount on Column 1*	*Rates in Excess*
50,000	100,000	4,300	7.8
100,000	200,000	8,200	7.2
200,000	300,000	15,400	6.8
300,000	400,000	22,200	6.5
400,000	500,000	28,700	6.3
500,000	600,000	35,000	6.0
600,000	700,000	41,000	5.9
700,000	800,000	46,900	5.8
800,000	900,000	52,700	5.7
900,000	1,000,000	58,400	5.6
1,000,000	1,500,000	64,000	5.6
1,500,000	2,000,000	92,000	5.6
2,000,000	2,500,000	120,000	5.5
2,500,000	3,000,000	147,550	5.5
3,000,000	3,500,000	175,000	5.4
3,500,000	4,000,000	202,000	5.3
4,000,000	4,500,000	228,500	5.2
4,500,000	5,000,000	254,500	5.1
5,000,000	6,000,000	280,000	5.0
6,000,000	7,000,000	330,000	4.9
7,000,000	8,000,000	379,000	4.8
8,000,000	9,000,000	427,000	4.7
9,000,000	10,000,000	474,000	4.6
10,000,000	-----	520,000	4.5

Several months after completing his duties and being discharged by the probate court, an executor received a check for three cents from the Internal Revenue Service with a note explaining that it represented a refund of an overpayment resulting from an error in addition which an audit had uncovered on the tax return he had filed. Wanting to be perfectly correct, he stopped in at the probate court and asked what he should do with it. The procedure was simple, he was told. They would reopen the estate, instruct him officially to pay the three cents to a specified heir, and then close the estate again. All this was done and a few days later he received his instruction from the court to pay the three cents to the heir. Enclosed with it was the probate court's bill for $8.78 for reopening the estate. There being no money left in the estate, he had to pay it out of his own pocket.

Now that we know what probate is, let's look at the abuses which make it important that we concern ourselves with its avoidance.

CHAPTER 3

Probate—The Ugly Side

Defend the fatherless;
Plead for the widow.
ISAIAH 1:17

The probate system, conceived generations ago as a device for protecting heirs, has now become their greatest enemy. Almost universally corrupt, it is essentially a form of private taxation levied by the legal profession upon the rest of the population. All across the land, both large and small estates are being plundered by lawyers specializing in "probate practice."

Traditionally, the system has operated in close cooperation with politicians who have been able to utilize some of its unconscionable profits to insure their own or their party's continuance in office. Local party bosses select candidates for the office of probate judge who will work along with them, and then put the party machinery to work to get their man elected.

In my own community, we had the same probate judge for nearly thirty years. The office had been "removed from politics"—meaning that he had been endorsed for reelection each year by both the Republican and Democratic parties, due, it was claimed, to his policy of being absolutely impartial. And he was. In the case of one estate I examined, he had appointed two appraisers, each of whom had received a fee of $3,600. One was the Democratic town chairman and the other was the Republican town chairman. The judge *was* quite impartial—he split the swag right down the middle!

Criticizing probate as costly and time consuming, the *New York Times* reported that "there is evidence—and general agreement among many top legal experts—that the probate procedures in many areas are woefully inefficient, inadequate, and . . . sometimes bordering on the scandalous."

First, consider the cost of probate. No respecter of persons, it afflicts the rich as well as those of modest means. It siphoned off 11 percent of Franklin D. Roosevelt's estate in the process of "protecting" his heirs. Dixie Lee Crosby left $1,300,000; probate grabbed 8½ percent. (Bing Crosby made sure it didn't happen to *his* estate; he utilized the plan described in this book.) Gertrude Strong Achilles, whose family backed George Eastman, of Eastman Kodak fame, died in California leaving $10,883,505; probate took 11 percent.

When Robert Sterling Clark died in New York, the administration expense was $856,747, the executor was paid $2,965,683, and the attorney grabbed a million dollars. It cost $4,822,430 to "protect" Clark's heirs. Mind you, none of these figures include taxes—they represent just the cost of the mechanical process of turning the money over to the heirs.

The estate of Arthur Vining Davis was put through the probate wringer in Florida. The First National Bank of Miami drew $2,512,500 as executor. Two co-executors, W. E. Dunwody, Jr., a Miami attorney, and Daniel Davis, a nephew of the dead man, drew $942,187 and $628,125 respectively for doing whatever they did. In addition, Dunwody's law firm, Mershon, Sawyer, Johnson, Dunwody and Cole, pulled out another $1,502,000. Still another law firm, Milbank, Tweed, Hadley and McCloy, was paid $236,000. There was no provision in Mr. Davis's will saying, "To the probate system, I bequeath six million dollars," but the system took it anyway.

It is common practice for lawyers drawing wills to ensure fat future fees by writing themselves in as executors, co-executors, or trustees of client's estates. Often, too, they insert clauses specifically directing that they or their law firms be hired to attend to probating the wills. I don't know who drew the Davis will but I'd be willing to wager that it was the same lawyer who collected almost a million dollars as co-executor and whose law firm collected another million and a half.

Law school students are taught to build a "will file," although the *New York Times* quoted a knowledgeable probate attorney as saying that there is no money in drawing wills. "The big money," he explained, "is in settling the estate after the death of the client."

Leo Kornfeld, former editor of *Trusts and Estates* magazine, the leading professional journal in the field of estate administration, wrote that the handling of most estates is "cut and dried. . . . Most of the work is done by the lawyer's secretary, problems are solved gratis by the clerks of the probate court, and very little of the lawyer's own time is consumed."

Explaining lawyers' "generosity" in drafting wills for $50 or $100, Mr. Kornfeld said:

It's really very simple. Wills are "loss leaders" for the lucrative probate which follows the client's death. The lawyer who drafts a will anticipates that he will be called upon to probate that will and handle the estate settlement. Here the customary percentage-based fees usually run into the thousands of dollars.

Many old lawyers look forward to finishing out the last years of their practice in the relative comfort and affluence of probating wills and settling estates. With two or three wills "maturing" each year, it works pretty much like an annuity policy. But it's obvious who's paying the premiums.

The legal fees earned in probate and estate settlement work are more often than not quite astronomical in relation to the time spent by the lawyer on the matter. It's time we got away from the unjust system of overcompensating lawyers for probate work, of the courts rubber-stamping (or not even being aware of) exorbitant fees which have absolutely no relationship to the time or effort expended by, or the competency of, the lawyer.

Now, perhaps as you read what I've written above, you've said to yourself: "Oh well, that doesn't apply to *my* estate. I'm no millionaire."

If that's what you think, disabuse yourself, for it does apply to you. Proportionately, the burden of probate expense falls heaviest on estates of modest size.

Before me as I write is a front-page clipping from a Missouri paper with a headline which reads: "Fees Eat Up Nearly Half of an Estate of $19,425." Two lawyers alone took 40 percent of the estate. Another story from the *Cincinnati Post* has a seven-column headline: "Another Case Uncovered: It *All* Goes to Fees." (While that may seem to be the maximum that can be taken from an estate, I shall not be surprised to read someday that a lawyer somewhere has submitted a bill for 110 percent of an estate he's been "protecting" via probate.)

In the Cincinnati case, schoolteacher Ruth Crittenden had died leaving a $38,000 estate. The local bar association's fee schedule called for a legal fee of $1,347. With the probate judge's approval, the lawyer took $8,625, which included pay for forty-nine hours allegedly spent "inspecting" the woman's small, dilapidated house. A petty, ambulance-chasing crook? No, he was the city solicitor—a respectable crook. He appraised the house at $12,000, which fattened his fee, and then sold it to a fellow lawyer for $5,000. He reported that he could find no heirs. By the time Miss Crittenden's relatives in another state learned that she was gone, the estate had been picked clean.

Sam Wilner died in a Chicago furnished room leaving a few bits of worn clothing, a handful of books, and $12,000 in a savings bank account. There were no debts and the only surviving relative was a niece in New York. The probate court appointed a local attorney as administrator. He promptly hired another attorney to advise him on the legal technicalities of withdrawing the $12,000 from the bank and sending it to New York. The problems loomed so large that the two of them petitioned the court to appoint yet another attorney to assist them. The administrator paid his brother-in-law $28.50 to "appraise" the few books, which he then sold for $2.00. (He could have saved the estate $26.50 if he had just dropped them into the nearest rubbish barrel—but then his brother-in-law wouldn't have gotten the price of a new pair of shoes out of poor Sam's estate.)

Five long years later, the niece, receiving no response to her repeated letters to the administrator, consulted a New York attorney to find out what she could do to get what was rightfully hers. But Chicago was 900 miles away, so the New York attorney hired a Chicago attorney to represent him in the matter. The niece waited another ten months and nothing happened. Finally, in desperation she telephoned me and asked if I had any suggestions. I was scheduled to debate a leading "probate specialist" on the Kup Show on Chicago TV the following Saturday night, and I promised her I'd cite her uncle's estate as an example of the way the probate system operated in the Windy City. I did, and on the following Wednesday she received a check for her uncle's estate—or rather, the $5,100 that was left of it. The three court-appointed Chicago banditti had taken the other 58 percent of Sam Wilner's estate, and the probate court had approved the theft. Out of her $5,100, she had to pay her New York attorney $1,400. Another estate "protected." If Al Capone could return to Chicago, he wouldn't bother with the beer business—he'd be a "specialist in probate practice."

One is reminded of the comment of a knowledgeable observer, Professor William Fratcher of the University of Missouri Law School: "We know that it's easier to take money from heirs before they get it and that the probate court lends itself to certain rackets that have to be eliminated."

Hyde Stewart, an Ohio postman, died leaving $22,864. The probate court appointed an administrator who by law should have been paid a fee of $874. He took $2,077—two and a half times the statutory fee—and the probate court approved it. He had hired an attorney whose fee also should have been $874, but who charged $3,500—four times what the law provided—and the probate court approved it. After twenty-five months, the two of them reported to the court that they could find no heirs and were directed by the judge to pay the remainder of the estate to the state. A reporter from the *Cleveland Plain Dealer,* checking local city directories in the public library, found five heirs in three days.

Another postal employee, Charles Guettinger, died leaving $4,500. Eight years later, his two sisters received $400 each. The probate system's vultures got the rest.

The point I want to make is that while the costs of probate are a drain on the estates of the wealthy, with smaller estates they are invariably a disaster.

Probate doesn't *have* to cost a great deal. It depends somewhat on who you are. Gordon Stouffer died in

Cleveland and the expense for probating his $1,937,477 estate was $97,323. At just about the same time and in the same city, Joseph C. Hostetler died leaving a similar sum, $1,780,394; probate cost: $2,798. Probating one estate cost thirty-five times the cost of probating the other. The explanation: Gordon Stouffer was an executive of a restaurant chain, while Joseph Hostetler was a partner in a Cleveland law firm. In Dallas, Robert G. Story died leaving $323,024. Administration costs totaled only ½ of 1 percent, $1,813. Happily for his heirs, Mr. Story, too, was a lawyer.

It isn't only the lawyers who profit, of course. In Connecticut, the state in which I live, there are 164 different fees a judge may collect for various probate procedures.

In attacking *How to Avoid Probate!,* lawyers commonly assert that my claim that their probate fees are excessive is baseless because such fees are "regulated" either by state statute or by bar association fee schedules. What they fail to mention is that the fees to which they refer are *minimum* fees. There is no such thing as a "maximum fee." The fees quoted are for completely routine paper-shuffling by their secretaries. They are permitted—and indeed, it is expected of them—that they will charge more for any "extraordinary services" they perform. The trouble is that in the field of probate practice, just about everything they do is now considered "extraordinary," justifying an inflated fee. Rarely is it possible for an aggrieved client to do something about such overcharging.

It *can* happen, though. In 1972, Walter E. Hermann died in Reno, Nevada, leaving a $3 million estate. His son, named as executor, hired the lawyer who drew the will to attend to its probating. To "guard" the interests of "absent heirs"—three adult daughters who'd been bequeathed $20,000 each—the executor's attorney asked the court to appoint an attorney who practiced in a city 500 miles away. That's equal to the distance from Boston, Massachusetts, to Richmond, Virginia—he was more "absent" than were the absent heirs! (The executor's attorney later explained his nomination by saying that he owed the distant attorney a favor.) But the distant lawyer didn't want to be traveling those 500 miles, so he persuaded the probate judge to appoint a third lawyer, who practiced in the city where the will was being probated, to represent him.

The Hermann estate finally emerged from the probate wringer in 1978. The executor's lawyer charged a fee of $250,000, and the probate court approved it. The two attorneys who were "guarding the interests of the daughters" asked for $210,000—*almost four times* what the daughters themselves were to get under the will. The probate court reduced it to $70,000. Among them, the three lawyers had asked for $460,000, or 16 percent of the estate.

At this, the executor "blew his top," going into civil court and demanding relief from the extortionate fees. Acknowledging that the lawyers' fee demands "shock

the conscience of the court," the judge there reduced the fee of the executor's attorney from the probate court-approved figure of $250,000 to $80,000, while the $70,000 court-approved fee of the daughters' attorneys was chopped to only $6,000. Mind you, these two were not fringe operators in the legal profession—they were two of the most distinguished lawyers in the State of Nevada, the type who assume an injured air when anyone suggests, as I do here, that probate practice is simply a racket.

In an editorial commenting on the Hermann case and hitting out at "grasping, money-grabbing attorneys," the *Reno Gazette* noted that "people in general distrust and doubt the motives of lawyers in general," adding that too many times in the settlement of an estate, "by the time the smoke clears, the lawyers have gathered in most of the money."

The sizable estate of inventor William B. Lear has been in litigation continuously since his death in 1978 due to the bungled preparation of his will by a leading Reno attorney. No settlement is yet in sight but the estate's lawyers have already claimed fees running into the hundreds of thousands.

Cleveland was the stamping ground of a particularly rapacious probate team, Probate Judge Frank L. Merrick and "probate specialist" Ellis V. Rippner. Rippner had been an aide to a previous probate judge who had been tried for embezzlement in a scandal in the Cuyahoga County probate court. Rippner was fired but soon became notorious for his handling of estates, working hand in hand with Merrick. Only a connecting door separated Rippner's law office from Merrick's probate court quarters. Together, the two wrote a handbook on probate practice which a Cleveland attorney described as a "real fee-maker." Here's a significant quotation from the book:

> The question as to what constitutes extraordinary and actual and necessary expenses is a matter to be determined by the probate court within its discretion and may not be determined by an appellate court on appeal, and once allowed, an appellate court is reluctant to set aside the amount allowed *even though the allowance appears unusually large in view of the services performed* (emphasis added).

What the two were saying was that if a lawyer submits a nice, juicy bill for approval by the probate court, and the judge approves it, it is useless for the heirs to appeal it to a higher court because the higher court would be "reluctant" to cut the fee regardless of how outrageously exorbitant it was.

Rippner wrote a particularly scathing denunciation of *How to Avoid Probate!* in a review of the book for a Cleveland newspaper. The seven-column headline read: "Book on Probate Is Called Dangerous." Noted Rippner: "He [Dacey] writes that it takes an average of two to five years to administer an estate in Ohio. In Ohio, by statute, the estate can be closed after nine months. Only where the estate is over $60,000 for a single person, or $120,000 for a married person, thus incurring a federal tax liability, will it be necessary to hold the estate open longer than a year. . . . There is no truth or foundation to the figures used by Dacey as to costs of administration. All of these are regulated either by statute or rule of court, and his suggestion that the administration expenses would amount to 20% is an out-and-out lie."

The discrepancy aroused the curiosity of the other newspaper in Cleveland, the *Plain Dealer,* which assigned two crack reporters to investigate estates passing through the local probate court. The results produced one of the major stories of the year in Cleveland. Their report, a series of articles, started with this page 1 streamer headline: "Estates of Dead Often Become Legal Prey." The documented series reported that "estates are kept open for years while lawyers build up their fees. Lawyers and administrators draw fees ranging up to 25% of the estate." It appeared that, if anything, my charges had been understated.

Concluded the *Plain Dealer:* "The probate court is archaic and tainted." In an editorial call for probate reform, the paper denounced the fact that in the local court, more than half of an estate could be "squandered" in the course of preserving it for the heirs. It assailed Judge Merrick, noting that in one case, two of his appointees who had made a one-hour trip were allowed to deduct a $400 fee, 10 percent of the $4,000 estate they were "protecting."

Probate practice is a happy hunting ground for dishonest lawyers. When Louis Moritz, an unmarried upholsterer, died in his home in a poor section of Chicago, police found $743,965 in brown paper bags on the premises. A first cousin, the closest of fourteen heirs, applied to be named administrator but the probate court refused, choosing instead to follow its usual pattern of naming a Chicago attorney who, in this case, promptly stole half of the assets. The probate court nevertheless accepted his final accounting (of what use is a probate court that doesn't even notice that a third of a million dollars is missing?), and it was only when the heirs filed a petition in the circuit court demanding to know what had become of the rest of the money that the embezzlement was made public. The circuit court ordered the bonding company to pay the estate $360,000, but significantly neither that court nor the probate court nor the Illinois Attorneys Disciplinary Registration Committee, which conducted an investigation into the theft, instituted any criminal action against the thief. Instead of being publicly disbarred, he was "permitted to remove his name from the rolls of attorneys in Illinois." It was another example of the doctrine that the disgrace of being found out is punishment enough for a lawyer.

A probate judge in my own city appointed a local undertaker, a political hack, as administrator of an estate. During the next five years, the man helped himself to $77,000 of the estate's assets. The heirs complained and he was arrested. His lawyer brought in the pastor of the man's church, the fire chief, and an assortment of other witnesses to testify that deep down in his heart the crook was a good man. The lawyer explained to the court that "Mr. X was incompetent to run his own business and suddenly he found himself administrator of a substantial estate." Apparently, no one thought to ask the probate judge to explain why he had appointed such an incompetent to handle the estate in the first place.

In Stratford, Connecticut, Probate Judge Thomas Coughlin drew a will for an elderly woman who had been brought to his office by a daughter. In it she left everything to her six children, with her daughter named as executrix. Not long afterward, without her family's knowledge, Coughlin went to the eighty-one-year-old woman's home with two of his probate court employees and had her sign a new will naming him as executor, disinheriting her children, and leaving everything, including the home the children had built for her, to a thirty-year-old roomer in the house. He later defended his action by producing a letter of instructions, perfectly phrased and professionally typed, allegedly written to him by the aged, foreign-born woman, who spoke only broken English, was semisenile, and under treatment by three doctors for five major diseases. He acknowledged that he had consulted with none of the doctors to confirm her mental capacity to make a valid will. When she died shortly afterward, he disqualified himself from serving as either probate judge or as executor under the will. Instead, he arranged for a friend who was judge of probate in an adjoining town to sit in his stead (a favorite ploy among judges with conflicts of interest). The visiting judge promptly appointed one of Judge Coughlin's lawyer friends as administrator of the estate. When the family opposed the acceptance of the will, the roomer hired the administrator's son and law partner as *his* counsel. It was cut and dried—the visiting judge decreed that everything should go to the roomer. When the family complained to the state's Council on Probate Judicial Conduct (a committee of probate lawyers and judges), that body found nothing to criticize about Judge Coughlin's conduct.

Another case which was the subject of a concurrent complaint to the council involved a seventy-three-year-old spinster, a home-owner and voter in Stratford all her life. After hospitalization in neighboring Bridgeport (Stratford had no hospital), the woman availed herself of her Medicare rights to a period in a Bridgeport convalescent home. While she was there, Judge Coughlin drew a will for her in which he named himself as executor. When she passed away unexpectedly a few weeks later, the death certificate properly identified her as a resident of Stratford. But if her will was presented for probate there, Coughlin would have had to disqualify himself from serving as executor, since he was the probate judge there before whom it would be presented. Accordingly, solely on the strength of her few weeks' stay in the Bridgeport hospital and convalescent home, he filed the will for probate in Bridgeport and the probate judge there went along with the deception, thus permitting Coughlin to serve as executor. The first thing he did was hire an attorney for the estate, the inference being that although he himself was a lawyer and probate judge, he knew too little about the probate process to handle it himself. But the lawyer he hired was—himself! As a result of these machinations, he collected a full executor's fee, a full attorney's fee, and then, just to illustrate that there is no limit to human greed, he sold the woman's Stratford home and charged the estate another $350 for handling the closing! Altogether, he collected nearly $5,000 for handling a $70,000 estate from the administration of which he had been absolutely disqualified by law. The Council on Probate Judicial Conduct considered all of these facts, too, and still found no reason to criticize him.

Incidental to his private practice of law on the side, the probate judge in another town near my home had occasion to represent a client seeking a zoning variance. In the weeks prior to his appearance before the zoning board, he appointed each of its members to a juicy appraisership. Not surprisingly, his client was granted the variance.

Joseph Bartz was an elderly retired man who roomed with a bailiff of the Common Pleas Court in Cleveland. Actually, he had escaped years before from an asylum to which he had been committed long ago when he was young. By hard work and frugal living, he had somehow accumulated an estate of $40,000.

The bailiff wrote a will naming himself as the old man's heir and persuaded him to sign it. Not long afterward, Bartz died. A doctor friend of the bailiff signed the death certificate, after which the bailiff had the old man's body hastily cremated. The will was presented in the probate court and accepted, and the bailiff got the $40,000. Nine months later, some relatives of Bartz discovered what had happened and appealed to the probate court to reopen the case, pointing out that the court had accepted a will executed under questionable circumstances by a man earlier adjudged legally incompetent and confined to an asylum, but the judge refused to reopen the case.

In one Connecticut probate court, a hearing took place on a request to sell a piece of property owned by an estate being administered by a local bank as executor under a will. The hearing was called to order and it was announced that a bid of $85,000 had been received from two local lawyers. Unexpectedly, a local automobile dealer arose and bid $125,000 for the property. Startled looks were exchanged, the hearing was hurriedly recessed, and the parties adjourned to the corridor. Five minutes later, the automobile dealer departed with a check for $25,000, pausing only long enough to stick his head into the judge's chambers and inform him he was withdrawing his bid. The hearing was reconvened and the bids were canvassed. The two lawyers were the only bidders and the property was sold to them for $85,000. True, the property cost the lawyers a total of $110,000—but it is also true that the heirs were robbed of $40,000. The probate judge knew it, the lawyers knew it, and the bank/executor knew it. In that court, a large American flag stands behind the judge. The Jolly Roger would be more appropriate.

The probate judge in another city owed a local man $5,000. The man died leaving a will in which his wife was appointed as executrix. The judge pretended to find a flaw in the will and rejected it. Officially, then, the man died intestate, and it was up to the judge to appoint an administrator—which he did, naming a friend. One of the first acts of the administrator was to waive the judge's indebtedness to the estate, and the judge approved it. When the heirs complained to the local bar association, it declined to take any action.

In Houston, a city which has required four bar grievance committees to run concurrently to deal with the flood of complaints of unprofessional conduct by members of the bar, a probate judge and two lawyers went to prison for looting estates. Happily for them, they were able to continue the practice of law from their prison cells, since in Texas a felony conviction is not regarded as sufficient grounds for disbarment.

I believe that the conduct of these probate judges is generally typical of the activities of all probate judges. That is the way things are done. It suggests the urgency with which we should all address ourselves to the problem of probate avoidance.

A special panel of Los Angeles jurists reported that "the authority of the courts and the rule of law are jeopardized by a mammoth bottleneck resulting from antiquated probate procedures and outmoded concepts. . . . The critical need for immediate and fundamental [probate] judicial reform is apparent." Some probate judges have sought to shift the blame to the lawyers, Probate Judge Earl F. Riley of Los Angeles warning the Lawyers' Club of that city that "probate courts were not created with the specific idea of making attorneys more wealthy."

Judge William T. Treat, who heads the probate court in Rockingham County, New Hampshire, also sees lawyers as the principal villains in the probate racket. "There are lawyers practicing in the probate field who are doing a great injustice to our profession and to their clients," he told a Washington conference. "Many are doing a shabby job, a few are dishonest, many are incompetent. A great many more are lazy, inefficient, and neglectful." Referring to Chief Justice Burger's criticism of widespread incompetence among lawyers practicing in our trial courts, Judge Treat said:

I'm not going to argue with the Chief Justice's priorities but he has an even more fertile field to plow in the probate world than he has in the trial court system. An experienced and conscientious probate lawyer is a very useful person to the community. What is regrettable is the small percentage of attorneys who qualify for that definition.

If we had not become by long experience accustomed to the inadequacies of our probate courts, surely by now there would have been a mass revolt. We hear much about the delays in trial courts, much about the faults of our district and municipal courts, but very little about the shocking failures of our probate courts. Is it maybe because the whole probate structure is so hopelessly confused that our judicial reformers recoil at the thought of making sense out of the whole mess?

Our Chief Justice should be devoting some of his time and his enormous influence toward the improvement of the probate court system. . . . The courts and the Bar Associations should . . . deal effectively with those lawyers who abuse the probate system by neglecting their practice and gouging their clients.

Lawyers considering disputing Judge Treat's conclusions may wish to take into account that he is the president of the National College of Probate Judges, a member of the advisory board of the National Center for State Courts, and the author of the three-volume work, *Treat on Probate*. Presumably, he knows whereof he speaks.

As I have traveled about the country discussing the abuses of probate, it has become commonplace for local lawyers to acknowledge that those abuses do exist *elsewhere*, in other cities or in other states. Always, the city I am visiting is pictured by the local lawyers as a legal Shangri-la where probate practitioners have no nasty habits. Invariably, however, when I return home I receive letters from people in that very area reciting their own probate horror stories.

The California bar has been particularly critical in its comments upon my claims of fee-charging excesses, citing over and over again that all of the fees incidental to probate in that state are set by statute. But those statutory fees are meaningless, for they are ignored. The $85,597 appraisers' fees assessed against the estate of Myford Irvine of Tustin, California, were *twelve times* the statutory amount. The $165,000 attorney's fee on the Gertrude Strong Achilles estate was $50,885 (45 percent) more than that called for by the statute. California law set the attorney's fee for probating Dixie Lee Crosby's estate at $18,605—but the attorney actually charged *three and a half times* that amount, $64,155, and the court approved it.

It is understandable why a group of California attorneys found occasion recently to complain that "the hard facts indicate that the trend away from probate—and probate courts—is reaching the point where the courts may have so little to supervise that the game may no longer be worth the candle."

So much for the costs of probate. Next, consider the delays involved.

In an address to the American Bar Association's Section of Real Property, Probate and Trust Law, Probate Judge David Brofman of Denver said:

I would like to see more businesslike administration and less cause for criticism in probate. Frankly, I cannot discredit too much the author of *How to Avoid Probate!* because . . . he has put the spotlight on an area where we are weak in probate, and perhaps this will result to the good of the public interest. This spotlighted area is that where we have failed to provide prompt termination and distribution of decedents' estates.

Citing a Colorado estate which had been in probate for thirty-three years, another in Nevada in which heirs had been waiting for twenty years, and two in New York which had run on for twenty-five and thirty-six years respectively, Judge Brofman said:

You can see from these examples that the public has a right to complain in this area; and likewise, any author is justified in taking the legal profession to task for the unwarranted long delays. I would dislike telling you how many man-hours are consumed in the court where I work in answering correspondence and setting up conferences where there has been undue delay in closing.

A most recent letter said: "He refuses to answer any mail sent to him. In your letter of a year ago you said that 'he anticipates being able to pay another partial advance on them in the near future.' Of course, the question is: 'What is the near future?' I still have heard nothing from him and I would like to know his present plans. I can only say that it is a pity that Norman Dacey's book, *How to Avoid Probate!* was not written and the advice heeded before Aunt Lillian passed away."

My files are jammed with similar letters, and I am certain it is repeated with as much or greater volume in many other probate jurisdictions. The evil of unreasonable delay must be eliminated from probate by us—the judges and lawyers—or we will be faced with other pressures in addition to the presently valid criticisms.

In Dallas, Billie Goff, sole heir to the $428,609 estate of her stepfather, had to apply for aid from the county welfare board because she couldn't obtain any money from his estate which had been in probate for several years.

During an appearance on a TV talk show in Boston, I took a call from a young man who explained that he'd had to drop out of college because he had had no funds with which to pay tuition. His father's estate of nearly $2 million had been in probate for four years and there was no sign of its early release.

Another man wrote me from San Francisco that his grandfather's estate had been in the probate court there for twenty-eight years!

I have already mentioned the undesirable publicity which attends probating. If I were so inclined, I could purchase a list of names and addresses of widows, compiled from probate court records and broken down into three groups. Names of those who have been widows for more than ten years sell for $25 per 1,000, while the names of those who have been widows for six years or three years sell for $35 and $40 per 1,000 respectively. What husband would knowingly permit his wife to become the target of the unscrupulous characters who purchase these lists of "hot prospects"? What wife could feel anything but foreboding that she might become the victim of these sharpsters? Too often, the appearance of the names of widows in the probate court records has been a prelude to financial disaster. If there was no other complaint, this alone would be sufficient reason to avoid probate.

Next to *being* a probate judge, the best thing is to have one in the family or as a friend. Chances are that you'll be named as an appraiser. Probate Judge Chase Davies of Cincinnati illustrates the point. Within the space of a relatively short time, his brother-in-law was given six appraiserships—on just one of them, his fee was $36,000. A son-in-law of the judge collected a fee of $6,584, among others. Another son-in-law pulled down $1,760. The judge's golf partner's name appeared frequently among the appraiser appointments. Another friend collected $36,000 for appraising the estate of Olivia P. Gamble, whose grandfather founded Proctor and Gamble. It was acknowledged that as appraiser he had done absolutely nothing except sign his name. The wives of three probate court employees hit the jackpot several times. Remember, every nickel of these fees was extorted from heirs who in most cases needed every cent that was left to them.

During an investigation made by local newspapers of the activities in Judge Davies's court, it was noted that a certain "Will Jackson" had been appointed an appraiser on an estate. At first reporters who sought to locate Jackson could find no trace of him, but then they discovered that "Will Jackson" was really Norman Payne, Judge Davies's assistant. Their continued search turned up more pay dirt—good old "Will Jackson" had been named as an appraiser by Judge Davies on a total of sixty-three estates. The judge found difficulty in explaining how he could appoint a nonexistent individual to serve.

An even more interesting fact of the Will Jackson affair was that more than fifty different Cincinnati lawyers had handled the sixty-three estates in which Jackson was named. Each of them had executed a document in which he said that Will Jackson had appeared personally before him, had identified the appraisal as his work, and had sworn that the signature beneath it was his. How does one attest to the signature of a nonexistent person?

What had happened, of course, was that the fifty-plus lawyers had committed perjury. Did the legal establish-

ment step in and disbar them, or suspend them, or otherwise discipline them? No, they *were* the legal establishment—and the bar doesn't punish itself.

Until the law was changed in Missouri, probate judges there regularly appointed themselves as appraisers—and collected that fee, too. One court clerk testified that she had made hundreds of appraisals, with the full fee "kicked back" to the judge who appointed her. Actually, there's nothing rare about appraiser fees being surrendered in whole or in part to the probate judge or to the political party in power—the practice has been quite common.

The average lawyer's attitude toward appraiserships was well illustrated in a Providence, Rhode Island, newspaper's interview with John M. Dring, who was the clerk of the Newport probate court for more than three decades. Said Mr. Dring: "The Newport County lawyers are a small, friendly group and they take care of their own. If a man needs a little extra money, he simply calls one of the top estate lawyers and asks to be remembered the next time appraiserships are being handed out." Mr. Dring himself had received fifty-three appraiserships during the forty-eight-month period preceding the interview. Even a court clerk needs a little "extra money" now and then. The "top estate lawyers" remember everybody—except, maybe, the widows.

Another dismal aspect of probate has to do with the appointment of "special guardians." Guardianship laws in the United States are a disaster. Probably in a majority of cases they result in an almost Dickensian deprivation of individual civil rights which would have been outlawed long ago were it not for the fact that they place their victims in a legal straitjacket. Such victims are generally powerless to extricate themselves without substantial outside help. Relatives, tired of caring for an aged member of the family or simply greedy to obtain possession of that person's assets, stream into probate courts with petitions to be appointed as conservator or guardian. The elderly, particularly those without surviving family members, become the objects of unbelievably outrageous conspiracies which are given probate court sanction simply because the individuals involved have no one to speak for them and defend their rights. Often, an unrelated "friend," a rest home operator, or simply a boardinghouse keeper, will make application for such appointment. A physician friend of the petitioner cheerfully certifies the old person as incompetent—even as insane—and the warehousing process gets under way. With a stroke of his pen, the probate judge strips the forlorn victim of his independence, his pride, his dignity—and his money. For all intents and purposes, the action is irrevocable. Frequently, the court appoints a local lawyer as special guardian. The inflexibility which characterizes guardianships imposes the necessity for making application to the court for approval of even the most routine transactions. Although these required filings are simply clerical work routinely handled by their secretaries, members of the bar serving as guardians use this court-imposed paper-shuffling as an excuse to inflate their fees unmercifully.

In Cleveland, Mrs. Amy C. Schunk had a "friend" who went into the probate court and claimed that Mrs. Schunk was incompetent. The court appointed attorney Joseph W. Bartunek as her guardian. Shortly thereafter, Bartunek himself won appointment to the probate bench, and he appointed another lawyer, Alvin Krenzler, to succeed him as guardian of Mrs. Schunk's $152,890 estate.

Krenzler promptly placed her in a nursing home, the charges for which included *all* care, according to the owner. Nevertheless, her ex-gardener, Joseph T. Castle, was hired to go to the nursing home three times each day to "feed" her. For this he was paid a salary of $100 per week—out of her estate, of course. In addition, he lived in her house rent-free for more than three years. Although he himself was a gardener, he hired a local landscaping firm to take care of the property, charging the cost to her estate. Apparently it was a chore for him to get to the nursing home, so he proposed that the estate buy him an automobile. Krenzler obtained Judge Bartunek's approval for the purchase of a new Buick, the court ruling that the car was "necessary for the health, welfare, and best interest of Mrs. Schunk."

Reporters from the *Cleveland Plain Dealer* who were making an investigation of probate court practices in the city kept tab on Mr. Castle's comings and goings—and found that he went only once each day, at noon, supposedly to feed Mrs. Schunk, not the three times daily for which he was collecting free rent, $100 per week salary, and a shiny new Buick.

When Mrs. Schunk died, lawyer Krenzler, who had been appointed as her guardian presumably because of his legal knowledge, hired as attorney for the estate another Cleveland lawyer, Ellis V. Rippner. They reported to the court that between them, they could find no heirs. But *Plain Dealer* reporters quickly found two heirs right there in Cleveland. Said Rippner: "I investigated and I didn't find any heirs. I won't say that we searched the highways and byways—but we looked."

The appointment of "special guardians" for children who have inherited money is one of the juiciest aspects of the probate racket. Two weeks after he left office, ex-Mayor Robert Wagner of New York was appointed as "special guardian" of eleven children, beneficiaries of a trust fund in a New York bank. None of the children lived in New York; three of them lived in Oregon, 3,000 miles away. Prior to the appointment, Wagner had never heard of them nor had they heard of him. In the probate court, the children's mothers protested the appointment of this total stranger as "guardian" but the court brushed aside their objection with the comment that there might be a "conflict of interest" between the mothers and their children. A knowledgeable probate attorney in New York called it "a nice going-away present for the Mayor" and estimated that his fees would approximate $50,000 for only token work, if any.

Don't assume that the guardian racket applies just to the wealthy. A Westchester couple received word that their two daughters had each been bequeathed $1,000 from the modest estate of their maternal grandmother. But the surrogate court would not allow the executor to pay the money to the children or to their parents. Instead, two local lawyers were appointed as "special guardians" for the girls. Each received a check for $1,000 from the executor, each deducted a $250 "guardian's fee" and sent the $750 balance along to the parents. It is sheer hypocrisy for the bar to pontificate about its Canons of Professional Responsibility when it countenances this kind of barefaced robbery.

When one of the two surrogate judges in Manhattan appointed the thirty-year-old son of the other as special guardian of thirty-five children who were among the beneficiaries of an estate which had come into his court, the newspapers questioned the propriety of the appointment. His explanation: "I did it as a wedding present for the young man."

A probate judge is as entitled as anyone else to give wedding presents. He is also entitled to pay for them out of his own pocket, instead of charging them to the widows and orphans whose estates come into his court to be "protected."

A former governor of Massachusetts appointed a member of the state legislature as a probate judge. When shortly afterward the governor's term expired, the probate judge promptly named his benefactor as special guardian in fifteen different estate matters.

Trust companies are disinclined to protest the fees demanded by the court-appointed special guardians. The *Wall Street Journal* quoted one of them as saying, "Sure, special guardians often are awarded fees that haven't any relation to the work performed. But these guardians can tie up an estate for years and I'm not going to make any of them or the judge mad at me." The *Journal* also quoted "lawyers knowledgeable in probate practice" as saying that needed reform could be accomplished simply by requiring the court to rotate appointments among lists of attorneys submitted by bar associations. Their idea of "reform" is to see to it that *they* get to ride the gravy train, too!

As the *New York Times* explained it, "The assumption is that the executors' lawyers would want to keep the guardians' fees low so that there would be more money for their clients and that the guardians would want to keep the lawyers' fees low so that there would be more money for the persons they are protecting. However . . . appeals from either side about exorbitant fees are rare, and some lawyers contend that informal agreements are often made allowing both sides to collect large fees." Quite obviously, lawyers in the probate field conspire with one another to mulct estates. If their honesty is questioned, they affect great indignation and deliver a brief sermon about the profession's high ethical standards.

Pennies From Heaven?
By Ray Osrin © *Cleveland Plain Dealer.*
Used with permission.

widespread use of the inter vivos trust as a means of bypassing the local probate tollbooth, it conspired with Connecticut's lawyer-legislators to insert into a new law, ostensibly intended to set uniform fees in the state's probate districts, a six-word hooker: "(or passing other than by will)." The effect of this is to require every person who files a Connecticut inheritance tax return directly with the state Tax Department to pay a fee of hundreds, even thousands, of dollars to the local probate court, even though that court had no jurisdiction over the estate and performed no service whatever. Any such improper demands should be utterly rejected, of course.

Marie M. Lambert's successful 1978 campaign to be elected the first woman surrogate judge in New York ended with a $175,000 deficit.

Not to worry: The law firm of which she was a partner, Katz, Shandell, Katz, Erasmous and Lambert, sent out invitations to a "birthday party" in her honor, invitees being told that a table for ten would cost $2,500. The invitation list was heavily weighted with lawyers specializing in trusts and estate work. As one of Manhattan's two surrogates, Mrs. Lambert supervises the distribution of estates and appoints lawyers as guardians of the young and incompetent, appointments which are highly prized by the same estate lawyers.

The president of the New York City Bar Association commented that the fund-raising scheme was "manifestly inappropriate," and State Supreme Court Justice James J. Leff told the *New York Times:* "Simply stated, it stinks." Since no action was taken against Surrogate Judge Lambert, we can only conclude that it is simply one more manifestation of the ethical level on which the probate system operates in New York City.

Some time earlier, an editorial in the *New York Post* noted that "reporters for this newspaper have found a clear pattern of patronage payments to Surrogate's relatives, political figures, former officeholders, and lawyers with good political connections."

Table for ten, sir? Right this way, sir!

Attempts by some states to regulate probate and guardian fees by requiring that lawyers file a report of such fees with a court-appointed probate officer have not been fully effective. In New York, for example, 20,000 of 100,000 lawyers' fees were not recorded.

People everywhere should be on the alert for local versions of a scheme hatched by the Connecticut probate establishment which has been described in an article in the *Journal of the American Bar Association* as "one of the most viciously corrupt systems ever devised by the inventive minds of the greedy." Furious at the reduction in its profits occasioned by the increasingly

The American Bar Association's answer to the abuses of probate is the Uniform Probate Code.

CHAPTER 4

The Uniform Probate Code

The Uniform Probate Code was conceived more than a decade ago as a joint project of the American Bar Association and the National Conference of Commissioners on Uniform State Laws, hopefully to bring about some measure of reform in what the sponsors called "the big mess of probate law."

Their intentions were good. The problem is that the probate apparatus is so utterly corrupt that as a reform vehicle the Code just could not deal with it adequately. Some structures—old, rickety, and dangerous—do not lend themselves to patchwork repair and repainting. Successful redevelopment begins with their demolition. That's what the probate system needs—demolition.

After its own survey of the institution, the *Wall Street Journal* concluded that "attempts to reform probate courts aren't new but rarely do they succeed because few lawyers and fewer judges want to disturb the gravy train dispensing them such huge favors."

The Code's sponsors report that from the start it has met with "determined opposition from those who profit, financially or politically, from the present system." Said the committee:

The greatest foot-dragging can be found among probate judges and their clerks and assistants. Although the Code would not eliminate these jobs, it would reduce the number of required contacts between each estate and the probate office. Judges tend to balk at this lessening of control. Lawyers, usually older than average, who specialize in probate work, resist any suggestions that would devaluate their training and experience. They can be counted on to follow the lead of the judges with whom they work.

Publishers of legal specialty newspapers that derive considerable revenue from published legal notices of probates oppose provisions in the Code that would reduce the number of required legal advertisements. They, too, side with the judges. Persons and corporations who sell the probate bonds now required by law line up in opposition to Code provisions which would relax bond requirements for administrators.

The political wallop of the local probate bureaucracy is bolstered by other facts, as well. Legislators, the very persons who will ultimately be responsible for changes or reforms in state laws, are accustomed to rely on probate "experts," usually including the probate judges, for advice on proposed changes in probate law. Also, existing rules give probate judges in many states a lot of power to do favors for others, including legislators. This power is based on the discretion of judges to appoint appraisers, special guardians, and administrators and to pass on applications of trustees and attorneys for compensation.

Committees of lawyers and law professors were established in each state and in the District of Columbia to organize the campaign to bring about the enactment of the Code in place of the existing probate laws of the state. Alas, in most states they ran into a stone wall of opposition which doomed their dreams of reform. In many cases, the opposition came not only from the probate establishment but from the entire state bar.

In an effort to win over these opponents, the state committees conceded point after point until each state's final version bore little resemblance to the Code as it had been drafted by the national body, which itself had been the product of a long series of compromises.

Although the sponsors now claim that twelve states (Alabama, Arizona, Colorado, Florida, Hawaii, Idaho, Minnesota, Montana, Nebraska, New Mexico, North Dakota, and Utah) have adopted the Code (South Dakota adopted and then repealed it), the statement is fallacious for there is certainly nothing "uniform" about the laws enacted. What was placed on the books was the remnant of the "reform" proposals after each pressure group had moved heaven and earth to insure that *its* ox was not the one being gored.

The "reform" turned out to be more apparent than real. With respect to the interminable delays which have always marked the operations of the probate system, the Code's framers made an effort to reduce them by eliminating some of the traditional ceremonial mumbo jumbo which everyone but the probate judges conceded is archaic. To overcome the obstinate objections of these reluctant dragons, the Code had to be so emasculated that the result was hardly calculated to cause dancing in the streets.

The American College of Probate Judges adopted a resolution opposing "any further spread of the Uniform Probate Code." The measure was introduced by a Michigan judge who argued that the Code would "jeopardize the power of probate judges everywhere." Obviously, the Code can't be all bad.

The California Bar, long a vigorous opponent of probate reform, appointed an ad hoc committee of eleven probate lawyers and a judge to study the proposal. As expected, the committee unanimously urged its rejection with the observation that it offered "a more sweeping substitute for our present law than is desirable to serve the public interest of Californians." What hypocrisy!

Harley J. Spitler, a San Francisco attorney who has advocated adoption of the Code, charged bitterly that under pressure of public demands for reform the state bar had "spawned" a reform bill which achieved only a slight loosening of court control over the processes of estate administration without actually ending or even reducing the abuses of exorbitant costs, protracted delays, and undesirable publicity. "Attorneys," he said, "will welcome the new act, for it cuts down some of the paper work without cutting the fee. The public? Well, the California public will continue to use inter vivos trusts, joint tenancies and other devices to avoid the entire court-supervised probate process."

The national committee sponsoring the Code reported that "in Ohio, probate court loyalists had little difficulty in passing their own relatively meaningless version of probate reform in 1975, a judge-backed bill, technically flawed and lacking any significant reform." Complaining that the Ohio Bar Association refused to support real reform, the Code sponsors charged that Ohio bar leaders were wary of "risking the ire of local judges, who have plenty of ways of hurting lawyers who must stand before them seeking approval of estate petitions." A spokesman for the Ohio probate establishment, Probate Judge Richard B. Metcalf of Columbus, rejected the Code as "pure junk."

How should one react to the disclosure that a widow, waiting patiently for the estate of her late husband to serve the two-to-five-year sentence imposed upon it by a local probate judge, faces the possibility of additional delay because the judge bears her lawyer a grudge in some matter unrelated to her husband's estate and is "punishing" the lawyer by withholding approval of the estate's settlement?

From the handful of states where some version of the Code, however emasculated, has been adopted have come many reports of bitter-enders on the probate bench who have simply refused to observe it and who continue doing business in the same old way. For them, it has been an easy transition from open disregard for the rights of heirs to open disregard for the law.

In Nevada, the state bar officially opposed the introduction of the Code. Ultimately, it succeeded in obtaining the enactment of a "reform" statute which appears at first glance to increase the costs of probate by 38 percent. Upon closer examination, however, the new law is revealed as having the effect of doubling or tripling the old costs which prevailed before "reform." The national sponsors of the Code suggested bitterly that Nevada adopt a new state motto: "Rip Thy Neighbor."

As for the effect of the Uniform Probate Code upon attorneys' fees, let us examine a few enlightening passages from an address on the subject delivered to a San Francisco symposium of the American College of Probate Counsel (a pretentious euphemism for "probate lawyers") by Malcolm A. Moore, a well-known Seattle attorney who led the unsuccessful effort to have the Code adopted in the State of Washington:

Nothing is said in the Code with respect to fees.

Under the Code, the attorney and the personal representative [the executor or administrator of an estate] both have more creative roles in handling estates because of the choice of procedures available. To the extent that choices between Code procedures are going to be made by personal representatives, presumably relying upon the advice of an attorney, more creativity is required of both the personal representative and the attorney.

All this means responsibility. Responsibility, one of the most important factors in determining what kind of fee an attorney is going to get, is certainly worth compensating. Under the Code, the personal representative and the attorney have more, not less responsibility because of the options available and the lack of court supervision. They've also got more liability, of course, and it seems to me that this deserves to be compensated. Under the Code, the attorney's role is a creative one, and it deserves a fair fee.

Any change that comes about with respect to minimum fee schedules would have come about anyway absent the Uniform Probate Code because of the mounting pressure epitomized by the Dacey book.

It's a lot easier to collect a fee from an estate when heirs have gotten windfalls, if you will, than to collect a fee—a fair fee, a compensatory fee—for drafting instruments during the client's life. That fact is not going to change.

What happens if the current trend toward avoidance of probate continues? I don't think anyone can deny that trend. When probate is avoided, so are lawyers. [The question is:] is there any way to prevent this from happening, even absent the Uniform Probate Code? Look at the trend. Look at the Dacey book. And look at the public's feelings as to avoidance of probate. It seems to me that quite apart from the Uniform Probate Code, this trend is going to continue and increase.

The Code makes probate respectable. It will make probate honest again; and to the extent that there are more probates, lawyers stand to gain for a variety of reasons. To the extent that probate avoidance continues and gets worse, lawyers in the estate field are going to find themselves more in the drafting end and less in the settlement category.

Banks have a very strong policy of utilizing the attorneys who drew the wills to probate the wills. The Code will not affect this. After all, attorneys are a major source of business for the bank.

What is your reaction? Do you have the impression that nothing in the Uniform Probate Code is going to reduce the take of the lawyers, "the hidden heirs in every estate"? Do not the references to "increased liability," "increased creativity," and "increased responsibility" allegedly required of lawyers by the Code warn us of *increased costs,* if anything? Did you notice the bit about probate avoidance "increasing and *getting worse?"* Worse for the American College of Probate Counsel, perhaps, but not worse for you and me.

Widows and orphans almost always inherit far too little for their needs, and every penny that they get is important to them. As to Mr. Moore's categorization of that meager inheritance as a "windfall" from which it is easy for an attorney to collect a fat fee—how does that set with you? Even if the Code fulfills his prediction that it will make probate "respectable" and "honest again," do you think that you will want any part of it?

The principal draftsman of, and spokesman for, the Uniform Probate Code has been Professor Richard V. Wellman of the University of Michigan Law School. In a speech to the St. Louis Bar Association he cited the increasing use of the inter vivos trust as a device to avoid probate, warning that:

> If this trend to use probate-avoiding devices continues for another 20 years or so, the will may become largely extinct. We may come to see [it] as another legal relic. Traditional probate practice may wither to the point where almost the only estates will be intestacies involving little money.
>
> If present probate practice declines markedly or disappears, the losers will be lawyers, probate court personnel, newspapers which lose legal advertising, and surety companies relying heavily on probate bonds. . . . But we must think about the public image of probate and estate lawyers, and of the bar in general. If the tendency to avoid wills and probate continues, lawyers will get no credit at all for the unorganized drift from probate to non-probate substitutes. If lawyer groups do nothing to change the status quo while property owners avoid probate with increasing regularity, it's going to make lawyers even less popular in a public sense.
>
> Lawyers who practice in poorer neighborhoods will be the last ones to counsel the use of will substitutes. If so, small property owners may be left in the backwater, out of the mainstream of probate avoid-

ance. In short, if lawyers ignore present trends, the law will be changed indirectly as portions of it simply become obsolete.

Dacey and others have challenged the entire legal profession with the charge that we keep probate laws rigged to protect fees. If he's right, and probate procedures can't be changed because of vested interests, all lawyers, whether handling probate work or not, will suffer loss of community respect, just as all lawyers are hurt when another member of the profession is dishonest or otherwise guilty of breaching the trust the public has bestowed upon us. . . .

We've been sustained over the years by little things like preparing deeds, simple tax returns and wills. Much of the deed and tax return business has slipped away from us. Let's do what we can to keep the will business from drifting away, too.

Let's not kid ourselves. Members of the public who think about estate planning will not continue to think of wills or lawyers unless something can be done about the apparently inflexible post-death costs.

Wellman warned that many lawyers may appear to be supporting the Code's objectives without any intention of observing its alleged reforms. "Lawyers may support the Code enthusiastically to get the benefit of the very favorable publicity for lawyers which should accompany such support. And then they may continue to handle estates as they have always done so that, in time, the public will realize that it has been shortchanged."

One of the sneakiest provisions of the Uniform Probate Code—and one which demonstrates the hypocrisy of its sponsors—is Section VII. Unlike the testamentary trust, the inter vivos trust has always been completely outside the jurisdiction of the probate court. One of the stated objectives of Section VII, according to Professor Wellman, is "to eliminate procedural distinctions between testamentary and inter vivos trusts by having trustees file written statements of acceptance of trusts with suitable courts, thereby acknowledging jurisdiction. This last objective is particularly important in this day of rash use of self-declared and family trusts by persons who are more concerned about avoiding probate than with being sensible in regard to the protection of their purposes and their beneficiaries. The [Code] creates a duty on trustees to register trusts with the estates court at the principal place of administration.

"We think that publicity about a new statutory duty to register trusts may put a slight damper on the tendency of persons to attempt to set up family trusts without advice."

Isn't that sickening? What Wellman is saying is: "This 'reform' plan we've cooked up [which doesn't reduce the lawyers' profits from probate by as much as ten cents] will catch the fish who've been getting through our nets by using the inter vivos trust to avoid probate. We'll pass a law requiring them to register their self-declared trust with the probate court and in that way their estate will become subject to that court's jurisdiction whether they like it or not. They won't be so quick to set up a trust without paying us a fee."

Explained Professor Wellman:

These provisions will mean much to the tens of thousands of little people who've been frightened by the recent literature about avoiding probate. But the new law for the average person won't deter people who consider themselves to be above average from seeking the advantages of planning for themselves and their families. Hence, *lawyers and professional fiduciaries will lose nothing* from enactment of provisions aiding the little fellow. Indeed, they should gain if general confidence in the probate system can be regenerated [emphasis added].

The important point, however, is that the portions of the Code which should have strong appeal for professional fiduciaries and attorneys may not win legislative approval except as part of a package which is clearly beneficial to the general public. Hence, it behooves us to argue the merits of the Code as a balanced document with advantages for all wealth levels.

If "lawyers and professional fiduciaries will lose nothing" from enactment of the Uniform Probate Code, how can it be regarded as a reform measure? Are not the present extortionate legal fees the No. 1 reason for reform?

Note Professor Wellman's explanation that the portions of the Code which will have "strong appeal" for lawyers "may not win legislative approval except as part of a package" which seems to offer the public "significant advantages." What the good professor is saying is that they'll be obliged to conceal the self-serving provisions of their "reform" plan in a pretty package which the public will think is intended to benefit those who have for so long suffered the wrongs of probate.

Obviously, the Code's "reform" is more apparent than real. One is reminded of the Ohio probate judge's rejection of it as "pure junk." It is not often that I find myself in agreement with a probate judge.

Let's not put our faith in reform then. Let's find an effective way of avoiding probate.

CHAPTER 5

Ways of Avoiding Probate

There are three kinds of property which can pass to your heirs at your death without going through the probate procedure. They are:

1. Life insurance payable to a named beneficiary.
2. Property jointly owned "with right of survivorship."
3. Property held in an inter vivos or "living" trust.

Life insurance policies payable to a named beneficiary are exempt from probate. If your policy is payable to your estate, it will be subject to probate. I know a lawyer who consistently advises his clients to make their insurance policies payable to their estate, the proceeds to be distributed in accordance with their wills. Like most of his colleagues, he derives a substantial part of his income from seeing the estates of deceased clients through probate. He fattens up the probatable estate of a client in every way possible, including dumping the life insurance into it unnecessarily. One widow complained to me that he had even inventoried her late husband's two fountain pens.

The circumstances in which it may be advisable to make life insurance payable to one's estate are relatively rare and the practice should be avoided, particularly in view of the fact that in most states life insurance payable to a named beneficiary is wholly or partially exempt from state inheritance taxes, an advantage denied policies payable to the insured's estate.

Many people use joint ownership as a substitute for a will. Indeed, lawyers often refer to it disdainfully as "the poor man's will." While it is true that it avoids the delay, expense, and publicity of probate, it frequently creates more problems than it solves.

In the first place, not all jointly owned property is probate-exempt. If the deed under which a husband and wife own a home jointly is an old one, they may be "tenants in common." If the husband dies first, his share of the house does not automatically pass to his spouse— its disposition is determined by his will. If he has left no will (and many people who use joint ownership don't bother making a will), his share will be distributed in accordance with the laws of the state in which he lives.

In many states, for example, if a childless, married man dies intestate (leaving no valid will), the first $5,000

of his estate goes to his widow. The balance of his estate she will share equally with her husband's parents. In the case of a couple with children, the widow will get one-third of his estate and the children will inherit the remaining two-thirds. If their joint ownership of their family residence is as "tenants in common," his share will go to his wife and children in those proportions. The children will then own part of the home and that makes a pretty messy title. If they are minors, the children cannot "sign off" in favor of their mother. Someone will have to apply to the probate court to be appointed their guardian. The guardian can then act for the children. The obvious guardian would be their mother but in such circumstances the propriety of the mother's acting as guardian to turn the children's property over to herself might well be questioned. All of this would be avoided by:

1. Having husband and wife hold the property under a survivorship deed which would provide that, upon the death of one, the property would revert in its entirety to the survivor, or
2. Making certain that each of the parties has made a valid will leaving his or her interest in the property to the other.

Under the survivorship deed arrangement, there will be no probating; if it passes under a will, that will must be probated.

If you must hold title to it jointly, at least make sure that the deed under which you hold it reads "John Smith and Mary Smith, or the survivor of them." If it doesn't, execute and file a new quit claim deed by which you deed the property to yourselves or the survivor of you. (In some states, the practice of joint owners quit-claiming a piece of property directly to themselves in survivorship is questioned. In such cases, they simply quit-claim the property to a third person, a "straw," who immediately quit-claims it back to them in survivorship.)

Many people have joint checking or savings accounts in banks. It is not uncommon for banks to block such accounts upon the death of one of the co-owners. It would be a good idea for the survivor to go to the bank promptly, withdraw the money, and transfer it to a new account in his or her name. Ask your bank to write you a letter stating what its policy is in this respect, so you'll be forewarned. (Note: The fact that such a transfer is effected does not eliminate any liability the estate of the deceased may have for state or federal death taxes.)

Now, don't get the idea that because I have *explained* joint ownership, I am recommending it, because I'm not. Joint *trusteeship,* yes; joint *ownership,* no.

In some states, safe deposit boxes of deceased persons can be opened only by a representative of a probate court or a state inheritance tax appraiser. In Illinois, such state appraisers were accused of looting deposit boxes of $40,000 in cash and securities over a period of only a few months.

In states having such requirements on safe deposit boxes, it may be desirable for husband and wife to have separate boxes in which the spouses' important papers (will, insurance policies, etc.) are kept. That way, they'll be freely available and not sealed in a safe deposit box until the judge of probate returns from his Caribbean cruise. Ready access to burial instructions, for example, is assured and prompt application may be made for urgently needed proceeds of life insurance policies. Remember, though, that the contents of such boxes must be taken into account in computing possible state or federal death tax liability.

Before you enter into joint ownership, consider the following cases:

MR. SMITH, a widower with two children, remarried. The second Mrs. Smith proved a fine mother to the children. Mr. Smith registered his securities in their joint names, knowing that his wife would see that the children were provided for. Vacationing together, their car rolled off a ferry and both were drowned. The law said that in the "common disaster," Mr. Smith died first, his securities reverting to his wife as co-owner. Unfortunately, Mrs. Smith hadn't made a will. By law, her estate went to her only surviving blood relative, a cousin whom she heartily disliked. None of Mr. Smith's estate went to his children—to whom she was not related except as stepmother.

MR. LITTLE thought that he had eliminated problems from his joint ownership by making certain that his wife had an appropriate will. Unfortunately, his wife's will was successfully contested after they were both gone and Mr. Little's plans were frustrated.

MR. JONES registered his securities jointly with his wife who later was in and out of sanitariums during periods of mental illness. Many securities which should have been disposed of remained in his portfolio simply because he couldn't sell without her approval and he disliked initiating formal proceedings to have her declared incompetent.

MR. GREEN registered his securities jointly with his wife, thus making her a gift of one-half of their value. He was penalized when a subsequent tax examination disclosed that he had failed to file an appropriate gift tax return. (The only property which Uncle Sam will let you place in joint ownership with your spouse without having to file a gift tax return is your residence.)

MR. BROWN, like Mr. Green, made his wife a gift of securities by registering her as joint owner. When they realized the gift tax implications, Mrs. Brown hurriedly turned the jointly owned property back to her husband. When a subsequent tax examination revealed the facts, a gift tax was assessed for Mr. Brown's "gift" to his wife—and another for her "gift" back to him.

MR. CARTER placed his securities in joint names. When he died, the tax people insisted that Mrs. Carter present documentary proof that she had provided half of the money to purchase the securities. When she could not, they taxed the whole lot as part of Mr. Carter's estate.

MR. WILSON, on the other hand, registered his security holdings similarly in joint names. When Mrs. Wilson died, 50 percent of the property was considered a part of her estate and Mr. Wilson paid a tax to get his own property back. (The stories of Mr. Carter and Mr. Wilson illustrate the fact that joint ownership creates a 150 percent tax liability—the property is 100 percent taxable if the husband dies and 50 percent taxable if the wife dies.)

MR. JAMISON placed his securities in joint ownership with his wife, intending that she should have the lifetime use of his estate but that upon her death it would revert to his two children. At his death, his property was automatically turned over to her as the surviving joint owner. A few years later she remarried. Her second husband was a well-meaning but impractical man who led his trusting spouse into unsound financial schemes. When she died, there was nothing left for the two Jamison children. In this instance, joint ownership was a poor substitute for a trust.

MR. ARMITAGE was forced into a disastrous marital settlement simply because it was the only way he could regain control of securities which, in an earlier, happier day, he had registered in joint names.

MR. ADAMS owned his securities jointly with his wife. Upon his death, his entire estate went to her. Upon her subsequent death, the same securities passed, together with her own personally owned securities, to their children. Mr. Adams's securities were taxed fully at his death and again upon his wife's death. If, instead of registering his securities jointly, he had left them in trust, one-half to his wife and one-half to his children with his wife enjoying the lifetime income from both halves, he would have avoided completely the second estate tax on the half designated for the children. In this case, joint ownership resulted in double taxation and a needless waste of many thousands of dollars.

MR. THOMPSON, thinking to avoid probate, placed some property in joint ownership with his brother. When the latter became the defendant in a legal action in which substantial damages were sought, his half interest in Mr. Thompson's property was attached, effectively preventing Mr. Thompson from disposing of it.

Many persons put securities in joint ownership in order to obtain a doubled $100 exemption on dividends received. As a professional estate planner, I recommend against this procedure. I don't think that the small tax benefit thus gained offsets the disadvantages which joint ownership not infrequently produces.

Conclusion:
1. Avoid making life insurance proceeds payable to your estate.
2. Avoid joint ownership.
Next, let's consider the third way of avoiding probate—through an inter vivos trust.

CHAPTER 6

The Inter Vivos or "Living" Trust

It is likely to be a long time before there is adequate probate reform in America. Don't be discouraged, though. You need not be the system's victim. There exists a magic key to probate exemption, a legal wonder drug which will give you permanent immunity from the racket.

The magic key is the inter vivos or "living" trust, a financial bridge from one generation to another.

There are two principal types of trusts. The most common, the "testamentary" trust, is so called because it is established under the provisions of your "last will and testament." You might, for example, direct the executor under your will to turn the net proceeds of your estate over to a local trust company which will invest the money and distribute income and principal in accordance with the instructions contained in your will.

A testamentary trust serves a very useful purpose when heirs are inexperienced or likely to be imprudent or profligate in their handling of the funds they are to receive. Large inheritances frequently fail to provide the lifetime security which the testators intended. Indeed, instances abound where sudden wealth has unhappily affected the lives of the beneficiaries. It almost always is better to leave a very large estate in the care of a responsible trustee. One way of doing this—the traditional way—has been a "testamentary trust" established under a will.

Our concern here, however, is with avoiding probate, and a testamentary trust does not avoid probate. With it, nothing happens until your will has cleared the probate court and your executor has been discharged. Thus, the testamentary trust is subject to all of the delay, expense, and publicity which ordinarily attaches to the probate process.

The second and far less well-known type is the inter vivos trust. (The legal term "inter vivos" refers to something that takes place during the lifetime of the persons involved, which explains why this type of trust is commonly referred to as a "living" trust.) When you set up a living trust, you create it now, while you are here, not through the instrumentality of your will after you are gone. No probate judge or other person ever has to check to determine whether it is genuine—you certified to its genuineness while you were living. No one has to turn the switch on and step on the accelerator; its engine is already running.

An inter vivos trust can be either revocable (you can cancel it or alter its terms) or irrevocable (you cannot change it). Our principal interest here is the revocable trust. It offers no lifetime tax advantages. On the other hand, it offers no disadvantage—all of the estate and income tax savings obtainable through a skillfully drawn testamentary trust are equally available in a well-drawn living trust.

There are many persons whose faculties or judgment are not so impaired as to justify an adjudication of incompetency but who nevertheless would be benefited if relieved of the details of handling investments or a business which age or ill health may make burdensome. The living trust offers an excellent solution.

By setting up a trust during his lifetime with someone else as a trustee, a person has an opportunity to observe the efficiency of the individual or institution whom he has named as trustee—it has been described as "an opportunity to see one's will in action."

If the laws of the state of his residence are not to an individual's liking, he can avoid them by setting up a living trust with a trustee institution in another state whose statutes he finds more palatable.

The exemption from probate accorded a properly drawn and executed revocable trust materially reduces, if it does not in fact completely eliminate, the likelihood of successful attack by disgruntled persons. Contested wills are an everyday occurrence and estates do not always go to those whom the testator has named to receive them. In the first place, the legal necessity for advertising the fact of a will's having been presented for probate invites the interest and attention of those who may feel that they have a legal basis for contesting the testamentary distribution. An inter vivos trust is distinguished by its privacy—parties likely to protest may not even learn of the death of the creator of the trust until long afterward when the transference of the property is a fait accompli. In a word, the publicity of probate invites attack upon a will; the privacy of an inter vivos trust discourages it.

Many patently unjustified will contests are initiated by claimants who recognize the weakness of their cause but who figure that the legitimate heirs, desperately in need of the money and wearying of the long legal delays, will agree to pay some amount of ransom in the interests of settling the claim and obtaining what is coming to them. The inter vivos trust makes the assets available to the rightful heirs immediately, thus eliminating the unfair pressures which a will contest might impose upon them.

I know of no instances of successful attack by a third party upon the legality or validity of a living trust. Of course, such a trust should not be used to deprive a spouse or creditors of sums to which they might rightfully be entitled. In *Smyth,* the Ohio Supreme Court ruled that property in a revocable inter vivos trust could not be reached by a surviving spouse, a useful protection for a man or woman who, separated but not divorced, wishes to insure that the estranged partner cannot make unsanctioned claims against the estate.

The inter vivos trust offers an important "bonus" advantage—exemption from attachment. Property held in trust for another is not subject to attachment by persons having a claim against the individual serving as trustee. The trusteeship must be a valid one evidenced by a written instrument, and title to the property must actually be vested in the trustee. Admittedly, this can be subject to misuse—investors lost millions in the operations of a bankrupt Denver promoter while he retired to a life of luxury on the income from the trusts he had set up at the height of his "success."

Every trust requires a trustee. The trustee of *your* living trust can be either a bank or an individual. The appointment of a bank as trustee will be discussed in a later chapter. If you choose to appoint an individual, it is important that the person selected be trustworthy and responsible and likely to live long enough to carry out your wishes, particularly where young children may be involved as beneficiaries.

While the withholding of assets from heirs who may be immature or profligate is oftentimes wise and prudent, the great majority of Americans are concerned simply with getting their estates to their families promptly and with the least possible wear and tear. For them, the answer is the unique "one-party trust." In this, the creator of the trust (called the "settlor") appoints an individual as trustee—but that individual is *himself.* In a "declaration of trust," he specifically identifies the asset involved and "declares" that he is holding it in trust for a specified beneficiary. That beneficiary is also named as his successor trustee with instructions that upon the settlor's death he is to turn the trust asset over to himself and thereby terminate the trust.

While officially there are four jobs, then, actually there are only two persons involved, the settlor and trustee being one and the same person, and the beneficiary and successor trustee being one and the same person.

If the trust asset is a savings account, for example, the beneficiary/successor trustee walks into the bank with the trust instrument and a copy of the settlor's death certificate—and walks out with the money. It's that simple. No lawyers, executors, administrators, or probate court. No two-to-five-year delay, no 10 percent or more in expenses, no publicity.

We have already noted that during the long-drawn-out probate procedure, the court will allow a limited payment of support to a widow. Children and other beneficiaries are not so entitled, however, and the death of a breadwinner frequently results in an interruption of income which works a hardship upon beneficiaries. In the case of an inter vivos trust, the trustee or successor trustee needs only a certification of the death of the settlor to fully activate the trust's income provisions in the interests of the heirs. There is no delay whatsoever. This assurance of uninterrupted income and access to the principal can be extremely important to a family beset by the uncertainties and financial problems ordinarily attending the death of the breadwinner.

This advantage of the living trust is particularly important when there is a business to be run or liquidated on favorable terms. The trustee can take action swiftly, without waiting for the ponderous machinery of probate to grind out an approval.

Frequently a great deal of undesirable publicity attaches to the probate of an estate. An inventory of what you own and what you owe, and who is to get what, is a matter of public record. When a business interest is involved, competitors may gain important information from such records, information which can adversely affect efforts to sell the business.

The inter vivos trust eliminates these disadvantages. It is a boon to those who seek privacy. Unlike a will, its terms are not disclosed to a probate court, and its assets and the identity of the persons to receive them are closely guarded secrets. If you resent the piece in the newspaper telling your business, this is the way to avoid it.

Not infrequently the individual drawing a will simply leaves "my estate" without actually inventorying it. The settlor under an inter vivos trust is called upon to list or identify the trust's assets. In the process of making such an inventory he is likely to become more conscious of any weak spots in his financial affairs. Scattered assets are more likely to be assembled. His attention is attracted to special problems attaching to certain assets. Not infrequently, he undertakes to resolve problems himself which might otherwise have been left to the executor of his will. Unsuitable or deteriorating investments are thus removed from the estate by the one person better qualified than the executor to correct the unsatisfactory conditions which may prevail.

In my view, however, the greatest advantage of the living trust lies in its saving of expenses. We noted earlier a quotation from an estate planning attorney who reported that administrative expenses on small estates of $10,000 to $20,000 are likely to be, on average, 20 percent. On medium-sized estates of, say, $100,000 they probably would be around 10 percent. On larger estates, they would be a smaller percentage.

This is an important proportion of your total estate. This is what the inter vivos trust can save you.

Let me emphasize again that we are not speaking here of taxes. At least, not taxes legally imposed by your government. Rather, it is a private tax, imposed by one group of citizens upon another, a form of tribute privately levied by the legal profession.

In the view of some lawyers, any attempt to pass property other than under a will amounts to a criminal conspiracy, but the Supreme Courts of many states have ruled that if an owner of property can dispose of it by means other than under his will, he has the right to do so. The fact that his purpose is to avoid probate is in no way prejudicial to that right.

If the inter vivos trust can, in fact, accomplish the wonderful end of avoiding probate, why is it not used more frequently? An article by Milton E. Meyer, Jr., at one time a distinguished Colorado attorney, appearing in the legal journal jointly sponsored by the Denver Bar Association, the Colorado Bar Association, and the University of Colorado College of Law, ascribed it to:

> 1. Unfamiliarity with the potentialities of the living trust on the part of many attorneys and financial advisors.
> 2. An unwillingness on the part of some clients, even after adequate explanation, to depart from patterns they consider familiar.
> 3. An overzealous preoccupation among some lawyers and some representatives of corporate fiduciaries with the perpetuation of the application to decedents' estates of tradition-hallowed, time-honored, but overly protective and elaborate judicial machinery, which application has the incidental effect of providing very handsome legal and executors' fees for the same lawyers and corporate fiduciaries for work that frequently is quite routine, if time consuming, in nature.

The point last made will be vehemently denied by many attorneys and trust officers. A number of "legal" arguments will be brought to bear for the purpose of demonstrating the dignity of and necessity for the formal administration of estates. There will, perhaps, even be vague references to "illegality," "sham," "fraud," and the like directed at efforts to by-pass probate through use of the living trust.

The late Professor Thomas E. Atkinson, in his authoritative *Wills* (2nd ed., 1953), wrote:

> In more than half of the cases in which people leave some property, it has been found possible to avoid administration.

After citing the expense, delays, and inconvenience of administration as being the causes for attempts to dispense with probate, he concluded:

> The popular demand for probate reform is largely inarticulate, but it is nonetheless real as shown by the efforts to shun the probate courts. Yet one who seeks to find a solution to the problems of dispensing with or shortening the administration of estates is literally a voice crying in the wilderness.

Commenting upon the likely reasons for the lack of support for such efforts from members of the bar and from corporate fiduciaries, Mr. Meyer ascribed it to the thinking described in paragraph 3 of his quotation reported above—that is, to the interest in continuing the "very handsome legal and executors' fees" which the present system begets. It is true that the fees involved are an important factor. The average attorney who has been practicing awhile has begun to derive a substantial proportion of his income from seeing the estates of deceased clients through probate. The inter vivos trust is exempt from probate. Seriously, now, do you expect one of them to tell you how to avoid probate?

To be fair, we must take into account that before publication of *How to Avoid Probate!,* very few attorneys knew about the living trust or understood its use. But, even now, most of the attorneys who know about it won't tell you or will strongly recommend against its use. I would put the proportion of lawyers who are both willing and competent to set up an inter vivos trust at 1 percent.

The American Bar Association agrees with the recommendation here that you utilize the living trust for probate avoidance. When some of its members launched violent attacks upon me for telling the public about it, it cautioned them that:

> Actually, what Mr. Dacey says is, in many respects, not dissimilar to the ideas urged by the Association. From the point of view of being critical of the basic purpose of Mr. Dacey's work, to wit, to further the use of the inter vivos trust, perhaps the American Bar Association is committed to a quite identical program.

The association followed this up with a training film, narrated by Professor James Casner of the Harvard Law School, to be shown to local bar associations across the country to acquaint the members with the advantages and mechanics of the living trust. Training films are not issued on subjects with which people are already familiar and the film's issuance confirmed the fact of the bar's ignorance on the subject of the living trust. Alas, little interest was displayed in the film and its limited showings were not well attended. Professor Casner's position that "it is generally correct to say that the revocable inter vivos trust may be a substitute for a will" apparently didn't set too well with the union's rank and file.

The magazine *Trusts and Estates,* the leading professional journal in the estate planning field, echoed the ABA's comment:

> We have to give Mr. Dacey credit for publicizing the advantages to be had by getting as much property as possible into a living trust. The Bar and the trust industry would do well to steal a page from Mr. Dacey—and do a much more aggressive job of informing the public of the many advantages of living trusts.

You may have occasion to observe that the subject of living trusts is one on which trust companies and banks exercising trust powers display a curious inconsistency rooted in self-interest. Go into a bank trust department and explain that you have about $250,000, that you are considering the creation of a living trust of which you will serve as your own trustee with members of your family as beneficiaries, and with one of them serving as successor trustee charged with distributing your estate among family members upon your death. Ask the trust officer for his unbiased opinion of your plan. The chances are 99 to 1 that he'll shake his head and advise you that your plan is a disaster.

But go back to the same bank the next day and talk with him again. Tell him that you've concluded that it would be better to have the bank serve as trustee. Observe the astonishing change when there's a fee in it for the bank. Yesterday's "disaster" will be hailed as a brilliant piece of estate planning upon your part, one in the accomplishment of which you may count on the bank's wholehearted support, et cetera, et cetera.

Lawyer critics of *How to Avoid Probate!* have charged repeatedly that my claim that the living trust eliminates the costs of probate is deceptive. The reason, they say, is that the establishment of a living trust with a bank will subject its creator to bank charges for its administration, beginning immediately and continuing during all the remaining years of his life. These charges, they assert, will aggregate more than the claimed probate savings.

This is a fabrication, deliberate and not one into which they have blundered through misunderstanding or ignorance. They know it's wrong. When you set up a "one-party trust," there is no trustee's fee, for you are your own trustee. The successor trustee who takes over when you are gone is the beneficiary—and he certainly is not going to charge himself a fee. This is equally true even if you have chosen to have a bank handle the distribution of your estate after you are gone. In that case, you simply cover each asset with a "one-party trust" naming the bank as beneficiary to receive it in its capacity as trustee under the trust agreement you have entered into with it. The bank's active service—and thus, its fee—does not begin until your death. Under the "one-party trust," your estate will pass to the bank twenty-four hours, not twenty-four months—or twenty-four years—after your death and with no probate costs incurred.

A living trust takes precedence over a will. If you bequeath an asset to someone in your will, and you name someone else to receive the same asset under a living trust, the individual named in the trust will get it. However, to avoid any problem with people who can't understand how you could make such a "mistake," *never mention in your will* an asset which you have already covered with an inter vivos trust.

Note that in all of the one-party trust forms contained in this book, provision is made for the successor trustee to assume active administration of the trust in the event the settlor becomes physically or mentally incapacitated. Such administration is limited to disbursing the trust's income or principal to assure the settlor's comfort and welfare. This provision eliminates the need for court-appointed guardianships or incompetency proceedings.

In the case of joint owners who create a trust of which they are co-trustees, upon the death or incompetency of one of them the survivor continues as sole trustee. The trust continues undisturbed.

A word about taxes: During the lifetime of the settlor under a revocable inter vivos trust, the income from the trust will be includable in such settlor's gross income for federal tax purposes. Banks, transfer agents, and the like should be provided with the settlor's Social Security number for tax reporting purposes. After the death of the settlor and the distribution of the assets, the income from those assets will be taxable to the beneficiary or beneficiaries. If pursuant to the terms of the trust, a third party continues to hold and administer it for a minor or other beneficiary, the trust will constitute a separate tax entity and the trustee is required to apply for an "employer's identification number" and file a Form 1041 annually.

Where the settlor is also the trustee, he has the same cost basis in the property as he had before establishing the trust. After the death of the settlor/trustee, the successor trustee's cost basis can be either (1) the value of the assets on the date of settlor/trustee's death, (2) the value on the date of distribution, or (3) their value six months after the date of the settlor/trustee's death. Thus, the fact that an asset under a living trust is made available promptly to the named beneficiary upon the death of the settlor/trustee does *not* deprive the estate of the right to claim the benefits of the alternate valuation dates.

In some states, federal and state death taxes are required to be computed upon the basis of appraisals made by persons appointed under the infamous probate court system. It has been established that 90 percent of such appraisers perform no actual service for the fee they receive. It is the obligation of every American to pay taxes for which he is liable. There is no obligation, however, to pay tribute to persons who actually perform no service. Heirs should be instructed to compute carefully any taxes due (if necessary, retaining the services of an accountant to assist in such computation),

and transmit a check for such ta   room for
state authority with an appropriate   sets. It is
an inventory.   uplicates

They should not permit themselv   ing ma-
submitting to an unconstitutional de   individ-
for services not rendered by court-a   rument
who are in most instances incompet
to perform such services.

Remember, the racket persists only   refer-
occurred to the public to call a halt   to be
estates.   quire additional
        ay use the order form at the
One final word: In *How to Avoid Pr*   ok to obtain them, or type new originals
were provided in duplicate in order tha   urself.
have a signed copy for handy reference   ginals   Now, let's put *your* assets in trust. We'll begin with
were deposited in a safe deposit box. In this book, such   your real estate.

A FEW DEFINITIONS TO REMEMBER:

"inter vivos"—during your lifetime
"settlor"—the person creating the trust
"primary beneficiary"—the person named as principal beneficiary
"contingent beneficiary"—a person named to receive the asset if the
    primary beneficiary is not living
"per stirpes"—in Latin, literally "in the stirrups of" or, as we would
    say, "in the shoes of—" it means that the children of a deceased
    beneficiary "stand in his shoes," that is, they take his share
"or the survivor of them"—if one beneficiary dies, the remaining
    beneficiary takes the share of such deceased beneficiary
"u/d/t"—under Declaration of Trust

CHAPTER 7

Avoiding Probate of Your Home

For most Americans, the family home is the single largest investment they will ever make, and thus it bulks large in the value of their estate and should not be permitted to become entangled in the probate web.

The inter vivos trust offers a simple solution. The property owner executes a "declaration of trust" which sets forth that he is holding the property "in trust" for the use and benefit of the beneficiary after the property owner's death.

He can, if he wishes, declare in the instrument that he is holding the property in trust for two or more persons whom he names. If, for example, he states that he is holding the property in trust for "John Smith and Mary Jones, in equal shares, or the survivor of them," the property will pass at his death to the two persons named. If one of these beneficiaries is not living at the time of his death, the property will pass in its entirety to the surviving beneficiary. If one of several beneficiaries dies, the property will pass to the surviving beneficiaries in equal shares.

If, on the other hand, he declares that he is holding the property in trust for "John Smith and Mary Jones, in equal shares, per stirpes," and one such beneficiary is not living at the time of his death, the deceased beneficiary's share will go to that beneficiary's "issue"— that is, his natural (not adopted) children.

It is essential that a successor trustee be named whose job it will be to turn the property over to the beneficiary. If one person has been named as beneficiary, that person is automatically named as successor trustee. If two or more persons are named to share equally, the one whose name is listed first serves as successor trustee. Under either arrangement, it is assumed that the beneficiary named is age 21 or over. If he or she is not, there is a space in which you should fill in the name of an adult who can act as trustee for such beneficiary until he or she attains age 21.

The declaration of trust completed, the property owner must next execute a quit claim deed transferring title to the property from himself as an individual to himself as trustee, i.e., from "John Smith" to "John Smith, Trustee under Declaration of Trust dated _____."

Both the quit claim deed and the declaration of trust should then be filed with the town or county clerk, or other office where real estate transfers in the area where the property is located are customarily recorded.

Upon the death of the property owner, the successor trustee establishes his authority simply by filing a copy of the death certificate with the office where the previous documents had been recorded, together with a quit claim deed which he executes in his capacity as successor trustee, turning the property over to himself as beneficiary. If there are two or more beneficiaries and the property is to be sold, he attends to such sale, distributes the proceeds, and the trust is terminated—all without any probating.

If the real estate involved is now jointly held, you may create a *joint trusteeship* by executing together a quite similar form of declaration of trust and a quit claim deed prepared for that purpose. If the property is now in only one name and you wish to create a joint trusteeship, you may do so—together you execute the same form of declaration of trust but the person who presently holds title to the property executes a somewhat different form of quit claim deed by which he deeds the property to the two joint trustees.

Whether you are one person putting the house in trust, or there are two of you proposing to create a joint trust, if you are just buying the property you can eliminate the necessity of executing the quit claim deeds mentioned above simply by having the seller make out the warranty deed to you as trustee(s), e.g., "John Smith, Trustee under his Declaration of Trust dated _____" or "John Smith and Mary Smith, Trustees under their Declaration of Trust dated _____." You are still going to make out and file the declaration of trust, of course, and it should bear the same date as the warranty deed, i.e., the date you "closed" on the real estate purchase.

Bear in mind that we are speaking here of a revocable trust. The property owner can cancel it at any time or amend it—to change the beneficiary, for example. The existence of the trust does not alter in the slightest degree the right and privilege of the property owner to sell or otherwise dispose of the property in any way he chooses during his lifetime.

If it is a joint trusteeship, upon the death of one of the co-owners, the surviving co-owner becomes the sole trustee with all of the rights and privileges which the two had as co-trustees, including the right to mortgage, sell, or otherwise dispose of the property and the right to cancel the trust or change the beneficiary. It is not necessary for the surviving trustee to do a thing because of the death of the co-trustee. If it is a husband and wife who are involved, for example, and the husband dies, the wife need take no action. The beneficiary designation they both had made earlier is still in full force and effect, and upon her death the property will pass to that beneficiary. On the other hand, if the two co-trustees should die together in a "common disaster," the property will pass immediately to the named beneficiary or beneficiaries.

Readers who are co-owners of real estate now but who aren't sure whether theirs is a survivorship deed can stop worrying about it the minute they create the joint trust which automatically provides the benefits of a survivorship deed. In addition, it eliminates the necessity for probating which would have been required if, under the old deed—even if it was a survivorship deed—they had died together in a "common disaster."

Because the trust is revocable, the transfer of title incidental to its establishment involves no gift and thus no gift tax liability. For the same reason, it does not remove the property from the estate of the owner for estate or inheritance tax purposes.

It is not necessary to revoke the trust in order to sell the property. The warranty deed which you give to the purchaser should simply be signed in your capacity as trustee, e.g., "John Smith, Trustee under his Declaration of Trust dated _____" or "John Smith and Mary Smith, Trustees under their Declaration of Trust dated _____." The sale of the house automatically revokes the trust without any further action on your part.

In some instances, apartment ownership is evidenced by issuance of shares of stock in the corporation owning the apartment and an assignment of a particular unit to the person holding the stock. Ownership of such apartments may be placed in trust by using one of the forms in Chapter 9.

On the following pages will be found copies of various declarations of trust and quit claim deeds which will be suitable for use in connection with the arrangements just described. The benefits and advantages described in this chapter apply *only* when these instruments are used.

The instruments provide for all furniture, fixtures, and personal property situated *on the premises* to pass to the beneficiary named. If you have such effects which are in storage and therefore not on the premises, use one of the declarations of trust in Chapter 17 to put them in trust.

Two Important Notes

NOTE A

To:

Residents of Alabama, Alaska, Arkansas, Delaware, District of Columbia, Florida, Georgia, Hawaii, Illinois, Kansas, Kentucky, Louisiana, Maryland, Michigan, Minnesota, Montana, New Hampshire, New Jersey, North Carolina, Ohio, Oregon, Pennsylvania, Puerto Rico, Rhode Island, South Carolina, Tennessee, Utah, Vermont, West Virginia, Wisconsin, and residents of New York married before September 1, 1930; also residents of the Canadian provinces of Manitoba, New Brunswick, Nova Scotia, Ontario, Prince Edward Island, and Quebec:

Under the law, your spouse has a legal claim upon your REAL ESTATE in the event of your death, that right being called "dower" in the case of a widow and "curtesy" in the case of a widower.

NOTE B

To:

Residents of Arizona, California, Idaho, Louisiana, Nevada, New Mexico, Texas, and Washington:

You live in a "community property" state. Under its laws, in the event of your death your spouse has a legal claim upon ALL OF YOUR PROPERTY acquired during the marriage.

In the case of either A or B above, if you are married and you have executed a declaration of trust covering an asset held in one name only naming as primary beneficiary a person *other than your spouse,* your spouse must join with you in signing the declaration of trust. A space for such signature is provided immediately beneath the line on which you sign as Settlor. If you are setting up a joint trust with someone *other than your spouse,* your spouse must sign the declaration of trust in the space provided. If the asset is real estate, your spouse must also sign the quit claim deed in the space provided.

CHAPTER 7

DECLARATION OF TRUST
For Naming
ONE BENEFICIARY
To Receive
REAL ESTATE
HELD IN ONE NAME

INSTRUCTIONS:

On the following pages will be found a declaration of trust (DT-101) suitable for use in connection with the establishment of an inter vivos trust covering real estate title to which is held in one name only, where it is desired to name some one person to receive the real estate upon the death of the owner.

Cross out *"city"* or *"town,"* leaving the appropriate designation of your community. If your house has no street number, cross out *"(and known as)."*

Enter the description of your property as it appears in the warranty deed or quit claim deed under which you acquired it. If it's too long to fit into the space, prune it judiciously to eliminate references to easements, rights of way, etc., and abbreviate wherever possible (e.g., *"SW"* for *"southwest"*). Next, enter in the space provided the date of that deed and the volume number and page number in the land records where it was recorded. (This information is generally to be found stamped in the upper margin of the old deed; sometimes *"Book"* or *"Liber"* is used instead of *"Vol."*)

Note that under this instrument, not only your house but also its entire contents—including your personal effects—will pass to the beneficiary named without going through probate. If you do *not* wish to include your furniture and personal effects in the trust, cross out *"and all furniture, fixtures and personal property situated therein"* and *initial it.*

Enter the name of the beneficiary in the appropriate place in Paragraph 1.

Note that Paragraph 7 designates as Successor Trustee *"whosoever shall at that time be beneficiary hereunder,"* which means that in most cases you don't need to fill anything in there. However, if there is any possibility of a beneficiary who has not attained the age of 21 years receiving the property, make certain that you name an adult in this paragraph who can act as trustee for such beneficiary. Avoid naming as trustee a person not likely to survive until the beneficiary has attained age 21.

When completed in the manner shown on the reverse side hereof, make several photocopies for reference purposes. The original of the declaration of trust and the quit claim deed (see page 55) should then be filed with the town or county clerk or other office where real estate transfers in the area where the property is located are customarily recorded. After they are recorded, they will be returned to you.

Important: Read carefully Notes A and B on page 38. *Both* apply to this declaration of trust.

DT-101

Declaration of Trust

DALEY TRUST

WHEREAS, I, __John J. Brown_____, County of __Fairfax__, State of __Connecticut__, of the

Town of __Milton__ am the owner of certain real property located at (and known as) __525 Main Street__

in the Town of __Milton__, State of __Connecticut__,

which property is described more fully in the Deed conveying it from __Henry B. Green__

to __John J. Brown__ as "that certain piece or parcel of land with buildings

thereon standing, located in said __Milton__, being

the rear portions of Lots #34 and 35, on Map of Building Lots of George Spooner, said map being dated May 3, 1952, and filed for record in the office of the Town Clerk, Milton, Connecticut in Book 5, Page 16 of said Maps. Said parcel of land is more particularly described as:

Beginning at a point on the south line of Lot #34, on said map, 73.5 feet East of the East line of Park Avenue -- running thence North along land of James E. Beach, 100 feet to a point on the North line of Lot #35 on said map, 70.44 feet East of the said line to Cornwall Street, thence East along land of the said James E. Beach (being Lot #51 on said map) 55 feet -- thence South along land of Thomas Cook (being Lot #56 on said map) 100 feet to the aforesaid North line of Bartram Street -- thence West to the point of beginning.

Being the same premises earlier conveyed to the Settlor by an instrument dated __June 22, 1972__ and recorded in Vol. __371__, Page __490__ of the __Milton__ Land Records.

NOW, THEREFORE, KNOW ALL MEN BY THESE PRESENTS, that I do hereby acknowledge and declare that I hold and will hold said real property and all my right, title and interest in and to said property and all furniture, fixtures and personal property situated therein on the date of my death, IN TRUST

1. For the use and benefit of

(Name) __Elizabeth A. Brown - my wife__

__Milton__ __Connecticut__ __06605__
City / State / Zip

(Address) __525__ __Main Street__
Number / Street

6. The death during my lifetime, or in a common accident or disaster with me, of the beneficiary designated hereunder shall revoke such designation, and in the former event, I reserve the right to designate a new beneficiary. Should I for any reason fail to designate such new beneficiary, this trust shall terminate upon my death and the trust property shall revert to my estate.

7. In the event of my physical or mental incapacity or my death, I hereby nominate and appoint as Successor Trustee hereunder whosoever shall at that time be beneficiary hereunder, unless such beneficiary shall not have attained the age of 21 years or is otherwise legally incapacitated in which event I hereby nominate and appoint

(Name) __Henry P. Adams__

__Milton__ __Conn.__ __06605__
City / State / Zip

(Address) __125__ __Barnum Street__
Number / Street

to be Successor Trustee.

8. This Declaration of Trust shall extend to and be binding upon the heirs, executors, administrators and assigns of the undersigned and upon the Successors to the Trustee.

9. The Trustee and his successors shall serve without bond.

10. This Declaration of Trust shall be construed and enforced in accordance with the laws of the State of __Connecticut__

Declaration of Trust

WHEREAS, I, _____ , of the

City/Town of _____ , County of _____ , State of _____ ,

am the owner of certain real property located at (and known as) _____ ,

in the City/Town of _____ , State of _____ ,

which property is described more fully in the Deed conveying it from _____

to _____ , as "that certain piece or parcel of land with buildings

thereon standing, located in said _____ , being

Being the same premises earlier conveyed to the Settlor by an instrument dated _____ and

recorded in Vol. _____ , Page _____ of the _____ Land Records.

NOW, THEREFORE, KNOW ALL MEN BY THESE PRESENTS, that I do hereby acknowledge and declare that I hold and will hold said real property and all my right, title and interest in and to said property and all furniture, fixtures and personal property situated therein on the date of my death, IN TRUST

1. For the use and benefit of

(Name) _____ , of

(Address) _____
    Number   *Street*   *City*   *State*   *Zip*

If because of my physical or mental incapacity certified in writing by a physician, the Successor Trustee hereinafter named shall assume active administration of this trust during my lifetime, such Successor Trustee shall be fully authorized to pay to me or disburse on my behalf such sums from income or principal as appear necessary or desirable for my comfort or welfare. Upon my death, unless the beneficiary shall predecease me or unless we both shall die as a result of a common accident or disaster, my Successor Trustee is hereby directed forthwith to transfer said property and all right, title and interest in and to said property unto the beneficiary absolutely and thereby terminate this trust; provided, however, that if the beneficiary hereunder shall not have attained the age of 21 years, the Successor Trustee shall hold the trust assets in continuing trust until such beneficiary shall have attained the age of 21 years. During such period of continuing trust the Successor Trustee, in his absolute discretion, may retain the specific trust property herein described if he believes it in the best interest of the beneficiary so to do, or he may sell or otherwise dispose of such specific trust property, investing and reinvesting the proceeds as he may deem appropriate. If the specific trust property shall be productive of income or if it be sold or otherwise disposed of, the Successor Trustee may apply or expend any or all of the income or principal directly for the maintenance, education and support of the beneficiary without the intervention of any guardian and without application to any court. Such payments of income or principal may be made to the parents of such beneficiary or to the person with whom the beneficiary is living without any liability upon the Successor Trustee to see to the application thereof. If such beneficiary survives me but dies before attaining the age of 21 years, at his or her death the Successor Trustee shall transfer, pay over and deliver the trust property to such beneficiary's personal representative, absolutely.

2. The beneficiary hereunder shall be liable for his proportionate share of any taxes levied upon the Settlor's total taxable estate by reason of the Settlor's death.

3. All interests of a beneficiary hereunder shall be inalienable and free from anticipation, assignment, attachment, pledge or control by creditors or a present or former spouse of such beneficiary in any proceedings at law or in equity.

4. I reserve unto myself the power and right during my lifetime (1) to place a mortgage or other lien upon the property, (2) to collect any rental or other income which may accrue from the trust property and to pay such income to myself as an individual. I shall be exclusively entitled to all such income accruing from the trust property during my lifetime, and no beneficiary named herein shall have any claim upon any such income and/or profits distributed to me.

5. I reserve unto myself the power and right at any time during my lifetime to amend or revoke in whole or in part the trust hereby created without the necessity of obtaining the consent of the beneficiary and without giving notice to the beneficiary. The sale or other disposition by me of the whole or any part of the property held hereunder shall constitute as to such whole or part a revocation of this trust.

6. The death during my lifetime, or in a common accident or disaster with me, of the beneficiary designated hereunder shall revoke such designation, and in the former event, I reserve the right to designate a new beneficiary. Should I for any reason fail to designate such new beneficiary, this trust shall terminate upon my death and the trust property shall revert to my estate.

7. In the event of my physical or mental incapacity or my death, I hereby nominate and appoint as Successor Trustee hereunder whosoever shall at that time be beneficiary hereunder, unless such beneficiary shall not have attained the age of 21 years or is otherwise legally incapacitated in which event I hereby nominate and appoint

(Name) _____, of

(Address) _____
        Number   *Street*   *City*   *State*   *Zip*

to be Successor Trustee.

8. This Declaration of Trust shall extend to and be binding upon the heirs, executors, administrators and assigns of the undersigned and upon the Successors to the Trustee.

9. The Trustee and his successors shall serve without bond.

10. This Declaration of Trust shall be construed and enforced in accordance with the laws of the State

of _____.

IN WITNESS WHEREOF, I have hereunto set my hand and seal this _____

day of _____, 19_____.

        (Settlor sign here) _____ L.S.

I, the undersigned legal spouse of the Settlor, hereby waive all community property, dower or curtesy rights which I may have in the hereinabove-described property and give my assent to the provisions of the trust and to the inclusion in it of the said property.

        (Spouse sign here) _____ L.S.

Witness: (1) _____   Witness: (2) _____

STATE OF _____   City

COUNTY OF _____   or Town _____

On the _____ day of _____, 19_____, personally appeared

_____

known to me to be the individual(s) who executed the foregoing instrument, and acknowledged the same to be _____ free act and deed, before me.

_____

(Notary Seal)   *Notary Public*

CHAPTER 7

DECLARATION OF TRUST

For Naming

ONE PRIMARY BENEFICIARY

And

ONE CONTINGENT BENEFICIARY

To Receive

REAL ESTATE HELD IN ONE NAME

INSTRUCTIONS:

On the following pages will be found a declaration of trust (DT-102) suitable for use in connection with the establishment of an inter vivos trust covering real estate title to which is held in one name only, where it is desired to name *one* person as primary beneficiary, with some *one* other person as contingent beneficiary to receive the real estate if the primary beneficiary be not surviving.

Cross out *"city"* or *"town,"* leaving the appropriate designation of your community. If your house has no street number, cross out *"(and known as)."*

Enter the description of your property as it appears in the warranty deed or quit claim deed under which you acquired it. If it's too long to fit into the space, prune it judiciously to eliminate references to easements, rights of way, etc., and abbreviate wherever possible (e.g., *"SW"* for *"southwest"*). Next, enter in the space provided the date of that deed and the volume number and page number in the land records where it was recorded. (This information is generally to be found stamped in the upper margin of the old deed; sometimes *"Book"* or *"Liber"* is used instead of *"Vol."*)

Note that under this instrument, not only your house but also its entire contents—including your personal effects—will pass to the beneficiary named without going through probate. If you do *not* wish to include your furniture and personal effects in the trust, cross out *"and all furniture, fixtures and personal property situated therein"* and *initial it.*

Enter the names of the beneficiaries in the appropriate places in Paragraph 1.

Note that Paragraph 7 designates as Successor Trustee *"whosoever shall at that time be beneficiary hereunder,"* which means that in most cases you don't need to fill anything in there. However, if there is any possibility of a beneficiary who has not attained the age of 21 years receiving property, make certain that you name an adult in this paragraph who can act as trustee for such beneficiary. Avoid naming as trustee a person not likely to survive until the beneficiary has attained age 21.

When completed in the manner shown on the reverse side hereof, make several photocopies for reference purposes. The original of the declaration of trust and quit claim deed (see page 55) should then be filed with the town or county clerk or other office where real estate transfers in the area where the property is located are customarily recorded. After they are recorded, they will be returned to you.

Important: Read carefully Notes A and B on page 38. *Both* apply to this declaration of trust.

Declaration of Trust

WHEREAS, I, __John J. Brown__, County of __Fairfax__, State of __Connecticut__, of the

Town of __Milton__, am the owner of certain real property located at (and known as) __525 Main Street__

in the Town of __Milton__, State of __Connecticut__

which property is described more fully in the Deed conveying it from __Henry B. Green__, as "that certain piece or parcel of land with buildings

to __John J. Brown__

thereon standing, located in said __Milton__, being

particularly described as:

the rear portions of Lots #34 and 35, on Map of Building Lots of George Spooner, said map being dated May 3, 1952, and filed for record in the office of the Town Clerk, Milton, Connecticut in Book 5, Page 16 of said Maps. Said parcel of land is more particularly described as:

Beginning at a point on the south line of Lot #34, on said map, 73.5 feet East of the East line of Park Avenue -- running thence North along land of James E. Beach, 100 feet to a point on the line of Lot #35 on said map, 70.44 feet East of the East line to Cornwall Street, thence East along land of the said James E. Beach (being Lot #51 on said map) 55 feet -- thence South along land of Thomas Cook (being Lot #56 on said map) 100 feet to the aforesaid North line of Bartram Street -- thence West to the point of beginning.

Being the same premises earlier conveyed to the Settlor by an instrument dated __June 22, 1972__ and recorded in Vol. __371__, Page __490__ of the __Milton__ Land Records.

NOW, THEREFORE, KNOW ALL MEN BY THESE PRESENTS, that I do hereby acknowledge and declare that I hold and will hold said real property and all my right, title and interest in and to said property and all furniture, fixtures and personal property situated therein on the date of my death, IN TRUST

1. For the use and benefit of

(Name) __Elizabeth A. Brown - my wife__

(Address) __525   Main Street__ __Milton__ __Connecticut__ __06605__
            Number   Street   City   State   Zip

or, if such beneficiary be not surviving, for the use and benefit of

(Name) __Dorothy Lynn - my niece__

(Address) __566   Midland Street__ __Portland__ __Wisconsin__ __53123__
            Number   Street   City   State   Zip

If because of my physical or mental incapacity certified in writing by a physician, the Successor Trustee hereinafter named shall assume active administration of this trust during my lifetime, such Successor Trustee shall be fully authorized to pay to me or disburse on my behalf such sums from income or principal as appear necessary or desirable for my comfort or welfare. Upon my death, unless the beneficiaries shall predecease me or unless we all shall die as a result of a common accident or disaster, my Successor Trustee is hereby directed forthwith to transfer said property and all my right, title and interest in and to said property unto the beneficiary absolutely and thereby terminate this trust; provided, however, that if the beneficiary hereunder shall not have attained the age of 21 years, the Successor Trustee shall hold the trust assets in continuing trust until such beneficiary shall

... hereunder shall revoke such designation, and in the former event, I reserve the right to designate a new beneficiary. Should I for any reason fail to designate such new beneficiary, this trust shall terminate upon my death and the trust property shall revert to my estate.

7. In the event of my death or legal incapacity, I hereby nominate and appoint as Successor Trustee hereunder whosoever shall at that time be beneficiary hereunder, unless such beneficiary shall not have attained the age of 21 years or is otherwise legally incapacitated in which event I hereby nominate and appoint

(Name) __Henry P. Adams__ __Milton__ __Connecticut__ __06605__
                                        City   State   Zip

(Address) __125   Barnum Street__
            Number   Street

to be Successor Trustee.

8. This Declaration of Trust shall extend to and be binding upon the heirs, executors, administrators and assigns of the undersigned and upon the Successors to the Trustee.

9. The Trustee and his successors shall serve without bond.

10. This Declaration of Trust shall be construed and enforced in accordance with the laws of the State of __Connecticut__

Declaration of Trust

WHEREAS, I, _____, of the

City/Town of _____, County of _____, State of _____,

am the owner of certain real property located at (and known as) _____,

in the City/Town of _____, State of _____,

which property is described more fully in the Deed conveying it from _____

to _____, as "that certain piece or parcel of land with buildings

thereon standing, located in said _____, being

Being the same premises earlier conveyed to the Settlor by an instrument dated _____ and

recorded in Vol. _____, Page _____ of the _____ Land Records.

NOW, THEREFORE, KNOW ALL MEN BY THESE PRESENTS, that I do hereby acknowledge and declare that I hold and will hold said real property and all my right, title and interest in and to said property and all furniture, fixtures and personal property situated therein on the date of my death, IN TRUST

1. For the use and benefit of

(Name) _____, of

(Address) _____
      Number   *Street*   *City*   *State*   *Zip*

or, if such beneficiary be not surviving, for the use and benefit of

(Name) _____, of

(Address) _____
      Number   *Street*   *City*   *State*   *Zip*

If because of my physical or mental incapacity certified in writing by a physician, the Successor Trustee hereinafter named shall assume active administration of this trust during my lifetime, such Successor Trustee shall be fully authorized to pay to me or disburse on my behalf such sums from income or principal as appear necessary or desirable for my comfort or welfare. Upon my death, unless the beneficiaries shall predecease me or unless we all shall die as a result of a common accident or disaster, my Successor Trustee is hereby directed forthwith to transfer said property and all my right, title and interest in and to said property unto the beneficiary absolutely and thereby terminate this trust; provided, however, that if the beneficiary hereunder shall not have attained the age of 21 years, the Successor Trustee shall hold the trust assets in continuing trust until such beneficiary shall have attained the age of 21 years. During such period of continuing trust the Successor Trustee, in his absolute discretion, may retain the specific trust property herein described if he believes it in the best interest of the beneficiary so to do, or he may sell or otherwise dispose of such specific trust property, investing and reinvesting the proceeds as he may deem appropriate. If the specific trust property shall be productive of income or if it be sold or otherwise disposed of, the Successor Trustee may apply or expend any or all of the income or principal directly for the maintenance, education and support of the beneficiary without the intervention of any guardian and without application to any court. Such payments of income or principal may be made to the parents of such beneficiary or to the person with whom the beneficiary is living without any liability upon the Successor Trustee to see to the application thereof. If such beneficiary survives me but dies before the age of 21 years, at his or her death the Successor Trustee shall transfer, pay over and deliver the trust property being held for such beneficiary to such beneficiary's personal representative, absolutely.

2. The beneficiary hereunder shall be liable for his proportionate share of any taxes levied upon the Settlor's total taxable estate by reason of the Settlor's death.

3. All interests of a beneficiary hereunder shall be inalienable and free from anticipation, assignment, attachment, pledge or control by creditors or a present or former spouse of such beneficiary in any proceedings at law or in equity.

4. I reserve unto myself the power and right during my lifetime (1) to place a mortgage or other lien upon the property, (2) to collect any rental or other income which may accrue from the trust property and to pay such income to myself as an individual. I shall be exclusively entitled to all such income accruing from the trust property during my lifetime, and no beneficiary named herein shall have any claim upon any such income and/or profits distributed to me.

5. I reserve unto myself the power and right at any time during my lifetime to amend or revoke in whole or in part the trust hereby created without the necessity of obtaining the consent of the beneficiaries and without giving notice to the beneficiaries. The sale or other disposition by me of the whole or any part of the property held hereunder shall constitute as to such whole or part a revocation of this trust.

6. The death during my lifetime, or in a common accident or disaster with me, of both of the beneficiaries designated hereunder shall revoke such designation, and in the former event, I reserve the right to designate a new beneficiary. Should I for any reason fail to designate such new beneficiary, this trust shall terminate upon my death and the trust property shall revert to my estate.

7. In the event of my death or legal incapacity, I hereby nominate and appoint as Successor Trustee hereunder whosoever shall at that time be beneficiary hereunder, unless such beneficiary shall not have attained the age of 21 years or is otherwise legally incapacitated in which event I hereby nominate and appoint

(Name) _____ , of

(Address) _____
           Number   *Street*   *City*   *State*   *Zip*

to be Successor Trustee.

8. This Declaration of Trust shall extend to and be binding upon the heirs, executors, administrators and assigns of the undersigned and upon the Successors to the Trustee.

9. The Trustee and his successors shall serve without bond.

10. This Declaration of Trust shall be construed and enforced in accordance with the laws of the State

of _____ .

IN WITNESS WHEREOF, I have hereunto set my hand and seal this _____

day of _____ , 19_____ .

          (Settlor sign here) _____ L.S.

I, the undersigned legal spouse of the Settlor, hereby waive all community property, dower or curtesy rights which I may have in the hereinabove-described property and give my assent to the provisions of the trust and to the inclusion in it of the said property.

        (Spouse sign here) _____ L.S.

Witness: (1) _____   Witness: (2) _____

STATE OF _____   City

                                      or

COUNTY OF _____   Town _____

On the _____ day of _____ , 19_____ , personally appeared

_____

known to me to be the individual(s) who executed the foregoing instrument, and acknowledged the same to be _____ free act and deed, before me.

(Notary Seal)   _____

                                                            Notary Public

CHAPTER 7

DECLARATION OF TRUST
For Naming
TWO OR MORE BENEFICIARIES,
SHARING EQUALLY,
To Receive
REAL ESTATE HELD IN ONE NAME

INSTRUCTIONS:

On the following pages will be found a declaration of trust (DT-103) suitable for use in connection with the establishment of an inter vivos trust covering real estate title to which is held in one name only, where it is desired to name two or more persons to share equally upon the death of the owner.

Cross out *"city"* or *"town,"* leaving the appropriate designation of your community. If your house has no street number, cross out *"(and known as)."*

Enter the description of your property as it appears in the warranty deed or quit claim deed under which you acquired it. If it's too long to fit into the space, prune it judiciously to eliminate references to easements, rights of way, etc., and abbreviate wherever possible (e.g., *"SW"* for *"southwest"*). Next, enter in the space provided the date of that deed and the volume number and page number in the land records where it was recorded. (This information is generally to be found stamped in the upper margin of the old deed; sometimes *"Book"* or *"Liber"* is used instead of *"Vol."*)

Note that under this instrument, not only your house but also its entire contents—including your personal effects—will pass to the beneficiaries named without going through probate. If you do *not* wish to include your furniture and personal effects in the trust, cross out *"and all furniture, fixtures and personal property situated therein"* and *initial it.*

Note that the instrument specifies that the named beneficiaries are to receive *"in equal shares, or the survivor of them/per stirpes."* Now, think carefully: If you have named three persons with the understanding that if one of them predeceases you, his children are to receive his share, cross out *"or the survivor of them"* and *initial it.* If that is *not* what you want—if, for example, you prefer that the share of the deceased person be divided between the two surviving persons, cross out *"per stirpes"* and *initial it.* Remember, you <u>must</u> cross out *"or the survivor of them"* or *"per stirpes"*— one or the other.

In Paragraph 1, enter the *number of persons* you are naming (to discourage unauthorized additions to the list) and then insert their names. The one whose name appears *first* will be the Successor Trustee responsible for seeing to the distribution of the trust property.

Whenever there is any possibility of a beneficiary who has not attained the age of 21 years receiving any portion of the property, make certain that you name an adult who can act as trustee for such beneficiary. The name of that adult should be inserted in Paragraph 7 of the instrument shown here. Avoid naming as trustee a person not likely to survive until the beneficiary has attained age 21.

When completed in the manner shown on the reverse side hereof, make several photocopies for reference purposes. The original of the declaration of trust and the quit claim deed (see page 55) should then be filed with the town or county clerk or other office where real estate transfers in the area where the property is located are customarily recorded. After they are recorded, they will be returned to you.

Important: Read carefully Notes A and B on page 38. *Both* apply to this declaration of trust.

DT-103

Declaration of Trust

WHEREAS, I, __John J. Brown__, County of __Fairfax__, State of __Connecticut__, of the

Town of __Milton__, am the owner of certain real property located at (and known as) __525 Main Street__, State of __Connecticut__

in the Town of __Milton__, which property is described more fully in the Deed conveying it from __Henry B. Green__, as "that certain piece or parcel of land with buildings

to __John J. Brown__ __Milton__, being thereon standing, located in said __John J. Brown__ __Milton__

particularly described as:

the rear portions of Lots #34 and 35, on Map of Building Lots of George Spooner, said map being dated May 3, 1952, and filed for record in the office of the Town Clerk, Milton, Connecticut in Book 5, Page 16 of said Maps. Said parcel of land is more particularly described as:

Beginning at a point on the south line of Lot #34, on said map, 73.5 feet East of the East line of Park Avenue -- running thence North along land of James E. Beach, 100 feet to a point on the North line of Lot #35 on said map, 70.44 feet East of the said line to Cornwall Street, thence East along land of the said James E. Beach (being Lot #51 on said map) 55 feet -- thence South along land of Thomas Cook (being Lot #56 on said map) 100 feet to the aforesaid North line of Bartram Street -- thence West to the point of beginning.

Being the same premises earlier conveyed to the Settlor by an instrument dated __June 22, 1972__ and recorded in Vol. __371__, Page __490__ of the __Milton__ Land Records.

NOW, THEREFORE, KNOW ALL MEN BY THESE PRESENTS, that I do hereby acknowledge and declare that I hold and will hold said real property and all my right, title and interest in and to said property and all furniture, fixtures and personal property situated therein on the date of my death, IN TRUST   __J.J.B.__   /per

1. For the use and benefit of the following __three (3)__ persons, in equal shares, /
stirpes:

> Thomas B. Brown - my brother
> Helen M. Brown - my sister
> Charles M. Brown - my brother

If because of my physical or mental incapacity certified in writing by a physician, the Successor Trustee hereinafter named shall assume active administration of this trust during my lifetime, such Successor Trustee shall be fully authorized to pay to me

my estate.

7. In the event of my physical or mental incapacity or my death, I hereby nominate and appoint as Successor Trustee hereunder the beneficiary named first above, unless such beneficiary shall not have attained the age of 21 years, or is otherwise legally incapacitated, in which event I hereby nominate and appoint as Successor Trustee hereunder the beneficiary named second above. If such beneficiary named second above shall not have attained the age of 21 years, or is otherwise legally incapacitated, then I nominate and appoint

(Name) __Henry P. Adams__   __Milton__ City   __Connecticut__ State   __06605__ Zip

(Address) __125__ Number   __Barnum Street__ Street

to be Successor Trustee.

8. This Declaration of Trust shall extend to and be binding upon the heirs, executors, administrators and assigns of the undersigned and upon the Successors to the Trustee.

9. The Trustee and his successors shall serve without bond.

10. This Declaration of Trust shall be construed and enforced in accordance with the laws of the State

of __Connecticut__

DACEY
TRUST

Declaration of Trust

WHEREAS, I, _____, of the

City/Town of _____, County of _____, State of _____,

am the owner of certain real property located at (and known as) _____,

in the City/Town of _____, State of _____,

which property is described more fully in the Deed conveying it from _____

to _____, as "that certain piece or parcel of land with buildings

thereon standing, located in said _____, being

Being the same premises earlier conveyed to the Settlor by an instrument dated _____ and

recorded in Vol. _____, Page _____ of the _____ Land Records.

NOW, THEREFORE, KNOW ALL MEN BY THESE PRESENTS, that I do hereby acknowledge and declare that I hold and will hold said real property and all my right, title and interest in and to said property and all furniture, fixtures and personal property situated therein on the date of my death, IN TRUST

1. For the use and benefit of the following _____ persons, in equal shares, or the survivor of them/per stirpes:

If because of my physical or mental incapacity certified in writing by a physician, the Successor Trustee hereinafter named shall assume active administration of this trust during my lifetime, such Successor Trustee shall be fully authorized to pay to me or disburse on my behalf such sums from income or principal as appear necessary or desirable for my comfort or welfare. Upon my death, unless all the beneficiaries shall predecease me or unless we all shall die as a result of a common accident or disaster, my Successor Trustee is hereby directed forthwith to transfer said property and all right, title and interest in and to said property unto the beneficiaries absolutely and thereby terminate this trust; provided, however, that if any beneficiary hereunder shall not have attained the age of 21 years, the Successor Trustee shall hold such beneficiary's share of the trust assets in continuing trust until such beneficiary shall have attained the age of 21 years. During such period of continuing trust the Successor Trustee, in his absolute discretion, may retain the specific trust property herein described if he believes it in the best interests of the beneficiary so to do, or he may sell or otherwise dispose of such specific trust property, investing and reinvesting the proceeds as he may deem appropriate. If the specific trust property shall be productive of income or if it be sold or otherwise disposed of, the Successor Trustee may apply or expend any or all of the income or principal directly for the maintenance, education and support of the beneficiary without the intervention of any guardian and without application to any court. Such payments of income or principal may be made to the parents of such beneficiary or to the person with whom the beneficiary is living without any liability upon the Successor Trustee to see to the application thereof. If such beneficiary survives me but dies before attaining the age of 21 years, at his or her death the Successor Trustee shall transfer, pay over and deliver the trust property being held for such beneficiary to such beneficiary's personal representative, absolutely.

    2. Each beneficiary hereunder shall be liable for his proportionate share of any taxes levied upon the Settlor's total taxable estate by reason of the Settlor's death.

    3. All interests of a beneficiary hereunder shall be inalienable and free from anticipation, assignment, attachment, pledge or control by creditors or by a present or former spouse of such beneficiary in any proceedings at law or in equity.

    4. I reserve unto myself the power and right during my lifetime (1) to place a mortgage or other lien upon the property, (2) to collect any rental or other income which may accrue from the trust property and to pay such income to myself as an individual. I shall be exclusively entitled to all such income accruing from the trust property during my lifetime, and no beneficiary named herein shall have any claim upon any such income and/or profits distributed to me.

    5. I reserve unto myself the power and right at any time during my lifetime to amend or revoke in whole or in part the trust hereby created without the necessity of obtaining the consent of any beneficiary and without giving notice to any beneficiary. The sale or other disposition by me of the whole or any part of the property held hereunder shall constitute as to such whole or part a revocation of this trust.

    6. The death during my lifetime, or in a common accident or disaster with me, of all of the beneficiaries designated hereunder shall revoke such designation, and in the former event, I reserve the right to designate new beneficiaries. Should I for any reason fail to designate such new beneficiaries, this trust shall terminate upon my death and the trust property shall revert to my estate.

    7. In the event of my physical or mental incapacity or my death, I hereby nominate and appoint as Successor Trustee hereunder the beneficiary named first above, unless such beneficiary shall not have attained the age of 21 years, or is otherwise legally incapacitated, in which event I hereby nominate and appoint as Successor Trustee hereunder the beneficiary named second above. If such beneficiary named second above shall not have attained the age of 21 years, or is otherwise legally incapacitated, then I nominate and appoint

(Name) _____ , of

(Address) _____
               Number   *Street*   *City*   *State*   *Zip*

to be Successor Trustee.

    8. This Declaration of Trust shall extend to and be binding upon the heirs, executors, administrators and assigns of the undersigned and upon the Successors to the Trustee.

    9. The Trustee and his successors shall serve without bond.

    10. This Declaration of Trust shall be construed and enforced in accordance with the laws of the State

of _____ .

    IN WITNESS WHEREOF, I have hereunto set my hand and seal this _____

day of _____ , 19_____ .

               (Settlor sign here) _____ L.S.

I, the undersigned legal spouse of the Settlor, hereby waive all community property, dower or curtesy rights which I may have in the hereinabove-described property and give my assent to the provisions of the trust and to the inclusion in it of the said property.

            (Spouse sign here) _____ L.S.

Witness: (1) _____   Witness: (2) _____

STATE OF _____   City
                                            or
COUNTY OF _____   Town _____

    On the _____ day of _____ , 19_____ , personally appeared

_____

known to me to be the individual(s) who executed the foregoing instrument, and acknowledged the same to be _____ free act and deed, before me.

_____

(Notary Seal)   *Notary Public*

CHAPTER 7

DECLARATION OF TRUST
For Naming
ONE PRIMARY BENEFICIARY WITH YOUR CHILDREN,
SHARING EQUALLY, AS CONTINGENT BENEFICIARIES
To Receive
REAL ESTATE HELD IN ONE NAME

INSTRUCTIONS:

On the following pages will be found a declaration of trust (DT-104) suitable for use in connection with the establishment of an inter vivos trust covering real estate title to which is held in one name only, where it is desired to name one person (ordinarily, but not necessarily, one's spouse) as primary beneficiary, with one's children as contingent beneficiaries to receive the real estate if the primary beneficiary be not surviving upon the death of the owner.

Cross out *"city"* or *"town,"* leaving the appropriate designation of your community. If your house has no street number, cross out *"(and known as)."*

Enter the description of your property as it appears in the warranty deed or quit claim deed under which you acquired it. If it's too long to fit into the space, prune it judiciously to eliminate references to easements, rights of way, etc., and abbreviate wherever possible (e.g., *"SW"* for *"southwest"*). Next, enter in the space provided the date of that deed and the volume number and page number in the land records where it was recorded. (This information is generally to be found stamped in the upper margin of the old deed; sometimes *"Book"* or *"Liber"* is used instead of *"Vol."*)

Note that under this instrument, not only your house but also its entire contents—including your personal effects—will pass to the beneficiary named without going through probate. If you do *not* wish to include your furniture and personal effects in the trust, cross out *"and all furniture, fixtures and personal property situated therein"* and *initial it.*

Enter the name of the primary beneficiary in the appropriate place in Paragraph 1. Note that the instrument first refers to your children as *"natural not/or adopted."* Now, decide: If you have an adopted child and you wish to *include* him, cross out the word *"not"* in the phrase *"natural not/or adopted"* and *initial it.* If you wish to *exclude* your adopted child, cross out the word *"or"* in the same phrase and *initial it.* Remember, you *must* cross out *"not"* or *"or"*—one or the other. If you have no adopted child, cross out *"not."*

Note next that the instrument specifies that your children are to receive *"in equal shares, or the survivor of them/per stirpes."* Now, think carefully: If it is your wish that if one of your children does not survive you, *his* share will revert to *his* children in equal shares, cross out *"or the survivor of them"* and *initial it.* If that is *not* what you want—that is, if you prefer that the share of any child of yours who predeceases you shall be divided between your other surviving children in equal shares, cross out *"per stirpes"* and *initial it.* Remember, you <u>must</u> cross out *"or the survivor of them"* or *"per stirpes"*—one or the other.

Note that in Paragraph 7, the "First Beneficiary" is designated as Successor Trustee, while a space is provided in which you should designate another person to act if the named Successor Trustee is not surviving or otherwise fails or ceases to act. This could be one of your children, for example, but it must be an adult who can act as trustee for any beneficiary who comes into a share of the trust before he reaches the age of 21 years. Bear in mind that if you have named your children to receive "in equal shares per stirpes," and one of them has died leaving children surviving, the Successor Trustee may be called upon to administer the funds for these, your grandchildren, until they reach age 21. Avoid naming someone not likely to survive until the youngest such beneficiary has attained age 21.

When completed in the manner shown on the reverse side hereof, make several photocopies for reference purposes. The original of the declaration of trust and the quit claim deed (see page 55) should then be filed with the town or county clerk or other office where real estate transfers in the area where the property is located are customarily recorded. After they are recorded, they will be returned to you.

Important: Read carefully Notes A and B on page 38. *Both* apply to this declaration of trust.

Declaration of Trust

WHEREAS, I, __John J. Brown__, County of __Fairfax__, State of __Connecticut__, of the Town of __Milton__,

am the owner of certain real property located at (and known as) __525 Main Street__

in the Town of __Milton__, State of __Connecticut__,

which property is described more fully in the Deed conveying it from __Henry B. Green__, as "that certain piece or parcel of land with buildings

to __John J. Brown__, being

thereon standing, located in said __Milton__

the rear portions of Lots #34 and 35, on Map of Building Lots of George Spooner, said map being dated May 3, 1952, and filed for record in the office of the Town Clerk, Milton, Connecticut in Book 5, Page 16 of said Maps. Said parcel of land is more particularly described as:

Beginning at a point on the south line of Lot #34, on said map, 73.5 feet East of the East line of Park Avenue -- running thence North along land of James E. Beach, 100 feet to a point on the North line of Lot #35 on said map, 70.44 feet East of the East line to Cornwall Street, thence East along land of the said James E. Beach (being Lot #51 on said map) 55 feet -- thence South along land of Thomas Cook (being Lot #56 on said map) 100 feet to the aforesaid North line of Bartram Street -- thence West to the point of beginning.

Being the same premises earlier conveyed to the Settlor by an instrument dated __June 22, 1972__ and recorded in Vol. __371__, Page __490__ of the __Milton__ Land Records.

NOW, THEREFORE, KNOW ALL MEN BY THESE PRESENTS, that I do hereby acknowledge and declare that I hold and will hold said real property and all my right, title and interest in and to said property and all furniture, fixtures and personal property situated therein on the date of my death, IN TRUST

1. For the use and benefit of

(Name) __Elizabeth A. Brown - my wife__ __Milton__ City __Connecticut__ State __06605__ Zip, of

(Address) __525__ Number __Main Street__ Street

(hereinafter referred to as the "First Beneficiary") and upon his or her death prior to the termination of the trust, for the use and benefit of my children, natural not adopted, in equal shares or the survivor of them.

If because of my physical or mental incapacity certified in writing by a physician, the Successor Trustee hereinafter named shall assume active administration of this trust during my lifetime, such Successor Trustee shall be fully authorized to pay to me or disburse on my behalf such sums from income or principal as appear necessary or desirable for my comfort or welfare. Upon my death, unless all the beneficiaries shall predecease me or unless we all shall die as a result of a common accident or disaster, my Successor Trustee is hereby directed forthwith to transfer said property and all right, title and interest in and to said property unto the beneficiary or beneficiaries absolutely and thereby terminate this trust; provided, however, that if any beneficiary hereunder shall not have attained the age of 21 years, the Successor Trustee shall hold such beneficiary's share of the trust assets

... revocation of this trust.

6. The death during my lifetime, or in a common accident or disaster with me, of all the beneficiaries designated hereunder shall revoke such designation, and in the former event, I reserve the right to designate a new beneficiary. Should I for any reason fail to designate such new beneficiary, this trust shall terminate upon my death and the trust property shall revert to my estate.

7. In the event of my death or legal incapacity, I hereby nominate and appoint as Successor Trustee hereunder the First Beneficiary, and upon his or her failure or ceasing to act, then I nominate and appoint

(Name) __Henry P. Adams__ __Milton__ City __Connecticut__ State __06605__ Zip, of

(Address) __125__ Number __Barnum Street__ Street

as Successor Trustee, and upon his or her failure or ceasing to act or should I for any reason fail to designate the person above intended to be nominated, then I nominate and appoint as such Successor Trustee hereunder whosoever shall qualify as executor, administrator or guardian, as the case may be, of my estate.

Declaration of Trust

WHEREAS, I, _____, of the

City/Town of _____, County of _____, State of _____,

am the owner of certain real property located at (and known as)_____,

in the City/Town of _____, State of _____,

which property is described more fully in the Deed conveying it from _____

to _____, as "that certain piece or parcel of land with buildings

thereon standing, located in said _____, being

Being the same premises earlier conveyed to the Settlor by an instrument dated _____ and

recorded in Vol. _____, Page _____ of the _____ Land Records.

NOW, THEREFORE, KNOW ALL MEN BY THESE PRESENTS, that I do hereby acknowledge and declare that I hold and will hold said real property and all my right, title and interest in and to said property and all furniture, fixtures and personal property situated therein on the date of my death, IN TRUST

1. For the use and benefit of

(Name) _____, of

(Address) _____

| Number | Street | City | State | Zip |

(hereinafter referred to as the "First Beneficiary") and upon his or her death prior to the termination of the trust, for the use and benefit of my children, natural not/or adopted, in equal shares or the survivor of them/per stirpes.

If because of my physical or mental incapacity certified in writing by a physician, the Successor Trustee hereinafter named shall assume active administration of this trust during my lifetime, such Successor Trustee shall be fully authorized to pay to me or disburse on my behalf such sums from income or principal as appear necessary or desirable for my comfort or welfare. Upon my death, unless all the beneficiaries shall predecease me or unless we all shall die as a result of a common accident or disaster, my Successor Trustee is hereby directed forthwith to transfer said property and all right, title and interest in and to said property unto the beneficiary or beneficiaries absolutely and thereby terminate this trust; provided, however, that if any beneficiary hereunder shall not have attained the age of 21 years, the Successor Trustee shall hold such beneficiary's share of the trust assets in continuing trust until such beneficiary shall have attained the age of 21 years. During such period of continuing trust the

Successor Trustee, in his absolute discretion, may retain the specific trust property herein described if he believes it in the best interests of the beneficiary so to do, or he may sell or otherwise dispose of such specific trust property, investing and reinvesting the proceeds as he may deem appropriate. If the specific trust property shall be productive of income or if it be sold or otherwise disposed of, the Successor Trustee may apply or expend any or all of the income or principal directly for the maintenance, education and support of the beneficiary without the intervention of any guardian and without application to any court. Such payments of income or principal may be made to the parents of such beneficiary or to the person with whom the beneficiary is living without any liability upon the Successor Trustee to see to the application thereof. If such beneficiary survives me but dies before attaining the age of 21 years, at his or her death the Successor Trustee shall transfer, pay over and deliver the trust property being held for such beneficiary to such beneficiary's personal representative, absolutely.

    2. Any beneficiary hereunder shall be liable for his proportionate share of any taxes levied upon the Settlor's total taxable estate by reason of the Settlor's death.

    3. All interests of a beneficiary hereunder shall be inalienable and free from anticipation, assignment, attachment, pledge or control by creditors or by a present or former spouse of such beneficiary in any proceedings at law or in equity.

    4. I reserve unto myself the power and right during my lifetime (1) to place a mortgage or other lien upon the property, (2) to collect any rental or other income which may accrue from the trust property and to pay such income to myself as an individual. I shall be exclusively entitled to all such income accruing from the trust property during my lifetime, and no beneficiary named herein shall have any claim upon any such income and/or profits distributed to me.

    5. I reserve unto myself the power and right at any time during my lifetime to amend or revoke in whole or in part the trust hereby created without the necessity of obtaining the consent of any beneficiary and without giving notice to any beneficiary. The sale or other disposition by me of the whole or any part of the property held hereunder shall constitute as to such whole or part a revocation of this trust.

    6. The death during my lifetime, or in a common accident or disaster with me, of all the beneficiaries designated hereunder shall revoke such designation, and in the former event, I reserve the right to designate a new beneficiary. Should I for any reason fail to designate such new beneficiary, this trust shall terminate upon my death and the trust property shall revert to my estate.

    7. In the event of my death or legal incapacity, I hereby nominate and appoint as Successor Trustee hereunder the First Beneficiary, and upon his or her failure or ceasing to act, then I nominate and appoint

(Name) _____, of

(Address) _____
             Number   *Street*   *City*   *State*   *Zip*

as Successor Trustee, and upon his or her failure or ceasing to act or should I for any reason fail to designate the person above intended to be nominated, then I nominate and appoint as such Successor Trustee hereunder whosoever shall qualify as executor, administrator or guardian, as the case may be, of my estate.

    8. This Declaration of Trust shall extend to and be binding upon the heirs, executors, administrators and assigns of the undersigned and upon the Successors to the Trustee.

    9. The Trustee and his successors shall serve without bond.

    10. This Declaration of Trust shall be construed and enforced in accordance with the laws of the State

of _____.

    IN WITNESS WHEREOF, I have hereunto set my hand and seal this _____

day of _____, 19_____.

               (Settlor sign here) _____ L.S.

I, the undersigned legal spouse of the Settlor, hereby waive all community property, dower or curtesy rights which I may have in the hereinabove-described property and give my assent to the provisions of the trust and to the inclusion in it of the said property.

               (Spouse sign here) _____ L.S.

Witness: (1) _____   Witness: (2) _____

STATE OF _____   City

COUNTY OF _____   or Town _____

    On the _____ day of _____, 19_____, personally appeared

_____

known to me to be the individual(s) who executed the foregoing instrument, and acknowledged the same to be _____ free act and deed, before me.

                        _____

(Notary Seal)   *Notary Public*

CHAPTER 7

QUIT CLAIM DEED,
COVERING REAL ESTATE
HELD IN ONE NAME
(FOR USE WITH DT-101, DT-102,
DT-103, or DT-104)

INSTRUCTIONS:

One or the other of two legal documents is ordinarily used to transfer title to real estate—a warranty deed or a quit claim deed.

When you buy a house, the owner gives you a warranty deed by which he "warrants" or guarantees that the house is his to sell. With that deed, you can hold him responsible if someone else turns up with a valid claim to ownership of the property.

If he gave you a quit claim deed, he would be providing no guarantee at all that he actually owned the property. He'd be saying: "Whatever title or claim I may have to this property I am turning over to you."

When you buy a house, then, you're not satisfied with a quit claim deed; you insist upon being given a warranty deed. The quit claim deed is used when property is being transferred from one member of a family to another, with no financial consideration being involved, or when one of two co-owners, not necessarily related, wishes to transfer his interest in the property to the other co-owner with or without a financial consideration being involved. They know each other and they know that they own the property between them, and there is no need for the retiring co-owner to "warrant" to the other that he owns one-half of the property.

In connection with the transfer of the title to your real estate from yourself as an individual to yourself as trustee, as explained in Chapter 7, a quit claim deed will be found on page 57 which will adequately serve your purpose.

Enter your name and the *date* of the declaration of trust (DT-101, DT-102, DT-103, or DT-104) which you have executed. In the large space provided, enter the description of the property as it appears in the declaration of trust. If it's too long to fit into the space, prune it judiciously to eliminate references to easements, rights of way, etc., and abbreviate wherever possible (e.g., "*SW*" for "*southwest*"). You are deeding it to yourself and you need only adequately identify the property. Below the description of the property is a place for you to insert the old deed's date and details of its recording. On the back of the quit claim deed, insert your name twice: first under "From," and again under "To."

After you have signed the quit claim deed as "Releasor" in the presence of two witnesses and had it notarized, make several photocopies for reference purposes. Thereafter, the original of the quit claim deed and the declaration of trust should be filed with the town or county clerk or other office where real estate transfers in the area where the property is located are customarily recorded. After they are recorded, they will be returned to you.

Important: Read carefully Notes A and B on page 38. *Both* apply to this quit claim deed.

QUIT CLAIM DEED

QCD

To All People To Whom These Presents Shall Come, Greetings;

, in conformity with the terms of a certain

KNOW YE, THAT I,

John J. Brown _____ April 2, 1980 , do by these presents release

(Name) _____ Declaration of Trust executed by me under date of _____ under the terms of such Declaration of Trust, and to my successors as Trustee under and forever Quit-Claim to myself as Trustee under the terms of such Declaration of Trust, all right, title, interest, claim and demand whatsoever which I as Releasor have or ought to have in or to the property located at:

525 Main Street, Milton, Connecticut, being the rear portions of Lots #34 and 35, on Map of Building Lots of George Spooner, said map being dated May 3, 1952, and filed for record in the office of the Town Clerk, Milton, Connecticut in Book 5, Page 15 of said maps. Said parcel of land is more particularly described as :

Beginning at a point on the south line of Lot #34, on said map, 73.5 feet East of the East line of Park Avenue -- running thence North along land of James E. Beach, 100 feet to a point on the North line of Lot #35 on said map, 70.44 feet East of the East line to Cornwall Street, thence East along land of the said James E.Beach (being Lot #51 on said map) 55 feet -- thence South along land of Thomas Cook (being Lot #56 on said map) 100 feet to the aforesaid North line of Bartram Street -- thence West to the point of beginning.

than One Dollar.

Being the same premises earlier conveyed to the Releasor by an instrument dated _____ July 14, 1960 _____ and

recorded in Vol. ___ 55 ___, Page ___ 613 ___ of the ___ Milton ___ Land Records.

QUIT CLAIM DEED

To All People To Whom These Presents Shall Come, Greetings;

KNOW YE, THAT I,

(Name) _____, in conformity with the terms of a certain

Declaration of Trust executed by me under date of _____, do by these presents release and forever Quit-Claim to myself as Trustee under the terms of such Declaration of Trust, and to my successors as Trustee under the terms of such Declaration of Trust, all right, title, interest, claim and demand whatsoever which I as Releasor have or ought to have in or to the property located at:

The consideration for this transfer is less than One Dollar.

Being the same premises earlier conveyed to the Releasor by an instrument dated _____ and

recorded in Vol. _____, Page _____ of the _____ Land Records.

To Have and to Hold the premises, with all the appurtenances, as such Trustee forever; and I declare and agree that neither I as an individual nor my heirs or assigns shall have or make any claim or demand upon such property.

IN WITNESS WHEREOF, I have hereunto set my hand and seal this _____

day of _____, 19_____.

_____ L.S.

Releasor (Owner)

I, the undersigned legal spouse of the above Releasor, hereby waive all community property, dower or curtesy rights which I may have in or to the hereinabove-described property.

(Spouse) _____ L.S.

Witness: (1) _____ Witness: (2) _____

STATE OF _____ City
or
COUNTY OF _____ Town _____

On the _____ day of _____, 19_____, personally appeared

_____

known to me to be the individual(s) who executed the foregoing instrument, and acknowledged the same to be _____ free act and deed, before me.

(Notary Seal)

_____
Notary Public

After recording, please return this instrument to:

State of _____

County of _____

The property affected by this instrument is situated in the City/Town of _____

by _____
Authorized Official

of the _____ Land Records

Vol. _____ on Page _____

at _____
Time
and recorded in

Received for record _____, 19_____

To

_____, Trustee

From

Quit Claim Deed

CHAPTER 7

DECLARATION OF TRUST
For Naming
ONE BENEFICIARY
To Receive
JOINTLY HELD REAL ESTATE

INSTRUCTIONS:

On the following pages will be found a declaration of trust (DT-101-J) suitable for use in connection with the establishment of an inter vivos trust covering real estate title to which is held in joint names, where it is desired to name one person to receive the real estate upon the death of the survivor of the two co-owners.

Enter the names of the two co-owners on the first line.

Cross out *"city"* or *"town,"* leaving the appropriate designation of your community. If your house has no street number, cross out *"(and known as)."*

Enter the description of your property as it appears in the warranty deed or quit claim deed under which you acquired it. If it's too long to fit into the space, prune it judiciously to eliminate references to easements, rights of way, etc., and abbreviate wherever possible (e.g., *"SW"* for *"southwest"*). Next, enter in the space provided the date of that deed and the volume number and page number in the land records where it was recorded. (This information is generally to be found stamped in the upper margin of the old deed; sometimes *"Book"* or *"Liber"* is used instead of *"Vol."*)

Note that under this instrument, not only your house but also its entire contents—including your personal effects—will pass to the beneficiary named without going through probate. If you do *not* wish to include your furniture and personal effects in the trust, cross out *"and all furniture, fixtures and personal property situated therein"* and *initial it.*

Enter the name of the beneficiary in the appropriate place in Paragraph 1.

Note that Paragraph 7 designates as Successor Trustee *"whosoever shall at that time be beneficiary hereunder,"* which means that in most cases you don't need to fill anything in there. However, if there is any possibility of a beneficiary who has not attained the age of 21 years receiving the property, make certain that you name an adult in this paragraph who can act as trustee for such beneficiary. Avoid naming as trustee a person not likely to survive until the beneficiary has attained age 21.

When completed in the manner shown on the reverse side hereof, make several photocopies for reference purposes. The original of the declaration of trust and the quit claim deed (see page 71) should then be filed with the town or county clerk or other office where real estate transfers in the area where the property is located are customarily recorded. After they are recorded, they will be returned to you.

Important: Read carefully Notes A and B on page 38. *Both* apply to this declaration of trust.

WHEREVER THE INSTRUCTION "INITIAL IT" APPEARS ABOVE,
IT MEANS THAT *BOTH* CO-OWNERS SHOULD INITIAL IT.

Declaration of Trust

WHEREAS, WE, __John J. Brown__ and __Elizabeth A. Brown__, of the City/Town, of __Milton__, County of __Fairfax__, State of __Connecticut__

are the owners as joint tenants of certain real property located at (and known as) __525 Main Street__

in the City/Town of __Milton__, State of __Connecticut__

which property is described more fully in the Deed conveying it from __Henry B. Green__

to __John J.Brown & Elizabeth A.Brown__, as "that certain piece or parcel of land with buildings thereon standing, located in said __Milton__, being

the rear portions of Lots #34 and 35, on Map of Building Lots of George Spooner, said map being dated May 3, 1952, and filed for record in the office of the Town Clerk, Milton, Connecticut in Book 5, Page 16 of said Maps. Said parcel of land is more particularly described as:

Beginning at a point on the south line of Lot #34, on said map, 73.5 feet East of the East line of Park Avenue -- running thence North along land of James E. Beach, 100 feet to a point on the line of Lot #35 on said map, 70.44 feet East of the said James E. Beach (being Lot #51 on said map) 55 feet -- thence South along land of Thomas Cook (being Lot #56 on said map) 100 feet to the aforesaid North line of Bartram Street -- thence West to the point of beginning.

Being the same premises earlier conveyed to the Settlors by an instrument dated __June 22, 1972__ and recorded in Vol. __371__, Page __490__ of the __Milton__ Land Records.

NOW, THEREFORE, KNOW ALL MEN BY THESE PRESENTS, that we do hereby acknowledge and declare that we hold and will hold said real property and all our right, title and interest in and to said property and all furniture, fixtures and personal property situated therein on the date of the death of the survivor of us, IN TRUST

1. For the use and benefit of __Jill A. Brown - our daughter__

(Name) _____ __Milton__ __Connecticut__ __06605__
City State Zip

(Address) __525__ __Main Street__
Number Street

If because of the physical or mental incapacity of both of us certified in writing by a physician, the Successor Trustee shall be fully hereinafter named shall assume active administration of this trust during our lifetime, such Successor Trustee shall be fully authorized to pay to us or disburse on our behalf such sums from income or principal as appear necessary or desirable for our comfort or welfare. Upon the death of the survivor of us, unless the beneficiary shall predecease us or unless we all die as a result of a common accident or disaster, our Successor Trustee is hereby directed forthwith to transfer said property and all right, title and interest in and to said property unto the beneficiary absolutely and thereby terminate this trust; provided, however, that if the beneficiary hereunder shall not have attained the age of 21 years, the Successor Trustee shall hold the trust in continuing trust until such beneficiary shall have attained the age of 21 years. During such period of continuing trust the Successor Trustee, in his absolute discretion, may retain the specific trust property herein described if he believes it in the best interest of the beneficiary so to do, or he may sell or otherwise dispose of such specific trust property, investing and reinvesting the proceeds as

part of the property, shall constitute as to such whole or part a revocation of this trust.

6. The death during our lifetime, or in a common accident or disaster with us, of the beneficiary designated hereunder shall revoke such designation, and in the former event, we reserve the right to designate a new beneficiary. Should we for any reason fail to designate such new beneficiary, this trust shall terminate upon the death of the survivor of us and the trust property shall revert to the estate of such survivor.

7. In the event of the physical or mental incapacity or death of one of us, the survivor shall continue as sole Trustee. In the event of the physical or mental incapacity or death of the survivor, or if we both shall die in a common accident, we hereby nominate and appoint as Successor Trustee hereunder whosoever shall at that time be beneficiary hereunder, unless such beneficiary shall not have attained the age of 21 years or is otherwise legally incapacitated, in which event we hereby nominate and appoint __Henry P. Adams__ __Milton__ __Connecticut__ __06605__
City State Zip

(Name) _____, of

(Address) __125__ __Barnum Street__
Number Street

to be Successor Trustee.

8. This Declaration of Trust shall extend to and be binding upon the heirs, executors, administrators and assigns of the undersigned and upon the Successors to the Trustees.

9. We as Trustees and our Successor Trustee shall serve without bond.

10. This Declaration of Trust shall be construed and enforced in accordance with the laws of the State of __Connecticut__

Declaration of Trust

WHEREAS, WE, _____ and _____, of the City/Town

of _____, County of _____, State of _____,

are the owners as joint tenants of certain real property located at (and known as) _____,

in the City/Town of _____, State of _____,

which property is described more fully in the Deed conveying it from _____

to _____, as "that certain piece or parcel of land with buildings thereon

standing, located in said _____, being

Being the same premises earlier conveyed to the Settlors by an instrument dated _____ and

recorded in Vol. _____, Page _____ of the _____ Land Records.

NOW, THEREFORE, KNOW ALL MEN BY THESE PRESENTS, that we do hereby acknowledge and declare that we hold and will hold said real property and all our right, title and interest in and to said property and all furniture, fixtures and personal property situated therein on the date of the death of the survivor of us, IN TRUST

    1. For the use and benefit of

(Name) _____, of

(Address) _____

              Number   *Street*   *City*   *State*   *Zip*

    If because of the physical or mental incapacity of both of us certified in writing by a physician, the Successor Trustee hereinafter named shall assume active administration of this trust during our lifetime, such Successor Trustee shall be fully authorized to pay to us or disburse on our behalf such sums from income or principal as appear necessary or desirable for our comfort or welfare. Upon the death of the survivor of us, unless the beneficiary shall predecease us or unless we all die as a result of a common accident or disaster, our Successor Trustee is hereby directed forthwith to transfer said property and all right, title and interest in and to said property unto the beneficiary absolutely and thereby terminate this trust; provided, however, that if the beneficiary hereunder shall not have attained the age of 21 years, the Successor Trustee shall hold such beneficiary's share of the trust assets in continuing trust until such beneficiary shall have attained the age of 21 years. During such period of continuing trust the Successor Trustee, in his absolute discretion, may retain the specific trust property herein described if he believes it in the best interest of the beneficiary so to do, or he may sell or otherwise dispose of such specific trust property, investing and reinvesting the proceeds as he may deem appropriate. If the specific trust property shall be productive of income or if it be sold or otherwise disposed of, the Successor Trustee may apply or expend any or all of the income or principal directly for the maintenance, education and support of the beneficiary without the intervention of any guardian and without application to any court. Such payments of income or principal may be made to the parents of such beneficiary or to the person with whom the beneficiary is living without any liability upon the Successor Trustee to see to the application thereof. If such beneficiary survives us but dies before attaining the age of 21 years, at his or her death the Successor Trustee shall transfer, pay over and deliver the trust property to such beneficiary's personal representative, absolutely.

2. The beneficiary hereunder shall be liable for his proportionate share of any taxes levied upon the total taxable estate of the survivor of us by reason of the death of such survivor.

3. All interests of the beneficiary hereunder shall be inalienable and free from anticipation, assignment, attachment, pledge or control by creditors or by a present or former spouse of such beneficiary in any proceedings at law or in equity.

4. We reserve unto ourselves the power and right during our lifetime (1) to place a mortgage or other lien upon the property, and (2) to collect any rental or other income which may accrue from the trust property and to pay such income to ourselves as individuals. We shall be exclusively entitled to all income accruing from the trust property during our lifetime and no beneficiary named herein shall have any claim upon any such income and/or profits distributed to us.

5. We reserve unto ourselves the power and right during our lifetime to amend or revoke in whole or in part the trust hereby created without the necessity of obtaining the consent of the beneficiary. The sale or other disposition by us of the whole or any part of the property shall constitute as to such whole or part a revocation of this trust.

6. The death during our lifetime, or in a common accident or disaster with us, of the beneficiary designated hereunder shall revoke such designation, and in the former event, we reserve the right to designate a new beneficiary. Should we for any reason fail to designate such new beneficiary, this trust shall terminate upon the death of the survivor of us and the trust property shall revert to the estate of such survivor.

7. In the event of the physical or mental incapacity or death of one of us, the survivor shall continue as sole Trustee. In the event of the physical or mental incapacity or death of the survivor, or if we both shall die in a common accident, we hereby nominate and appoint as Successor Trustee hereunder whosoever shall at that time be beneficiary hereunder, unless such beneficiary shall not have attained the age of 21 years or is otherwise legally incapacitated, in which event we hereby nominate and appoint

(Name) _____, of

(Address) _____
        Number   *Street*   *City*   *State*   *Zip*

to be Successor Trustee.

8. This Declaration of Trust shall extend to and be binding upon the heirs, executors, administrators and assigns of the undersigned and upon the Successors to the Trustees.

9. We as Trustees and our Successor Trustee shall serve without bond.

10. This Declaration of Trust shall be construed and enforced in accordance with the laws of the State

of _____.

IN WITNESS WHEREOF, we have hereunto set our hands and seals this _____

day of _____, 19_____.

        (First Settlor sign here) _____ L.S.

        (Second Settlor sign here) _____ L.S.

I, the undersigned legal spouse of one of the above Settlors, hereby waive all community property, dower or curtesy rights which I may have in the hereinabove-described property and give my assent to the provisions of the trust and to the inclusion in it of the said property.

        (Spouse sign here) _____ L.S.

Witness: (1) _____   Witness: (2) _____

STATE OF _____   City

COUNTY OF _____   or

                          Town _____

On the _____ day of _____, 19_____, personally appeared

_____ and _____

known to me to be the individuals who executed the foregoing instrument, and acknowledged the same to be their free act and deed, before me.

_____

(Notary Seal)   *Notary Public*

CHAPTER 7

DECLARATION OF TRUST

For Naming

ONE PRIMARY BENEFICIARY

And

ONE CONTINGENT BENEFICIARY

To Receive

JOINTLY HELD REAL ESTATE

INSTRUCTIONS:

On the following pages will be found a declaration of trust (DT-102-J) suitable for use in connection with the establishment of an inter vivos trust covering real estate title to which is held in joint names, where it is desired to name *one* person as primary beneficiary to receive jointly owned real estate, with some *one* other person as contingent beneficiary to receive the property if the primary beneficiary be not living upon the death of the surviving co-owner.

Enter the names of the two co-owners on the first line.

Cross out *"city"* or *"town,"* leaving the appropriate designation of your community. If your house has no street number, cross out *"(and known as)."*

Enter the description of your property as it appears in the warranty deed or quit claim deed under which you acquired it. If it's too long to fit into the space, prune it judiciously to eliminate references to easements, rights of way, etc., and abbreviate wherever possible (e.g., *"SW"* for *"southwest"*). Next, enter in the space provided the date of that deed and the volume number and page number in the land records where it was recorded. (This information is generally to be found stamped in the upper margin of the old deed; sometimes *"Book"* or *"Liber"* is used instead of *"Vol."*)

Note that under this instrument, not only your house but also its entire contents—including your personal effects—will pass to the beneficiary named without going through probate. If you do not wish to include your furniture and personal effects in the trust, cross out *"and all furniture, fixtures and personal property situated therein"* and *initial it.*

Enter the names of the beneficiaries in the appropriate places in Paragraph 1.

Note that Paragraph 7 designates as Successor Trustee *"whosoever shall at that time be beneficiary hereunder,"* which means that in most cases you don't need to fill anything in there. However, if there is any possibility of a beneficiary who has not attained the age of 21 years receiving the property, make certain that you name an adult in this paragraph who can act as trustee for such beneficiary. Avoid naming as trustee a person not likely to survive until the beneficiary has attained age 21.

When completed in the manner shown on the reverse side hereof, make several photocopies for reference purposes. The original of the declaration of trust and the quit claim deed (see page 71) should then be filed with the town or county clerk or other office where real estate transfers in the area where the property is located are customarily recorded. After they are recorded, they will be returned to you.

Important: Read carefully Notes A and B on page 38. *Both* apply to this declaration of trust.

WHEREVER THE INSTRUCTION "INITIAL IT" APPEARS ABOVE,
IT MEANS THAT *BOTH* CO-OWNERS SHOULD INITIAL IT.

Declaration of Trust

WHEREAS, WE, **John J. Brown** _____ and **Elizabeth A. Brown** _____, of the ~~City~~/Town

of _____, County of **Fairfax** _____, State of **Connecticut** _____

Milton

are the owners as joint tenants of certain real property located at (and known as) **525 Main Street** _____

in the ~~City~~/Town of **Milton** _____, State of **Connecticut** _____

which property is described more fully in the Deed conveying it from **Henry B. Green** _____

to **John J. Brown & Elizabeth A.Brown** _____ as "that certain piece or parcel of land with buildings thereon

standing, located in said **Milton** _____, being

the rear portions of Lots #34 and 35, on Map of Building Lots
of George Spooner, said map being dated May 3, 1952, and filed
for record in the office of the Town Clerk, Milton, Connecticut
in Book 5, Page 16 of said Maps. Said parcel of land is more
particularly described as:

Beginning at a point on the south line of Lot #34, on said map,
73.5 feet East of the East line of Park Avenue -- running thence
North along land of James E. Beach, 100 feet to a point on the
North line of Lot #35 on said map, 70.44 feet East of the East.
line to Cornwall Street, thence East along land of the said
James E. Beach (being Lot #51 on said map) 55 feet -- thence
South along land of Thomas Cook (being Lot #56 on said map)
100 feet to the aforesaid North line of Bartram Street --
thence West to the point of beginning.

Being the same premises earlier conveyed to the Settlors by an instrument dated **June 22, 1972** _____ and

recorded in Vol. **371** ___, Page **490** ___ of the **Milton** _____ Land Records.

NOW, THEREFORE, KNOW ALL MEN BY THESE PRESENTS, that we do hereby acknowledge and declare that we
hold and will hold said real property and all our right, title and interest in and to said property and all furniture, fixtures and
personal property situated therein on the date of the death of the survivor of us, IN TRUST

1. For the use and benefit of

(Name) **Jill A. Brown -our daughter** _____ **Milton** _____ **Connecticut** ___ **06605** ___, of
        City   State   Zip

(Address) **525** ___ **Main Street** _____
          Number   Street

or, if such beneficiary be not surviving, for the use and benefit of

(Name) **Dorothy Lynn - our niece** _____ **Portland** _____ **Wisconsin** ___ **53123** ___, of
        City   State   Zip

(Address) **566** ___ **Midland Street** _____
          Number   Street

hereunder shall revoke such designation, and in the former event, we reserve the right to designate a new beneficiary. Should we
for any reason fail to designate such new beneficiary, this trust shall terminate upon the death of the survivor of us and the trust
property shall revert to the estate of such survivor.

7. In the event of the physical or mental incapacity or death of one of us, the survivor shall continue as sole Trustee. In the
event of the physical or mental incapacity or death of the survivor, or if we both shall die in a common accident, we hereby
nominate and appoint as Successor Trustee hereunder whosoever shall at that time be beneficiary hereunder, unless such
beneficiary shall not have attained the age of 21 years or is otherwise legally incapacitated, in which event we hereby nominate
and appoint

(Name) **Henry P. Adams** _____ **Milton** _____ **Connecticut** ___ **06605** ___, of
        City   State   Zip

(Address) **125** ___ **Barnum Street** _____
          Number   Street

to be Successor Trustee.

8. This Declaration of Trust shall extend to and be binding upon the heirs, executors, administrators and assigns of the

Declaration of Trust

WHEREAS, WE, _____ and _____, of the City/Town

of _____, County of _____, State of _____,

are the owners as joint tenants of certain real property located at (and known as) _____,

in the City/Town of _____, State of _____,

which property is described more fully in the Deed conveying it from _____

to _____ as "that certain piece or parcel of land with buildings thereon

standing, located in said _____, being

Being the same premises earlier conveyed to the Settlors by an instrument dated _____ and

recorded in Vol. _____, Page _____ of the _____ Land Records.

NOW, THEREFORE, KNOW ALL MEN BY THESE PRESENTS, that we do hereby acknowledge and declare that we hold and will hold said real property and all our right, title and interest in and to said property and all furniture, fixtures and personal property situated therein on the date of the death of the survivor of us, IN TRUST

1. For the use and benefit of

(Name) _____, of

(Address) _____
        Number   Street   City   State   Zip

or, if such beneficiary be not surviving, for the use and benefit of

(Name) _____, of

(Address) _____
        Number   Street   City   State   Zip

If because of the physical or mental incapacity of both of us certified in writing by a physician, the Successor Trustee hereinafter named shall assume active administration of this trust during our lifetime, such Successor Trustee shall be fully authorized to pay to us or disburse on our behalf such sums from income or principal as appear necessary or desirable for our comfort or welfare. Upon the death of the survivor of us, unless the beneficiaries shall predecease us or unless we all shall die as a result of a common accident or disaster, our Successor Trustee is hereby directed forthwith to transfer said property and all right, title and interest in and to said property unto the beneficiary absolutely and thereby terminate this trust; provided, however, that if the beneficiary hereunder shall not have attained the age of 21 years, the Successor Trustee shall hold the trust assets in continuing trust until such beneficiary shall have attained the age of 21 years. During such period of continuing trust the Successor Trustee, in his absolute discretion, may retain the specific trust property herein described if he believes it in the best interest of the beneficiary so to do, or he may sell or otherwise dispose of such specific trust property, investing and reinvesting the proceeds as he may deem appropriate. If the specific trust property shall be productive of income or if it be sold or otherwise disposed of, the Successor Trustee may apply or expend any or all of the income or principal directly for the maintenance, education and support of the beneficiary without the intervention of any guardian and without application to any court. Such payments of income or principal may be made to the parents of such beneficiary or to the person with whom the beneficiary is living without any liability upon the Successor Trustee to see to the application thereof. If such beneficiary survives us but dies before attaining the age of 21 years, at his or her death the Successor Trustee shall transfer, pay over and deliver the trust property to such beneficiary's personal representative, absolutely.

2. Any beneficiary hereunder shall be liable for his proportionate share of any taxes levied upon the total taxable estate of the survivor of us by reason of the death of such survivor.

3. All interests of a beneficiary hereunder shall be inalienable and free from anticipation, assignment, attachment, pledge or control by creditors or by a present or former spouse of such beneficiary in any proceedings at law or in equity.

4. We reserve unto ourselves the power and right during our lifetime (1) to place a mortgage or other lien upon the property, (2) to collect any rental or other income which may accrue from the trust property and to pay such income to ourselves as individuals. We shall be exclusively entitled to all income accruing from the trust property during our lifetime, and no beneficiary named herein shall have any claim upon any such income and/or profits distributed to us.

5. We reserve unto ourselves the power and right at any time during our lifetime to amend or revoke in whole or in part the trust hereby created without the necessity of obtaining the consent of any beneficiary and without giving notice to any beneficiary. The sale or other disposition by us of the whole or any part of the property held hereunder shall constitute as to such whole or part a revocation of this trust.

6. The death during our lifetime, or in a common accident or disaster with us, of both of the beneficiaries designated hereunder shall revoke such designation, and in the former event, we reserve the right to designate a new beneficiary. Should we for any reason fail to designate such new beneficiary, this trust shall terminate upon the death of the survivor of us and the trust property shall revert to the estate of such survivor.

7. In the event of the physical or mental incapacity or death of one of us, the survivor shall continue as sole Trustee. In the event of the physical or mental incapacity or death of the survivor, or if we both shall die in a common accident, we hereby nominate and appoint as Successor Trustee hereunder whosoever shall at that time be beneficiary hereunder, unless such beneficiary shall not have attained the age of 21 years or is otherwise legally incapacitated, in which event we hereby nominate and appoint

(Name) _____, of

(Address) _____
          Number   Street   City   State   Zip

to be Successor Trustee.

8. This Declaration of Trust shall extend to and be binding upon the heirs, executors, administrators and assigns of the undersigned and upon the Successors to the Trustees.

9. We as Trustees and our Successor Trustee shall serve without bond.

10. This Declaration of Trust shall be construed and enforced in accordance with the laws of the State

of _____.

IN WITNESS WHEREOF, we have hereunto set our hands and seals this _____

day of _____, 19_____.

(First Settlor sign here) _____ L.S.

(Second Settlor sign here) _____ L.S.

I, the undersigned legal spouse of one of the above Settlors, hereby waive all community property, dower or curtesy rights which I may have in the hereinabove-described property and give my assent to the provisions of the trust and to the inclusion in it of the said property.

(Spouse sign here) _____ L.S.

Witness: (1) _____   Witness: (2) _____

STATE OF _____   City
                                                or
COUNTY OF _____   Town _____

On the _____ day of _____ , 19_____, personally appeared

_____ and _____

known to me to be the individuals who executed the foregoing instrument, and acknowledged the same to be their free act and deed, before me.

_____

(Notary Seal)   Notary Public

CHAPTER 7

DECLARATION OF TRUST
For Naming
TWO OR MORE BENEFICIARIES,
SHARING EQUALLY,
To Receive
JOINTLY HELD REAL ESTATE

INSTRUCTIONS:

On the following pages will be found a declaration of trust (DT-103-J) suitable for use where it is desired to name two or more persons, sharing equally, to receive jointly owned real estate upon the death of the survivor of the two co-owners.

Enter the names of the two co-owners on the first line.

Cross out *"city"* or *"town,"* leaving the appropriate designation of your community. If your house has no street number, cross out *"(and known as)."*

Enter the description of your property as it appears in the warranty deed or quit claim deed by which you acquired it. If it's too long to fit into the space, prune it judiciously to eliminate references to easements, rights of way, etc., and abbreviate wherever possible (e.g., *"SW"* for *"southwest"*). Next, enter in the space provided the date of that deed and the volume number and page number in the land records where it was recorded. (This information is generally to be found stamped in the upper margin of the old deed; sometimes *"Book"* or *"Liber"* is used instead of *"Vol."*)

Note that under this instrument, not only your house but also its entire contents—including your personal effects—will pass to the beneficiaries named without going through probate. If you do not wish to include your furniture and personal effects in the trust, cross out *"and all furniture, fixtures and personal property situated therein"* and *initial it.*

In Paragraph 1, indicate the *number of persons* you are naming (to discourage unauthorized additions to the list) and then insert their names. The one whose name appears *first* will be the Successor Trustee responsible for seeing to the distribution of the trust property.

Note that the instrument specifies that the named beneficiaries are to receive *"in equal shares, or the survivor of them/per stirpes."* Now, think carefully: If you have named three persons to share equally with the intention that if one of them predeceases you, *his* children will take *his* share, cross out *"or the survivor of them"* and *initial it.* If that is *not* what you want—if, for example, you prefer that the share of the deceased person be divided between the two surviving persons, cross out *"per stirpes"* and *initial it.* Remember, you <u>must</u> cross out either *"or the survivor of them"* or *"per stirpes"*—one or the other.

Note that Paragraph 7 designates as Successor Trustee *"the beneficiary named first above,"* which means that in most cases you don't need to fill anything in there. However, if there is any possibility of a beneficiary who has not attained the age of 21 years receiving the property, make certain that you name an adult in this paragraph who can act as trustee for such beneficiary. Avoid naming as trustee a person not likely to survive until the beneficiary has attained age 21.

When completed in the manner shown on the reverse side hereof, make several photocopies for reference purposes. The original of the declaration of trust and the quit claim deed (see page 71) should then be filed with the town or county clerk or other office where real estate transfers in the area where the property is located are customarily recorded. After they are recorded they will be returned to you.

Important: Read carefully Notes A and B on page 38. *Both* apply to this declaration of trust.

WHEREVER THE INSTRUCTION "INITIAL IT" APPEARS ABOVE,
IT MEANS THAT *BOTH* CO-OWNERS SHOULD INITIAL IT.

DACEY TRUST

Declaration of Trust

WHEREAS, WE **John J. Brown** and **Elizabeth A. Brown**, of the City/Town

of **Milton**, County of **Fairfax**, State of **Connecticut**,

are the owners as joint tenants of certain real property located at (and known as) **525 Main Street**

in the City/Town of **Milton**, State of **Connecticut**,

which property is described more fully in the Deed conveying it from **Henry B. Green**

to **John J. Brown & Elizabeth A. Brown** as "that certain piece or parcel of land with buildings thereon

standing, located in said **Milton**", being

the rear portions of Lots #34 and 35, on Map of Building Lots of George Spooner, said map being dated May 3, 1952, and filed for record in the office of the Town Clerk, Milton, Connecticut in Book 5, Page 16 of said Maps. Said parcel of land is more particularly described as:

Beginning at a point on the south line of Lot #34, on said map, 73.5 feet East of the East line of Park Avenue -- running thence North along land of James E. Beach, 100 feet to a point on the North line of Lot #35 on said map, 70.44 feet East of the said line to Cornwall Street, thence East along land of the said James E. Beach (being Lot #51 on said map) 55 feet -- thence South along land of Thomas Cook (being Lot #56 on said map) 100 feet to the aforesaid North line of Bartram Street -- thence West to the point of beginning.

Being the same premises earlier conveyed to the Settlors by an instrument dated **June 22, 1972** and

recorded in Vol. **371**, Page **490** of the **Milton** Land Records.

NOW, THEREFORE, KNOW ALL MEN BY THESE PRESENTS, that we do hereby acknowledge and declare that we hold and will hold said real property and all our right, title and interest in and to said property and all furniture, fixtures and personal property situated therein on the date of the death of the survivor of us, IN TRUST

1. For the use and benefit of the following **three (3)** persons, in equal shares, ~~either/per~~ **2-2-0** stirpes:

Thomas B. Brown - our brother
Helen M. Brown - our sister
Charles M. Brown - our brother

If because of the physical or mental incapacity of both of us certified in writing by a physician, the Successor Trustee hereinafter named shall assume active administration of this trust during our lifetime, such Successor Trustee shall be fully authorized to pay to us or disburse on our behalf such sums from income or principal as appear necessary or desirable for our comfort or welfare. Upon the death of the survivor of us, unless the beneficiaries shall predecease us or unless we all shall die as a result of a common accident or disaster, our Successor Trustee is hereby directed forthwith to transfer said property and all right, title and interest in and to said property unto the beneficiaries absolutely and thereby terminate this trust; provided, however, that if any beneficiary hereunder shall not have attained the age of 21 years, the Successor Trustee shall hold such beneficiary's share of the trust assets in continuing trust until such beneficiary shall have attained the age of 21 years. During such period of continuing trust the Successor Trustee, in his absolute discretion, may retain the specific trust property herein described if he believes it in the best interest of the beneficiary so to do, or he may sell or otherwise dispose of such specific trust property, investing and reinvesting the proceeds as he may deem appropriate. If the specific trust property shall be productive of income or if it be sold or otherwise disposed of, the Successor Trustee may apply or expend any or all of the income or principal directly for the maintenance, education and support of the beneficiary without the intervention of any guardian and without application to any court. Such payments of income or principal may be made to the parents of such beneficiary or to the person

7. In the event of the physical or mental incapacity or death of one of us, the survivor shall continue as sole Trustee. In the event of the physical or mental incapacity or death of the survivor, or if we both shall die in a common accident, we hereby nominate and appoint as Successor Trustee hereunder the beneficiary named first above, unless such beneficiary named first above, above shall not have attained the age of 21 years or is otherwise legally incapacitated, in which event we hereby nominate second appoint as such Successor Trustee the beneficiary named second above, unless such beneficiary shall not have attained the age of 21 years or is otherwise legally incapacitated, in which event we hereby nominate and appoint

Henry P. Adams, of

Milton   **Connecticut 06605**
                              City   State   Zip

(Name)

(Address) **125**   **Barnum Street**
          Number   Street

to be Successor Trustee.

8. This Declaration of Trust shall extend to and be binding upon the heirs, executors, administrators and assigns of the

Declaration of Trust

WHEREAS, WE, _____ and _____, of the City/Town

of _____, County of _____, State of _____,

are the owners as joint tenants of certain real property located at (and known as) _____,

in the City/Town of _____, State of _____,

which property is described more fully in the Deed conveying it from _____

to _____ as "that certain piece or parcel of land with buildings thereon

standing, located in said _____, being

Being the same premises earlier conveyed to the Settlors by an instrument dated _____ and

recorded in Vol. _____, Page _____ of the _____ Land Records.

    NOW, THEREFORE, KNOW ALL MEN BY THESE PRESENTS, that we do hereby acknowledge and declare that we hold and will hold said real property and all our right, title and interest in and to said property and all furniture, fixtures and personal property situated therein on the date of the death of the survivor of us, IN TRUST

    1. For the use and benefit of the following _____ persons, in equal shares, or the survivor of them/per stirpes:

    If because of the physical or mental incapacity of both of us certified in writing by a physician, the Successor Trustee hereinafter named shall assume active administration of this trust during our lifetime, such Successor Trustee shall be fully authorized to pay to us or disburse on our behalf such sums from income or principal as appear necessary or desirable for our comfort or welfare. Upon the death of the survivor of us, unless the beneficiaries shall predecease us or unless we all shall die as a result of a common accident or disaster, our Successor Trustee is hereby directed forthwith to transfer said property and all right, title and interest in and to said property unto the beneficiaries absolutely and thereby terminate this trust; provided, however, that if any beneficiary hereunder shall not have attained the age of 21 years, the Successor Trustee shall hold such beneficiary's share of the trust assets in continuing trust until such beneficiary shall have attained the age of 21 years. During such period of continuing trust the Successor Trustee, in his absolute discretion, may retain the specific trust property herein described if he believes it in the best interest of the beneficiary so to do, or he may sell or otherwise dispose of such specific trust property, investing and reinvesting the proceeds as he may deem appropriate. If the specific trust property shall be productive of income or if it be sold or otherwise disposed of, the Successor Trustee may apply or expend any or all of the income or principal directly for the maintenance, education and support of the beneficiary without the intervention of any guardian and without application to any court. Such payments of income or principal may be made to the parents of such beneficiary or to the person with whom the beneficiary is living without any liability upon the Successor Trustee to see to the application thereof. If such beneficiary survives us but dies before attaining the age of 21 years, at his or her death the Successor Trustee shall transfer, pay over and deliver the trust property being held for such beneficiary to such beneficiary's personal representative, absolutely.

2. Each beneficiary hereunder shall be liable for his proportionate share of any taxes levied upon the total taxable estate of the survivor of us by reason of the death of such survivor.

3. All interests of a beneficiary hereunder shall be inalienable and free from anticipation, assignment, attachment, pledge or control by creditors or by a present or former spouse of such beneficiary in any proceedings at law or in equity.

4. We reserve unto ourselves the power and right during our lifetime (1) to place a mortgage or other lien upon the property, (2) to collect any rental or other income which may accrue from the trust property and to pay such income to ourselves as individuals. We shall be exclusively entitled to all income accruing from the trust property during our lifetime, and no beneficiary named herein shall have any claim upon any such income and/or profits distributed to us.

5. We reserve unto ourselves the power and right at any time during our lifetime to amend or revoke in whole or in part the trust hereby created without the necessity of obtaining the consent of any beneficiary and without giving notice to any beneficiary. The sale or other disposition by us of the whole or any part of the property held hereunder shall constitute as to such whole or part a revocation of this trust.

6. The death during our lifetime, or in a common accident or disaster with us, of all of the beneficiaries designated hereunder shall revoke such designation, and in the former event, we reserve the right to designate a new beneficiary. Should we for any reason fail to designate such new beneficiary, this trust shall terminate upon the death of the survivor of us and the trust property shall revert to the estate of such survivor.

7. In the event of the physical or mental incapacity or death of one of us, the survivor shall continue as sole Trustee. In the event of the physical or mental incapacity or death of the survivor, or if we both shall die in a common accident, we hereby nominate and appoint as Successor Trustee hereunder the beneficiary named first above, unless such beneficiary shall not have attained the age of 21 years or is otherwise legally incapacitated, in which event we hereby nominate and appoint as such Successor Trustee the beneficiary named second above, unless such beneficiary named second above shall not have attained the age of 21 years or is otherwise legally incapacitated, in which event we hereby nominate and appoint

(Name) _____, of

(Address) _____
Number   Street   City   State   Zip

to be Successor Trustee.

8. This Declaration of Trust shall extend to and be binding upon the heirs, executors, administrators and assigns of the undersigned and upon the Successors to the Trustees.

9. We as Trustee and our Successor Trustee shall serve without bond.

10. This Declaration of Trust shall be construed and enforced in accordance with the laws of the State of _____.

IN WITNESS WHEREOF, we have hereunto set our hands and seals this _____

day of _____, 19_____.

(First Settlor sign here) _____ L.S.

(Second Settlor sign here) _____ L.S.

I, the undersigned legal spouse of one of the above Settlors, hereby waive all community property, dower or curtesy rights which I may have in the hereinabove-described property and give my assent to the provisions of the trust and to the inclusion in it of the said property.

(Spouse sign here) _____ L.S.

Witness: (1) _____ Witness: (2) _____

STATE OF _____ City

COUNTY OF _____ or Town _____

On the _____ day of _____, 19_____, personally appeared

_____ and _____

known to me to be the individuals who executed the foregoing instrument, and acknowledged the same to be their free act and deed, before me.

_____

(Notary Seal)   Notary Public

CHAPTER 7

QUIT CLAIM DEED—JOINT,
COVERING REAL ESTATE
HELD IN JOINT NAMES
(FOR USE WITH DT-101-J, DT-102-J, OR DT-103-J)

INSTRUCTIONS:

One or the other of two legal documents is ordinarily used to transfer title to real estate—a warranty deed or a quit claim deed.

When you buy a house, the owner gives you a warranty deed by which he "warrants" or guarantees that the house is his to sell. With that deed, you can hold him responsible if someone else turns up with a valid claim to ownership of the property.

If he gave you a quit claim deed, he would be providing no guarantee at all that he actually owned the property. He'd be saying: "Whatever title or claim I may have to this property I am turning over to you."

When you buy a house, then, you're not satisfied with a quit claim deed; you insist upon being given a warranty deed. The quit claim deed is used when property is being transferred from one member of a family to another, with no financial consideration being involved, or when one of two co-owners, not necessarily related, wishes to transfer his interest in the property to the other co-owner with or without a financial consideration being involved. They know each other and they know that they own the property between them, and there is no need for the retiring co-owner to "warrant" to the other that he owns one-half of the property.

In connection with the transfer of the title to your real estate from yourselves as individuals to yourselves as trustees, as explained in Chapter 7, a quit claim deed will be found on page 73 which will adequately serve your purpose.

As co-owners, enter at the top your names and the date of the declaration of trust (DT-101-J, DT-102-J, or DT-103-J) which you have executed. Then, in the large space provided, enter the description of the property as it appears in the deed by which you acquired it. If it's too long to fit into the space, prune it judiciously to eliminate references to easements, rights of way, etc., and abbreviate wherever possible (e.g., "*SW*" for "*southwest*"). You are deeding it to yourselves and you need only adequately identify the property. Below the description of the property is a place for you to insert details of the deed by which you acquired it. In the end panel on the reverse side, insert your name and that of the co-owner twice: first under "From," and again under "To."

When you have both signed the quit claim deed as "Releasors" in the presence of two witnesses and had it notarized, make several photocopies for reference purposes. The original of the quit claim deed and the declaration of trust should then be filed with the town or county clerk or other office where property transfers in the area where the property is located are customarily recorded. After they are recorded, they will be returned to you.

Important: Read carefully Notes A and B on page 38. *Both* apply to this quit claim deed.

QUIT CLAIM DEED

To All People To Whom These Presents Shall Come, Greetings;

KNOW YE, THAT WE,   Elizabeth A. Brown   April 2, 1980

(Name) ___John J. Brown___   and (Name) _____ under date of _____ and

in conformity with the terms of a certain Declaration of Trust executed by us under date of such Declaration of Trust, and

do by these presents release and forever Quit-Claim to ourselves as Trustees under the terms of such Declaration of Trust, and

to our successors as Trustee under the terms of such Declaration of Trust, all right, title, interest, claim and demand whatsoever

which we as Releasors have or ought to have in or to the property located at:

525 Main Street, Milton, Connecticut, being
the rear portions of Lots #34 and 35, on Map of Building Lots
of George Spooner, said map being dated May 3, 1952, and filed
for record in the office of the Town Clerk, Milton, Connecticut
in Book 5, Page 16 of said Maps.   Said parcel of land is more
particularly described as:

Beginning at a point on the south line of Lot #34, on said map,
73.5 feet East of the East line of Park Avenue -- running thence
North along land of James E. Beach, 100 feet to a point on the
North line of Lot #35 on said map, 70.44 feet East of the East
line to Cornwall Street, thence East along land of the said
James E. Beach (being Lot #51 on said map) 55 feet -- thence
South along land of Thomas Cook (being Lot #56 on said map)
100 feet to the aforesaid North line of Bartram Street --
thence West to the point of beginning.

than One Dollar

Being the same premises earlier conveyed to the Releasor by an instrument dated ___July 14, 1960___ and

recorded in Vol. __55__, Page __613__ of the ___Milton___ Land Records.

After recording. Please return this instrument to:

State of

County of

The property affected by this instrument
is situated in the City/Town of

by

Authorized Official

Vol. _____ of the _____ Land Records

Time _____ on Page _____ and recorded in

Received for record _____ at _____

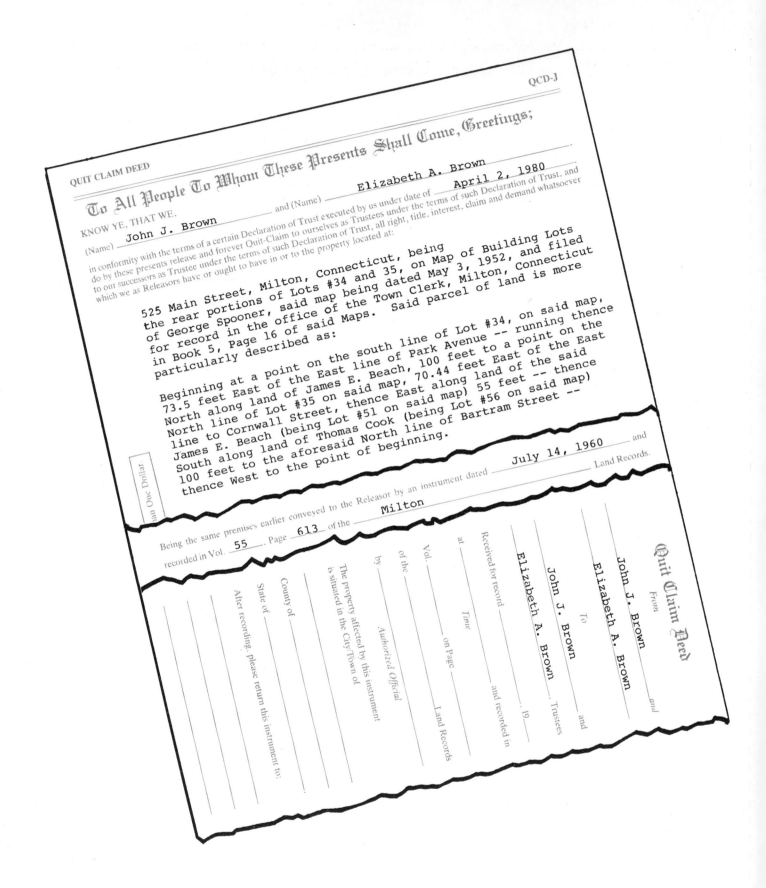

QUIT CLAIM DEED

To All People To Whom These Presents Shall Come, Greetings;

KNOW YE, THAT WE,

(Name) _____ and (Name) _____,

in conformity with the terms of a certain Declaration of Trust executed by us under date of _____,
do by these presents release and forever Quit-Claim to ourselves as Trustees under the terms of such Declaration of Trust, and to our successors as Trustee under the terms of such Declaration of Trust, all right, title, interest, claim and demand whatsoever which we as Releasors have or ought to have in or to the property located at:

The consideration for this transfer is less than One Dollar.

Being the same premises earlier conveyed to the Releasors by an instrument dated _____ and

recorded in Vol. _____, Page _____ of the _____ Land Records.

To Have and to Hold the premises, with all the appurtenances, as such Trustees forever; and we declare and agree that neither we as individuals nor our heirs or assigns shall have or make any claim or demand upon such property.

IN WITNESS WHEREOF, we have hereunto set our hands and seals this _____

day of _____ , 19_____ .

_____ L.S.

Releasor (First co-owner)

_____ L.S.

Releasor (Second co-owner)

I, the undersigned legal spouse of one of the above Releasors, hereby waive all community property, dower or curtesy rights which I may have in or to the hereinabove-described property.

(Spouse) _____ L.S.

Witness: (1) _____   Witness: (2) _____

STATE OF _____ }   City
                                                        or
COUNTY OF _____   Town _____

On the _____ day of _____ , 19____ , personally appeared

_____ and _____

known to me to be the individuals who executed the foregoing instrument, and acknowledged the same to be their free act and deed, before me.

(Notary Seal)

_____

Notary Public

Quit Claim Deed

From

_____

and

_____

To

_____

and

_____ , Trustees

Received for record _____ , 19____

at _____ and recorded in

Time

Vol. _____ on Page _____

of the _____ Land Records

by _____

Authorized Official

The property affected by this instrument is situated in the City/Town of _____

County of _____

State of _____

After recording, please return this instrument to:

CHAPTER 7

SPECIAL QUIT CLAIM DEED,
For Use Where It Is Desired To Create
A JOINT TRUST
With Real Estate Now Held In
ONE NAME
(FOR USE ONLY WITH DT-101-J, DT-102-J, OR DT-103-J)

INSTRUCTIONS:

One or the other of two legal documents is ordinarily used to transfer title to real estate—a warranty deed or a quit claim deed.

When you buy a house, the owner gives you a warranty deed by which he "warrants" or guarantees that the house is his to sell. With that deed, you can hold him responsible if someone else turns up with a valid claim to ownership of the property.

If he gave you a quit claim deed, he would be providing no guarantee at all that he actually owned the property. He'd be saying: "Whatever title or claim I may have to this property I am turning over to you."

When you buy a house, then, you're not satisfied with a quit claim deed; you insist upon being given a warranty deed. The quit claim deed is used when property is being transferred from one member of a family to another with no financial consideration being involved, or when one of two co-owners, not necessarily related, wishes to transfer his interest in the property to the other co-owner with or without a financial consideration being involved. They know each other and they know that they own the property between them, and there is no need for the retiring co-owner to "warrant" to the other that he owns one-half of the property.

There are situations where it is desired to create a joint trust covering real estate which until now has been held in one name only. A property owner who marries, for example, may wish to place such property in a joint trust with his or her spouse.

On the following pages will be found a Special Quit Claim Deed suitable for use in such situations. It should be executed by the individual who *now* owns the real estate after the two persons who are to hold it as joint trustees have executed DT-101-J, DT-102-J, or DT-103-J.

Enter in order, your name, the name of the joint trustee, the date of the declaration of trust which you have jointly executed, the name of the joint trustee again, and then in the large space, the description of the property as it appears in the declaration of trust. If it's too long to fit into the space, prune it judiciously to eliminate references to easements, rights of way, etc., and abbreviate wherever possible (e.g., "*SW*" for "*southwest*"). You are deeding it to yourself and you need only adequately identify the property. Below the description of the property is a place for you to insert details of the deed by which you acquired it. In the end panel on the reverse side, insert your name under "*From*" and your name and that of your new Co-Trustee under "*To.*"

When the document has been executed, witnessed, and notarized, make several photocopies for reference purposes. The original of the quit claim deed and the declaration of trust should then be filed with the town or county clerk or other office where property transfers in the area in which the property is located are customarily recorded. After they have been recorded, they will be returned to you.

Important: Read carefully Notes A and B on page 38. *Both* apply to this quit claim deed.

QUIT CLAIM DEED—SPEC.

QCD-SPEC.

To All People To Whom These Presents Shall Come, Greetings;

, in conformity with the terms of a certain

Know Ye, That I, **John J. Brown**

(Name) _____ and by _____ **Elizabeth A. Brown**

Declaration of Trust executed by me and by _____, do by these presents release and forever Quit-Claim to myself and to the

under date of **April 2, 1980**

said **Elizabeth A. Brown**

as Joint Trustees under the terms of such Declaration of Trust, all right, title, interest, claim and demand whatsoever which I as
Releasor have or ought to have in or to the property located at:

525 Main Street, Milton, Connecticut, being
the rear portions of Lots #34 and 35, on Map of Building Lots
of George Spooner, said map being dated May 3, 1952, and filed
for record in the office of the Town Clerk, Milton, Connecticut
in Book 5, Page 16 of said Maps.   Said parcel of land is more
particularly described as:

Beginning at a point on the south line of Lot #34, on said map,
73.5 feet East of the East line of Park Avenue -- running thence
North along land of James E. Beach, 100 feet to a point on the
line to Cornwall Street, thence East along land of the said
James E. Beach (being Lot #35 on said map, 70.44 feet East of the
South along land of Thomas Cook (being Lot #51 on said map) 55 feet -- thence
100 feet to the aforesaid North line of Bartram Street --
thence West to the point of beginning.

transfer is less than One Dollar.

Being the same premises earlier conveyed to the Releasor by an instrument dated **July 14, 1960** and

recorded in Vol. **71** Page **613** of the **Milton** Land Records.

Elizabeth A. Brown
John J. Brown Trustees

To

and

From

John J. Brown

Quit Claim Deed

QUIT CLAIM DEED—SPEC.

To All People To Whom These Presents Shall Come, Greetings;

Know Ye, That I,

(Name) _____ , in conformity with the terms of a certain

Declaration of Trust executed by me and by _____

under date of _____ , do by these presents release and forever Quit-Claim to myself and to the

said _____

as Joint Trustees under the terms of such Declaration of Trust, all right, title, interest, claim and demand whatsoever which I as Releasor have or ought to have in or to the property located at:

The consideration for this transfer is less than One Dollar.

Being the same premises earlier conveyed to the Releasor by an instrument dated _____ and

recorded in Vol. _____ , Page _____ of the _____ Land Records.

To Have and to Hold the premises, with all the appurtenances, as such joint Trustees forever; and I declare and agree that neither I as an individual nor my heirs or assigns shall have or make any claim or demand upon such property.

IN WITNESS WHEREOF, I have hereunto set my hand and seal this _____

day of _____ , 19_____.

_____ L.S.

Releasor (Owner)

I, the undersigned legal spouse of the above Releasor, hereby waive all community property, dower or curtesy rights in or to the hereinabove-described property.

(Spouse) _____ L.S.

Witness: (1) _____   Witness: (2) _____

STATE OF _____   City
                                                 or
COUNTY OF _____   Town _____

On the _____ day of _____ , 19_____, personally appeared

_____

known to me to be the individual(s) who executed the foregoing instrument, and acknowledged the same to be _____
free act and deed, before me.

(Notary Seal)   *Notary Public*

Quit Claim Deed

From

To

_____ and _____ Trustees

Received for record _____ , 19_____

at _____ and recorded in

Time

Vol. _____ on Page _____

of the _____ Land Records

by _____

Authorized Official

The property affected by this instrument is situated in the City/Town of _____

County of _____

State of _____

After recording, please return this instrument to:

Avoiding Probate of a Bank Account

Checking and savings bank accounts ordinarily are registered in one of five principal ways:

1. In the name of the individual owner;
2. In the names of two persons jointly on a "one or the other" basis;
3. In the name of one individual as trustee for another;
4. In the name of one individual as guardian for another;
5. In the name of one individual as custodian for another.

Before we address ourselves to the first type, which represents our principal interest here, let us briefly consider the other four. No. 2, joint registration, is a very common form, particularly with husband and wife. It is importantly different from joint registration of securities—the latter is always "John Smith *and* Mary Smith," never "John Smith *or* Mary Smith." Jointly registered securities therefore require the action of *both* parties to effect a sale or process a dividend payment, whereas in the case of a joint bank account, either party may act alone in connection with the account.

Jointly held bank accounts have one very important drawback mentioned in an earlier chapter. Many banks will block such an account upon receipt of notification of the death of one of the joint owners. A client of my firm suffered a severe heart attack and was hospitalized. His wife reported a need for extra funds for hospital bills, etc., and we quickly arranged a $10,000 partial withdrawal from his trust account with us. The check was drawn in his name and his wife deposited it in their joint checking account. He died the following day. Not only would the bank not let her draw any of the $10,000, but it also declined to honor the checks which she had hurriedly drawn the previous day in payment of pressing bills. This practice of blocking accounts is not universal. It would be well to ask your bank to write you a letter stating that it will not block your jointly owned account upon the death of one of the joint owners. Failing this, the survivor should promptly arrange the transfer of any balance into a new account in his name. A bereaved person is frequently in no frame of mind to hurry down

to a bank to transfer funds. In such circumstances, a third party should be dispatched with a check if it be a checking account, or with the simple authorization for payment to a third party which generally is illustrated in every savings bank book.

The third common form of registration—as trustee for another—also involves conditions peculiar to bank accounts, conditions which differ from those attending trustee registration of securities. If you register common stock in your name as trustee, there must be a written trust instrument in existence. The stock's transfer agent may not require you to display the written instrument when you *buy* the stock, but it will almost certainly demand to see it when you want to sell it.

Accounts in savings banks require no such written instrument. Savings accounts in commercial banks are a different story; they generally want a copy of a proper trust instrument on file.

The so-called "Totten trust" is worth mentioning here, since it is the commonest form of savings bank trust account. In the early years of this century, an individual named Totten opened a bank account in his name ostensibly as trustee for a relative. The validity of the trust was challenged after his death, eventually receiving reluctant court approval. That was long ago, however, when trusts were even more of a mystery than they are to most lawyers today, and over the years the Totten trust has been successfully challenged so many times that it should be against the law for savings banks to offer them. The banks do, however, and if you go in to open an inter vivos trust, you'll have to be very careful or they'll palm off a Totten trust on you. The distinguishing characteristic is that there isn't any trust instrument, only a signature card, and the account is opened in some such form as "John Smith in trust for Willie Smith."

With an ordinary trustee registration, many banks will deliver up the proceeds to the beneficiary if the trustee's death certificate is presented, provided the beneficiary has reached the age of reason. If John Smith opens a savings account for his 15-year-old son and dies, in most cases the bank will deliver the money to the son. If the child is quite young, the bank will probably ask that someone obtain a court appointment as guardian. Remember those "special guardianships" we discussed earlier?

Guardians are appointed by the probate court. For example, a child might be awarded a court or insurance company settlement for injuries suffered in an accident. The probate court would appoint a guardian, not necessarily a parent, who would receive and hold the money for the minor. In his capacity as guardian, he could open a bank account. If he died, the court would be called upon to appoint a new guardian who would have access to the money upon presentation to the bank of his credentials from the probate court.

A parent wishing simply to make a cash gift to a child might deposit it in a bank account which he holds as "custodian."

None of these accounts (2 through 5) is subject to probate. The joint account is exempt because there is a surviving co-owner. The others are exempt because the funds are actually not the property of the deceased but rather belong to the beneficiary.

No claim is made here that the conditions and circumstances described represent ironclad and inflexible law in effect everywhere. There are exceptions to almost every rule and there are bound to be areas where local custom or the policy of an institution differs from that described here. What I am trying to do is alert you to some of the pitfalls which may cause you trouble. Knowing of them, you can make careful inquiry to discover what ground rules apply in your own area.

Like other forms of property, the individually registered savings or checking account will fall within the jurisdiction of the probate court—if you let it. You can avoid it by using the same "magic key" to probate exemption, the inter vivos trust.

On the following pages will be found forms which may be used to establish an inter vivos trust covering a checking or savings account in one name alone, or in the names of two persons as "joint trustees." Don't try it with more than two.

There are two points which can prove troublesome in some cases. In the first place, bank personnel whose duties include the opening of new accounts ordinarily do not know much about living trusts. Just remember that you now know far more about the subject of trusts than they do. Don't ask them whether you've done the right thing in setting up the trust—decide that for yourself. And don't ask them whether you've made the forms out correctly. Just approach them confidently, saying: "I'd like to open an account registered exactly as I've written it out on this piece of paper. I'll be holding it under a declaration of trust. Here's a copy of that declaration, in case you'd like to keep it in your files." Write out the registration ahead of time: "John Smith, Trustee under his Declaration of Trust dated _____," or "John Smith and Mary Smith, Trustees under their Declaration of Trust dated _____." If you already have an account, hand them the passbook and the declaration of trust and ask them to change the name on the account "exactly as I've written it here."

Some banks prefer not to be responsible for the safekeeping of the trust instrument. No problem: Just hold onto it yourself.

The other possibility is that you'll run into a savings banker who, not understanding trusts, decides to refer it to the bank's lawyer. We've already noted that lawyers will do just about anything to keep you from having a trust. This one may advise the bank not to accept it but instead to offer you a Totten trust. At that point you should ask yourself two simple questions. First, "whose money is it?" Second, "if it is *my* money, shouldn't *I* be the one to decide how it is to be held?" Then just walk across the street to another bank which appreciates your business and which will open the account as you want it. One large savings bank in Brooklyn has lost hundreds of accounts by listening to a staff lawyer who hates trusts.

CHAPTER 8

DECLARATION OF TRUST
For Naming
ONE BENEFICIARY
To Receive
A BANK ACCOUNT HELD IN ONE NAME

INSTRUCTIONS:

On the following pages will be found a declaration of trust (DT-105) suitable for use in connection with the establishment of an inter vivos trust covering a checking or savings account held in one name only, where it is desired to name some one person to receive the account upon the death of the owner.

Cross out *"city"* or *"town,"* leaving the appropriate designation of your community. Next, cross out *"checking"* or *"savings,"* leaving the appropriate designation of the bank account. Then, name the bank; if it's a branch, identify the location.

Enter the name of the beneficiary in the appropriate place in Paragraph 1.

Note that Paragraph 8 designates as Successor Trustee *"whosoever shall at that time be beneficiary hereunder,"* which means that in most cases you don't need to fill anything in there. However, if there is any possibility of a beneficiary who has not attained the age of 21 years receiving the bank account, make certain that you name an adult in this paragraph who can act as trustee for such beneficiary. Avoid naming as trustee a person not likely to survive until the beneficiary has attained age 21.

When completed in the manner shown on the reverse side hereof, make several photocopies for reference purposes. Hold the original in safekeeping and offer a copy to the bank when you open the account. Instruct them to identify the account in this manner: *"(your name), Trustee u/d/t dated _____."*

Important: Read carefully Note B on page 38, which applies to this declaration of trust.

Declaration of Trust

DACEY TRUST

WHEREAS, I, __John J. Brown__ , County of __Fairfax__ , State of __Connecticut__ of the Town of __Milton__ am the owner of a checking account in the __Milton Savings Bank__ (name of Bank) , State of __Connecticut__ located in the Town of __Milton__

NOW, THEREFORE, KNOW ALL MEN BY THESE PRESENTS, that I do hereby acknowledge and declare that I hold and will hold said bank account and all my right, title and interest in and to said account IN TRUST

1. For the use and benefit of:

(Name) __Elizabeth A. Brown - my wife__

(Address) __525__ __Main Street__ __Milton__ __Connecticut__ __06605__
Number / Street / City / State / Zip

If because of my physical or mental incapacity certified in writing by a physician, the Successor Trustee hereinafter named shall assume active administration of this trust during my lifetime, such Successor Trustee shall be fully authorized to pay to me or disburse on my behalf such sums from income or principal as appear necessary or desirable for my comfort or welfare. Upon my death, unless the beneficiary shall predecease me or unless we both shall die as a result of a common accident or disaster, my Successor Trustee is hereby directed forthwith to transfer said bank account and all right, title and interest in and to said account unto the beneficiary absolutely and thereby terminate this trust; _provided_, however, that if the beneficiary hereunder shall not have attained the age of 21 years, the Successor Trustee shall hold the trust assets in continuing trust until such beneficiary shall terminate it, investing and reinvesting the proceeds as he may deem appropriate. Prior to the date upon which such beneficiary attains the age of 21 years, the Successor Trustee may apply or expend any or all of the income or principal directly for the maintenance, education and support of the beneficiary without the intervention of any guardian and without application to any court. Such payments of income or principal may be made to the parents of such beneficiary or to the person with whom the beneficiary is living without any liability upon the Successor Trustee to see to the application thereof. If such beneficiary survives me but dies before attaining the age of 21 years, at his or her death the Successor Trustee shall transfer, pay over and deliver the trust property to such beneficiary's personal representative, absolutely.

2. The beneficiary hereunder shall be liable for his proportionate share of any taxes levied upon the Settlor's total taxable estate by reason of the Settlor's death.

3. All interests of a beneficiary hereunder shall be inalienable and free from anticipation, assignment, attachment, pledge or control by creditors or a present or former spouse of such beneficiary in any proceedings at law or in equity.

4. This trust is created with the express understanding that the bank at which the account is maintained shall be under no liability whatsoever to see to its proper administration. On the contrary, upon the transfer of the right, title and interest in and to such account by any trustee hereunder, said bank shall conclusively treat the transferee as the sole owner of said account. As and if I shall elect from time to time to cause interest payments on said account to be distributed rather than compounded, the bank shall be fully authorized to pay such interest direct to me individually unless there shall have been filed with it written notice of my death or incapacity satisfactory to it. Until the bank shall receive from some person interested in this trust, written notice of any death or other event upon which the right to receive may depend, the bank shall incur no liability for payments made in good faith to persons whose interests shall have been affected by such event. The bank shall be protected in acting upon any notice or other instrument or document believed by it to be genuine and to have been signed or presented by the proper party or parties.

5. I reserve unto myself the power and right to collect any interest or other income which may accrue from the trust property and, in my sole discretion as Trustee, either to accumulate such interest or income as an addition to the trust assets being held hereunder or pay such interest or income to myself as an individual. I shall be exclusively entitled to all income accruing from the trust property during my lifetime, and no beneficiary named herein shall have any claim upon any such income distributed to me.

6. I reserve unto myself the power and right at any time during my lifetime to amend or revoke in whole or in part the trust hereby created without the necessity of obtaining the consent of the beneficiary and without giving notice to the beneficiary. The withdrawal by me of the whole or any part of the bank account held hereunder shall constitute as to such whole or part a revocation of this trust.

7. The death during my lifetime, or in a common accident or disaster with me, of the beneficiary designated hereunder shall revoke such designation. and in the former event, this trust shall terminate upon my death and the trust property shall revert to my estate. to designate such new beneficiary, this trust shall terminate upon my death, I hereby nominate and appoint as Successor Trustee

8. In the event of my physical or mental incapacity or my death, I hereby nominate and appoint hereunder whosoever shall at that time be beneficiary hereunder, unless such beneficiary shall not have attained the age of 21 years or is otherwise legally incapacitated, in which event I hereby nominate and appoint

(Name) __Henry P. Adams__ __Milton__ __Connecticut__ __06605__
City / State / Zip

(Address) __125__ __Barnum Street__
Number / Street

to be Successor Trustee.

9. This Declaration of Trust shall extend to and be binding upon the heirs, executors, administrators and assigns of the undersigned and upon the Successors to the Trustee.

10. The Trustee and his successors shall serve without bond.

11. This Declaration of Trust shall be construed and enforced in accordance with the laws of the State of __Connecticut__

Declaration of Trust

WHEREAS, I, _____, of the

City/Town of _____, County of _____, State of _____,

am the owner of a checking/savings account in the _____,
(name of Bank)

located in the City/Town of _____, State of _____;

    NOW, THEREFORE, KNOW ALL MEN BY THESE PRESENTS, that I do hereby acknowledge and declare that I hold and will hold said bank account and all my right, title and interest in and to said account IN TRUST

    1. For the use and benefit of:

(Name) _____, of

(Address) _____
      Number   *Street*   *City*   *State*   *Zip*

    If because of my physical or mental incapacity certified in writing by a physician, the Successor Trustee hereinafter named shall assume active administration of this trust during my lifetime, such Successor Trustee shall be fully authorized to pay to me or disburse on my behalf such sums from income or principal as appear necessary or desirable for my comfort or welfare. Upon my death, unless the beneficiary shall predecease me or unless we both shall die as a result of a common accident or disaster, my Successor Trustee is hereby directed forthwith to transfer said bank account and all right, title and interest in and to said account unto the beneficiary absolutely and thereby terminate this trust; provided, however, that if the beneficiary hereunder shall not have attained the age of 21 years, the Successor Trustee shall hold the trust assets in continuing trust until such beneficiary shall have attained the age of 21 years. During such period of continuing trust the Successor Trustee, in his absolute discretion, may retain the specific bank account herein described if he believes it to be in the best interests of the beneficiary so to do, or he may terminate it, investing and reinvesting the proceeds as he may deem appropriate. Prior to the date upon which such beneficiary attains the age of 21 years, the Successor Trustee may apply or expend any or all of the income or principal directly for the maintenance, education and support of the beneficiary without the intervention of any guardian and without application to any court. Such payments of income or principal may be made to the parents of such beneficiary or to the person with whom the beneficiary is living without any liability upon the Successor Trustee to see to the application thereof. If such beneficiary survives me but dies before attaining the age of 21 years, at his or her death the Successor Trustee shall transfer, pay over and deliver the trust property to such beneficiary's personal representative, absolutely.

    2. The beneficiary hereunder shall be liable for his proportionate share of any taxes levied upon the Settlor's total taxable estate by reason of the Settlor's death.

    3. All interests of a beneficiary hereunder shall be inalienable and free from anticipation, assignment, attachment, pledge or control by creditors or a present or former spouse of such beneficiary in any proceedings at law or in equity.

    4. This trust is created with the express understanding that the bank at which the account is maintained shall be under no liability whatsoever to see to its proper administration. On the contrary, upon the transfer of the right, title and interest in and to such account by any trustee hereunder, said bank shall conclusively treat the transferee as the sole owner of said account. Until the bank shall receive from some person interested in this trust, written notice of any death or other event upon which the right to receive may depend, the bank shall incur no liability for payments made in good faith to persons whose interests shall have been affected by such event. The bank shall be protected in acting upon any notice or other instrument or document believed by it to be genuine and to have been signed or presented by the proper party or parties.

    5. I reserve unto myself the power and right to collect any interest or other income which may accrue from the trust property and, in my sole discretion as Trustee, either to accumulate such interest or income as an addition to the trust assets being held hereunder or pay such interest or income to myself as an individual. I shall be exclusively entitled to all income accruing from the trust property during my lifetime, and no beneficiary named herein shall have any claim upon any such income distributed to me.

    6. I reserve unto myself the power and right at any time during my lifetime to amend or revoke in whole or in part the trust hereby created without the necessity of obtaining the consent of the beneficiary and without giving notice to the beneficiary. The withdrawal by me of the whole or any part of the bank account held hereunder shall constitute as to such whole or part a revocation of this trust.

    7. The death during my lifetime, or in a common accident or disaster with me, of the beneficiary designated hereunder shall revoke such designation, and in the former event, I reserve the right to designate a new beneficiary. Should I for any reason fail to designate such new beneficiary, this trust shall terminate upon my death and the trust property shall revert to my estate.

    8. In the event of my physical or mental incapacity or my death, I hereby nominate and appoint as Successor Trustee hereunder whosoever shall at that time be beneficiary hereunder, unless such beneficiary shall not have attained the age of 21 years or is otherwise legally incapacitated, in which event I hereby nominate and appoint

(Name) _____, of

(Address) _____
      Number   *Street*   *City*   *State*   *Zip*

to be Successor Trustee.

9. This Declaration of Trust shall extend to and be binding upon the heirs, executors, administrators and assigns of the undersigned and upon the Successors to the Trustee.

10. The Trustee and his successors shall serve without bond.

11. This Declaration of Trust shall be construed and enforced in accordance with the laws of the State

of _____.

IN WITNESS WHEREOF, I have hereunto set my hand and seal this _____

day of _____, 19_____.

(Settlor sign here) _____ L.S.

I, the undersigned legal spouse of the above Settlor, hereby waive all community property rights which I may have in the hereinabove-described account and give my assent to the provisions of the trust and to the inclusion in it of the said account.

(Spouse sign here) _____ L.S.

Witness: (1) _____   Witness: (2) _____

STATE OF _____ ⎫   City
                                      ⎬   or
COUNTY OF _____ ⎭   Town _____

On the _____ day of _____, 19_____, personally appeared

_____

known to me to be the individual(s) who executed the foregoing instrument, and acknowledged the same to be _____ free act and deed, before me.

(Notary Seal)   _____

                                                 Notary Public

---

DECLARATION OF TRUST

For Naming

ONE PRIMARY BENEFICIARY

And

ONE CONTINGENT BENEFICIARY

To Receive

A BANK ACCOUNT HELD IN ONE NAME

INSTRUCTIONS:

On the following pages will be found a declaration of trust (DT-106) suitable for use in connection with the establishment of an inter vivos trust covering a checking or savings account held in one name only, where it is desired to name some *one* person as primary beneficiary, with some *one* other person as contingent beneficiary to receive the account if the primary beneficiary be not surviving upon the death of the owner.

Cross out *"city"* or *"town,"* leaving the appropriate designation of your community. Next, cross out *"checking"* or *"savings,"* leaving the appropriate designation of the bank account. Then, name the bank; if it's a branch, identify the location.

Enter the names of the beneficiaries in the appropriate place in Paragraph 1.

Note that Paragraph 8 designates as Successor Trustee *"whosoever shall at that time be beneficiary hereunder,"* which means that in most cases you don't need to fill anything in there. However, if there is any possibility of a beneficiary who has not attained the age of 21 years receiving the bank account, make certain that you name an adult in this paragraph who can act as trustee for such beneficiary. Avoid naming as trustee a person not likely to survive until the beneficiary has attained age 21.

When completed in the manner shown on the reverse side hereof, make several photocopies for reference purposes. Hold the original in safekeeping and offer a copy to the bank when you open the account. Instruct them to identify the account in this manner: *"(your name), Trustee u/d/t dated _____."*

Important: Read carefully Note B on page 38, which applies to this declaration of trust.

DT-106

Declaration of Trust

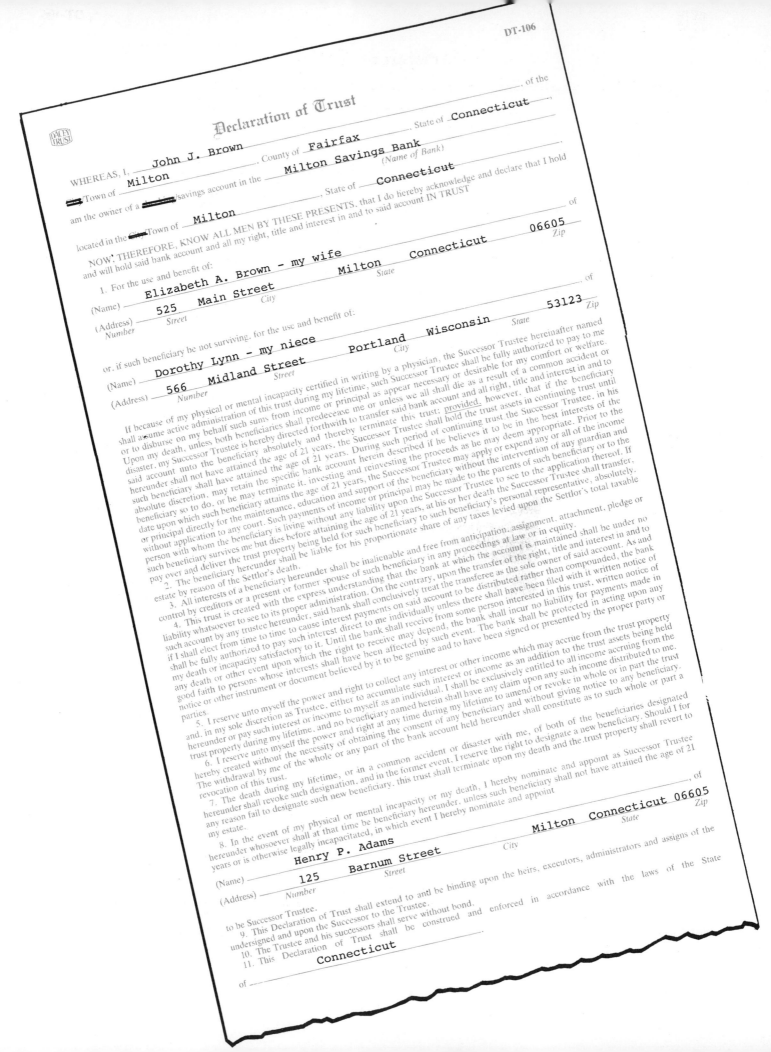

WHEREAS, I, __John J. Brown__, County of __Fairfax__, State of __Connecticut__, of the

Town of __Milton__ am the owner of a ~~checking~~/savings account in the __Milton Savings Bank__ (Name of Bank)

located in the City/Town of __Milton__, State of __Connecticut__,

NOW, THEREFORE, KNOW ALL MEN BY THESE PRESENTS, that I do hereby acknowledge and declare that I hold and will hold said bank account and all my right, title and interest in and to said account IN TRUST

1. For the use and benefit of:

(Name) __Elizabeth A. Brown - my wife__ __Milton__ __Connecticut__ __06605__
City State Zip

(Address) __525__ __Main Street__
Number Street

or, if such beneficiary be not surviving, for the use and benefit of:

(Name) __Dorothy Lynn - my niece__ __Portland__ __Wisconsin__ __53123__ of
City State Zip

(Address) __566__ __Midland Street__
Number Street

If because of my physical or mental incapacity certified in writing by a physician, the Successor Trustee hereinafter named shall assume active administration of this trust during my lifetime, such Successor Trustee shall be fully authorized to pay to me or to disburse on my behalf such sums from income or principal as appear necessary or desirable for my comfort or welfare. Upon my death, unless both beneficiaries shall predecease me or unless we all shall die as a result of a common accident or disaster, my Successor Trustee is hereby directed forthwith to transfer said bank account and all right, title and interest in and to said account unto the beneficiary absolutely and thereby terminate this trust; provided, however, that if the beneficiary hereunder shall not have attained the age of 21 years, the Successor Trustee shall hold the trust assets in continuing trust until such beneficiary shall have attained the age of 21 years. During such period of continuing trust, the Successor Trustee, in his absolute discretion, may retain the specific bank account herein described if he believes it to be in the best interests of the beneficiary so to do, or he may terminate it, investing and reinvesting the proceeds as he may deem appropriate. Prior to the date upon which such beneficiary attains the age of 21 years, the Successor Trustee may apply or expend any or all of the income or principal directly for the maintenance, education and support of the beneficiary without the intervention of any guardian and without application to any court. Such payments of income or principal may be made to the parents of such beneficiary or to the person with whom the beneficiary is living without any liability upon the Successor Trustee to see to the application thereof. If such beneficiary survives me but dies before attaining the age of 21 years, at his or her death the Successor Trustee shall transfer, pay over and deliver the trust property to such beneficiary's personal representative, absolutely.

2. The beneficiary hereunder shall be liable for his proportionate share of any taxes levied upon the Settlor's total taxable estate by reason of the Settlor's death.

3. All interests of a beneficiary hereunder shall be inalienable and free from anticipation, assignment, attachment, pledge or control by creditors or a present or former spouse of such beneficiary in any proceedings at law or in equity.

4. This trust is created with the express understanding that the bank at which the account is maintained shall be under no liability whatsoever to see to its proper administration. On the contrary, upon the transfer of the right, title and interest in and to such account by any trustee hereunder, said bank shall conclusively treat the transferee as the sole owner of said account. As and if I shall elect from time to time to cause interest payments on said account to be distributed rather than compounded, the bank shall be fully authorized to pay such interest direct to me individually unless there shall have been filed with it written notice of my death or incapacity satisfactory to it. Until the bank shall receive from some person interested in this trust, written notice of any death or other event upon which the right to receive may depend, the bank shall incur no liability for payments made in good faith to persons whose interests shall have been affected by such event. The bank shall be protected in acting upon any notice or other instrument or document believed by it to be genuine and to have been signed or presented by the proper party or parties.

5. I reserve unto myself the power and right to collect any interest or other income which may accrue from the trust property and, in my sole discretion as Trustee, either to accumulate such interest or income as an addition to the trust assets being held hereunder or pay such interest or income to myself as an individual. I shall be exclusively entitled to all income accruing from the trust property during my lifetime, and no beneficiary named herein shall have any claim upon any such income distributed to me.

6. I reserve unto myself the power and right at any time during my lifetime to amend or revoke in whole or in part the trust hereby created without the necessity of obtaining the consent of any beneficiary and without giving notice to any beneficiary. The withdrawal by me of the whole or any part of the bank account held hereunder shall constitute as to such whole or part a revocation of this trust.

7. The death during my lifetime, or in a common accident or disaster with me, of both of the beneficiaries designated hereunder shall revoke such designation, and in the former event, I reserve the right to designate a new beneficiary. Should I for any reason fail to designate such new beneficiary, this trust shall terminate upon my death and the trust property shall revert to my estate.

8. In the event of my physical or mental incapacity or my death, I hereby nominate and appoint as Successor Trustee hereunder whosoever shall at that time be beneficiary hereunder, unless such beneficiary shall not have attained the age of 21 years or is otherwise legally incapacitated, in which event I hereby nominate and appoint

(Name) __Henry P. Adams__ __Milton__ __Connecticut__ __06605__ of
City State Zip

(Address) __125__ __Barnum Street__
Number Street

to be Successor Trustee.

9. This Declaration of Trust shall extend to and be binding upon the heirs, executors, administrators and assigns of the undersigned and upon the Successor to the Trustee.

10. The Trustee and his successors shall serve without bond.

11. This Declaration of Trust shall be construed and enforced in accordance with the laws of the State of __Connecticut__.

Declaration of Trust

WHEREAS, I, _____, of the

City/Town of _____, County of _____, State of _____,

am the owner of a checking/savings account in the _____,
(Name of Bank)

located in the City/Town of _____, State of _____;

NOW, THEREFORE, KNOW ALL MEN BY THESE PRESENTS, that I do hereby acknowledge and declare that I hold and will hold said bank account and all my right, title and interest in and to said account IN TRUST

1. For the use and benefit of:

(Name) _____, of

(Address) _____
Number   Street   City   State   Zip

or, if such beneficiary be not surviving, for the use and benefit of:

(Name) _____, of

(Address) _____
Number   Street   City   State   Zip

If because of my physical or mental incapacity certified in writing by a physician, the Successor Trustee hereinafter named shall assume active administration of this trust during my lifetime, such Successor Trustee shall be fully authorized to pay to me or to disburse on my behalf such sums from income or principal as appear necessary or desirable for my comfort or welfare. Upon my death, unless both beneficiaries shall predecease me or unless we all shall die as a result of a common accident or disaster, my Successor Trustee is hereby directed forthwith to transfer said bank account and all right, title and interest in and to said account unto the beneficiary absolutely and thereby terminate this trust; <u>provided,</u> however, that if the beneficiary hereunder shall not have attained the age of 21 years, the Successor Trustee shall hold the trust assets in continuing trust until such beneficiary shall have attained the age of 21 years. During such period of continuing trust the Successor Trustee, in his absolute discretion, may retain the specific bank account herein described if he believes it to be in the best interests of the beneficiary so to do, or he may terminate it, investing and reinvesting the proceeds as he may deem appropriate. Prior to the date upon which such beneficiary attains the age of 21 years, the Successor Trustee may apply or expend any or all of the income or principal directly for the maintenance, education and support of the beneficiary without the intervention of any guardian and without application to any court. Such payments of income or principal may be made to the parents of such beneficiary or to the person with whom the beneficiary is living without any liability upon the Successor Trustee to see to the application thereof. If such beneficiary survives me but dies before attaining the age of 21 years, at his or her death the Successor Trustee shall transfer, pay over and deliver the trust property being held for such beneficiary to such beneficiary's personal representative, absolutely.

2. The beneficiary hereunder shall be liable for his proportionate share of any taxes levied upon the Settlor's total taxable estate by reason of the Settlor's death.

3. All interests of a beneficiary hereunder shall be inalienable and free from anticipation, assignment, attachment, pledge or control by creditors or a present or former spouse of such beneficiary in any proceedings at law or in equity.

4. This trust is created with the express understanding that the bank at which the account is maintained shall be under no liability whatsoever to see to its proper administration. On the contrary, upon the transfer of the right, title and interest in and to such account by any trustee hereunder, said bank shall conclusively treat the transferee as the sole owner of said account. Until the bank shall receive from some person interested in this trust, written notice of any death or other event upon which the right to receive may depend, the bank shall incur no liability for payments made in good faith to persons whose interests shall have been affected by such event. The bank shall be protected in acting upon any notice or other instrument or document believed by it to be genuine and to have been signed or presented by the proper party or parties.

5. I reserve unto myself the power and right to collect any interest or other income which may accrue from the trust property and, in my sole discretion as Trustee, either to accumulate such interest or income as an addition to the trust assets being held hereunder or pay such interest or income to myself as an individual. I shall be exclusively entitled to all income accruing from the trust property during my lifetime, and no beneficiary named herein shall have any claim upon any such income distributed to me.

6. I reserve unto myself the power and right at any time during my lifetime to amend or revoke in whole or in part the trust hereby created without the necessity of obtaining the consent of any beneficiary and without giving notice to any beneficiary. The withdrawal by me of the whole or any part of the bank account held hereunder shall constitute as to such whole or part a revocation of this trust.

7. The death during my lifetime, or in a common accident or disaster with me, of both of the beneficiaries designated hereunder shall revoke such designation, and in the former event, I reserve the right to designate a new beneficiary. Should I for any reason fail to designate such new beneficiary, this trust shall terminate upon my death and the trust property shall revert to my estate.

8. In the event of my physical or mental incapacity or my death, I hereby nominate and appoint as Successor Trustee hereunder whosoever shall at that time be beneficiary hereunder, unless such beneficiary shall not have attained the age of 21 years or is otherwise legally incapacitated, in which event I hereby nominate and appoint

(Name) _____ , of

(Address) _____
      Number   *Street*   *City*   *State*   *Zip*

to be Successor Trustee.

9. This Declaration of Trust shall extend to and be binding upon the heirs, executors, administrators and assigns of the undersigned and upon the Successor to the Trustee.

10. The Trustee and his successors shall serve without bond.

11. This Declaration of Trust shall be construed and enforced in accordance with the laws of the State

of _____ .

IN WITNESS WHEREOF, I have hereunto set my hand and seal this _____

day of _____ , 19 _____ .

(Settlor sign here) _____ L.S.

I, the undersigned legal spouse of the above Settlor, hereby waive all community property rights which I may have in the hereinabove-described account and give my assent to the provisions of the trust and to the inclusion in it of the said account.

(Spouse sign here) _____ L.S.

Witness: (1) _____   Witness: (2) _____

STATE OF _____   City
or

COUNTY OF _____   Town _____

On the _____ day of _____ , 19 _____ , personally appeared

_____

known to me to be the individual(s) who executed the foregoing instrument, and acknowledged the same to be _____ free act and deed, before me.

(Notary Seal)   _____
                                           Notary Public

CHAPTER 8

DECLARATION OF TRUST
For Naming
TWO OR MORE BENEFICIARIES, SHARING EQUALLY,
To Receive
A BANK ACCOUNT HELD IN ONE NAME

INSTRUCTIONS:

On the following pages will be found a declaration of trust (DT-107) suitable for use in connection with the establishment of an inter vivos trust covering a checking or savings account held in one name only, where it is desired to name two or more persons to share the account equally upon the death of the owner.

Cross out *"city"* or *"town,"* leaving the appropriate designation of your community. Next, cross out *"checking"* or *"savings,"* leaving the appropriate designation of the bank account. Then, name the bank; if it's a branch, identify the location.

In Paragraph 1, indicate the *number of persons* you are naming (to discourage unauthorized additions to the list) and then insert their names. The one whose name appears *first* will be the Successor Trustee responsible for seeing to the distribution of the trust property.

Note that the instrument specifies that the named beneficiaries are to receive *"in equal shares, or the survivor of them/per stirpes."* Now, think carefully: If you have named three persons with the understanding that if one of them predeceases you, *his* children will take *his* share, cross out *"or the survivor of them"* and *initial it.* If that is *not* what you want—if, for example, you prefer that the share of the deceased person be divided between the two surviving persons, cross out *"per stirpes"* and *initial it.* Remember, you <u>must</u> cross out either *"or the survivor of them"* or *"per stirpes"*—one or the other.

Note that Paragraph 8 designates as Successor Trustee *"the beneficiary named first above."* Wherever there is any possibility of a beneficiary who has not attained the age of 21 years receiving the bank account, make certain that you name an adult in this paragraph who can act as trustee for such beneficiary. Avoid naming as trustee a person not likely to survive until the beneficiary has attained age 21.

When completed in the manner shown on the reverse side hereof, make several photocopies for reference purposes. Hold the original in safekeeping and offer a copy to the bank when you open the account. Instruct them to identify the account in this manner: *"(your name), Trustee u/d/t dated _____."*

Important: Read carefully Note B on page 38, which applies to this declaration of trust.

Declaration of Trust

WHEREAS, I, __John J. Brown__ _____, of the

__Town of__ __Milton__ , County of __Fairfax__ , State of __Connecticut__

am the owner of a _____ savings account in the __Milton Savings Bank__
(Name of Bank)

located in the __Town of__ __Milton__ , State of __Connecticut__

NOW, THEREFORE, KNOW ALL MEN BY THESE PRESENTS, that I do hereby acknowledge and declare that I hold and will hold said bank account and all my right, title and interest in and to said account IN TRUST __J.J.B.__ per

1. For the use and benefit of the following __three (3)__ persons, in equal shares, stirpes:

Thomas B. Brown - my brother
Helen M. Brown - my sister
Charles M. Brown - my brother

If because of my physical or mental incapacity certified in writing by a physician, the Successor Trustee hereinafter named shall assume active administration of this trust during my lifetime, such Successor Trustee shall be fully authorized to pay to me or disburse on my behalf such sums from income or principal as appear necessary or desirable for my comfort or welfare. Upon my death, unless all of the beneficiaries shall predecease me or unless we all shall die as a result of a common accident or disaster, my Successor Trustee is hereby directed forthwith to transfer said bank account and all right, title and interest in and to said account unto the beneficiaries absolutely and thereby terminate this trust; provided, however, that if any beneficiary hereunder shall not have attained the age of 21 years, the Successor Trustee shall hold such beneficiary's share of the trust assets in continuing trust until such beneficiary shall have attained the age of 21 years. During such period of continuing trust the Successor Trustee, in his absolute discretion, may retain the specific bank account herein described if he believes it to be in the best interests of the beneficiary so to do, or he may terminate it, investing and reinvesting the proceeds as he may deem appropriate. Prior to the date upon which such beneficiary attains the age of 21 years, the Successor Trustee may apply or expend any or all of the income or principal directly for the maintenance, education and support of the beneficiary without the intervention of any guardian and without application to any court. Such payments of income or principal may be made to the parents of such beneficiary or to the person with whom the beneficiary is living without any liability upon the Successor Trustee to see to the application thereof. If such beneficiary survives me but dies before attaining the age of 21 years, at his or her death the Successor Trustee shall transfer, pay over and deliver the trust property being held for such beneficiary to such beneficiary's personal representative, absolutely.

2. Each beneficiary hereunder shall be liable for his proportionate share of any taxes levied upon the Settlor's total taxable estate by reason of the Settlor's death.

3. All interests of a beneficiary hereunder shall be inalienable and free from anticipation, assignment, attachment, pledge or control by creditors or a present or former spouse of such beneficiary in any proceedings at law or in equity.

4. This trust is created with the express understanding that the bank at which the account is maintained shall be under no liability whatsoever to see to its proper administration, and upon the transfer of the right, title and interest in and to such account by any trustee hereunder, said bank shall conclusively treat the transferee as the sole owner of said account. As and if I shall elect from time to time to cause interest payments on said account to be distributed rather than compounded, the bank shall be fully authorized to pay such interest direct to me individually unless there shall have been filed with it written notice of my death or other event upon which the right to receive may depend, the bank shall incur no liability for payments made in good faith to persons whose interests shall have been affected by it to be genuine and to have been signed or presented by the proper party or parties, other instrument or document believed by it to collect any interest or other income which may accrue from the trust property

5. I reserve unto myself the power and right to collect any interest or other income as an addition to the trust assets being held hereunder or and, in my sole discretion as Trustee, either to accumulate such income as an addition to all income accruing from the trust property during pay such income to myself as an individual. I shall be exclusively entitled to all income accruing from the trust property during my lifetime, and no beneficiary named herein shall have any claim upon any such income distributed to me.

8. In the event of my physical or mental incapacity or my death, I hereby nominate and appoint as Successor Trustee the beneficiary named first above, unless such beneficiary shall not have attained the age of 21 years or is otherwise legally incapacitated in which event I hereby nominate and appoint as Successor Trustee the beneficiary named second above, unless such beneficiary named second above shall not have attained the age of 21 years or is otherwise legally incapacitated, in which latter event I hereby nominate and appoint

__Henry P. Adams__ , __Milton__ , __Connecticut__ __06605__ , of
(Name)   City   State   Zip

__125 Barnum Street__
(Address) — Number   Street

to be Successor Trustee.

9. This Declaration of Trust shall extend to and be binding upon the heirs, executors, administrators and assigns of the undersigned and upon the Successors to the Trustee.

10. The Trustee and his successors shall serve without bond.

11. This Declaration of Trust shall be construed and enforced in accordance with the laws of the State of __Connecticut__

Declaration of Trust

WHEREAS, I, _____, of the

City/Town of _____, County of _____, State of _____,

am the owner of a checking/savings account in the _____,
(Name of Bank)

located in the City/Town of _____, State of _____;

NOW, THEREFORE, KNOW ALL MEN BY THESE PRESENTS, that I do hereby acknowledge and declare that I hold and will hold said bank account and all my right, title and interest in and to said account IN TRUST

1. For the use and benefit of the following _____ persons, in equal shares, or the survivor of them/per stirpes:

If because of my physical or mental incapacity certified in writing by a physician, the Successor Trustee hereinafter named shall assume active administration of this trust during my lifetime, such Successor Trustee shall be fully authorized to pay to me or disburse on my behalf such sums from income or principal as appear necessary or desirable for my comfort or welfare. Upon my death, unless all of the beneficiaries shall predecease me or unless we all shall die as a result of a common accident or disaster, my Successor Trustee is hereby directed forthwith to transfer said bank account and all right, title and interest in and to said account unto the beneficiaries absolutely and thereby terminate this trust; <u>provided</u>, however, that if any beneficiary hereunder shall not have attained the age of 21 years, the Successor Trustee shall hold such beneficiary's share of the trust assets in continuing trust until such beneficiary shall have attained the age of 21 years. During such period of continuing trust the Successor Trustee, in his absolute discretion, may retain the specific bank account herein described if he believes it to be in the best interests of the beneficiary so to do, or he may terminate it, investing and reinvesting the proceeds as he may deem appropriate. Prior to the date upon which such beneficiary attains the age of 21 years, the Successor Trustee may apply or expend any or all of the income or principal directly for the maintenance, education and support of the beneficiary without the intervention of any guardian and without application to any court. Such payments of income or principal may be made to the parents of such beneficiary or to the person with whom the beneficiary is living without any liability upon the Successor Trustee to see to the application thereof. If such beneficiary survives me but dies before attaining the age of 21 years, at his or her death the Successor Trustee shall transfer, pay over and deliver the trust property being held for such beneficiary to such beneficiary's personal representative, absolutely.

2. Each beneficiary hereunder shall be liable for his proportionate share of any taxes levied upon the Settlor's total taxable estate by reason of the Settlor's death.

3. All interests of a beneficiary hereunder shall be inalienable and free from anticipation, assignment, attachment, pledge or control by creditors or a present or former spouse of such beneficiary in any proceedings at law or in equity.

4. This trust is created with the express understanding that the bank at which the account is maintained shall be under no liability whatsoever to see to its proper administration, and upon the transfer of the right, title and interest in and to such account by any trustee hereunder, said bank shall conclusively treat the transferee as the sole owner of said account. Until the bank shall receive from some person interested in this trust, written notice of any death or other event upon which the right to receive may depend, the bank shall incur no liability for payments made in good faith to persons whose interests shall have been affected by such event. The bank shall be protected in acting upon any notice or other instrument or document believed by it to be genuine and to have been signed or presented by the proper party or parties.

5. I reserve unto myself the power and right to collect any interest or other income which may accrue from the trust property and, in my sole discretion as Trustee, either to accumulate such income as an addition to the trust assets being held hereunder or pay such income to myself as an individual. I shall be exclusively entitled to all income accruing from the trust property during my lifetime, and no beneficiary named herein shall have any claim upon any such income distributed to me.

6. I reserve unto myself the power and right at any time during my lifetime to amend or revoke in whole or in part the trust hereby created without the necessity of obtaining the consent of the beneficiaries and without giving notice to the beneficiaries. The withdrawal by me of the whole or any part of the bank account held hereunder shall constitute as to such whole or part a revocation of this trust.

7. The death during my lifetime, or in a common accident or disaster with me, of all of the beneficiaries designated hereunder shall revoke such designation, and in the former event, I reserve the right to designate a new beneficiary. Should I for any reason fail to designate such new beneficiary, this trust shall terminate upon my death and the trust property shall revert to my estate.

8. In the event of my physical or mental incapacity or my death, I hereby nominate and appoint as Successor Trustee the beneficiary named first above, unless such beneficiary shall not have attained the age of 21 years or is otherwise legally incapacitated in which event I hereby nominate and appoint as Successor Trustee the beneficiary named second above, unless such beneficiary named second above shall not have attained the age of 21 years or is otherwise legally incapacitated, in which latter event I hereby nominate and appoint

(Name) _____ , of

(Address) _____

      Number   *Street*   *City*   *State*   *Zip*

to be Successor Trustee.

9. This Declaration of Trust shall extend to and be binding upon the heirs, executors, administrators and assigns of the undersigned and upon the Successors to the Trustee.

10. The Trustee and his successors shall serve without bond.

11. This Declaration of Trust shall be construed and enforced in accordance with the laws of the State

of _____ .

IN WITNESS WHEREOF, I have hereunto set my hand and seal this _____

day of _____ , 19_____ .

      (Settlor sign here) _____ L.S.

I, the undersigned legal spouse of the Settlor, hereby waive all community property rights which I may have in the hereinabove-described account and give my assent to the provisions of the trust and to the inclusion in it of the said account.

      (Spouse sign here) _____ L.S.

Witness: (1) _____   Witness: (2) _____

STATE OF _____   City

      or

COUNTY OF _____   Town _____

On the _____ day of _____ , 19_____ , personally appeared

_____

known to me to be the individual(s) who executed the foregoing instrument, and acknowledged the same to be _____ free act and deed, before me.

_____

(Notary Seal)   *Notary Public*

CHAPTER 8

DECLARATION OF TRUST
For Naming
ONE PRIMARY BENEFICIARY WITH YOUR CHILDREN,
SHARING EQUALLY, AS CONTINGENT BENEFICIARIES
To Receive
A BANK ACCOUNT HELD IN ONE NAME

INSTRUCTIONS:

On the following pages will be found a declaration of trust (DT-108) suitable for use in connection with the establishment of an inter vivos trust covering a checking or savings account held in one name only, where it is desired to name one person (ordinarily, but not necessarily, one's spouse) as primary beneficiary, with one's children as contingent beneficiaries to receive the account if the primary beneficiary be not surviving.

Cross out *"city"* or *"town,"* leaving the appropriate designation of your community. Next, cross out *"checking"* or *"savings,"* leaving the appropriate designation of the bank account. Then, name the bank; if it's a branch, identify the location.

Enter the name of the primary beneficiary (called the "First Beneficiary") in the appropriate place in Paragraph 1. Note that the instrument first refers to your children as *"natural not/or adopted."* Now, decide: If you have an adopted child and you wish to include him, cross out the word *"not"* in the phrase *"natural not/or adopted"* and *initial it.* If you wish to *exclude* your adopted child, cross out the word *"or"* in the same phrase and *initial it.* Remember, you <u>must</u> cross out *"not"* or *"or"*—one or the other. If you have no adopted child, simply cross out *"not."*

Note next that the instrument specifies that your children are to receive *"in equal shares, or the survivor of them/per stirpes."* Now, think carefully: If it is your wish that if one of your children does not survive you, *his* share will revert to *his* children in equal shares, cross out *"or the survivor of them"* and *initial it.* If that is *not* what you want—if, for example, you prefer that the share of any child of yours who predeceases you shall be divided between your other surviving children in equal shares, cross out *"per stirpes"* and *initial it.* Remember, you <u>must</u> cross out *"or the survivor of them"* or *"per stirpes"*—one or the other.

Note that in Paragraph 8, the First Beneficiary is designated as Successor Trustee, while a space is provided in which you should designate another person to so act if the named Successor Trustee is not surviving or otherwise fails or ceases to act. This could be one of your children, for example, but it must be an adult who can act as trustee for any beneficiary who comes into a share of the trust before attaining the age of 21. Avoid naming someone not likely to survive until the youngest such beneficiary has attained age 21.

When completed in the manner shown on the reverse side hereof, make several photocopies for reference purposes. Hold the original in safekeeping and offer a copy to the bank when you open the account. Instruct them to identify the account in this manner: *"(your name), Trustee u/d/t dated _____."*

Important: Read carefully Note B on page 38, which applies to this declaration of trust.

Declaration of Trust

WHEREAS, I, __John J. Brown__, County of __Fairfax__, State of __Connecticut__, of the Town of __Milton__, am the owner of a ~~savings~~ savings account in the __Milton Savings Bank__ (Name of Bank) located in the ~~Town~~ Town of __Milton__, State of __Connecticut__;

NOW, THEREFORE, KNOW ALL MEN BY THESE PRESENTS, that I do hereby acknowledge and declare that I hold and will hold said bank account and all my right, title and interest in and to said account IN TRUST

1. For the use and benefit of:

(Name) __Elizabeth A. Brown - my wife__

(Address) __525__ __Main Street__ __Milton__ __Connecticut 06605__
Number   Street   City   State   Zip

J.J.B.   *J.J.B.*

(hereinafter referred to as the "First Beneficiary"), and upon his or her death prior to the termination of the trust, for the use and benefit of my children, natural not adopted, in equal shares, or the survivor of them, per stirpes.

If because of my physical or mental incapacity certified in writing by a physician, the Successor Trustee hereinafter named shall assume active administration of this trust during my lifetime, such Successor Trustee shall be fully authorized to pay to me or disburse on my behalf such sums from income or principal as appear necessary or desirable for my comfort or welfare. Upon my death, unless all of the beneficiaries shall predecease me or unless we all shall die as a result of a common accident or disaster, my Successor Trustee is hereby directed forthwith to transfer said bank account and all right, title and interest in and to said account unto the beneficiary or beneficiaries absolutely and thereby terminate this trust; _provided_, however, that if any beneficiary hereunder shall not have attained the age of 21 years, the Successor Trustee shall hold such beneficiary's share of the trust assets in continuing trust until such beneficiary shall have attained the age of 21 years. During such period of continuing trust the Successor Trustee, in his absolute discretion, may retain the specific bank account herein described if he believes it to be in the best interests of the beneficiary so to do, or he may terminate it, investing and reinvesting the proceeds as he may deem appropriate. Prior to the date upon which such beneficiary attains the age of 21 years, the Successor Trustee may apply or expend any or all of the income or principal directly for the maintenance, education and support of the beneficiary without the intervention of any guardian and without application to any court. Such payments of income or principal may be made to the parents of such beneficiary or to the person with whom the beneficiary is living without any liability upon the Successor Trustee to see to the application thereof. If such beneficiary survives me but dies before attaining the age of 21 years, at his or her death the Successor Trustee shall transfer, pay over and deliver the trust property being held for such beneficiary to such beneficiary's personal representative, absolutely.

2. Each beneficiary hereunder shall be liable for his proportionate share of any taxes levied upon the Settlor's total taxable estate by reason of the Settlor's death.

3. All interests of a beneficiary hereunder shall be inalienable and free from anticipation, assignment, attachment, pledge or control by creditors or a present or former spouse of such beneficiary in any proceedings at law or in equity.

4. This trust is created with the express understanding that the bank at which the account is maintained shall be under no liability whatsoever to see to its proper administration. On the contrary, upon the transfer of the right, title and interest in and to such account by any trustee hereunder, said bank shall conclusively treat the transferee as the sole owner of said account. As and if I shall elect from time to time to cause interest payments on said account to be distributed rather than compounded, the bank shall be fully authorized to pay such interest direct to me individually unless there shall have been filed with it written notice of my death or incapacity satisfactory to it. Until the bank shall receive from some person interested in this trust, written notice of any death or other event upon which the right to receive may depend, the bank shall incur no liability for payments made in good faith to persons whose interests shall have been affected by such event. The bank shall be protected in acting upon any notice or other instrument or document believed by it to be genuine and to have been signed or presented by the proper party or parties.

5. I reserve unto myself the power and right to collect any interest or other income which may accrue from the trust property and, in my sole discretion as Trustee, either to accumulate such interest or income as an addition to the trust assets being held hereunder or pay such income to myself as an individual. I shall be exclusively entitled to all income accruing from the trust property during my lifetime, and no beneficiary named herein shall have any claim upon any such income distributed to me.

6. I reserve unto myself the power and right at any time during my lifetime to amend or revoke in whole or in part the trust hereby created without the necessity of obtaining the consent of the beneficiaries and without giving notice to the beneficiaries. The withdrawal by me of the whole or any part of the bank account held hereunder shall constitute as to such whole or part a revocation of this trust.

7. The death during my lifetime, or in a common accident or disaster with me, of all of the beneficiaries designated hereunder shall revoke such designation, and in the former event, I reserve the right to designate a new beneficiary. Should I for any reason fail to designate such beneficiary, this ~~shall~~ ... my death and the trust property shall revert to

8. In the event of my physical or mental incapacity or my death, I hereby nominate and appoint as Successor Trustee hereunder the First Beneficiary, or if such First Beneficiary be not surviving or fails or ceases to act. I nominate and appoint

(Name) __Henry P. Adams__ __Milton__ __Connecticut__ __06605__
City   State   Zip

(Address) __125__ __Barnum Street__
Number   Street

to be Successor Trustee. If such person fails or ceases to act or should I for any reason fail to designate the person above intended to be nominated, then I nominate and appoint as such Successor Trustee hereunder whosoever shall qualify as executor, administrator or guardian, as the case may be, of my estate.

9. This Declaration of Trust shall extend to and be binding upon the heirs, executors, administrators and assigns of the undersigned and upon the Successors to the Trustee.

10. The Trustee and his successors shall serve without bond.

11. This Declaration of Trust shall be construed and enforced in accordance with the laws of the State of __Connecticut__.

Declaration of Trust

WHEREAS, I, _____, of the

City/Town of _____, County of _____, State of _____,

am the owner of a checking/savings account in the _____,

(Name of Bank)

located in the City/Town of _____, State of _____;

NOW, THEREFORE, KNOW ALL MEN BY THESE PRESENTS, that I do hereby acknowledge and declare that I hold and will hold said bank account and all my right, title and interest in and to said account IN TRUST

1. For the use and benefit of:

(Name) _____, of

(Address) _____

| Number | Street | City | State | Zip |

(hereinafter referred to as the "First Beneficiary"), and upon his or her death prior to the termination of the trust, for the use and benefit of my children, natural not/or adopted, in equal shares, or the survivor of them/per stirpes.

If because of my physical or mental incapacity certified in writing by a physician, the Successor Trustee hereinafter named shall assume active administration of this trust during my lifetime, such Successor Trustee shall be fully authorized to pay to me or disburse on my behalf such sums from income or principal as appear necessary or desirable for my comfort or welfare. Upon my death, unless all of the beneficiaries shall predecease me or unless we all shall die as a result of a common accident or disaster, my Successor Trustee is hereby directed forthwith to transfer said bank account and all right, title and interest in and to said account unto the beneficiary or beneficiaries absolutely and thereby terminate this trust; provided, however, that if any beneficiary hereunder shall not have attained the age of 21 years, the Successor Trustee shall hold such beneficiary's share of the trust assets in continuing trust until such beneficiary shall have attained the age of 21 years. During such period of continuing trust the Successor Trustee, in his absolute discretion, may retain the specific bank account herein described if he believes it to be in the best interests of the beneficiary so to do, or he may terminate it, investing and reinvesting the proceeds as he may deem appropriate. Prior to the date upon which such beneficiary attains the age of 21 years, the Successor Trustee may apply or expend any or all of the income or principal directly for the maintenance, education and support of the beneficiary without the intervention of any guardian and without application to any court. Such payments of income or principal may be made to the parents of such beneficiary or to the person with whom the beneficiary is living without any liability upon the Successor Trustee to see to the application thereof. If such beneficiary survives me but dies before attaining the age of 21 years, at his or her death the Successor Trustee shall transfer, pay over and deliver the trust property being held for such beneficiary to such beneficiary's personal representative, absolutely.

2. Each beneficiary hereunder shall be liable for his proportionate share of any taxes levied upon the Settlor's total taxable estate by reason of the Settlor's death.

3. All interests of a beneficiary hereunder shall be inalienable and free from anticipation, assignment, attachment, pledge or control by creditors or a present or former spouse of such beneficiary in any proceedings at law or in equity.

4. This trust is created with the express understanding that the bank at which the account is maintained shall be under no liability whatsoever to see to its proper administration. On the contrary, upon the transfer of the right, title and interest in and to such account by any trustee hereunder, said bank shall conclusively treat the transferee as the sole owner of said account. Until the bank shall receive from some person interested in this trust, written notice of any death or other event upon which the right to receive may depend, the bank shall incur no liability for payments made in good faith to persons whose interests shall have been affected by such event. The bank shall be protected in acting upon any notice or other instrument or document believed by it to be genuine and to have been signed or presented by the proper party or parties.

5. I reserve unto myself the power and right to collect any interest or other income which may accrue from the trust property and, in my sole discretion as Trustee, either to accumulate such interest or income as an addition to the trust assets being held hereunder or pay such income to myself as an individual. I shall be exclusively entitled to all income accruing from the trust property during my lifetime, and no beneficiary named herein shall have any claim upon any such income distributed to me.

6. I reserve unto myself the power and right at any time during my lifetime to amend or revoke in whole or in part the trust hereby created without the necessity of obtaining the consent of the beneficiaries and without giving notice to the beneficiaries. The withdrawal by me of the whole or any part of the bank account held hereunder shall constitute as to such whole or part a revocation of this trust.

7. The death during my lifetime, or in a common accident or disaster with me, of all of the beneficiaries designated hereunder shall revoke such designation, and in the former event, I reserve the right to designate a new beneficiary. Should I for any reason fail to designate such new beneficiary, this trust shall terminate upon my death and the trust property shall revert to my estate.

8. In the event of my physical or mental incapacity or my death, I hereby nominate and appoint as Successor Trustee hereunder the First Beneficiary, or if such First Beneficiary be not surviving or fails or ceases to act, I nominate and appoint

(Name) _____, of

(Address) _____

           Number   *Street*   *City*   *State*   *Zip*

to be Successor Trustee. If such person fails or ceases to act or should I for any reason fail to designate the person above intended to be nominated, then I nominate and appoint as such Successor Trustee hereunder whosoever shall qualify as executor, administrator or guardian, as the case may be, of my estate.

9. This Declaration of Trust shall extend to and be binding upon the heirs, executors, administrators and assigns of the undersigned and upon the Successors to the Trustee.

10. The Trustee and his successors shall serve without bond.

11. This Declaration of Trust shall be construed and enforced in accordance with the laws of the State

of _____.

IN WITNESS WHEREOF, I have hereunto set my hand and seal this _____

day of _____, 19_____.

          (Settlor sign here) _____ L.S.

I, the undersigned legal spouse of the Settlor, hereby waive all community property rights which I may have in the hereinabove-described account and give my assent to the provisions of the trust and to the inclusion in it of the said account.

          (Spouse sign here) _____ L.S.

Witness: (1) _____   Witness: (2) _____

STATE OF _____   City
                                            or
COUNTY OF _____   Town _____

On the _____ day of _____, 19_____, personally appeared

_____

known to me to be the individual(s) who executed the foregoing instrument, and acknowledged the same to be _____ free act and deed, before me.

          _____

(Notary Seal)   *Notary Public*

CHAPTER 8

DECLARATION OF TRUST
For Naming
ONE BENEFICIARY
To Receive
A BANK ACCOUNT HELD IN JOINT NAMES

INSTRUCTIONS:

On the following pages will be found a declaration of trust (DT-105-J) suitable for use in connection with the establishment of an inter vivos trust covering a checking or savings account held in joint names where it is desired to name one person to receive the account upon the death of the survivor of the two joint owners.

Enter the names of the two co-owners on the first line.

Cross out *"city"* or *"town,"* leaving the appropriate designation of your community. Next, cross out *"checking"* or *"savings,"* leaving the appropriate designation of the bank account. Then, name the bank; if it's a branch, identify the location.

Enter the name of the beneficiary in the appropriate place in Paragraph 1.

Note that Paragraph 8 designates as Successor Trustee *"whosoever shall at that time be beneficiary hereunder,"* which means that in most cases you don't need to fill anything in there. However, if there is any possibility of a beneficiary who has not attained the age of 21 years receiving the property, make certain that you name an adult in this paragraph who can act as trustee for such beneficiary. Avoid naming as trustee a person not likely to survive until the beneficiary has attained age 21.

When completed in the manner shown on the reverse side hereof, make several photocopies for reference purposes. Hold the original in safekeeping and offer a copy to the bank when you open the account. Instruct them to identify the account in this manner: *"(your name) and (your co-owner's name), Trustees u/d/t dated _____."*

Important: Read carefully Note B on page 38, which applies to this declaration of trust.

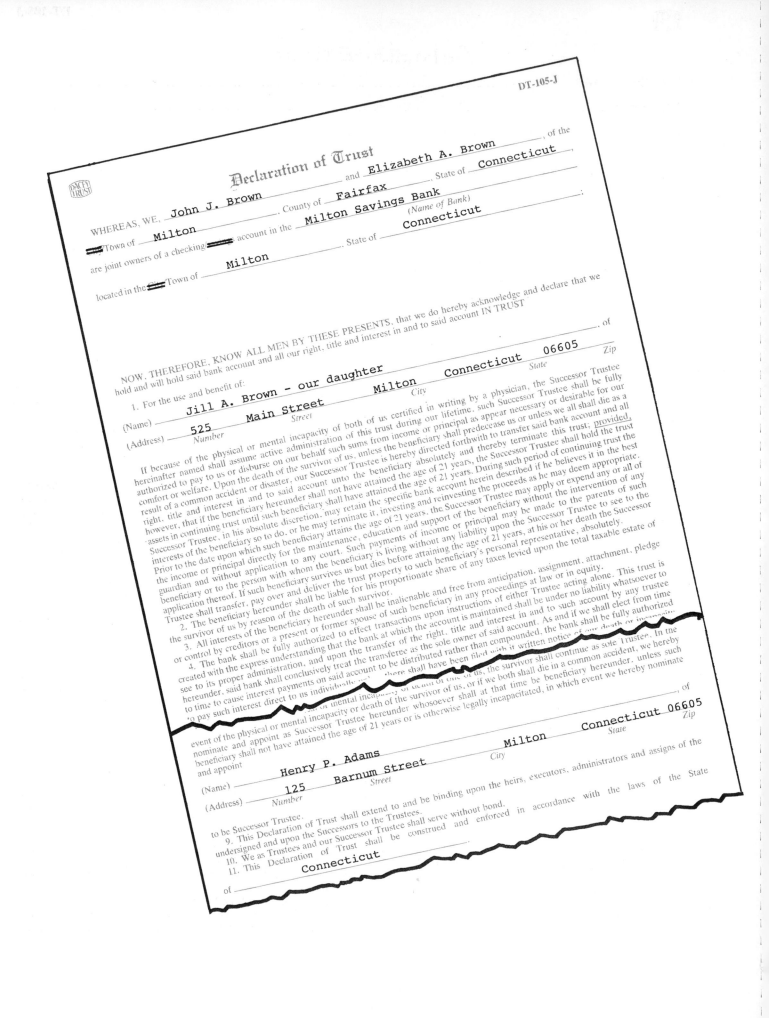

DT-105-J

Declaration of Trust

WHEREAS, WE, **John J. Brown** and **Elizabeth A. Brown**, of the County of **Fairfax**, State of **Connecticut**, Town of **Milton** are joint owners of a checking/savings account in the **Milton Savings Bank** (Name of Bank) located in the Town of **Milton**, State of **Connecticut**:

NOW, THEREFORE, KNOW ALL MEN BY THESE PRESENTS, that we do hereby acknowledge and declare that we hold and will hold said bank account and all our right, title and interest in and to said account IN TRUST

1. For the use and benefit of:

(Name) **Jill A. Brown - our daughter**

(Address) **525** **Main Street** **Milton** **Connecticut** **06605**
Number Street City State Zip

If because of the physical or mental incapacity of both of us certified in writing by a physician, the Successor Trustee hereinafter named shall assume active administration of this trust during our lifetime, such Successor Trustee shall be fully authorized to pay to us or disburse on our behalf such sums from income or principal as appear necessary or desirable for our comfort or welfare. Upon the death of the survivor of us, unless the beneficiary shall predecease us or unless we all shall die as a result of a common accident or disaster, our Successor Trustee is hereby directed forthwith to transfer said bank account and all right, title and interest in and to said account unto the beneficiary absolutely and thereby terminate this trust; provided, however, that if the beneficiary hereunder shall not have attained the age of 21 years, the Successor Trustee shall hold the trust assets in continuing trust until such beneficiary shall have attained the age of 21 years. During such period of continuing trust the Successor Trustee, in his absolute discretion, may retain the specific bank account herein described if he believes it in the best interests of the beneficiary so to do, or he may terminate it, investing and reinvesting the proceeds as he may deem appropriate. Prior to the date upon which such beneficiary attains the age of 21 years, the Successor Trustee may apply or expend any or all of the income or principal directly for the maintenance, education and support of the beneficiary without the intervention of any guardian and without application to any court. Such payments of income or principal may be made to the parents of such beneficiary or to the person with whom the beneficiary is living without any liability upon the Successor Trustee to see to the application thereof. If such beneficiary survives us but dies before attaining the age of 21 years, at his or her death the Successor Trustee shall transfer, pay over and deliver the trust property to such beneficiary's personal representative, absolutely.

2. The beneficiary hereunder shall be liable for his proportionate share of any taxes levied upon the total taxable estate of the survivor of us by reason of the death of such survivor.

3. All interests of the beneficiary hereunder shall be inalienable and free from anticipation, assignment, attachment, pledge or control by creditors or a present or former spouse of such beneficiary in any proceedings at law or in equity. This trust is created with the express understanding that the bank at which the account is maintained shall be under no liability whatsoever to see to its proper administration, and upon the transfer of the right, title and interest in and to such account by any trustee hereunder, said bank shall conclusively treat the transferee as the sole owner of said account. As and if we shall elect from time to time to cause interest payments on said account to be distributed rather than compounded, the bank shall be fully authorized to pay such interest direct to us individually, ~~...there shall have been filed with it written notice of our death or incapaci...~~

...or mental incapacity or death of one of us, or if we both shall die in a common accident, the survivor shall continue as sole Trustee. In the event of the physical or mental incapacity or death of the survivor of us, or if we both shall die in a common accident, we hereby nominate and appoint as Successor Trustee hereunder whosoever shall at that time be beneficiary hereunder, unless such beneficiary shall not have attained the age of 21 years or is otherwise legally incapacitated, in which event we hereby nominate and appoint

(Name) **Henry P. Adams** **Milton** **Connecticut** **06605**
City State Zip

(Address) **125** **Barnum Street**
Number Street

to be Successor Trustee.

9. This Declaration of Trust shall extend to and be binding upon the heirs, executors, administrators and assigns of the undersigned and upon the Successors to the Trustees.

10. We as Trustees and our Successor Trustee shall serve without bond.

11. This Declaration of Trust shall be construed and enforced in accordance with the laws of the State of **Connecticut**

Declaration of Trust

WHEREAS, WE, _____ and _____, of the

City/Town of _____, County of _____, State of _____,

are joint owners of a checking/savings account in the _____,
(Name of Bank)

located in the City/Town of _____, State of _____;

NOW, THEREFORE, KNOW ALL MEN BY THESE PRESENTS, that we do hereby acknowledge and declare that we hold and will hold said bank account and all our right, title and interest in and to said account IN TRUST

1. For the use and benefit of:

(Name) _____, of

(Address) _____
Number   Street   City   State   Zip

If because of the physical or mental incapacity of both of us certified in writing by a physician, the Successor Trustee hereinafter named shall assume active administration of this trust during our lifetime, such Successor Trustee shall be fully authorized to pay to us or disburse on our behalf such sums from income or principal as appear necessary or desirable for our comfort or welfare. Upon the death of the survivor of us, unless the beneficiary shall predecease us or unless we all shall die as a result of a common accident or disaster, our Successor Trustee is hereby directed forthwith to transfer said bank account and all right, title and interest in and to said account unto the beneficiary absolutely and thereby terminate this trust; provided, however, that if the beneficiary hereunder shall not have attained the age of 21 years, the Successor Trustee shall hold the trust assets in continuing trust until such beneficiary shall have attained the age of 21 years. During such period of continuing trust the Successor Trustee, in his absolute discretion, may retain the specific bank account herein described if he believes it in the best interests of the beneficiary so to do, or he may terminate it, investing and reinvesting the proceeds as he may deem appropriate. Prior to the date upon which such beneficiary attains the age of 21 years, the Successor Trustee may apply or expend any or all of the income or principal directly for the maintenance, education and support of the beneficiary without the intervention of any guardian and without application to any court. Such payments of income or principal may be made to the parents of such beneficiary or to the person with whom the beneficiary is living without any liability upon the Successor Trustee to see to the application thereof. If such beneficiary survives us but dies before attaining the age of 21 years, at his or her death the Successor Trustee shall transfer, pay over and deliver the trust property to such beneficiary's personal representative, absolutely.

2. The beneficiary hereunder shall be liable for his proportionate share of any taxes levied upon the total taxable estate of the survivor of us by reason of the death of such survivor.

3. All interests of the beneficiary hereunder shall be inalienable and free from anticipation, assignment, attachment, pledge or control by creditors or a present or former spouse of such beneficiary in any proceedings at law or in equity.

4. The bank shall be fully authorized to effect transactions upon instructions of either Trustee acting alone. This trust is created with the express understanding that the bank at which the account is maintained shall be under no liability whatsoever to see to its proper administration, and upon the transfer of the right, title and interest in and to such account by any trustee hereunder, said bank shall conclusively treat the transferee as the sole owner of said account. Until the bank shall receive from some person interested in this trust, written notice of any death or other event upon which the right to receive may depend, the bank shall incur no liability for payments made in good faith to persons whose interest shall have been affected by such event. The bank shall be protected in acting upon any notice or other instrument or document believed by it to be genuine and to have been signed or presented by the proper party or parties.

5. We reserve unto ourselves the power and right to collect any interest or other income which may accrue from the trust property and, in our sole discretion as Trustees, either to accumulate such interest or income as an addition to the trust assets being held hereunder or pay such interest or income to ourselves as individuals. We shall be exclusively entitled to all dividends, interest or other income from the trust property during our lifetime, and no beneficiary named herein shall have any claim upon any such income distributed to us.

6. We reserve unto ourselves the power and right at any time during our lifetime to amend or revoke in whole or in part the trust hereby created without the necessity of obtaining the consent of the beneficiary and without giving notice to the beneficiary. The withdrawal by us of the whole or any part of the bank account held hereunder shall constitute as to such whole or part a revocation of this trust.

7. The death during our lifetime, or in a common accident or disaster with us, of the beneficiary designated hereunder shall revoke such designation, and in the former event, we reserve the right to designate a new beneficiary. Should we for any reason fail to designate such new beneficiary, this trust shall terminate upon the death of the survivor of us and the trust property shall revert to the estate of such survivor.

8. In the event of the physical or mental incapacity or death of one of us, the survivor shall continue as sole Trustee. In the event of the physical or mental incapacity or death of the survivor of us, or if we both shall die in a common accident, we hereby nominate and appoint as Successor Trustee hereunder whosoever shall at that time be beneficiary hereunder, unless such beneficiary shall not have attained the age of 21 years or is otherwise legally incapacitated, in which event we hereby nominate and appoint

(Name) _____, of

(Address) _____
        Number   *Street*   *City*   *State*   *Zip*

to be Successor Trustee.

9. This Declaration of Trust shall extend to and be binding upon the heirs, executors, administrators and assigns of the undersigned and upon the Successors to the Trustees.

10. We as Trustees and our Successor Trustee shall serve without bond.

11. This Declaration of Trust shall be construed and enforced in accordance with the laws of the State

of _____.

IN WITNESS WHEREOF, we have hereunto set our hands and seals this _____

day of _____, 19_____.

        (First Settlor sign here) _____ L.S.

      (Second Settlor sign here) _____ L.S.

I, the undersigned legal spouse of one of the above Settlors, hereby waive all community property rights which I may have in the hereinabove-described trust property and give my assent to the provisions of the trust and to the inclusion in it of the said property.

        (Spouse sign here) _____ L.S.

Witness: (1) _____   Witness: (2) _____

STATE OF _____ } City

COUNTY OF _____   or
                                        Town _____

On the _____ day of _____, 19_____, personally appeared

_____ and _____

known to me to be the individuals who executed the foregoing instrument, and acknowledged the same to be their free act and deed, before me.

_____

(Notary Seal)   *Notary Public*

CHAPTER 8

DECLARATION OF TRUST
For Naming
ONE PRIMARY BENEFICIARY
And
ONE CONTINGENT BENEFICIARY
To Receive
A BANK ACCOUNT HELD IN JOINT NAMES

INSTRUCTIONS:

On the following pages will be found a declaration of trust (DT-106-J) suitable for use in connection with the estabiishment of an inter vivos trust covering a checking or savings account held in joint names, where it is desired to name some *one* person as primary beneficiary with some *one* other person as contingent beneficiary to receive the account upon the death of the survivor of the two joint owners.

Enter the names of the two co-owners on the first line.

Cross out *"city"* or *"town,"* leaving the appropriate designation of your community. Next, cross out *"checking"* or *"savings,"* leaving the appropriate designation of the bank account. Then, name the bank; if it's a branch, identify the location.

Enter the names of the beneficiaries in the appropriate place in Paragraph 1.

Note that Paragraph 8 designates as Successor Trustee *"whosoever shall at that time be beneficiary hereunder,"* which means that in most cases you don't need to fill anything in there. However, if there is any possibility of a beneficiary who has not attained the age of 21 years receiving the property, make certain that you name an adult in this paragraph who can act as trustee for such beneficiary. Avoid naming as trustee a person not likely to survive until the beneficiary has attained age 21.

When completed in the manner shown on the reverse side hereof, make several photocopies for reference purposes. Hold the original in safekeeping and offer a copy to the bank when you open the account. Instruct them to identify the account in this manner: *"(your name) and (your co-owner's name), Trustees u/d/t dated _____."*

Important: Read carefully Note B on page 38, which applies to this declaration of trust.

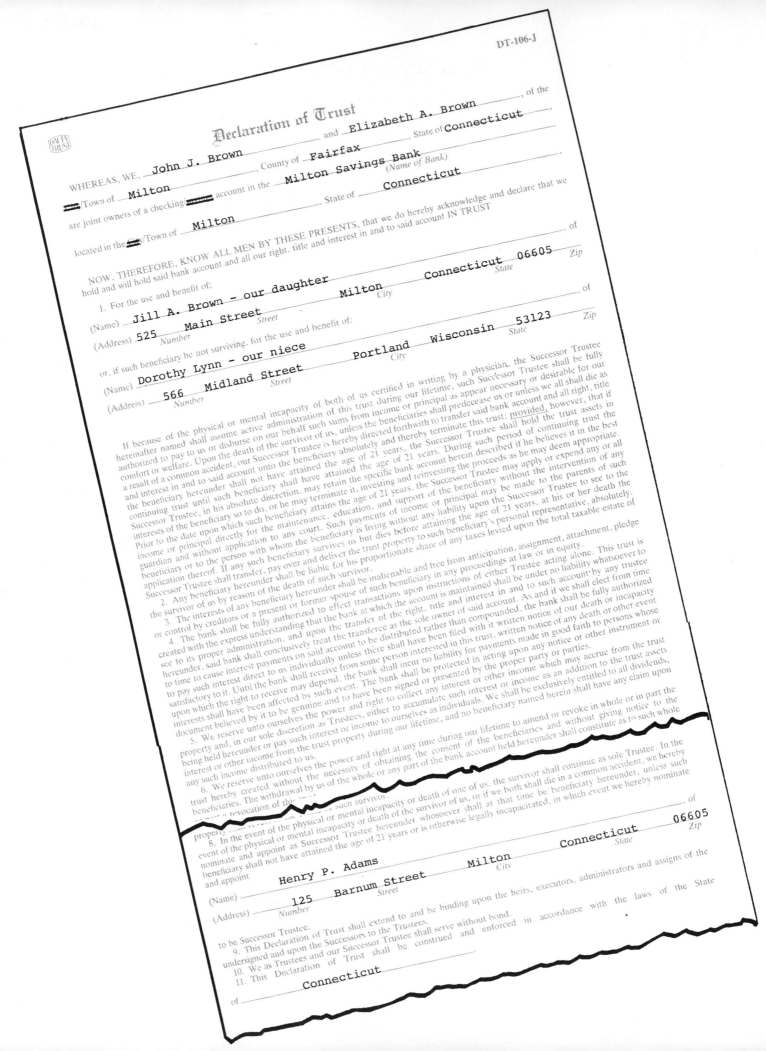

Declaration of Trust

WHEREAS, WE, __John J. Brown__ and __Elizabeth A. Brown__, of the __City/Town of __Milton__, County of __Fairfax__, State of __Connecticut__, are joint owners of a checking/savings account in the __Milton Savings Bank__ (Name of Bank) located in the City/Town of __Milton__, State of __Connecticut__,

NOW, THEREFORE, KNOW ALL MEN BY THESE PRESENTS, that we do hereby acknowledge and declare that we hold and will hold said bank account and all our right, title and interest in and to said account IN TRUST

1. For the use and benefit of:

(Name) __Jill A. Brown - our daughter__ __Milton__ City __Connecticut__ State __06605__ Zip, of

(Address) __525__ Number __Main Street__ Street

or, if such beneficiary be not surviving, for the use and benefit of:

(Name) __Dorothy Lynn - our niece__ __Portland__ City __Wisconsin__ State __53123__ Zip, of

(Address) __566__ Number __Midland Street__ Street

If because of the physical or mental incapacity of both of us certified in writing by a physician, the Successor Trustee hereinafter named shall assume active administration of this trust during our lifetime, such Successor Trustee shall be fully authorized to pay to us or disburse on our behalf such sums from income or principal as appear necessary or desirable for our comfort or welfare. Upon the death of the survivor of us, unless the beneficiaries shall predecease us or unless we all shall die as a result of a common accident, our Successor Trustee is hereby directed forthwith to transfer said bank account and all right, title and interest in and to said account unto the beneficiary absolutely and thereby terminate this trust; provided, however, that if the beneficiary hereunder shall not have attained the age of 21 years, the Successor Trustee shall hold the trust assets in continuing trust until such beneficiary shall have attained the age of 21 years. During such period of continuing trust the Successor Trustee, in his absolute discretion, may retain the specific bank account herein described if he believes it in the best interests of the beneficiary so to do, or he may terminate it, investing and reinvesting the proceeds as he may deem appropriate. Prior to the date upon which such beneficiary attains the age of 21 years, the Successor Trustee may apply or expend any or all income or principal directly for the maintenance, education, and support of the beneficiary without the intervention of any guardian and without application to any court. Such payments of income or principal may be made to the parents of such beneficiary or to the person with whom the beneficiary is living without any liability upon the Successor Trustee to see to the application thereof. If any such beneficiary survives us but dies before attaining the age of 21 years, at his or her death the Successor Trustee shall transfer, pay over and deliver the trust property to such beneficiary's personal representative, absolutely.

2. Any beneficiary hereunder shall be liable for his proportionate share of any taxes levied upon the total taxable estate of the survivor of us by reason of the death of such survivor.

3. The interests of any beneficiary hereunder shall be inalienable and free from anticipation, assignment, attachment, pledge or control by creditors or a present or former spouse of such beneficiary in any proceedings at law or in equity. This trust is created with the express understanding that the bank at which the account is maintained shall be under no liability whatsoever to see to its proper administration, and upon the transfer of the right, title and interest in and to such account by any trustee hereunder, said bank shall be fully authorized to effect transactions upon instructions of either Trustee acting alone. As and if we shall elect from time to time to cause interest payments on said account to be distributed rather than compounded, the bank shall be fully authorized to pay such interest direct to us individually unless there shall have been filed with it written notice of our death or incapacity satisfactory to it. Until the bank shall receive from some person interested in this trust, written notice of any death or other event upon which the right to receive may depend, the bank shall be protected in acting upon any notice or other instrument or document believed by it to be genuine and to have been signed or presented by the proper party or parties.

4. The bank shall be fully authorized to effect transactions upon instructions of either Trustee acting alone. The bank shall conclusively treat the transferee as the sole owner of said account. We shall be exclusively entitled to all dividends, interests shall have been affected by such event. The bank shall receive no liability for payments made in good faith to persons whose interests or income to ourselves as individuals. We shall be exclusively entitled to all dividends,

5. We reserve unto ourselves the power and right to collect any interest or other income as an addition to the trust assets being held hereunder or pay such interest or income to ourselves as individuals. We shall be exclusively entitled to all dividends, interest or other income from the trust property during our lifetime, and no beneficiary named herein shall have any claim upon any such income distributed to us.

6. We reserve unto ourselves the power and right at any time during our lifetime to amend or revoke in whole or in part the trust hereby created without the necessity of obtaining the consent of the beneficiaries and without giving notice to the beneficiaries. The withdrawal by us of the whole or any part of the bank account held hereunder shall constitute as to such whole or part a revocation of this trust.

8. In the event of the physical or mental incapacity or death of one of us, the survivor shall continue as sole Trustee. In the event of the physical or mental incapacity or death of the survivor of us, or if we both shall die in a common accident, we hereby nominate and appoint as Successor Trustee hereunder whosoever shall at that time be beneficiary hereunder, unless such beneficiary shall not have attained the age of 21 years or is otherwise legally incapacitated, in which event we hereby nominate and appoint

(Name) __Henry P. Adams__ __Milton__ City __Connecticut__ State __06605__ Zip, of

(Address) __125__ Number __Barnum Street__ Street

to be Successor Trustee.

9. This Declaration of Trust shall extend to and be binding upon the heirs, executors, administrators and assigns of the undersigned and upon the Successors to the Trustees.

10. We as Trustees and our Successor Trustee shall serve without bond.

11. This Declaration of Trust shall be construed and enforced in accordance with the laws of the State of __Connecticut__.

Declaration of Trust

WHEREAS, WE, _____ and _____, of the

City/Town of _____, County of _____, State of _____,

are joint owners of a checking/savings account in the _____,
(Name of Bank)

located in the City/Town of _____, State of _____;

NOW, THEREFORE, KNOW ALL MEN BY THESE PRESENTS, that we do hereby acknowledge and declare that we hold and will hold said bank account and all our right, title and interest in and to said account IN TRUST

1. For the use and benefit of:

(Name) _____, of

(Address) _____
        Number   Street   City   State   Zip

or, if such beneficiary be not surviving, for the use and benefit of:

(Name) _____, of

(Address) _____
        Number   Street   City   State   Zip

If because of the physical or mental incapacity of both of us certified in writing by a physician, the Successor Trustee hereinafter named shall assume active administration of this trust during our lifetime, such Successor Trustee shall be fully authorized to pay to us or disburse on our behalf such sums from income or principal as appear necessary or desirable for our comfort or welfare. Upon the death of the survivor of us, unless the beneficiaries shall predecease us or unless we all shall die as a result of a common accident, our Successor Trustee is hereby directed forthwith to transfer said bank account and all right, title and interest in and to said account unto the beneficiary absolutely and thereby terminate this trust; provided, however, that if the beneficiary hereunder shall not have attained the age of 21 years, the Successor Trustee shall hold the trust assets in continuing trust until such beneficiary shall have attained the age of 21 years. During such period of continuing trust the Successor Trustee, in his absolute discretion, may retain the specific bank account herein described if he believes it in the best interests of the beneficiary so to do, or he may terminate it, investing and reinvesting the proceeds as he may deem appropriate. Prior to the date upon which such beneficiary attains the age of 21 years, the Successor Trustee may apply or expend any or all income or principal directly for the maintenance, education, and support of the beneficiary without the intervention of any guardian and without application to any court. Such payments of income or principal may be made to the parents of such beneficiary or to the person with whom the beneficiary is living without any liability upon the Successor Trustee to see to the application thereof. If any such beneficiary survives us but dies before attaining the age of 21 years, at his or her death the Successor Trustee shall transfer, pay over and deliver the trust property to such beneficiary's personal representative, absolutely.

2. Any beneficiary hereunder shall be liable for his proportionate share of any taxes levied upon the total taxable estate of the survivor of us by reason of the death of such survivor.

3. The interests of any beneficiary hereunder shall be inalienable and free from anticipation, assignment, attachment, pledge or control by creditors or a present or former spouse of such beneficiary in any proceedings at law or in equity.

4. The bank shall be fully authorized to effect transactions upon instructions of either Trustee acting alone. This trust is created with the express understanding that the bank at which the account is maintained shall be under no liability whatsoever to see to its proper administration, and upon the transfer of the right, title and interest in and to such account by any trustee hereunder, said bank shall conclusively treat the transferee as the sole owner of said account. Until the bank shall receive from some person interested in this trust, written notice of any death or other event upon which the right to receive may depend, the bank shall incur no liability for payments made in good faith to persons whose interests shall have been affected by such event. The bank shall be protected in acting upon any notice or other instrument or document believed by it to be genuine and to have been signed or presented by the proper party or parties.

5. We reserve unto ourselves the power and right to collect any interest or other income which may accrue from the trust property and, in our sole discretion as Trustees, either to accumulate such interest or income as an addition to the trust assets being held hereunder or pay such interest or income to ourselves as individuals. We shall be exclusively entitled to all dividends, interest or other income from the trust property during our lifetime, and no beneficiary named herein shall have any claim upon any such income distributed to us.

6. We reserve unto ourselves the power and right at any time during our lifetime to amend or revoke in whole or in part the trust hereby created without the necessity of obtaining the consent of the beneficiaries and without giving notice to the beneficiaries. The withdrawal by us of the whole or any part of the bank account held hereunder shall constitute as to such whole or part a revocation of this trust.

7. The death during our lifetime, or in a common accident or disaster with us, of both of the beneficiaries designated hereunder shall revoke such designation, and in the former event, we reserve the right to designate a new beneficiary. Should we

for any reason fail to designate such new beneficiary, this trust shall terminate upon the death of the survivor of us and the trust property shall revert to the estate of such survivor.

8. In the event of the physical or mental incapacity or death of one of us, the survivor shall continue as sole Trustee. In the event of the physical or mental incapacity or death of the survivor of us, or if we both shall die in a common accident, we hereby nominate and appoint as Successor Trustee hereunder whosoever shall at that time be beneficiary hereunder, unless such beneficiary shall not have attained the age of 21 years or is otherwise legally incapacitated, in which event we hereby nominate and appoint

(Name) _____ , of

(Address) _____
　　　　　　　　 Number 　　　　 *Street* 　　　　 *City* 　　　　 *State* 　　　 *Zip*

to be Successor Trustee.

9. This Declaration of Trust shall extend to and be binding upon the heirs, executors, administrators and assigns of the undersigned and upon the Successors to the Trustees.

10. We as Trustees and our Successor Trustee shall serve without bond.

11. This Declaration of Trust shall be construed and enforced in accordance with the laws of the State

of _____ .

IN WITNESS WHEREOF, we have hereunto set our hands and seals this _____

day of _____ , 19_____ .

　　　　　　　　　　 (First Settlor sign here) _____ L.S.

　　　　　　　　 (Second Settlor sign here) _____ L.S.

I, the undersigned legal spouse of one of the above Settlors, hereby waive all community property rights which I may have in the hereinabove-described trust property and give my assent to the provisions of the trust and to the inclusion in it of the said trust property.

　　　　　　　　　　 (Spouse sign here) _____ L.S.

Witness: (1) _____ 　 Witness: (2) _____

STATE OF _____ 　 City
　　　　　　　　　　　　　　　　　　　　　　　　　 or
COUNTY OF _____ 　 Town _____

On the _____ day of _____ , 19_____ , personally appeared

_____ and _____

known to me to be the individuals who executed the foregoing instrument, and acknowledged the same to be their free act and deed, before me.

(Notary Seal) 　　　　　　　　　　　　　　　　　 _____
　　　　　　　　　　　　　　　　　　　　　　　　　　　　 Notary Public

CHAPTER 8

DECLARATION OF TRUST

For Naming

TWO OR MORE BENEFICIARIES, SHARING EQUALLY,

To Receive

A BANK ACCOUNT HELD IN JOINT NAMES

INSTRUCTIONS:

On the following pages will be found a declaration of trust (DT-107-J) suitable for use in connection with the establishment of an inter vivos trust covering a checking or savings account held in joint names where it is desired to name two or more persons, sharing equally, to receive the account upon the death of the survivor of the two owners.

Enter the names of the two co-owners on the first line.

Cross out *"city"* or *"town,"* leaving the appropriate designation of your community. Next, cross out *"checking"* or *"savings,"* leaving the appropriate designation of the bank account. Then, name the bank; if it's a branch, identify the location.

In Paragraph 1, indicate the *number of persons* you are naming (to discourage unauthorized additions to the list) and then insert their names. The one whose name appears *first* will be the Successor Trustee responsible for seeing to the distribution of the trust property.

Note that the instrument specifies that the named beneficiaries are to receive *"in equal shares, or the survivor of them/per stirpes."* Now, think carefully: If you have named three persons with the intention that if one of them predeceases you, *his* children will take *his* share, cross out *"or the survivor of them"* and *initial it.* If that is *not* what you want—if, for example, you prefer that the share of the deceased person be divided between the two surviving persons, cross out *"per stirpes"* and *initial it.* Remember, you <u>must</u> cross out either *"or the survivor of them"* or *"per stirpes"*—one or the other.

Note that Paragraph 8 designates as Successor Trustee *"the beneficiary named first above."* Whenever there is a possibility of a beneficiary who has not attained the age of 21 years receiving a share of the trust property, make certain that you name an adult in this paragraph who can act as trustee for such beneficiary. Avoid naming as trustee a person not likely to survive until the beneficiary has attained age 21.

When completed in the manner shown on the reverse side hereof, make several photocopies of the declaration of trust. Hold the original in safekeeping and offer a copy to the bank when you open the account. Instruct them to identify the account in this manner: *"(your name) and (your co-owner's name), Trustees u/d/t dated _____."*

Important: Read carefully Note B on page 38, which applies to this declaration of trust.

WHEREVER THE INSTRUCTION "INITIAL IT" APPEARS ABOVE,
IT MEANS THAT *BOTH* CO-OWNERS SHOULD INITIAL IT.

DT-107-J

Declaration of Trust

WHEREAS, WE, __John J. Brown__ and __Elizabeth A. Brown__, of the __Town of__ __Milton__, County of __Fairfax__, State of __Connecticut__,

are joint owners of a ~~checking~~/savings account in the __Midland Savings Bank__
(Name of Bank)

located in the ~~City~~/Town of __Milton__, State of __Connecticut__, that we do hereby acknowledge and declare that we

J.J.B.
E.A.B.

NOW, THEREFORE, KNOW ALL MEN BY THESE PRESENTS, that we do hereby acknowledge and declare that we hold and will hold said bank account and all our right, title and interest in and to said account IN TRUST

1. For the use and benefit of the following __three (3)__ persons, in equal shares, or the survivor of them:

> Thomas B. Brown - our brother
> Helen M. Brown - our sister
> Charles M. Brown - our brother

If because of the physical or mental incapacity of both of us certified in writing by a physician, the Successor Trustee hereinafter named shall assume active administration of this trust during our lifetime, such Successor Trustee shall be fully authorized to pay to us or disburse on our behalf such sums from income or principal as appear necessary or desirable for our comfort or welfare. Upon the death of the survivor of us, unless all the beneficiaries shall predecease us or unless we all shall die as a result of a common accident or disaster, our Successor Trustee is hereby directed forthwith to transfer said bank account and all right, title and interest in and to said account unto the beneficiaries absolutely and thereby terminate this trust; provided, however, that if any beneficiary hereunder shall not have attained the age of 21 years, the Successor Trustee shall hold such beneficiary's share of the trust assets in continuing trust until such beneficiary shall have attained the age of 21 years. During such period of continuing trust the Successor Trustee, in his absolute discretion, may retain the specific bank account herein described if he believes it in the best interests of the beneficiary so to do, or he may terminate or otherwise dispose of it, investing and reinvesting the proceeds as he may deem appropriate. Prior to the date upon which such beneficiary attains the age of 21 years, the Successor Trustee may apply or expend any or all of the income or principal directly for the maintenance, education and support of the beneficiary without the intervention of any guardian and without application to any court. Such payments of income or principal may be made to the parents of such beneficiary or to the person with whom the beneficiary is living without any liability upon the Successor Trustee to see to the application thereof. If any such beneficiary survives us but dies before the age of 21 years, at his or her death the Successor Trustee shall transfer, pay over and deliver the trust property being held for such beneficiary to said beneficiary's personal representative, absolutely.

2. Each beneficiary hereunder shall be liable for his proportionate share of any taxes levied upon the total taxable estate of the survivor of us by reason of the death of such survivor.

3. The interests of any beneficiary hereunder shall be inalienable and free from anticipation, assignment, attachment, pledge or control by creditors or a present or former spouse of such beneficiary in any proceedings at law or in equity. This trust is created with the express understanding that the bank at which the account is maintained shall be under no liability whatsoever to see to its proper administration, and upon the transfer of the right, title and interest in and to such account by any trustee hereunder, said bank shall be fully authorized to treat the transferee as the sole owner of said account. As and if we shall elect from time to time to cause interest payments on said account to be distributed rather than compounded, the bank shall be fully authorized to pay such interest direct to us individually unless there shall have been filed with it written notice of our death or incapacity satisfactory to it. Until the bank shall receive from some person interested in this trust, written notice of any death or other event upon which the right to receive may depend, the bank shall be protected in acting upon any notice or other instrument or document believed by it to be genuine and to have been signed or presented by the proper party or parties.

4. The bank shall be fully authorized to affect transactions upon instructions of either Trustee acting alone, and if we shall elect to collect any interest or other income as an addition to the trust assets being held hereunder or pay such income to ourselves during our lifetime, we shall be exclusively entitled to all dividends, interest or other income from the trust property during our lifetime, and no beneficiary named herein shall have any claim upon any such income distributed to us.

5. We reserve unto ourselves the power and right at any time during our lifetime to amend or revoke in whole or in part the trust hereby created without the necessity of obtaining the consent of any beneficiary and without giving notice to any beneficiary. The withdrawal by us of the whole or any part of the bank account held hereunder shall constitute as to such whole or part a revocation of this trust.

6. We reserve unto ourselves the power and right at any time during our lifetime to designate new beneficiaries. Should we for any reason in our sole discretion as Trustees, either to accumulate such income as an addition to the trust assets being held

7. The death during our lifetime, or in a common accident or disaster with us, of all of the beneficiaries designated hereunder shall revoke such designation, and in the former event, we reserve the right to designate new beneficiaries. Should we for any ~~property shall revoke~~ ... of such survivor.

8. In the event of the physical or mental incapacity or death of one of us, the survivor shall continue as sole Trustee. In the event of the physical or mental incapacity or death of the survivor of us, we hereby nominate and appoint as Successor Trustee hereunder the beneficiary named first above, unless such beneficiary shall not have attained the age of 21 years or is otherwise legally incapacitated, in which event we hereby nominate and appoint as Successor Trustee hereunder the beneficiary named second above. If such beneficiary named second above shall not have attained the age of 21 years, or is otherwise legally incapacitated, in which event we hereby nominate and appoint

__Henry P. Adams__ __Milton__ __Connecticut__ __06605__
(Name) *City* *State* *Zip*

(Address) __125__ __Barnum Street__
Number *Street*

to be Successor Trustee.

9. This Declaration of Trust shall extend to and be binding upon the heirs, executors, administrators and assigns of the undersigned and upon the Successors to the Trustees.

10. We as Trustees and our Successor Trustee shall serve without bond.

11. This Declaration of Trust shall be construed and enforced in accordance with the laws of the State of __Connecticut__

Declaration of Trust

WHEREAS, WE, _____ and _____, of the

City/Town of _____, County of _____ State of _____,

are joint owners of a checking/savings account in the _____,

(Name of Bank)

located in the City/Town of _____, State of _____;

NOW, THEREFORE, KNOW ALL MEN BY THESE PRESENTS, that we do hereby acknowledge and declare that we hold and will hold said bank account and all our right, title and interest in and to said account IN TRUST

    1. For the use and benefit of the following _____ persons, in equal shares, or the survivor of them/per stirpes:

If because of the physical or mental incapacity of both of us certified in writing by a physician, the Successor Trustee hereinafter named shall assume active administration of this trust during our lifetime, such Successor Trustee shall be fully authorized to pay to us or disburse on our behalf such sums from income or principal as appear necessary or desirable for our comfort or welfare. Upon the death of the survivor of us, unless all the beneficiaries shall predecease us or unless we all shall die as a result of a common accident or disaster, our Successor Trustee is hereby directed forthwith to transfer said bank account and all right, title and interest in and to said account unto the beneficiaries absolutely and thereby terminate this trust; <u>provided</u>, however, that if any beneficiary hereunder shall not have attained the age of 21 years, the Successor Trustee shall hold such beneficiary's share of the trust assets in continuing trust until such beneficiary shall have attained the age of 21 years. During such period of continuing trust the Successor Trustee, in his absolute discretion, may retain the specific bank account herein described if he believes it in the best interests of the beneficiary so to do, or he may terminate or otherwise dispose of it, investing and reinvesting the proceeds as he may deem appropriate. Prior to the date upon which such beneficiary attains the age of 21 years, the Successor Trustee may apply or expend any or all of the income or principal directly for the maintenance, education and support of the beneficiary without the intervention of any guardian and without application to any court. Such payments of income or principal may be made to the parents of such beneficiary or to the person with whom the beneficiary is living without any liability upon the Successor Trustee to see to the application thereof. If any such beneficiary survives us but dies before the age of 21 years, at his or her death the Successor Trustee shall transfer, pay over and deliver the trust property being held for such beneficiary to said beneficiary's personal representative, absolutely.

    2. Each beneficiary hereunder shall be liable for his proportionate share of any taxes levied upon the total taxable estate of the survivor of us by reason of the death of such survivor.

    3. The interests of any beneficiary hereunder shall be inalienable and free from anticipation, assignment, attachment, pledge or control by creditors or a present or former spouse of such beneficiary in any proceedings at law or in equity.

    4. The bank shall be fully authorized to affect transactions upon instructions of either Trustee acting alone. This trust is created with the express understanding that the bank at which the account is maintained shall be under no liability whatsoever to see to its proper administration, and upon the transfer of the right, title and interest in and to such account by any trustee hereunder, said bank shall conclusively treat the transferee as the sole owner of said account. Until the bank shall receive from some person interested in this trust, written notice of any death or other event upon which the right to receive may depend, the bank shall incur no liability for payments made in good faith to persons whose interest shall have been affected by such event. The bank shall be protected in acting upon any notice or other instrument or document believed by it to be genuine and to have been signed or presented by the proper party or parties.

    5. We reserve unto ourselves the power and right to collect any interest or other income which may accrue from the trust property and, in our sole discretion as Trustees, either to accumulate such income as an addition to the trust assets being held hereunder or pay such income to ourselves as individuals. We shall be exclusively entitled to all dividends, interest or other income from the trust property during our lifetime, and no beneficiary named herein shall have any claim upon any such income distributed to us.

    6. We reserve unto ourselves the power and right at any time during our lifetime to amend or revoke in whole or in part the trust hereby created without the necessity of obtaining the consent of any beneficiary and without giving notice to any beneficiary. The withdrawal by us of the whole or any part of the bank account held hereunder shall constitute as to such whole or part a revocation of this trust.

7. The death during our lifetime, or in a common accident or disaster with us, of all of the beneficiaries designated hereunder shall revoke such designation, and in the former event, we reserve the right to designate new beneficiaries. Should we for any reason fail to designate such new beneficiaries, this trust shall terminate upon the death of the survivor of us and the trust property shall revert to the estate of such survivor.

8. In the event of the physical or mental incapacity or death of one of us, the survivor shall continue as sole Trustee. In the event of the physical or mental incapacity or death of the survivor of us, we hereby nominate and appoint as Successor Trustee hereunder the beneficiary named first above, unless such beneficiary shall not have attained the age of 21 years or is otherwise legally incapacitated, in which event we hereby nominate and appoint as Successor Trustee hereunder the beneficiary named second above. If such beneficiary named second above shall not have attained the age of 21 years, or is otherwise legally incapacitated, we hereby nominate and appoint

(Name) _____, of

(Address) _____
    Number   *Street*   *City*   *State*   *Zip*

to be Successor Trustee.

9. This Declaration of Trust shall extend to and be binding upon the heirs, executors, administrators and assigns of the undersigned and upon the Successors to the Trustees.

10. We as Trustees and our Successor Trustee shall serve without bond.

11. This Declaration of Trust shall be construed and enforced in accordance with the laws of the State

of _____.

IN WITNESS WHEREOF, we have hereunto set our hands and seals this _____

day of _____, 19_____.

      (First Settlor sign here) _____ L.S.

     (Second Settlor sign here) _____ L.S.

I, the undersigned legal spouse of one of the above Settlors, hereby waive all community property rights which I may have in the hereinabove-described trust property and give my assent to the provisions of the trust and to the inclusion in it of the said trust property.

       (Spouse sign here) _____ L.S.

Witness: (1) _____   Witness: (2) _____

STATE OF _____ ⎫   City

                 ⎬   or

COUNTY OF _____ ⎭   Town _____

On the _____ day of _____, 19_____, personally appeared

_____ and _____

known to me to be the individuals who executed the foregoing instrument, and acknowledged the same to be their free act and deed, before me.

_____

(Notary Seal)   *Notary Public*

CHAPTER 9

Avoiding Probate of Securities

We have observed earlier that many persons seek to avoid probate of the securities they own by registering them in joint names. Some of the pitfalls of such joint ownership as a solution to the problem of probate avoidance have already been noted. It is important that those who use it understand clearly that while it does establish beyond question to whom the property is to pass at death, it does not assure that it will pass to the surviving co-owner without having been subject to the jurisdiction of the probate court. Many issuers of stock or transfer agents insist upon "clearance" in the form of documents from the probate court indicating the court's knowledge of and lack of objection to the proposed transfer of the property to the surviving co-owner.

Joint ownership of real estate, we noted, was characterized by having the title read: *"John Smith and Mary Smith, or the survivor of them."* The equivalent, when it comes to securities registration, is *"John Smith and Mary Smith, as joint tenants with right of survivorship and not as tenants in common."* All this is generally compressed by transfer agents into *"John Smith and Mary Smith, JTWROS."* That *"tenants in common"* business is the thing to watch out for.

Let's illustrate the kind of problem it can create in securities ownership: John Smith registers his securities jointly with his wife under a "tenancy in common" registration. He dies leaving three minor children and no will. The one-half of the securities represented by the wife's joint ownership continues to be her property. Her intestate husband's half of the property passes under the laws of the state which decree that one-third of his share will go to his widow and two-thirds to his children collectively. The net result: The widow now owns two-thirds of the stock and the children one-third. Unless there is some very special circumstance justifying tenancy in common, it should be avoided. Few brokers or others responsible for securities registration would deliberately initiate such a form of ownership. It is worth making certain that you don't have it, though. Indeed, one of the messages of this book is to avoid joint ownership completely.

To avoid these headaches let us turn once again to that legal "wonder drug," the inter vivos trust, which is readily adaptable for use in connection with the registration of securities. By executing a relatively simple declaration of trust, the owner of securities may thereby not only clearly establish who is to receive such securities upon his death but he can also insure that they will pass to that beneficiary without having become subject to the jurisdiction of the probate court.

We are speaking, again, of a revocable trust, one which may be altered or cancelled completely at any time. The securities will remain a part of your taxable estate so far as both income and death taxes are concerned. Their registration under the declaration of trust will not alter in the slightest degree your right to do with them as you wish during your lifetime. In a word, you have nothing to lose, no possible disadvantage— and everything to gain by placing your securities holdings beyond the reach of the probate court.

On the following pages will be found several trust instruments which will prove useful in implementing the suggestions made here. There are forms for covering securities held in one name alone, and other forms for use by persons who have been using joint ownership and who can now substitute a joint trusteeship.

Please understand that it is not enough simply to fill out the forms—the securities you buy must be registered so as to reflect the existence of the trust. If you already own the securities, you must send them in to the transfer agent and have them reregistered to indicate that they are covered by the trust.

If you don't follow these registration instructions, you won't have a trust—and the probate demons will get'cha!

A word about mutual funds:

Millions of Americans now own mutual fund shares— reflecting, no doubt, a belief that as more and more of the wealth of the country has gravitated toward the funds, more and more of the top investment brains must necessarily have gravitated in the same direction. Certainly the funds' advantages of wide diversification, professional selection, and continuous supervision have wide appeal.

Mutual funds fall into two general categories—those which have a sales charge or "load" and those which do not, the latter being referred to as "no-load" funds. Load funds are generally purchased through an investment dealer who is compensated for his services from the sales charge. Shares of no-load funds must be purchased directly from the fund.

Like stocks or bonds, mutual fund shares are securities and may be put in trust in the same fashion. In the case of load funds, the registration instructions are given to the investment dealer, while in the case of no-load funds they are given directly to the fund.

There is one significant difference between ownership of individual stocks or bonds and ownership of mutual fund shares. When you buy the former, you are issued a certificate. The great majority of today's mutual fund shareholders do not take a certificate, though, electing instead to leave their shares on deposit with the fund's custodian bank. Most investors choose to reinvest all dividends and capital gains distributions and each time such a dividend or distribution is paid, the custodian bank sends a confirmation. This "accumulation account" share balance grows steadily as these sums are reinvested in additional shares, even in fractional shares for which certificates could not be issued.

Obviously, if you have such an account, you aren't going to have any certificate to which to attach a declaration of trust. Just make sure that you keep the original declaration in a secure place and offer the fund a photocopy for its files.

CHAPTER 9

DECLARATION OF TRUST
For Naming
ONE BENEFICIARY
To Receive
SECURITIES HELD IN ONE NAME

INSTRUCTIONS:

On the following pages will be found a declaration of trust (DT-109) suitable for use in connection with the establishment of an inter vivos trust covering stocks, bonds, or mutual fund shares now held in one name, where it is desired to name some one person to receive the securities upon the death of the owner.

Cross out *"city"* or *"town,"* leaving the appropriate designation of your community.

In Paragraph 1 enter the name of the beneficiary in the place provided.

In Paragraph 2, enter your name and the date you are executing the declaration of trust.

Note that Paragraph 10 designates as Successor Trustee *"whosoever shall at that time be beneficiary hereunder,"* which means that in most cases you don't need to fill anything in there. However, if there is any possibility of a beneficiary who has not attained the age of 21 years receiving the trust assets, make certain that you name an adult in this paragraph who can act as trustee for such beneficiary. Avoid naming as trustee a person not likely to survive until the beneficiary has attained age 21.

When completed in the manner shown on the reverse side, make one photocopy of the declaration of trust for each separate stock or bond you own, plus sufficient additional copies to take care of future securities purchases. Then, put the original in safekeeping.

It is absolutely essential that you instruct your broker or mutual fund to register or reregister your securities in this form: *"(your name), Trustee u/d/t dated* (date you have signed the declaration of trust)." It will not be necessary to file the declaration of trust with the issuer at the time you purchase the securities. However, if and when you sell any of them, the issuer, transfer agent, or custodian will almost certainly require you to display the instrument. If you die, the beneficiary will be required to produce it in order to obtain possession of the securities. In the circumstances, the safest thing to do is to staple a copy of it to *each* of the securities when the latter are issued. The stapling procedure should also be followed in the case of unregistered bonds. If you fail to follow these instructions in registering or reregistering your securities, they will be subject to probate.

Important: Read carefully Note B on page 38, which applies to this declaration of trust.

Declaration of Trust

WHEREAS, I, _____ John J. Brown _____, County of _____ Fairfax _____, State of _____ Connecticut _____, of the /Town of _____ Milton _____

am the owner of certain securities including common and preferred stocks, bonds, debentures and mutual fund shares;

NOW, THEREFORE, KNOW ALL MEN BY THESE PRESENTS, that I do hereby acknowledge and declare that I hold and will hold said securities and all my right, title and interest in and to said securities IN TRUST

1. For the use and benefit of:

(Name) _____ Elizabeth A. Brown - my wife _____ Milton _____ City _____ Connecticut _____ State _____ 06605 _____ Zip

(Address) _____ 525 _____ Number _____ Main Street _____ Street

If because of my physical or mental incapacity certified in writing by a physician, the Successor Trustee shall assume active administration of this trust during my lifetime, such Successor Trustee shall be fully authorized to pay to me or disburse on my behalf such sums from income or principal as appear necessary or desirable for my comfort or welfare. Upon my death, unless the beneficiary shall predecease me or unless we both shall die as a result of a common accident or disaster, my Successor Trustee is hereby directed forthwith to transfer said securities and all right, title and interest in and to said securities unto the beneficiary absolutely and thereby terminate this trust: provided, however, that if the beneficiary hereunder shall not have attained the age of 21 years, the Successor Trustee shall hold the trust assets in continuing trust until such beneficiary shall have attained the age of 21 years. During such period of continuing trust the Successor Trustee, in his absolute discretion, may retain the specific securities herein described if he believes it to be in the best interests of the beneficiary so to do, or he may sell or otherwise dispose of any or all of them, investing and reinvesting the proceeds as he may deem appropriate. Prior to the date upon which such beneficiary attains the age of 21 years, the Successor Trustee may apply or expend any or all of the income or principal of the trust directly for the maintenance, education and support of the beneficiary without the intervention of any guardian and without application to any court. Such payments of income or principal may be made to the parents of such beneficiary or to the person with whom the beneficiary is living without any liability upon the Successor Trustee to see to the application thereof. If such beneficiary survives me but dies before attaining the age of 21 years, at his or her death the Successor Trustee shall transfer, pay over and deliver the trust property to such beneficiary's personal representative, absolutely.

2. For purposes of specific identification, the assets held pursuant to this trust shall be all those securities registered in the name of: _____, Trustee u/d/t (or "Trustee U-A")

_____ John J. Brown _____

dated _____ February 2, 1980 _____

3. The beneficiary hereunder shall be liable for his proportionate share of any taxes levied upon the Settlor's total taxable estate by reason of the Settlor's death.

4. All interests of a beneficiary hereunder shall be inalienable and free from anticipation, assignment, attachment, pledge or control by creditors or a present or former spouse of such beneficiary in any proceedings at law or in equity.

5. This trust is created upon the express understanding that the issuer, transfer agent or custodian of any securities hereunder shall be under no liability whatsoever to see to its proper administration, and that upon the transfer of the right, title and interest in and to said securities by any Trustee hereunder, said issuer, transfer agent or custodian shall conclusively treat the

_____ death or other event upon which the right to receive may depend, the said issuer, transfer agent or custodian shall incur no liability for payments made in good faith to persons whose interests shall have been affected by such event. The issuer, transfer agent or custodian shall be protected in acting upon any notice or other instrument or document believed by it to be genuine and to have been signed or presented by the proper party or parties.

6. I reserve unto myself the right to pledge any of the securities held hereunder as collateral for a loan.

7. I reserve unto myself exclusively the power and right to collect any dividends, interest, capital gain distributions or other income which may accrue from the trust property during my lifetime and to pay such income to myself as an individual, and no beneficiary named herein shall have any claim upon any such income and/or profits distributed to me.

8. I reserve unto myself the power and right at any time during my lifetime to amend or revoke in whole or in part the trust hereby created without the necessity of obtaining the consent of the beneficiary and without giving notice to the beneficiary. The sale by me of the whole or any part of the portfolio of securities held hereunder shall constitute as to such whole or part a revocation of this trust.

9. The death during my lifetime, or in a common accident or disaster with me, of the beneficiary designated hereunder shall revoke such designation, and in the former event, this trust shall terminate upon my death and the assets held hereunder shall revert to my estate.

10. In the event of my physical or mental incapacity or my death, I hereby nominate and appoint as Successor Trustee hereunder whosoever shall at that time be beneficiary hereunder, unless such beneficiary shall not have attained the age of 21 years, or is otherwise legally incapacitated, in which event I hereby nominate and appoint

(Name) _____ Henry P. Adams _____ Milton _____ City _____ Connecticut _____ State _____ 06605 _____ Zip

(Address) _____ 125 _____ Number _____ Barnum Street _____ Street

to be Successor Trustee.

11. This Declaration of Trust shall extend to and be binding upon the heirs, executors, administrators and assigns of the undersigned and upon the Successors to the Trustee.

12. The Trustee and his successors shall serve without bond.

13. This Declaration of Trust shall be construed and enforced in accordance with the laws of the State

of _____ Connecticut _____

IN WITNESS WHEREOF, I have hereunto set my hand and seal this _____ second _____

day of _____ February _____, 19 80.

DACEY TRUST

Declaration of Trust

WHEREAS, I, _____, of the

City/Town of _____, County of _____, State of _____,

am the owner of certain securities including common and preferred stocks, bonds, debentures and mutual fund shares;

NOW, THEREFORE, KNOW ALL MEN BY THESE PRESENTS, that I do hereby acknowledge and declare that I hold and will hold said securities and all my right, title and interest in and to said securities IN TRUST

1. For the use and benefit of:

(Name) _____, of

(Address) _____

| Number | Street | City | State | Zip |

If because of my physical or mental incapacity certified in writing by a physician, the Successor Trustee shall assume active administration of this trust during my lifetime, such Successor Trustee shall be fully authorized to pay to me or disburse on my behalf such sums from income or principal as appear necessary or desirable for my comfort or welfare. Upon my death, unless the beneficiary shall predecease me or unless we both shall die as a result of a common accident or disaster, my Successor Trustee is hereby directed forthwith to transfer said securities and all right, title and interest in and to said securities unto the beneficiary absolutely and thereby terminate this trust; provided, however, that if the beneficiary hereunder shall not have attained the age of 21 years, the Successor Trustee shall hold the trust assets in continuing trust until such beneficiary shall have attained the age of 21 years. During such period of continuing trust the Successor Trustee, in his absolute discretion, may retain the specific securities herein described if he believes it to be in the best interests of the beneficiary so to do; or he may sell or otherwise dispose of any or all of them, investing and reinvesting the proceeds as he may deem appropriate. Prior to the date upon which such beneficiary attains the age of 21 years, the Successor Trustee may apply or expend any or all of the income or principal of the trust directly for the maintenance, education and support of the beneficiary without the intervention of any guardian and without application to any court. Such payments of income or principal may be made to the parents of such beneficiary or to the person with whom the beneficiary is living without any liability upon the Successor Trustee to see to the application thereof. If such beneficiary survives me but dies before attaining the age of 21 years, at his or her death the Successor Trustee shall transfer, pay over and deliver the trust property to such beneficiary's personal representative, absolutely.

2. For purposes of specific identification, the assets held pursuant to this trust shall be all those securities registered in the name of:

"_____, *Trustee u/d/t* (or *"Trustee U-A"*)

dated _____."

3. The beneficiary hereunder shall be liable for his proportionate share of any taxes levied upon the Settlor's total taxable estate by reason of the Settlor's death.

4. All interests of a beneficiary hereunder shall be inalienable and free from anticipation, assignment, attachment, pledge or control by creditors or a present or former spouse of such beneficiary in any proceedings at law or in equity.

5. This trust is created upon the express understanding that the issuer, transfer agent or custodian of any securities held hereunder shall be under no liability whatsoever to see to its proper administration, and that upon the transfer of the right, title and interest in and to said securities by any Trustee hereunder, said issuer, transfer agent or custodian shall conclusively treat the transferee as the sole owner of said securities. In the event that any shares, cash or other property shall be distributable at any time under the terms of said securities the said issuer, transfer agent or custodian is fully authorized to transfer, pay over and deliver the same to whosoever shall then be Trustee hereunder, and shall be under no liability to see to the proper application thereof. Until the issuer, transfer agent or custodian shall receive from some person interested in this trust, written notice of any death or other event upon which the right to receive may depend, the said issuer, transfer agent or custodian shall incur no liability for payments made in good faith to persons whose interests shall have been affected by such event. The issuer, transfer agent or custodian shall be protected in acting upon any notice or other instrument or document believed by it to be genuine and to have been signed or presented by the proper party or parties.

6. I reserve unto myself the right to pledge any of the securities held hereunder as collateral for a loan.

7. I reserve unto myself exclusively the power and right to collect any dividends, interest, capital gain distributions or other income which may accrue from the trust property during my lifetime and to pay such income to myself as an individual, and no beneficiary named herein shall have any claim upon any such income and/or profits distributed to me.

8. I reserve unto myself the power and right at any time during my lifetime to amend or revoke in whole or in part the trust hereby created without the necessity of obtaining the consent of the beneficiary and without giving notice to the beneficiary. The sale by me of the whole or any part of the portfolio of securities held hereunder shall constitute as to such whole or part a revocation of this trust.

9. The death during my lifetime, or in a common accident or disaster with me, of the beneficiary designated hereunder shall revoke such designation, and in the former event, I reserve the right to designate a new beneficiary. Should I for any reason fail to designate such new beneficiary, this trust shall terminate upon my death and the assets held hereunder shall revert to my estate.

10. In the event of my physical or mental incapacity or my death, I hereby nominate and appoint as Successor Trustee hereunder whosoever shall at that time be beneficiary hereunder, unless such beneficiary shall not have attained the age of 21 years, or is otherwise legally incapacitated, in which event I hereby nominate and appoint

(Name) _____ , of

(Address) _____
                Number   Street   City   State   Zip

to be Successor Trustee.

11. This Declaration of Trust shall extend to and be binding upon the heirs, executors, administrators and assigns of the undersigned and upon the Successors to the Trustee.

12. The Trustee and his successors shall serve without bond.

13. This Declaration of Trust shall be construed and enforced in accordance with the laws of the State

of _____ .

IN WITNESS WHEREOF, I have hereunto set my hand and seal this _____

day of _____ , 19_____ .

                    (Settlor sign here) _____ L.S.

I, the undersigned legal spouse of the above Settlor, hereby waive all community property rights which I may have in the hereinabove-described securities and give my assent to the provisions of the trust and to the inclusion in it of the said securities.

                    (Spouse sign here) _____ L.S.

Witness: (1) _____   Witness: (2) _____

STATE OF _____ ⎫   City

COUNTY OF _____ ⎬   or
                                                     Town _____

On the _____ day of _____ , 19_____ , personally appeared

_____

known to me to be the individual(s) who executed the foregoing instrument, and acknowledged the same to be _____ free act and deed, before me.

_____

(Notary Seal)   Notary Public

CHAPTER 9

DECLARATION OF TRUST
For Naming
ONE PRIMARY BENEFICIARY
And
ONE CONTINGENT BENEFICIARY
To Receive
SECURITIES HELD IN ONE NAME

INSTRUCTIONS:

On the following pages will be found a declaration of trust (DT-110) suitable for use in connection with the establishment of an inter vivos trust covering stocks, bonds, or mutual fund shares now held in one name, where it is desired to name some *one* person as primary beneficiary, with some *one* other person as contingent beneficiary to receive the securities if the primary beneficiary be not surviving upon the death of the owner.

Cross out *"city"* or *"town,"* leaving the appropriate designation of your community. In Paragraph 1, enter the names of the beneficiaries in the place provided. In Paragraph 2, enter your name and the date you are executing the declaration of trust.

Note that Paragraph 10 designates as Successor Trustee *"whosoever shall at that time be beneficiary hereunder,"* which means that in most cases you don't need to fill anything in there. However, if there is any possibility of a beneficiary who has not attained the age of 21 years receiving the trust assets, make certain that you name an adult in this paragraph who can act as trustee for such beneficiary. Avoid naming as trustee a person not likely to survive until the beneficiary has attained age 21.

When completed in the manner shown on the reverse side, make one photocopy of the declaration of trust for each separate stock or bond you own, plus sufficient additional copies to take care of future securities purchases. Then, put the original in safekeeping.

It is absolutely essential that you instruct your broker or mutual fund to register your securities in this form: *"(your name), Trustee u/d/t dated* (date you have signed the declaration of trust)." It will not be necessary to file the declaration of trust with the issuer at the time you purchase the securities. However, if and when you sell any of them, the issuer or transfer agent will almost certainly require you to display the instrument. If you die, the beneficiary will be required to produce it in order to obtain possession of the securities. In the circumstances, the safest thing to do is to staple a copy of it to *each* of the securities when the latter are issued. This stapling procedure should also be followed in the case of unregistered bonds. If you fail to follow these instructions in registering or reregistering your securities, they will be subject to probate.

Important: Read carefully Note B on page 38, which applies to this declaration of trust.

Declaration of Trust

DACEY TRUST

WHEREAS, I, _____ John J. Brown _____, County of _____ Fairfax _____, State of _____ Connecticut _____, of the Town of _____ Milton _____,

am the owner of certain securities, including common and preferred stocks, bonds, debentures and mutual fund shares;

NOW, THEREFORE, KNOW ALL MEN BY THESE PRESENTS, that I do hereby acknowledge and declare that I hold and will hold said securities and all my right, title and interest in and to said securities IN TRUST

1. For the use and benefit of:

(Name) _____ Elizabeth A. Brown – my wife _____, of _____ Milton _____ City _____ Connecticut _____ State _____ 06605 _____ Zip

(Address) _____ 525 _____ Number _____ Main Street _____ Street

or, if he or she be not surviving, for the use and benefit of:

(Name) _____ Jill A. Brown – my daughter _____, of _____ Milton _____ City _____ Connecticut _____ State _____ 06605 _____ Zip

(Address) _____ 525 _____ Number _____ Main Street _____ Street

If because of my physical or mental incapacity certified in writing by a physician, the Successor Trustee hereinafter named shall assume active administration of this trust during my lifetime, such Successor Trustee shall be fully authorized to pay to me or disburse on my behalf such sums from income or principal as appear necessary or desirable for my comfort or welfare. Upon my death, unless both the beneficiaries shall predecease me or unless we all shall die as a result of a common accident or disaster, my Successor Trustee is hereby directed forthwith to transfer said securities and all right, title and interest in and to said securities unto the beneficiary absolutely and thereby terminate this trust; provided, however, that if the beneficiary hereunder ... the income or principal directly for the maintenance, education and support of the beneficiar... ... the parents of such beneficiary or to the person with whom the beneficiary is living without any liability upon the Successor Trustee to see to the application thereof. If such beneficiary survives me but dies before attaining the age of 21 years, at his or her death the Successor Trustee shall transfer, pay over and deliver the trust property to such beneficiary's personal representative, absolutely.

2. For the purposes of specific identification, the assets held pursuant to this trust shall be all those securities registered in the name of:

_____ John J. Brown _____, Trustee udit (or "Trustee U-A")

dated _____ February 2, 1980 _____

3. The beneficiary hereunder shall be liable for his proportionate share of any taxes levied upon the Settlor's total taxable estate by reason of the Settlor's death.

4. All interests of a beneficiary hereunder shall be inalienable and free from anticipation, assignment, attachment, pledge or control by creditors or a present or former spouse of such beneficiary in any proceedings at law or in equity.

5. This trust is created upon the express understanding that the issuer, transfer agent or custodian of any securities hereunder shall be under no liability whatsoever to see to its proper administration, and that upon the transfer of the right, title and interest in and to said securities by any Trustee hereunder, said issuer, transfer agent or other property shall be distributable at any time under the terms of said securities. In the event that any shares, cash or other property shall be distributable at transferee as the sole owner of the said securities, the said issuer, transfer agent or custodian is fully authorized to transfer, pay over and deliver the same to whosoever shall then be Trustee hereunder, and shall be under no liability to see to the proper application thereof. Until the issuer, transfer agent or custodian shall receive from some person interested in this trust, written notice of any death or other event upon which the right to receive may depend, said issuer, transfer agent or custodian shall incur no liability for payments made in good faith to persons whose interests shall have been affected by such event. The issuer, transfer agent or custodian shall be protected in acting upon any notice or other instrument or document believed by it to be genuine and to have been signed or presented by the proper party or parties.

6. I reserve unto myself the right to pledge any of the securities held hereunder as collateral for a loan.

7. I reserve unto myself exclusively the power and right at any time during my lifetime and to collect any dividends, interest, capital gain distributions or other income which may accrue from the trust property during my lifetime and/or profits distributed to me, and no beneficiary named herein shall have any claim upon any such income to myself as an individual, and no beneficiary named herein shall have any claim upon any such income to myself as an individual, and no

8. I reserve unto myself the power and right at any time during my lifetime to amend or revoke in whole or in part the trust hereby created without the necessity of obtaining the consent of the beneficiaries and without giving notice to the beneficiaries. The sale by me of the whole or any part of the portfolio of securities held hereunder shall constitute as to such whole or part a revocation of this trust.

9. The death during my lifetime, or in a common accident or disaster with me, of both of the beneficiaries designated hereunder shall revoke such designation, and in the former event, I reserve the right to designate a new beneficiary. Should I for any reason fail to designate such new beneficiary, this trust shall terminate upon my death and the assets held hereunder shall revert to my estate.

10. In the event of my physical or mental incapacity or my death, I hereby nominate and appoint as Successor Trustee hereunder whosoever shall at that time be beneficiary hereunder, unless such beneficiary shall not have attained the age of 21 years or is otherwise legally incapacitated, in which event I hereby nominate and appoint

(Name) _____ Henry P. Adams _____, of _____ Milton _____ City _____ Connecticut _____ State _____ 06605 _____ Zip

(Address) _____ 125 _____ Number _____ Barnum Street _____ Street

to be Successor Trustee.

11. This Declaration of Trust shall extend to and be binding upon the heirs, executors, administrators and assigns of the undersigned and upon the Successors to the Trustee.

12. The Trustee and his successors shall serve without bond.

13. This Declaration of Trust shall be construed and enforced in accordance with the laws of the State of _____ Connecticut _____

Declaration of Trust

WHEREAS, I, _____, of the

City/Town of _____, County of _____, State of _____,

am the owner of certain securities, including common and preferred stocks, bonds, debentures and mutual fund shares;

NOW, THEREFORE, KNOW ALL MEN BY THESE PRESENTS, that I do hereby acknowledge and declare that I hold and will hold said securities and all my right, title and interest in and to said securities IN TRUST

1. For the use and benefit of:

(Name) _____, of

(Address) _____
               Number   Street   City   State   Zip

or, if he or she be not surviving, for the use and benefit of:

(Name) _____, of

(Address) _____
               Number   Street   City   State   Zip

If because of my physical or mental incapacity certified in writing by a physician, the Successor Trustee hereinafter named shall assume active administration of this trust during my lifetime, such Successor Trustee shall be fully authorized to pay to me or disburse on my behalf such sums from income or principal as appear necessary or desirable for my comfort or welfare. Upon my death, unless both the beneficiaries shall predecease me or unless we all shall die as a result of a common accident or disaster, my Successor Trustee is hereby directed forthwith to transfer said securities and all right, title and interest in and to said securities unto the beneficiary absolutely and thereby terminate this trust; provided, however, that if the beneficiary hereunder shall not have attained the age of 21 years, the Successor Trustee shall hold the trust assets in continuing trust until such beneficiary shall have attained the age of 21 years. During such period of continuing trust the Successor Trustee, in his absolute discretion, may retain the specific securities herein described if he believes it to be in the best interests of the beneficiary so to do, or he may sell or otherwise dispose of any or all of them, investing and reinvesting the proceeds as he may deem appropriate. Prior to the date upon which such beneficiary attains the age of 21 years, the Successor Trustee may apply or expend any or all of the income or principal directly for the maintenance, education and support of the beneficiary without the intervention of any guardian and without application to any court. Such payments of income or principal may be made to the parents of such beneficiary or to the person with whom the beneficiary is living without any liability upon the Successor Trustee to see to the application thereof. If such beneficiary survives me but dies before attaining the age of 21 years, at his or her death the Successor Trustee shall transfer, pay over and deliver the trust property to such beneficiary's personal representative, absolutely.

2. For the purposes of specific identification, the assets held pursuant to this trust shall be all those securities registered in the name of:

"_____, Trustee u/d/t (or "Trustee U-A")

    dated _____."

3. The beneficiary hereunder shall be liable for his proportionate share of any taxes levied upon the Settlor's total taxable estate by reason of the Settlor's death.

4. All interests of a beneficiary hereunder shall be inalienable and free from anticipation, assignment, attachment, pledge or control by creditors or a present or former spouse of such beneficiary in any proceedings at law or in equity.

5. This trust is created upon the express understanding that the issuer, transfer agent or custodian of any securities held hereunder shall be under no liability whatsoever to see to its proper administration, and that upon the transfer of the right, title and interest in and to said securities by any Trustee hereunder, said issuer, transfer agent or custodian shall conclusively treat the transferee as the sole owner of the said securities. In the event that any shares, cash or other property shall be distributable at any time under the terms of said securities, the said issuer, transfer agent or custodian is fully authorized to transfer, pay over and deliver the same to whosoever shall then be Trustee hereunder, and shall be under no liability to see to the proper application thereof. Until the issuer, transfer agent or custodian shall receive from some person interested in this trust, written notice of any death or other event upon which the right to receive may depend, said issuer, transfer agent or custodian shall incur no liability for payments made in good faith to persons whose interests shall have been affected by such event. The issuer, transfer agent or custodian shall be protected in acting upon any notice or other instrument or document believed by it to be genuine and to have been signed or presented by the proper party or parties.

6. I reserve unto myself the right to pledge any of the securities held hereunder as collateral for a loan.

7. I reserve unto myself exclusively the power and right to collect any dividends, interest, capital gain distributions or other income which may accrue from the trust property during my lifetime and to pay such income to myself as an individual, and no beneficiary named herein shall have any claim upon any such income and/or profits distributed to me.

8. I reserve unto myself the power and right at any time during my lifetime to amend or revoke in whole or in part the trust hereby created without the necessity of obtaining the consent of the beneficiaries and without giving notice to the beneficiaries. The sale by me of the whole or any part of the portfolio of securities held hereunder shall constitute as to such whole or part a revocation of this trust.

9. The death during my lifetime, or in a common accident or disaster with me, of both of the beneficiaries designated hereunder shall revoke such designation, and in the former event, I reserve the right to designate a new beneficiary. Should I for any reason fail to designate such new beneficiary, this trust shall terminate upon my death and the assets held hereunder shall revert to my estate.

10. In the event of my physical or mental incapacity or my death, I hereby nominate and appoint as Successor Trustee hereunder whosoever shall at that time be beneficiary hereunder, unless such beneficiary shall not have attained the age of 21 years or is otherwise legally incapacitated, in which event I hereby nominate and appoint

(Name) _____ , of

(Address) _____
           Number   *Street*   *City*   *State*   *Zip*

to be Successor Trustee.

11. This Declaration of Trust shall extend to and be binding upon the heirs, executors, administrators and assigns of the undersigned and upon the Successors to the Trustee.

12. The Trustee and his successors shall serve without bond.

13. This Declaration of Trust shall be construed and enforced in accordance with the laws of the State

of _____ .

IN WITNESS WHEREOF, I have hereunto set my hand and seal this _____

day of _____ , 19_____ .

(Settlor sign here) _____ L.S.

I, the undersigned legal spouse of the above Settlor, hereby waive all community property rights which I may have in the hereinabove-described securities and give my assent to the provisions of the trust and to the inclusion in it of the said securities.

(Spouse sign here) _____ L.S.

Witness: (1) _____   Witness: (2) _____

STATE OF _____   City
                                         or
COUNTY OF _____   Town _____

On the _____ day of _____ , 19_____ , personally appeared

_____

known to me to be the individual(s) who executed the foregoing instrument, and acknowledged the same to be _____ free act and deed, before me.

_____
                                   Notary Public

(Notary Seal)

CHAPTER 9

DECLARATION OF TRUST
For Naming
TWO OR MORE PERSONS, SHARING EQUALLY,
To Receive
SECURITIES HELD IN ONE NAME

INSTRUCTIONS:

On the following pages will be found a declaration of trust (DT-111) suitable for use in connection with the establishment of an inter vivos trust covering stocks, bonds, or mutual fund shares now held in one name, where it is desired to name two or more persons, sharing equally, to receive the securities upon the death of the owner.

Cross out *"city"* or *"town,"* leaving the appropriate designation of your community.

In Paragraph 1, indicate the *number of persons* you are naming (to discourage unauthorized additions to the list) and then insert their names. The one whose name appears *first* will be the Successor Trustee responsible for seeing to the distribution of the trust property.

Note that the instrument specifies that the named beneficiaries are to receive *"in equal shares, or the survivor of them/per stirpes."* Now, think carefully: If you have named three persons with the understanding that if one of them predeceases you, *his* children will take *his* share, cross out *"or the survivor of them"* and *initial it.* If that is *not* what you want—if, for example, you prefer that the share of the deceased person be divided between the two surviving persons, cross out *"per stirpes"* and *initial it.* Remember, you <u>must</u> cross out either *"or the survivor of them"* or *"per stirpes"*—one or the other.

In Paragraph 2, enter your name and the date you are executing the declaration of trust.

Note next that Paragraph 10 designates as Successor Trustee *"the beneficiary named first above,"* which means that in most cases you don't need to fill anything in there. However, if there is any possibility of a beneficiary who has not attained the age of 21 years receiving the assets, make certain that you name an adult in this paragraph who can act as trustee for such beneficiary. Avoid naming as trustee a person not likely to survive until the beneficiary has attained age 21.

When completed in the manner shown on the reverse side, make one photocopy of the declaration of trust for *each* separate stock or bond you own, plus sufficient additional copies to take care of future securities purchases. Then, put the original in safekeeping.

It is absolutely essential that you instruct your broker or mutual fund to register your securities in this form: *"(your name), Trustee u/d/t dated* (date you have signed the declaration of trust)." It will not be necessary to file the declaration of trust with the issuer at the time you purchase the securities. However, if and when you sell any of them, the issuer, transfer agent or custodian will almost certainly require you to display the instrument. If you die, the beneficiary will be required to produce it in order to obtain possession of the securities. In the circumstances, the safest thing to do is to staple a copy of it to *each* of the securities when the latter are issued. This stapling procedure should also be followed in the case of unregistered bonds. If you fail to follow these instructions in registering or reregistering your securities, they will be subject to probate.

Important: Read carefully Note B on page 38, which applies to this declaration of trust.

DT-111

Declaration of Trust

WHEREAS, I, __John J. Brown__, County of __Fairfax__, State of __Connecticut__, of the Town of __Milton__, am the owner of certain securities, including common and preferred stocks, bonds, debentures and mutual fund shares;

NOW, THEREFORE, KNOW ALL MEN BY THESE PRESENTS, that I do hereby acknowledge and declare that I hold and will hold said securities and all my right, title and interest in and to said securities IN TRUST   *J.J.B.*

1. For the use and benefit of the following __three (3)__ persons, in equal shares, _____ stirpes:

    Thomas B. Brown - my brother
    Helen M. Brown - my sister
    Charles M. Brown - my brother

If because of my physical or mental incapacity certified in writing by a physician, the Successor Trustee hereinafter named shall assume active administration of this trust during my lifetime, such Successor Trustee shall be fully authorized to pay to me or disburse on my behalf such sums from income or principal as appear necessary or desirable for my comfort or welfare. Upon my death, unless the beneficiaries all shall predecease me or unless we all shall die as a result of a common accident or disaster, my Successor Trustee is hereby directed forthwith to transfer said securities and all right, title and interest in and to said ... beneficiary without the intervention of any guardian and without application to any court. Such payments of income or principal may be made to the parents of such beneficiary or to the person with whom the beneficiary is living without any liability upon the Successor Trustee to see to the application thereof. If such beneficiary survives me but dies before attaining the age of 21 years, at his or her death the Successor Trustee shall transfer, pay over and deliver the trust property being held for such beneficiary to such beneficiary's personal representative, absolutely.

2. For purposes of specific identification, the assets held pursuant to this trust shall be all those securities registered in the name of: __John J. Brown__, Trustee, u/d/t (or "Trustee U-A")

dated __February 2, 1980__

3. Each beneficiary hereunder shall be liable for his proportionate share of any taxes levied upon the Settlor's total taxable estate by reason of the Settlor's death.

4. The interests of a beneficiary hereunder shall be inalienable and free from anticipation, assignment, attachment, pledge or control by creditors or a present or former spouse of such beneficiary in any proceeding at law or in equity.

5. This trust is created upon the express understanding that the issuer, transfer agent or custodian of any securities hereunder shall be under no liability whatsoever to see to its proper administration, and that upon the transfer of the right, title and interest in and to said securities by any Trustee hereunder, said issuer, transfer agent or custodian shall conclusively treat the ... revert to my estate.

10. In the event of my physical or mental incapacity or my death, I hereby nominate and appoint as Successor Trustee hereunder the beneficiary named first above, unless such beneficiary shall not have attained the age of 21 years or is otherwise legally incapacitated, in which event I hereby nominate and appoint as Successor Trustee the beneficiary whose name appears second above. If such beneficiary whose name appears second above shall not have attained the age of 21 years or is otherwise legally incapacitated, I nominate and appoint

(Name) __Henry P. Adams__

(Address) __125__ __Barnum Street__ __Milton__ __Connecticut__ __06605__
      Number   Street   City   State   Zip

to be Successor Trustee.

11. The Declaration of Trust shall extend to and be binding upon the heirs, executors, administrators and assigns of the

𝔇𝔢𝔠𝔩𝔞𝔯𝔞𝔱𝔦𝔬𝔫 𝔬𝔣 𝔗𝔯𝔲𝔰𝔱

WHEREAS, I, _____, of the

City/Town of _____, County of _____, State of _____,

am the owner of certain securities, including common and preferred stocks, bonds, debentures and mutual fund shares;

   NOW, THEREFORE, KNOW ALL MEN BY THESE PRESENTS, that I do hereby acknowledge and declare that I hold and will hold said securities and all my right, title and interest in and to said securities IN TRUST

   1. For the use and benefit of the following _____ persons, in equal shares, or the survivor of them/per stirpes:

   If because of my physical or mental incapacity certified in writing by a physician, the Successor Trustee hereinafter named shall assume active administration of this trust during my lifetime, such Successor Trustee shall be fully authorized to pay to me or disburse on my behalf such sums from income or principal as appear necessary or desirable for my comfort or welfare. Upon my death, unless the beneficiaries all shall predecease me or unless we all shall die as a result of a common accident or disaster, my Successor Trustee is hereby directed forthwith to transfer said securities and all right, title and interest in and to said securities unto the beneficiaries absolutely and thereby terminate this trust; provided, however, that if any beneficiary hereunder shall not have attained the age of 21 years, the Successor Trustee shall hold such beneficiary's share of the trust assets in continuing trust until such beneficiary shall have attained the age of 21 years. During such period of continuing trust the Successor Trustee, in his absolute discretion, may retain the specific securities herein described if he believes it to be in the best interest of the beneficiary so to do, or he may sell or otherwise dispose of any or all of them, investing and reinvesting the proceeds as he may deem appropriate. Prior to the date upon which such beneficiary attains the age of 21 years, the Successor Trustee may apply or expend any or all of the income or principal directly for the maintenance, education and support of the beneficiary without the intervention of any guardian and without application to any court. Such payments of income or principal may be made to the parents of such beneficiary or to the person with whom the beneficiary is living without any liability upon the Successor Trustee to see to the application thereof. If such beneficiary survives me but dies before attaining the age of 21 years, at his or her death the Successor Trustee shall transfer, pay over and deliver the trust property being held for such beneficiary to such beneficiary's personal representative, absolutely.

   2. For purposes of specific identification, the assets held pursuant to this trust shall be all those securities registered in the name of:

   "_____, *Trustee, u/d/t* (or *"Trustee U-A"*)

   dated _____."

   3. Each beneficiary hereunder shall be liable for his proportionate share of any taxes levied upon the Settlor's total taxable estate by reason of the Settlor's death.

   4. The interests of a beneficiary hereunder shall be inalienable and free from anticipation, assignment, attachment, pledge or control by creditors or a present or former spouse of such beneficiary in any proceeding at law or in equity.

   5. This trust is created upon the express understanding that the issuer, transfer agent or custodian of any securities held hereunder shall be under no liability whatsoever to see to its proper administration, and that upon the transfer of the right, title and interest in and to said securities by any Trustee hereunder, said issuer, transfer agent or custodian shall conclusively treat the transferee as the sole owner of said securities. In the event that any shares, cash or other property shall be distributable at any time under the terms of said securities, the said issuer, transfer agent or custodian is fully authorized to transfer, pay over and deliver the same to whosoever shall then be Trustee hereunder, and shall be under no liability to see to the proper application thereof. Until the issuer, transfer agent or custodian shall receive from some person interested in this trust, written notice of any death or other event upon which the right to receive may depend, said issuer, transfer agent or custodian shall incur no liability for payments made in good faith to persons whose interests shall have been affected by such event. The issuer, transfer agent or custodian shall be protected in acting upon any notice or other instrument or document believed by it to be genuine and to have been signed or presented by the proper party or parties.

   6. I reserve unto myself the power and right to pledge any of the securities held hereunder as collateral for a loan.

   7. I reserve unto myself exclusively the power and right to collect any dividends, interest, capital gain distributions or other income which may accrue from the trust property during my lifetime and to pay such income to myself as an individual, and no beneficiary named herein shall have any claim upon any such income and/or profits distributed to me.

8. I reserve unto myself the power and right at any time during my lifetime to amend or revoke in whole or in part the trust hereby created without the necessity of obtaining the consent of the beneficiaries and without giving notice to the beneficiaries. The sale by me of the whole or any part of the portfolio of securities held hereunder shall constitute as to such whole or part a revocation of this trust.

9. The death during my lifetime, or in a common accident or disaster with me, of all of the beneficiaries designated hereunder shall revoke such designation, and in the former event, I reserve the right to designate a new beneficiary. Should I for any reason fail to designate such new beneficiary, this trust shall terminate upon my death and the assets held hereunder shall revert to my estate.

10. In the event of my physical or mental incapacity or my death, I hereby nominate and appoint as Successor Trustee hereunder the beneficiary named first above, unless such beneficiary shall not have attained the age of 21 years or is otherwise legally incapacitated, in which event I hereby nominate and appoint as Successor Trustee the beneficiary whose name appears second above. If such beneficiary whose name appears second above shall not have attained the age of 21 years or is otherwise legally incapacitated, I nominate and appoint

(Name) _____ , of

(Address) _____

         Number   *Street*   *City*   *State*   *Zip*

to be Successor Trustee.

11. This Declaration of Trust shall extend to and be binding upon the heirs, executors, administrators and assigns of the undersigned and upon the Successors to the Trustee.

12. The Trustee and his successors shall serve without bond.

13. This Declaration of Trust shall be construed and enforced in accordance with the laws of the State

of _____ .

IN WITNESS WHEREOF, I have hereunto set my hand and seal this _____

day of _____ , 19_____ .

        (Settlor sign here) _____ L.S.

I, the undersigned legal spouse of the above Settlor, hereby waive all community property rights which I may have in the hereinabove-described securities and give my assent to the provisions of the trust and to the inclusion in it of the said securities.

        (Spouse sign here) _____ L.S.

Witness: (1) _____   Witness: (2) _____

STATE OF _____   City

COUNTY OF _____   or

                                     Town _____

On the _____ day of _____ , 19_____ , personally appeared

_____

known to me to be the individual(s) who executed the foregoing instrument, and acknowledged the same to be _____ free act and deed, before me.

_____

(Notary Seal)   *Notary Public*

CHAPTER 9

DECLARATION OF TRUST
For Naming
**ONE PRIMARY BENEFICIARY WITH YOUR CHILDREN,
SHARING EQUALLY, AS CONTINGENT BENEFICIARIES**
To Receive
SECURITIES HELD IN ONE NAME

INSTRUCTIONS:

On the following pages will be found a declaration of trust (DT-112) suitable for use in connection with the establishment of an inter vivos trust covering stocks, bonds, or mutual fund shares now held in one name, where it is desired to name some *one* person (ordinarily, but not necessarily, one's spouse) as primary beneficiary, with one's children as contingent beneficiaries to receive the securities upon the death of the owner.

Cross out *"city"* or *"town,"* leaving the appropriate designation of your community.

In Paragraph 1, enter the name of the primary beneficiary (called the "First Beneficiary") in the place provided. Note that the instrument refers to your children as *"natural not/or adopted."* Now, decide: If you have an adopted child and you wish to *include* him, cross out the word *"not"* in the phrase *"natural not/or adopted"* and *initial it.* If you wish to *exclude* your adopted child, cross out the word *"or"* in the same phrase and *initial it.* Remember, you <u>must</u> cross out *"not"* or *"or"*—one or the other. If you have no adopted child, simply cross out *"not."*

Note next that the instrument specifies that your children are to receive *"in equal shares, or the survivor of them/per stirpes."* Now, think carefully: If it is your wish that if one of your children does not survive you, *his* share shall be paid to *his* children in equal shares, cross out *"or the survivor of them"* and *initial it.* If that is *not* what you want—if, for example, you prefer that the share of your deceased child be divided among your surviving children, cross out *"per stirpes"* and *initial it.* Remember, you <u>must</u> cross out *"or the survivor of them"* or *"per stirpes"*—one or the other.

In Paragraph 2, enter your name and the date you are executing the Declaration of Trust.

Note that Paragraph 10 designates as Successor Trustee *"whosoever shall at that time be beneficiary hereunder,"* which means that in most cases you don't need to fill anything in there. However, if there is any possibility of a beneficiary who has not attained the age of 21 years receiving the trust assets, make certain you name an adult in this paragraph who can act as trustee for such beneficiary. Avoid naming as trustee a person not likely to survive until the beneficiary has attained age 21.

When completed in the manner shown on the reverse side, make one photocopy of the declaration of trust for each separate stock or bond you own, plus sufficient additional copies to take care of future securities purchases. Then, put the original in safekeeping.

It is absolutely essential that you instruct your broker or mutual fund to register or reregister your securities in this form: *"(your name), Trustee u/d/t dated* (date you have signed the declaration of trust)." It will not be necessary to file the declaration of trust with the issuer at the time you purchase the securities. However, if and when you sell any of them, the issuer, transfer agent, or custodian will almost certainly require you to display the instrument. If you die, the beneficiary will be required to produce it in order to obtain possession of the securities. In the circumstances, the safest thing to do is to staple a copy of it to *each* of the securities when the latter are issued. This stapling procedure should also be followed in the case of unregistered bonds. If you fail to follow these instructions in registering or reregistering your securities, they will be subject to probate.

Important: Read carefully Note B on page 38, which applies to this declaration of trust.

Declaration of Trust

WHEREAS, I, _____ John J. Brown _____, of the _____, County of _____ Fairfax _____, State of _____ Connecticut

City/Town of _____ Milton _____

am the owner of certain securities, including common and preferred stocks, bonds, debentures and mutual fund shares;

NOW, THEREFORE, KNOW ALL MEN BY THESE PRESENTS, that I do hereby acknowledge and declare that I hold and will hold said securities and all my right, title and interest in and to said securities IN TRUST

1. For the use and benefit of:

(Name) _____ Elizabeth A. Brown – my wife _____

(Address) _____ 525 _____ Main Street _____ ʃʃ.ð. _____ Milton _____ Connecticut _____ 06605
　　　　　　　Number　　　　　　Street　　　　　　　　　　　　　City　　　　　　　　State　　　　　　　Zip

(hereinafter referred to as the "First Beneficiary") and upon his or her death prior to the termination of the trust, for the use and benefit of my children, natural and/or adopted, in equal shares, or the survivor of them, per stirpes.

ʃʃ.ð.

parents of such beneficiary or to the person with whom the beneficiary is living without any liability upon the Successor Trustee to see to the application thereof. If such beneficiary survives me but dies before attaining the age of 21 years, at his or her death the Successor Trustee shall transfer, pay over and deliver the trust property being held for such beneficiary to such beneficiary's personal representative, absolutely.

2. For the purposes of specific identification, the assets held pursuant to this trust shall be all those securities registered in the name of:

"_____ John J. Brown _____", Trustee u/d/t/ (or "Trustee U-A")

dated _____ April 2, 1980 _____

3. Each beneficiary hereunder shall be liable for his proportionate share of any taxes levied upon the Settlor's total taxable estate by reason of the Settlor's death.

4. All interests of a beneficiary hereunder shall be inalienable and free from anticipation, assignment, attachment, pledge or control by creditors or a present or former spouse of such beneficiary in any proceedings at law or in equity.

5. This trust is created upon the express understanding that the issuer, transfer agent or custodian of any securities

revert to my estate.

10. In the event of my physical or mental incapacity or my death, I hereby nominate and appoint as Successor Trustee hereunder the First Beneficiary unless such beneficiary shall not have attained the age of 21 years or is otherwise legally incapacitated, in which event I hereby nominate and appoint

(Name) _____ Henry P. Adams _____, of

(Address) _____ 125 _____ Barnum Street _____ Milton _____ Connecticut _____ 06605
　　　　　　　Number　　　　　　Street　　　　　　　　City　　　　　　　State　　　　　　Zip

to be Successor Trustee.

11. This Declaration of Trust shall extend to and be binding upon the heirs, executors, administrators and assigns of the undersigned and upon the Successors to the Trustee.

12. The Trustee and his successors shall serve without bond.

13. This Declaration of Trust shall be construed and enforced in accordance with the laws of the State

of _____ Connecticut

Declaration of Trust

WHEREAS, I, _____, of the

City/Town of _____, County of _____, State of _____,

am the owner of certain securities, including common and preferred stocks, bonds, debentures and mutual fund shares;

NOW, THEREFORE, KNOW ALL MEN BY THESE PRESENTS, that I do hereby acknowledge and declare that I hold and will hold said securities and all my right, title and interest in and to said securities IN TRUST

    1. For the use and benefit of:

(Name) _____, of

(Address) _____

| Number | Street | City | State | Zip |

(hereinafter referred to as the "First Beneficiary") and upon his or her death prior to the termination of the trust, for the use and benefit of my children, natural not/or adopted, in equal shares, or the survivor of them/per stirpes.

    If because of my physical or mental incapacity certified in writing by a physician, the Successor Trustee hereinafter named shall assume active administration of this trust during my lifetime, such Successor Trustee shall be fully authorized to pay to me or disburse on my behalf such sums from income or principal as appear necessary or desirable for my comfort or welfare. Upon my death, unless the beneficiaries shall predecease me or unless we all shall die as a result of a common accident or disaster, my Successor Trustee is hereby directed forthwith to transfer said securities and all right, title and interest in and to said securities unto the beneficiary absolutely and thereby terminate this trust; provided, however, that if any beneficiary hereunder shall not have attained the age of 21 years, the Successor Trustee shall hold such beneficiary's share of the trust assets in continuing trust until such beneficiary shall have attained the age of 21 years. During such period of continuing trust the Successor Trustee, in his absolute discretion, may retain the specific securities herein described if he believes it to be in the best interest of the beneficiary so to do, or he may sell or otherwise dispose of any or all of them, investing and reinvesting the proceeds as he may deem appropriate. Prior to the date upon which such beneficiary attains the age of 21 years, the Successor Trustee may apply or expend any or all of the income or principal directly for the maintenance, education and support of the beneficiary without the intervention of any guardian and without application to any court. Such payments of income or principal may be made to the parents of such beneficiary or to the person with whom the beneficiary is living without any liability upon the Successor Trustee to see to the application thereof. If such beneficiary survives me but dies before attaining the age of 21 years, at his or her death the Successor Trustee shall transfer, pay over and deliver the trust property being held for such beneficiary to such beneficiary's personal representative, absolutely.

    2. For the purposes of specific identification, the assets held pursuant to this trust shall be all those securities registered in the name of:

"_____, *Trustee u/d/t/* (or *"Trustee U-A"*)

    *dated*_____."

    3. Each beneficiary hereunder shall be liable for his proportionate share of any taxes levied upon the Settlor's total taxable estate by reason of the Settlor's death.

    4. All interests of a beneficiary hereunder shall be inalienable and free from anticipation, assignment, attachment, pledge or control by creditors or a present or former spouse of such beneficiary in any proceedings at law or in equity.

    5. This trust is created upon the express understanding that the issuer, transfer agent or custodian of any securities hereunder shall be under no liability whatsoever to see to its proper administration, and that upon the transfer of the right, title and interest in and to said securities by any Trustee hereunder, said issuer, transfer agent or custodian shall conclusively treat the transferee as the sole owner of said securities. In the event that any shares, cash or other property shall be distributable at any time under the terms of said securities, the said issuer, transfer agent or custodian is fully authorized to transfer, pay over and deliver the same to whosoever shall then be Trustee hereunder, and shall be under no liability to see to the proper application thereof. Until the issuer, transfer agent or custodian shall receive from some person interested in this trust, written notice of any death or other event upon which the right to receive may depend, said issuer, transfer agent or custodian shall incur no liability for payments made in good faith to persons whose interests shall have been affected by such event. The issuer, transfer agent or custodian shall be protected in acting upon any notice or other instrument or document believed by it to be genuine and to have been signed or presented by the proper party or parties.

    6. I reserve unto myself the right to pledge any of the securities held hereunder as collateral for a loan.

    7. I reserve unto myself exclusively the power and right to collect any dividends, interest, capital gain distributions or other income which may accrue from the trust property during my lifetime and to pay such income to myself as an individual, and no beneficiary named herein shall have any claim upon any such income and/or profits distributed to me.

8. I reserve unto myself the power and right at any time during my lifetime to amend or revoke in whole or in part the trust hereby created without the necessity of obtaining the consent of the beneficiaries and without giving notice to the beneficiaries. The sale by me of the whole or any part of the portfolio of securities held hereunder shall constitute as to such whole or part a revocation of this trust.

9. The death during my lifetime, or in a common accident or disaster with me, of all of the beneficiaries designated hereunder shall revoke such designation, and in the former event, I reserve the right to designate a new beneficiary. Should I for any reason fail to designate such new beneficiary, this trust shall terminate upon my death and the assets held hereunder shall revert to my estate.

10. In the event of my physical or mental incapacity or my death, I hereby nominate and appoint as Successor Trustee hereunder the First Beneficiary unless such beneficiary shall not have attained the age of 21 years or is otherwise legally incapacitated, in which event I hereby nominate and appoint

(Name) _____, of

(Address) _____

      Number   *Street*   *City*   *State*   *Zip*

to be Successor Trustee.

11. This Declaration of Trust shall extend to and be binding upon the heirs, executors, administrators and assigns of the undersigned and upon the Successors to the Trustee.

12. The Trustee and his successors shall serve without bond.

13. This Declaration of Trust shall be construed and enforced in accordance with the laws of the State

of _____.

IN WITNESS WHEREOF, I have hereunto set my hand and seal this _____

day of _____, 19_____.

        (Settlor sign here) _____ L.S.

I, the undersigned legal spouse of the above Settlor, hereby waive all community property rights which I may have in the hereinabove-described securities and give my assent to the provisions of the trust and to the inclusion in it of the said securities.

        (Spouse sign here) _____ L.S.

Witness: (1) _____   Witness: (2) _____

STATE OF _____   City

COUNTY OF _____   or

                           Town _____

On the _____ day of _____, 19_____, personally appeared

_____

known to me to be the individual(s) who executed the foregoing instrument, and acknowledged the same to be _____ free act and deed, before me.

(Notary Seal)

                         _____

                              Notary Public

CHAPTER 9

DECLARATION OF TRUST
For Naming
ONE BENEFICIARY
To Receive
SECURITIES HELD IN JOINT NAMES

INSTRUCTIONS:

On the following pages will be found a declaration of trust (DT-109-J) suitable for use in connection with the establishment of an inter vivos trust covering stocks, bonds, or mutual fund shares now held in joint names, where it is desired to name some *one* person to receive the securities upon the death of the survivor of the two joint owners.

Cross out *"city"* or *"town,"* leaving the appropriate designation of your community.

In Paragraph 1, enter the name of the beneficiary in the place provided.

In Paragraph 2, enter the names of the joint owners and the date that you are executing the declaration of trust.

Note that Paragraph 10 designates as Successor Trustee *"whosoever shall at that time be beneficiary hereunder,"* which means that in most cases you don't need to fill anything in there. However, if there is any possibility of a beneficiary who has not attained the age of 21 years receiving the trust assets, make certain that you name an adult in this paragraph who can act as trustee for such beneficiary. Avoid naming as trustee a person not likely to survive until the beneficiary has attained age 21.

When completed in the manner shown on the reverse side, make one photocopy of the declaration of trust for *each* separate stock or bond you own, plus sufficient additional copies to take care of future securities purchases. Then, put the original in safekeeping.

It is absolutely essential that you instruct your broker or mutual fund to register your securities in this form: *"(your name) and (your co-owner's name), Trustees u/d/t dated* (date you have signed the declaration of trust)." It will not be necessary to file the declaration of trust with the issuer at the time you purchase the securities. However, if and when you sell any of them, the issuer, transfer agent, or custodian will almost certainly require you to display the instrument. If you die, the beneficiary will be required to produce it in order to obtain possession of the securities. In the circumstances, the safest thing to do is to staple a copy of it to *each* of the securities when the latter are issued. This stapling procedure should also be followed in the case of unregistered bonds. If you fail to follow these instructions in registering or reregistering your securities, they will be subject to probate.

Important: Read carefully Note B on page 38, which applies to this declaration of trust.

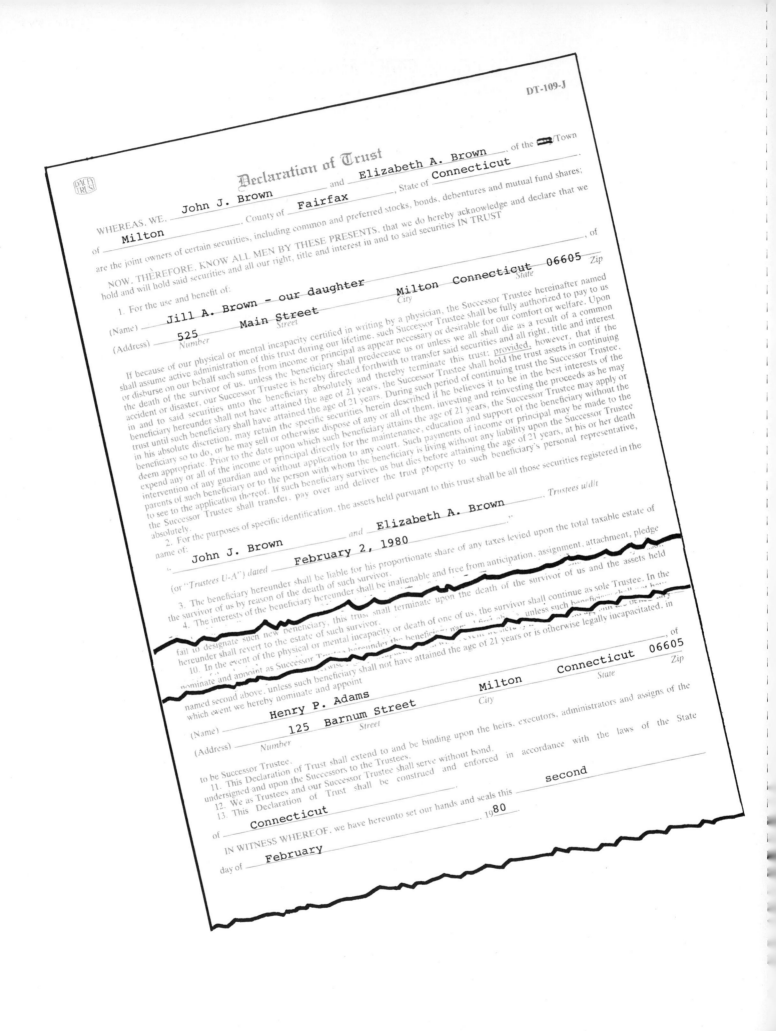

DT-109-J

Declaration of Trust

WHEREAS, WE, __John J. Brown__ and __Elizabeth A. Brown__, of the ~~City~~/Town of __Milton__, County of __Fairfax__, State of __Connecticut__ are the joint owners of certain securities, including common and preferred stocks, bonds, debentures and mutual fund shares;

NOW, THEREFORE, KNOW ALL MEN BY THESE PRESENTS, that we do hereby acknowledge and declare that we hold and will hold said securities and all our right, title and interest in and to said securities IN TRUST

1. For the use and benefit of:

(Name) __Jill A. Brown – our daughter__

(Address) __525__ __Main Street__ __Milton__ __Connecticut__ __06605__
          Number   Street   City   State   Zip

If because of our physical or mental incapacity certified in writing by a physician, the Successor Trustee hereinafter named shall assume active administration of this trust during our lifetime, such Successor Trustee shall be fully authorized to pay to us or disburse on our behalf such sums from income or principal as appear necessary or desirable for our comfort or welfare. Upon the death of the survivor of us, unless the beneficiary shall predecease us or unless we all shall die as a result of a common accident or disaster, our Successor Trustee is hereby directed forthwith to transfer said securities and all right, title and interest in and to said securities unto the beneficiary absolutely and thereby terminate this trust: provided, however, that if the beneficiary hereunder shall not have attained the age of 21 years, the Successor Trustee shall hold the trust assets in continuing trust until such beneficiary shall have attained the age of 21 years. During such period of continuing trust the Successor Trustee, in his absolute discretion, may retain the specific securities herein described if he believes it to be in the best interests of the beneficiary so to do, or he may sell or otherwise dispose of any or all of them, investing and reinvesting the proceeds as he may deem appropriate. Prior to the date upon which such beneficiary attains the age of 21 years, the Successor Trustee may apply or expend any or all of the income or principal directly for the maintenance, education and support of the beneficiary without the intervention of any guardian and without application to any court. Such payments of income or principal may be made to the parents of such beneficiary or to the person with whom the beneficiary is living without any liability upon the Successor Trustee to see to the application thereof. If such beneficiary survives us but dies before attaining the age of 21 years, at his or her death the Successor Trustee shall transfer, pay over and deliver the trust property to such beneficiary's personal representative, absolutely.

2. For the purposes of specific identification, the assets held pursuant to this trust shall be all those securities registered in the name of:

"__John J. Brown__ and __Elizabeth A. Brown__, Trustees u/d/t

(or "Trustees U-A") dated __February 2, 1980__

3. The beneficiary hereunder shall be liable for his proportionate share of any taxes levied upon the total taxable estate of the survivor of us by reason of the death of such survivor.

4. The interests of the beneficiary hereunder shall be inalienable and free from anticipation, assignment, attachment, pledge

fail to designate such new beneficiary, this trust shall terminate upon the death of the survivor of us and the assets held hereunder shall revert to the estate of such survivor. In the event of the physical or mental incapacity or death of one of us, the survivor shall continue as sole Trustee. In the

10. In the event ... unless such beneficiary ... shall not have attained the age of 21 years or is otherwise legally incapacitated, in which event we hereby nominate and appoint

(Name) __Henry P. Adams__

(Address) __125__ __Barnum Street__ __Milton__ __Connecticut__ __06605__
          Number   Street   City   State   Zip

to be Successor Trustee.

11. This Declaration of Trust shall extend to and be binding upon the heirs, executors, administrators and assigns of the undersigned and upon the Successors to the Trustees.

12. We as Trustees and our Successor Trustee shall serve without bond.

13. This Declaration of Trust shall be construed and enforced in accordance with the laws of the State of __Connecticut__.

IN WITNESS WHEREOF, we have hereunto set our hands and seals this __second__ day of __February__, 19__80__.

Declaration of Trust

WHEREAS, WE, _____ and _____, of the City/Town

of _____, County of _____, State of _____,

are the joint owners of certain securities, including common and preferred stocks, bonds, debentures and mutual fund shares;

NOW, THEREFORE, KNOW ALL MEN BY THESE PRESENTS, that we do hereby acknowledge and declare that we hold and will hold said securities and all our right, title and interest in and to said securities IN TRUST

1. For the use and benefit of:

(Name) _____, of

(Address) _____
           Number   Street   City   State   Zip

If because of our physical or mental incapacity certified in writing by a physician, the Successor Trustee hereinafter named shall assume active administration of this trust during our lifetime, such Successor Trustee shall be fully authorized to pay to us or disburse on our behalf such sums from income or principal as appear necessary or desirable for our comfort or welfare. Upon the death of the survivor of us, unless the beneficiary shall predecease us or unless we all shall die as a result of a common accident or disaster, our Successor Trustee is hereby directed forthwith to transfer said securities and all right, title and interest in and to said securities unto the beneficiary absolutely and thereby terminate this trust; provided, however, that if the beneficiary hereunder shall not have attained the age of 21 years, the Successor Trustee shall hold the trust assets in continuing trust until such beneficiary shall have attained the age of 21 years. During such period of continuing trust the Successor Trustee, in his absolute discretion, may retain the specific securities herein described if he believes it to be in the best interests of the beneficiary so to do, or he may sell or otherwise dispose of any or all of them, investing and reinvesting the proceeds as he may deem appropriate. Prior to the date upon which such beneficiary attains the age of 21 years, the Successor Trustee may apply or expend any or all of the income or principal directly for the maintenance, education and support of the beneficiary without the intervention of any guardian and without application to any court. Such payments of income or principal may be made to the parents of such beneficiary or to the person with whom the beneficiary is living without any liability upon the Successor Trustee to see to the application thereof. If such beneficiary survives us but dies before attaining the age of 21 years, at his or her death the Successor Trustee shall transfer, pay over and deliver the trust property to such beneficiary's personal representative, absolutely.

2. For the purposes of specific identification, the assets held pursuant to this trust shall be all those securities registered in the name of:

"_____ and _____, Trustees u/d/t

(or "Trustees U-A") dated _____."

3. The beneficiary hereunder shall be liable for his proportionate share of any taxes levied upon the total taxable estate of the survivor of us by reason of the death of such survivor.

4. The interests of the beneficiary hereunder shall be inalienable and free from anticipation, assignment, attachment, pledge or control by creditors or a present or former spouse of such beneficiary in any proceedings at law or in equity.

5. This trust is created upon the express understanding that the issuer, transfer agent or custodian of any securities held hereunder shall be under no liability whatsoever to see to its proper administration, and that upon the transfer of the right, title and interest in and to said securities by any Trustee hereunder, said issuer, transfer agent or custodian shall conclusively treat the transferee as the sole owner of said securities. In the event that any shares, cash or other property shall be distributable at any time under the terms of said securities, said issuer, transfer agent or custodian is fully authorized to transfer, pay over and deliver the same to whosoever shall then be Trustee hereunder, and shall be under no liability to see to the proper application thereof. Until the issuer, transfer agent or custodian shall receive from some person interested in this trust, written notice of any death or other event upon which the right to receive may depend, said issuer, transfer agent or custodian shall incur no liability for payments made in good faith to persons whose interests shall have been affected by such event. The issuer, transfer agent or custodian shall be protected in acting upon any notice or other instrument or document believed by it to be genuine and to have been signed or presented by the proper party or parties.

6. We reserve unto ourselves the right to pledge any of the securities held hereunder as collateral for a loan.

7. We reserve unto ourselves exclusively the power and right to collect any dividends, interest, capital gain distributions or other income which may accrue from the trust property during our lifetime and to pay such income to ourselves as individuals, and no beneficiary named herein shall have any claim upon any such income and/or profits distributed to us.

8. We reserve unto ourselves the power and right at any time during our lifetime to amend or revoke in whole or in part the trust hereby created without the necessity of obtaining the consent of the beneficiary and without giving notice to the beneficiary. The sale by us of the whole or any part of the portfolio of securities held hereunder shall constitute as to such whole or part a revocation of this trust.

9. The death during our lifetime, or in a common accident or disaster with us, of the beneficiary designated hereunder shall revoke such designation, and in the former event, we reserve the right to designate a new beneficiary. Should we for any reason fail to designate such new beneficiary, this trust shall terminate upon the death of the survivor of us and the assets held hereunder shall revert to the estate of such survivor.

10. In the event of the physical or mental incapacity or death of one of us, the survivor shall continue as sole Trustee. In the event of the physical or mental incapacity or death of the survivor of us, or if we both shall die in a common accident, we hereby nominate and appoint as Successor Trustee whosoever shall at that time be beneficiary hereunder, unless such beneficiary shall not have attained the age of 21 years or is otherwise legally incapacitated, in which event we hereby nominate and appoint

(Name) _____, of

(Address) _____
       Number   *Street*   *City*   *State*   *Zip*

to be Successor Trustee.

11. This Declaration of Trust shall extend to and be binding upon the heirs, executors, administrators and assigns of the undersigned and upon the Successors to the Trustees.

12. We as Trustees and our Successor Trustee shall serve without bond.

13. This Declaration of Trust shall be construed and enforced in accordance with the laws of the State

of _____.

IN WITNESS WHEREOF, we have hereunto set our hands and seals this _____

day of _____, 19_____.

                 (First Settlor sign here) _____ L.S.

           (Second Settlor sign here) _____ L.S.

I, the undersigned legal spouse of one of the above Settlors, hereby waive all community property rights which I may have in the hereinabove-described securities and give my assent to the provisions of the trust and to the inclusion in it of the said securities.

             (Spouse sign here) _____ L.S.

Witness: (1) _____   Witness: (2) _____

STATE OF _____   City

COUNTY OF _____   or Town _____

On the _____ day of _____, 19_____, personally appeared

_____ and _____

known to me to be the individuals who executed the foregoing instrument, and acknowledged the same to be their free act and deed, before me.

_____

(Notary Seal)   *Notary Public*

CHAPTER 9

DECLARATION OF TRUST

For Naming

ONE PRIMARY BENEFICIARY

And

ONE CONTINGENT BENEFICIARY

To Receive

SECURITIES HELD IN JOINT NAMES

INSTRUCTIONS:

On the following pages will be found a declaration of trust (DT-110-J) suitable for use in connection with the establishment of an inter vivos trust covering stocks, bonds, or mutual fund shares now held in joint names, where it is desired to name some *one* person as primary beneficiary, with some *one* other person as contingent beneficiary, to receive the securities upon the death of the survivor of the two joint owners.

Cross out *"city"* or *"town,"* leaving the appropriate designation of your community.

In Paragraph 1, enter the name of the beneficiaries in the place provided.

In Paragraph 2, enter the names of the joint owners and the date you are executing the declaration of trust.

Note that Paragraph 10 designates as Successor Trustee *"whosoever shall at that time be beneficiary hereunder,"* which means that in most cases you don't need to fill anything in there. However, if there is any possibility of a beneficiary who has not attained the age of 21 years receiving the trust assets, make certain that you name an adult in this paragraph who can act as trustee for such beneficiary. Avoid naming as trustee a person not likely to survive until the beneficiary has attained age 21.

When completed in the manner shown on the reverse side, make one photocopy of the declaration of trust for each separate stock or bond you own, plus sufficient additional copies to take care of future securities purchases. Then, put the original in safekeeping.

It is absolutely essential that you instruct your broker or mutual fund to register your securities in this form: *"(your name) and (your co-owner's name), Trustees u/d/t dated* (date you have signed the declaration of trust)." It will not be necessary to file the declaration of trust with the issuer at the time you purchase the securities. However, if and when you sell any of them, the issuer, transfer agent, or custodian will almost certainly require you to display the instrument. If you die, the beneficiary will be required to produce it in order to obtain possession of the securities. In the circumstances, the safest thing to do is to staple a copy of it to *each* of the securities when the latter are issued. This stapling procedure should also be followed in the case of unregistered bonds. If you fail to follow these instructions in registering or reregistering your securities, they will be subject to probate.

Important: Read carefully Note B on page 38, which applies to this declaration of trust.

DACEY TRUST

Declaration of Trust

WHEREAS, WE, __John J. Brown__ and __Elizabeth A. Brown__, of the ~~City~~ Town

of __Milton__, County of __Fairfax__, State of __Connecticut__,

are the joint owners of certain securities, including common and preferred stocks, bonds, debentures and mutual fund shares;

NOW, THEREFORE, KNOW ALL MEN BY THESE PRESENTS, that we do hereby acknowledge and declare that we

hold and will hold said securities and all our right, title and interest in and to said securities IN TRUST

1. For the use and benefit of:

(Name) __Jill A. Brown - our daughter__, of

(Address) __525__   __Main Street__   __Milton__   __Connecticut__   __06605__
      Number   Street   City   State   Zip

if he or she be not surviving, for the use and benefit of:

(Name) __Dorothy Lynn - our niece__

(Address) __566__   __Midland Street__   __Portland__   __Wisconsin__   __53123__
      Number   Street   City   State   Zip

If because of our physical or mental incapacity certified in writing by a physician, the Successor Trustee hereinafter named shall assume active administration of ... the beneficiary ... our lifetime, such Successor Trustee ... authorized to ...

... beneficiary hereunder shall not have attained the age of 21 years. During such period of continuing trust the Successor Trustee shall hold the trust assets in continuing trust until the beneficiary shall have attained the age of 21 years, investing and reinvesting the proceeds as he may believe it to be in the best interest of the his absolute discretion, may retain the specific securities herein described if he believes it to be in the best interest of the beneficiary so to do, or he may sell or otherwise dispose of any or all of them, the Successor Trustee may apply or deem appropriate. Prior to the date upon which such beneficiary attains the age of 21 years, the Successor Trustee may apply or expend any or all of the income or principal of the trust directly for the maintenance, education and support of the beneficiary without the intervention of any guardian and without application to any court. Such payments of income or principal may be made to the parents of such beneficiary or to the person with whom the beneficiary is living without any liability upon the Successor Trustee to see to the application thereof. If such beneficiary survives us but dies before attaining the age of 21 years, at his or her death the Successor Trustee shall transfer, pay over and deliver the trust property to such beneficiary's personal representative, absolutely.

2. For purposes of specific identification, the assets held pursuant to this trust shall be all those securities registered in the names of:

"__John J. Brown__ and __Elizabeth A. Brown__, Trustees

udit (or "Trustees U-A") dated __February 2, 1980__

3. The beneficiary hereunder shall be liable for his proportionate share of any taxes levied upon the total taxable estate of the survivor of us by reason of the death of such survivor.

4. All interests of a beneficiary hereunder shall be inalienable and free from anticipation, assignment, attachment, pledge or control by creditors or a present or former spouse of such beneficiary in any proceedings at law or in equity.

5. This trust is created upon the express understanding that the issuer, transfer agent or custodian shall incur no liability hereunder shall ... for no liability ...

... deliver the same to whosoever shall then be Trustee hereunder, and shall be under no liability to see to the proper application thereof. Until the issuer, transfer agent or custodian shall receive from some person interested in this trust, written notice of any death or other event upon which the right to receive may depend, said issuer, transfer agent or custodian shall incur no liability for payments made in good faith to persons whose interests shall have been affected by such event. The issuer, transfer agent or custodian shall be protected by acting upon any notice or other instrument or document believed by it to be genuine and to have been signed or presented by the proper party or parties.

6. We reserve unto ourselves exclusively the right to pledge any of the securities held hereunder as collateral for a loan.

7. We reserve unto ourselves the right to collect any dividends, interest, capital gain distributions or other income which may accrue from the trust property during our lifetime and to pay such income to ourselves as individuals, and no beneficiary named herein shall have any claim upon any such income and/or profits distributed to us.

8. We reserve unto ourselves the power and right at any time during our lifetime to amend or revoke in whole or in part the trust hereby created without the necessity of obtaining the consent of the beneficiaries and without giving notice to such beneficiaries. The sale by us of the whole or any part of the portfolio of securities held hereunder shall constitute as to such whole or part a revocation of this trust.

10. In the event of the physical or mental incapacity or death of one of us, the survivor shall continue as sole Trustee. In the event of the or physical or mental incapacity or death of the survivor, or if we both shall die in a common accident or disaster, we hereby nominate and appoint as Successor Trustee hereunder whosoever shall at that time be beneficiary hereunder, unless such beneficiary shall not have attained the age of 21 years or is otherwise legally incapacitated, in which event we hereby nominate

and appoint __Henry P. Adams__   __Milton__   __Connecticut__   __06605__, of
                                City   State   Zip

(Name)

(Address) __125__   __Barnum Street__
      Number   Street

to be Successor Trustee.

11. This Declaration of Trust shall extend to and be binding upon the heirs, executors, administrators and assigns of the undersigned and upon the Successors to the Trustees.

12. We as Trustees and our Successor Trustee shall serve without bond.

13. This Declaration of Trust shall be construed and enforced in accordance with the laws of the State

of __Connecticut__

Declaration of Trust

WHEREAS, WE, _____ and _____, of the City/Town

of _____, County of _____, State of _____,

are the joint owners of certain securities, including common and preferred stocks, bonds, debentures and mutual fund shares;

NOW, THEREFORE, KNOW ALL MEN BY THESE PRESENTS, that we do hereby acknowledge and declare that we hold and will hold said securities and all our right, title and interest in and to said securities IN TRUST

    1. For the use and benefit of:

(Name) _____, of

(Address) _____
          Number   *Street*   *City*   *State*   *Zip*

or, if he or she be not surviving, for the use and benefit of:

(Name) _____, of

(Address) _____
          Number   *Street*   *City*   *State*   *Zip*

If because of our physical or mental incapacity certified in writing by a physician, the Successor Trustee hereinafter named shall assume active administration of this trust during our lifetime, such Successor Trustee shall be fully authorized to pay to us or disburse on our behalf such sums from income or principal as appear necessary or desirable for our comfort and welfare. Upon the death of the survivor of us, unless the beneficiaries both shall predecease us or unless we all shall die as a result of a common accident or disaster, our Successor Trustee is hereby directed forthwith to transfer said securities and all right, title and interest in and to said securities unto the beneficiary absolutely and thereby terminate this trust; provided, however, that if the beneficiary hereunder shall not have attained the age of 21 years, the Successor Trustee shall hold the trust assets in continuing trust until the beneficiary shall have attained the age of 21 years. During such period of continuing trust the Successor Trustee, in his absolute discretion, may retain the specific securities herein described if he believes it to be in the best interest of the beneficiary so to do, or he may sell or otherwise dispose of any or all of them, investing and reinvesting the proceeds as he may deem appropriate. Prior to the date upon which such beneficiary attains the age of 21 years, the Successor Trustee may apply or expend any or all of the income or principal of the trust directly for the maintenance, education and support of the beneficiary without the intervention of any guardian and without application to any court. Such payments of income or principal may be made to the parents of such beneficiary or to the person with whom the beneficiary is living without any liability upon the Successor Trustee to see to the application thereof. If such beneficiary survives us but dies before attaining the age of 21 years, at his or her death the Successor Trustee shall transfer, pay over and deliver the trust property to such beneficiary's personal representative, absolutely.

    2. For purposes of specific identification, the assets held pursuant to this trust shall be all those securities registered in the names of:

"_____ and _____, *Trustees u/d/t*

(or *"Trustees U-A"*) dated _____."

    3. The beneficiary hereunder shall be liable for his proportionate share of any taxes levied upon the total taxable estate of the survivor of us by reason of the death of such survivor.

    4. All interests of a beneficiary hereunder shall be inalienable and free from anticipation, assignment, attachment, pledge or control by creditors or a present or former spouse of such beneficiary in any proceedings at law or in equity.

    5. This trust is created upon the express understanding that the issuer, transfer agent or custodian of any securities held hereunder shall be under no liability whatsoever to see to its proper administration, and that upon the transfer of the right, title and interest in and to said securities by any Trustee hereunder, said issuer, transfer agent or custodian shall conclusively treat the transferee as the sole owner of said securities. In the event that any shares, cash or other property shall be distributable at any time under the terms of said securities, said issuer, transfer agent or custodian is fully authorized to transfer, pay over and deliver the same to whosoever shall then be Trustee hereunder, and shall be under no liability to see to the proper application thereof. Until the issuer, transfer agent or custodian shall receive from some person interested in this trust, written notice of any death or other event upon which the right to receive may depend, said issuer, transfer agent or custodian shall incur no liability for payments made in good faith to persons whose interests shall have been affected by such event. The issuer, transfer agent or custodian shall be protected in acting upon any notice or other instrument or document believed by it to be genuine and to have been signed or presented by the proper party or parties.

    6. We reserve unto ourselves the right to pledge any of the securities held hereunder as collateral for a loan.

7. We reserve unto ourselves exclusively the power and right to collect any dividends, interest, capital gain distributions or other income which may accrue from the trust property during our lifetime and to pay such income to ourselves as individuals, and no beneficiary named herein shall have any claim upon any such income and/or profits distributed to us.

8. We reserve unto ourselves the power and right at any time during our lifetime to amend or revoke in whole or in part the trust hereby created without the necessity of obtaining the consent of the beneficiaries and without giving notice to the beneficiaries. The sale by us of the whole or any part of the portfolio of securities held hereunder shall constitute as to such whole or part a revocation of this trust.

9. The death during our lifetime, or in a common accident or disaster with us, of both of the beneficiaries designated hereunder shall revoke such designation, and in the former event, we reserve the right to designate a new beneficiary. Should we for any reason fail to designate such new beneficiary, this trust shall terminate upon the death of the survivor of us and the assets held hereunder shall revert to the estate of such survivor.

10. In the event of the physical or mental incapacity or death of one of us, the survivor shall continue as sole Trustee. In the event of the physical or mental incapacity or death of the survivor, or if we both shall die in a common accident or disaster, we hereby nominate and appoint as Successor Trustee hereunder whosoever shall at that time be beneficiary hereunder, unless such beneficiary shall not have attained the age of 21 years or is otherwise legally incapacitated, in which event we hereby nominate and appoint

(Name) _____ , of

(Address) _____

             Number   *Street*   *City*   *State*   *Zip*

to be Successor Trustee.

11. This Declaration of Trust shall extend to and be binding upon the heirs, executors, administrators and assigns of the undersigned and upon the Successors to the Trustees.

12. We as Trustees and our Successor Trustee shall serve without bond.

13. This Declaration of Trust shall be construed and enforced in accordance with the laws of the State

of _____ .

IN WITNESS WHEREOF, we have hereunto set our hands and seals this _____

day of _____ , 19_____ .

        (First Settlor sign here) _____ L.S.

        (Second Settlor sign here) _____ L.S.

I, the undersigned legal spouse of one of the above Settlors, hereby waive all community property rights which I may have in the hereinabove-described securities and give my assent to the provisions of the trust and to the inclusion in it of the said securities.

        (Spouse sign here) _____ L.S.

Witness: (1) _____   Witness: (2) _____

STATE OF _____ ⎫ City

                                  ⎬ or

COUNTY OF _____ ⎭ Town _____

On the _____ day of _____ , 19_____ , personally appeared

_____ and _____

known to me to be the individuals who executed the foregoing instrument, and acknowledged the same to be their free act and deed, before me.

_____

(Notary Seal)   *Notary Public*

CHAPTER 9

DECLARATION OF TRUST
For Naming
TWO OR MORE BENEFICIARIES, SHARING EQUALLY,
To Receive
SECURITIES HELD IN JOINT NAMES

INSTRUCTIONS:

On the following pages will be found a declaration of trust (DT-111-J) suitable for use in connection with the establishment of an inter vivos trust covering stocks, bonds, or mutual fund shares now held in joint names, where it is desired to name two or more persons, sharing equally, to receive the securities upon the death of the survivor of the two joint owners.

Cross out *"city"* or *"town,"* leaving the appropriate designation of your community.

In Paragraph 1, indicate the *number of persons* you are naming (to discourage unauthorized additions to the list) and then insert their names. The one whose name appears *first* will be the Successor Trustee responsible for seeing to the distribution of the trust property.

Note that the instrument specifies that the named beneficiaries are to receive *"in equal shares, or the survivor of them/per stirpes."* Now, think carefully: If you have named three persons with the understanding that if one of them predeceases you, *his* children will take *his* share, cross out *"or the survivor of them"* and *initial it.* If that is *not* what you want—if, for example, you prefer that the share of the deceased person be divided between the two surviving persons, cross out *"per stirpes"* and *initial it.* Remember, you <u>must</u> cross out either *"or the survivor of them"* or *"per stirpes"*—one or the other.

In Paragraph 2, enter the names of the joint owners and the date you are executing the declaration of trust.

Note that Paragraph 10 designates as Successor Trustee *"the beneficiary named first above,"* which means that in most cases you don't need to fill anything in there. However, if there is any possibility of a beneficiary who has not attained the age of 21 years receiving the trust assets, make certain that you name an adult in this paragraph who can act as trustee for such beneficiary. Avoid naming as trustee a person not likely to survive until the beneficiary has attained age 21.

When completed in the manner shown on the reverse side, make one photocopy of the declaration of trust for *each* separate stock or bond you own, plus sufficient additional copies to take care of future securities purchases. Then, put the original in safekeeping.

It is absolutely essential that you instruct your broker or mutual fund to register your securities in this form: *"(your name) and (your co-owner's name), Trustees u/d/t dated* (date you have signed the declaration of trust)." It will not be necessary to file the declaration of trust with the issuer at the time you purchase the securities. However, if and when you sell any of them, the issuer, transfer agent, or custodian will almost certainly require you to display the instrument. If you die, the beneficiary will be required to produce it in order to obtain possession of the securities. In the circumstances, the safest thing to do is to staple a copy of it to *each* of the securities when the latter are issued. This stapling procedure should also be followed in the case of unregistered bonds. If you fail to follow these instructions in registering or reregistering your securities, they will be subject to probate.

Important: Read carefully Note B on page 38, which applies to this declaration of trust.

WHEREVER THE INSTRUCTION "INITIAL IT" APPEARS ABOVE,
IT MEANS THAT *BOTH* CO-OWNERS SHOULD INITIAL IT.

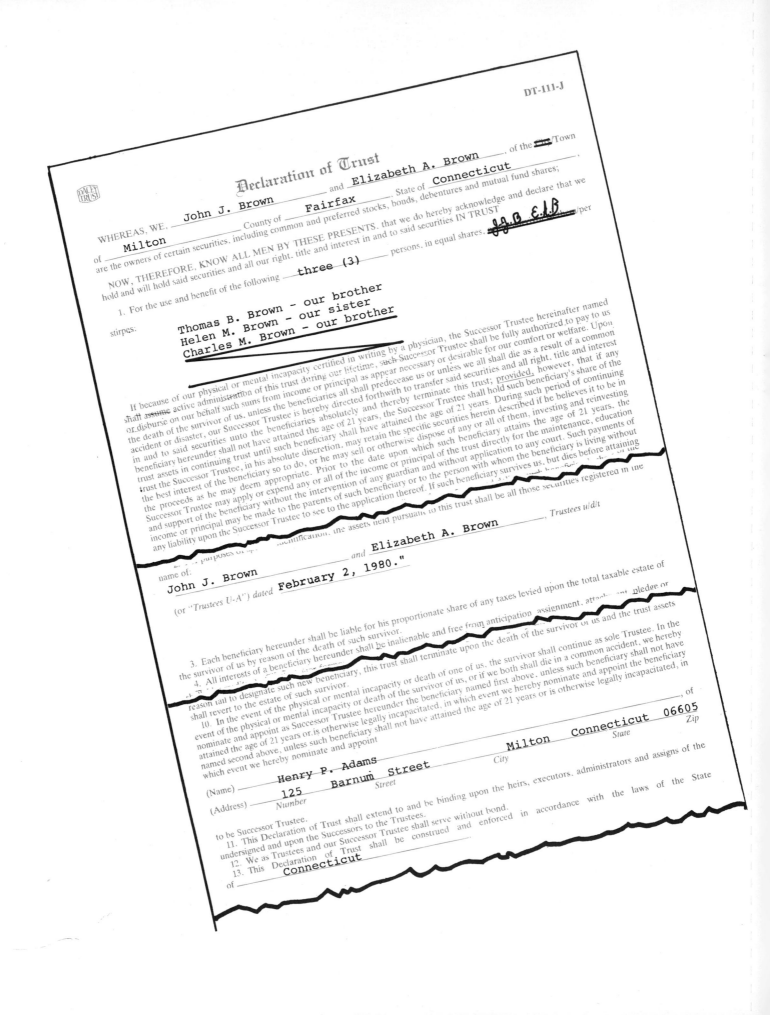

Declaration of Trust

WHEREAS, WE, **John J. Brown** and **Elizabeth A. Brown**, of the Town
of **Milton**, County of **Fairfax**, State of **Connecticut**
are the owners of certain securities, including common and preferred stocks, bonds, debentures and mutual fund shares;

NOW, THEREFORE, KNOW ALL MEN BY THESE PRESENTS, that we do hereby acknowledge and declare that we
hold and will hold said securities and all our right, title and interest in and to said securities IN TRUST

1. For the use and benefit of the following **three (3)** persons, in equal shares, per
stirpes:

Thomas B. Brown - our brother
Helen M. Brown - our sister
~~Charles M. Brown - our brother~~

If because of our physical or mental incapacity certified in writing by a physician, the Successor Trustee shall be fully authorized to pay to us
shall assume active administration of this trust during our lifetime, such Successor Trustee shall be fully authorized to pay to us
or disburse on our behalf such sums from income or principal as appear necessary or desirable for our comfort or welfare. Upon
the death of the survivor of us. unless the beneficiaries all shall predecease us or unless we all shall die as a result of a common
accident or disaster, our Successor Trustee is hereby directed forthwith to transfer said securities and all right, title and interest
in and to said securities unto the beneficiaries absolutely and thereby terminate this trust; provided, however, that if any
beneficiary hereunder shall not have attained the age of 21 years, the Successor Trustee shall hold such beneficiary's share of the
trust the Successor Trustee, in his absolute discretion, may retain the specific securities herein described if he believes it to be in
the best interest of the beneficiary so to do, or he may sell or otherwise dispose of any or all of them, investing and reinvesting
the proceeds as he may deem appropriate. Prior to the date upon which such beneficiary attains the age of 21 years, the
Successor Trustee may apply or expend any or all of the income or principal of the trust directly for the maintenance, education
and support of the beneficiary without the intervention of any guardian and without application to any court. Such payments of
income or principal may be made to the parents of such beneficiary or to the person with whom the beneficiary is living without
any liability upon the Successor Trustee to see to the application thereof. If such beneficiary survives us, but dies before attaining

purposes of identification, the assets held pursuant to this trust shall be all those securities registered in the

name of: **John J. Brown** and **Elizabeth A. Brown**, Trustees u/d t

(or "Trustees U-A") dated **February 2, 1980."**

3. Each beneficiary hereunder shall be liable for his proportionate share of any taxes levied upon the total taxable estate of
the survivor of us by reason of the death of such survivor.

4. All interests of a beneficiary hereunder shall be inalienable and free from anticipation, assignment, attachment, pledge or

reason fail to designate such new beneficiary, this trust shall terminate upon the death of the survivor of us and the trust assets
shall revert to the estate of such survivor.

10. In the event of the physical or mental incapacity or death of one of us, the survivor shall continue as sole Trustee. In the
event of the physical or mental incapacity or death of the survivor of us, or if we both shall die in a common accident, we hereby
nominate and appoint as Successor Trustee hereunder the beneficiary named first above. unless such beneficiary shall not have
attained the age of 21 years or is otherwise legally incapacitated, in which event we hereby nominate and appoint the beneficiary
named second above, unless such beneficiary shall not have attained the age of 21 years or is otherwise legally incapacitated, in
which event we hereby nominate and appoint

(Name) **Henry P. Adams**, of **Milton**, **Connecticut** **06605**
(Address) **125** **Barnum** **Street**

to be Successor Trustee.
11. This Declaration of Trust shall extend to and be binding upon the heirs, executors, administrators and assigns of the
undersigned and upon the Successors to the Trustees.
12. We as Trustees and our Successor Trustee shall serve without bond.
13. This Declaration of Trust shall be construed and enforced in accordance with the laws of the State
of **Connecticut**

Declaration of Trust

WHEREAS, WE, _____ and _____, of the City/Town of _____, County of _____, State of _____,

are the owners of certain securities, including common and preferred stocks, bonds, debentures and mutual fund shares;

NOW, THEREFORE, KNOW ALL MEN BY THESE PRESENTS, that we do hereby acknowledge and declare that we hold and will hold said securities and all our right, title and interest in and to said securities IN TRUST

    1. For the use and benefit of the following _____ persons, in equal shares, or the survivor of them/per stirpes:

If because of our physical or mental incapacity certified in writing by a physician, the Successor Trustee hereinafter named shall assume active administration of this trust during our lifetime, such Successor Trustee shall be fully authorized to pay to us or disburse on our behalf such sums from income or principal as appear necessary or desirable for our comfort or welfare. Upon the death of the survivor of us, unless the beneficiaries all shall predecease us or unless we all shall die as a result of a common accident or disaster, our Successor Trustee is hereby directed forthwith to transfer said securities and all right, title and interest in and to said securities unto the beneficiaries absolutely and thereby terminate this trust; provided, however, that if any beneficiary hereunder shall not have attained the age of 21 years, the Successor Trustee shall hold such beneficiary's share of the trust assets in continuing trust until such beneficiary shall have attained the age of 21 years. During such period of continuing trust the Successor Trustee, in his absolute discretion, may retain the specific securities herein described if he believes it to be in the best interest of the beneficiary so to do, or he may sell or otherwise dispose of any or all of them, investing and reinvesting the proceeds as he may deem appropriate. Prior to the date upon which such beneficiary attains the age of 21 years, the Successor Trustee may apply or expend any or all of the income or principal of the trust directly for the maintenance, education and support of the beneficiary without the intervention of any guardian and without application to any court. Such payments of income or principal may be made to the parents of such beneficiary or to the person with whom the beneficiary is living without any liability upon the Successor Trustee to see to the application thereof. If such beneficiary survives us, but dies before attaining the age of 21 years, at his or her death the Successor Trustee shall transfer, pay over and deliver such beneficiary's share of the trust property to such beneficiary's personal representative, absolutely.

    2. For purposes of specific identification, the assets held pursuant to this trust shall be all those securities registered in the name of:

"_____ and _____, Trustees u/d/t

(or "Trustees U-A") dated _____."

    3. Each beneficiary hereunder shall be liable for his proportionate share of any taxes levied upon the total taxable estate of the survivor of us by reason of the death of such survivor.

    4. All interests of a beneficiary hereunder shall be inalienable and free from anticipation, assignment, attachment, pledge or control by creditors or a present or former spouse of such beneficiary in any proceedings at law or in equity.

    5. This trust is created upon the express understanding that the issuer, transfer agent or custodian of any securities held hereunder shall be under no liability whatsoever to see to its proper administration, and that upon the transfer of the right, title and interest in and to said securities by any Trustee hereunder, said issuer, transfer agent or custodian shall conclusively treat the transferee as sole owner of the shares. In the event that any shares, cash or other property shall be distributable at any time under the terms of said securities, said issuer, transfer agent or custodian is fully authorized to transfer, pay over and deliver the same to whosoever shall then be Trustee hereunder, and shall be under no liability to see to the proper application thereof. Until the issuer, transfer agent or custodian shall receive from some person interested in this trust, written notice of any death or other event upon which the right to receive may depend, said issuer, transfer agent or custodian shall incur no liability for payments made in good faith to persons whose interests shall have been affected by such event. The issuer, transfer agent or custodian shall be protected in acting upon any notice or other instrument or document believed by it to be genuine and to have been signed or presented by the proper party or parties.

    6. We reserve unto ourselves the right to pledge any of the securities held hereunder as collateral for a loan.

7. We reserve unto ourselves exclusively the power and right to collect any dividends, interest, capital gain distributions or other income which may accrue from the trust property during our lifetime and to pay such income to ourselves as individuals, and no beneficiary named herein shall have any claim upon any such income and/or profits distributed to us.

8. We reserve unto ourselves the power and right at any time during our lifetime to amend or revoke in whole or in part the trust hereby created without the necessity of obtaining the consent of the beneficiary and without giving notice to the beneficiary. The sale by us of the whole or any part of the portfolio of securities held hereunder shall constitute as to such whole or part a revocation of this trust.

9. The death during our lifetime, or in a common accident or disaster with us, of all of the beneficiaries designated hereunder shall revoke such designation, and in the former event, we reserve the right to designate a new beneficiary. Should we for any reason fail to designate such new beneficiary, this trust shall terminate upon the death of the survivor of us and the trust assets shall revert to the estate of such survivor.

10. In the event of the physical or mental incapacity or death of one of us, the survivor shall continue as sole Trustee. In the event of the physical or mental incapacity or death of the survivor of us, or if we both shall die in a common accident, we hereby nominate and appoint as Successor Trustee hereunder the beneficiary named first above, unless such beneficiary shall not have attained the age of 21 years or is otherwise legally incapacitated, in which event we hereby nominate and appoint the beneficiary named second above, unless such beneficiary shall not have attained the age of 21 years or is otherwise legally incapacitated, in which event we hereby nominate and appoint

(Name) _____, of

(Address) _____
Number   Street   City   State   Zip

to be Successor Trustee.

11. This Declaration of Trust shall extend to and be binding upon the heirs, executors, administrators and assigns of the undersigned and upon the Successors to the Trustees.

12. We as Trustees and our Successor Trustee shall serve without bond.

13. This Declaration of Trust shall be construed and enforced in accordance with the laws of the State of _____.

IN WITNESS WHEREOF, we have hereunto set our hands and seals this _____

day of _____, 19_____.

(First Settlor sign here) _____ L.S.

(Second Settlor sign here) _____ L.S.

I, the undersigned legal spouse of one of the above Settlors, hereby waive all community property rights which I may have in the hereinabove-described securities and give my assent to the provisions of the trust and to the inclusion in it of the said securities.

(Spouse sign here) _____L.S.

Witness: (1) _____   Witness: (2) _____

STATE OF _____   City

COUNTY OF _____   or Town _____

On the _____ day of _____, 19 ____, personally appeared

_____ and _____

known to me to be the individuals who executed the foregoing instrument, and acknowledged the same to be their free act and deed, before me.

(Notary Seal)   _____
                                     Notary Public

CHAPTER 10

Avoiding Probate of a Brokerage Account

Some investors, particularly those who are traders, leave their securities on deposit with a brokerage firm. The individual stocks or bonds are then registered in the broker's or "street" name, rather than in the name of the investor. In such cases, it is the brokerage account itself, not the underlying securities, which should be placed in an inter vivos trust. On the following pages will be found declarations of trust which will be suitable for this purpose.

With some brokerage firms, innovation and change are suspect. Not understanding the inter vivos trust, they may give you an argument or perhaps refer it to their lawyer. My advice: Don't argue. Don't allow a stranger in a brokerage firm to dictate how you will leave your estate. If they choose to give you a hard time now, chances are that they'll give your heirs the same hard time. If you detect an attitude of indifference or any unwillingness to cooperate with you in your careful planning of your estate, simply take your account elsewhere.

CHAPTER 10

DECLARATION OF TRUST
For Naming
ONE BENEFICIARY
To Receive
A BROKERAGE ACCOUNT HELD IN ONE NAME

INSTRUCTIONS:

On the following pages will be found a declaration of trust (DT-113) suitable for use in connection with the establishment of an inter vivos trust covering a brokerage account held in one name, where it is desired to name some *one* person to receive the account upon the death of the owner.

Cross out *"city"* or *"town,"* leaving the appropriate designation of your community.

Enter the name of the firm where the brokerage account is maintained in the space provided near the top, and the name of the beneficiary in the appropriate place in Paragraph 1.

Note that Paragraph 8 designates as Successor Trustee *"whosoever shall at that time be beneficiary hereunder,"* which means that in most cases you don't need to fill anything in there. However, if there is any possibility of a beneficiary who has not attained the age of 21 years receiving the brokerage account, make certain that you name an adult in this paragraph who can act as trustee for such beneficiary. Avoid naming as trustee a person not likely to survive until the beneficiary has attained age 21.

When completed in the manner shown on the reverse side hereof, make several photocopies for reference purposes. Place the original in safekeeping and file a copy with the investment firm with whom the brokerage account is maintained. Ask the firm to give you a written confirmation that in the event of your death it will recognize the trust and promptly turn the securities over to the Successor Trustee whom you have named. Insist that henceforth all communications from the firm be sent to *"(your name), Trustee u/d/t dated _____."*

Important: Read carefully Note B on page 38, which applies to this declaration of trust.

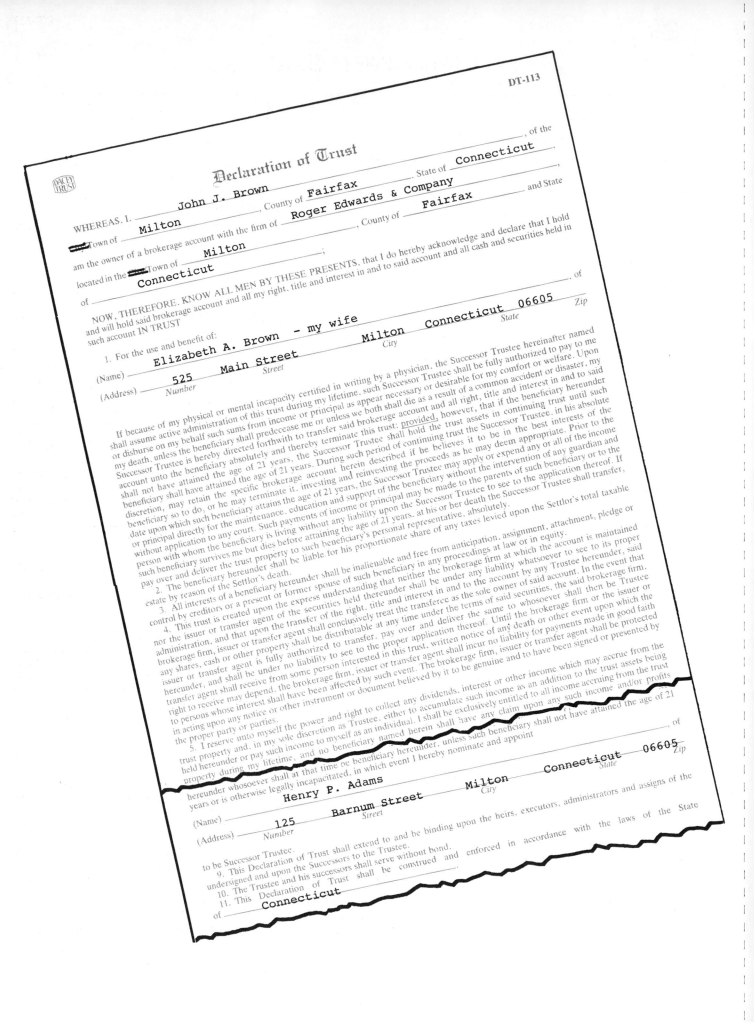

DT-113

Declaration of Trust

WHEREAS, I, __John J. Brown__, County of __Fairfax__, State of __Connecticut__, of the Town of __Milton__, am the owner of a brokerage account with the firm of __Roger Edwards & Company__, County of __Fairfax__ and State located in the Town of __Milton__, __Connecticut__ of ;

NOW, THEREFORE, KNOW ALL MEN BY THESE PRESENTS, that I do hereby acknowledge and declare that I hold and will hold said brokerage account and all my right, title and interest in and to said account and all cash and securities held in such account IN TRUST

1. For the use and benefit of:

(Name) __Elizabeth A. Brown — my wife__

__525__   __Main Street__   __Milton__   __Connecticut__   __06605__
(Address) __Number__   __Street__   __City__   __State__   __Zip__

If because of my physical or mental incapacity certified in writing by a physician, such Successor Trustee shall assume active administration of this trust during my lifetime, such Successor Trustee shall be fully authorized to pay to me or disburse on my behalf such sums from income or principal as appear necessary or desirable for my comfort or welfare. Upon my death, unless the beneficiary shall predecease me or unless we both shall die as a result of a common accident or disaster, my Successor Trustee is hereby directed forthwith to transfer said brokerage account and all right, title and interest in and to said account unto the beneficiary absolutely and thereby terminate this trust: provided, however, that if the beneficiary hereunder shall not have attained the age of 21 years, the Successor Trustee shall hold the trust assets in continuing trust until such beneficiary shall have attained the age of 21 years. During such period of continuing trust the Successor Trustee, in his absolute discretion, may retain the specific brokerage account herein described if he believes it to be in the best interests of the beneficiary so to do, or he may terminate it, investing and reinvesting the proceeds as he may deem appropriate. Prior to the date upon which such beneficiary attains the age of 21 years, the Successor Trustee may apply or expend any or all of the income or principal directly for the maintenance, education and support of the beneficiary without the intervention of any guardian and without application to any court. Such payments of income or principal may be made to the parents of such beneficiary or to the person with whom the beneficiary is living without any liability upon the Successor Trustee to see to the application thereof. If such beneficiary survives me but dies before attaining the age of 21 years, at his or her death the Successor Trustee shall transfer, pay over and deliver the trust property to such beneficiary's personal representative, absolutely.

2. The beneficiary hereunder shall be liable for his proportionate share of any taxes levied upon the Settlor's total taxable estate by reason of the Settlor's death.

3. All interests of a beneficiary hereunder shall be inalienable and free from anticipation, assignment, attachment, pledge or control by creditors or a present or former spouse of such beneficiary in any proceedings at law or in equity.

4. This trust is created upon the express understanding that neither the brokerage firm at which the account is maintained nor the issuer or transfer agent of the securities held thereunder shall be under any liability whatsoever to see to its proper administration, and that upon the transfer of the right, title and interest in and to the account by any Trustee hereunder, said brokerage firm, issuer or transfer agent shall conclusively treat the transferee as the sole owner of said account. In the event that any shares, cash or other property shall be distributable at any time under the terms of said securities, the said brokerage firm, issuer or transfer agent is fully authorized to transfer, pay over and deliver the same to whosoever shall then be Trustee hereunder, and shall be under no liability to see to the proper application thereof. Until the brokerage firm or the issuer or transfer agent shall receive from some person interested in this trust, written notice of any death or other event upon which the right to receive may depend, the brokerage firm, issuer or transfer agent shall incur no liability for payments made in good faith to persons whose interest shall have been affected by such event. The brokerage firm, issuer or transfer agent shall be protected in acting upon any notice or other instrument or document believed by it to be genuine and to have been signed or presented by the proper party or parties.

5. I reserve unto myself the power and right to collect any dividends, interest or other income which may accrue from the trust property and, in my sole discretion as Trustee, either to accumulate such income as an addition to the trust assets being held hereunder or pay such income to myself as an individual. I shall be exclusively entitled to all income accruing from the trust property during my lifetime, and no beneficiary named herein shall have any claim upon any such income and/or profits

hereunder whosoever shall at that time be beneficiary hereunder, unless such beneficiary shall not have attained the age of 21 years or is otherwise legally incapacitated, in which event I hereby nominate and appoint

(Name) __Henry P. Adams__   __Milton__   __Connecticut__   __06605__
(Address) __125__   __Barnum Street__   __City__   __State__   __Zip__
__Number__   __Street__

to be Successor Trustee.

9. This Declaration of Trust shall extend to and be binding upon the heirs, executors, administrators and assigns of the undersigned and upon the Successors to the Trustee.

10. The Trustee and his successors shall serve without bond.

11. This Declaration of Trust shall be construed and enforced in accordance with the laws of the State of __Connecticut__

Declaration of Trust

WHEREAS, I, _____, of the

City/Town of _____, County of _____, State of _____,

am the owner of a brokerage account with the firm of _____,

located in the City/Town of _____, County of _____ and State

of _____ ;

NOW, THEREFORE, KNOW ALL MEN BY THESE PRESENTS, that I do hereby acknowledge and declare that I hold and will hold said brokerage account and all my right, title and interest in and to said account and all cash and securities held in such account IN TRUST

1. For the use and benefit of:

(Name) _____, of

(Address) _____
   Number   Street   City   State   Zip

If because of my physical or mental incapacity certified in writing by a physician, the Successor Trustee hereinafter named shall assume active administration of this trust during my lifetime, such Successor Trustee shall be fully authorized to pay to me or disburse on my behalf such sums from income or principal as appear necessary or desirable for my comfort or welfare. Upon my death, unless the beneficiary shall predecease me or unless we both shall die as a result of a common accident or disaster, my Successor Trustee is hereby directed forthwith to transfer said brokerage account and all right, title and interest in and to said account unto the beneficiary absolutely and thereby terminate this trust; provided, however, that if the beneficiary hereunder shall not have attained the age of 21 years, the Successor Trustee shall hold the trust assets in continuing trust until such beneficiary shall have attained the age of 21 years. During such period of continuing trust the Successor Trustee, in his absolute discretion, may retain the specific brokerage account herein described if he believes it to be in the best interests of the beneficiary so to do, or he may terminate it, investing and reinvesting the proceeds as he may deem appropriate. Prior to the date upon which such beneficiary attains the age of 21 years, the Successor Trustee may apply or expend any or all of the income or principal directly for the maintenance, education and support of the beneficiary without the intervention of any guardian and without application to any court. Such payments of income or principal may be made to the parents of such beneficiary or to the person with whom the beneficiary is living without any liability upon the Successor Trustee to see to the application thereof. If such beneficiary survives me but dies before attaining the age of 21 years, at his or her death the Successor Trustee shall transfer, pay over and deliver the trust property to such beneficiary's personal representative, absolutely.

2. The beneficiary hereunder shall be liable for his proportionate share of any taxes levied upon the Settlor's total taxable estate by reason of the Settlor's death.

3. All interests of a beneficiary hereunder shall be inalienable and free from anticipation, assignment, attachment, pledge or control by creditors or a present or former spouse of such beneficiary in any proceedings at law or in equity.

4. This trust is created upon the express understanding that neither the brokerage firm at which the account is maintained nor the issuer or transfer agent of the securities held hereunder shall be under any liability whatsoever to see to its proper administration, and that upon the transfer of the right, title and interest in and to the account by any Trustee hereunder, said brokerage firm, issuer or transfer agent shall conclusively treat the transferee as the sole owner of said account. In the event that any shares, cash or other property shall be distributable at any time under the terms of said securities, the said brokerage firm, issuer or transfer agent is fully authorized to transfer, pay over and deliver the same to whosoever shall then be Trustee hereunder, and shall be under no liability to see to the proper application thereof. Until the brokerage firm or the issuer or transfer agent shall receive from some person interested in this trust, written notice of any death or other event upon which the right to receive may depend, the brokerage firm, issuer or transfer agent shall incur no liability for payments made in good faith to persons whose interest shall have been affected by such event. The brokerage firm, issuer or transfer agent shall be protected in acting upon any notice or other instrument or document believed by it to be genuine and to have been signed or presented by the proper party or parties.

5. I reserve unto myself the power and right to collect any dividends, interest or other income which may accrue from the trust property and, in my sole discretion as Trustee, either to accumulate such income as an addition to the trust assets being held hereunder or pay such income to myself as an individual. I shall be exclusively entitled to all income accruing from the trust property during my lifetime, and no beneficiary named herein shall have any claim upon any such income and/or profits distributed to me.

6. I reserve unto myself the power and right at any time during my lifetime to amend or revoke in whole or in part the trust hereby created without the necessity of obtaining the consent of the beneficiary and without giving notice to the beneficiary. The sale by me of the whole or any part of the said brokerage account held hereunder shall constitute as to such whole or part a revocation of this trust.

7. The death during my lifetime, or in a common accident or disaster with me, of the beneficiary designated hereunder shall revoke such designation, and in the former event, I reserve the right to designate a new beneficiary. Should I for any reason fail to designate such new beneficiary, this trust shall terminate upon my death and the trust property shall revert to my estate.

8. In the event of my physical or mental incapacity or my death, I hereby nominate and appoint as Successor Trustee hereunder whosoever shall at that time be beneficiary hereunder, unless such beneficiary shall not have attained the age of 21 years or is otherwise legally incapacitated, in which event I hereby nominate and appoint

(Name) _____ , of

(Address) _____
              Number   *Street*   *City*   *State*   *Zip*

to be Successor Trustee.

9. This Declaration of Trust shall extend to and be binding upon the heirs, executors, administrators and assigns of the undersigned and upon the Successors to the Trustee.

10. The Trustee and his successors shall serve without bond.

11. This Declaration of Trust shall be construed and enforced in accordance with the laws of the State of _____ .

IN WITNESS WHEREOF, I have hereunto set my hand and seal this _____

day of _____ , 19_____ .

          (Settlor sign here) _____ L.S.

I, the undersigned legal spouse of the above Settlor, hereby waive all community property rights which I may have in the hereinabove-described account and give my assent to the provisions of the trust and to the inclusion in it of the said account.

          (Spouse sign here) _____ L.S.

Witness: (1) _____   Witness: (2) _____

STATE OF _____   City
                                       or
COUNTY OF _____   Town _____

On the _____ day of _____ , 19_____ , personally appeared

_____

known to me to be the individual(s) who executed the foregoing instrument, and acknowledged the same to be _____ free act and deed, before me.

(Notary Seal)   _____
                                               Notary Public

CHAPTER 10

DECLARATION OF TRUST
For Naming
ONE PRIMARY BENEFICIARY
And
ONE CONTINGENT BENEFICIARY
To Receive
A BROKERAGE ACCOUNT HELD IN ONE NAME

INSTRUCTIONS:

On the following pages will be found a declaration of trust (DT-114) suitable for use in connection with the establishment of an inter vivos trust covering a brokerage account held in one name, where it is desired to name some *one* person as primary beneficiary, with some *one* other person as contingent beneficiary to receive the account if the primary beneficiary be not surviving upon the death of the owner.

Cross out *"city"* or *"town,"* leaving the appropriate designation of your community.

Enter the name of the firm where the brokerage account is maintained in the space provided near the top, and the names of the beneficiaries in the appropriate places in Paragraph 1.

Note that Paragraph 8 designates as Successor Trustee *"whosoever shall at that time be beneficiary hereunder,"* which means that in most cases you don't need to fill anything in there. However, if there is any possibility of a beneficiary who has not attained the age of 21 years receiving the brokerage account, make certain that you name an adult in this paragraph who can act as trustee for such beneficiary. Avoid naming as trustee a person not likely to survive until the beneficiary has attained age 21.

When completed in the manner shown on the reverse side hereof, make several photocopies for reference purposes. Place the original in safekeeping and file one copy with the investment firm with whom the brokerage account is maintained. Ask the firm to give you a written confirmation that in the event of your death it will recognize the trust and promptly turn the securities over to the Successor Trustee whom you have named. Insist that henceforth all communications from the firm be sent to *"(your name), Trustee u/d/t dated _____."*

Important: Read carefully Note B on page 38, which applies to this declaration of trust.

Declaration of Trust

DACEY TRUST

WHEREAS, I, __John J. Brown__, County of __Fairfax__, State of __Connecticut__, of the

Town of __Milton__ am the owner of a brokerage account with the firm of __Roger Edwards & Company__, County of __Fairfax__ and State

located in the Town of __Milton__ of __Connecticut__

NOW, THEREFORE, KNOW ALL MEN BY THESE PRESENTS, that I do hereby acknowledge and declare that I hold and will hold said brokerage account and all my right, title and interest in and to said account and all cash and securities held in such account IN TRUST

1. For the use and benefit of:

(Name) __Elizabeth A. Brown - my wife__ __Milton__ City __Connecticut__ State __06605__ Zip , of

(Address) __525 Main Street__ Number __Street__

or, if he or she be not surviving, for the use and benefit of:

(Name) __Dorothy Lynn - my niece__ __Portland__ City __Wisconsin__ State __53123__ Zip , of

(Address) __566 Midland Street__ Number __Street__

If because of my physical or mental incapacity certified in writing by a physician, the Successor Trustee hereinafter named shall assume active administration of this trust during my lifetime, such Successor Trustee shall be fully authorized to pay to me or disburse on my behalf such sums from income or principal as appear necessary or desirable for my comfort or welfare. Upon my death, unless both beneficiaries shall predecease me or unless we all shall die as a result of a common accident or disaster, my Successor Trustee is hereby directed forthwith to transfer said brokerage account and all right, title and interest in and to said account unto the beneficiary absolutely and thereby terminate this trust; provided, however, that if the beneficiary hereunder shall not have attained the age of 21 years, the Successor Trustee shall hold the trust assets in continuing trust until such beneficiary shall have attained the age of 21 years. During said period of continuing trust the Successor Trustee, in his absolute discretion, may retain the specific brokerage account herein described if he believes it to be in the best interests of the beneficiary so to do, or he may terminate it, investing and reinvesting the proceeds as he may deem appropriate. Prior to the date upon which such beneficiary attains the age of 21 years, the Successor Trustee may apply or expend any or all of the income or principal directly for the maintenance, education and support of the beneficiary without the intervention of any guardian and without application to any court. Such payments of income or principal may be made to the parents of such beneficiary or to the person with whom the beneficiary is living without any liability upon the Successor Trustee to see to the application thereof. If such beneficiary survives me but dies before attaining the age of 21 years, at his or her death the Successor Trustee shall transfer, pay over and deliver the trust property to such beneficiary's personal representative, absolutely.

2. The beneficiary shall be liable for his proportionate share of any taxes levied upon the Settlor's total taxable estate by reason of the Settlor's death.

3. All interests of a beneficiary hereunder shall be inalienable and free from anticipation, assignment, attachment, pledge or control by creditors or a present or former spouse of such beneficiary in any proceedings at law or in equity.

4. This trust is created upon the express understanding that neither the brokerage firm at which the account is maintained nor the issuer or transfer agent of the securities held hereunder shall be under any liability whatsoever to see to its proper administration, and that upon the transfer of the right, title and interest in and to the account by any Trustee hereunder, said brokerage firm, issuer or other property shall be distributable at any time under the terms of said securities, the said brokerage firm, any shares, cash or other property shall be distributable at any time under the terms of said securities, the said brokerage firm, issuer or transfer agent is fully authorized to transfer, pay over and deliver the same to whosoever shall then be Trustee hereunder, and shall be under no liability to see to the proper application thereof. Until the brokerage firm or the issuer or transfer agent shall receive from some person interested in this trust, written notice of any death or other event upon which the right to receive may depend, the brokerage firm, issuer or transfer agent shall incur no liability for payments made in good faith to persons whose interests shall have been affected by such event. The brokerage firm, issuer or transfer agent shall be protected in acting upon any notice or other instrument or document believed by it to be genuine and to have been signed or presented by

7. The death during my lifetime, or in a common accident or disaster with me, of both the beneficiaries designated hereunder shall revoke such designation, and in the former event, I reserve the right to designate a new beneficiary. Should I for any reason fail to designate such new beneficiary, this trust shall terminate upon my death and the trust property shall revert to my estate.

8. In the event of my physical or mental incapacity or my death, I hereby nominate and appoint as Successor Trustee hereunder whosoever shall at that time be beneficiary hereunder, unless such beneficiary shall not have attained the age of 21 years or is otherwise legally incapacitated, in which event I hereby nominate and appoint

_____, of

(Name) __Henry P. Adams__ __Milton__ City __Connecticut__ State __06605__ Zip

(Address) __125 Barnum Street__ Number __Street__

to be Successor Trustee.

9. This Declaration of Trust shall extend to and be binding upon the heirs, executors, administrators and assigns of the undersigned and upon the Successors to the Trustee.

10. The Trustee and his successors shall serve without bond.

11. This Declaration of Trust shall be construed and enforced in accordance with the laws of the State of __Connecticut__

Declaration of Trust

WHEREAS, I, _____, of the

City/Town of _____, County of _____, State of _____,

am the owner of a brokerage account with the firm of _____,

located in the City/Town of _____, County of _____

and State of _____ ;

NOW, THEREFORE, KNOW ALL MEN BY THESE PRESENTS, that I do hereby acknowledge and declare that I hold and will hold said brokerage account and all my right, title and interest in and to said account and all cash and securities held in such account IN TRUST

1. For the use and benefit of:

(Name) _____, of

(Address) _____
      Number   Street   City   State   Zip

or, if he or she be not surviving, for the use and benefit of:

(Name) _____, of

(Address) _____
      Number   Street   City   State   Zip

If because of my physical or mental incapacity certified in writing by a physician, the Successor Trustee hereinafter named shall assume active administration of this trust during my lifetime, such Successor Trustee shall be fully authorized to pay to me or disburse on my behalf such sums from income or principal as appear necessary or desirable for my comfort or welfare. Upon my death, unless both beneficiaries shall predecease me or unless we all shall die as a result of a common accident or disaster, my Successor Trustee is hereby directed forthwith to transfer said brokerage account and all right, title and interest in and to said account unto the beneficiary absolutely and thereby terminate this trust; provided, however, that if the beneficiary hereunder shall not have attained the age of 21 years, the Successor Trustee shall hold the trust assets in continuing trust until such beneficiary shall have attained the age of 21 years. During said period of continuing trust the Successor Trustee, in his absolute discretion, may retain the specific brokerage account herein described if he believes it to be in the best interests of the beneficiary so to do, or he may terminate it, investing and reinvesting the proceeds as he may deem appropriate. Prior to the date upon which such beneficiary attains the age of 21 years, the Successor Trustee may apply or expend any or all of the income or principal directly for the maintenance, education and support of the beneficiary without the intervention of any guardian and without application to any court. Such payments of income or principal may be made to the parents of such beneficiary or to the person with whom the beneficiary is living without any liability upon the Successor Trustee to see to the application thereof. If such beneficiary survives me but dies before attaining the age of 21 years, at his or her death the Successor Trustee shall transfer, pay over and deliver the trust property to such beneficiary's personal representative, absolutely.

2. The beneficiary hereunder shall be liable for his proportionate share of any taxes levied upon the Settlor's total taxable estate by reason of the Settlor's death.

3. All interests of a beneficiary hereunder shall be inalienable and free from anticipation, assignment, attachment, pledge or control by creditors or a present or former spouse of such beneficiary in any proceedings at law or in equity.

4. This trust is created upon the express understanding that neither the brokerage firm at which the account is maintained nor the issuer or transfer agent of the securities held hereunder shall be under any liability whatsoever to see to its proper administration, and that upon the transfer of the right, title and interest in and to the account by any Trustee hereunder, said brokerage firm, issuer or transfer agent shall conclusively treat the transferee as the sole owner of said account. In the event that any shares, cash or other property shall be distributable at any time under the terms of said securities, the said brokerage firm, issuer or transfer agent is fully authorized to transfer, pay over and deliver the same to whosoever shall then be Trustee hereunder, and shall be under no liability to see to the proper application thereof. Until the brokerage firm or the issuer transfer agent shall receive from some person interested in this trust, written notice of any death or other event upon which the right to receive may depend, the brokerage firm, issuer or transfer agent shall incur no liability for payments made in good faith to persons whose interests shall have been affected by such event. The brokerage firm, issuer or transfer agent shall be protected in acting upon any notice or other instrument or document believed by it to be genuine and to have been signed or presented by the proper party or parties.

5. I reserve unto myself the power and right to collect any dividends, interest or other income which may accrue from the trust property and, in my sole discretion as Trustee, either to accumulate such income as an addition to the trust assets being held hereunder or pay such income to myself as an individual. I shall be exclusively entitled to all income accruing from the trust property during my lifetime, and no beneficiary named herein shall have any claim upon any such income and/or profits distributed to me.

6. I reserve unto myself the power and right at any time during my lifetime to amend or revoke in whole or in part the trust hereby created without the necessity of obtaining the consent of the beneficiaries and without giving notice to the beneficiaries. The sale by me of the whole or any part of the said brokerage account held hereunder shall constitute as to such whole or part a revocation of this trust.

7. The death during my lifetime, or in a common accident or disaster with me, of both the beneficiaries designated hereunder shall revoke such designation, and in the former event, I reserve the right to designate a new beneficiary. Should I for any reason fail to designate such new beneficiary, this trust shall terminate upon my death and the trust property shall revert to my estate.

8. In the event of my physical or mental incapacity or my death, I hereby nominate and appoint as Successor Trustee hereunder whosoever shall at that time be beneficiary hereunder, unless such beneficiary shall not have attained the age of 21 years or is otherwise legally incapacitated, in which event I hereby nominate and appoint

(Name) _____, of

(Address) _____
           Number   *Street*   *City*   *State*   *Zip*

to be Successor Trustee.

9. This Declaration of Trust shall extend to and be binding upon the heirs, executors, administrators and assigns of the undersigned and upon the Successors to the Trustee.

10. The Trustee and his successors shall serve without bond.

11. This Declaration of Trust shall be construed and enforced in accordance with the laws of the State

of _____.

IN WITNESS WHEREOF, I have hereunto set my hand and seal this _____

day of _____, 19_____.

(Settlor sign here) _____ L.S.

I, the undersigned legal spouse of the above Settlor, hereby waive all community property rights which I may have in the hereinabove-described account and give my assent to the provisions of the trust and to the inclusion in it of the said account.

(Spouse sign here) _____ L.S.

Witness: (1) _____ Witness: (2) _____

STATE OF _____ City

COUNTY OF _____ or Town _____

On the _____ day of _____, 19_____, personally appeared

_____

known to me to be the individual(s) who executed the foregoing instrument, and acknowledged the same to be _____ free act and deed, before me.

_____

(Notary Seal)   *Notary Public*

CHAPTER 10

DECLARATION OF TRUST

For Naming

TWO OR MORE BENEFICIARIES, SHARING EQUALLY,

To Receive

A BROKERAGE ACCOUNT HELD IN ONE NAME

INSTRUCTIONS:

On the following pages will be found a declaration of trust (DT-115), suitable for use in connection with the establishment of an inter vivos trust covering a brokerage account held in one name, where it is desired to name two or more persons, sharing equally, to receive the account upon the death of the owner.

Cross out *"city"* or *"town,"* leaving the appropriate designation of your community.

Enter the name of the firm where the brokerage account is maintained in the space provided near the top.

In Paragraph 1, indicate the *number of persons* you are naming (to discourage unauthorized additions to the list) and then insert their names. The one whose name appears *first* will be the Successor Trustee responsible for seeing to the distribution of the trust property.

Note that the instrument specifies that the named beneficiaries are to receive *"in equal shares, or the survivor of them/per stirpes."* Now, think carefully: If you have named three persons with the understanding that if one of them predeceases you, his children will take his share, cross out *"or the survivor of them"* and *initial it.* If that is *not* what you want—if, for example, you prefer that the share of the deceased person be divided between the two surviving persons, cross out *"per stirpes"* and *initial it.* Remember, you <u>must</u> cross out *"or the survivor of them"* or *"per stirpes"*—one or the other.

Note that Paragraph 8 designates as Successor Trustee *"the beneficiary named first above,"* which means that in most cases you don't need to fill anything in there. However, if there is any possibility of a beneficiary who has not attained the age of 21 years receiving the brokerage account, make certain that you name an adult in this paragraph who can act as trustee for such beneficiary. Avoid naming as trustee a person not likely to survive until the beneficiary has attained age 21.

When completed in the manner shown on the reverse side hereof, make several photocopies for reference purposes. Place the original in safekeeping and file one copy with the investment firm with whom the brokerage account is maintained. Ask the firm to give you a written confirmation that in the event of your death it will recognize the trust and promptly turn the securities over to the Successor Trustee whom you have named. Insist that henceforth all communications from the firm be sent to *"(your name), Trustee u/d/t dated _____."*

Important: Read carefully Note B on page 38, which applies to this declaration of trust.

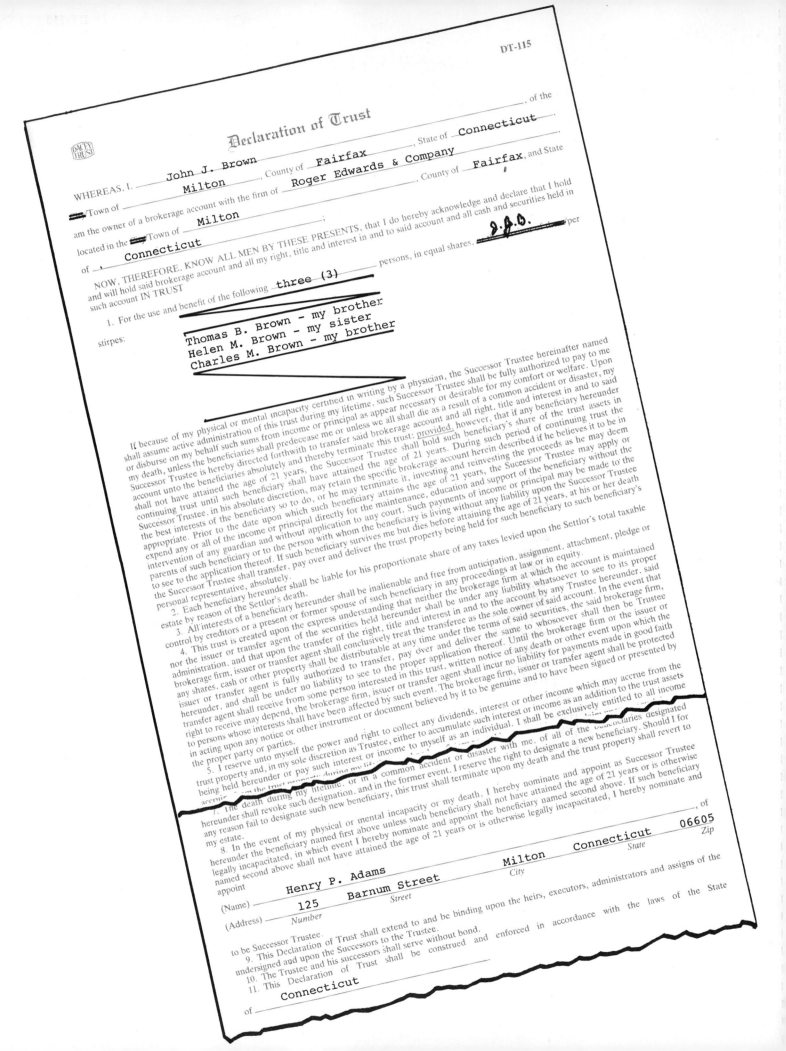

Declaration of Trust

DT-115

WHEREAS, I, _____ John J. Brown _____, State of _____ Connecticut _____, of the

Town of _____ Milton _____, County of _____ Fairfax _____, Roger Edwards & Company, County of _____ Fairfax _____, and State

am the owner of a brokerage account with the firm of _____

located in the _____ Town of _____ Milton _____;

of _____ Connecticut _____;

NOW, THEREFORE, KNOW ALL MEN BY THESE PRESENTS, that I do hereby acknowledge and declare that I hold
and will hold said brokerage account and all my right, title and interest in and to said account and all cash and securities held in
such account IN TRUST

1. For the use and benefit of the following _____ three (3) _____ persons, in equal shares,

stirpes:

Thomas B. Brown - my brother
Helen M. Brown - my sister
Charles M. Brown - my brother

If because of my physical or mental incapacity certified in writing by a physician, the Successor Trustee hereinafter named
shall assume active administration of this trust during my lifetime, such Successor Trustee shall be fully authorized to pay to me
or disburse on my behalf such sums from income or principal as appear necessary or desirable for my comfort or welfare. Upon
my death, unless the beneficiaries shall predecease me or unless we all shall die as a result of a common accident or disaster, my
Successor Trustee is hereby directed forthwith to transfer said brokerage account and all right, title and interest in and to said
account unto the beneficiaries absolutely and thereby terminate this trust; provided, however, that if any beneficiary hereunder
shall not have attained the age of 21 years, the Successor Trustee shall hold such beneficiary's share of the trust assets in
continuing trust until such beneficiary shall have attained the age of 21 years. During such period of continuing trust the
Successor Trustee, in his absolute discretion, may retain the specific brokerage account herein described if he believes it to be in
the best interests of the beneficiary so to do, or he may terminate it, investing and reinvesting the proceeds as he may deem
appropriate. Prior to the date upon which such beneficiary attains the age of 21 years, the Successor Trustee may apply or
expend any or all of the income or principal directly for the maintenance, education and support of the beneficiary without the
intervention of any guardian and without application to any court. Such payments of income or principal may be made to the
parents of such beneficiary or to the person with whom the beneficiary is living without any liability upon the Successor Trustee
to see to the application thereof. If such beneficiary survives me but dies before attaining the age of 21 years, at his or her death
the Successor Trustee shall transfer, pay over and deliver the trust property being held for such beneficiary to such beneficiary's
personal representative, absolutely.

2. Each beneficiary hereunder shall be liable for his proportionate share of any taxes levied upon the Settlor's total taxable
estate by reason of the Settlor's death.

3. All interests of a beneficiary hereunder shall be inalienable and free from anticipation, assignment, attachment, pledge or
control by creditors or a present or former spouse of such beneficiary in any proceedings at law or in equity.

4. This trust is created upon the express understanding that neither the brokerage firm at which the account is maintained
nor the issuer or transfer agent of the securities held hereunder shall be under any liability whatsoever to see to its proper
administration, and that upon the transfer of the right, title and interest in and to the account by any Trustee hereunder, said
brokerage firm, issuer or other property shall be distributable at any time under the terms of said securities, the said brokerage firm,
any shares, cash or other property shall be distributable at any time under the terms of said securities, the said brokerage firm,
issuer or transfer agent is fully authorized to transfer, pay over and deliver the same to whosoever shall then be Trustee
hereunder, and shall be under no liability to see to the proper application thereof. Until the brokerage firm or the issuer or
transfer agent shall receive from some person interested in this trust, written notice of any death or other event upon which the
right to receive may depend, the brokerage firm, issuer or transfer agent shall incur no liability for payments made in good faith
to persons whose interests shall have been affected by such event. The brokerage firm, issuer or transfer agent shall be protected
in acting upon any notice or other instrument or document believed by it to be genuine and to have been signed or presented by
the proper party or parties.

5. I reserve unto myself the power and right to collect any dividends, interest or other income which may accrue from the
trust property and, in my sole discretion as Trustee, either to accumulate such interest or income as an addition to the trust assets
being held hereunder or pay such interest or income to myself as an individual. I shall be exclusively entitled to all income
accruing from the trust property during my lifetime, or in a common accident or disaster with me, of all of the beneficiaries designated

7. The death during my lifetime, or in a common accident or disaster with me, of all of the beneficiaries designated
hereunder shall revoke such designation, and in the former event. I reserve the right to designate a new beneficiary. Should I for
any reason fail to designate such new beneficiary, this trust shall terminate upon my death and the trust property shall revert to
my estate.

8. In the event of my physical or mental incapacity or my death, I hereby nominate and appoint as Successor Trustee
hereunder the beneficiary named first above unless such beneficiary shall not have attained the age of 21 years or is otherwise
legally incapacitated, in which event I hereby nominate and appoint the beneficiary named second above. If such beneficiary
named second above shall not have attained the age of 21 years or is otherwise legally incapacitated, I hereby nominate and
appoint

_____ Henry P. Adams _____ Milton _____ Connecticut _____ 06605 _____, of
(Name) _____ 125 _____ Barnum Street _____ City _____ State _____ Zip

(Address) _____ Number _____ Street

to be Successor Trustee.

9. This Declaration of Trust shall extend to and be binding upon the heirs, executors, administrators and assigns of the
undersigned and upon the Successors to the Trustee.

10. The Trustee and his successors shall serve without bond.

11. This Declaration of Trust shall be construed and enforced in accordance with the laws of the State

of _____ Connecticut _____

Declaration of Trust

WHEREAS, I, _____, of the

City/Town of _____, County of _____, State of _____,

am the owner of a brokerage account with the firm of _____,

located in the City/Town of _____, County of _____

and State of _____;

NOW, THEREFORE, KNOW ALL MEN BY THESE PRESENTS, that I do hereby acknowledge and declare that I hold and will hold said brokerage account and all my right, title and interest in and to said account and all cash and securities held in such account IN TRUST

1. For the use and benefit of the following _____ persons, in equal shares, or the survivor of them/per stirpes:

If because of my physical or mental incapacity certified in writing by a physician, the Successor Trustee hereinafter named shall assume active administration of this trust during my lifetime, such Successor Trustee shall be fully authorized to pay to me or disburse on my behalf such sums from income or principal as appear necessary or desirable for my comfort or welfare. Upon my death, unless the beneficiaries shall predecease me or unless we all shall die as a result of a common accident or disaster, my Successor Trustee is hereby directed forthwith to transfer said brokerage account and all right, title and interest in and to said account unto the beneficiaries absolutely and thereby terminate this trust; provided, however, that if any beneficiary hereunder shall not have attained the age of 21 years, the Successor Trustee shall hold such beneficiary's share of the trust assets in continuing trust until such beneficiary shall have attained the age of 21 years. During such period of continuing trust the Successor Trustee, in his absolute discretion, may retain the specific brokerage account herein described if he believes it to be in the best interests of the beneficiary so to do, or he may terminate it, investing and reinvesting the proceeds as he may deem appropriate. Prior to the date upon which such beneficiary attains the age of 21 years, the Successor Trustee may apply or expend any or all of the income or principal directly for the maintenance, education and support of the beneficiary without the intervention of any guardian and without application to any court. Such payments of income or principal may be made to the parents of such beneficiary or to the person with whom the beneficiary is living without any liability upon the Successor Trustee to see to the application thereof. If such beneficiary survives me but dies before attaining the age of 21 years, at his or her death the Successor Trustee shall transfer, pay over and deliver the trust property being held for such beneficiary to such beneficiary's personal representative, absolutely.

2. Each beneficiary hereunder shall be liable for his proportionate share of any taxes levied upon the Settlor's total taxable estate by reason of the Settlor's death.

3. All interests of a beneficiary hereunder shall be inalienable and free from anticipation, assignment, attachment, pledge or control by creditors or a present or former spouse of such beneficiary in any proceedings at law or in equity.

4. This trust is created upon the express understanding that neither the brokerage firm at which the account is maintained nor the issuer or transfer agent of the securities held hereunder shall be under any liability whatsoever to see to its proper administration, and that upon the transfer of the right, title and interest in and to the account by any Trustee hereunder, said brokerage firm, issuer or transfer agent shall conclusively treat the transferee as the sole owner of said account. In the event that any shares, cash or other property shall be distributable at any time under the terms of said securities, the said brokerage firm, issuer or transfer agent is fully authorized to transfer, pay over and deliver the same to whosoever shall then be Trustee hereunder, and shall be under no liability to see to the proper application thereof. Until the brokerage firm or the issuer or transfer agent shall receive from some person interested in this trust, written notice of any death or other event upon which the right to receive may depend, the brokerage firm, issuer or transfer agent shall incur no liability for payments made in good faith to persons whose interests shall have been affected by such event. The brokerage firm, issuer or transfer agent shall be protected in acting upon any notice or other instrument or document believed by it to be genuine and to have been signed or presented by the proper party or parties.

5. I reserve unto myself the power and right to collect any dividends, interest or other income which may accrue from the trust property and, in my sole discretion as Trustee, either to accumulate such interest or income as an addition to the trust assets being held hereunder or pay such interest or income to myself as an individual. I shall be exclusively entitled to all income accruing from the trust property during my lifetime, and no beneficiary named herein shall have any claim upon any such income and/or profits distributed to me.

6. I reserve unto myself the power and right at any time during my lifetime to amend or revoke in whole or in part the trust hereby created without the necessity of obtaining the consent of the beneficiaries and without giving notice to the beneficiaries. The sale by me of the whole or any part of the brokerage account held hereunder shall constitute as to such whole or part a revocation of this trust.

7. The death during my lifetime, or in a common accident or disaster with me, of all of the beneficiaries designated hereunder shall revoke such designation, and in the former event, I reserve the right to designate a new beneficiary. Should I for any reason fail to designate such new beneficiary, this trust shall terminate upon my death and the trust property shall revert to my estate.

8. In the event of my physical or mental incapacity or my death, I hereby nominate and appoint as Successor Trustee hereunder the beneficiary named first above unless such beneficiary shall not have attained the age of 21 years or is otherwise legally incapacitated, in which event I hereby nominate and appoint the beneficiary named second above. If such beneficiary named second above shall not have attained the age of 21 years or is otherwise legally incapacitated, I hereby nominate and appoint

(Name) _____, of

(Address) _____

             Number   *Street*   *City*   *State*   *Zip*

to be Successor Trustee.

9. This Declaration of Trust shall extend to and be binding upon the heirs, executors, administrators and assigns of the undersigned and upon the Successors to the Trustee.

10. The Trustee and his successors shall serve without bond.

11. This Declaration of Trust shall be construed and enforced in accordance with the laws of the State

of _____.

IN WITNESS WHEREOF, I have hereunto set my hand and seal this _____

day of _____, 19_____.

        (Settlor sign here) _____ L.S.

I, the undersigned legal spouse of the above Settlor, hereby waive all community property rights which I may have in the hereinabove-described account and give my assent to the provisions of the trust and to the inclusion in it of the said account.

        (Spouse sign here) _____ L.S.

Witness: (1) _____   Witness: (2) _____

STATE OF _____   City

COUNTY OF _____   or

                                            Town _____

On the _____ day of _____, 19_____, personally appeared

_____

known to me to be the individual(s) who executed the foregoing instrument, and acknowledged the same to be _____ free act and deed, before me.

(Notary Seal)   _____

                                                  Notary Public

CHAPTER 10

DECLARATION OF TRUST

For Naming

ONE PRIMARY BENEFICIARY WITH YOUR CHILDREN,

SHARING EQUALLY, AS CONTINGENT BENEFICIARIES

To Receive

A BROKERAGE ACCOUNT HELD IN ONE NAME

INSTRUCTIONS:

On the following pages will be found a declaration of trust (DT-116) suitable for use in connection with the establishment of an inter vivos trust covering a brokerage account held in one name, where it is desired to name one person. (ordinarily, but not necessarily, one's spouse) as primary beneficiary, with one's children as contingent beneficiaries to receive the account upon the death of the owner.

Cross out *"city"* or *"town,"* leaving the appropriate designation of your community.

Enter the name of the firm where the brokerage account is maintained in the space provided near the top.

Enter the name of the primary beneficiary (called the "First Beneficiary") in the appropriate place in Paragraph 1. Note that the instrument refers to your children as *"natural not/or adopted."* Now, decide: If you have an adopted child and you wish to include him, cross out the word *"not"* in the phrase *"natural not/or adopted"* and *initial it.* If you wish to *exclude* your adopted child, cross out the word *"or"* in the same phrase and *initial it.* Remember you <u>must</u> cross out *"not"* or *"or"*—one or the other. If you have no adopted child, simply cross out *"not."*

Note next that the instrument specifies that your children are to receive *"in equal shares, or the survivor of them/per stirpes."* Now, think carefully: If it is your wish that, if one of your children does not survive you, *his* share will revert to *his* children in equal shares, cross out *"or the survivor of them"* and *initial it.* If that is *not* what you want—if, for example, you prefer that the share of your deceased child be divided among your surviving children, cross out *"per stirpes"* and *initial it.* Remember, you <u>must</u> cross out *"or the survivor of them"* or *"per stirpes"*—one or the other.

Note that in Paragraph 8, the First Beneficiary is designated as Successor Trustee, while a space is provided in which you should designate another person to so act if the named Successor Trustee is not surviving or otherwise fails or ceases to act. This could be one of your children, for example, but it must be an adult who can act as trustee for any beneficiary who has not attained the age of 21 years who comes into a share of the trust. Avoid naming someone not likely to survive until the youngest such beneficiary has attained age 21.

When completed in the manner shown on the reverse side hereof, make several photocopies of the declaration of trust for reference purposes. Place the original in safekeeping and file one copy with the investment firm where the account is maintained. Insist that henceforth all communications from the firm be sent to *"(your name), Trustee u/d/t dated _____."*

Important: Read carefully Note B on page 38, which applies to this declaration of trust.

DT-116

Declaration of Trust

WHEREAS, I, **John J. Brown**, County of **Fairfax**, State of **Connecticut**,
Town of **Milton** am the owner of a brokerage account with the firm of **Roger Edwards & Company**, County of **Fairfax** and State
located in the Town of **Milton**
of **Connecticut**;

NOW, THEREFORE, KNOW ALL MEN BY THESE PRESENTS, that I do hereby acknowledge and declare that I hold and will hold said brokerage account and all my right, title and interest in and to said account and all cash and securities held in such account IN TRUST

1. For the use and benefit of:

Elizabeth A. Brown - my wife   **Milton**   **Connecticut**   **06605**
(Name)   City   State   Zip

525   **Main Street**
(Address) Number   Street

(hereinafter referred to as the "First Beneficiary") and, upon his or her death prior to the termination of the trust, for the use and benefit of my children, natural not or adopted, in equal shares, or the survivor of them, absolutely.

If because of my physical or mental incapacity certified in writing by a physician, such Successor Trustee hereinafter named shall assume active administration of this trust during my lifetime, such Successor Trustee shall be fully authorized to pay to me or disburse on my behalf such sums from income or principal as appear necessary or desirable for my comfort or welfare. Upon my death, unless the beneficiaries all shall predecease me or unless we all shall die as a result of a common accident or disaster, my Successor Trustee is hereby directed forthwith to transfer said brokerage account and all right, title and interest in and to said account unto the beneficiary absolutely and thereby terminate this trust; *provided, however,* that if any beneficiary hereunder shall not have attained the age of 21 years, the Successor Trustee shall hold such beneficiary's share of the trust assets in continuing trust until such beneficiary shall have attained the age of 21 years. During such period of continuing trust the Successor Trustee, in his absolute discretion, may retain the specific brokerage account herein described if he believes it to be in the best interests of the beneficiary so to do, or he may terminate it, investing and reinvesting the proceeds as he may deem appropriate. Prior to the date upon which such beneficiary attains the age of 21 years, the Successor Trustee may apply or expend any or all of the income or principal directly for the maintenance, education and support of such beneficiary without the intervention of any guardian and without application to any court. Such payments of income or principal may be made to the parents of such beneficiary or to the person with whom the beneficiary is living without any liability upon the Successor Trustee to see to the application thereof. If such beneficiary survives me but dies before attaining the age of 21 years, at his or her death the Successor Trustee shall transfer, pay over and deliver the trust property being held for such beneficiary to such beneficiary's personal representative, absolutely.

2. Each beneficiary hereunder shall be liable for his proportionate share of any taxes levied upon the Settlor's total taxable estate by reason of the Settlor's death.

3. All interests of a beneficiary hereunder shall be inalienable and free from anticipation, assignment, attachment, pledge or control by creditors or a present or former spouse of such beneficiary in any proceedings at law or in equity.

4. This trust is created upon the express understanding that neither the brokerage firm at which the account is maintained nor the issuer or transfer agent of the securities held thereunder shall be under any liability whatsoever to see to its proper administration, and that upon the transfer of the right, title and interest in and to said account by any Trustee hereunder, said brokerage firm, issuer or transfer agent shall conclusively treat the transferee as the sole owner of said account. In the event that any shares, cash or other property shall be distributable at any time under the terms of said securities, the said brokerage firm shall then be Trustee issuer or transfer agent is fully authorized to transfer, pay over and deliver the same to whosoever shall then be Trustee hereunder, and shall be under no liability to see to the proper application thereof. Until the brokerage firm or the issuer or transfer agent shall receive from some person interested in this trust, written notice of any death or other event upon which the right to receive may depend, the brokerage firm, issuer or transfer agent shall incur no liability for payments made in good faith to persons whose interests shall have been affected by such event. The brokerage firm, issuer or transfer agent shall be protected in acting upon any notice or other instrument or document believed by it to be genuine and to have been signed or presented by the proper party or parties.

5. I reserve unto myself the power and right to collect any dividends, interest or other income which may accrue from the trust property and, in my sole discretion as Trustee, either to accumulate such income as an addition to the trust assets being held hereunder or pay such income to myself as an individual. I shall be exclusively entitled to all income accruing from the trust property during my lifetime, and no beneficiary named herein shall have any claim upon any such income and/or profits distributed to me.

6. I reserve unto myself the power and right at any time during my lifetime to amend or revoke in whole or in part the trust hereby created without the necessity of obtaining the consent of the beneficiary and without giving notice to the beneficiary. The sale by me of the whole or any part of the brokerage account held hereunder shall constitute as to such whole or part a revocation of this trust.

7. The death during my lifetime, or in a common accident or disaster with me, of all the beneficiaries designated hereunder shall revoke such designation, and in the former event, this trust shall terminate upon my death and the trust property shall revert to my estate. Should I for any reason fail to designate such new beneficiary, this trust shall terminate upon my death and the trust property shall revert to my estate.

8. In the event of my physical or mental incapacity or my death, I hereby nominate and appoint as Successor Trustee hereunder the First Beneficiary or, if such First Beneficiary be not surviving or fails or ceases to act, I nominate and appoint

Henry P. Adams   **Milton**   **Connecticut**   **06605**
(Name)   City   State   Zip

125   **Barnum Street**
(Address) Number   Street

to be Successor Trustee. If such person fails or ceases to act or should I for any reason fail to designate the person above intended to be nominated, then I nominate and appoint as such Successor Trustee whosoever shall qualify as executor, administrator or guardian, as the case may be, of my estate.

10. The Trustee and his successors shall serve without bond.

11. This Declaration of Trust shall be construed and enforced in accordance with the laws of the State of **Connecticut**

Declaration of Trust

WHEREAS, I, _____, of the

City/Town of _____, County of _____, State of _____,

am the owner of a brokerage account with the firm of _____,

located in the City/Town of _____, County of _____

and State of _____;

NOW, THEREFORE, KNOW ALL MEN BY THESE PRESENTS, that I do hereby acknowledge and declare that I hold and will hold said brokerage account and all my right, title and interest in and to said account and all cash and securities held in such account IN TRUST

    1. For the use and benefit of:

(Name) _____, of

(Address) _____

          Number   *Street*   *City*   *State*   *Zip*

(hereinafter referred to as the "First Beneficiary") and, upon his or her death prior to the termination of the trust, for the use and benefit of my children, natural not/or adopted, in equal shares, or the survivor of them/per stirpes.

    If because of my physical or mental incapacity certified in writing by a physician, the Successor Trustee hereinafter named shall assume active administration of this trust during my lifetime, such Successor Trustee shall be fully authorized to pay to me or disburse on my behalf such sums from income or principal as appear necessary or desirable for my comfort or welfare. Upon my death, unless the beneficiaries all shall predecease me or unless we all shall die as a result of a common accident or disaster, my Successor Trustee is hereby directed forthwith to transfer said brokerage account and all right, title and interest in and to said account unto the beneficiary absolutely and thereby terminate this trust; provided, however, that if any beneficiary hereunder shall not have attained the age of 21 years, the Successor Trustee shall hold such beneficiary's share of the trust assets in continuing trust until such beneficiary shall have attained the age of 21 years. During such period of continuing trust the Successor Trustee, in his absolute discretion, may retain the specific brokerage account herein described if he believes it to be in the best interests of the beneficiary so to do, or he may terminate it, investing and reinvesting the proceeds as he may deem appropriate. Prior to the date upon which such beneficiary attains the age of 21 years, the Successor Trustee may apply or expend any or all of the income or principal directly for the maintenance, education and support of such beneficiary without the intervention of any guardian and without application to any court. Such payments of income or principal may be made to the parents of such beneficiary or to the person with whom the beneficiary is living without any liability upon the Successor Trustee to see to the application thereof. If such beneficiary survives me but dies before attaining the age of 21 years, at his or her death the Successor Trustee shall transfer, pay over and deliver the trust property being held for such beneficiary to such beneficiary's personal representative, absolutely.

    2. Each beneficiary hereunder shall be liable for his proportionate share of any taxes levied upon the Settlor's total taxable estate by reason of the Settlor's death.

    3. All interests of a beneficiary hereunder shall be inalienable and free from anticipation, assignment, attachment, pledge or control by creditors or a present or former spouse of such beneficiary in any proceedings at law or in equity.

    4. This trust is created upon the express understanding that neither the brokerage firm at which the account is maintained nor the issuer or transfer agent of the securities held hereunder shall be under any liability whatsoever to see to its proper administration, and that upon the transfer of the right, title and interest in and to said account by any Trustee hereunder, said brokerage firm, issuer or transfer agent shall conclusively treat the transferee as the sole owner of said account. In the event that any shares, cash or other property shall be distributable at any time under the terms of said securities, the said brokerage firm, issuer or transfer agent is fully authorized to transfer, pay over and deliver the same to whosoever shall then be Trustee hereunder, and shall be under no liability to see to the proper application thereof. Until the brokerage firm or the issuer or transfer agent shall receive from some person interested in this trust, written notice of any death or other event upon which the right to receive may depend, the brokerage firm, issuer or transfer agent shall incur no liability for payments made in good faith to persons whose interests shall have been affected by such event. The brokerage firm, issuer or transfer agent shall be protected in acting upon any notice or other instrument or document believed by it to be genuine and to have been signed or presented by the proper party or parties.

    5. I reserve unto myself the power and right to collect any dividends, interest or other income which may accrue from the trust property and, in my sole discretion as Trustee, either to accumulate such income as an addition to the trust assets being held hereunder or pay such income to myself as an individual. I shall be exclusively entitled to all income accruing from the trust property during my lifetime, and no beneficiary named herein shall have any claim upon any such income and/or profits distributed to me.

6. I reserve unto myself the power and right at any time during my lifetime to amend or revoke in whole or in part the trust hereby created without the necessity of obtaining the consent of the beneficiary and without giving notice to the beneficiary. The sale by me of the whole or any part of the brokerage account held hereunder shall constitute as to such whole or part a revocation of this trust.

7. The death during my lifetime, or in a common accident or disaster with me, of all the beneficiaries designated hereunder shall revoke such designation, and in the former event, I reserve the right to designate a new beneficiary. Should I for any reason fail to designate such new beneficiary, this trust shall terminate upon my death and the trust property shall revert to my estate.

8. In the event of my physical or mental incapacity or my death, I hereby nominate and appoint as Successor Trustee hereunder the First Beneficiary or, if such First Beneficiary be not surviving or fails or ceases to act, I nominate and appoint

(Name) _____ , of

(Address) _____

Number   Street   City   State   Zip

to be Successor Trustee. If such person fails or ceases to act or should I for any reason fail to designate the person above intended to be nominated, then I nominate and appoint as such Successor Trustee whosoever shall qualify as executor, administrator or guardian, as the case may be, of my estate.

9. This Declaration of Trust shall extend to and be binding upon the heirs, executors, administrators and assigns of the undersigned and you the Successors to the Trustee.

10. The Trustee and his successors shall serve without bond.

11. This Declaration of Trust shall be construed and enforced in accordance with the laws of the State

of _____ .

IN WITNESS WHEREOF, I have hereunto set my hand and seal this _____

day of _____ , 19_____ .

(Settlor sign here) _____ L.S.

I, the undersigned legal spouse of the above Settlor, hereby waive all community property rights which I may have in the hereinabove-described account and give my assent to the provisions of the trust and to the inclusion in it of the said account.

(Spouse sign here) _____ L.S.

Witness: (1) _____   Witness: (2) _____

STATE OF _____   City
                                     or
COUNTY OF _____   Town _____

On the _____ day of _____ , 19_____ , personally appeared

_____

known to me to be the individual(s) who executed the foregoing instrument, and acknowledged the same to be _____ free act and deed, before me.

_____

(Notary Seal)   Notary Public

CHAPTER 10

DECLARATION OF TRUST
For Naming
ONE BENEFICIARY
To Receive
A BROKERAGE ACCOUNT HELD IN JOINT NAMES

INSTRUCTIONS:

On the following pages will be found a declaration of trust (DT-113-J) suitable for use in connection with the establishment of an inter vivos trust covering a brokerage account held in joint names, where it is desired to name some *one* person to receive the account upon the death of the survivor of the two joint owners.

Cross out *"city"* or *"town,"* leaving the appropriate designation of your community.

Enter the name of the firm where the brokerage account is maintained in the space provided near the top, and name of the beneficiary in the appropriate place in Paragraph 1.

Note that Paragraph 8 designates as Successor Trustee *"whosoever shall at that time be beneficiary hereunder,"* which means that in most cases you don't need to fill anything in there. However, if there is any possibility of a beneficiary who has not attained the age of 21 years receiving the brokerage account, make certain that you name an adult in this paragraph who can act as trustee for such beneficiary. Avoid naming as trustee a person not likely to survive until the beneficiary has attained age 21.

When completed in the manner shown on the reverse side hereof, make several photocopies for reference purposes. Place the original in safekeeping and file one copy with the investment firm with whom the brokerage account is maintained. Ask the firm to give you a written confirmation that in the event of your death it will recognize the trust and promptly turn the securities over to the Successor Trustee whom you have named. Insist that henceforth all communications from the firm be to *"(your name) and (your co-owner's name), Trustees u/d/t dated _____."*

Important: Read carefully Note B on page 38, which applies to this declaration of trust.

DT-113-J

Declaration of Trust

WHEREAS, We, __John J. Brown__ and __Elizabeth A. Brown__, of the __City/Town of Milton__, County of __Fairfax__, State of __Connecticut__

are the joint owners of a brokerage account with the firm of __Roger Edwards & Company__, County of __Fairfax__ and State

located in the __City/Town of Milton__

of __Connecticut__:

NOW, THEREFORE, KNOW ALL MEN BY THESE PRESENTS, that we do hereby acknowledge and declare that we hold said brokerage account and all our right, title and interest in and to said account and all cash and securities held in such account IN TRUST

1. For the use and benefit of:

(Name) __Jill A. Brown – our daughter__ __Milton__ City __Connecticut 06605__ State Zip

(Address) __525__ Number __Main Street__ Street

If because of our physical or mental incapacity certified in writing by a physician, the Successor Trustee hereinafter named shall assume active administration of this trust during our lifetime, such Successor Trustee shall be fully authorized to pay to us or disburse on our behalf such sums from income or principal as appear necessary or desirable for our comfort or welfare. Upon the death of the survivor of us, unless the beneficiary shall predecease us or unless we all shall die as a result of a common accident or disaster, our Successor Trustee is hereby directed forthwith to transfer said brokerage account and all right, title and interest in and to said account unto the beneficiary absolutely and thereby terminate this trust; provided, however, that if the beneficiary hereunder shall not have attained the age of 21 years, the Successor Trustee shall hold the trust assets in continuing trust until such beneficiary shall have attained the age of 21 years. During such period of continuing trust the Successor Trustee, in his absolute discretion, may retain the specific brokerage account herein described if he believes it to be in the best interests of the beneficiary so to do, or he may terminate it, investing and reinvesting the proceeds as he may deem appropriate. Prior to the date upon which such beneficiary attains the age of 21 years, the Successor Trustee may apply or expend any or all of the income or principal directly for the maintenance, education and support of such beneficiary without the intervention of any guardian and without application to any court. Such payments of income or principal may be made to the parents of such beneficiary or to the person with whom the beneficiary is living without any liability upon the Successor Trustee to see to the application thereof. If such beneficiary survives us but dies before attaining the age of 21 years, at his or her death the Successor Trustee shall transfer, pay over and deliver the trust property to such beneficiary's personal representative, absolutely.

2. The beneficiary hereunder shall be liable for his proportionate share of any taxes levied upon the total taxable estate of the survivor of us by reason of the death of such survivor.

3. The interest of the beneficiary hereunder shall be inalienable and free from anticipation, assignment, attachment, pledge or control by creditors or a present or former spouse of such beneficiary in any proceedings at law or in equity.

4. This trust is created upon the express understanding that neither the brokerage firm at which the account is maintained nor the issuer or transfer agent of the securities held hereunder shall be under any liability whatsoever to see to its proper administration, and that upon the transfer of the right, title and interest in and to the account by any Trustee hereunder, said brokerage firm, issuer or transfer agent shall conclusively treat the transferee as the sole owner of said account. In the event that any shares, cash or other property shall be distributable at any time under the terms of said securities, the said brokerage firm, issuer or transfer agent is fully authorized to transfer, pay over and deliver the same to whosoever shall then be Trustee hereunder, and shall be under no liability to see to the proper application thereof. Until the brokerage firm or other event upon which the transfer agent shall receive from some person interested in this trust, written notice of any death or other event upon which the right to receive may depend, the brokerage firm, issuer or transfer agent shall incur no liability for payments made in good faith to persons whose interests shall have been affected by such event. The brokerage firm, issuer or transfer agent shall be protected by in acting upon any notice or other instrument or document believed by it to be genuine and to have been signed or presented by the proper party or parties.

5. We reserve unto ourselves the power and right to collect any dividends, interest or other income which may accrue from the trust property and, in our sole discretion as Trustees, either to accumulate such interest or income as an addition to the trust assets being held hereunder or pay such interest or income to ourselves as individuals. We shall be exclusively entitled to all income accruing from the trust property during our lifetime, and no beneficiary named herein shall have any claim upon any such income and/or profits distributed to us.

6. We reserve unto ourselves the power and right at any time during our lifetime to amend or revoke in whole or in part the trust hereby created without the necessity of obtaining the consent of the beneficiary and without giving notice to the beneficiary. The sale by us of the whole or any part of the brokerage account held hereunder shall constitute as to such whole or part a revocation of this trust.

7. The death during our lifetime, or in a common accident or disaster with us, of the beneficiary designated hereunder shall revoke such designation, and in the former event, we reserve the right to designate a new beneficiary. Should we for any reason fail to designate such new beneficiary, this trust shall terminate upon the death of the survivor of us and the trust property shall revert to the estate of such survivor.

8. In the event of the physical or mental incapacity or death of one of us, the survivor shall continue as sole Trustee. In the event of the physical or mental incapacity or death of the survivor of us, or if we both shall die in a common accident, we hereby nominate and appoint as Successor Trustee hereunder whosoever shall act that time be beneficiary hereunder unless such beneficiary shall not have attained the age of 21 years or is otherwise legally incapacitated, in which event we hereby nominate and appoint __Henry P. Adams__ __Milton__ City __Connecticut 06605__ State Zip , of

(Name) __125__ Number __Barnum Street__ Street

(Address)

as such Successor Trustee.

9. This Declaration of Trust shall extend to and be binding upon the heirs, executors, administrators and assigns of the undersigned and upon the Successors to the Trustees.

10. We as Trustees and our Successor Trustee shall serve without bond.

11. This Declaration of Trust shall be construed and enforced in accordance with the laws of the State of __Connecticut__

Declaration of Trust

WHEREAS, WE, _____ and _____, of the

City/Town of _____, County of _____, State of _____,

are the joint owners of a brokerage account with the firm of _____,

located in the City/Town of _____, County of _____

and State of_____;

NOW, THEREFORE, KNOW ALL MEN BY THESE PRESENTS, that we do hereby acknowledge and declare that we hold said brokerage account and all our right, title and interest in and to said account and all cash and securities held in such account IN TRUST

1. For the use and benefit of:

(Name) _____, of

(Address) _____

| Number | Street | City | State | Zip |

If because of our physical or mental incapacity certified in writing by a physician, the Successor Trustee hereinafter named shall assume active administration of this trust during our lifetime, such Successor Trustee shall be fully authorized to pay to us or disburse on our behalf such sums from income or principal as appear necessary or desirable for our comfort or welfare. Upon the death of the survivor of us, unless the beneficiary shall predecease us or unless we all shall die as a result of a common accident or disaster, our Successor Trustee is hereby directed forthwith to transfer said brokerage account and all right, title and interest in and to said account unto the beneficiary absolutely and thereby terminate this trust; provided, however, that if the beneficiary hereunder shall not have attained the age of 21 years, the Successor Trustee shall hold the trust assets in continuing trust until such beneficiary shall have attained the age of 21 years. During such period of continuing trust the Successor Trustee, in his absolute discretion, may retain the specific brokerage account herein described if he believes it to be in the best interests of the beneficiary so to do, or he may terminate it, investing and reinvesting the proceeds as he may deem appropriate. Prior to the date upon which such beneficiary attains the age of 21 years, the Successor Trustee may apply or expend any or all of the income or principal directly for the maintenance, education and support of such beneficiary without the intervention of any guardian and without application to any court. Such payments of income or principal may be made to the parents of such beneficiary or to the person with whom the beneficiary is living without any liability upon the Successor Trustee to see to the application thereof. If such beneficiary survives us but dies before attaining the age of 21 years, at his or her death the Successor Trustee shall transfer, pay over and deliver the trust property to such beneficiary's personal representative, absolutely.

2. The beneficiary hereunder shall be liable for his proportionate share of any taxes levied upon the total taxable estate of the survivor of us by reason of the death of such survivor.

3. The interest of the beneficiary hereunder shall be inalienable and free from anticipation, assignment, attachment, pledge or control by creditors or a present or former spouse of such beneficiary in any proceedings at law or in equity.

4. This trust is created upon the express understanding that neither the brokerage firm at which the account is maintained nor the issuer or transfer agent of the securities held hereunder shall be under any liability whatsoever to see to its proper administration, and that upon the transfer of the right, title and interest in and to the account by any Trustee hereunder, said brokerage firm, issuer or transfer agent shall conclusively treat the transferee as the sole owner of said account. In the event that any shares, cash or other property shall be distributable at any time under the terms of said securities, the said brokerage firm, issuer or transfer agent is fully authorized to transfer, pay over and deliver the same to whosoever shall then be Trustee hereunder, and shall be under no liability to see to the proper application thereof. Until the brokerage firm or the issuer or transfer agent shall receive from some person interested in this trust, written notice of any death or other event upon which the right to receive may depend, the brokerage firm, issuer or transfer agent shall incur no liability for payments made in good faith to persons whose interests shall have been affected by such event. The brokerage firm, issuer or transfer agent shall be protected in acting upon any notice or other instrument or document believed by it to be genuine and to have been signed or presented by the proper party or parties.

5. We reserve unto ourselves the power and right to collect any dividends, interest or other income which may accrue from the trust property and, in our sole discretion as Trustees, either to accumulate such interest or income as an addition to the trust assets being held hereunder or pay such interest or income to ourselves as individuals. We shall be exclusively entitled to all income accruing from the trust property during our lifetime, and no beneficiary named herein shall have any claim upon any such income and/or profits distributed to us.

6. We reserve unto ourselves the power and right at any time during our lifetime to amend or revoke in whole or in part the trust hereby created without the necessity of obtaining the consent of the beneficiary and without giving notice to the beneficiary. The sale by us of the whole or any part of the brokerage account held hereunder shall constitute as to such whole or part a revocation of this trust.

7. The death during our lifetime, or in a common accident or disaster with us, of the beneficiary designated hereunder shall revoke such designation, and in the former event, we reserve the right to designate a new beneficiary. Should we for any reason fail to designate such new beneficiary, this trust shall terminate upon the death of the survivor of us and the trust property shall revert to the estate of such survivor.

8. In the event of the physical or mental incapacity or death of one of us, the survivor shall continue as sole Trustee. In the event of the physical or mental incapacity or death of the survivor of us, or if we both shall die in a common accident, we hereby nominate and appoint as Successor Trustee hereunder whosoever shall at that time be beneficiary hereunder unless such beneficiary shall not have attained the age of 21 years or is otherwise legally incapacitated, in which event we hereby nominate and appoint

(Name) _____, of

(Address) _____
　　　　　Number　　　　　　　Street　　　　　　　City　　　　　　　State　　　　　Zip

to be Successor Trustee.

9. This Declaration of Trust shall extend to and be binding upon the heirs, executors, administrators and assigns of the undersigned and upon the Successors to the Trustees.

10. We as Trustees and our Successor Trustee shall serve without bond.

11. This Declaration of Trust shall be construed and enforced in accordance with the laws of the State

of _____.

IN WITNESS WHEREOF, we have hereunto set our hands and seals this _____

day of _____, 19_____.

　　　　　　　　　(First Settlor sign here) _____ L.S.

　　　　　　　　(Second Settlor sign here) _____ L.S.

I, the undersigned legal spouse of one of the above Settlors, hereby waive all community property rights which I may have in the hereinabove-described account and give my assent to the provisions of the trust and to the inclusion in it of the said account.

　　　　　　　　　(Spouse sign here) _____ L.S.

Witness: (1) _____　　Witness: (2) _____

STATE OF _____　　City
　　　　　　　　　　　　　　　　　　　　　　　or
COUNTY OF _____　　Town _____

On the _____ day of _____, 19_____, personally appeared

_____ and _____

known to me to be the individuals who executed the foregoing instrument, and acknowledged the same to be their free act and deed, before me.

(Notary Seal)　　　　　　　　　　　　　　　　_____
　　　　　　　　　　　　　　　　　　　　　　　　　　　Notary Public

CHAPTER 10

DECLARATION OF TRUST
For Naming
ONE PRIMARY BENEFICIARY
And
ONE CONTINGENT BENEFICIARY
To Receive
A BROKERAGE ACCOUNT HELD IN JOINT NAMES

INSTRUCTIONS:

On the following pages will be found a declaration of trust (DT-114-J) suitable for use in connection with the establishment of an inter vivos trust covering a brokerage account held in joint names, where it is desired to name some *one* person as primary beneficiary, with some *one* other person as contingent beneficiary to receive the account if the primary beneficiary be not surviving upon the death of the survivor of the two joint owners.

Cross out *"city"* or *"town,"* leaving the appropriate designation of your community.

Enter the name of the firm where the brokerage account is maintained in the space provided near the top, and the names of the beneficiaries in the appropriate places in Paragraph 1.

Note that Paragraph 8 designates as Successor Trustee *"whosoever shall at that time be beneficiary hereunder,"* which means that in most cases you don't need to fill anything in there. However, if there is any possibility of a beneficiary who has not attained the age of 21 years receiving the trust assets, make certain that you name an adult in this paragraph who can act as trustee for such beneficiary. Avoid naming as trustee a person not likely to survive until the beneficiary has attained age 21.

When completed in the manner shown on the reverse side hereof, make several photocopies for reference purposes. Place the original in safekeeping and file one copy with the investment firm with whom the brokerage account is maintained. Ask the firm to give you a written confirmation that in the event of your death it will recognize the trust and promptly turn the securities over to the Successor Trustee whom you have named. Insist that henceforth all communications from the firm be sent to *"(your name) and (your co-owner's name), Trustees u/d/t dated _____."*

Important: Read carefully Note B on page 38, which applies to this declaration of trust.

Declaration of Trust

DACEY TRUST

WHEREAS, We __John J. Brown__ and __Elizabeth A. Brown__, of the __Town of__ __Milton__, County of __Fairfax__, State of __Connecticut__, are the joint owners of a brokerage account with the firm of __Roger Edwards & Company__, and State of located in the __Town of__ __Milton__, County of __Fairfax__,
__Connecticut__;

NOW, THEREFORE, KNOW ALL MEN BY THESE PRESENTS, that we do hereby acknowledge and declare that we hold and will hold said brokerage account and all our right, title and interest in and to said account and all cash and securities held in such account IN TRUST

1. For the use and benefit of:

(Name) __Jill A. Brown - our daughter__, of

(Address) __525__ __Main Street__ __Milton__ __Connecticut__ __06605__
Number Street City State Zip

or, if he or she be not surviving, for the use and benefit of:

(Name) __Dorothy Lynn - our niece__, of

(Address) __566__ __Midland Street__ __Portland__ __Wisconsin__ __53123__
Number Street City State Zip

If because of our physical or mental incapacity certified in writing by a physician, the Successor Trustee hereinafter named shall assume active administration of this trust during our lifetime, such Successor Trustee shall be fully authorized to pay to us or disburse on our behalf such sums from income or principal as may appear necessary or desirable for our comfort or welfare. Upon the death of the survivor of us, unless both beneficiaries shall predecease us or unless we all shall die as a result of a common accident or disaster, our Successor Trustee is hereby directed forthwith to transfer said account and all right, title and interest in and to said account unto the beneficiary absolutely and thereby terminate this trust; provided, however, that if the beneficiary hereunder shall not have attained the age of 21 years, the Successor Trustee shall hold the trust assets in continuing trust until such beneficiary shall have attained the age of 21 years. During such period of continuing trust the Successor Trustee, in his absolute discretion, may retain the specific brokerage account herein described if he believes it to be in the best interests of the beneficiary so to do, or he may terminate it, investing and reinvesting the proceeds as he may deem appropriate. Prior to the date upon which such beneficiary attains the age of 21 years, the Successor Trustee may apply or expend any or all of the income or principal directly for the maintenance, education and support of the beneficiary without the intervention of any guardian and without application to any court. Such payments of income or principal may be made to the parents of such beneficiary or to the person with whom such beneficiary is living without any liability upon the Successor Trustee to see to the application thereof. If such beneficiary survives us but dies before attaining the age of 21 years, at his or her death the Successor Trustee shall transfer, pay over and deliver the trust property to such beneficiary's personal representative, absolutely.

2. The beneficiary hereunder shall be liable for his proportionate share of any taxes levied upon the total taxable estate of the survivor of us by reason of the death of such survivor.

3. All interests of a beneficiary hereunder shall be inalienable and free from anticipation, assignment, attachment, pledge or control by creditors or a present or former spouse of such beneficiary in any proceedings at law or in equity.

4. This trust is created upon the express understanding that neither the brokerage firm at which the account is maintained nor the issuer or transfer agent of the securities held thereunder shall be under any liability whatsoever to see to its proper administration, and that upon transfer of the right, title and interest in and to said account by any Trustee hereunder, said brokerage firm, issuer or transfer agent shall conclusively treat the transferee as the sole owner of said securities, the said brokerage firm, any shares, cash or other property shall be distributable at any time under the terms of said account. In the event that issuer or transfer agent is fully authorized to transfer, pay over and deliver the same to whosoever shall then be Trustee hereunder, and shall be under no liability to see to the proper application thereof. Until the brokerage firm or the issuer or transfer agent shall receive from some person interested in this trust, written notice of any death or other event upon which the right to receive may depend, the brokerage firm, issuer or transfer agent shall incur no liability for payments made in good faith to persons whose interests shall have been affected by such event. The brokerage firm, issuer or transfer agent shall be protected in acting upon any notice or other instrument or document believed by it to be genuine and to have been signed or presented by the proper party or parties.

5. We reserve unto ourselves the power and right to collect any interest or other income which may accrue from the trust property and, in our sole discretion as Trustees, either to accumulate such interest or income as an addition to the trust assets. being held hereunder or pay such interest or income to ourselves as individuals. We shall be exclusively entitled to all income accruing from the trust property during our lifetime, and no beneficiary named herein shall have any claim upon any such income and/or profits distributed to us.

6. We reserve unto ourselves the ~~... at any time during our life... with us, or both of the beneficiaries designated~~ hereunder shall revoke such designation, and in the former event, we reserve the right to designate a new beneficiary. Should we for any reason fail to designate such new beneficiary, this trust shall terminate upon the death of the survivor of us and the trust property shall revert to the estate of such survivor.

8. In the event of the physical or mental incapacity or death of one of us, the survivor shall continue as sole Trustee. In the event of the physical or mental incapacity or death of the survivor of us, or if we both shall die in a common accident, we hereby nominate and appoint as Successor Trustee hereunder whosoever shall at that time be beneficiary hereunder, unless such beneficiary shall not have attained the age of 21 years or is otherwise legally incapacitated, in which event we hereby nominate and appoint

(Name) __Henry P. Adams__, of

(Address) __125__ __Barnum Street__ __Milton__ __Connecticut__ __06605__
Number Street City State Zip

to be Successor Trustee.

9. This Declaration of Trust shall extend to and be binding upon the heirs, executors, administrators and assigns of the undersigned and upon the Successors to the Trustees.

10. We as Trustees and our Successor Trustee shall serve without bond.

11. This Declaration of Trust shall be construed and enforced in accordance with the laws of the State of __Connecticut__

Declaration of Trust

WHEREAS, WE, _____ and _____, of the

City/Town of _____, County of _____, State of _____

are the joint owners of a brokerage account with the firm of _____,

located in the City/Town of _____, County of _____ and State of

_____;

NOW, THEREFORE, KNOW ALL MEN BY THESE PRESENTS, that we do hereby acknowledge and declare that we hold and will hold said brokerage account and all our right, title and interest in and to said account and all cash and securities held in such account IN TRUST

    1. For the use and benefit of:

(Name) _____, of

(Address) _____

              Number   *Street*   *City*   *State*   *Zip*

or, if he or she be not surviving, for the use and benefit of:

(Name) _____, of

(Address) _____

              Number   *Street*   *City*   *State*   *Zip*

If because of our physical or mental incapacity certified in writing by a physician, the Successor Trustee hereinafter named shall assume active administration of this trust during our lifetime, such Successor Trustee shall be fully authorized to pay to us or disburse on our behalf such sums from income or principal as appear necessary or desirable for our comfort or welfare. Upon the death of the survivor of us, unless both beneficiaries shall predecease us or unless we all shall die as a result of a common accident or disaster, our Successor Trustee is hereby directed forthwith to transfer said account and all right, title and interest in and to said account unto the beneficiary absolutely and thereby terminate this trust; provided, however, that if the beneficiary hereunder shall not have attained the age of 21 years, the Successor Trustee shall hold the trust assets in continuing trust until such beneficiary shall have attained the age of 21 years. During such period of continuing trust the Successor Trustee, in his absolute discretion, may retain the specific brokerage account herein described if he believes it to be in the best interests of the beneficiary so to do, or he may terminate it, investing and reinvesting the proceeds as he may deem appropriate. Prior to the date upon which such beneficiary attains the age of 21 years, the Successor Trustee may apply or expend any or all of the income or principal directly for the maintenance, education and support of the beneficiary without the intervention of any guardian and without application to any court. Such payments of income or principal may be made to the parents of such beneficiary or to the person with whom such beneficiary is living without any liability upon the Successor Trustee to see to the application thereof. If such beneficiary survives us but dies before attaining the age of 21 years, at his or her death the Successor Trustee shall transfer, pay over and deliver the trust property to such beneficiary's personal representative, absolutely.

    2. The beneficiary hereunder shall be liable for his proportionate share of any taxes levied upon the total taxable estate of the survivor of us by reason of the death of such survivor.

    3. All interests of a beneficiary hereunder shall be inalienable and free from anticipation, assignment, attachment, pledge or control by creditors or a present or former spouse of such beneficiary in any proceedings at law or in equity.

    4. This trust is created upon the express understanding that neither the brokerage firm at which the account is maintained nor the issuer or transfer agent of the securities held hereunder shall be under any liability whatsoever to see to its proper administration, and that upon transfer of the right, title and interest in and to said account by any Trustee hereunder, said brokerage firm, issuer or transfer agent shall conclusively treat the transferee as the sole owner of said account. In the event that any shares, cash or other property shall be distributable at any time under the terms of said securities, the said brokerage firm, issuer or transfer agent is fully authorized to transfer, pay over and deliver the same to whosoever shall then be Trustee hereunder, and shall be under no liability to see to the proper application thereof. Until the brokerage firm or the issuer or transfer agent shall receive from some person interested in this trust, written notice of any death or other event upon which the right to receive may depend, the brokerage firm, issuer or transfer agent shall incur no liability for payments made in good faith to persons whose interests shall have been affected by such event. The brokerage firm, issuer or transfer agent shall be protected in acting upon any notice or other instrument or document believed by it to be genuine and to have been signed or presented by the proper party or parties.

5. We reserve unto ourselves the power and right to collect any interest or other income which may accrue from the trust property and, in our sole discretion as Trustees, either to accumulate such interest or income as an addition to the trust assets being held hereunder or pay such interest or income to ourselves as individuals. We shall be exclusively entitled to all income accruing from the trust property during our lifetime, and no beneficiary named herein shall have any claim upon any such income and/or profits distributed to us.

6. We reserve unto ourselves the power and right at any time during our lifetime to amend or revoke in whole or in part the trust hereby created without the necessity of obtaining the consent of the beneficiaries and without giving notice to the beneficiaries. The sale by us of the whole or any part of the brokerage account held hereunder shall constitute as to such whole or part a revocation of this trust.

7. The death during our lifetime, or in a common accident or disaster with us, of both of the beneficiaries designated hereunder shall revoke such designation, and in the former event, we reserve the right to designate a new beneficiary. Should we for any reason fail to designate such new beneficiary, this trust shall terminate upon the death of the survivor of us and the trust property shall revert to the estate of such survivor.

8. In the event of the physical or mental incapacity or death of one of us, the survivor shall continue as sole Trustee. In the event of the physical or mental incapacity or death of the survivor of us, or if we both shall die in a common accident, we hereby nominate and appoint as Successor Trustee hereunder whosoever shall at that time be beneficiary hereunder, unless such beneficiary shall not have attained the age of 21 years or is otherwise legally incapacitated, in which event we hereby nominate and appoint

(Name) _____ , of

(Address) _____
　　　　　　　　Number　　　　　　Street　　　　　　　City　　　　　　　State　　　　　Zip

to be Successor Trustee.

9. This Declaration of Trust shall extend to and be binding upon the heirs, executors, administrators and assigns of the undersigned and upon the Successors to the Trustees.

10. We as Trustees and our Successor Trustee shall serve without bond.

11. This Declaration of Trust shall be construed and enforced in accordance with the laws of the State

of _____ .

IN WITNESS WHEREOF, we have hereunto set our hands and seals this _____

day of _____ , 19_____ .

(First Settlor sign here) _____ L.S.

(Second Settlor sign here) _____ L.S.

I, the undersigned legal spouse of one of the above Settlors, hereby waive all community property rights which I may have in the hereinabove-described account and give my assent to the provisions of the trust and to the inclusion in it of the said account.

(Spouse sign here) _____ L.S.

Witness: (1) _____　　　Witness: (2) _____

STATE OF _____　　City

COUNTY OF _____　　or
　　　　　　　　　　　　　　　　　　　　　　　Town _____

On the _____ day of _____ , 19_____ , personally appeared

_____ and _____

known to me to be the individuals who executed the foregoing instrument, and acknowledged the same to be their free act and deed, before me.

(Notary Seal)

_____
　　　　　　　　　　　　　　　Notary Public

CHAPTER 10

DECLARATION OF TRUST
For Naming
TWO OR MORE BENEFICIARIES, SHARING EQUALLY,
To Receive
A BROKERAGE ACCOUNT HELD IN JOINT NAMES

INSTRUCTIONS:

On the following pages will be found a declaration of trust (DT-115-J) suitable for use in connection with the establishment of an inter vivos trust covering a brokerage account held in joint names where it is desired to name two or more persons, sharing equally, to receive the account upon the death of the survivor of the two joint owners.

Cross out *"city"* or *"town,"* leaving the appropriate designation of your community.

Enter the name of the firm where the brokerage account is maintained in the space provided near the top.

In Paragraph 1, indicate the *number of persons* you are naming (to discourage unauthorized additions to the list) and then insert their names. The one whose name appears *first* will be the Successor Trustee responsible for seeing to the distribution of the trust property.

Note that the instrument specifies that the named beneficiaries are to receive *"in equal shares, or the survivor of them/per stirpes."* Now, think carefully: If you have named three persons with the understanding that if one of them predeceases you, *his* children will take *his* share, cross out *"or the survivor of them"* and *initial it.* If that is *not* what you want—if, for example, you prefer that the share of the deceased person be divided between the two surviving persons, cross out *"per stirpes"* and *initial it.* Remember, you <u>must</u> cross out *"or the survivor of them"* or *"per stirpes"*—one or the other.

Note that Paragraph 8 designates as Successor Trustee *"the beneficiary named first above,"* which means that in most cases you don't need to fill anything in there. However, if there is any possibility of a beneficiary who has not attained the age of 21 years receiving the brokerage account, make certain that you name an adult in this paragraph who can act as trustee for such beneficiary. Avoid naming as trustee a person not likely to survive until the beneficiary has attained age 21.

When completed in the manner shown on the reverse side hereof, make several photocopies of the declaration of trust. Place the original in safekeeping and file one copy with the investment firm with whom the brokerage account is maintained. Ask the firm to give you a written confirmation that in the event of your death it will recognize the trust and promptly turn the securities over to the Successor Trustee whom you have named. Insist that henceforth all communications from the firm be sent to *"(your name) and (your co-owner's name), Trustees u/d/t dated _____."*

Important: Read carefully Note B on page 38, which applies to this declaration of trust.

WHEREVER THE INSTRUCTION "INITIAL IT" APPEARS ABOVE,
IT MEANS THAT *BOTH* CO-OWNERS SHOULD INITIAL IT.

DT-115-J

Declaration of Trust

WHEREAS, We **John J. Brown** and **Elizabeth A. Brown**, of the Town of **Milton**, County of **Fairfax**, State of **Connecticut**, are the joint owners of a brokerage account with the firm of **Roger Edwards & Company**, County of **Fairfax** and State of located in the Town of **Milton**;

NOW, THEREFORE, KNOW ALL MEN BY THESE PRESENTS, that we do hereby acknowledge and declare that we hold, **Connecticut** and will hold said brokerage account and all our right, title and interest in and to said account and all cash and securities held in such account IN TRUST

1. For the use and benefit of the following **three (3)** persons, in equal shares, stirpes:

> Thomas B. Brown - our brother
> Helen M. Brown - our sister
> Charles M. Brown - our brother

If because of our physical or mental incapacity certified in writing by a physician, the Successor Trustee hereinafter named shall assume active administration of this trust during our lifetime, such Successor Trustee shall be fully authorized to pay to us or disburse in our behalf such sums from income or principal as appear necessary or desirable for our comfort or welfare. Upon the death of the survivor of us, unless the beneficiaries shall all predecease us or unless we all shall die as a result of a common accident, our Successor Trustee is hereby directed forthwith to transfer said brokerage account and all right, title and interest in and to said account unto the beneficiaries absolutely and thereby terminate this trust; provided, however, that if any beneficiary hereunder shall not have attained the age of 21 years, the Successor Trustee shall hold such beneficiary's share of the trust assets in continuing trust until such beneficiary shall have attained the age of 21 years. During such period of continuing trust the Successor Trustee, in his absolute discretion, may retain the specific brokerage account herein described if he believes it to be in the best interests of the beneficiary so to do, or he may terminate it, investing and reinvesting the proceeds as he may deem appropriate. Prior to the date upon which such beneficiary attains the age of 21 years, the Successor Trustee may apply or expend any or all of the income or principal directly for the maintenance, education and support of such beneficiary without the intervention of any guardian and without application to any court. Such payments of income or principal may be made to the parents of such beneficiary or to the person with whom the beneficiary is living without any liability upon the Successor Trustee to see to the application thereof. If such beneficiary survives us but dies before attaining the age of 21 years, at his or her death the Successor Trustee shall transfer, pay over and deliver the trust property being held for such beneficiary to the beneficiary's personal representative, absolutely.

2. Each beneficiary hereunder shall be liable for his proportionate share of any taxes levied upon the total taxable estate of the survivor of us by reason of the death of such survivor.

3. All interests of a beneficiary or a present or former spouse of such beneficiary in any proceedings at law or in equity. control by creditors or the issuer or transfer agent of the securities held thereunder shall be inalienable and free from anticipation, assignment, attachment, pledge or

4. This trust is created upon the express understanding that neither the brokerage firm at which the account is maintained administration, and that upon the transfer of the right, title and interest in and to the account by any Trustee hereunder, said brokerage firm, issuer or transfer agent shall conclusively treat the transferee as the sole owner of said account. In the event that any shares, cash or other property shall be distributable at any time under the terms of said securities, the said brokerage firm, issuer or transfer agent is fully authorized to transfer, pay over and deliver the same to whosoever shall then be Trustee hereunder, and shall be under no liability to see to the proper application thereof. Until the brokerage firm or the issuer or right to receive may depend, the brokerage firm, issuer or transfer agent shall incur no liability for payments made in good faith transfer agent shall receive from some person interested in this trust, written notice of any death or other event upon which the in acting upon any notice or other instrument or document believed by it to be genuine and to have been signed or presented by the proper party or parties.

5. We reserve unto ourselves the power and right to collect any interest or other income which may accrue from the trust property and, in our sole discretion as Trustees, either to accumulate such interest or income as an addition to the trust assets being held hereunder or pay such interest or income to ourselves as individuals. We shall be exclusively entitled to all income accruing from the trust property during our lifetime, and no beneficiary named herein shall have any claim upon any such income and/or profits distributed to us.

shall revoke such designation, and in the former event, we reserve the right to designate a new beneficiary. Should we for any reason fail to designate such new beneficiary, this trust shall terminate upon the death of the survivor of us and the trust property shall revert to the estate of such survivor.

8. In the event of the physical or mental incapacity or death of the survivor of us, or if we both shall die in a common accident, we hereby nominate and appoint as Successor Trustee hereunder the beneficiary named first above, unless such beneficiary shall not have attained the age of 21 years or is otherwise legally incapacitated, in which event we hereby nominate and appoint the beneficiary named second above, unless such beneficiary shall not have attained the age of 21 years or is otherwise legally incapacitated, in which event we hereby nominate and appoint

(Name) **Henry P. Adams**
(Address) **125 Barnum Street** **Milton** **Connecticut** **06605**
Number Street City State Zip

as such Successor Trustee.

9. This Declaration of Trust shall extend to and be binding upon the heirs, executors, administrators and assigns of the undersigned and upon the Successors to the Trustees.

10. We as Trustees and our Successor Trustee shall serve without bond.

11. This Declaration of Trust shall be construed and enforced in accordance with the laws of the State of **Connecticut**

Declaration of Trust

WHEREAS, WE, _____ and _____, of the

City/Town of _____, County of _____, State of _____,

are the joint owners of a brokerage account with the firm of _____,

located in the City/Town of _____, County of _____ and State

of _____;

NOW, THEREFORE, KNOW ALL MEN BY THESE PRESENTS, that we do hereby acknowledge and declare that we hold and will hold said brokerage account and all our right, title and interest in and to said account and all cash and securities held in such account IN TRUST

1. For the use and benefit of the following _____ persons, in equal shares, or the survivor of them/per stirpes:

If because of our physical or mental incapacity certified in writing by a physician, the Successor Trustee hereinafter named shall assume active administration of this trust during our lifetime, such Successor Trustee shall be fully authorized to pay to us or disburse in our behalf such sums from income or principal as appear necessary or desirable for our comfort or welfare. Upon the death of the survivor of us, unless the beneficiaries shall all predecease us or unless we all shall die as a result of a common accident, our Successor Trustee is hereby directed forthwith to transfer said brokerage account and all right, title and interest in and to said account unto the beneficiaries absolutely and thereby terminate this trust; provided, however, that if any beneficiary hereunder shall not have attained the age of 21 years, the Successor Trustee shall hold such beneficiary's share of the trust assets in continuing trust until such beneficiary shall have attained the age of 21 years. During such period of continuing trust the Successor Trustee, in his absolute discretion, may retain the specific brokerage account herein described if he believes it to be in the best interests of the beneficiary so to do, or he may terminate it, investing and reinvesting the proceeds as he may deem appropriate. Prior to the date upon which such beneficiary attains the age of 21 years, the Successor Trustee may apply or expend any or all of the income or principal directly for the maintenance, education and support of such beneficiary without the intervention of any guardian and without application to any court. Such payments of income or principal may be made to the parents of such beneficiary or to the person with whom the beneficiary is living without any liability upon the Successor Trustee to see to the application thereof. If such beneficiary survives us but dies before attaining the age of 21 years, at his or her death the Successor Trustee shall transfer, pay over and deliver the trust property being held for such beneficiary to the beneficiary's personal representative, absolutely.

2. Each beneficiary hereunder shall be liable for his proportionate share of any taxes levied upon the total taxable estate of the survivor of us by reason of the death of such survivor.

3. All interests of a beneficiary hereunder shall be inalienable and free from anticipation, assignment, attachment, pledge or control by creditors or a present or former spouse of such beneficiary in any proceedings at law or in equity.

4. This trust is created upon the express understanding that neither the brokerage firm at which the account is maintained nor the issuer or transfer agent of the securities held hereunder shall be under any liability whatsoever to see to its proper administration, and that upon the transfer of the right, title and interest in and to the account by any Trustee hereunder, said brokerage firm, issuer or transfer agent shall conclusively treat the transferee as the sole owner of said account. In the event that any shares, cash or other property shall be distributable at any time under the terms of said securities, the said brokerage firm, issuer or transfer agent is fully authorized to transfer, pay over and deliver the same to whosoever shall then be Trustee hereunder, and shall be under no liability to see to the proper application thereof. Until the brokerage firm or the issuer or transfer agent shall receive from some person interested in this trust, written notice of any death or other event upon which the right to receive may depend, the brokerage firm, issuer or transfer agent shall incur no liability for payments made in good faith to persons whose interests shall have been affected by such event. The brokerage firm, issuer or transfer agent shall be protected in acting upon any notice or other instrument or document believed by it to be genuine and to have been signed or presented by the proper party or parties.

5. We reserve unto ourselves the power and right to collect any interest or other income which may accrue from the trust property and, in our sole discretion as Trustees, either to accumulate such interest or income as an addition to the trust assets being held hereunder or pay such interest or income to ourselves as individuals. We shall be exclusively entitled to all income accruing from the trust property during our lifetime, and no beneficiary named herein shall have any claim upon any such income and/or profits distributed to us.

6. We reserve unto ourselves the power and right at any time during our lifetime to amend or revoke in whole or in part the trust hereby created without the necessity of obtaining the consent of the beneficiaries and without giving notice to the beneficiaries. The sale by us of the whole or any part of the brokerage account held hereunder shall constitute as to such whole or part a revocation of this trust.

7. The death during our lifetime, or in a common accident or disaster with us, of all of the beneficiaries designated hereunder shall revoke such designation, and in the former event, we reserve the right to designate a new beneficiary. Should we for any reason fail to designate such new beneficiary, this trust shall terminate upon the death of the survivor of us and the trust property shall revert to the estate of such survivor.

8. In the event of the physical or mental incapacity or death of one of us, the survivor shall continue as sole Trustee. In the event of the physical or mental incapacity or death of the survivor of us, or if we both shall die in a common accident, we hereby nominate and appoint as Successor Trustee hereunder the beneficiary named first above, unless such beneficiary shall not have attained the age of 21 years or is otherwise legally incapacitated, in which event we hereby nominate and appoint the beneficiary named second above, unless such beneficiary shall not have attained the age of 21 years or is otherwise legally incapacitated, in which event we hereby nominate and appoint

(Name) _____ , of

(Address) _____

          Number   *Street*   *City*   *State*   *Zip*

to be Successor Trustee.

9. This Declaration of Trust shall extend to and be binding upon the heirs, executors, administrators and assigns of the undersigned and upon the Successors to the Trustees.

10. We as Trustees and our Successor Trustee shall serve without bond.

11. This Declaration of Trust shall be construed and enforced in accordance with the laws of the State

of _____ .

IN WITNESS WHEREOF, we have hereunto set our hands and seals this _____

day of _____ , 19_____ .

          (First Settlor sign here) _____ L.S.

          (Second Settlor sign here) _____ L.S.

I, the undersigned legal spouse of one of the above Settlors, hereby waive all community property rights which I may have in the hereinabove-described account and give my assent to the provisions of the trust and to the inclusion in it of the said account.

          (Spouse sign here) _____ L.S.

Witness: (1) _____   Witness: (2) _____

STATE OF _____   City

COUNTY OF _____   or
Town _____

On the _____ day of _____ , 19_____ , personally appeared

_____ and _____

known to me to be the individuals who executed the foregoing instrument, and acknowledged the same to be their free act and deed, before me.

_____

(Notary Seal)   *Notary Public*

CHAPTER 11

Avoiding Probate of
a Safe Deposit Box

In an earlier chapter we detailed some of the problems which can arise with safe deposit boxes upon the death of the owner, and noted that such problems were not necessarily eliminated by having the box in joint names. Such boxes are frequently blocked if the bank learns of the death of a joint owner who is the family breadwinner.

It was explained that one solution is to have separate "his" and "her" boxes, into which each puts the spouse's assets and important papers such as burial instructions, will, life insurance policies, and other documents which are likely to be needed immediately.

The disadvantage of this arrangement, of course, is that both boxes are tied up if the parties die in a common accident or disaster, a very real possibility in these days of increasing travel to far places.

The solution is a simple one: Put the safe deposit box in a trust similar to those you have established to cover your other assets.

It is important that you understand that giving someone ready access to a safe deposit box does not mean that such person is automatically able to obtain use and control of the contents. If included in the contents are deeds to real estate held in your name, for example, or securities registered in your name, the person whom you have named to receive the contents of the box can legally transfer title to such assets to himself only if you have covered them with one or another of the declarations of trust in this book and named him as beneficiary. The beneficiary whom you have named to receive the box and its contents *can* assume use and control of such of the assets as are *not* registered in your name (bearer bonds, cash, jewelry, rare coins or stamps, etc.).

Needless to say, the ready access thus assured should never be regarded or used as a means of evading the payment of estate taxes. The beneficiary has both a moral and a legal obligation to see to it that all of the assets found in the box are taken into account in computing any taxes for which the owner's estate may be liable by reason of the owner's death.

Declarations of trust designed for this purpose will be found on the pages immediately following. Some are intended for use with boxes held in one name, others are suitable for jointly held safe deposit boxes.

CHAPTER 11

DECLARATION OF TRUST

For Naming

ONE BENEFICIARY

To Receive

A SAFE DEPOSIT BOX HELD IN ONE NAME

INSTRUCTIONS:

On the following pages will be found a declaration of trust (DT-117) suitable for use in connection with the establishment of an inter vivos trust covering a safe deposit box held in one name only, where it is desired to name some one person to receive the box and its contents upon the death of the owner.

Cross out *"city"* or *"town,"* leaving the appropriate designation of your community. Next, enter the name of the bank where the safe deposit box is maintained in the space provided near the top, and the name of the beneficiary in the appropriate place in Paragraph 1.

Note that Paragraph 8 designates as Successor Trustee *"whosoever shall at that time be beneficiary hereunder,"* which means that in most cases you don't need to fill anything in there. However, if there is any possibility of a beneficiary who has not attained the age of 21 years receiving the safe deposit box, make certain that you name an adult in this paragraph who can act as trustee for such beneficiary. Avoid naming as trustee a person not likely to survive until the beneficiary has attained age 21.

When completed in the manner shown on the reverse side hereof, make several photocopies for reference purposes. Hold the original in safekeeping and offer a copy to the bank where the safe deposit box is maintained. Instruct them to identify the box holder in this manner: *"(your name), Trustee u/d/t dated _____."*

Important: Read carefully Note B on page 38, which applics to this declaration of trust.

DT-117

Declaration of Trust

, of the

WHEREAS, I, **John J. Brown** , County of **Fairfax** , State of **Connecticut**

Town of **Milton** **Milton Savings Bank** , State of **Connecticut**
(Name of Bank)

am the holder of a safe deposit box in the

located in the Town of **Milton** , of

NOW, THEREFORE. KNOW ALL MEN BY THESE PRESENTS, that I do hereby acknowledge and declare that I hold and will hold said safe deposit box and all my right. title and interest in and to said safe deposit box and its contents IN TRUST

1. For the use and benefit of:

Elizabeth A. Brown — my wife **Milton** **Connecticut** **06605**
(Name) City State Zip

(Address) **525** **Main Street**
Number Street

If because of my physical or mental incapacity certified in writing by a physician. the Successor Trustee hereinafter named shall assume active administration of this trust during my lifetime, such Successor Trustee shall be fully authorized to pay to me or disburse on my behalf such sums from income or principal generated by or constituting the contents of said box as appear necessary or desirable for my comfort or welfare. Upon my death, unless the beneficiary shall predecease me or unless we both shall die as a result of a common accident or disaster. my Successor Trustee is hereby directed forthwith to transfer said safe deposit box and all right. title and interest in and to said box and its contents unto the beneficiary absolutely and thereby terminate this trust; provided, however, that if the beneficiary hereunder shall not have attained the age of 21 years, the Successor Trustee shall hold the trust assets in continuing trust until such beneficiary shall have attained the age of 21 years.

During such period of continuing trust the Successor Trustee, in his absolute discretion, may retain the specific safe deposit box and contents herein described if he believes it to be in the best interests of the beneficiary so to do, or he may terminate the box such beneficiary attains the age of 21 years, the Successor Trustee may apply or expend any or all of the contents of the box or, if such contents have been disposed of, any or all of the income or principal derived from such disposition, directly for the maintenance, education and support of the beneficiary without the intervention of any guardian and without application to any court. Such payments of income or principal may be made to the parents of such beneficiary or to the person with whom the beneficiary is living without any liability upon the Successor Trustee to see to the application thereof. If such beneficiary survives me but dies before attaining the age of 21 years, at his or her death the Successor Trustee shall transfer, pay over and deliver the trust property to such beneficiary's personal representative, absolutely.

If among the contents of the safe deposit box held hereunder there be any asset identifiable as having been covered by a declaration of trust in connection with which a beneficiary other than the one named in this trust has been designated, the Successor Trustee of this trust shall assert no claim to such asset but shall promptly deliver up the same to the individual named as Successor Trustee of such other trust.

2. The beneficiary hereunder shall be liable for his proportionate share of any taxes levied upon the Settlor's total taxable estate by reason of the Settlor's death.

3. All interests of a beneficiary hereunder shall be inalienable and free from anticipation, assignment, attachment, pledge or control by creditors or a present or former spouse of such beneficiary in any proceedings at law or in equity.

4. This trust is created with the express understanding that the bank at which the safe deposit box is maintained shall be under no liability whatsoever to see to its proper administration. On the contrary, upon the presentation by the Successor

. . . . . death . . . . . income, or in a common accident or disaster . . . . . die, or the beneficiary designated hereunder shall revoke such designation, and in the former event, I reserve the right to designate a new beneficiary. Should I for any reason fail to designate such new beneficiary, this trust shall terminate upon my death, I hereby nominate and appoint as Successor Trustee

8. In the event of my physical or mental incapacity or my death, I hereby nominate and appoint hereunder whosoever shall at that time be beneficiary hereunder, unless such beneficiary shall not have attained the age of 21 years or is otherwise legally incapacitated, in which event I hereby nominate and appoint

Henry P. Adams **Milton** **Connecticut** **06605**
(Name) City State Zip

(Address) **125** **Barnum** **Street**
Number Street

to be Successor Trustee.

This Declaration of Trust shall extend to and be binding upon the heirs, executors, administrators and assigns of the undersigned and upon the Successors to the Trustee.

9. This Declaration of Trust shall extend to and be binding upon the heirs, executors, administrators and assigns of the undersigned and upon the Successors to the Trustee.

10. The Trustee and his successors shall serve without bond.

11. This Declaration of Trust shall be construed and enforced in accordance with the laws of the State

of **Connecticut**

Declaration of Trust

WHEREAS, I, ———————————————————————————————————, of the

City/Town of ———————————————, County of —————————, State of —————————,

am the holder of a safe deposit box in the ———————————————————————,
(Name of Bank)

located in the City/Town of ———————————————, State of ——————————;

NOW, THEREFORE, KNOW ALL MEN BY THESE PRESENTS, that I do hereby acknowledge and declare that I hold and will hold said safe deposit box and all my right, title and interest in and to said safe deposit box and its contents IN TRUST

1. For the use and benefit of:

(Name) ———————————————————————————————————, of

(Address) ———————————————————————————————————
Number   Street   City   State   Zip

If because of my physical or mental incapacity certified in writing by a physician, the Successor Trustee hereinafter named shall assume active administration of this trust during my lifetime, such Successor Trustee shall be fully authorized to pay to me or disburse on my behalf such sums from income or principal generated by or constituting the contents of said box as appear necessary or desirable for my comfort or welfare. Upon my death, unless the beneficiary shall predecease me or unless we both shall die as a result of a common accident or disaster, my Successor Trustee is hereby directed forthwith to transfer said safe deposit box and all right, title and interest in and to said box and its contents unto the beneficiary absolutely and thereby terminate this trust; provided, however, that if the beneficiary hereunder shall not have attained the age of 21 years, the Successor Trustee shall hold the trust assets in continuing trust until such beneficiary shall have attained the age of 21 years. During such period of continuing trust the Successor Trustee, in his absolute discretion, may retain the specific safe deposit box and contents herein described if he believes it to be in the best interests of the beneficiary so to do, or he may terminate the box and dispose of its contents, investing and reinvesting the proceeds as he may deem appropriate. Prior to the date upon which such beneficiary attains the age of 21 years, the Successor Trustee may apply or expend any or all of the contents of the box or, if such contents have been disposed of, any or all of the income or principal derived from such disposition, directly for the maintenance, education and support of the beneficiary without the intervention of any guardian and without application to any court. Such payments of income or principal may be made to the parents of such beneficiary or to the person with whom the beneficiary is living without any liability upon the Successor Trustee to see to the application thereof. If such beneficiary survives me but dies before attaining the age of 21 years, at his or her death the Successor Trustee shall transfer, pay over and deliver the trust property to such beneficiary's personal representative, absolutely.

If among the contents of the safe deposit box held hereunder there be any asset identifiable as having been covered by a declaration of trust in connection with which a beneficiary other than the one named in this trust has been designated, the Successor Trustee of this trust shall assert no claim to such asset but shall promptly deliver up the same to the individual named as Successor Trustee of such other trust.

2. The beneficiary hereunder shall be liable for his proportionate share of any taxes levied upon the Settlor's total taxable estate by reason of the Settlor's death.

3. All interests of a beneficiary hereunder shall be inalienable and free from anticipation, assignment, attachment, pledge or control by creditors or a present or former spouse of such beneficiary in any proceedings at law or in equity.

4. This trust is created with the express understanding that the bank at which the safe deposit box is maintained shall be under no liability whatsoever to see to its proper administration. On the contrary, upon the presentation by the Successor Trustee to the bank of proper evidence of my death, the bank shall thereafter treat such Successor Trustee as the one solely entitled to the box and its contents. The bank shall be protected in acting upon any notice or other instrument or document believed by it to be genuine and to have been signed or presented by the proper party or parties.

5. I reserve unto myself the power and right at any time to remove all or any portion of the contents of the box, or to add to such contents.

6. I reserve unto myself the power and right at any time during my lifetime to amend or revoke in whole or in part the trust hereby created without the necessity of obtaining the consent of the beneficiary and without giving notice to the beneficiary. The withdrawal by me of the whole or any part of the contents of the safe deposit box held hereunder shall constitute as to such whole or part a revocation of this trust.

7. The death during my lifetime, or in a common accident or disaster with me, of the beneficiary designated hereunder shall revoke such designation, and in the former event, I reserve the right to designate a new beneficiary. Should I for any reason fail to designate such new beneficiary, this trust shall terminate upon my death and the trust property shall revert to my estate.

8. In the event of my physical or mental incapacity or my death, I hereby nominate and appoint as Successor Trustee hereunder whosoever shall at that time be beneficiary hereunder, unless such beneficiary shall not have attained the age of 21 years or is otherwise legally incapacitated, in which event I hereby nominate and appoint

(Name) _____ , of

(Address) _____
          Number   *Street*   *City*   *State*   *Zip*

to be Successor Trustee.

9. This Declaration of Trust shall extend to and be binding upon the heirs, executors, administrators and assigns of the undersigned and upon the Successors to the Trustee.

10. The Trustee and his successors shall serve without bond.

11. This Declaration of Trust shall be construed and enforced in accordance with the laws of the State

of _____ .

 IN WITNESS WHEREOF, I have hereunto set my hand and seal this _____

day of _____ , 19_____ .

          (Settlor sign here) _____ L.S.

I, the undersigned legal spouse of the above Settlor, hereby waive all community property rights which I may have in the contents of the hereinabove-described safe deposit box and give my assent to the provisions of the trust and to the inclusion in it of the said box and its contents.

          (Spouse sign here) _____ L.S.

Witness: (1) _____   Witness: (2) _____

STATE OF _____ ⎫   City
                 or
COUNTY OF _____ ⎭   Town _____

 On the _____ day of _____ , 19_____ , personally appeared

_____

known to me to be the individual(s) who executed the foregoing instrument, and acknowledged the same to be _____ free act and deed, before me.

_____

(Notary Seal)   *Notary Public*

CHAPTER 11

DECLARATION OF TRUST

For Naming

ONE PRIMARY BENEFICIARY

And

ONE CONTINGENT BENEFICIARY

To Receive

A SAFE DEPOSIT BOX HELD IN ONE NAME

INSTRUCTIONS:

On the following pages will be found a declaration of trust (DT-118) suitable for use in connection with the establishment of an inter vivos trust covering a safe deposit box held in one name only, where it is desired to name some *one* person as primary beneficiary, with some *one* other person as contingent beneficiary to receive the box and its contents if the primary beneficiary be not surviving upon the death of the owner.

Cross out *"city"* or *"town,"* leaving the appropriate designation of your community. Next, enter the name of the bank where the safe deposit box is maintained in the space provided near the top, and the names of the beneficiaries in the appropriate place in Paragraph 1.

Note that Paragraph 8 designates as Successor Trustee *"whosoever shall at that time be beneficiary hereunder,"* which means that in most cases you don't need to fill anything in there. However, if there is any possibility of a beneficiary who has not attained the age of 21 years receiving the safe deposit box, make certain that you name an adult in this paragraph who can act as trustee for such beneficiary. Avoid naming as trustee a person not likely to survive until the beneficiary has attained age 21.

When completed in the manner shown on the reverse side hereof, make several photocopies for reference purposes. Hold the original in safekeeping and offer a copy to the bank where the safe deposit box is maintained. Instruct them to identify the box holder in this manner: *"(your name), Trustee u/d/t dated _____."*

Important: Read carefully Note B on page 38, which applies to this declaration of trust.

DT-118

Declaration of Trust

DACEY TRUST

WHEREAS, I, __John J. Brown__, County of __Fairfax__, State of __Connecticut__, of the Town of __Milton__ am the holder of a safe deposit box in the __Milton Savings Bank__ (Name of Bank), State of __Connecticut__ located in the Town of __Milton__

NOW, THEREFORE, KNOW ALL MEN BY THESE PRESENTS, that I do hereby acknowledge and declare that I hold and will hold said safe deposit box and all my right, title and interest in and to said safe deposit box and its contents IN TRUST

1. For the use and benefit of:

(Name) __Elizabeth A. Brown – my wife__ __Milton__ City __Connecticut__ State __06605__ Zip

(Address) __525 Main Street__ Number Street

or, if such beneficiary be not surviving, for the use and benefit of:

(Name) __Jill A. Brown – my daughter__ __Milton__ City __Connecticut__ State __06605__ Zip

(Address) __525 Main Street__ Number Street

If because of my physical or mental incapacity certified in writing by a physician, the Successor Trustee hereinafter named shall assume active administration of this trust during my lifetime, such Successor Trustee shall be fully authorized to pay to me or disburse on my behalf such sums from income or principal generated by or constituting the contents of said box as appear necessary or desirable for my comfort or welfare. Upon my death, unless both beneficiaries shall predecease me or unless we all shall die as a result of a common accident or disaster, my Successor Trustee is hereby directed forthwith to transfer said safe deposit box and all right, title and interest in and to said box and its contents unto the beneficiary absolutely and thereby terminate this trust; provided, however, that if the beneficiary hereunder shall not have attained the age of 21 years, the Successor Trustee shall hold the trust assets in continuing trust until such beneficiary shall have attained the age of 21 years. During such period of continuing trust the Successor Trustee, in his absolute discretion, may retain the specific safe deposit box and its contents herein described if he believes it to be in the best interests of the beneficiary so to do, or he may terminate the box and dispose of its contents, investing and reinvesting the proceeds as he may deem appropriate. Prior to the date upon which such beneficiary attains the age of 21 years, the Successor Trustee may apply or expend any or all of the income or principal derived from such disposition, directly for the maintenance, education and support of the beneficiary without the intervention of any guardian and without application to any court. Such payments of income or principal may be made to the parents of such beneficiary or to the person with whom the beneficiary is living without any liability upon the Successor Trustee to see to the application thereof. If such beneficiary survives me but dies before attaining the age of 21 years, at his or her death the Successor Trustee shall transfer, pay over and deliver the trust property being held for such beneficiary to such beneficiary's personal representative, absolutely.

If among the contents of the safe deposit box held hereunder there be any asset identifiable as having been covered by a declaration of trust in connection with which beneficiaries other than those named in this trust have been designated, the Successor Trustee of such other trust shall assert no claim to such asset but shall promptly deliver up the same to the individual named as Successor Trustee of such other trust.

2. The beneficiary hereunder shall be liable for his proportionate share of any taxes levied upon the Settlor's total taxable estate by reason of the Settlor's death.

3. All interests of a beneficiary hereunder shall be inalienable and free from anticipation, assignment, attachment, pledge or control by creditors or a present or former spouse of such beneficiary in any proceedings at law or in equity.

4. This trust is created with the express understanding that the bank at which the safe deposit box is maintained shall be under no liability whatsoever to see to its proper administration. On the contrary, upon the presentation by the Successor Trustee to the bank of proper evidence of my death, the bank shall thereafter treat such Successor Trustee as the one solely entitled to the box and its contents. The bank shall be protected in acting upon any notice or other instrument or document believed by it to be genuine and to have been signed or presented by the proper party or parties.

8. In the event of my physical or mental incapacity or my death, I hereby nominate and appoint as Successor Trustee hereunder whosoever shall at that time be beneficiary hereunder, unless such beneficiary shall not have attained the age of 21 years or is otherwise legally incapacitated, in which event I hereby nominate and appoint _____, of

(Name) __Henry P. Adams__ __Milton__ City __Connecticut__ State __06605__ Zip

(Address) __125 Barnum Street__ Number Street

to be Successor Trustee.

9. This Declaration of Trust shall extend to and be binding upon the heirs, executors, administrators and assigns of the undersigned and upon the Successors to the Trustee.

10. The Trustee and his successors shall serve without bond.

11. This Declaration of Trust shall be construed and enforced in accordance with the laws of the State of __Connecticut__

Declaration of Trust

WHEREAS, I, _____, of the

City/Town of _____, County of _____, State of _____;

am the holder of a safe deposit box in the _____,

(Name of Bank)

located in the City/Town of _____, State of _____;

NOW, THEREFORE, KNOW ALL MEN BY THESE PRESENTS, that I do hereby acknowledge and declare that I hold and will hold said safe deposit box and all my right, title and interest in and to said safe deposit box and its contents IN TRUST

1. For the use and benefit of:

(Name) _____, of

(Address) _____
         Number   Street   City   State   Zip

or, if such beneficiary be not surviving, for the use and benefit of:

(Name) _____, of

(Address) _____
         Number   Street   City   State   Zip

If because of my physical or mental incapacity certified in writing by a physician, the Successor Trustee hereinafter named shall assume active administration of this trust during my lifetime, such Successor Trustee shall be fully authorized to pay to me or disburse on my behalf such sums from income or principal generated by or constituting the contents of said box as appear necessary or desirable for my comfort or welfare. Upon my death, unless both beneficiaries shall predecease me or unless we all shall die as a result of a common accident or disaster, my Successor Trustee is hereby directed forthwith to transfer said safe deposit box and all right, title and interest in and to said box and its contents unto the beneficiary absolutely and thereby terminate this trust; provided, however, that if the beneficiary hereunder shall not have attained the age of 21 years, the Successor Trustee shall hold the trust assets in continuing trust until such beneficiary shall have attained the age of 21 years. During such period of continuing trust the Successor Trustee, in his absolute discretion, may retain the specific safe deposit box and its contents herein described if he believes it to be in the best interests of the beneficiary so to do, or he may terminate the box and dispose of its contents, investing and reinvesting the proceeds as he may deem appropriate. Prior to the date upon which such beneficiary attains the age of 21 years, the Successor Trustee may apply or expend any or all of the contents of the box or, if such contents have been disposed of, any or all of the income or principal derived from such disposition, directly for the maintenance, education and support of the beneficiary without the intervention of any guardian and without application to any court. Such payments of income or principal may be made to the parents of such beneficiary or to the person with whom the beneficiary is living without any liability upon the Successor Trustee to see to the application thereof. If such beneficiary survives me but dies before attaining the age of 21 years, at his or her death the Successor Trustee shall transfer, pay over and deliver the trust property being held for such beneficiary to such beneficiary's personal representative, absolutely.

If among the contents of the safe deposit box held hereunder there be any asset identifiable as having been covered by a declaration of trust in connection with which beneficiaries other than those named in this trust have been designated, the Successor Trustee of this trust shall assert no claim to such asset but shall promptly deliver up the same to the individual named as Successor Trustee of such other trust.

2. The beneficiary hereunder shall be liable for his proportionate share of any taxes levied upon the Settlor's total taxable estate by reason of the Settlor's death.

3. All interests of a beneficiary hereunder shall be inalienable and free from anticipation, assignment, attachment, pledge or control by creditors or a present or former spouse of such beneficiary in any proceedings at law or in equity.

4. This trust is created with the express understanding that the bank at which the safe deposit box is maintained shall be under no liability whatsoever to see to its proper administration. On the contrary, upon the presentation by the Successor Trustee to the bank of proper evidence of my death, the bank shall thereafter treat such Successor Trustee as the one solely entitled to the box and its contents. The bank shall be protected in acting upon any notice or other instrument or document believed by it to be genuine and to have been signed or presented by the proper party or parties.

5. I reserve unto myself the power and right at any time to remove all or any portion of the contents of the box, or to add to such contents.

6. I reserve unto myself the power and right at any time during my lifetime to amend or revoke in whole or in part the trust hereby created without the necessity of obtaining the consent of any beneficiary and without giving notice to any beneficiary. The withdrawal by me of the whole or any part of the contents of the safe deposit box held hereunder shall constitute as to such whole or part a revocation of this trust.

7. The death during my lifetime, or in a common accident or disaster with me, of both of the beneficiaries designated hereunder shall revoke such designation, and in the former event, I reserve the right to designate a new beneficiary. Should I for any reason fail to designate such new beneficiary, this trust shall terminate upon my death and the trust property shall revert to my estate.

8. In the event of my physical or mental incapacity or my death, I hereby nominate and appoint as Successor Trustee hereunder whosoever shall at that time be beneficiary hereunder, unless such beneficiary shall not have attained the age of 21 years or is otherwise legally incapacitated, in which event I hereby nominate and appoint

(Name) _____ , of

(Address) _____
         Number   *Street*   *City*   *State*   *Zip*

to be Successor Trustee.

9. This Declaration of Trust shall extend to and be binding upon the heirs, executors, administrators and assigns of the undersigned and upon the Successors to the Trustee.

10. The Trustee and his successors shall serve without bond.

11. This Declaration of Trust shall be construed and enforced in accordance with the laws of the State

of _____ .

IN WITNESS WHEREOF, I have hereunto set my hand and seal this _____

day of _____ , 19_____ .

        (Settlor sign here) _____ L.S.

I, the undersigned legal spouse of the above Settlor, hereby waive all community property rights which I may have in the contents of the hereinabove-described safe deposit box and give my assent to the provisions of the trust and to the inclusion in it of the said box and its contents.

        (Spouse sign here) _____ L.S.

Witness: (1) _____   Witness: (2) _____

STATE OF _____   City

COUNTY OF _____   or

                         Town _____

On the _____ day of _____ , 19_____ , personally appeared

_____

known to me to be the individual(s) who executed the foregoing instrument, and acknowledged the same to be _____ free act and deed, before me.

_____

(Notary Seal)   *Notary Public*

DECLARATION OF TRUST
For Naming
TWO OR MORE BENEFICIARIES, SHARING EQUALLY,
To Receive
A SAFE DEPOSIT BOX HELD IN ONE NAME

INSTRUCTIONS:

On the following pages will be found a declaration of trust (DT-119) suitable for use in connection with the establishment of an inter vivos trust covering a safe deposit box held in one name only, where it is desired to name two or more persons to share the box and its contents equally upon the death of the owner.

Cross out *"city"* or *"town,"* leaving the appropriate designation of your community. Next, enter the name of the bank where the safe deposit box is maintained in the space provided near the top.

In Paragraph 1, indicate the *number of persons* you are naming (to discourage unauthorized additions to the list) and then insert their names. The one whose name appears *first* will be the Successor Trustee responsible for seeing to the distribution of the trust property.

Note that the instrument specifies that the named beneficiaries are to receive *"in equal shares, or the survivor of them/per stirpes."* Now, think carefully: If you have named three persons with the understanding that if one of them predeceases you, *his* children will take *his* share, cross out *"or the survivor of them"* and *initial it.* If that is *not* what you want—if, for example, you prefer that the share of the deceased person be divided between the two surviving persons, cross out *"per stirpes"* and *initial it.* Remember, you <u>must</u> cross out either *"or the survivor of them"* or *"per stirpes"*—one or the other.

Note that Paragraph 8 designates as Successor Trustee *"the beneficiary named first above,"* which means that in most cases you don't need to fill anything in there. However, if there is any possibility of a beneficiary who has not attained the age of 21 years receiving the safe deposit box, make certain that you name an adult in this paragraph who can act as trustee for such beneficiary. Avoid naming as trustee a person not likely to survive until the beneficiary has attained age 21.

When completed in the manner shown on the reverse side hereof, make several photocopies for reference purposes. Hold the original in safekeeping and offer a copy to the bank where the safe deposit box is maintained. Instruct them to identify the box holder in this manner: *"(your name), Trustee u/d/t dated _____."*

Important: Read carefully Note B on page 38, which applies to this declaration of trust.

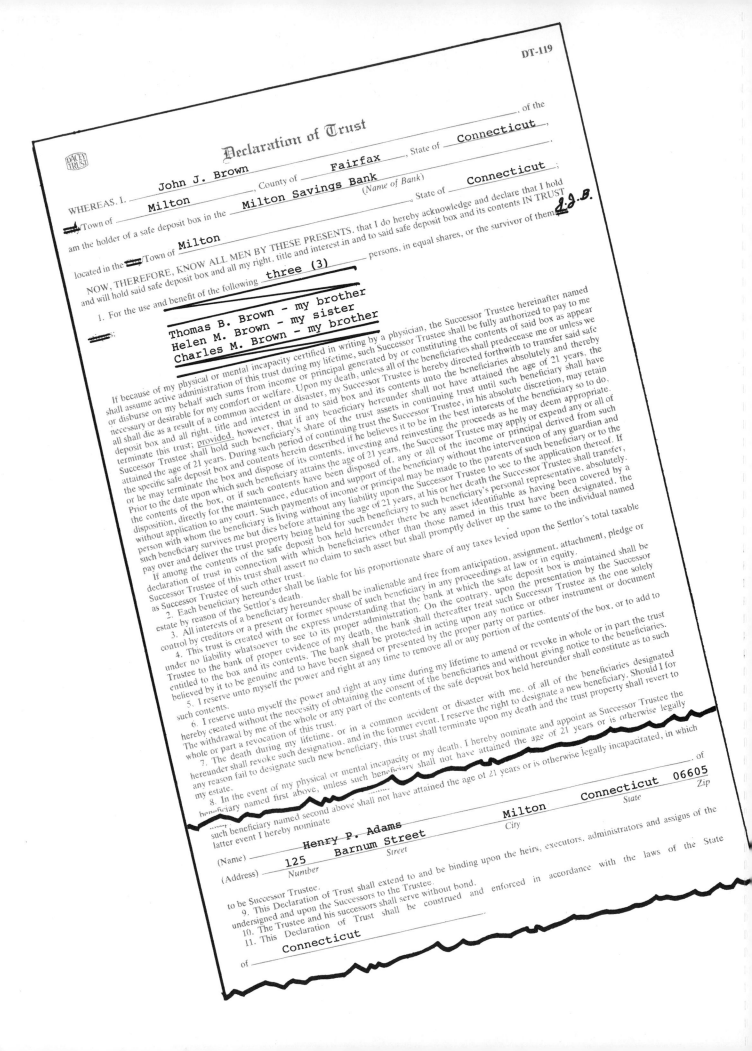

Declaration of Trust

DT-119

WHEREAS, I, __John J. Brown__ , County of __Fairfax__ , State of __Connecticut__ , of the ☒ Town of __Milton__ am the holder of a safe deposit box in the __Milton Savings Bank__ (Name of Bank), State of __Connecticut__ , located in the ☒ Town of __Milton__

NOW, THEREFORE, KNOW ALL MEN BY THESE PRESENTS, that I do hereby acknowledge and declare that I hold and will hold said safe deposit box and all my right, title and interest in and to said safe deposit box and its contents IN TRUST   _J.J.B._

1. For the use and benefit of the following __three (3)__ persons, in equal shares, or the survivor of them:

__Thomas B. Brown – my brother__
__Helen M. Brown – my sister__
__Charles M. Brown – my brother__

If because of my physical or mental incapacity certified in writing by a physician, the Successor Trustee hereinafter named shall assume active administration of this trust during my lifetime, such Successor Trustee shall be fully authorized to pay to me or disburse on my behalf such sums from income or principal generated by or constituting the contents of said box as appear necessary or desirable for my comfort or welfare. Upon my death, unless all of the beneficiaries shall predecease me or unless we all shall die as a result of a common accident or disaster, my Successor Trustee is hereby directed forthwith to transfer said safe deposit box and all right, title and interest in and to said box and its contents unto the beneficiaries absolutely and thereby terminate this trust; provided, however, that if any beneficiary hereunder shall not have attained the age of 21 years, the Successor Trustee shall hold such beneficiary's share of the trust assets in continuing trust until such beneficiary shall have attained the age of 21 years. During such period of continuing trust the Successor Trustee, in his absolute discretion, may retain the specific safe deposit box and contents herein described if he believes it to be in the best interests of the beneficiary so to do, or he may terminate the box and dispose of its contents, investing and reinvesting the proceeds as he may deem appropriate. Prior to the date upon which such beneficiary attains the age of 21 years, the Successor Trustee may apply or expend any or all of the contents of the box, or if such contents have been disposed of, any or all of the income or principal derived from such disposition, directly for the maintenance, education and support of the beneficiary without the intervention of any guardian and without application to any court. Such payments of income or principal may be made to the parents of such beneficiary or to the person with whom the beneficiary is living without any liability upon the Successor Trustee to see to the application thereof. If such beneficiary survives me but dies before attaining the age of 21 years, at his or her death the Successor Trustee shall transfer, pay over and deliver the trust property being held for such beneficiary to such beneficiary's personal representative, absolutely.

If among the contents of the safe deposit box held hereunder there be any asset identifiable as having been covered by a declaration of trust in connection with which beneficiaries other than those named in this trust have been designated, the Successor Trustee of this trust shall assert no claim to such asset but shall promptly deliver up the same to the individual named as Successor Trustee of such other trust.

2. Each beneficiary hereunder shall be liable for his proportionate share of any taxes levied upon the Settlor's total taxable estate by reason of the Settlor's death.

3. All interests of a beneficiary hereunder shall be inalienable and free from anticipation, assignment, attachment, pledge or control by creditors or a present or former spouse of such beneficiary in any proceedings at law or in equity.

4. This trust is created with the express understanding that the bank at which the safe deposit box is maintained shall be under no liability whatsoever to see to its proper administration. On the contrary, upon the presentation by the Successor Trustee to the bank of proper evidence of my death, the bank shall thereafter treat such Successor Trustee as the one solely entitled to the box and its contents. The bank shall be protected in acting upon any notice or other instrument or document believed by it to be genuine and to have been signed or presented by the proper party or parties.

5. I reserve unto myself the power and right at any time to remove all or any portion of the contents of the box, or to add to such contents.

6. I reserve unto myself the power and right at any time during my lifetime to amend or revoke in whole or in part the trust hereby created without the necessity of obtaining the consent of the beneficiaries and without giving notice to the beneficiaries. The withdrawal by me of the whole or any part of the contents of the safe deposit box held hereunder shall constitute as to such whole or part a revocation of this trust.

7. The death during my lifetime, or in a common accident or disaster with me, of all of the beneficiaries designated hereunder shall revoke such designation, and in the former event, I reserve the right to designate a new beneficiary. Should I for any reason fail to designate such new beneficiary, this trust shall terminate upon my death and the trust property shall revert to my estate.

8. In the event of my physical or mental incapacity or my death, I hereby nominate and appoint as Successor Trustee the beneficiary named first above, unless such beneficiary shall not have attained the age of 21 years or is otherwise legally incapacitated, in which such beneficiary named second above shall not have attained the age of 21 years or is otherwise legally incapacitated, in which latter event I hereby nominate __Henry P. Adams__ .... __Milton__ , __Connecticut__ __06605__
(Name)   City   State   Zip
(Address) __125__   __Barnum Street__
Number   Street

to be Successor Trustee.

9. This Declaration of Trust shall extend to and be binding upon the heirs, executors, administrators and assigns of the undersigned and upon the Successors to the Trustee.

10. The Trustee and his successors shall serve without bond.

11. This Declaration of Trust shall be construed and enforced in accordance with the laws of the State of __Connecticut__

Declaration of Trust

WHEREAS, I, _____, of the

City/Town of _____, County of _____, State of _____,

am the holder of a safe deposit box in the _____,

(Name of Bank)

located in the City/Town of _____, State of _____;

NOW, THEREFORE, KNOW ALL MEN BY THESE PRESENTS, that I do hereby acknowledge and declare that I hold and will hold said safe deposit box and all my right, title and interest in and to said safe deposit box and its contents IN TRUST

1. For the use and benefit of the following _____ persons, in equal shares, or the survivor of them/per stirpes:

If because of my physical or mental incapacity certified in writing by a physician, the Successor Trustee hereinafter named shall assume active administration of this trust during my lifetime, such Successor Trustee shall be fully authorized to pay to me or disburse on my behalf such sums from income or principal generated by or constituting the contents of said box as appear necessary or desirable for my comfort or welfare. Upon my death, unless all of the beneficiaries shall predecease me or unless we all shall die as a result of a common accident or disaster, my Successor Trustee is hereby directed forthwith to transfer said safe deposit box and all right, title and interest in and to said box and its contents unto the beneficiaries absolutely and thereby terminate this trust; provided, however, that if any beneficiary hereunder shall not have attained the age of 21 years, the Successor Trustee shall hold such beneficiary's share of the trust assets in continuing trust until such beneficiary shall have attained the age of 21 years. During such period of continuing trust the Successor Trustee, in his absolute discretion, may retain the specific safe deposit box and contents herein described if he believes it to be in the best interests of the beneficiary so to do, or he may terminate the box and dispose of its contents, investing and reinvesting the proceeds as he may deem appropriate. Prior to the date upon which such beneficiary attains the age of 21 years, the Successor Trustee may apply or expend any or all of the contents of the box, or if such contents have been disposed of, any or all of the income or principal derived from such disposition, directly for the maintenance, education and support of the beneficiary without the intervention of any guardian and without application to any court. Such payments of income or principal may be made to the parents of such beneficiary or to the person with whom the beneficiary is living without any liability upon the Successor Trustee to see to the application thereof. If such beneficiary survives me but dies before attaining the age of 21 years, at his or her death the Successor Trustee shall transfer, pay over and deliver the trust property being held for such beneficiary to such beneficiary's personal representative, absolutely.

If among the contents of the safe deposit box held hereunder there be any asset identifiable as having been covered by a declaration of trust in connection with which beneficiaries other than those named in this trust have been designated, the Successor Trustee of this trust shall assert no claim to such asset but shall promptly deliver up the same to the individual named as Successor Trustee of such other trust.

2. Each beneficiary hereunder shall be liable for his proportionate share of any taxes levied upon the Settlor's total taxable estate by reason of the Settlor's death.

3. All interests of a beneficiary hereunder shall be inalienable and free from anticipation, assignment, attachment, pledge or control by creditors or a present or former spouse of such beneficiary in any proceedings at law or in equity.

4. This trust is created with the express understanding that the bank at which the safe deposit box is maintained shall be under no liability whatsoever to see to its proper administration. On the contrary, upon the presentation by the Successor Trustee to the bank of proper evidence of my death, the bank shall thereafter treat such Successor Trustee as the one solely entitled to the box and its contents. The bank shall be protected in acting upon any notice or other instrument or document believed by it to be genuine and to have been signed or presented by the proper party or parties.

5. I reserve unto myself the power and right at any time to remove all or any portion of the contents of the box, or to add to such contents.

6. I reserve unto myself the power and right at any time during my lifetime to amend or revoke in whole or in part the trust hereby created without the necessity of obtaining the consent of the beneficiaries and without giving notice to the beneficiaries. The withdrawal by me of the whole or any part of the contents of the safe deposit box held hereunder shall constitute as to such whole or part a revocation of this trust.

7. The death during my lifetime, or in a common accident or disaster with me, of all of the beneficiaries designated hereunder shall revoke such designation, and in the former event, I reserve the right to designate a new beneficiary. Should I for any reason fail to designate such new beneficiary, this trust shall terminate upon my death and the trust property shall revert to my estate.

8. In the event of my physical or mental incapacity or my death, I hereby nominate and appoint as Successor Trustee the beneficiary named first above, unless such beneficiary shall not have attained the age of 21 years or is otherwise legally incapacitated, in which event I hereby nominate and appoint as Successor Trustee the beneficiary named second above, unless such beneficiary named second above shall not have attained the age of 21 years or is otherwise legally incapacitated, in which latter event I hereby nominate

(Name) _____ , of

(Address) _____
        Number   *Street*   *City*   *State*   *Zip*

to be Successor Trustee.

9. This Declaration of Trust shall extend to and be binding upon the heirs, executors, administrators and assigns of the undersigned and upon the Successors to the Trustee.

10. The Trustee and his successors shall serve without bond.

11. This Declaration of Trust shall be construed and enforced in accordance with the laws of the State

of _____ .

IN WITNESS WHEREOF, I have hereunto set my hand and seal this _____

day of _____ , 19_____ .

        (Settlor sign here) _____ L.S.

I, the undersigned legal spouse of the above Settlor, hereby waive all community property rights which I may have in the contents of the hereinabove-described safe deposit box and give my assent to the provisions of the trust and to the inclusion in it of the said box and its contents.

        (Spouse sign here) _____ L.S.

Witness: (1) _____   Witness: (2) _____

STATE OF _____ ⎫ City

COUNTY OF _____ ⎬ or
                                          ⎭ Town _____

On the _____ day of _____ , 19_____ , personally appeared

_____

known to me to be the individual(s) who executed the foregoing instrument, and acknowledged the same to be _____ free act and deed, before me.

(Notary Seal)

                                    _____
                                         Notary Public

CHAPTER 11

DECLARATION OF TRUST

For Naming

**ONE PRIMARY BENEFICIARY WITH YOUR CHILDREN,
SHARING EQUALLY, AS CONTINGENT BENEFICIARIES**

To Receive

A SAFE DEPOSIT BOX HELD IN ONE NAME

INSTRUCTIONS:

On the following pages will be found a declaration of trust (DT-120) suitable for use in connection with the establishment of an inter vivos trust covering a safe deposit box held in one name only, where it is desired to name one person (ordinarily, but not necessarily, one's spouse) as primary beneficiary, with one's children as contingent beneficiaries to receive the safe deposit box and its contents if the primary beneficiary be not surviving upon the death of the owner.

Cross out *"city"* or *"town,"* leaving the appropriate designation of your community. Next, enter the name of the bank where the safe deposit box is maintained in the space provided near the top, and the name of the primary beneficiary (called the "First Beneficiary") in the appropriate place in Paragraph 1. Note that the instrument first refers to your children as *"natural not/or adopted."* Now, decide: If you have an adopted child and you wish to include him, cross out the word *"not"* in the phrase *"natural not/or adopted"* and *initial it.* If you wish to *exclude* your adopted child, cross out the word *"or"* in the same phrase and *initial it.* Remember, you <u>must</u> cross out *"not"* or *"or"*— one or the other. If you have no adopted child, simply cross out *"not."*

Note next that the instrument specifies that your children are to receive *"in equal shares, or the survivor of them/per stirpes."* Now, think carefully: If it is your wish that if one of your children does not survive you, *his* share will revert to *his* children in equal shares, cross out *"or the survivor of them"* and *initial it.* If that is *not* what you want—if, for example, you prefer that the share of any child of yours who predeceases you shall be divided between your other surviving children in equal shares, cross out *"per stirpes"* and *initial it.* Remember, you <u>must</u> cross out *"or the survivor of them"* or *"per stirpes"*—one or the other.

Note that in Paragraph 8, the First Beneficiary is designated as Successor Trustee, while a space is provided in which you should designate another person to so act if the named Successor Trustee is not surviving or otherwise fails or ceases to act. This could be one of your children, for example, but it must be an adult who can act as trustee for any beneficiary who comes into a share of the trust before attaining the age of 21. Avoid naming someone not likely to survive until the youngest such beneficiary has attained age 21.

When completed in the manner shown on the reverse side hereof, make several photocopies. Hold the original in safekeeping and offer a copy to the bank where the box is maintained. Instruct them to identify the box holder in this manner: *"(your name), Trustee u/d/t dated _____."*

Important: Read carefully Note B on page 38, which applies to this declaration of trust.

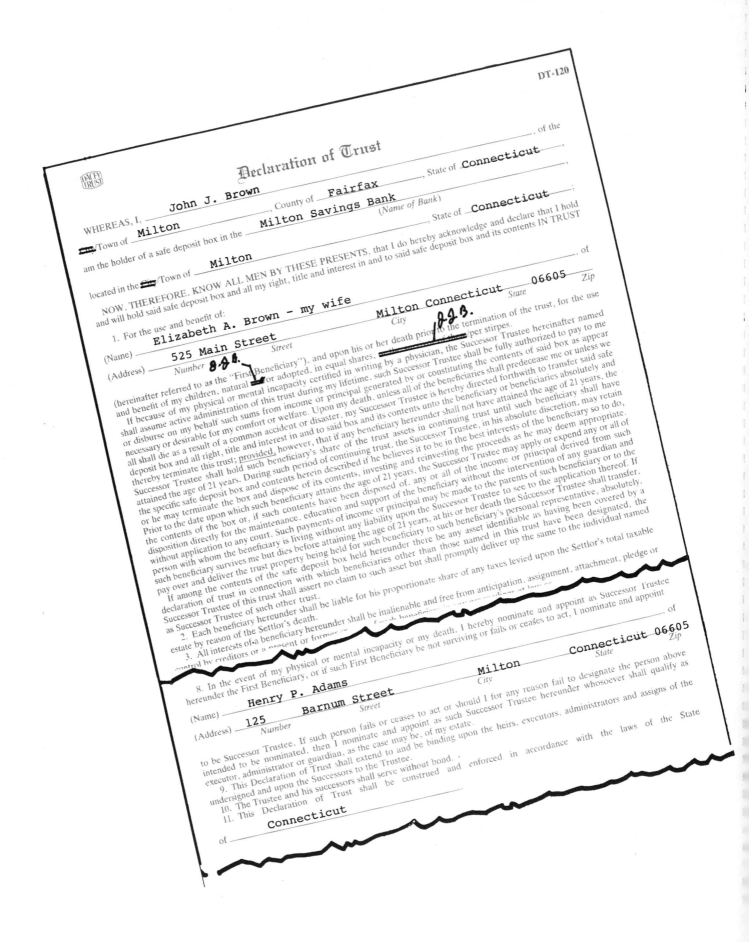

Declaration of Trust

DACEY TRUST

WHEREAS, I, __John J. Brown__, County of __Fairfax__, State of __Connecticut__,

Town of __Milton__ am the holder of a safe deposit box in the __Milton Savings Bank__ (Name of Bank), State of __Connecticut__,

located in the City/Town of __Milton__,

NOW, THEREFORE, KNOW ALL MEN BY THESE PRESENTS, that I do hereby acknowledge and declare that I hold and will hold said safe deposit box and all my right, title and interest in and to said safe deposit box and its contents IN TRUST

1. For the use and benefit of:

__Elizabeth A. Brown - my wife__   __Milton Connecticut__   __06605__ Zip

(Name)   City   State

__525 Main Street__

(Address)   Number   Street   *J.J.B.*   *J.J.B.*

(hereinafter referred to as the "First Beneficiary"), and upon his or her death prior to the termination of the trust, for the use and benefit of my children, natural or adopted, in equal shares, the survivor/per stirpes.

If because of my physical or mental incapacity certified in writing by a physician, such Successor Trustee hereinafter named shall assume active administration of this trust during my lifetime, such Successor Trustee shall be fully authorized to pay to me or disburse on my behalf such sums from income or principal generated by or constituting the contents of said box as appear necessary or desirable for my comfort or welfare. Upon my death, unless all of the beneficiaries shall predecease me or unless we all shall die as a result of a common accident or disaster, my Successor Trustee is hereby directed forthwith to transfer said safe deposit box and all right, title and interest in and to said box and its contents unto the beneficiary or beneficiaries absolutely and thereby terminate this trust; provided, however, that if any beneficiary hereunder shall not have attained the age of 21 years, the Successor Trustee shall hold such beneficiary's share of the trust assets in continuing trust until such beneficiary shall have attained the age of 21 years. During such period of continuing trust, the Successor Trustee, in his absolute discretion, may retain the specific safe deposit box and contents herein described if he believes it to be in the best interests of the beneficiary so to do, or he may terminate the box and dispose of its contents, investing and reinvesting the proceeds as he may deem appropriate. Prior to the date upon which such beneficiary attains the age of 21 years, the Successor Trustee may apply or expend any or all of the contents of the box or, if such contents have been disposed of, any or all of the income or principal derived from such disposition directly for the maintenance, education and support of the beneficiary without the intervention of any guardian and without application to any court. Such payments of income or principal may be made to the parents of such beneficiary or to the person with whom the beneficiary is living without any liability upon the Successor Trustee to see to the application thereof. If such beneficiary survives me but dies before attaining the age of 21 years, at his or her death the Successor Trustee shall transfer, pay over and deliver the trust property being held for such beneficiary to such beneficiary's personal representative, absolutely.

If among the contents of the safe deposit box held hereunder there be any asset identifiable as having been covered by a declaration of trust in connection with which beneficiaries other than those named in this trust have been designated, the Successor Trustee of this trust shall assert no claim to such asset but shall promptly deliver up the same to the individual named as Successor Trustee of such other trust.

2. Each beneficiary hereunder shall be liable for his proportionate share of any taxes levied upon the Settlor's total taxable estate by reason of the Settlor's death.

3. All interests of a beneficiary hereunder shall be inalienable and free from anticipation, assignment, attachment, pledge or control by creditors or a present or former _____ ... such benefic ...

8. In the event of my physical or mental incapacity or my death, I hereby nominate and appoint as Successor Trustee hereunder the First Beneficiary, or if such First Beneficiary be not surviving or fails or ceases to act, I nominate and appoint

__Henry P. Adams__   __Milton__   __Connecticut__ __06605__

(Name)   City   State   Zip

__125__   __Barnum Street__

(Address)   Number   Street

to be Successor Trustee. If such person fails or ceases to act or should I for any reason fail to designate the person above intended to be nominated, then I nominate and appoint as such Successor Trustee hereunder whosoever shall qualify as executor, administrator or guardian, as the case may be, of my estate.

9. This Declaration of Trust shall extend to and be binding upon the heirs, executors, administrators and assigns of the undersigned and upon the Successors to the Trustee.

10. The Trustee and his successors shall serve without bond.

11. This Declaration of Trust shall be construed and enforced in accordance with the laws of the State of __Connecticut__

Declaration of Trust

WHEREAS, I, _____, of the

City/Town of _____, County of _____, State of _____,

am the holder of a safe deposit box in the _____,
(Name of Bank)

located in the City/Town of _____, State of _____;

    NOW, THEREFORE, KNOW ALL MEN BY THESE PRESENTS, that I do hereby acknowledge and declare that I hold and will hold said safe deposit box and all my right, title and interest in and to said safe deposit box and its contents IN TRUST

    1. For the use and benefit of:

(Name) _____, of

(Address) _____
Number   Street   City   State   Zip

(hereinafter referred to as the "First Beneficiary"), and upon his or her death prior to the termination of the trust, for the use and benefit of my children, natural not/or adopted, in equal shares, or the survivor of them/per stirpes.

    If because of my physical or mental incapacity certified in writing by a physician, the Successor Trustee hereinafter named shall assume active administration of this trust during my lifetime, such Successor Trustee shall be fully authorized to pay to me or disburse on my behalf such sums from income or principal generated by or constituting the contents of said box as appear necessary or desirable for my comfort or welfare. Upon my death, unless all of the beneficiaries shall predecease me or unless we all shall die as a result of a common accident or disaster, my Successor Trustee is hereby directed forthwith to transfer said safe deposit box and all right, title and interest in and to said box and its contents unto the beneficiary or beneficiaries absolutely and thereby terminate this trust; <u>provided,</u> however, that if any beneficiary hereunder shall not have attained the age of 21 years, the Successor Trustee shall hold such beneficiary's share of the trust assets in continuing trust until such beneficiary shall have attained the age of 21 years. During such period of continuing trust, the Successor Trustee, in his absolute discretion, may retain the specific safe deposit box and contents herein described if he believes it to be in the best interests of the beneficiary so to do, or he may terminate the box and dispose of its contents, investing and reinvesting the proceeds as he may deem appropriate. Prior to the date upon which such beneficiary attains the age of 21 years, the Successor Trustee may apply or expend any or all of the contents of the box or, if such contents have been disposed of, any or all of the income or principal derived from such disposition directly for the maintenance, education and support of the beneficiary without the intervention of any guardian and without application to any court. Such payments of income or principal may be made to the parents of such beneficiary or to the person with whom the beneficiary is living without any liability upon the Successor Trustee to see to the application thereof. If such beneficiary survives me but dies before attaining the age of 21 years, at his or her death the Successor Trustee shall transfer, pay over and deliver the trust property being held for such beneficiary to such beneficiary's personal representative, absolutely.

    If among the contents of the safe deposit box held hereunder there be any asset identifiable as having been covered by a declaration of trust in connection with which beneficiaries other than those named in this trust have been designated, the Successor Trustee of this trust shall assert no claim to such asset but shall promptly deliver up the same to the individual named as Successor Trustee of such other trust.

    2. Each beneficiary hereunder shall be liable for his proportionate share of any taxes levied upon the Settlor's total taxable estate by reason of the Settlor's death.

    3. All interests of a beneficiary hereunder shall be inalienable and free from anticipation, assignment, attachment, pledge or control by creditors or a present or former spouse of such beneficiary in any proceedings at law or in equity.

    4. This trust is created with the express understanding that the bank at which the safe deposit box is maintained shall be under no liability whatsoever to see to its proper administration. On the contrary, upon the presentation by the Successor Trustee to the bank of proper evidence of my death, the bank shall thereafter treat such Successor Trustee as the one solely entitled to the box and its contents. The bank shall be protected in acting upon any notice or other instrument or document believed by it to be genuine and to have been signed or presented by the proper party or parties.

    5. I reserve unto myself the power and right at any time to remove all or any portion of the contents of the box, or to add to such contents.

    6. I reserve unto myself the power and right at any time during my lifetime to amend or revoke in whole or in part the trust hereby created without the necessity of obtaining the consent of the beneficiaries and without giving notice to the beneficiaries. The withdrawal by me of the whole or any part of the contents of the safe deposit box held hereunder shall constitute as to such whole or part a revocation of this trust.

    7. The death during my lifetime, or in a common accident or disaster with me, of all of the beneficiaries designated hereunder shall revoke such designation, and in the former event, I reserve the right to designate a new beneficiary. Should I for any reason fail to designate such new beneficiary, this trust shall terminate upon my death and the trust property shall revert to my estate.

8. In the event of my physical or mental incapacity or my death, I hereby nominate and appoint as Successor Trustee hereunder the First Beneficiary, or if such First Beneficiary be not surviving or fails or ceases to act, I nominate and appoint

(Name) _____ , of

(Address) _____
      Number   *Street*   *City*   *State*   *Zip*

to be Successor Trustee. If such person fails or ceases to act or should I for any reason fail to designate the person above intended to be nominated, then I nominate and appoint as such Successor Trustee hereunder whosoever shall qualify as executor, administrator or guardian, as the case may be, of my estate.

9. This Declaration of Trust shall extend to and be binding upon the heirs, executors, administrators and assigns of the undersigned and upon the Successors to the Trustee.

10. The Trustee and his successors shall serve without bond.

11. This Declaration of Trust shall be construed and enforced in accordance with the laws of the State

of _____ .

IN WITNESS WHEREOF, I have hereunto set my hand and seal this _____

day of _____ , 19_____ .

           (Settlor sign here) _____ L.S.

I, the undersigned legal spouse of the Settlor, hereby waive all community property rights which I may have in the contents of the hereinabove-described safe deposit box and give my assent to the provisions of the trust and to the inclusion in it of the said safe deposit box and its contents.

           (Spouse sign here) _____ L.S.

Witness: (1) _____   Witness: (2) _____

STATE OF _____ ⎱   City

COUNTY OF _____ ⎰ or
                                 Town _____

On the _____ day of _____ , 19_____ , personally appeared

_____

known to me to be the individual(s) who executed the foregoing instrument, and acknowledged the same to be _____ free act and deed, before me.

(Notary Seal)

_____
                Notary Public

CHAPTER 11

DECLARATION OF TRUST
For Naming
ONE BENEFICIARY
To Receive
A SAFE DEPOSIT BOX HELD IN JOINT NAMES

INSTRUCTIONS:

On the following pages will be found a declaration of trust (DT-117-J) suitable for use in connection with the establishment of an inter vivos trust covering a safe deposit box held in joint names where it is desired to name one person to receive the box and its contents upon the death of the survivor of the two joint owners.

Enter the names of the two co-owners on the first line.

Cross out *"city"* or *"town,"* leaving the appropriate designation of your community. Next, enter the name of the bank where the safe deposit box is maintained in the space provided near the top, and the name of the beneficiary in the appropriate place in Paragraph 1.

Note that Paragraph 8 designates as Successor Trustee *"whosoever shall at that time be beneficiary hereunder,"* which means that in most cases you don't need to fill anything in there. However, if there is any possibility of a beneficiary who has not attained the age of 21 years receiving the safe deposit box, make certain that you name an adult in this paragraph who can act as trustee for such beneficiary. Avoid naming as trustee a person not likely to survive until the beneficiary has attained age 21.

When completed in the manner shown on the reverse side hereof, make several photocopies for reference purposes. Hold the original in safekeeping and offer a copy to the bank where the safe deposit box is maintained. Instruct them to identify the box holders in this manner: *"(your name) and (your co-owner's name), Trustees u/d/t dated _____."*

Important: Read carefully Note B on page 38, which applies to this declaration of trust.

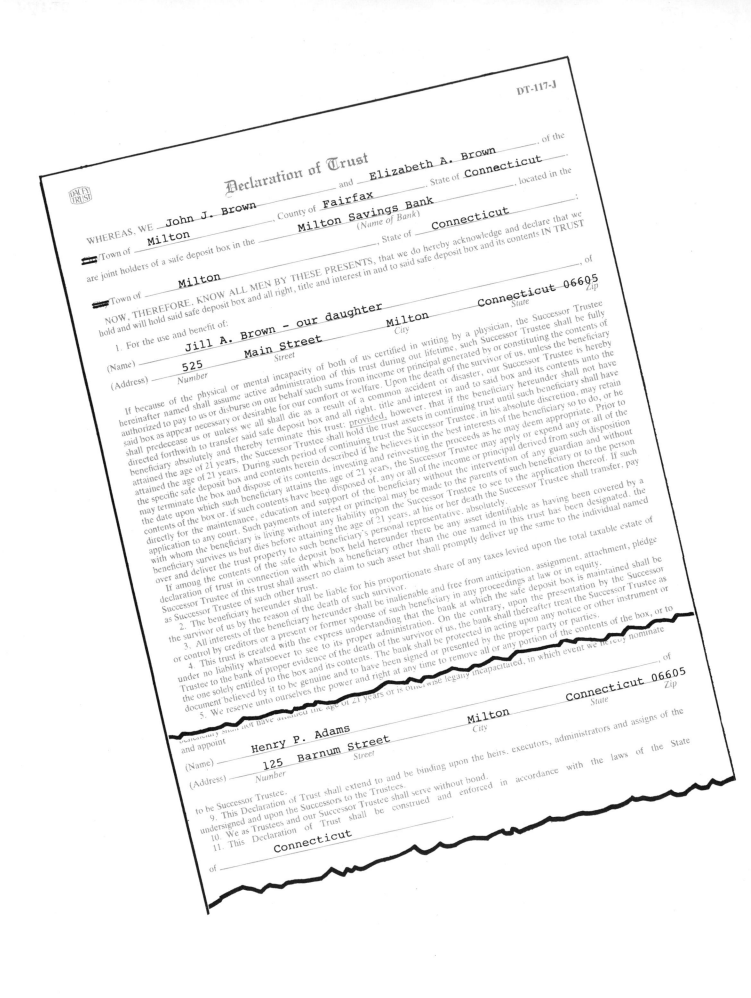

DT-117-J

Declaration of Trust

WHEREAS, WE __John J. Brown__ and __Elizabeth A. Brown__, of the Town of __Milton__, County of __Fairfax__, State of __Connecticut__, located in the __Milton Savings Bank__ (Name of Bank), State of __Connecticut__, are joint holders of a safe deposit box in the

NOW, THEREFORE, KNOW ALL MEN BY THESE PRESENTS, that we do hereby acknowledge and declare that we hold and will hold said safe deposit box and all right, title and interest in and to said safe deposit box and its contents IN TRUST

Town of __Milton__

1. For the use and benefit of:

(Name) __Jill A. Brown - our daughter__ __Milton__ City __Connecticut 06605__ State Zip

(Address) __525__ Number __Main Street__ Street

If because of the physical or mental incapacity of both of us certified in writing by a physician, the Successor Trustee shall be fully hereinafter named shall assume active administration of this trust during our lifetime, such Successor Trustee shall be fully authorized to pay to us or disburse on our behalf such sums from income or principal generated by or constituting the contents of said box as appear necessary or desirable for our comfort or welfare. Upon the death of the survivor of us, unless the beneficiary shall predecease us or unless we all shall die as a result of a common accident or disaster, our Successor Trustee is hereby directed forthwith to transfer said safe deposit box and all right, title and interest in and to said box and its contents unto the beneficiary absolutely and thereby terminate this trust: provided, however, that if the beneficiary hereunder shall not have attained the age of 21 years, the Successor Trustee shall hold the trust assets in continuing trust until such beneficiary shall have the specific safe deposit box and contents herein described if he believes it in the best interests of the beneficiary so to do, or he may terminate the box and dispose of its contents, investing and reinvesting the proceeds as he may deem appropriate. Prior to the date upon which such beneficiary attains the age of 21 years, the Successor Trustee may apply or expend any or all of the contents of the box or, if such contents have been disposed of, any or all of the income or principal derived from such disposition directly for the maintenance, education and support of the beneficiary without the intervention of any guardian and without application to any court. Such payments of interest or principal may be made to the parents of such beneficiary or to the person with whom the beneficiary is living without any liability upon the Successor Trustee to see to the application thereof. If such beneficiary survives us but dies before attaining the age of 21 years, at his or her death the Successor Trustee shall transfer, pay over and deliver the trust property to such beneficiary's personal representative, absolutely.

If among the contents of the safe deposit box held hereunder there be any asset identifiable as having been covered by a declaration of trust in connection with which a beneficiary other than the one named in this trust has been designated, the Successor Trustee of this trust shall assert no claim to such asset but shall promptly deliver up the same to the individual named as Successor Trustee of such other trust.

2. The beneficiary hereunder shall be liable for his proportionate share of any taxes levied upon the total taxable estate of the survivor of us by the reason of the death of such survivor.

3. All interests of the beneficiary hereunder shall be inalienable and free from anticipation, assignment, attachment, pledge or control by creditors or a present or former spouse of such beneficiary in any proceedings at law or in equity.

4. This trust is created with the express understanding that the bank at which the safe deposit box is maintained shall be under no liability whatsoever to see to its proper administration. On the contrary, upon the presentation by the Successor Trustee to the bank of proper evidence of the death of the survivor of us, the bank shall thereafter treat the Successor Trustee as the one solely entitled to the box and its contents. The bank shall be protected in acting upon any notice or other instrument or document believed by it to be genuine and to have been signed or presented by the proper party or parties.

5. We reserve unto ourselves the power and right at any time to remove all or any portion of the contents of the box, or to beneficiary shall not have attained the age of 21 years or is otherwise legally incapacitated, in which event we hereby nominate

and appoint __Henry P. Adams__ __Milton__ City __Connecticut 06605__ State Zip

(Name) __Henry P. Adams__

(Address) __125__ Number __Barnum Street__ Street

to be Successor Trustee.

9. This Declaration of Trust shall extend to and be binding upon the heirs, executors, administrators and assigns of the undersigned and upon the Successors to the Trustees.

10. We as Trustees and our Successor Trustee shall serve without bond.

11. This Declaration of Trust shall be construed and enforced in accordance with the laws of the State of __Connecticut__.

Declaration of Trust

WHEREAS, WE, ＿＿＿＿＿＿＿＿＿＿＿ and ＿＿＿＿＿＿＿＿＿＿＿, of the

City/Town of ＿＿＿＿＿＿＿＿＿, County of ＿＿＿＿＿＿, State of ＿＿＿＿＿＿,

are joint holders of a safe deposit box in the ＿＿＿＿＿＿＿＿＿＿＿, located in the
(Name of Bank)

City/Town of ＿＿＿＿＿＿＿＿＿＿＿, State of ＿＿＿＿＿＿＿＿＿;

NOW, THEREFORE, KNOW ALL MEN BY THESE PRESENTS, that we do hereby acknowledge and declare that we hold and will hold said safe deposit box and all our right, title and interest in and to said safe deposit box and its contents IN TRUST

1. For the use and benefit of:

(Name) ＿＿＿＿＿＿＿＿＿＿＿＿＿＿＿, of

(Address) ＿＿＿＿＿＿＿＿＿＿＿＿＿＿＿
      Number   *Street*   *City*   *State*   *Zip*

If because of the physical or mental incapacity of both of us certified in writing by a physician, the Successor Trustee hereinafter named shall assume active administration of this trust during out lifetime, such Successor Trustee shall be fully authorized to pay to us or disburse on our behalf such sums from income or principal generated by or constituting the contents of said box as appear necessary or desirable for our comfort or welfare. Upon the death of the survivor of us, unless the beneficiary shall predecease us or unless we all shall die as a result of a common accident or disaster, our Successor Trustee is hereby directed forthwith to transfer said safe deposit box and all right, title and interest in and to said box and its contents unto the beneficiary absolutely and thereby terminate this trust; provided, however, that if the beneficiary hereunder shall not have attained the age of 21 years, the Successor Trustee shall hold the trust assets in continuing trust until such beneficiary shall have attained the age of 21 years. During such period of continuing trust the Successor Trustee, in his absolute discretion, may retain the specific safe deposit box and contents herein described if he believes it in the best interests of the beneficiary so to do, or he may terminate the box and dispose of its contents, investing and reinvesting the proceeds as he may deem appropriate. Prior to the date upon which such beneficiary attains the age of 21 years, the Successor Trustee may apply or expend any or all of the contents of the box or, if such contents have been disposed of, any or all of the income or principal derived from such disposition directly for the maintenance, education and support of the beneficiary without the intervention of any guardian and without application to any court. Such payments of income or principal may be made to the parents of such beneficiary or to the person with whom the beneficiary is living without any liability upon the Successor Trustee to see to the application thereof. If such beneficiary survives us but dies before attaining the age of 21 years, at his or her death the Successor Trustee shall transfer, pay over and deliver the trust property to such beneficiary's personal representative, absolutely.

If among the contents of the safe deposit box held hereunder there be any asset identifiable as having been covered by a declaration of trust in connection with which a beneficiary other than the one named in this trust has been designated, the Successor Trustee of this trust shall assert no claim to such asset but shall promptly deliver up the same to the individual named as Successor Trustee of such other trust.

2. The beneficiary hereunder shall be liable for his proportionate share of any taxes levied upon the total taxable estate of the survivor of us by the reason of the death of such survivor.

3. All interests of the beneficiary hereunder shall be inalienable and free from anticipation, assignment, attachment, pledge or control by creditors or a present or former spouse of such beneficiary in any proceedings at law or in equity.

4. This trust is created with the express understanding that the bank at which the safe deposit box is maintained shall be under no liability whatsoever to see to its proper administration. On the contrary, upon the presentation by the Successor Trustee to the bank of proper evidence of the death of the survivor of us, the bank shall thereafter treat the Successor Trustee as the one solely entitled to the box and its contents. The bank shall be protected in acting upon any notice or other instrument or document believed by it to be genuine and to have been signed or presented by the proper party or parties.

5. We reserve unto ourselves the power and right at any time to remove all or any portion of the contents of the box, or to add to such contents.

6. We reserve unto ourselves the power and right at any time during our lifetime to amend or revoke in whole or in part the trust hereby created without the necessity of obtaining the consent of the beneficiary and without giving notice to the beneficiary. The withdrawal by us of the whole or any part of the contents of the safe deposit box held hereunder shall constitute as to such whole or part a revocation of this trust.

7. The death during our lifetime, or in a common accident or disaster with us, of the beneficiary designated hereunder shall revoke such designation, and in the former event, we reserve the right to designate a new beneficiary. Should we for any reason fail to designate such new beneficiary, this trust shall terminate upon the death of the survivor of us and the trust property shall revert to the estate of such survivor.

8. In the event of the physical or mental incapacity or death of one of us, the survivor shall continue as sole Trustee. In the event of the physical or mental incapacity or death of the survivor of us, or if we both shall die in a common accident, we hereby nominate and appoint as Successor Trustee hereunder whosoever shall at that time be beneficiary hereunder, unless such

beneficiary shall not have attained the age of 21 years or is otherwise legally incapacitated, in which event we hereby nominate and appoint

(Name) _____ , of

(Address) _____

            Number   *Street*   *City*   *State*   *Zip*

to be Successor Trustee.

    9. This Declaration of Trust shall extend to and be binding upon the heirs, executors, administrators and assigns of the undersigned and upon the Successors to the Trustees.

    10. We as Trustees and our Successor Trustee shall serve without bond.

    11. This Declaration of Trust shall be construed and enforced in accordance with the laws of the State

of _____ .

    IN WITNESS WHEREOF, we have hereunto set our hands and seals this _____

day of _____ , 19_____ .

                       (First Settlor sign here) _____ L.S.

                   (Second Settlor sign here) _____ L.S.

I, the undersigned legal spouse of one of the above Settlors, hereby waive all community property rights which I may have in the contents of the hereinabove-described safe deposit box and give my assent to the provisions of the trust and to the inclusion in it of the said box and its contents.

                    (Spouse sign here) _____ L.S.

Witness: (1) _____   Witness: (2) _____

STATE OF _____ ⎱   City

COUNTY OF _____ ⎰   or Town _____

    On the _____ day of_____ , 19_____ , personally appeared

_____ and _____

known to me to be the individuals who executed the foregoing instrument, and acknowledged the same to be their free act and deed, before me.

                                  _____

(Notary Seal)   *Notary Public*

CHAPTER 11

DECLARATION OF TRUST
For Naming
ONE PRIMARY BENEFICIARY
And
ONE CONTINGENT BENEFICIARY
To Receive
A SAFE DEPOSIT BOX HELD IN JOINT NAMES

INSTRUCTIONS:

On the following pages will be found a declaration of trust (DT-118-J) suitable for use in connection with the establishment of an inter vivos trust covering a safe deposit box held in joint names where it is desired to name some *one* person as primary beneficiary, with some *one* other person as contingent beneficiary to receive the box and its contents if the primary beneficiary be not living upon the death of the survivor of the two joint owners.

Enter the names of the two co-owners on the first line.

Cross out *"city"* or *"town,"* leaving the appropriate designation of your community. Next, enter the name of the bank where the safe deposit box is maintained in the space provided near the top, and the names of the beneficiaries in the appropriate place in Paragraph 1.

Note that Paragraph 8 designates as Successor Trustee *"whosoever shall at that time be beneficiary hereunder,"* which means that in most cases you don't need to fill anything in there. However, if there is any possibility of a beneficiary who has not attained the age of 21 years receiving the safe deposit box, make certain that you name an adult in this paragraph who can act as trustee for such beneficiary. Avoid naming as trustee a person not likely to survive until the beneficiary has attained age 21.

When completed in the manner shown on the reverse side hereof, make several photocopies for reference purposes. Hold the original in safekeeping and offer a copy to the bank where the safe deposit box is maintained. Instruct them to identify the box holders in this manner: *"(your name) and (your co-owner's name), Trustees u/d/t dated _____."*

Important: Read carefully Note B on page 38, which applies to this declaration of trust.

Declaration of Trust

WHEREAS, WE __John J. Brown__ and __Elizabeth A. Brown__, of the __Town of__ __Milton__, County of __Fairfax__, State of __Connecticut__, located in the __Milton Savings Bank__ (Name of Bank), State of __Connecticut__, are joint holders of a safe deposit box in the __Town of__ __Milton__,

NOW, THEREFORE, KNOW ALL MEN BY THESE PRESENTS, that we do hereby acknowledge and declare that we hold and will hold said safe deposit box and all our right, title and interest in and to said safe deposit box and its contents IN TRUST

1. For the use and benefit of:

(Name) __Jill A. Brown - our daughter__

(Address) __525   Main   Street__, __Milton__ City, __Connecticut__ State, __06605__ Zip
Number   Street

or, if such beneficiary be not surviving, for the use and benefit of:

(Name) __Dorothy Lynn - our niece__

(Address) __566 Midland Street__, __Portland   Wisconsin__ City State, __53123__ Zip
Number   Street

If because of the physical or mental incapacity of both of us certified in writing by a physician, the Successor Trustee hereinafter named shall assume active administration of this trust during our lifetime, such Successor Trustee shall be fully authorized to pay to us or disburse on our behalf such sums from income or principal generated by or constituting the contents of said box as appear necessary or desirable for our comfort or welfare. Upon the death of the survivor of us, unless the beneficiaries shall predecease us or unless we all shall die as a result of a common accident, our Successor Trustee is hereby directed forthwith to transfer said safe deposit box and all right, title and interest in and to said box and its contents unto the beneficiary absolutely and thereby terminate this trust; provided, however, that if the beneficiary hereunder shall not have attained the age of 21 years, the Successor Trustee shall hold the trust assets in continuing trust until such beneficiary shall have the specific safe deposit box and its contents herein described if he believes it in the best interests of the beneficiary so to do, or he may terminate the box or, if such contents have been disposed of, any or all of the income or principal derived from such contents of the box or, if such contents have been disposed of, any or all of the income or principal derived from such disposition, directly for the maintenance, education, and support of the beneficiary without the intervention of any guardian and without application to any court. Such payments of income or principal may be made to the parents of such beneficiary or to the person with whom the beneficiary is living without any liability upon the Successor Trustee to see to the application thereof. If such beneficiary survives us but dies before attaining the age of 21 years, at his or her death the Successor Trustee shall transfer, pay over and deliver the trust property to such beneficiary's personal representative, absolutely.

If among the contents of the safe deposit box held hereunder there be any asset identifiable as having been covered by a declaration of trust in connection with which beneficiaries other than those named in this trust have been designated, the Successor Trustee of this trust shall assert no claim to such asset but shall promptly deliver up the same to the individual named ~~Successor Trustee of such other's~~

8. In the event of the physical or mental incapacity or death of one of us, the survivor shall continue as sole Trustee. In the event of the physical or mental incapacity or death of the survivor of us, or if we both shall die in a common accident, we hereby nominate and appoint as Successor Trustee hereunder whosoever shall at that time be beneficiary hereunder, unless such beneficiary shall not have attained the age of 21 years, or is otherwise legally incapacitated, in which event we hereby nominate and appoint

(Name) __Henry P. Adams__, __Milton__ City, __Connecticut__ State __06605__ Zip, of

(Address) __125 Barnum Street__
Number   Street

to be Successor Trustee.

9. This Declaration of Trust shall extend to and be binding upon the heirs, executors, administrators and assigns of the undersigned and upon the Successors to the Trustees.

10. We as Trustees and our Successor Trustee shall serve without bond.

11. This Declaration of Trust shall be construed and enforced in accordance with the laws of the State of __Connecticut__

Declaration of Trust

WHEREAS, WE, _____ and _____, of the

City/Town of _____, County of _____, State of _____,

are joint holders of a safe deposit box in the _____, located in the
(Name of Bank)

City/Town of _____, State of _____;

NOW, THEREFORE, KNOW ALL MEN BY THESE PRESENTS, that we do hereby acknowledge and declare that we hold and will hold said safe deposit box and all our right, title and interest in and to said safe deposit box and its contents IN TRUST

1. For the use and benefit of:

(Name) _____, of

(Address) _____
     Number   Street   City   State   Zip

or, if such beneficiary be not surviving, for the use and benefit of:

(Name) _____, of

(Address) _____
     Number   Street   City   State   Zip

If because of the physical or mental incapacity of both of us certified in writing by a physician, the Successor Trustee hereinafter named shall assume active administration of this trust during our lifetime, such Successor Trustee shall be fully authorized to pay to us or disburse on our behalf such sums from income or principal generated by or constituting the contents of said box as appear necessary or desirable for our comfort or welfare. Upon the death of the survivor of us, unless the beneficiaries shall predecease us or unless we all shall die as a result of a common accident, our Successor Trustee is hereby directed forthwith to transfer said safe deposit box and all right, title and interest in and to said box and its contents unto the beneficiary absolutely and thereby terminate this trust; provided, however, that if the beneficiary hereunder shall not have attained the age of 21 years, the Successor Trustee shall hold the trust assets in continuing trust until such beneficiary shall have attained the age of 21 years. During such period of continuing trust the Successor Trustee, in his absolute discretion, may retain the specific safe deposit box and its contents herein described if he believes it in the best interests of the beneficiary so to do, or he may terminate the box and dispose of its contents, investing and reinvesting the proceeds as he may deem appropriate. Prior to the date upon which such beneficiary attains the age of 21 years, the Successor Trustee may apply or expend any or all of the contents of the box or, if such contents have been disposed of, any or all of the income or principal derived from such disposition, directly for the maintenance, education, and support of the beneficiary without the intervention of any guardian and without application to any court. Such payments of income or principal may be made to the parents of such beneficiary or to the person with whom the beneficiary is living without any liability upon the Successor Trustee to see to the application thereof. If such beneficiary survives us but dies before attaining the age of 21 years, at his or her death the Successor Trustee shall transfer, pay over and deliver the trust property to such beneficiary's personal representative, absolutely.

If among the contents of the safe deposit box held hereunder there be any asset identifiable as having been covered by a declaration of trust in connection with which beneficiaries other than those named in this trust have been designated, the Successor Trustee of this trust shall assert no claim to such asset but shall promptly deliver up the same to the individual named as Successor Trustee of such other trust.

2. Each beneficiary hereunder shall be liable for his proportionate share of any taxes levied upon the total taxable estate of the survivor of us by reason of the death of such survivor.

3. The interests of any beneficiary hereunder shall be inalienable and free from anticipation, assignment, attachment, pledge or control by creditors or a present or former spouse of such beneficiary in any proceedings at law or in equity.

4. This trust is created with the express understanding that the bank at which the safe deposit box is maintained shall be under no liability whatsoever to see to its proper administration. On the contrary, upon the presentation by the Successor Trustee to the bank of proper evidence of the death of the survivor of us, the bank shall hereafter treat the Successor Trustee as the one solely entitled to the box and its contents. The bank shall be protected in acting upon any notice or other instrument or document believed by it to be genuine and to have been signed or presented by the proper party or parties.

5. We reserve unto ourselves the power and right at any time to remove all or any portion of the contents of the box, or to add to such contents.

6. We reserve unto ourselves the power and right at any time during our lifetime to amend or revoke in whole or in part the trust hereby created without the necessity of obtaining the consent of the beneficiaries and without giving notice to the beneficiaries. The withdrawal by us of the whole or any part of the contents of the safe deposit box held hereunder shall constitute as to such whole or part a revocation of this trust.

7. The death during our lifetime, or in a common accident or disaster with us, of both of the beneficiaries designated hereunder shall revoke such designation, and in the former event, we reserve the right to designate a new beneficiary. Should we for any reason fail to designate such new beneficiary, this trust shall terminate upon the death of the survivor of us and the trust property shall revert to the estate of such survivor.

8. In the event of the physical or mental incapacity or death of one of us, the survivor shall continue as sole Trustee. In the event of the physical or mental incapacity or death of the survivor of us, or if we both shall die in a common accident, we hereby nominate and appoint as Successor Trustee hereunder whosoever shall at that time be beneficiary hereunder, unless such beneficiary shall not have attained the age of 21 years, or is otherwise legally incapacitated, in which event we hereby nominate and appoint

(Name) _____, of

(Address) _____
  Number   Street   City   State   Zip

to be Successor Trustee.

9. This Declaration of Trust shall extend to and be binding upon the heirs, executors, administrators and assigns of the undersigned and upon the Successors to the Trustees.

10. We as Trustees and our Successor Trustee shall serve without bond.

11. This Declaration of Trust shall be construed and enforced in accordance with the laws of the State

of _____.

IN WITNESS WHEREOF, we have hereunto set our hands and seals this _____

day of _____, 19_____.

(First Settlor sign here) _____ L.S.

(Second Settlor sign here) _____ L.S.

I, the undersigned legal spouse of one of the above Settlors, hereby waive all community property rights which I may have in the contents of the hereinabove-described safe deposit box and give my assent to the provisions of the trust and to the inclusion in it of the said box and its contents.

(Spouse sign here) _____ L.S.

Witness: (1) _____   Witness: (2) _____

STATE OF _____ ⎤   City
                                         ⎥   or
COUNTY OF _____ ⎦   Town _____

On the _____ day of _____, 19_____, personally appeared

_____ and _____

known to me to be the individuals who executed the foregoing instrument, and acknowledged the same to be their free act and deed, before me.

_____
(Notary Seal)   Notary Public

CHAPTER 11

DECLARATION OF TRUST
For Naming
TWO OR MORE BENEFICIARIES, SHARING EQUALLY,
To Receive
A SAFE DEPOSIT BOX HELD IN JOINT NAMES

INSTRUCTIONS:

On the following pages will be found a declaration of trust (DT-119-J) suitable for use in connection with the establishment of an inter vivos trust covering a safe deposit box held in joint names where it is desired to name two or more persons, sharing equally, to receive the box and its contents upon the death of the survivor of the two owners.

Enter the names of the two co-owners on the first line.

Cross out *"city"* or *"town,"* leaving the appropriate designation of your community. Next, enter the name of the bank where the safe deposit box is maintained.

In Paragraph 1, indicate the *number of persons* you are naming (to discourage unauthorized additions to the list) and then insert their names. The one whose name appears *first* will be the Successor Trustee responsible for seeing to the distribution of the trust property.

Note that the instrument specifies that the named beneficiaries are to receive *"in equal shares, or the survivor of them/per stirpes."* Now, think carefully: If you have named three persons with the intention that if one of them predeceases you, *his* children will take *his* share, cross out *"or the survivor of them"* and *initial it.* If that is *not* what you want—if, for example, you prefer that the share of the deceased person be divided between the two surviving persons, cross out *"per stirpes"* and *initial it.* Remember, you <u>must</u> cross out either *"or the survivor of them"* or *"per stirpes"*—one or the other.

Note that Paragraph 8 designates as Successor Trustee *"the beneficiary named first above,"* which means that in most cases you don't need to fill anything in there. However, if there is a possibility of a beneficiary who has not attained the age of 21 years receiving a share of the trust property, make certain that you name an adult in this paragraph who can act as trustee for such beneficiary. Avoid naming as trustee a person not likely to survive until the beneficiary has attained age 21.

When completed in the manner shown on the reverse side hereof, make several photocopies. Hold the original in safekeeping and offer a copy to the bank where the safe deposit box is maintained. Instruct them to identify the box holders in this manner: *"(your name) and (your co-owner's name), Trustees u/d/t dated _____."*

Important: Read carefully Note B on page 38, which applies to this declaration of trust.

WHEREVER THE INSTRUCTION *"INITIAL IT"* APPEARS ABOVE,
IT MEANS THAT *BOTH* CO-OWNERS SHOULD INITIAL IT.

DT-119-J

Declaration of Trust

WHEREAS. WE ___John J. Brown___ and ___Elizabeth A. Brown___, of the ___Town of ___Milton___, County of ___Fairfax___, State of ___Connecticut___,

are joint holders of a safe deposit box in the ___Milton Savings Bank___ (Name of Bank), State of ___Connecticut___

located in the ___Town of ___Milton___

NOW, THEREFORE, KNOW ALL MEN BY THESE PRESENTS, that we do hereby acknowledge and declare that we hold and will hold said safe deposit box and all our right, title and interest in and to said safe deposit box and its contents IN TRUST

1. For the use and benefit of the following ___three (3)___ persons, in equal shares, or the survivor of them

Thomas B. Brown - our brother
Helen M. Brown - our sister
Charles M. Brown - our brother

If because of the physical or mental incapacity of both of us certified in writing by a physician, the Successor Trustee hereinafter named shall assume active administration of this trust during our lifetime, such Successor Trustee shall be fully authorized to pay to us or disburse on our behalf such sums from income or principal generated by or constituting the contents of said box as appear necessary or desirable for our comfort or welfare. Upon the death of the survivor of us, unless all the beneficiaries shall predecease us or unless we all shall die as a result of a common accident or disaster, our Successor Trustee is hereby directed forthwith to transfer said safe deposit box and all right, title and interest in and to said box and its contents unto the beneficiaries absolutely and thereby terminate this trust; provided, however, that if any beneficiary hereunder shall not have attained the age of 21, the Successor Trustee shall hold such beneficiary's share of the trust assets in continuing trust until such beneficiary shall have attained the age of 21 years. During such period of continuing trust the Successor Trustee, in his absolute discretion, may retain the specific safe deposit box and its contents herein described if he believes it in the best interests of the beneficiary so to do, or he may terminate the box and dispose of its contents, investing and reinvesting the proceeds as he may deem appropriate. Prior to the date upon which such beneficiary attains the age of 21 years, the Successor Trustee may apply or expend any or all of the contents of the box or, if such contents have been disposed of, any or all of the income or principal derived from such disposition directly for the maintenance, education and support of the beneficiary without the intervention of any guardian and without application to any court. Such payments of income or principal may be made to the parents of such beneficiary or to the person with whom the beneficiary is living without any liability upon the Successor Trustee to see to the application thereof. If any such beneficiary survives us but dies before attaining the age of 21 years, at his or her death the Successor Trustee shall transfer, pay over and deliver the trust property being held for such beneficiary to said beneficiary's personal representative, absolutely.

If among the contents of the safe deposit box held hereunder there be any asset identifiable as having been covered by a declaration of trust in connection with which beneficiaries other than those named in this trust have been designated, the Successor Trustee of this trust shall assert no claim to such asset but shall promptly deliver up the same to the individual named as Successor Trustee of such other trust.

2. Each beneficiary hereunder shall be liable for his proportionate share of any taxes levied upon the total taxable estate of the survivor of us by reason of the death of such survivor.

nominate and appoint as Successor Trustee hereunder the beneficiary named first above, unless such beneficiary shall not have attained the age of 21 years, or is otherwise legally incapacitated, in which event we hereby nominate and appoint as Successor Trustee hereunder the beneficiary whose name appears second above. If such beneficiary named second above shall not have attained the age of 21 years, or is otherwise legally incapacitated, then we nominate and appoint ___Henry P. Adams___ of ___Milton___ City, ___Connecticut 06605___ State Zip

(Name) ___Henry P. Adams___

(Address) ___125___ Number ___Barnum Street___ Street

to be Successor Trustee

9. This Declaration of Trust shall extend to and be binding upon the heirs, executors, administrators and assigns of the undersigned and upon the Successors to the Trustees.
10. We as Trustees and our Successor Trustee shall serve without bond.
11. This Declaration of Trust shall be construed and enforced in accordance with the laws of the State of ___Connecticut___

Declaration of Trust

WHEREAS, WE, _____ and _____, of the

City/Town of _____, County of _____, State of _____,

are joint holders of a safe deposit box in the _____,

(Name of Bank)

located in the City/Town of _____, State of _____;

NOW, THEREFORE, KNOW ALL MEN BY THESE PRESENTS, that we do hereby acknowledge and declare that we hold and will hold said safe deposit box and all our right, title and interest in and to said safe deposit box and its contents IN TRUST

1. For the use and benefit of the following _____ persons, in equal shares, or the survivor of them/per stirpes:

If because of the physical or mental incapacity of both of us certified in writing by a physician, the Successor Trustee hereinafter named shall assume active administration of this trust during our lifetime, such Successor Trustee shall be fully authorized to pay to us or disburse on our behalf such sums from income or principal generated by or constituting the contents of said box as appear necessary or desirable for our comfort or welfare. Upon the death of the survivor of us, unless all the beneficiaries shall predecease us or unless we all shall die as a result of a common accident or disaster, our Successor Trustee is hereby directed forthwith to transfer said safe deposit box and all right, title and interest in and to said box and its contents unto the beneficiaries absolutely and thereby terminate this trust; provided, however, that if any beneficiary hereunder shall not have attained the age of 21, the Successor Trustee shall hold such beneficiary's share of the trust assets in continuing trust until such beneficiary shall have attained the age of 21 years. During such period of continuing trust the Successor Trustee, in his absolute discretion, may retain the specific safe deposit box and its contents herein described if he believes it in the best interests of the beneficiary so to do, or he may terminate the box and dispose of its contents, investing and reinvesting the proceeds as he may deem appropriate. Prior to the date upon which such beneficiary attains the age of 21 years, the Successor Trustee may apply or expend any or all of the contents of the box or, if such contents have been disposed of, any or all of the income or principal derived from such disposition directly for the maintenance, education and support of the beneficiary without the intervention of any guardian and without application to any court. Such payments of income or principal may be made to the parents of such beneficiary or to the person with whom the beneficiary is living without any liability upon the Successor Trustee to see to the application thereof. If any such beneficiary survives us but dies before attaining the age of 21 years, at his or her death the Successor Trustee shall transfer, pay over and deliver the trust property being held for such beneficiary to said beneficiary's personal representative, absolutely.

If among the contents of the safe deposit box held hereunder there be any asset identifiable as having been covered by a declaration of trust in connection with which beneficiaries other than those named in this trust have been designated, the Successor Trustee of this trust shall assert no claim to such asset but shall promptly deliver up the same to the individual named as Successor Trustee of such other trust.

2. Each beneficiary hereunder shall be liable for his proportionate share of any taxes levied upon the total taxable estate of the survivor of us by reason of the death of such survivor.

3. The interests of any beneficiary hereunder shall be inalienable and free from anticipation, assignment, attachment, pledge or control by creditors or a present or former spouse of such beneficiary in any proceedings at law or in equity.

4. This trust is created with the express understanding that the bank at which the safe deposit box is maintained shall be under no liability whatsoever to see to its proper administration. On the contrary, upon the presentation by the Successor Trustee to the bank of proper evidence of the death of the survivor of us, the bank shall thereafter treat the Successor Trustee as the one solely entitled to the box and its contents. The bank shall be protected in acting upon any notice or other instrument or document believed by it to be genuine and to have been signed or presented by the proper party or parties.

5. We reserve unto ourselves the power and right at any time to remove all or any portion of the contents of the box, or to add to such contents.

6. We reserve unto ourselves the power and right at any time during our lifetime to amend or revoke in whole or in part the trust hereby created without the necessity of obtaining the consent of any beneficiary and without giving notice to any beneficiary. The withdrawal by us of the whole or any part of the contents of the safe deposit box held hereunder shall constitute as to such whole or part a revocation of this trust.

7. The death during our lifetime, or in a common accident or disaster with us, of all of the beneficiaries designated hereunder shall revoke such designation, and in the former event, we reserve the right to designate new beneficiaries. Should we for any reason fail to designate such new beneficiaries, this trust shall terminate upon the death of the survivor of us and the trust property shall revert to the estate of such survivor.

8. In the event of the physical or mental incapacity or death of one of us, the survivor shall continue as sole Trustee. In the event of the physical or mental incapacity or death of the survivor of us, or if we both shall die in a common accident, we hereby nominate and appoint as Successor Trustee hereunder the beneficiary named first above, unless such beneficiary shall not have attained the age of 21 years, or is otherwise legally incapacitated, in which event we hereby nominate and appoint as Successor Trustee hereunder the beneficiary whose name appears second above. If such beneficiary named second above shall not have attained the age of 21 years, or is otherwise legally incapacitated, then we nominate and appoint

(Name) _____, of

(Address) _____

| Number | Street | City | State | Zip |

to be Successor Trustee.

9. This Declaration of Trust shall extend to and be binding upon the heirs, executors, administrators and assigns of the undersigned and upon the Successors to the Trustees.

10. We as Trustees and our Successor Trustee shall serve without bond.

11. This Declaration of Trust shall be construed and enforced in accordance with the laws of the State

of _____.

IN WITNESS WHEREOF, we have hereunto set our hands and seals this _____

day of _____, 19____.

(First Settlor sign here) _____ L.S.

(Second Settlor sign here) _____ L.S.

I, the undersigned legal spouse of one of the above Settlors, hereby waive all community property rights which I may have in the contents of the hereinabove-described safe deposit box and give my assent to the provisions of the trust and to the inclusion in it of the said box and its contents.

(Spouse sign here) _____ L.S.

Witness: (1) _____   Witness: (2) _____

STATE OF _____   City
                                     or
COUNTY OF _____   Town _____

On the _____ day of _____, 19____, personally appeared

_____ and _____

known to me to be the individuals who executed the foregoing instrument, and acknowledged the same to be their free act and deed, before me.

(Notary Seal)   _____
                                                      Notary Public

Avoiding Probate of a Mortgage, First Trust Deed, or Real Estate Sales Contract

Generally speaking, "mortgage," "first trust deed," or "real estate sales contract" are simply different regional names for the same thing. In each case, the name signifies an indebtedness collaterized by real estate. Just as you can bequeath such an asset in your will, so you can utilize an inter vivos trust to transfer title to the asset in the event of your death.

On the following pages will be found declarations of trust which will be suitable for use in creating a living trust to cover (a) a mortgage, first trust deed, or real estate sales contract held in one name, or (b) the same type of asset held in joint names. You will recall that in the case of trusts covering your *ownership* of real estate, in addition to the declaration of trust it was necessary to execute and file a quit claim deed by which you transferred title from yourself as an individual to yourself as trustee. A somewhat similar requirement applies to the asset here being discussed—in addition to the declaration of trust, you must execute and file an "Assignment of Mortgage" from yourself as an individual to yourself as trustee. Accordingly, after the four forms of declaration of trust to cover a mortgage held in one name, you will find an "Assignment of Mortgage" (AM) to be used *only* with those forms. After the three forms designed for putting in trust a mortgage held in joint names, you will find an "Assignment of Mortgage" (AM-J) for use only with a jointly held mortgage. Make certain that you match them correctly.

It is possible for a mortgage held in one name to be put into a joint trust but neither the AM nor the AM-J forms may be used for this purpose. Instead, at the very end of this chapter you will find a special assignment form (AM-SPEC) which you may use for that purpose.

CHAPTER 12

DECLARATION OF TRUST

For Naming

ONE BENEFICIARY

To Receive

A MORTGAGE, FIRST TRUST DEED, OR REAL ESTATE

SALES CONTRACT HELD IN ONE NAME

INSTRUCTIONS:

On the following pages will be found a declaration of trust (DT-121) suitable for use in connection with the establishment of an inter vivos trust covering a mortgage, first trust deed, or real estate sales contract held in one name, where it is desired to name some one person to receive the asset upon the death of the owner.

Cross out *"city"* or *"town,"* leaving the appropriate designation of your community. Next, insert the address of the property; if it has no street number, cross out *"(and known as),"* and follow it with the description of the property as it appears in the mortgage deed.

Enter the name of the beneficiary in the appropriate place in Paragraph 1.

Note that Paragraph 7 designates as Successor Trustee *"whosoever shall at that time be beneficiary hereunder,"* which means that in most cases you don't need to fill anything in there. However, if there is any possibility of a beneficiary who has not attained the age of 21 years receiving the trust property, make certain that you name an adult in this paragraph who can act as trustee for such beneficiary. Avoid naming as trustee a person not likely to survive until the beneficiary has attained age 21.

Next, execute the "Assignment of Mortgage, First Trust Deed, or Real Estate Sales Contract" (AM) to be found on page 217.

When completed, make several photocopies for reference purposes, and then file the original of both documents with the town or county clerk or other office where real estate transfers in the area where the property is located are customarily recorded. After they are recorded, they will be returned to you.

Important: Read carefully Note B on page 38, which applies to this declaration of trust.

Declaration of Trust

WHEREAS, I, __John J. Brown__, County of __Fairfax__, State of __Connecticut__, of the City/Town of __Milton__, am the holder of a mortgage, first trust deed or real estate sales contract on certain real property located at (and known as) __525 Main Street__, State of __Connecticut__, which property is described more fully in such mortgage, first trust deed or real estate sales contract as "that certain piece of parcel of land with any buildings thereon standing, located in said __Milton__ __Milton__, being in the City/Town of __Milton__, particularly described as:

the rear portions of Lots #34 and 35, on Map of Building Lots of George Spooner, said map being dated May 3, 1952, and filed for record in the office of the Town Clerk, Milton, Connecticut in Book 5, Page 16 of said Maps. Said parcel of land is more particularly described as:

Beginning at a point on the south line of Lot #34, on said map, 73.5 feet East of the East line of Park Avenue -- running thence North along land of James E. Beach, 100 feet to a point on the East line of Lot #35 on said map, 70.44 feet East of the said line to Cornwall Street, thence East along land of the said James E. Beach (being Lot #51 on said map) 55 feet -- thence South along land of Thomas Cook (being Lot #56 on said map) 100 feet to the aforesaid North line of Bartram Street -- thence West to the point of beginning.

NOW, THEREFORE, KNOW ALL MEN BY THESE PRESENTS, that I do hereby acknowledge and declare that I hold and will hold said mortgage, first trust deed or real estate sales contract and all my right, title and interest in and to said mortgage, first trust deed or real estate sales contract IN TRUST

1. For the use and benefit of: __Elizabeth A. Brown -- my wife__, __Milton__ __Connecticut 06605__, of

(Name) ____ City ____ State ____ Zip

(Address) __525__ __Main Street__
Number Street

If because of my physical or mental incapacity certified in writing by a physician, the Successor Trustee hereinafter named shall assume active administration of this trust during my lifetime, such Successor Trustee shall be fully authorized to pay to me or disburse on my behalf such sums from income or principal as appear necessary or desirable for my comfort or welfare. Upon my death, unless the beneficiary shall predecease me or unless we both shall die as a result of a common accident or disaster, my Successor Trustee is hereby directed forthwith to transfer the trust property and all right, title and interest in and to said property unto the beneficiary absolutely and hereby terminate this trust; provided, however, that if the beneficiary hereunder

[...] Prior to the date upon which such beneficiary attains the age of 21 years, the Successor Trustee may apply or expend any or all of the income or principal directly for the maintenance, education and support of the beneficiary without the intervention of any guardian and without application to any court. Such payments of income or principal may be made to the parents of such beneficiary or to the person with whom the beneficiary is living without any liability upon the Successor Trustee to see to the application thereof. If such beneficiary survives me but dies before attaining the age of 21 years, at his or her death the Successor Trustee shall transfer, pay over and deliver the trust property to such beneficiary's personal representative, absolutely.

2. The beneficiary hereunder shall be liable for his proportionate share of any taxes levied upon the Settlor's total taxable estate by reason of the Settlor's death.

3. All interests of a beneficiary hereunder shall be inalienable and free from anticipation, assignment, attachment, pledge or control by creditors or a present or former spouse of such beneficiary in any proceedings at law or in equity.

4. I reserve unto myself the power and right to collect any interest or payments constituting amortization which may accrue from the trust property and to pay them to myself as an individual. I shall be exclusively entitled to all such income accruing from the trust property during my lifetime, and no beneficiary named herein shall have any claim upon any such income distributed to me.

5. I reserve unto myself the power and right at any time during my lifetime to amend or revoke in whole or in part the trust hereby created without the necessity of obtaining the consent of the beneficiary and without giving notice to the beneficiary. The transfer of the trust property by me to another person shall constitute a revocation of this trust.

6. The death during my lifetime, or in a common accident or disaster with me, of the beneficiary designated hereunder shall revoke such designation, and in the former event, I reserve the right to designate a new beneficiary. Should I for any reason fail to designate such new beneficiary, this trust shall terminate upon my death and the trust property shall revert to my estate.

7. In the event of my physical or mental incapacity or death, I hereby nominate and appoint as Successor Trustee hereunder whosoever shall at that time be beneficiary hereunder, unless such beneficiary shall not have attained the age of 21 years, or is otherwise legally incapacitated, in which event I hereby nominate and appoint

__Henry P. Adams__, __Milton__ __Connecticut 06605__, of

(Name) ____ City ____ State ____ Zip

(Address) __125__ __Barnum Street__
Number Street

to be Successor Trustee.

8. This Declaration of Trust shall extend to and be binding upon the heirs, executors, administrators and assigns of the undersigned and upon the Successors to the Trustee.

9. The Trustee and his successors shall serve without bond.

10. This Declaration of Trust shall be construed and enforced in accordance with the laws of the State of __Connecticut__.

Declaration of Trust

WHEREAS, I, _____, of the

City/Town of _____, County of _____, State of _____,

am the holder of a mortgage, first trust deed or real estate sales contract on certain real property located at (and known

as) _____,

in the City/Town of _____, State of _____, which property is

described more fully in such mortgage, first trust deed or real estate sales contract as "that certain piece or parcel of land with

any buildings thereon standing, located in said _____, being

NOW, THEREFORE, KNOW ALL MEN BY THESE PRESENTS, that I do hereby acknowledge and declare that I hold and will hold said mortgage, first trust deed or real estate sales contract and all my right, title and interest in and to said mortgage, first trust deed or real estate sales contract IN TRUST

1. For the use and benefit of:

(Name) _____, of

(Address) _____
　　　　　　　　Number　　　　　　　Street　　　　　　　City　　　　　　　State　　　　　Zip

If because of my physical or mental incapacity certified in writing by a physician, the Successor Trustee hereinafter named shall assume active administration of this trust during my lifetime, such Successor Trustee shall be fully authorized to pay to me or disburse on my behalf such sums from income or principal as appear necessary or desirable for my comfort or welfare. Upon my death, unless the beneficiary shall predecease me or unless we both shall die as a result of a common accident or disaster, my Successor Trustee is hereby directed forthwith to transfer the trust property and all right, title and interest in and to said property unto the beneficiary absolutely and hereby terminate this trust; provided, however, that if the beneficiary hereunder shall not have attained the age of 21 years, the Successor Trustee shall hold the trust assets in continuing trust until such beneficiary shall have attained the age of 21 years. During such period of continuing trust the Successor Trustee, in his absolute discretion, may retain the specific trust property herein described if he believes it in the best interest of the beneficiary so to do, or he may sell or otherwise dispose of such specific trust property, investing and reinvesting the proceeds as he may deem appropriate. Prior to the date upon which such beneficiary attains the age of 21 years, the Successor Trustee may apply or expend any or all of the income or principal directly for the maintenance, education and support of the beneficiary without the intervention of any guardian and without application to any court. Such payments of income or principal may be made to the parents of such beneficiary or to the person with whom the beneficiary is living without any liability upon the Successor Trustee to see to the application thereof. If such beneficiary survives me but dies before attaining the age of 21 years, at his or her death the Successor Trustee shall transfer, pay over and deliver the trust property to such beneficiary's personal representative, absolutely.

2. The beneficiary hereunder shall be liable for his proportionate share of any taxes levied upon the Settlor's total taxable estate by reason of the Settlor's death.

3. All interests of a beneficiary hereunder shall be inalienable and free from anticipation, assignment, attachment, pledge or control by creditors or a present or former spouse of such beneficiary in any proceedings at law or in equity.

4. I reserve unto myself the power and right to collect any interest or payments constituting amortization which may accrue from the trust property and to pay them to myself as an individual. I shall be exclusively entitled to all such income accruing from the trust property during my lifetime, and no beneficiary named herein shall have any claim upon any such income distributed to me.

5. I reserve unto myself the power and right at any time during my lifetime to amend or revoke in whole or in part the trust hereby created without the necessity of obtaining the consent of the beneficiary and without giving notice to the beneficiary. The transfer of the trust property by me to another person shall constitute a revocation of this trust.

6. The death during my lifetime, or in a common accident or disaster with me, of the beneficiary designated hereunder shall revoke such designation, and in the former event, I reserve the right to designate a new beneficiary. Should I for any reason fail to designate such new beneficiary, this trust shall terminate upon my death and the trust property shall revert to my estate.

7. In the event of my physical or mental incapacity or death, I hereby nominate and appoint as Successor Trustee hereunder whosoever shall at that time be beneficiary hereunder, unless such beneficiary shall not have attained the age of 21 years, or is otherwise legally incapacitated, in which event I hereby nominate and appoint

(Name) _____ _____, of

(Address) _____
  Number   Street   City   State   Zip

to be Successor Trustee.

8. This Declaration of Trust shall extend to and be binding upon the heirs, executors, administrators and assigns of the undersigned and upon the Successors to the Trustee.

9. The Trustee and his successors shall serve without bond.

10. This Declaration of Trust shall be construed and enforced in accordance with the laws of the State

of _____.

IN WITNESS WHEREOF, I have hereunto set my hand and seal this _____

day of _____, 19____.

(Settlor sign here) _____ L.S.

I, the undersigned legal spouse of the above Settlor, hereby waive all community property rights which I may have in the hereinabove-described trust property and give my assent to the provisions of the trust and to the inclusion in it of the said property.

(Spouse sign here) _____ L.S.

Witness: (1) _____   Witness: (2) _____

STATE OF _____   City
                                     or
COUNTY OF _____   Town _____

On the _____ day of _____, 19____, personally appeared

_____

known to me to be the individual(s) who executed the foregoing instrument, and acknowledged the same to be _____ free act and deed, before me.

_____

(Notary Seal)   Notary Public

CHAPTER 12

DECLARATION OF TRUST

For Naming

ONE PRIMARY BENEFICIARY

And

ONE CONTINGENT BENEFICIARY

To Receive

A MORTGAGE, FIRST TRUST DEED, OR REAL ESTATE

SALES CONTRACT HELD IN ONE NAME

INSTRUCTIONS:

On the following pages will be found a declaration of trust (DT-122) suitable for use in connection with the establishment of an inter vivos trust covering a mortgage, first trust deed, or real estate sales contract held in one name, where it is desired to name some *one* person as primary beneficiary with some *one* other person as contingent beneficiary to receive the asset if the primary beneficiary be not surviving upon the death of the owner.

Cross out *"city"* or *"town,"* leaving the appropriate designation of your community. Insert the address of the property; if it has no street number, cross out *"(and known as)"* and follow it with the description of the property as it appears in the mortgage deed.

Enter the names of the beneficiaries in the appropriate place in Paragraph 1.

Note that Paragraph 7 designates as Successor Trustee *"whosoever shall at that time be beneficiary hereunder,"* which means that in most cases you don't need to fill anything in there. However, if there is any possibility of a beneficiary who has not attained the age of 21 years receiving the trust property, make certain that you name an adult in this paragraph who can act as trustee for such beneficiary. Avoid naming as trustee a person not likely to survive until the beneficiary has attained age 21.

Next, execute the "Assignment of Mortgage, First Trust Deed, or Real Estate Sales Contract" (AM) to be found on page 217.

When completed, make several photocopies for reference purposes, and then file the original of both documents with the town or county clerk or other office where real estate transfers in the area where the property is located are customarily recorded. After they are recorded, they will be returned to you.

Important: Read carefully Note B on page 38, which applies to this declaration of trust.

DT-122

Declaration of Trust

WHEREAS, I, __John J. Brown__, County of __Fairfax__, State of __Connecticut__, of the Town of __Milton__, am the holder of a mortgage, first trust deed or real estate sales contract on certain real property located at (and known as) __525 Main Street__, State of __Connecticut__ which property is in the Town of __Milton__, described more fully in such mortgage, first trust deed or real estate sales contract as "that certain piece or parcel of land with any buildings thereon standing, located in said __Milton__, being

the rear portions of Lots #34 and 35, on Map of Building Lots of George Spooner, said map being dated May 3, 1952, and filed for record in the office of the Town Clerk, Milton, Connecticut in Book 5, Page 16 of said Maps. Said parcel of land is more particularly described as:

Beginning at a point on the south line of Lot #34, on said map, 73.5 feet East of the East line of Park Avenue -- running thence North along land of James E. Beach, 100 feet to a point on the North line of Lot #35 on said map, 70.44 feet East of the said line to Cornwall Street, thence East along land of the said James E. Beach (being Lot #51 on said map) 55 feet -- thence South along land of Thomas Cook (being Lot #56 on said map) 100 feet to the aforesaid North line of Bartram Street -- thence West to the point of beginning.

NOW, THEREFORE, KNOW ALL MEN BY THESE PRESENTS, that I do hereby acknowledge and declare that I hold and will hold said mortgage, first trust deed or real estate sales contract and all my right, title and interest in and to said mortgage, first trust deed or real estate sales contract IN TRUST

1. For the use and benefit of:

(Name) __Elizabeth A. Brown - my wife__ __Milton__ City __Connecticut__ State __06605__ Zip, of
(Address) __525   Main Street__ Street
        Number

or, if such beneficiary be not surviving, for the use and benefit of:

(Name) __Jill A. Brown - my daughter__ __Milton__ City __Connecticut__ State __06605__ Zip, of
(Address) __525 Main Street__ Street
        Number

If because of my physical or mental incapacity certified in writing by a physician, the Successor Trustee hereinafter named shall assume active administration of this trust during my lifetime, such Successor Trustee shall be fully authorized to pay to me or disburse on my behalf such sums from income or principal as appear necessary or desirable for my comfort or welfare. Upon my death, unless the beneficiaries both shall predecease me or unless we all shall die as a result of a common accident or disaster, my Successor Trustee is hereby directed forthwith to transfer the trust property and all right, title and interest in and to said property unto the beneficiary absolutely and _____ terminate this _____ _____ _____ _____ _____ of the beneficiary hereunder

_____ the beneficiary hereunder _____ be _____ for his proportionate share of any taxes levied upon the Settlor's total taxable estate by reason of the Settlor's death.

3. All interests of a beneficiary hereunder shall be inalienable and free from anticipation, assignment, attachment, pledge or control by creditors or a present or former spouse of such beneficiary in any proceedings at law or in equity.

4. I reserve unto myself the power and right to collect any interest or payments constituting amortization which may accrue from the trust property during my lifetime, and no beneficiary named herein shall have any claim upon such income accruing from the trust property during my lifetime, and to pay them to myself as an individual. I shall be exclusively entitled to all such income distributed to me.

5. I reserve unto myself the power and right at any time during my lifetime to amend or revoke in whole or in part the trust hereby created without the necessity of obtaining the consent of the beneficiaries and without giving notice to the beneficiaries. The transfer of the trust property by me to another person shall constitute a revocation of this trust.

6. The death during my lifetime, or in a common accident or disaster with me, of both of the beneficiaries designated hereunder shall revoke such designation, and in the former event, I reserve the right to designate a new beneficiary. Should I for any reason fail to designate such new beneficiary, this trust shall terminate upon my death and the trust property shall revert to my estate.

7. In the event of my physical or mental incapacity or death, I hereby nominate and appoint as Successor Trustee hereunder whosoever shall at that time be beneficiary hereunder, unless such beneficiary shall not have attained the age of 21 years or is otherwise legally incapacitated, in which event I hereby nominate and appoint

(Name) __Henry P. Adams__ __Milton__ City __Connecticut__ State __06605__ Zip, of
(Address) __125   Barnum Street__ Street
        Number

to be Successor Trustee.
8. This Declaration of Trust shall extend to and be binding upon the heirs, executors, administrators and assigns of the undersigned and upon the Successors to the Trustee.
9. The Trustee and his successors shall serve without bond.
10. This Declaration of Trust shall be construed and enforced in accordance with the laws of the State of __Connecticut__

Declaration of Trust

WHEREAS, I, _____, of the

City/Town of _____, County of _____, State of _____,

am the holder of a mortgage, first trust deed or real estate sales contract on certain real property located at (and known

as) _____,

in the City/Town of _____, State of _____, which property is

described more fully in such mortgage, first trust deed or real estate sales contract as "that certain piece or parcel of land with

any buildings thereon standing, located in said _____, being

NOW, THEREFORE, KNOW ALL MEN BY THESE PRESENTS, that I do hereby acknowledge and declare that I hold and will hold said mortgage, first trust deed or real estate sales contract and all my right, title and interest in and to said mortgage, first trust deed or real estate sales contract IN TRUST

1. For the use and benefit of:

(Name) _____, of

(Address) _____
        Number   Street   City   State   Zip

or, if such beneficiary be not surviving, for the use and benefit of:

(Name) _____, of

(Address) _____
        Number   Street   City   State   Zip

If because of my physical or mental incapacity certified in writing by a physician, the Successor Trustee hereinafter named shall assume active administration of this trust during my lifetime, such Successor Trustee shall be fully authorized to pay to me or disburse on my behalf such sums from income or principal as appear necessary or desirable for my comfort or welfare. Upon my death, unless the beneficiaries both shall predecease me or unless we all shall die as a result of a common accident or disaster, my Successor Trustee is hereby directed forthwith to transfer the trust property and all right, title and interest in and to said property unto the beneficiary absolutely and hereby terminate this trust; provided, however, that if the beneficiary hereunder shall not have attained the age of 21 years, the Successor Trustee shall hold the trust assets in continuing trust until such beneficiary shall have attained the age of 21 years. During such period of continuing trust the Successor Trustee, in his absolute discretion, may retain the specific trust property herein described if he believes it in the best interest of the beneficiary so to do, or he may sell or otherwise dispose of such specific trust property, investing and reinvesting the proceeds as he may deem appropriate. Prior to the date upon which such beneficiary attains the age of 21 years, the Successor Trustee may apply or expend any or all of the income or principal directly for the maintenance, education and support of the beneficiary without the intervention of any guardian and without application to any court. Such payments of income or principal may be made to the parents of such beneficiary or to the person with whom the beneficiary is living without any liability upon the Successor Trustee to see to the application thereof. If such beneficiary survives me but dies before attaining the age of 21 years, at his or her death the Successor Trustee shall transfer, pay over and deliver the trust property to such beneficiary's personal representative, absolutely.

2. The beneficiary hereunder shall be liable for his proportionate share of any taxes levied upon the Settlor's total taxable estate by reason of the Settlor's death.

3. All interests of a beneficiary hereunder shall be inalienable and free from anticipation, assignment, attachment, pledge or control by creditors or a present or former spouse of such beneficiary in any proceedings at law or in equity.

4. I reserve unto myself the power and right to collect any interest or payments constituting amortization which may accrue from the trust property and to pay them to myself as an individual. I shall be exclusively entitled to all such income accruing from the trust property during my lifetime, and no beneficiary named herein shall have any claim upon such income distributed to me.

5. I reserve unto myself the power and right at any time during my lifetime to amend or revoke in whole or in part the trust hereby created without the necessity of obtaining the consent of the beneficiaries and without giving notice to the beneficiaries. The transfer of the trust property by me to another person shall constitute a revocation of this trust.

6. The death during my lifetime, or in a common accident or disaster with me, of both of the beneficiaries designated hereunder shall revoke such designation, and in the former event, I reserve the right to designate a new beneficiary. Should I for any reason fail to designate such new beneficiary, this trust shall terminate upon my death and the trust property shall revert to my estate.

7. In the event of my physical or mental incapacity or death, I hereby nominate and appoint as Successor Trustee hereunder whosoever shall at that time be beneficiary hereunder, unless such beneficiary shall not have attained the age of 21 years or is otherwise legally incapacitated, in which event I hereby nominate and appoint

(Name) _____, of

(Address) _____

| Number | Street | City | State | Zip |

to be Successor Trustee.

8. This Declaration of Trust shall extend to and be binding upon the heirs, executors, administrators and assigns of the undersigned and upon the Successors to the Trustee.

9. The Trustee and his successors shall serve without bond.

10. This Declaration of Trust shall be construed and enforced in accordance with the laws of the State of

_____.

IN WITNESS WHEREOF, I have hereunto set my hand and seal this _____

day of _____, 19_____.

(Settlor sign here) _____ L.S.

I, the undersigned legal spouse of the above Settlor, hereby waive all community property rights which I may have in the hereinabove-described trust property and give my assent to the provisions of the trust and to the inclusion in it of the said property.

(Spouse sign here) _____ L.S.

Witness: (1) _____   Witness: (2) _____

STATE OF _____   City
or
COUNTY OF _____   Town _____

On the _____ day of _____, 19_____, personally appeared

_____

known to me to be the individual(s) who executed the foregoing instrument, and acknowledged the same to be _____ free act and deed, before me.

_____

(Notary Seal)   Notary Public

CHAPTER 12

DECLARATION OF TRUST

For Naming

TWO OR MORE BENEFICIARIES, SHARING EQUALLY,

To Receive

A MORTGAGE, FIRST TRUST DEED, OR REAL ESTATE

SALES CONTRACT HELD IN ONE NAME

INSTRUCTIONS:

On the following pages will be found a declaration of trust (DT-123) suitable for use in connection with the establishment of an inter vivos trust covering a mortgage, first trust deed, or real estate sales contract held in one name only, where it is desired to name two or more persons to share the asset equally upon the death of the owner.

Cross out *"city"* or *"town,"* leaving the appropriate designation of your community. Next, insert the address of the property; if it has no street number, cross out *"(and known as)"* and follow it with the description of the property as it appears in the mortgage deed.

In Paragraph 1, indicate the *number of persons* you are naming (to discourage unauthorized additions to the list) and then insert their names. The one whose name appears *first* will be the Successor Trustee responsible for seeing to the distribution of the trust property.

Note that the instrument specifies that the named beneficiaries are to receive *"in equal shares, or the survivor of them/per stirpes."* Now, think carefully: If you have named three persons with the understanding that if one of them predeceases you, *his* children will take *his* share, cross out *"or the survivor of them"* and *initial it.* If that is *not* what you want—if, for example, you prefer that the share of the deceased person be divided between the two surviving persons, cross out *"per stirpes"* and *initial it.* Remember, you <u>must</u> cross out either *"or the survivor of them"* or *"per stirpes"*—one or the other.

Note that Paragraph 7 designates as Successor Trustee *"the beneficiary named first above,"* which means that in most cases you don't have to fill anything in there. However, if there is any possibility of a beneficiary who has not attained the age of 21 years receiving the trust property, make certain that you name an adult in this paragraph who can act as trustee for such beneficiary. Avoid naming as trustee a person not likely to survive until the beneficiary has attained age 21.

Next, execute the "Assignment of Mortgage, First Trust Deed, or Real Estate Sales Contract" (AM) to be found on page 217.

When completed, make several photocopies for reference purposes and file the original of both documents with the town or county clerk or other office where real estate transfers in the area where the property is located are customarily recorded. After they are recorded, they will be returned to you.

Important: Read carefully Note B on page 38, which applies to this declaration of trust.

Declaration of Trust

DALEY TRUST

WHEREAS, I, __John J. Brown__, County of __Fairfax__, State of __Connecticut__, of the City/Town of __Milton__, am the holder of a mortgage, first trust deed or real estate sales contract on certain real property located at (and known as) __525 Main Street__, State of __Connecticut__, which property is, in the City/Town of __Milton__, described more fully in such mortgage, first trust deed or real estate sales contract as "that certain piece or parcel of land with any buildings thereon standing, located in said __Milton__, being

the rear portions of Lots #34 and 35, on Map of Building Lots of George Spooner, said map being dated May 3, 1952, and filed for record in the office of the Town Clerk, Milton, Connecticut in Book 5, Page 16 of said Maps. Said parcel of land is more particularly described as:

Beginning at a point on the south line of Lot #34, on said map, 73.5 feet East of the East line of Park Avenue -- running thence North along land of James E. Beach, 100 feet to a point on the North line of Lot #35 on said map, 70.44 feet East of the said line to Cornwall Street, thence East along land of the said James E. Beach (being Lot #51 on said map) 55 feet -- thence South along land of Thomas Cook (being Lot #56 on said map) 100 feet to the aforesaid North line of Cornwall Street.

NOW, THEREFORE, KNOW ALL MEN BY THESE PRESENTS, that I do hereby acknowledge and declare that I hold and will hold said mortgage, first trust deed or real estate sales contract and all my right, title and interest in and to said mortgage, first trust deed or real estate sales contract IN TRUST   _J.J.B._

1. For the use and benefit of the following __three (3)__ persons, in equal shares, or the survivor of them/per stirpes:

Thomas B. Brown - my brother
Helen M. Brown - my sister
Charles M. Brown - my brother

If because of my physical or mental incapacity certified in writing by a physician, the Successor Trustee hereinafter named shall assume active administration of this trust during my lifetime, such Successor Trustee shall be fully authorized to pay to me or disburse on my behalf such sums from income or principal as appear necessary or desirable for my comfort or welfare. Upon my death, my Successor Trustee is hereby directed forthwith to transfer the trust property and all right, title and interest in and to said property unto the beneficiaries absolutely and thereby terminate this trust; provided, however, that if any beneficiary hereunder shall not have attained the age of 21 years, the Successor Trustee shall hold such beneficiary's share of the trust assets in continuing trust until such beneficiary shall have attained the age of 21 years. During such period of continuing trust the Successor Trustee, in his absolute discretion, may retain the specific trust property herein described if he believes it to be in the

7. In the event of my physical or mental incapacity or my death, I hereby nominate and appoint as Successor Trustee the beneficiary named first above, unless such beneficiary shall not have attained the age of 21 years or is otherwise legally incapacitated in which event I hereby nominate and appoint as Successor Trustee the beneficiary named second above, unless such beneficiary named second above shall not have attained the age of 21 years or is otherwise legally incapacitated, in which latter event I hereby nominate and appoint

(Name) __Henry P. Adams__ , __Milton__ , __Connecticut__ __06605__ , of
                                                    City   State   Zip

(Address) __125 Barnum Street__
              Number   Street

to be Successor Trustee.
8. This Declaration of Trust shall extend to and be binding upon the heirs, executors, administrators and assigns of the undersigned and upon the Successors to the Trustee.
9. The Trustee and his successors shall serve without bond.
10. This Declaration of Trust shall be construed and enforced in accordance with the laws of the State of

__Connecticut__ .

Declaration of Trust

WHEREAS, I, _____, of the

City/Town of _____, County of _____, State of _____,

am the holder of a mortgage, first trust deed or real estate sales contract on certain real property located at (and known

as) _____,

in the City/Town of _____, State of _____, which property is

described more fully in such mortgage, first trust deed or real estate sales contract as "that certain piece or parcel of land with

any buildings thereon standing, located in said _____, being

NOW, THEREFORE, KNOW ALL MEN BY THESE PRESENTS, that I do hereby acknowledge and declare that I hold and will hold said mortgage, first trust deed or real estate sales contract and all my right, title and interest in and to said mortgage, first trust deed or real estate sales contract IN TRUST

1. For the use and benefit of the following _____ persons, in equal shares, or the survivor of them/per stirpes:

If because of my physical or mental incapacity certified in writing by a physician, the Successor Trustee hereinafter named shall assume active administration of this trust during my lifetime, such Successor Trustee shall be fully authorized to pay to me or disburse on my behalf such sums from income or principal as appear necessary or desirable for my comfort or welfare. Upon my death, unless all of the beneficiaries shall predecease me or unless we all shall die as a result of a common accident or disaster, my Successor Trustee is hereby directed forthwith to transfer the trust property and all right, title and interest in and to said property unto the beneficiaries absolutely and thereby terminate this trust; provided, however, that if any beneficiary hereunder shall not have attained the age of 21 years, the Successor Trustee shall hold such beneficiary's share of the trust assets in continuing trust until such beneficiary shall have attained the age of 21 years. During such period of continuing trust the Successor Trustee, in his absolute discretion, may retain the specific trust property herein described if he believes it to be in the best interests of the beneficiary so to do, or he may sell or otherwise dispose of it, investing and reinvesting the proceeds as he may deem appropriate. Prior to the date upon which such beneficiary attains the age of 21 years, the Successor Trustee may apply or expend any or all of the income or principal directly for the maintenance, education and support of the beneficiary without the intervention of any guardian and without application to any court. Such payments of income or principal may be made to the parents of such beneficiary or to the person with whom the beneficiary is living without any liability upon the Successor Trustee to see to the application thereof. If such beneficiary survives me but dies before attaining the age of 21 years, at his or her death the Successor Trustee shall transfer, pay over and deliver the trust property being held for such beneficiary to such beneficiary's personal representative, absolutely.

2. Each beneficiary hereunder shall be liable for his proportionate share of any taxes levied upon the Settlor's total taxable estate by reason of the Settlor's death.

3. All interests of a beneficiary hereunder shall be inalienable and free from anticipation, assignment, attachment, pledge or control by creditors or a present or former spouse of such beneficiary in any proceedings at law or in equity.

4. I reserve unto myself the power and right to collect any interest or payments constituting amortization which may accrue from the trust property and to pay such income to myself as an individual. I shall be exclusively entitled to all income accruing from the trust property during my lifetime, and no beneficiary named herein shall have any claim upon any such income distributed to me.

5. I reserve unto myself the power and right at any time during my lifetime to amend or revoke in whole or in part the trust hereby created without the necessity of obtaining the consent of the beneficiaries and without giving notice to the beneficiaries. The transfer of the trust property by me to another person shall constitute a revocation of this trust.

6. The death during my lifetime, or in a common accident or disaster with me, of all of the beneficiaries designated hereunder shall revoke such designation, and in the former event, I reserve the right to designate a new beneficiary. Should I for any reason fail to designate such new beneficiary, this trust shall terminate upon my death and the trust property shall revert to my estate.

7. In the event of my physical or mental incapacity or my death, I hereby nominate and appoint as Successor Trustee the beneficiary named first above, unless such beneficiary shall not have attained the age of 21 years or is otherwise legally incapacitated in which event I hereby nominate and appoint as Successor Trustee the beneficiary named second above, unless such beneficiary named second above shall not have attained the age of 21 years or is otherwise legally incapacitated, in which latter event I hereby nominate and appoint

(Name) _____ , of

(Address) _____
        Number   *Street*   *City*   *State*   *Zip*

to be Successor Trustee.

8. This Declaration of Trust shall extend to and be binding upon the heirs, executors, administrators and assigns of the undersigned and upon the Successors to the Trustee.

9. The Trustee and his successors shall serve without bond.

10. This Declaration of Trust shall be construed and enforced in accordance with the laws of the State of

_____.

IN WITNESS WHEREOF, I have hereunto set my hand and seal this _____

day of _____ , 19_____ .

               (Settlor sign here) _____ L.S.

I, the undersigned legal spouse of the above Settlor, hereby waive all community property rights which I may have in the hereinabove-described trust property and give my assent to the provisions of the trust and to the inclusion in it of the said property.

          (Spouse sign here) _____ L.S.

Witness: (1) _____   Witness: (2) _____

STATE OF _____   City

COUNTY OF _____   or Town _____

On the _____ day of _____ , 19_____ , personally appeared

_____

known to me to be the individual(s) who executed the foregoing instrument, and acknowledged the same to be _____ free act and deed, before me.

_____
(Notary Seal)   *Notary Public*

CHAPTER 12

DECLARATION OF TRUST
For Naming
**ONE PRIMARY BENEFICIARY WITH YOUR CHILDREN,
SHARING EQUALLY, AS CONTINGENT BENEFICIARIES**
To Receive
**A MORTGAGE, FIRST TRUST DEED, OR REAL ESTATE
SALES CONTRACT HELD IN ONE NAME**

INSTRUCTIONS:

On the following pages will be found a declaration of trust (DT-124) suitable for use in connection with the establishment of an inter vivos trust covering a mortgage, first trust deed, or real estate sales contract held in one name only, where it is desired to name one person (ordinarily, but not necessarily, one's spouse) as primary beneficiary with one's children sharing equally as contingent beneficiaries to receive the asset if the primary beneficiary be not surviving.

Cross out *"city"* or *"town,"* leaving the appropriate designation of your community. Next, insert the address of the property; if it has no street number, cross out *"(and known as)"* and follow it with the description of the property as it appears in the mortgage deed.

Enter the name of the primary beneficiary (called the "First Beneficiary") in the appropriate place in Paragraph 1. Note that the instrument first refers to your children as *"natural not/or adopted."* Now, decide: If you have an adopted child and you wish to include him, cross out the word *"not"* in the phrase *"natural not/or adopted"* and *initial it.* If you wish to *exclude* your adopted child, cross out the word *"or"* in the same phrase and *initial it.* Remember, you <u>must</u> cross out *"not"* or *"or"*—one or the other. If you have no adopted child, simply cross out *"not."*

Note next that the instrument specifies that your children are to receive *"in equal shares, or the survivor of them/per stirpes."* Now, think carefully: If it is your wish that if one of your children does not survive you, *his* share will revert to *his* children in equal shares, cross out *"or the survivor of them"* and *initial it.* If that is *not* what you want—if, for example, you prefer that the share of any child of yours who predeceases you shall be divided between your other surviving children in equal shares, cross out *"per stirpes"* and *initial it.* Remember, you <u>must</u> cross out *"or the survivor of them"* or *"per stirpes"*—one or the other.

Note that in Paragraph 7, the First Beneficiary is designated as Successor Trustee, while a space is provided in which you should designate another person to so act if the named Successor Trustee is not surviving or otherwise fails or ceases to act. This could be one of your children, for example, but it must be an adult who can act as trustee for any beneficiary who comes into a share of the trust before attaining the age of 21. Avoid naming someone not likely to survive until the youngest such beneficiary has attained age 21.

Next, execute the "Assignment of Mortgage, First Trust Deed, or Real Estate Sales Contract" (AM) to be found on page 217.

When completed, make several photocopies for reference purposes, and then file the original of both documents with the town or county clerk or other office where real estate transfers in the area where the property is located are customarily recorded. After they are recorded, they will be returned to you.

Important: Read carefully Note B on page 38, which applies to this declaration of trust.

Declaration of Trust

WHEREAS, I, _____ John J. Brown _____, County of _Fairfax_, State of _Connecticut_, of the
Town of _Milton_
am the holder of a mortgage, first trust deed or real estate sales contract on certain real property located at (and known
as) _525 Main Street_, State of _Connecticut_, which property is
in the City/Town of _Milton_ _Milton_, being
described more fully in such mortgage, first trust deed or real estate sales contract as "that certain piece or parcel of land with
any buildings thereon standing, located in said _Milton_

the rear portions of Lots #34 and 35, on Map of Building Lots
of George Spooner, said map being dated May 3, 1952, and filed
for record in the office of the Town Clerk, Milton, Connecticut
in Book 5, Page 16 of said Maps. Said parcel of land is more
particularly described as:

Beginning at a point on the south line of Lot #34, on said map,
73.5 feet East of the East line of Park Avenue -- running thence
North along land of James E. Beach, 100 feet to a point on the
North line of Lot #35 on said map, 70.44 feet East of the East
line to Cornwall Street, thence East along land of the said
James E. Beach (being Lot #51 on said map) 55 feet -- thence
South along land of Thomas Cook (being Lot #56 on said map)
100 feet to the aforesaid North line of Bartram Street --
thence West to the point of beginning.

NOW, THEREFORE, KNOW ALL MEN BY THESE PRESENTS, that I do hereby acknowledge and declare that I hold
and will hold said mortgage, first trust deed or real estate sales contract and all my right, title and interest in and to said
mortgage, first trust deed or real estate sales contract IN TRUST

1. For the use and benefit of: _____, of

(Name) _Elizabeth A. Brown - my wife_ _Milton_ _Connecticut_ _06605_
City _State_ _Zip_
(Address) _525_ _Main Street_
Number _Street_

(hereinafter referred to as the "First Beneficiary"), and upon his or her death prior to the termination of the trust, for the use
and benefit of my children, natural not/or adopted, in equal shares, or the survivor of them/per stirpes.
If because of my physical or mental incapacity certified in writing by a physician, the Successor Trustee hereinafter named
shall assume active administration of this trust during my lifetime, such Successor Trustee shall be fully authorized to pay to me
or disburse on my behalf such sums from income or principal as appear necessary or desirable for my comfort or welfare. Upon
my death, unless all of the beneficiaries shall predecease me or unless we all shall die as a result of a common accident or
disaster, my Successor Trustee is hereby directed forthwith to transfer the trust property and all right, title and interest in and to
said property unto the beneficiary absolutely and thereby terminate this trust; provided, however, that if any beneficiary
[text obscured] the Successor Trustee shall hold such benef[iciary's share of the trust assets]

upon the Successor Trustee to see to the application thereof. If such beneficiary survives me but dies before attaining the age of
21 years, at his or her death the Successor Trustee shall transfer, pay over and deliver the trust property being held for such
beneficiary to such beneficiary's personal representative, absolutely.

2. Each beneficiary hereunder shall be liable for his proportionate share of any taxes levied upon the Settlor's total taxable
estate by reason of the Settlor's death.

3. All interests of a beneficiary hereunder shall be inalienable and free from anticipation, assignment, attachment, pledge or
control by creditors or a present or former spouse of such beneficiary in any proceedings at law or in equity.

4. I reserve unto myself the power and right to collect any interest or payments constituting amortization which may accrue
from the trust property and to pay them to myself as an individual. I shall be exclusively entitled to all such income accruing from
the trust property during my lifetime, and no beneficiary named herein shall have any claim upon such income distributed to me.

5. I reserve unto myself the power and right at any time during my lifetime to amend or revoke in whole or in part the trust
hereby created without the necessity of obtaining the consent of the beneficiaries and without giving notice to the beneficiaries.
The transfer of the trust property by me to another person shall constitute a revocation of this trust.

6. The death during my lifetime, or in a common accident or disaster with me, of all of the beneficiaries designated
hereunder shall revoke such designation, and in the former event, I reserve the right to designate a new beneficiary. Should I for
any reason fail to designate such new beneficiary, this trust shall terminate upon my death and the trust property shall revert to
my estate.

7. In the event of my physical or mental incapacity or death, I hereby nominate and appoint as Successor Trustee hereunder
the First Beneficiary, or if such First Beneficiary be not surviving or fails or ceases to act. I nominate and appoint
_____, of

(Name) _Henry P. Adams_ _Milton_ _Connecticut_ _06605_
City _State_ _Zip_
(Address) _125_ _Barnum Street_
Number _Street_

to be Successor Trustee. If such person fails or ceases to act or should I for any reason fail to designate the person above
intended to be nominated, then I nominate and appoint as such Successor Trustee hereunder whosoever shall qualify as
executor, administrator or guardian, as the case may be, of my estate.

8. This Declaration of Trust shall extend to and be binding upon the heirs, executors, administrators and assigns of the
undersigned and upon the Successors to the Trustee.

9. The Trustee and his successors shall serve without bond.

10. This Declaration of Trust shall be construed and enforced in accordance with the laws of the State of
Connecticut

Declaration of Trust

WHEREAS, I, _____ , of the

City/Town of _____ , County of _____ , State of _____ ,

am the holder of a mortgage, first trust deed or real estate sales contract on certain real property located at (and known

as) _____ ,

in the City/Town of _____ , State of _____ , which property is

described more fully in such mortgage, first trust deed or real estate sales contract as "that certain piece or parcel of land with

any buildings thereon standing, located in said _____ , being

NOW, THEREFORE, KNOW ALL MEN BY THESE PRESENTS, that I do hereby acknowledge and declare that I hold and will hold said mortgage, first trust deed or real estate sales contract and all my right, title and interest in and to said mortgage, first trust deed or real estate sales contract IN TRUST

1. For the use and benefit of:

(Name) _____ , of

(Address) _____

      Number   *Street*   *City*   *State*   *Zip*

(hereinafter referred to as the "First Beneficiary"), and upon his or her death prior to the termination of the trust, for the use and benefit of my children, natural not/or adopted, in equal shares, or the survivor of them/per stirpes.

If because of my physical or mental incapacity certified in writing by a physician, the Successor Trustee hereinafter named shall assume active administration of this trust during my lifetime, such Successor Trustee shall be fully authorized to pay to me or disburse on my behalf such sums from income or principal as appear necessary or desirable for my comfort or welfare. Upon my death, unless all of the beneficiaries shall predecease me or unless we all shall die as a result of a common accident or disaster, my Successor Trustee is hereby directed forthwith to transfer the trust property and all right, title and interest in and to said property unto the beneficiary absolutely and thereby terminate this trust; <u>provided</u>, however, that if any beneficiary hereunder shall not have attained the age of 21 years, the Successor Trustee shall hold such beneficiary's share of the trust assets in continuing trust until such beneficiary shall have attained the age of 21 years. During such period of continuing trust the Successor Trustee, in his absolute discretion, may retain the specific trust property herein described if he believes it in the best interest of the beneficiary so to do, or he may sell or otherwise dispose of such specific trust property, investing and reinvesting the proceeds as he may deem appropriate. Prior to the date upon which such beneficiary attains the age of 21 years, the Successor Trustee may apply or expend any or all of the income or principal directly for the maintenance, education and support of the beneficiary without the intervention of any guardian and without application to any court. Such payments of income or principal may be made to the parents of such beneficiary or to the person with whom the beneficiary is living without any liability upon the Successor Trustee to see to the application thereof. If such beneficiary survives me but dies before attaining the age of 21 years, at his or her death the Successor Trustee shall transfer, pay over and deliver the trust property being held for such beneficiary to such beneficiary's personal representative, absolutely.

2. Each beneficiary hereunder shall be liable for his proportionate share of any taxes levied upon the Settlor's total taxable estate by reason of the Settlor's death.

3. All interests of a beneficiary hereunder shall be inalienable and free from anticipation, assignment, attachment, pledge or control by creditors or a present or former spouse of such beneficiary in any proceedings at law or in equity.

4. I reserve unto myself the power and right to collect any interest or payments constituting amortization which may accrue from the trust property and to pay them to myself as an individual. I shall be exclusively entitled to all such income accruing from the trust property during my lifetime, and no beneficiary named herein shall have any claim upon any such income distributed to me.

5. I reserve unto myself the power and right at any time during my lifetime to amend or revoke in whole or in part the trust hereby created without the necessity of obtaining the consent of the beneficiaries and without giving notice to the beneficiaries. The transfer of the trust property by me to another person shall constitute a revocation of this trust.

6. The death during my lifetime, or in a common accident or disaster with me, of all of the beneficiaries designated hereunder shall revoke such designation, and in the former event, I reserve the right to designate a new beneficiary. Should I for any reason fail to designate such new beneficiary, this trust shall terminate upon my death and the trust property shall revert to my estate.

7. In the event of my physical or mental incapacity or death, I hereby nominate and appoint as Successor Trustee hereunder the First Beneficiary, or if such First Beneficiary be not surviving or fails or ceases to act, I nominate and appoint

(Name) _____ , of

(Address) _____
      Number   *Street*   *City*   *State*   *Zip*

to be Successor Trustee. If such person fails or ceases to act or should I for any reason fail to designate the person above intended to be nominated, then I nominate and appoint as such Successor Trustee hereunder whosoever shall qualify as executor, administrator or guardian, as the case may be, of my estate.

8. This Declaration of Trust shall extend to and be binding upon the heirs, executors, administrators and assigns of the undersigned and upon the Successors to the Trustee.

9. The Trustee and his successors shall serve without bond.

10. This Declaration of Trust shall be construed and enforced in accordance with the laws of the State of

_____.

IN WITNESS WHEREOF, I have hereunto set my hand and seal this _____

day of _____ , 19_____.

(Settlor sign here) _____ L.S.

I, the undersigned legal spouse of the above Settlor, hereby waive all community property rights which I may have in the hereinabove-described trust property and give my assent to the provisions of the trust and to the inclusion in it of the said property.

(Spouse sign here) _____ L.S.

Witness: (1) _____   Witness: (2) _____

STATE OF _____   City

COUNTY OF _____   or
                                       Town _____

On the _____ day of _____ , 19_____, personally appeared

_____

known to me to be the individual(s) who executed the foregoing instrument, and acknowledged the same to be _____ free act and deed, before me.

(Notary Seal)   _____
                                                                  Notary Public

---

ASSIGNMENT OF
MORTGAGE, FIRST TRUST DEED,
OR REAL ESTATE SALES CONTRACT
HELD IN ONE NAME

INSTRUCTIONS:

Having executed a declaration of trust to establish that henceforth you will hold the mortgage, first trust deed, or real estate sales contract in trust, you next must complete a formal transfer or assignment of such contract to yourself as trustee. This can be accomplished through use of the form on the following pages.

At ①, enter your name. At ②, enter the name of the other party to the mortgage, first trust deed, or real estate sales contract. At ③, enter the place where the contract was recorded. At ④, enter the date of the declaration of trust which you have just executed. In the three places where the identification of the specific contract you hold is indicated as "Mortgage," "First Trust Deed," or "Real Estate Sales Contract," one above the other, cross out the descriptions not applicable.

If you are just entering into the mortgage, first trust deed, or real estate sales contract and it has not yet been recorded, you can eliminate the need for this assignment form by simply having your name appear on the mortgage, first trust deed, or real estate sales contract in this fashion: "*(your name), Trustee u/d/t dated* (date of the declaration of trust)."

After your signatures have been witnessed and notarized, make several photocopies for reference purposes, and then file the originals of both documents with the town or county clerk or other office where real estate transfers in the area where the property is located are customarily recorded. After they are recorded, they will be returned to you.

This form is intended for use with a mortgage, first trust deed, or real estate sales contract which is held in *one name only;* it may *not* be used where the mortgage, first trust deed, or real estate sales contract is held jointly. For these latter, use Form AM-J on page 233.

Important: Read carefully Note B on page 38, which applies to this instrument.

ASSIGNMENT OF MORTGAGE,
FIRST TRUST DEED,
OR REAL ESTATE SALES CONTRACT

AM

To All People To Whom These Presents Shall Come, Greetings;

① KNOW YE, THAT I, _John J. Brown_ _____ , the individual named

as the owner and holder of a certain | Mortgage / ~~First Trust Deed~~ / ~~Real Estate Sales Contract~~ | from _____ to me, recorded in the

② _Donald Jordan_ _____ Land Records, Volume __71__ , Page __613__ , do hereby assign,

③ _Milton_ _____ transfer and set over unto myself as Trustee under the terms of a certain _____ , all my right, title and interest in and to said

④ Declaration of Trust dated _April 2, 1980_ _____ and to the note or other evidence of indebtedness intended to be secured by such

| Mortgage / ~~First Trust Deed~~ / ~~Real Estate Sales Contract~~ |

| Mortgage / ~~First Trust Deed~~ / ~~Real Estate Sales Contract~~ |

TO HAVE AND TO HOLD as such Trustee forever, and I declare that neither I as an individual nor my heirs or assigns shall have or make any claim or demand pursuant to such instrument.

IN WITNESS WHEREOF, I have hereunto set my hand and seal this ____ **second** ____ , 19_80_ .

day of ____ **April** ____   (Assignor sign here) _____ _John J. Brown_ _____ L.S.

I, the undersigned legal spouse of the above Assignor, do hereby waive all community property rights which I may have in the hereinabove-described trust property and give my assent to the provisions of the trust and to the inclusion in it of the said property.

(Spouse sign here) _____ L.S.

Witness: (2) _____ _Helene Strey_

Witness: (1) _Dorothy Lynn_

STATE OF __Connecticut__

COUNTY OF __Fairfax__

City or Town __Milton__ , 19 _80_ , personally appeared

On the __second__ day of __April__   _John J. Brown_

known to me to be the individual(s) who executed the foregoing instrument, and acknowledged the same to be __his__ free act and deed, before me.

_____ _Anna Beck_ _____
Notary Public

(Notary Seal)

ASSIGNMENT OF MORTGAGE,
FIRST TRUST DEED,
OR REAL ESTATE SALES CONTRACT

To All People To Whom These Presents Shall Come, Greetings;

① KNOW YE, THAT I, _____, the individual named

as the owner and holder of a certain { Mortgage / First Trust Deed / Real Estate Sales Contract } from

② _____ to me, recorded in the

③ _____ Land Records, Volume _____, Page _____, do hereby assign,

transfer and set over unto myself as Trustee under the terms of a certain

④ Declaration of Trust dated _____, all my right, title and interest in and to said

{ Mortgage / First Trust Deed / Real Estate Sales Contract } and to the note or other evidence of indebtedness intended to be secured by such

{ Mortgage / First Trust Deed / Real Estate Sales Contract }

    TO HAVE AND TO HOLD as such Trustee forever, and I declare that neither I as an individual nor my heirs or assigns
shall have or make any claim or demand pursuant to such instrument.

    IN WITNESS WHEREOF, I have hereunto set my hand and seal this _____

day of _____, 19_____.

                        (Assignor sign here) _____ L.S.

I, the undersigned legal spouse of the above Assignor, do hereby waive all community property rights which I may have in
the hereinabove-described trust property and give my assent to the provisions of the trust and to the inclusion in it of the
said property.

                        (Spouse sign here) _____ L.S.

Witness: (1) _____ Witness: (2) _____

STATE OF _____ City or Town _____

COUNTY OF _____

    On the _____ day of _____, 19_____, personally appeared

_____

known to me to be the individual(s) who executed the foregoing instrument, and acknowledged the same to be _____ free
act and deed, before me.

_____

(Notary Seal)   *Notary Public*

Assignment of
Mortgage,
First Trust Deed,
or
Real Estate Sales Contract

FROM

_____

TO

_____, Trustee

DATED _____, 19 ____

Received _____, 19 ____

At _____ M

Recorded in the _____

LAND RECORDS

Vol. _____, Page _____

_____
Authorized Signature

This instrument relates to property located at

Number   Street
_____

City   State
_____

After recording, return to:

_____

_____

_____

CHAPTER 12

DECLARATION OF TRUST

For Naming

ONE BENEFICIARY

To Receive

A MORTGAGE, FIRST TRUST DEED, OR REAL ESTATE
SALES CONTRACT HELD IN JOINT NAMES

INSTRUCTIONS:

On the following pages will be found a declaration of trust (DT-121-J) suitable for use in connection with the establishment of an inter vivos trust covering a mortgage, first trust deed, or real estate sales contract held in joint names where it is desired to name some one person to receive the asset upon the death of the survivor of the two joint owners.

Cross out *"city"* or *"town,"* leaving the appropriate designation of your community. Insert the address of the property; if it has no street number, cross out "*(and known as)*" and follow it with the description of the property as it appears in the mortgage deed.

Enter the name of the beneficiary in the appropriate place in Paragraph 1.

Note that Paragraph 7 designates as Successor Trustee *"whosoever shall at that time be beneficiary hereunder,"* which means that in most cases you don't need to fill anything in there. However, if there is any possibility of a beneficiary who has not attained the age of 21 years receiving the trust property, make certain that you name an adult in this paragraph who can act as trustee for such beneficiary. Avoid naming as trustee a person not likely to survive until the beneficiary has attained age 21.

Next, execute the "Assignment of Mortgage, First Trust Deed, or Real Estate Sales Contract" (AM-J) to be found on page 233.

When completed, make several photocopies for reference purposes, and then file the original of both documents with the town or county clerk or other office where real estate transfers in the area where the property is located are customarily recorded. After they are recorded, they will be returned to you.

Important: Read carefully Note B on page 38, which applies to this declaration of trust.

Declaration of Trust

WHEREAS, We, **John J. Brown** and **Elizabeth A. Brown**, of the City/Town of **Milton**, County of **Fairfax**, State of **Connecticut**, are the holders of a mortgage, first trust deed or real estate sales contract on certain real property located at (and known as) **525 Main Street**, which property is in the City/Town of **Milton**, State of **Connecticut**, being described more fully in such mortgage, first trust deed or real estate sales contract as "that certain piece or parcel of land with any buildings thereon standing, located in said **Milton**:

the rear portions of Lots #34 and 35, on Map of Building Lots of George Spooner, said map being dated May 3, 1952, and filed for record in the office of the Town Clerk, Milton, Connecticut in Book 5, Page 16 of said Maps. Said parcel of land is more particularly described as:

Beginning at a point on the south line of Lot #34, on said map, 73.5 feet East of the East line of Park Avenue -- running thence North along land of James E. Beach, 100 feet to a point on the North line of Lot #35 on said map, 70.44 feet East of the said line to Cornwall Street, thence East along land of the said James E. Beach (being Lot #51 on said map) 55 feet -- thence South along land of Thomas Cook (being Lot #56 on said map) 100 feet to the aforesaid North line of Bartram Street -- thence West to the point of beginning.

1. For the use and benefit of:

(Name) **Jill A. Brown - our daughter** **Milton** City **Connecticut 06605** State Zip

(Address) **525 Main Street** Street Number

If because of our physical or mental incapacity certified in writing by a physician, the Successor Trustee hereinafter named shall assume active administration of this trust during our lifetime, such Successor Trustee shall be fully authorized to pay to us or disburse on our behalf such sums from income or principal as appear necessary or desirable for our comfort or welfare. Upon the death of the survivor of us, unless the beneficiary shall predecease us or unless we all shall die as a result of a common accident appropriate. Prior to the date upon which the beneficiary attains the age of 21 years, the Successor Trustee may apply or expend any or all of the income or principal directly for the maintenance, education and support of the beneficiary without the intervention of any guardian and without application to any court. Such payments of income or principal may be made to the parents of such beneficiary or to the person with whom the beneficiary is living without any liability upon the Successor Trustee to see to the application thereof. If such beneficiary survives us but dies before attaining the age of 21 years, at his or her death the Successor Trustee shall transfer, pay over and deliver the trust property to such beneficiary's personal representative, absolutely.

2. The beneficiary hereunder shall be liable for his proportionate share of any taxes levied upon the total taxable estate of the survivor of us by reason of the death of such survivor.

3. All interests of the beneficiary hereunder shall be inalienable and free from anticipation, assignment, attachment, pledge or control by creditors or a present or former spouse of such beneficiary in any proceedings at law or in equity.

4. We reserve unto ourselves the power and right to collect any interest or payments constituting amortization which may accrue from the trust property and to pay them to ourselves as individuals. We shall be exclusively entitled to all such income accruing from the trust property during our lifetime, and no beneficiary named herein shall have any claim upon such income distributed to us.

5. We reserve unto ourselves the power and right at any time during our lifetime to amend or revoke in whole or in part the trust hereby created without the necessity of obtaining the consent of the beneficiary and without giving notice to the beneficiary. The transfer of the trust property by us to another person shall constitute a revocation of this trust.

6. The death during our lifetime, or in a common accident or disaster with us, of the beneficiary designated hereunder shall revoke such designation, and in the former event, we reserve the right to designate a new beneficiary. Should we for any reason fail to designate such new beneficiary, this trust shall terminate upon the death of the survivor of us and the trust property shall revert to the estate of such survivor.

7. In the event of the physical or mental incapacity or death of one of us, the survivor shall continue as sole Trustee. In the event of the physical or mental incapacity or death of the survivor of us, or if we both shall die in a common accident or disaster, we hereby nominate and appoint as Successor Trustee whosoever shall at that time be beneficiary hereunder, unless such beneficiary shall not have attained the age of 21 years or is otherwise legally incapacitated, in which event we hereby nominate and appoint

(Name) **Henry P. Adams** **Milton** City **Connecticut 06605** State Zip

(Address) **125 Barnum Street** Street Number

to be Successor Trustee.

8. This Declaration of Trust shall extend to and be binding upon the heirs, executors, administrators and assigns of the undersigned and upon the Successors to the Trustee.

Declaration of Trust

WHEREAS, WE, _____ and _____, of the

City/Town of _____, County of _____, State of _____,

are the holders of a mortgage, first trust deed or real estate sales contract on certain real property located at (and known

as) _____,

in the City/Town of _____, State of _____, which property is

described more fully in such mortgage, first trust deed or real estate sales contract as "that certain piece or parcel of land with

any buildings thereon standing, located in said _____, being

NOW, THEREFORE, KNOW ALL MEN BY THESE PRESENTS, that we do hereby acknowledge and declare that we hold and will hold said mortgage, first trust deed or real estate sales contract and all our right, title and interest in and to said mortgage, first trust deed or real estate sales contract IN TRUST

1. For the use and benefit of:

(Name) _____, of

(Address) _____
               Number   *Street*   *City*   *State*   *Zip*

If because of our physical or mental incapacity certified in writing by a physician, the Successor Trustee hereinafter named shall assume active administration of this trust during our lifetime, such Successor Trustee shall be fully authorized to pay to us or disburse on our behalf such sums from income or principal as appear necessary or desirable for our comfort or welfare. Upon the death of the survivor of us, unless the beneficiary shall predecease us or unless we all shall die as a result of a common accident, our Successor Trustee is hereby directed forthwith to transfer the trust property and all right, title and interest in and to said property unto the beneficiary absolutely and thereby terminate this trust; provided, however, that if the beneficiary hereunder shall not have attained the age of 21 years, the Successor Trustee shall hold the trust assets in continuing trust until such beneficiary shall have attained the age of 21 years. During such period of continuing trust the Successor Trustee, in his absolute discretion, may retain the specific trust property herein described if he believes it in the best interest of the beneficiary so to do, or he may sell or otherwise dispose of such specific trust property, investing and reinvesting the proceeds as he may deem appropriate. Prior to the date upon which the beneficiary attains the age of 21 years, the Successor Trustee may apply or expend any or all of the income or principal directly for the maintenance, education and support of the beneficiary without the intervention of any guardian and without application to any court. Such payments of income or principal may be made to the parents of such beneficiary or to the person with whom the beneficiary is living without any liability upon the Successor Trustee to see to the application thereof. If such beneficiary survives us but dies before attaining the age of 21 years, at his or her death the Successor Trustee shall transfer, pay over and deliver the trust property to such beneficiary's personal representative, absolutely.

2. The beneficiary hereunder shall be liable for his proportionate share of any taxes levied upon the total taxable estate of the survivor of us by reason of the death of such survivor.

3. All interests of the beneficiary hereunder shall be inalienable and free from anticipation, assignment, attachment, pledge or control by creditors or a present or former spouse of such beneficiary in any proceedings at law or in equity.

4. We reserve unto ourselves the power and right to collect any interest or payments constituting amortization which may accrue from the trust property and to pay them to ourselves as individuals. We shall be exclusively entitled to all such income accruing from the trust property during our lifetime, and no beneficiary named herein shall have any claim upon any such income distributed to us.

5. We reserve unto ourselves the power and right at any time during our lifetime to amend or revoke in whole or in part the trust hereby created without the necessity of obtaining the consent of the beneficiary and without giving notice to the beneficiary. The transfer of the trust property by us to another person shall constitute a revocation of this trust.

6. The death during our lifetime, or in a common accident or disaster with us, of the beneficiary designated hereunder shall revoke such designation, and in the former event, we reserve the right to designate a new beneficiary. Should we for any reason fail to designate such new beneficiary, this trust shall terminate upon the death of the survivor of us and the trust property shall revert to the estate of such survivor.

7. In the event of the physical or mental incapacity or death of one of us, the survivor shall continue as sole Trustee. In the event of the physical or mental incapacity or death of the survivor of us, or if we both shall die in a common accident or disaster, we hereby nominate and appoint as Successor Trustee whosoever shall at that time be beneficiary hereunder, unless such beneficiary shall not have attained the age of 21 years or is otherwise legally incapacitated, in which event we hereby nominate and appoint

(Name) _____ , of

(Address) _____

| Number | Street | City | State | Zip |

to be Successor Trustee.

8. This Declaration of Trust shall extend to and be binding upon the heirs, executors, administrators and assigns of the undersigned and upon the Successors to the Trustee.

9. We as Trustees and our Successor Trustee shall serve without bond.

10. This Declaration of Trust shall be construed and enforced in accordance with the laws of the State of

_____ .

IN WITNESS WHEREOF, we have hereunto set our hands and seals this _____

day of _____ , 19_____ .

(First Settlor sign here) _____ L.S.

(Second Settlor sign here) _____ L.S.

I, the undersigned legal spouse of one of the above Settlors, hereby waive all community property rights which I may have in the hereinabove-described trust property and give my assent to the provisions of the trust and to the inclusion in it of the said property.

(Spouse sign here) _____ L.S.

Witness: (1) _____   Witness: (2) _____

STATE OF _____   City

COUNTY OF _____   or
Town _____

On the _____ day of _____ , 19_____ , personally appeared

_____ and _____

known to me to be the individuals who executed the foregoing instrument, and acknowledged the same to be their free act and deed, before me.

_____

(Notary Seal)   Notary Public

CHAPTER 12

DECLARATION OF TRUST

For Naming

ONE PRIMARY BENEFICIARY

And

ONE CONTINGENT BENEFICIARY

To Receive

A MORTGAGE, FIRST TRUST DEED, OR REAL ESTATE

SALES CONTRACT HELD IN JOINT NAMES

INSTRUCTIONS:

On the following pages will be found a declaration of trust (DT-122-J) suitable for use in connection with the establishment of an inter vivos trust covering a mortgage, first trust deed, or real estate sales contract held in joint names, where it is desired to name some *one* person as primary beneficiary, with some *one* other person as contingent beneficiary to receive the asset if the primary beneficiary be not surviving upon the death of the survivor of the two joint owners.

Cross out *"city"* or *"town,"* leaving the appropriate designation of your community. Insert the address of the property; if it has no street number, cross out *"(and known as)"* and follow it with the description of the property as it appears in the mortgage deed.

Enter the names of the beneficiaries in the appropriate place in Paragraph 1.

Note that Paragraph 7 designates as Successor Trustee *"whosoever shall at that time be beneficiary hereunder,"* which means that in most cases you don't need to fill anything in there. However, if there is any possibility of a beneficiary who has not attained the age of 21 years receiving the trust property, make certain that you name an adult in this paragraph who can act as trustee for such beneficiary. Avoid naming as trustee a person not likely to survive until the beneficiary has attained age 21.

Next, execute the "Assignment of Mortgage, First Trust Deed, or Real Estate Sales Contract" (AM-J) to be found on page 233.

When completed, make several photocopies for reference purposes, and then file the original of both documents with the town or county clerk or other office where real estate transfers in the area where the property is located are customarily recorded. After they are recorded, they will be returned to you.

Important: Read carefully Note B on page 38, which applies to this declaration of trust.

Declaration of Trust

WHEREAS, We, __John J. Brown__ and __Elizabeth A. Brown__, of the

__Town of Milton__, County of __Fairfax__, State of __Connecticut__,

are the holders of a mortgage, first trust deed or real estate sales contract on certain real property located at (and known

as) __525 Main Street__, which property is

in the __Town of Milton__, State of __Connecticut__, being

described more fully in such mortgage, first trust deed or real estate sales contract as "that certain piece or parcel of land with

any buildings thereon standing, located in said __Milton__:

the rear portions of Lots #34 and 35, on Map of Building Lots of George Spooner, said map being dated May 3, 1952, and filed for record in the office of the Town Clerk, Milton, Connecticut in Book 5, Page 16 of said Maps. Said parcel of land is more particularly described as:

Beginning at a point on the south line of Lot #34, on said map, 73.5 feet East of the East line of Park Avenue -- running thence North along land of James E. Beach, 100 feet to a point on the line to Cornwall Street, 70.44 feet East of the East line of Lot #35 on said map, thence East along land of the said James E. Beach (being Lot #51 on said map) 55 feet -- thence South along land of Thomas Cook (being Lot #56 on said map) 100 feet to the aforesaid North line of Bartram Street -- thence West to the point of beginning.

NOW, THEREFORE, KNOW ALL MEN BY THESE PRESENTS, that we do hereby acknowledge and declare that we hold and will hold said mortgage, first trust deed or real estate sales contract and all our right, title and interest in and to said mortgage, first trust deed or real estate sales contract IN TRUST

1. For the use and benefit of:

(Name) __Jill A. Brown - our daughter__, of __Milton__, __Connecticut__ __06605__
City   State   Zip

(Address) __525__ __Main Street__
Number   Street

or, if such beneficiary be not surviving, for the use and benefit of:

(Name) __Dorothy Lynn - our niece__, of __Portland__, __Wisconsin__ __53123__
City   State   Zip

(Address) __566__ __Midland Street__
Number   Street

If because of our physical or mental incapacity certified in writing by a physician, the Successor Trustee hereinafter named shall assume active administration of this trust during our lifetime, such Successor Trustee shall be fully authorized to pay to us or disburse on our behalf such sums from income or principal as appear necessary or desirable for our comfort or welfare. Upon the death of the survivor of us, unless both the beneficiaries shall predecease us or unless we all shall die as a result of a common accident, our Successor Trustee is hereby directed forthwith to transfer the trust property and all right, title and interest in and to said property unto the beneficiary absolutely and hereby terminate this trust; provided, however, that if the beneficiary hereunder shall not have attained the age of 21 years, the Successor Trustee shall hold the trust assets in continuing trust until such beneficiary shall have attained the age of 21 years. During such period of continuing trust the Successor Trustee, in his absolute discretion, may retain the specific trust property herein described if he believes it in the best interest of the beneficiary

6. The death during our lifetime, or in a common accident or disaster with us, of both of the beneficiaries designated hereunder shall revoke such designation, and in the former event, we reserve the right to designate a new beneficiary. Should we for any reason fail to designate such new beneficiary, this trust shall terminate upon the death of the survivor of us and the trust property shall revert to the estate of such survivor.

7. In the event of the physical or mental incapacity or death of one of us, the survivor shall continue as sole Trustee. In the event of the physical or mental incapacity or death of the survivor of us, or if we both shall die in a common accident, we hereby nominate and appoint as Successor Trustee whosoever shall at that time be beneficiary hereunder, unless such beneficiary shall not have attained the age of 21 years or is otherwise legally incapacitated, in which event we hereby nominate and appoint

(Name) __Henry P. Adams__, of __Milton__, __Connecticut__ __06605__
City   State   Zip

(Address) __125__ __Barnum Street__
Number   Street

to be Successor Trustee.

8. This Declaration of Trust shall extend to and be binding upon the heirs, executors, administrators and assigns of the undersigned and upon the Successors to the Trustees.

9. We as Trustees and our Successor Trustee shall serve without bond.

10. This Declaration of Trust shall be construed and enforced in accordance with the laws of the State of __Connecticut__.

Declaration of Trust

WHEREAS, WE, _____ and _____, of the

City/Town of _____, County of _____, State of _____,

are the holders of a mortgage, first trust deed or real estate sales contract on certain real property located at (and known

as) _____,

in the City/Town of _____, State of _____, which property is

described more fully in such mortgage, first trust deed or real estate sales contract as "that certain piece or parcel of land with

any buildings thereon standing, located in said _____, being

NOW, THEREFORE, KNOW ALL MEN BY THESE PRESENTS, that we do hereby acknowledge and declare that we hold and will hold said mortgage, first trust deed or real estate sales contract and all our right, title and interest in and to said mortgage, first trust deed or real estate sales contract IN TRUST

    1. For the use and benefit of:

(Name) _____, of

(Address) _____
          Number   Street   City   State   Zip

or, if such beneficiary be not surviving, for the use and benefit of:

(Name) _____, of

(Address) _____
          Number   Street   City   State   Zip

    If because of our physical or mental incapacity certified in writing by a physician, the Successor Trustee hereinafter named shall assume active administration of this trust during our lifetime, such Successor Trustee shall be fully authorized to pay to us or disburse on our behalf such sums from income or principal as appear necessary or desirable for our comfort or welfare. Upon the death of the survivor of us, unless both the beneficiaries shall predecease us or unless we all shall die as a result of a common accident, our Successor Trustee is hereby directed forthwith to transfer the trust property and all right, title and interest in and to said property unto the beneficiary absolutely and hereby terminate this trust; <u>provided,</u> however, that if the beneficiary hereunder shall not have attained the age of 21 years, the Successor Trustee shall hold the trust assets in continuing trust until such beneficiary shall have attained the age of 21 years. During such period of continuing trust the Successor Trustee, in his absolute discretion, may retain the specific trust property herein described if he believes it in the best interest of the beneficiary so to do, or he may sell or otherwise dispose of such specific trust property, investing and reinvesting the proceeds as he may deem appropriate. Prior to the date upon which such beneficiary attains the age of 21 years, the Successor Trustee may apply or expend any or all of the income or principal directly for the maintenance, education and support of the beneficiary without the intervention of any guardian and without application to any court. Such payments of income or principal may be made to the parents of such beneficiary or to the person with whom the beneficiary is living without any liability upon the Successor Trustee to see to the application thereof. If such beneficiary survives us but dies before attaining the age of 21 years, at his or her death the Successor Trustee shall transfer, pay over and deliver the trust property to such beneficiary's personal representative, absolutely.

    2. The beneficiary hereunder shall be liable for his proportionate share of any taxes levied upon the total taxable estate of the survivor of us by reason of the death of such survivor.

    3. All interests of a beneficiary hereunder shall be inalienable and free from anticipation, assignment, attachment, pledge or control by creditors or a present or former spouse of such beneficiary in any proceedings at law or in equity.

    4. We reserve unto ourselves the power and right to collect any interest or payments constituting amortization which may accrue from the trust property and to pay them to ourselves as individuals. We shall be exclusively entitled to all such income accruing from the trust property during our lifetime, and no beneficiary named herein shall have any claim upon any such income distributed to us.

    5. We reserve unto ourselves the power and right at any time during our lifetime to amend or revoke in whole or in part the trust hereby created without the necessity of obtaining the consent of the beneficiaries and without giving notice to the beneficiaries. The transfer of the trust property by us to another person shall constitute a revocation of this trust.

    6. The death during our lifetime, or in a common accident or disaster with us, of both of the beneficiaries designated hereunder shall revoke such designation, and in the former event, we reserve the right to designate a new beneficiary. Should we for any reason fail to designate such new beneficiary, this trust shall terminate upon the death of the survivor of us and the trust property shall revert to the estate of such survivor.

    7. In the event of the physical or mental incapacity or death of one of us, the survivor shall continue as sole Trustee. In the event of the physical or mental incapacity or death of the survivor of us, or if we both shall die in a common accident, we hereby nominate and appoint as Successor Trustee whosoever shall at that time be beneficiary hereunder, unless such beneficiary shall not have attained the age of 21 years or is otherwise legally incapacitated, in which event we hereby nominate and appoint

(Name) _____, of

(Address) _____
            Number   *Street*   *City*   *State*   *Zip*

to be Successor Trustee.

    8. This Declaration of Trust shall extend to and be binding upon the heirs, executors, administrators and assigns of the undersigned and upon the Successors to the Trustees.

    9. We as Trustees and our Successor Trustee shall serve without bond.

    10. This Declaration of Trust shall be construed and enforced in accordance with the laws of the State of

_____.

    IN WITNESS WHEREOF, we have hereunto set our hands and seals this _____

day of _____, 19_____.

                          (First Settlor sign here) _____ L.S.

                       (Second Settlor sign here) _____ L.S.

I, the undersigned legal spouse of one of the above Settlors, hereby waive all community property rights which I may have in the hereinabove-described trust property and give my assent to the provisions of the trust and to the inclusion in it of the said property.

                         (Spouse sign here) _____ L.S.

Witness: (1) _____   Witness: (2) _____

STATE OF _____   City

COUNTY OF _____   or
                                    Town _____

    On the _____ day of _____, 19_____, personally appeared

_____ and _____

known to me to be the individuals who executed the foregoing instrument, and acknowledged the same to be their free act and deed, before me.

_____

(Notary Seal)   *Notary Public*

CHAPTER 12

DECLARATION OF TRUST

For Naming

TWO OR MORE BENEFICIARIES, SHARING EQUALLY,

To Receive

**A MORTGAGE, FIRST TRUST DEED, OR REAL ESTATE
SALES CONTRACT HELD IN JOINT NAMES**

INSTRUCTIONS:

On the following pages will be found a declaration of trust (DT-123-J) suitable for use in connection with the establishment of an inter vivos trust covering a mortgage, first trust deed, or real estate sales contract held in joint names, where it is desired to name two or more persons to receive the asset upon the death of the survivor of the two joint owners.

Cross out *"city"* or *"town,"* leaving the appropriate designation of your community. Insert the address of the property; if it has no street number, cross out *"(and known as)"* and follow it with the description of the property as it appears in the mortgage deed.

In Paragraph 1, indicate the *number of persons* you are naming (to discourage unauthorized additions to the list) and then insert their names. The one whose name appears *first* will be the Successor Trustee responsible for seeing to the distribution of the trust property.

Note that the instrument specifies that the named beneficiaries are to receive *"in equal shares, or the survivor of them/per stirpes."* Now, think carefully: If you have named three persons with the understanding that if one of them predeceases you, *his* children will take *his* share, cross out *"or the survivor of them"* and *initial it.* If that is *not* what you want—if, for example, you prefer that the share of the deceased person be divided between the two surviving persons, cross out *"per stirpes"* and *initial it.* Remember, you <u>must</u> cross out either *"or the survivor of them"* or *"per stirpes"*—one or the other.

Note that Paragraph 7 designates as Successor Trustee *"the beneficiary named first above,"* which means that in most cases you don't need to fill anything in there. However, if there is any possibility of a beneficiary who has not attained the age of 21 years receiving the trust property, make certain that you name an adult in this paragraph who can act as trustee for such beneficiary. Avoid naming as trustee a person not likely to survive until the beneficiary has attained age 21.

Next, execute the "Assignment of Mortgage, First Trust Deed, or Real Estate Sales Contract" (AM-J) to be found on page 233.

When completed, make several photocopies for reference purposes, and then file the originals of both documents with the town or county clerk or other office where real estate transfers in the area where the property is located are customarily recorded. After they are recorded, they will be returned to you.

Important: Read carefully Note B on page 38, which applies to this declaration of trust.

Declaration of Trust

WHEREAS, We, __John J. Brown__ and __Elizabeth A. Brown__ , of the

~~City~~/Town of __Milton__ , County of __Fairfax__ , State of __Connecticut__ ,

are the holders of a mortgage, first trust deed or real estate sales contract on certain real property located at (and known

as) __525 Main Street__ __Milton__ , State of __Connecticut__ which property is

in the ~~City~~/Town of __Milton__ described more fully in such mortgage, first trust deed or real estate sales contract as "that certain piece or parcel of land with

any buildings thereon standing, located in said __Milton__ , being

the rear portions of Lots #34 and 35, on Map of Building Lots of George Spooner, said map being dated May 3, 1952, and filed for record in the office of the Town Clerk, Milton, Connecticut in Book 5, Page 16 of said Maps. Said parcel of land is more particularly described as:

Beginning at a point on the south line of Lot #34, on said map, 73.5 feet East of the East line of Park Avenue -- running thence North along land of James E. Beach, 100 feet to a point on the North line of Lot #35 on said map, 70.44 feet East of the said line to Cornwall Street, thence East along land of the said James E. Beach (being Lot #51 on said map) 55 feet -- thence South along land of Thomas Cook (being Lot #56 on said map) 100 feet to the aforesaid North line of Bartram Street -- thence West to the point of beginning.

NOW, THEREFORE, KNOW ALL MEN BY THESE PRESENTS, that we do hereby acknowledge and declare that we hold and will hold said mortgage, first trust deed or real estate sales contract and all our right, title and interest in and to said mortgage, first trust deed or real estate sales contract IN TRUST *J.J.B. E.A.B.* per

1. For the use and benefit of the following __three (3)__ persons, in equal shares,

stirpes:

> __Thomas B. Brown - our brother__
> __Helen M. Brown - our sister__
> __Charles M. Brown - our brother__

If because of our physical or mental incapacity certified in writing by a physician, the Successor Trustee hereinafter named shall assume active administration of this trust during our lifetime, such Successor Trustee shall be fully authorized to pay to us or disburse on our behalf such sums from income or principal as appear necessary or desirable for our comfort or welfare. Upon the death of the survivor of us, unless we all shall die as a result of a common accident, our Successor Trustee is hereby directed forthwith to transfer the trust property and all right, title and interest in and to ... which may

... reserve unto ourselves the power and right to ... any interest or payments constituting ... entitled to all such income accrue from the trust property and to pay them to ourselves as individuals. We shall be exclusively entitled to all such income accruing from the trust property during our lifetime, and no beneficiary named herein shall have any claim upon any such income distributed to us.

5. We reserve unto ourselves the power and right at any time during our lifetime to amend or revoke in whole or in part the trust hereby created without the necessity of obtaining the consent of the beneficiaries and without giving notice to the beneficiaries. The transfer of the trust property by us to another person or disaster with us, of all of the beneficiaries designated hereunder

6. The death during our lifetime, or in a common accident or disaster with us, of all of the beneficiaries designated hereunder shall revoke such designation, and in the former event, this trust shall terminate upon the death of the survivor of us and the trust property shall revert to the estate of such survivor.

7. In the event of the physical or mental incapacity or death of one of us, the survivor shall continue as sole Trustee. In the event of the physical or mental incapacity or death of the survivor, or if we both shall die in a common accident or disaster, we hereby nominate and appoint as Successor Trustee the beneficiary named first above unless such beneficiary shall not have attained the age of 21 years or is otherwise legally incapacitated, in which event we nominate and appoint as Successor Trustee the beneficiary whose name appears second above. If such beneficiary named second above shall not have attained the age of 21 years or is otherwise legally incapacitated, we hereby nominate and appoint

__Henry P. Adams__ __Milton__ __Connecticut__ __06605__
(Name) City State Zip

(Address) __125__ __Barnum Street__
Number Street

to be Successor Trustee.

8. This Declaration of Trust shall extend to and be binding upon the heirs, executors, administrators and assigns of the undersigned and upon the Successors to the Trustees.

9. We as Trustees and our Successor Trustee shall serve without bond.

10. This Declaration of Trust shall be construed and enforced in accordance with the laws of the State of __Connecticut__

Declaration of Trust

WHEREAS, WE, _____ and _____, of the

City/Town of _____, County of _____, State of _____,

are the holders of a mortgage, first trust deed or real estate sales contract on certain real property located at (and known

as) _____,

in the City/Town of _____, State of _____, which property is

described more fully in such mortgage, first trust deed or real estate sales contract as "that certain piece or parcel of land with

any buildings thereon standing, located in said _____, being

NOW, THEREFORE, KNOW ALL MEN BY THESE PRESENTS, that we do hereby acknowledge and declare that we hold and will hold said mortgage, first trust deed or real estate sales contract and all our right, title and interest in and to said mortgage, first trust deed or real estate sales contract IN TRUST

    1. For the use and benefit of the following _____ persons, in equal shares, or the survivor of them/per stirpes:

If because of our physical or mental incapacity certified in writing by a physician, the Successor Trustee hereinafter named shall assume active administration of this trust during our lifetime, such Successor Trustee shall be fully authorized to pay to us or disburse on our behalf such sums from income or principal as appear necessary or desirable for our comfort or welfare. Upon the death of the survivor of us, unless all of the beneficiaries shall predecease us or unless we all shall die as a result of a common accident, our Successor Trustee is hereby directed forthwith to transfer the trust property and all right, title and interest in and to said property unto the beneficiaries absolutely and hereby terminate this trust; provided, however, that if any beneficiary hereunder shall not have attained the age of 21 years, the Successor Trustee shall hold such beneficiary's share of the trust assets in continuing trust until such beneficiary shall have attained the age of 21 years. During such period of continuing trust the Successor Trustee, in his absolute discretion, may retain the specific trust property herein described if he believes it in the best interest of the beneficiary so to do, or he may sell or otherwise dispose of such specific trust property, investing and reinvesting the proceeds as he may deem appropriate. Prior to the date upon which such beneficiary attains the age of 21 years, the

Successor Trustee may apply or expend any or all of the income or principal directly for the maintenance, education and support of the beneficiary without the intervention of any guardian and without application to any court. Such payments of income or principal may be made to the parents of such beneficiary or to the person with whom the beneficiary is living without any liability upon the Successor Trustee to see to the application thereof. If such beneficiary survives us but dies before attaining the age of 21 years, at his or her death the Successor Trustee shall transfer, pay over and deliver the trust property being held for such beneficiary to such beneficiary's personal representative, absolutely.

2. Each beneficiary hereunder shall be liable for his proportionate share of any taxes levied upon the total taxable estate of the survivor of us by reason of the death of such survivor.

3. All interests of a beneficiary hereunder shall be inalienable and free from anticipation, assignment, attachment, pledge or control by creditors or a present or former spouse of such beneficiary in any proceedings at law or in equity.

4. We reserve unto ourselves the power and right to collect any interest or payments constituting amortization which may accrue from the trust property and to pay them to ourselves as individuals. We shall be exclusively entitled to all such income accruing from the trust property during our lifetime, and no beneficiary named herein shall have any claim upon any such income distributed to us.

5. We reserve unto ourselves the power and right at any time during our lifetime to amend or revoke in whole or in part the trust hereby created without the necessity of obtaining the consent of the beneficiaries and without giving notice to the beneficiaries. The transfer of the trust property by us to another person shall constitute a revocation of this trust.

6. The death during our lifetime, or in a common accident or disaster with us, of all of the beneficiaries designated hereunder shall revoke such designation, and in the former event, we reserve the right to designate a new beneficiary. Should we for any reason fail to designate such new beneficiary, this trust shall terminate upon the death of the survivor of us and the trust property shall revert to the estate of such survivor.

7. In the event of the physical or mental incapacity or death of one of us, the survivor shall continue as sole Trustee. In the event of the physical or mental incapacity or death of the survivor, or if we both shall die in a common accident or disaster, we hereby nominate and appoint as Successor Trustee the beneficiary named first above unless such beneficiary shall not have attained the age of 21 years or is otherwise legally incapacitated, in which event we nominate and appoint as Successor Trustee the beneficiary whose name appears second above. If such beneficiary named second above shall not have attained the age of 21 years or is otherwise legally incapacitated, we hereby nominate and appoint

(Name) _____ , of

(Address) _____

Number   Street   City   State   Zip

to be Successor Trustee.

8. This Declaration of Trust shall extend to and be binding upon the heirs, executors, administrators and assigns of the undersigned and upon the Successors to the Trustees.

9. We as Trustees and our Successor Trustee shall serve without bond.

10. This Declaration of Trust shall be construed and enforced in accordance with the laws of the State of

_____ .

IN WITNESS WHEREOF, we have hereunto set our hands and seals this _____

day of _____ , 19_____ .

(First Settlor sign here) _____ L.S.

(Second Settlor sign here) _____ L.S.

I, the undersigned legal spouse of one of the above Settlors, hereby waive all community property rights which I may have in the hereinabove-described trust property and give my assent to the provisions of the trust and to the inclusion in it of the said property.

(Spouse sign here) _____ L.S.

Witness: (1) _____   Witness: (2) _____

STATE OF _____   City

COUNTY OF _____   or Town _____

On the _____ day of _____ , 19_____ , personally appeared

_____ and _____

known to me to be the individuals who executed the foregoing instrument, and acknowledged the same to be their free act and deed, before me.

_____

(Notary Seal)   Notary Public

ASSIGNMENT OF
MORTGAGE, FIRST TRUST DEED,
OR REAL ESTATE SALES CONTRACT
HELD IN JOINT NAMES

INSTRUCTIONS:

Having executed a declaration of trust to establish that henceforth you will hold the mortgage, first trust deed, or real estate sales contract in trust, you next must complete a formal transfer or assignment of such contract to yourselves as trustees. This can be accomplished through use of the form on the following pages.

At ①, enter your name and that of your co-trustee. At ②, enter the name of the other party to the mortgage, first trust deed, or real estate sales contract. At ③, enter the place where the contract was recorded. At ④, enter the date of the declaration of trust which you have just executed. In the three places where the identification of the specific contract you hold is indicated as "Mortgage," "First Trust Deed," or "Real Estate Sales Contract," one above the other, cross out the descriptions not applicable.

If you are just entering into the mortgage, first trust deed, or real estate sales contract and it has not yet been recorded, you can eliminate the need for this assignment form by simply having your name appear on the mortgage, first trust deed, or real estate sales contract in this fashion: "*(your name) and (your co-trustee's name), Trustees u/d/t dated* (date of the declaration of trust)."

Finally, have your signatures witnessed and notarized. Make several photocopies for reference purposes and then file the original with the declaration of trust with the town or county clerk or other office where real estate transfers in the area where the property is located are customarily recorded. After they have been recorded, they will be returned to you.

This form is intended for use with a mortgage, first trust deed, or real estate sales contract which is held in *joint names only;* it may not be used where the mortgage, first trust deed, or real estate sales contract is held in one name. For these latter, use Form AM on page 217.

Important: Read carefully Note B on page 38, which applies to this instrument.

ASSIGNMENT OF MORTGAGE,
FIRST TRUST DEED,
OR REAL ESTATE SALES CONTRACT

AM-J

To All People To Whom These Presents Shall Come, Greetings;

① KNOW YE, THAT WE, __John J. Brown__ and __Elizabeth A. Brown__

as the owners and holders of a certain {Mortgage / ~~First Trust Deed~~ / ~~Real Estate Sales Contract~~} from _____ to me, recorded in the

② __Donald Jordan__ Land Records, Volume __71__ Page __613__ do hereby

③ __Milton__ assign, transfer and set over unto ourselves as Trustees under the terms of a certain _____, all my right, title and interest in and to said

④ Declaration of Trust dated __April 2, 1980__ and to the note or other evidence of indebtedness intended to be secured by such

{Mortgage / ~~First Trust Deed~~ / ~~Real Estate Sales Contract~~}

{Mortgage / ~~First Trust Deed~~ / ~~Real Estate Sales Contract~~}

TO HAVE AND TO HOLD as such Trustees forever, and we declare that neither we as individuals nor our heirs or assigns shall have or make any claim or demand pursuant to such instrument.

IN WITNESS WHEREOF. we have hereunto set our hands and seals this __second__ _____ L.S.

day of __April__ , 19 __80__ (First Assignor sign here) _John J. Brown_ L.S.

(Second Assignor sign here) _Elizabeth A. Brown_

I, the undersigned legal spouse of one of the above Assignors, do hereby waive all community property rights which I may have in the hereinabove-described trust property and give my assent to the provisions of the trust and to the inclusion in it of the said property.

(Spouse sign here) _____ L.S.

Witness: (2) _Helene Storey_

Witness: (1) _Dorothy Lynne_

City or Town __Milton__ , 19 __80__ personally appeared

STATE OF __Connecticut__

COUNTY OF __Fairfax__ day of __April__ and __Elizabeth A. Brown__

On the __second__ __John J. Brown__ and Elizabeth A. Brown known to me to be the individuals who executed the foregoing instrument. and acknowledged the same to be their free act and deed, before me.

Anna Beck
Notary Public

(Notary Seal)

**ASSIGNMENT OF MORTGAGE,
FIRST TRUST DEED,
OR REAL ESTATE SALES CONTRACT**

To All People To Whom These Presents Shall Come, Greetings;

① KNOW YE, THAT WE, _____ and _____,

as the owners and holders of a certain { Mortgage / First Trust Deed / Real Estate Sales Contract } from

② _____ to me, recorded in the

③ _____ Land Records, Volume _____, Page_____, do hereby

assign, transfer and set over unto ourselves as Trustees under the terms of a certain

④ Declaration of Trust dated _____, all our right, title and interest in and to said

{ Mortgage / First Trust Deed / Real Estate Sales Contract }   and to the note or other evidence of indebtedness intended to be secured by such

{ Mortgage / First Trust Deed / Real Estate Sales Contract }

TO HAVE AND TO HOLD as such Trustees forever, and we declare that neither we as individuals nor our heirs or assigns shall have or make any claim or demand pursuant to such instrument.

IN WITNESS WHEREOF, we have hereunto set our hands and seals this _____

day of _____, 19____.

(First Assignor sign here) _____ L.S.

(Second Assignor sign here) _____ L.S.

I, the undersigned legal spouse of one of the above Assignors, do hereby waive all community property rights which I may have in the hereinabove-described trust property and give my assent to the provisions of the trust and to the inclusion in it of the said property.

(Spouse sign here) _____ L.S.

Witness: (1) _____   Witness: (2) _____

STATE OF _____ } City
                                        or
COUNTY OF _____ } Town _____

On the _____ day of _____, 19____, personally appeared

_____ and _____

known to me to be the individuals who executed the foregoing instrument, and acknowledged the same to be their free act and deed, before me.

_____

(Notary Seal)   Notary Public

Assignment of
Mortgage,
First Trust Deed,
or
Real Estate Sales Contract

FROM

_____

(Your Co-Owner)

_____

(Yourself)

and

TO

_____

(Yourself)

and

_____

(Your Co-Trustee)

, Trustees

DATED _____, 19 ____

Received _____, 19 ____

At _____ M

Recorded in the _____

LAND RECORDS

Vol. _____, Page _____

Authorized Signature

This instrument relates to property located at

Number   Street

_____

City   State

After recording, return to:

_____

_____

_____

CHAPTER 12

ASSIGNMENT TO A <u>JOINTLY</u> HELD TRUST
Of A
MORTGAGE, FIRST TRUST DEED,
OR REAL ESTATE SALES CONTRACT
HELD IN <u>ONE</u> NAME

INSTRUCTIONS:

Having executed a declaration of trust to establish that henceforth you will hold in *joint trust* a mortgage, first trust deed, or real estate sales contract *now held in one name,* you next must complete a formal transfer or assignment of such contract from yourself as an individual to yourself and the co-trustee. This can be accomplished through use of the form on the following pages.

At ①, enter your name. At ②, enter the name of the other party to the mortgage, first trust deed, or real estate sales contract. At ③, enter the place where the contract was recorded. At ④, enter the name of the person who is to be co-trustee with you. At ⑤, enter the date of the declaration of trust which you and your co-trustee have just executed.

In the three places where the identification of the specific contract you hold is indicated as "Mortgage," "First Trust Deed," or "Real Estate Sales Contract," one above the other, cross out the descriptions not applicable.

Finally, have your signature witnessed and notarized, make several photocopies for reference purposes and file the original with the original of the declaration of trust with the town or county clerk or other office where real estate transfers in the area where the property is located are customarily recorded. After they have been recorded, they will be returned to you.

Important: Read carefully Note B on page 38, which applies to this instrument.

ASSIGNMENT OF MORTGAGE,
FIRST TRUST DEED,
OR REAL ESTATE SALES CONTRACT

AM-SPECIAL

To All People To Whom These Presents Shall Come, Greetings;

① KNOW YE. THAT I, ____John J. Brown____ , the individual named

as the owner and holder of a certain | Mortgage / ~~First Trust Deed~~ / ~~Real Estate Sales Contract~~ | from _____ to me, recorded in the _____, Page __613__ , do hereby

Land Records, Volume __71__

② ____Donald Jordan____ ____Elizabeth A. Brown__ , as co-Trustees under the terms of a certain

③ ____Milton____ assign, transfer and set over unto myself and _____, all my right, title and interest in and to said

④ assign, transfer and set over unto myself and _____

⑤ Declaration of Trust dated ____April 4, 1980____ and to the note or other evidence of indebtedness intended to be secured by such

| Mortgage / ~~First Trust Deed~~ / ~~Real Estate Sales Contract~~ |

| Mortgage / ~~First Trust Deed~~ / ~~Real Estate Sales Contract~~ |

TO HAVE AND TO HOLD as such Trustees forever, and I declare that neither I as an individual nor my heirs or assigns shall have or make any claim or demand pursuant to such instrument.

IN WITNESS WHEREOF, I have hereunto set my hand and seal this ____fourth____

day of ____April____ , 19 __80__   (Assignor sign here) ____*John J Brown*____ L.S.

I, the undersigned legal spouse of the above Assignor, do hereby waive all community property rights which I may have in the hereinabove-described trust property and give my assent to the provisions of the trust and to the inclusion in it of the said property. L.S.

(Spouse sign here) _____   Witness: (2) ____*Hilene Storey*____

Witness: (1) ____*Dorothy Lynn*____

STATE OF ____Connecticut____   City or Town ____Milton____

COUNTY OF ____Fairfax____   day of ____April____ , 19__80__ , personally appeared

On the ____fourth____

____John J Brown____ known to me to be the individual(s) who executed the foregoing instrument, and acknowledged the same to be __his__ free act and deed. before me.

____*Anna Beck*____ Notary Public

(Notary Seal)

**ASSIGNMENT OF MORTGAGE,
FIRST TRUST DEED,
OR REAL ESTATE SALES CONTRACT**

To All People To Whom These Presents Shall Come, Greetings;

① KNOW YE, THAT I, _____, the individual named

    as the owner and holder of a certain { Mortgage / First Trust Deed / Real Estate Sales Contract } from

② _____ to me, recorded in the

③ _____ Land Records, Volume _____, Page _____, do hereby

④ assign, transfer and set over unto myself and _____, as co-Trustees under the terms of a certain

⑤ Declaration of Trust dated _____, all my right, title and interest in and to said

{ Mortgage / First Trust Deed / Real Estate Sales Contract } and to the note or other evidence of indebtedness intended to be secured by such

{ Mortgage / First Trust Deed / Real Estate Sales Contract }

    TO HAVE AND TO HOLD as such Trustees forever, and I declare that neither I as an individual nor my heirs or assigns shall have or make any claim or demand pursuant to such instrument.

    IN WITNESS WHEREOF, I have hereunto set my hand and seal this _____

day of _____, 19____.

        (Assignor sign here) _____ L.S.

I, the undersigned legal spouse of the above Assignor, do hereby waive all community property rights which I may have in the hereinabove-described trust property and give my assent to the provisions of the trust and to the inclusion in it of the said property.

        (Spouse sign here) _____ L.S.

Witness: (1) _____   Witness: (2) _____

STATE OF _____   City
                                        or
COUNTY OF _____   Town _____

    On the _____ day of _____, 19____, personally appeared

_____

known to me to be the individual(s) who executed the foregoing instrument, and acknowledged the same to be _____ free act and deed, before me.

_____

(Notary Seal)   *Notary Public*

Assignment of
Mortgage,
First Trust Deed,
or
Real Estate Sales Contract

FROM

_____

(Yourself)

and

_____

(Yourself)

TO

_____

(Your Co-Trustee), Trustees

DATED _____, 19 ___

Received _____, 19 ___

At _____, M

Recorded in the _____

Vol. _____, Page _____

L A N D   R E C O R D S

Authorized Signature

This instrument relates to property located at

Number _____ Street _____

City _____ State _____

After recording, return to:

_____

_____

Avoiding Probate of a Contract Covering a Literary Work or Musical Composition

By reason of their creation of a literary work or musical composition, many persons receive a royalty income which may be expected to continue after their death. This type of asset frequently goes unidentified in a will and is not bequeathed to a specific beneficiary. Instead it simply becomes a part of the general estate, oftentimes creating problems for an executor charged with dividing the assets among several beneficiaries. Since future royalties cannot be determined, it is difficult to assign a present value to such an asset, and beneficiaries are frequently loathe to agree to an estate settlement which involves their acceptance of such an asset as part of their inheritance.

To avoid such problems, it behooves the creator of the property to specifically identify the beneficiary who is to receive it upon his death. If he chooses to do this via his will, it becomes subject to the traditional delay, expense, and publicity of probate.

The copyright of a literary work is generally owned by the author who then enters into a _contract_ with a publisher to produce and sell the work, paying the author a royalty. Occasionally, however, the copyright is owned by the publisher, particularly in those cases where the publisher commissioned the author to produce the work. In this latter case, too, the author has a _contract_ with the publisher under which he is paid an agreed royalty for the sale of the work.

A somewhat different situation applies with respect to musical compositions. While composers who have not yet developed a market for their works may own and control a copyright for which they have personally made application, nearly all composers whose works are being marketed have either assigned their copyright to their publisher or have allowed their works to be copyrighted directly by the publisher. Such composers receive royalties under the terms of a _contract_ with the publisher.

Composers may derive additional benefits from individual performances of their works under a _contract_ with ASCAP, BMI, or SESAC which provides that those organizations will collect fees for such performance rights and will divide them between the composer and the publisher who owns the copyright.

The word "contract" is stressed in the paragraphs above to emphasize that in the case of published authors or composers, it is not the copyright-holding but the _contract_ under which they receive royalties which is significant. The contract is the property the disposition of which in the event of death should be the subject of thought and careful planning.

As with any other form of property, these contracts may be covered with an inter vivos trust that will exempt them from probate and simplify their transfer to heirs. On the following pages will be found several declarations of trust suitable for such purpose.

CHAPTER 13

DECLARATION OF TRUST
For Naming
ONE BENEFICIARY
To Receive
**ROYALTIES FROM A LITERARY WORK
OR MUSICAL COMPOSITION HELD IN ONE NAME**

INSTRUCTIONS:

On the following pages will be found a declaration of trust (DT-125) suitable for use in connection with the establishment of an inter vivos trust covering rights to receive royalties on a literary work or musical composition held in one name, where it is desired to name some one person to receive such rights upon the death of the owner.

Cross out *"city"* or *"town,"* leaving the appropriate designation of your community. Next, cross out *"author"* or *"composer"* and *"literary works"* or *"musical compositions."* Then, insert the date of the contract under which you receive royalties. Finally, enter the name and address of the individual or firm with whom you have entered into the contract.

Enter the name of the beneficiary in the appropriate place in Paragraph 1.

Note that Paragraph 8 designates as Successor Trustee *"whosoever shall at that time be beneficiary hereunder,"* which means that in most cases you don't need to fill anything in there. However, if there is any possibility of a beneficiary who has not attained the age of 21 years receiving the contract rights upon your death, make certain that you name an adult in this paragraph who can act as trustee for such beneficiary. Avoid naming as trustee a person not likely to survive until the beneficiary has attained age 21.

When completed in the manner shown on the reverse side hereof, make several photocopies for reference purposes. Hold the original in safekeeping and provide a copy to the other party to the contract with instructions to hereafter identify the contract owner as: *"(your name), Trustee u/d/t dated* (date you are executing this declaration of trust)." The "Trustee" designation need *not* go on your royalty checks, however.

Important: Read carefully Note B on page 38, which applies to this declaration of trust.

DT-125

Declaration of Trust

of the

WHEREAS, I, **John J. Brown**, County of **Fairfax**, State of **Connecticut**,

City/Town of **Milton**, am the (composer) of certain (musical compositions) which are published, distributed and/or performed pursuant to a contract (hereinafter called "the Contract") entered into by me under date of **January 20, 1980**, with:

(Name) **Music Master Inc.** **Chicago** City **Illinois** State **60411** Zip

(Address) **371** Number **Broadway** Street , of

under the terms of which royalty payments accrue to me from the publication, distribution and/or performance of such works;

NOW, THEREFORE, KNOW ALL MEN BY THESE PRESENTS, that I do hereby acknowledge and declare that I hold and will hold my ownership of the above-described property and all my right, title and interest in and to the benefits payable to me under the said Contract IN TRUST

1. For the use and benefit of:

(Name) **Elizabeth A. Brown – my wife** **Milton** City **Connecticut** State **06605** Zip , of

(Address) **525** Number **Main Street** Street

If because of my physical or mental incapacity certified in writing by a physician, the Successor Trustee hereinafter named shall assume active administration of this trust during my lifetime, such Successor Trustee shall be fully authorized to pay to me or disburse on my behalf such sums from income or principal as appear necessary or desirable for my comfort or welfare. Upon my death, unless the beneficiary shall predecease me or unless we both shall die as a result of a common accident, my Successor Trustee is hereby directed forthwith to transfer said Contract and all my right, title and interest in and to all benefits payable to me under said Contract unto the beneficiary absolutely and thereby terminate this trust; provided, however, that if the beneficiary hereunder shall not have attained the age of 21 years, the Successor Trustee shall hold the trust assets in continuing trust until such beneficiary shall have attained the age of 21 years. During such period of continuing trust the Successor Trustee, in his absolute discretion, may retain the specific Contract herein described if he believes it to be in the best interests of the beneficiary so to do, or, subject to its terms, he may terminate it in whole or in part, investing and reinvesting the proceeds as he may deem appropriate. Prior to the date upon which such beneficiary attains the age of 21 years, the Successor Trustee may apply or expend any or all of the income or principal directly for the maintenance, education and support of the beneficiary without the intervention of any guardian and without application to any court. Such payments of income or principal may be made to the parents of such beneficiary or to the person with whom the beneficiary is living without any liability upon the Successor Trustee to see to the application thereof. If such beneficiary survives me but dies before attaining the age of 21 years, at his or her death the Successor Trustee shall transfer, pay over and deliver the trust property being held for such beneficiary to such beneficiary's personal representative, absolutely.

2. The beneficiary hereunder shall be liable for his proportionate share of any taxes levied upon the Settlor's total taxable estate by reason of the Settlor's death.

3. All interests of a beneficiary hereunder shall be inalienable and free from anticipation, assignment, attachment, pledge or control by creditors or a present or former spouse of such beneficiary in any proceedings at law or in equity.

4. This trust is created with the express understanding that the other party to the Contract shall be under no liability whatsoever to see to its proper administration, and upon the transfer of the right, title and interest in and to such Contract by any trustee hereunder, said other party to the Contract shall conclusively treat the transferee as the sole owner of all of my rights in the Contract. The other party shall receive from some person interested in this trust, written notice of any death or other event upon which the right to receive may depend. Such other party shall be protected in acting upon any notice or other instrument or document believed by it to be genuine and to have been signed or presented by the proper party or parties.

Until such other party shall receive from some person interested in this trust, written notice of any death or other event shall have been affected by such event. Such other party shall be fully authorized to pay all royalties or other income direct to me individually.

5. I reserve unto myself the power and right to collect any royalties or other income which may accrue from the trust property and to pay such income to myself as an individual. I shall have any claim upon any such income accruing from the trust property during my lifetime, and no beneficiary named herein shall have any claim upon any such income distributed to me.

6. I reserve unto myself the power and right at any time during my lifetime to amend or revoke in whole or in part the trust hereby created without the necessity of obtaining the consent of the beneficiary and without giving notice to the beneficiary. The cancellation of the whole or any part of the Contract held hereunder shall constitute as to such whole or part a revocation of this trust.

7. The death during my lifetime, or in a common accident or disaster with me, of the beneficiary designated hereunder shall revoke such designation, and in the former event, I reserve the right to designate a new beneficiary. Should I for any reason fail to designate such new beneficiary, this trust shall terminate upon my death and the trust property shall revert to my estate.

8. In the event of my physical or mental incapacity or my death, I hereby nominate and appoint as Successor Trustee hereunder whosoever shall at that time be beneficiary hereunder, unless such beneficiary shall not have attained the age of 21 years or is otherwise legally incapacitated, in which event I hereby nominate and appoint

(Name) **Henry P. Adams** **Milton** City **Connecticut** State **06605** Zip , of

(Address) **125** Number **Barnum Street** Street

to be Successor Trustee.

9. This Declaration of Trust shall extend to and be binding upon the heirs, executors, administrators and assigns of the undersigned and upon the Successors to the Trustee.

10. The Trustee and his successors shall serve without bond.

11. This Declaration of Trust shall be construed and enforced in accordance with the laws of the State of **Connecticut**

Declaration of Trust

WHEREAS, I, _____, of the

City/Town of _____, County of _____, State of _____,

am the (author) of certain (literary works) which are published,
       (composer)   (musical compositions)

distributed and/or performed pursuant to a contract (hereinafter called "the Contract")

entered into by me under date of _____, with:

(Name) _____, of

(Address) _____
         Number   *Street*   *City*   *State*   *Zip*

under the terms of which royalty payments accrue to me from the publication, distribution and/or performance of such works;

NOW, THEREFORE, KNOW ALL MEN BY THESE PRESENTS, that I do hereby acknowledge and declare that I hold and will hold my ownership of the above-described property and all my right, title and interest in and to the benefits payable to me under the said Contract IN TRUST

1. For the use and benefit of:

(Name) _____, of

(Address) _____
         Number   *Street*   *City*   *State*   *Zip*

If because of my physical or mental incapacity certified in writing by a physician, the Successor Trustee hereinafter named shall assume active administration of this trust during my lifetime, such Successor Trustee shall be fully authorized to pay to me or disburse on my behalf such sums from income or principal as appear necessary or desirable for my comfort or welfare. Upon my death, unless the beneficiary shall predecease me or unless we both shall die as a result of a common accident, my Successor Trustee is hereby directed forthwith to transfer said Contract and all my right, title and interest in and to all benefits payable to me under said Contract unto the beneficiary absolutely and thereby terminate this trust; provided, however, that if the beneficiary hereunder shall not have attained the age of 21 years, the Successor Trustee shall hold the trust assets in continuing trust until such beneficiary shall have attained the age of 21 years. During such period of continuing trust the Successor Trustee, in his absolute discretion, may retain the specific Contract herein described if he believes it to be in the best interests of the beneficiary so to do, or, subject to its terms, he may terminate it in whole or in part, investing and reinvesting the proceeds as he may deem appropriate. Prior to the date upon which such beneficiary attains the age of 21 years, the Successor Trustee may apply or expend any or all of the income or principal directly for the maintenance, education and support of the beneficiary without the intervention of any guardian and without application to any court. Such payments of income or principal may be made to the parents of such beneficiary or to the person with whom the beneficiary is living without any liability upon the Successor Trustee to see to the application thereof. If such beneficiary survives me but dies before attaining the age of 21 years, at his or her death the Successor Trustee shall transfer, pay over and deliver the trust property being held for such beneficiary to such beneficiary's personal representative, absolutely.

2. The beneficiary hereunder shall be liable for his proportionate share of any taxes levied upon the Settlor's total taxable estate by reason of the Settlor's death.

3. All interests of a beneficiary hereunder shall be inalienable and free from anticipation, assignment, attachment, pledge or control by creditors or a present or former spouse of such beneficiary in any proceedings at law or in equity.

4. This trust is created with the express understanding that the other party to the Contract shall be under no liability whatsoever to see to its proper administration, and upon the transfer of the right, title and interest in and to such Contract by any trustee hereunder, said other party shall conclusively treat the transferee as the sole owner of all of my rights in the Contract. Until such other party shall receive from some person interested in this trust, written notice of any death or other event upon which the right to receive may depend, it shall incur no liability for payments made in good faith to persons whose interests shall have been affected by such event. Such other party shall be protected in acting upon any notice or other instrument or document believed by it to be genuine and to have been signed or presented by the proper party or parties.

5. I reserve unto myself the power and right to collect any royalties or other income which may accrue from the trust property and to pay such income to myself as an individual. I shall be exclusively entitled to all income accruing from the trust property during my lifetime, and no beneficiary named herein shall have any claim upon any such income distributed to me.

6. I reserve unto myself the power and right at any time during my lifetime to amend or revoke in whole or in part the trust hereby created without the necessity of obtaining the consent of the beneficiary and without giving notice to the beneficiary. The cancellation of the whole or any part of the Contract held hereunder shall constitute as to such whole or part a revocation of this trust.

7. The death during my lifetime, or in a common accident or disaster with me, of the beneficiary designated hereunder shall revoke such designation, and in the former event, I reserve the right to designate a new beneficiary. Should I for any reason fail to designate such new beneficiary, this trust shall terminate upon my death and the trust property shall revert to my estate.

8. In the event of my physical or mental incapacity or my death, I hereby nominate and appoint as Successor Trustee hereunder whosoever shall at that time be beneficiary hereunder, unless such beneficiary shall not have attained the age of 21 years or is otherwise legally incapacitated, in which event I hereby nominate and appoint

(Name) _____ , of

(Address) _____
   Number   Street   City   State   Zip

to be Successor Trustee.

9. This Declaration of Trust shall extend to and be binding upon the heirs, executors, administrators and assigns of the undersigned and upon the Successors to the Trustee.

10. The Trustee and his successors shall serve without bond.

11. This Declaration of Trust shall be construed and enforced in accordance with the laws of the State of

_____ .

IN WITNESS WHEREOF, I have hereunto set my hand and seal this _____

day of _____ , 19_____ .

(Settlor sign here) _____ L.S.

I, the undersigned legal spouse of the above Settlor, hereby waive all community property rights which I may have in the hereinabove-described Contract and give my assent to the provisions of the trust and to the inclusion in it of the said Contract.

(Spouse sign here) _____ L.S.

Witness: (1) _____   Witness: (2) _____

STATE OF _____⎫   City
                                          ⎬   or
COUNTY OF _____⎭   Town _____

On the _____ day of _____ , 19_____ , personally appeared

_____

known to me to be the individual(s) who executed the foregoing instrument, and acknowledged the same to be _____ free act and deed, before me.

(Notary Seal)   _____
                                                          Notary Public

CHAPTER 13

DECLARATION OF TRUST

For Naming

ONE PRIMARY BENEFICIARY

And

ONE CONTINGENT BENEFICIARY

To Receive

ROYALTIES FROM A LITERARY WORK

OR MUSICAL COMPOSITION HELD IN ONE NAME

INSTRUCTIONS:

On the following pages will be found a declaration of trust (DT-126) suitable for use in connection with the establishment of an inter vivos trust covering rights to receive royalties on a literary work or musical composition held in one name, where it is desired to name some *one* person as primary beneficiary, with some *one* other person as contingent beneficiary to receive the asset if the primary beneficiary be not surviving upon the death of the owner.

Cross out *"city"* or *"town,"* leaving the appropriate designation of your community. Next, cross out *"author"* or *"composer"* and *"literary works"* or *"musical compositions."* Then, insert the date of the contract under which you receive royalties. Finally, enter the name and address of the individual or firm with whom you have entered into the contract.

Enter the names of the beneficiaries in the appropriate place in Paragraph 1.

Note that Paragraph 8 designates as Successor Trustee *"whosoever shall at that time be beneficiary hereunder,"* which means that in most cases you don't need to fill anything in there. However, if there is any possibility of a beneficiary who has not attained the age of 21 years receiving the contract rights upon your death, make certain that you name an adult in this paragraph who can act as trustee for such beneficiary. Avoid naming as trustee a person not likely to survive until the beneficiary has attained age 21.

When completed in the manner shown on the reverse side hereof, make several photocopies for reference purposes. Hold the original in safekeeping and provide a copy to the other party to the contract with instructions to hereafter identify the contract owner as: *"(your name), Trustee u/d/t dated* (date you are executing this declaration of trust)." The "Trustee" designation need *not* go on your royalty checks, however.

Important: Read carefully Note B on page 38, which applies to this declaration of trust.

Declaration of Trust

WHEREAS, I, __John J. Brown__, County of __Fairfax__, State of __Connecticut__ of the City/Town of __Milton__, am the (composer) of certain (musical compositions) which are published, distributed and/or performed pursuant to a contract (hereinafter called "the Contract") entered into by me under date of __January 20, 1980__, with:

(Name) __Music Master Inc.__

(Address) __371__ __Broadway__ __Chicago__ __Illinois__ __60411__
            Number   Street   City   State   Zip

under the terms of which royalty payments accrue to me from the publication, distribution and/or performance of such works;

NOW, THEREFORE, KNOW ALL MEN BY THESE PRESENTS, that I do hereby acknowledge and declare that I hold and will hold my ownership of the above-described property and all my right, title and interest in and to the benefits payable to me under the said Contract IN TRUST

1. For the use and benefit of:

(Name) __Elizabeth A. Brown – my wife__

(Address) __525__ __Main Street__ __Milton__ __Connecticut__ __06605__
            Number   Street   City   State   Zip

or, if such beneficiary be not surviving, for the use and benefit of:

(Name) __Jill A. Brown – my daughter__

(Address) __525__ __Main Street__ __Milton__ __Connecticut__ __06605__
            Number   Street   City   State   Zip

If because of my physical or mental incapacity certified in writing by a physician, the Successor Trustee hereinafter named shall assume active administration of this trust during my lifetime, such Successor Trustee shall be fully authorized to pay to me or disburse on my behalf such sums from income or principal as appear necessary or desirable for my comfort or welfare. Upon my death, unless both beneficiaries shall predecease me or unless we all shall die as a result of a common accident, my Successor Trustee is hereby directed forthwith to transfer said Contract and all my right, title and interest in and to the benefits payable to me under said Contract unto the beneficiary absolutely and thereby terminate this trust: provided, however, that if the beneficiary hereunder shall not have attained the age of 21 years, the Successor Trustee shall hold the trust assets in continuing trust until such beneficiary shall have attained the specific Contract herein described if he believes it to be in the best interests of the in his absolute discretion, may retain the specific Contract herein described if he believes it to be in the best interests of the beneficiary so to do, or, subject to its terms, he may terminate it in whole or in part, investing and reinvesting the proceeds as he may deem appropriate. Prior to the date upon which such beneficiary attains the age of 21 years, the Successor Trustee may apply or expend any or all of the income or principal directly for the maintenance, education and support of the beneficiary without the intervention of any guardian and without application to any court. Such payments of income or principal may be made to the parents of such beneficiary or to the person with whom the beneficiary is living without any liability upon the Successor Trustee to see to the application thereof. If such beneficiary survives me but dies before attaining the age of 21 years, at his or her death the Successor Trustee shall transfer, pay over and deliver the trust property being held for such beneficiary to such beneficiary's personal representative, absolutely.

2. Each beneficiary hereunder shall be liable for his proportionate share of any taxes levied upon the Settlor's total taxable estate by reason of the Settlor's death.

3. All interests of a beneficiary hereunder shall be inalienable and free from anticipation, assignment, attachment, pledge or control by creditors or a present or former spouse of such beneficiary in any proceedings at law or in equity.

4. This trust is created with the express understanding that the other party to the Contract shall be under no liability whatsoever to see to its proper administration, and upon the transfer of the right, title and interest in and to such Contract by any trustee hereunder, said other party shall conclusively treat the transferee as the sole owner of all of my rights in the Contract. The other party to the Contract shall be fully authorized to pay all royalties or other income direct to me individually. Until such other party shall receive from some person interested in this trust, written notice of any death or event upon which the right to receive may depend, it shall incur no liability for payments made in good faith to persons whose interests shall have been affected by such event. Such other party shall be protected in acting upon any notice or other instrument or document believed by it to be genuine and to have been signed or presented by the proper party or parties.

5. I reserve unto myself the power and right to collect any royalties or other income which may accrue from the trust property and to pay such income to myself as an individual. I shall be exclusively entitled to all income accruing from the trust property during my lifetime, and no beneficiary named herein shall have any claim upon any such income distributed to me.

6. I reserve unto myself the power and right at any time during my lifetime to amend or revoke in whole or in part the trust hereby created without the necessity of ~~...~~ the consent of the beneficiary ~~...~~ without giv~~...~~ to the b~~...~~

~~...~~ reby revoke such designation, and in the former event, I reserve the right to designate a new beneficiary. Should I for any reason fail to designate such new beneficiary, this trust shall terminate upon my death and the trust property shall revert to my estate.

8. In the event of my physical or mental incapacity or my death, I hereby nominate and appoint as Successor Trustee hereunder whosoever shall at that time be beneficiary hereunder, unless such beneficiary shall not have attained the age of 21 years or is otherwise legally incapacitated, in which event I hereby nominate and appoint

(Name) __Henry P. Adams__ __Milton__ __Connecticut__ __06605__
                                City   State   Zip

(Address) __125__ __Barnum Street__
            Number   Street

9. This Declaration of Trust shall extend to and be binding upon the heirs, executors, administrators and assigns of the undersigned and upon the Successors to the Trustee.

10. The Trustee and his successors shall serve without bond.

11. This Declaration of Trust shall be construed and enforced in accordance with the laws of the State of __Connecticut__

Declaration of Trust

WHEREAS, I, _____, of the

City/Town of _____, County of _____, State of _____,

am the (author) of certain (literary works) which are published,
(composer) (musical compositions)

distributed and/or performed pursuant to a contract (hereinafter called "the Contract")

entered into by me under date of _____, with:

(Name) _____, of

(Address) _____
Number   Street   City   State   Zip

under the terms of which royalty payments accrue to me from the publication, distribution and/or performance of such works;

NOW, THEREFORE, KNOW ALL MEN BY THESE PRESENTS, that I do hereby acknowledge and declare that I hold and will hold my ownership of the above-described property and all my right, title and interest in and to the benefits payable to me under the said Contract IN TRUST

1. For the use and benefit of:

(Name) _____, of

(Address) _____
Number   Street   City   State   Zip

or, if such beneficiary be not surviving, for the use and benefit of:

(Name) _____, of

(Address) _____
Number   Street   City   State   Zip

If because of my physical or mental incapacity certified in writing by a physician, the Successor Trustee hereinafter named shall assume active administration of this trust during my lifetime, such Successor Trustee shall be fully authorized to pay to me or disburse on my behalf such sums from income or principal as appear necessary or desirable for my comfort or welfare. Upon my death, unless both beneficiaries shall predecease me or unless we all shall die as a result of a common accident, my Successor Trustee is hereby directed forthwith to transfer said Contract and all my right, title and interest in and to the benefits payable to me under said Contract unto the beneficiary absolutely and thereby terminate this trust; provided, however, that if the beneficiary hereunder shall not have attained the age of 21 years, the Successor Trustee shall hold the trust assets in continuing trust until such beneficiary shall have attained the age of 21 years. During such period of continuing trust the Successor Trustee, in his absolute discretion, may retain the specific Contract herein described if he believes it to be in the best interests of the beneficiary so to do, or, subject to its terms, he may terminate it in whole or in part, investing and reinvesting the proceeds as he may deem appropriate. Prior to the date upon which such beneficiary attains the age of 21 years, the Successor Trustee may apply or expend any or all of the income or principal directly for the maintenance, education and support of the beneficiary without the intervention of any guardian and without application to any court. Such payments of income or principal may be made to the parents of such beneficiary or to the person with whom the beneficiary is living without any liability upon the Successor Trustee to see to the application thereof. If such beneficiary survives me but dies before attaining the age of 21 years, at his or her death the Successor Trustee shall transfer, pay over and deliver the trust property being held for such beneficiary to such beneficiary's personal representative, absolutely.

2. Each beneficiary hereunder shall be liable for his proportionate share of any taxes levied upon the Settlor's total taxable estate by reason of the Settlor's death.

3. All interests of a beneficiary hereunder shall be inalienable and free from anticipation, assignment, attachment, pledge or control by creditors or a present or former spouse of such beneficiary in any proceedings at law or in equity.

4. This trust is created with the express understanding that the other party to the Contract shall be under no liability whatsoever to see to its proper administration, and upon the transfer of the right, title and interest in and to such Contract by any trustee hereunder, said other party shall conclusively treat the transferee as the sole owner of all of my rights in the Contract. Until such other party shall receive from some person interested in this trust, written notice of any death or event upon which the right to receive may depend, it shall incur no liability for payments made in good faith to persons whose interests shall have been affected by such event. Such other party shall be protected in acting upon any notice or other instrument or document believed by it to be genuine and to have been signed or presented by the proper party or parties.

5. I reserve unto myself the power and right to collect any royalties or other income which may accrue from the trust property and to pay such income to myself as an individual. I shall be exclusively entitled to all income accruing from the trust property during my lifetime, and no beneficiary named herein shall have any claim upon any such income distributed to me.

6. I reserve unto myself the power and right at any time during my lifetime to amend or revoke in whole or in part the trust hereby created without the necessity of obtaining the consent of the beneficiaries and without giving notice to the beneficiaries. The cancellation of the whole or any part of the Contract held hereunder shall constitute as to such whole or part a revocation of this trust.

7. The death during my lifetime, or in a common accident or disaster with me, of both of the beneficiaries designated hereunder shall revoke such designation, and in the former event, I reserve the right to designate a new beneficiary. Should I for any reason fail to designate such new beneficiary, this trust shall terminate upon my death and the trust property shall revert to my estate.

8. In the event of my physical or mental incapacity or my death, I hereby nominate and appoint as Successor Trustee hereunder whosoever shall at that time be beneficiary hereunder, unless such beneficiary shall not have attained the age of 21 years or is otherwise legally incapacitated, in which event I hereby nominate and appoint

(Name) _____ , of

(Address) _____
    Number   Street   City   State   Zip

9. This Declaration of Trust shall extend to and be binding upon the heirs, executors, administrators and assigns of the undersigned and upon the Successors to the Trustee.

10. The Trustee and his successors shall serve without bond.

11. This Declaration of Trust shall be construed and enforced in accordance with the laws of the State of

_____ .

IN WITNESS WHEREOF, I have hereunto set my hand and seal this _____

day of _____ , 19_____ .

(Settlor sign here) _____ L.S.

I, the undersigned legal spouse of the above Settlor, hereby waive all community property rights which I may have in the hereinabove-described Contract and give my assent to the provisions of the trust and to the inclusion in it of the said Contract.

(Spouse sign here) _____ L.S.

Witness: (1) _____   Witness: (2) _____

STATE OF _____ ⎫   City
                                          ⎬   or
COUNTY OF _____ ⎭   Town _____

On the _____ day of _____ , 19_____ , personally appeared

_____

known to me to be the individual(s) who executed the foregoing instrument, and acknowledged the same to be _____ free act and deed, before me.

_____

(Notary Seal)   Notary Public

CHAPTER 13

DECLARATION OF TRUST
For Naming
TWO OR MORE BENEFICIARIES, SHARING EQUALLY,
To Receive
ROYALTIES FROM A LITERARY WORK
OR MUSICAL COMPOSITION HELD IN ONE NAME

INSTRUCTIONS:

On the following pages will be found a declaration of trust (DT-127) suitable for use in connection with the establishment of an inter vivos trust covering rights to receive royalties on a literary work or musical composition held in one name, where it is desired to name two or more persons to receive such rights upon the death of the owner.

Cross out *"city"* or *"town,"* leaving the appropriate designation of your community. Next, cross out *"author"* or *"composer"* and *"literary works"* or *"musical compositions."* Then, insert the date of the contract under which you receive royalties. Finally, enter the name and address of the individual or firm with whom you have entered into the contract.

In Paragraph 1, indicate the *number of persons* you are naming (to discourage unauthorized additions to the list) and then insert their names. The one whose name appears *first* will be the Successor Trustee responsible for seeing to the distribution of the trust property.

Note that the instrument specifies that the named beneficiaries are to receive *"in equal shares, or the survivor of them/per stirpes."* Now, think carefully: If you have named three persons with the understanding that if one of them predeceases you, *his* children will take *his* share, cross out *"or the survivor of them"* and *initial it.* If that is *not* what you want—if, for example, you prefer that the share of the deceased person be divided between the two surviving persons, cross out *"per stirpes"* and *initial it.* Remember, you <u>must</u> cross out either *"or the survivor of them"* or *"per stirpes"*—one or the other.

Note that Paragraph 8 designates as Successor Trustee *"the beneficiary named first above."* Whenever there is any possibility of a beneficiary who has not attained the age of 21 years receiving the contract rights upon your death, make certain that you name an adult in this paragraph who can act as trustee for such beneficiary. Avoid naming as trustee a person not likely to survive until the beneficiary has attained age 21.

When completed in the manner shown on the reverse side hereof, make several photocopies for reference purposes. Hold the original in safekeeping and provide a copy to the other party to the contract with instructions to hereafter identify the contract owner as: *"(your name), Trustee u/d/t dated* (date you are executing this declaration of trust)." The "Trustee" designation need *not* go on your royalty checks, however.

Important: Read carefully Note B on page 38, which applies to this declaration of trust.

Declaration of Trust

WHEREAS, I, __John J. Brown__, County of __Fairfax__, State of __Connecticut__, of the

City/Town of __Milton__ (~~~~~~~~) which are published,

am the (composer) of certain (musical compositions) , with: , of

distributed and/or performed pursuant to a contract (hereinafter called "the Contract")

entered into by me under date of __January 20, 1980__

(Name) __Music Master, Inc.__   __Chicago__ City   __Illinois__ State   __60411__ Zip

(Address) __371__ Number   __Broadway__ Street   *J.J.B.*

under the terms of which royalty payments accrue to me from the publication, distribution and/or performance of such works;

NOW, THEREFORE, KNOW ALL MEN BY THESE PRESENTS, that I do hereby acknowledge and declare that I hold and will hold my ownership of the above-described property and all my right, title and interest in and to the benefits payable to me under the said Contract IN TRUST

1. For the use and benefit of the following __three (3)__ persons, in equal shares, or the survivor of them:

   Thomas B. Brown - my brother
   Helen M. Brown - my sister
   Charles M. Brown - my brother

If because of my physical or mental incapacity certified in writing by a physician, the Successor Trustee hereinafter named shall assume active administration of this trust during my lifetime, such Successor Trustee shall be fully authorized to pay to me or disburse on my behalf such sums from income or principal as appear necessary or desirable for my comfort or welfare. Upon my death, unless all the beneficiaries shall predecease me or unless we all shall die as a result of a common accident, my Successor Trustee is hereby directed forthwith to transfer said Contract and all my right, title and interest in and to the benefits payable to me under said Contract unto the beneficiaries absolutely and thereby terminate this trust; provided, however, that if any beneficiary hereunder shall not have attained the age of 21 years, the Successor Trustee shall hold the trust assets in continuing trust until such beneficiary shall have attained the age of 21 years. During such period of continuing trust the Successor Trustee, in his absolute discretion, may retain the specific Contract herein described if he believes it to be in the best interests of the beneficiary so to do, or, subject to its terms, he may terminate it in whole or in part, investing and reinvesting the proceeds as he may deem appropriate. Prior to the date upon which such beneficiary attains the age of 21 years, the Successor Trustee may apply or expend any or all of the income or principal directly for the maintenance, education and support of the beneficiary without the intervention of any guardian and without application to any court. Such payments of income or principal may be made to the parents of such beneficiary or to the person with whom the beneficiary is living without any liability upon the Successor Trustee to see to the application thereof. If such beneficiary survives me but dies before attaining the age of 21 years, at his or her death the Successor Trustee shall transfer, pay over and deliver the trust property being held for such beneficiary to such beneficiary's personal representative, absolutely.

2. Each beneficiary hereunder shall be liable for his proportionate share of any taxes levied upon the Settlor's total taxable estate by reason of the Settlor's death.

3. All interests of a beneficiary hereunder shall be inalienable and free from anticipation, assignment, attachment, pledge or control by creditors or a present or former spouse of such beneficiary in any proceedings at law or in equity.

7. The death during my lifetime, or in a common accident or disaster with me, of all of the beneficiaries designated hereunder shall revoke such designation, and in the former event, this trust shall terminate upon my death and the trust property shall revert to my estate.

8. In the event of my physical or mental incapacity or my death, I hereby nominate and appoint as Successor Trustee the beneficiary named first above, unless such beneficiary shall not have attained the age of 21 years or is otherwise legally incapacitated, in which event I hereby nominate and appoint as Successor Trustee the beneficiary named second above, unless such beneficiary named second above shall not have attained the age of 21 years or is otherwise legally incapacitated, in which latter event I hereby nominate and appoint

__Henry P. Adams__   __Milton__ City   __Connecticut__ State   __06605__ Zip

(Name)

(Address) __125__ Number   __Barnum Street__ Street

to be Successor Trustee.

9. This Declaration of Trust shall extend to and be binding upon the heirs, executors, administrators and assigns of the undersigned and upon the Successors to the Trustee.

10. The Trustee and his successors shall serve without bond.

11. This Declaration of Trust shall be construed and enforced in accordance with the laws of the State of __Connecticut__

Declaration of Trust

WHEREAS, I, _____, of the

City/Town of _____, County of _____, State of _____,

am the (author)/(composer) of certain (literary works)/(musical compositions) which are published,

distributed and/or performed pursuant to a contract (hereinafter called "the Contract")

entered into by me under date of _____, with:

(Name) _____, of

(Address) _____

| Number | Street | City | State | Zip |

under the terms of which royalty payments accrue to me from the publication, distribution and/or performance of such works;

NOW, THEREFORE, KNOW ALL MEN BY THESE PRESENTS, that I do hereby acknowledge and declare that I hold and will hold my ownership of the above-described property and all my right, title and interest in and to the benefits payable to me under the said Contract IN TRUST

1. For the use and benefit of the following _____ persons, in equal shares, or the survivor of them/per stirpes:

If because of my physical or mental incapacity certified in writing by a physician, the Successor Trustee hereinafter named shall assume active administration of this trust during my lifetime, such Successor Trustee shall be fully authorized to pay to me or disburse on my behalf such sums from income or principal as appear necessary or desirable for my comfort or welfare. Upon my death, unless all the beneficiaries shall predecease me or unless we all shall die as a result of a common accident, my Successor Trustee is hereby directed forthwith to transfer said Contract and all my right, title and interest in and to the benefits payable to me under said Contract unto the beneficiaries absolutely and thereby terminate this trust; provided, however, that if any beneficiary hereunder shall not have attained the age of 21 years, the Successor Trustee shall hold such beneficiary's share of the trust assets in continuing trust until such beneficiary shall have attained the age of 21 years. During such period of continuing trust the Successor Trustee, in his absolute discretion, may retain the specific Contract herein described if he believes it to be in the best interests of the beneficiary so to do, or, subject to its terms, he may terminate it in whole or in part, investing and reinvesting the proceeds as he may deem appropriate. Prior to the date upon which such beneficiary attains the age of 21 years, the Successor Trustee may apply or expend any or all of the income or principal directly for the maintenance, education and support of the beneficiary without the intervention of any guardian and without application to any court. Such payments of income or principal may be made to the parents of such beneficiary or to the person with whom the beneficiary is living without any liability upon the Successor Trustee to see to the application thereof. If such beneficiary survives me but dies before attaining the age of 21 years, at his or her death the Successor Trustee shall transfer, pay over and deliver the trust property being held for such beneficiary to such beneficiary's personal representative, absolutely.

2. Each beneficiary hereunder shall be liable for his proportionate share of any taxes levied upon the Settlor's total taxable estate by reason of the Settlor's death.

3. All interests of a beneficiary hereunder shall be inalienable and free from anticipation, assignment, attachment, pledge or control by creditors or a present or former spouse of such beneficiary in any proceedings at law or in equity.

4. This trust is created with the express understanding that the other party to the Contract shall be under no liability whatsoever to see to its proper administration, and upon the transfer of the right, title and interest in and to such Contract by any trustee hereunder, said other party shall conclusively treat the transferee as the sole owner of all of my rights in the Contract. Until such other party shall receive from some person interested in this trust, written notice of any death or other

event upon which the right to receive may depend, it shall incur no liability for payments made in good faith to persons whose interests shall have been affected by such event. Such other party shall be protected in acting upon any notice or other instrument or document believed by it to be genuine and to have been signed or presented by the proper party or parties.

5. I reserve unto myself the power and right to collect any royalties or other income which may accrue from the trust property and to pay such income to myself as an individual. I shall be exclusively entitled to all income accruing from the trust property during my lifetime, and no beneficiary named herein shall have any claim upon any such income distributed to me.

6. I reserve unto myself the power and right at any time during my lifetime to amend or revoke in whole or in part the trust hereby created without the necessity of obtaining the consent of the beneficiaries and without giving notice to the beneficiaries. The cancellation of the whole or any part of the Contract held hereunder shall constitute as to such whole or part a revocation of this trust.

7. The death during my lifetime, or in a common accident or disaster with me, of all of the beneficiaries designated hereunder shall revoke such designation, and in the former event, I reserve the right to designate a new beneficiary. Should I for any reason fail to designate such new beneficiary, this trust shall terminate upon my death and the trust property shall revert to my estate.

8. In the event of my physical or mental incapacity or my death, I hereby nominate and appoint as Successor Trustee the beneficiary named first above, unless such beneficiary shall not have attained the age of 21 years or is otherwise legally incapacitated, in which event I hereby nominate and appoint as Successor Trustee the beneficiary named second above, unless such beneficiary named second above shall not have attained the age of 21 years or is otherwise legally incapacitated, in which latter event I hereby nominate and appoint

(Name) _____, of

(Address) _____

             Number   *Street*   *City*   *State*   *Zip*

to be Successor Trustee.

9. This Declaration of Trust shall extend to and be binding upon the heirs, executors, administrators and assigns of the undersigned and upon the Successors to the Trustee.

10. The Trustee and his successors shall serve without bond.

11. This Declaration of Trust shall be construed and enforced in accordance with the laws of the State of

_____.

IN WITNESS WHEREOF, I have hereunto set my hand and seal this _____

day of _____, 19_____.

        (Settlor sign here) _____ L.S.

I, the undersigned legal spouse of the above Settlor, hereby waive all community property rights which I may have in the hereinabove-described Contract and give my assent to the provisions of the trust and to the inclusion in it of the said Contract.

        (Spouse sign here) _____ L.S.

Witness: (1) _____   Witness: (2) _____

STATE OF _____   City

COUNTY OF _____   or

                               Town _____

On the _____ day of _____, 19_____, personally appeared

_____

known to me to be the individual(s) who executed the foregoing instrument, and acknowledged the same to be _____ free act and deed, before me.

(Notary Seal)   _____

                                                           Notary Public

CHAPTER 13

DECLARATION OF TRUST

For Naming

ONE PRIMARY BENEFICIARY WITH YOUR CHILDREN, SHARING EQUALLY, AS CONTINGENT BENEFICIARIES

To Receive

ROYALTIES FROM A LITERARY WORK OR MUSICAL COMPOSITION HELD IN ONE NAME

INSTRUCTIONS:

On the following pages will be found a declaration of trust (DT-128) suitable for use in connection with the establishment of an inter vivos trust covering rights to receive royalties on a literary work or musical composition held in one name, where it is desired to name some one person (ordinarily, but not necessarily, one's spouse) as primary beneficiary with one's children, sharing equally, as contingent beneficiaries to receive such rights upon the death of the owner.

Cross out *"city"* or *"town,"* leaving the appropriate designation of your community. Next, cross out *"author"* or *"composer"* and *"literary works"* or *"musical compositions."* Then, insert the date of the contract under which you receive royalties. Finally, enter the name and address of the individual or firm with whom you have entered into the contract.

Enter the name of the primary beneficiary (called the "First Beneficiary") in the appropriate place in Paragraph 1. Note that the instrument first refers to your children as *"natural not/or adopted."* Now, decide: If you have an adopted child and you wish to include him, cross out the word *"not"* in the phrase *"natural not/or adopted"* and *initial it.* If you wish to *exclude* your adopted child, cross out the word *"or"* in the same phrase and *initial it.* Remember, you <u>must</u> cross out *"not"* or *"or"*—one or the other. If you have no adopted child, simply cross out *"not."*

Note next that the instrument specifies that your children are to receive *"in equal shares, or the survivor of them/per stirpes."* Now, think carefully: If it is your wish that if one of your children does not survive you, *his* share will revert to *his* children in equal shares, cross out *"or the survivor of them"* and *initial it.* If that is *not* what you want—if, for example, you prefer that the share of any child of yours who predeceases you shall be divided between your other surviving children in equal shares, cross out *"per stirpes"* and *initial it.* Remember, you <u>must</u> cross out *"or the survivor of them"* or *"per stirpes"*—one or the other.

Note that in Paragraph 8, the First Beneficiary is designated as Successor Trustee, while a space is provided in which you should designate another person to so act if the named Successor Trustee is not surviving or otherwise fails or ceases to act. This could be one of your children, for example, but it must be an adult who can act as trustee for any beneficiary who comes into a share of the trust before attaining the age of 21. Avoid naming someone not likely to survive until the youngest such beneficiary has attained age 21.

When completed in the manner shown on the reverse side hereof, make several photocopies for reference purposes. Hold the original in safekeeping and provide a copy to the other party to the contract with instructions to hereafter identify the contract owner as: *"(your name), Trustee u/d/t dated* (date you are executing this declaration of trust)." The "Trustee" designation need *not* go on your royalty checks, however.

Important: Read carefully Note B on page 38, which applies to this declaration of trust.

DT-128

Declaration of Trust

_____, of the

WHEREAS, I, __John J. Brown__, County of __Fairfax__, State of __Connecticut__

am the ~~(author)~~/Town of __Milton__ of certain ~~(literary works)~~ (musical compositions) which are published, _____, with:

(composer)

distributed and/or performed pursuant to a contract (hereinafter called "the Contract")

entered into by me under date of __January 20, 1980__

(Name) __Music Master, Inc.__ __Chicago__ __Illinois__ __60411__
City State Zip

(Address) __371__ __Broadway__
Number Street

under the terms of which royalty payments accrue to me from the publication, distribution and/or performance of such works;

NOW, THEREFORE, KNOW ALL MEN BY THESE PRESENTS, that I do hereby acknowledge and declare that I hold and will hold my ownership of the above-described property and all my right, title and interest in and to the benefits payable to me under the said Contract IN TRUST

1. For the use and benefit of:

(Name) __Elizabeth A. Brown - my wife__ __Milton__ __Connecticut__ __06605__
City State Zip

(Address) __525__ __Main Street__
Number Street

(hereinafter referred to as the "First Beneficiary"), and upon his or her death prior to the termination of the trust, for the use and benefit of my children, natural or adopted, in equal shares, the survivor of them/per stirpes.

If because of my physical or mental incapacity certified in writing by a physician, the Successor Trustee hereinafter named shall assume active administration of this trust during my lifetime, such Successor Trustee shall be fully authorized to pay to me or disburse on my behalf such sums from income or principal as appear necessary or desirable for my comfort or welfare. Upon my death, unless the beneficiary or beneficiaries all shall predecease me or unless we all shall die as a result of a common accident or disaster, my Successor Trustee is hereby directed forthwith to transfer said Contract and all my right, title and interest in and to the benefits payable to me under said Contract unto the beneficiary or beneficiaries absolutely and thereby terminate this trust; _provided_, however, that if any beneficiary hereunder shall not have attained the age of 21 years, the Successor Trustee shall hold such beneficiary's share of the trust assets in continuing trust until such beneficiary shall have attained the age of 21 years. During such period of continuing trust the Successor Trustee, in his absolute discretion, may retain the specific Contract herein described if he believes it to be in the best interests of the beneficiary so to do, or, subject to its terms, he may terminate it in whole or in part, investing and reinvesting the proceeds as he may deem appropriate. Prior to the date upon which such beneficiary attains the age of 21 years, the Successor Trustee may apply or expend any or all of the income or principal directly for the maintenance, education and support of the beneficiary without the intervention of any guardian and without application to any court. Such payments of income or principal may be made to the parents of such beneficiary or to the person with whom the beneficiary is living without any liability upon the Successor Trustee to see to the application thereof. If such beneficiary survives me but dies before attaining the age of 21 years, at his or her death the Successor Trustee shall transfer, pay over and deliver the trust property being held for such beneficiary to such beneficiary's personal representative, absolutely.

2. Each beneficiary hereunder shall be liable for his proportionate share of any taxes levied upon the Settlor's total taxable estate by reason of the Settlor's death.

3. All interests of a beneficiary hereunder shall be inalienable and free from anticipation, assignment, attachment, pledge or control by creditors or a present or former spouse of such beneficiary in any proceedings at law or in equity.

4. This trust is created with the express understanding that the other party to the Contract shall be under no liability whatsoever to see to its proper administration, and upon the transfer of the right, title and interest in and to such Contract by any trustee hereunder, said other party shall be fully authorized to treat the transferee as the sole owner of all of my rights in the Contract. The other party to the Contract shall receive from some person interested in this trust, written notice of any death or other event upon which the right to receive may depend, it shall incur no liability for payments made in good faith to persons whose interests shall have been affected by such event. Such other party shall be protected in acting upon any notice or other instrument or document believed by it to be genuine and to have been signed or presented by the proper party or parties.

5. I reserve unto myself the power and right to collect any royalties or other income which may accrue from the trust property and to pay such income to myself as an individual. I shall be exclusively entitled to all income accruing from the trust property during my lifetime, and no beneficiary named herein shall have any claim upon any such income distributed to me.

6. I reserve unto myself the power and right at any time during my lifetime to amend or revoke in whole or in part the trust hereby created without the necessity of obtaining the consent of the beneficiaries and without giving notice to the beneficiaries of The cancellation of the whole or any part of the Contract held hereunder shall constitute as to such whole or part a revocation of this trust.

any reason fail to designate such new beneficiary, this trust shall terminate upon my death and the trust property shall revert to my estate.

8. In the event of my physical or mental incapacity or my death, I hereby nominate and appoint as Successor Trustee hereunder the First Beneficiary, or if such First Beneficiary be not surviving or fails or ceases to act. I nominate and appoint _____, of

(Name) __Henry P. Adams__ __Milton__ __Connecticut__ __06605__
City State Zip

(Address) __125__ __Barnum Street__
Number Street

to be Successor Trustee. If such person fails or ceases to act or should I for any reason fail to designate the person above intended to be nominated, then I nominate and appoint as such Successor Trustee hereunder whosoever shall qualify as executor, administrator or guardian, as the case may be, of my estate.

9. This Declaration of Trust shall extend to and be binding upon the heirs, executors, administrators and assigns of the undersigned and upon the Successors to the Trustee.

10. The Trustee and his successors shall serve without bond.

11. This Declaration of Trust shall be construed and enforced in accordance with the laws of the State

of __Connecticut__

Declaration of Trust

WHEREAS, I, _____, of the

City/Town of _____, County of _____, State of _____,

am the (author) (composer) of certain (literary works) (musical compositions) which are published,

distributed and/or performed pursuant to a contract (hereinafter called "the Contract")

entered into by me under date of _____, with:

(Name) _____, of

(Address) _____
Number   Street   City   State   Zip

under the terms of which royalty payments accrue to me from the publication, distribution and/or performance of such works;

NOW, THEREFORE, KNOW ALL MEN BY THESE PRESENTS, that I do hereby acknowledge and declare that I hold and will hold my ownership of the above-described property and all my right, title and interest in and to the benefits payable to me under the said Contract IN TRUST

1. For the use and benefit of:

(Name) _____, of

(Address) _____
Number   Street   City   State   Zip

(hereinafter referred to as the "First Beneficiary"), and upon his or her death prior to the termination of the trust, for the use and benefit of my children, natural not/or adopted, in equal shares, or the survivor of them/per stirpes.

If because of my physical or mental incapacity certified in writing by a physician, the Successor Trustee hereinafter named shall assume active administration of this trust during my lifetime, such Successor Trustee shall be fully authorized to pay to me or disburse on my behalf such sums from income or principal as appear necessary or desirable for my comfort or welfare. Upon my death, unless the beneficiary or beneficiaries all shall predecease me or unless we all shall die as a result of a common accident or disaster, my Successor Trustee is hereby directed forthwith to transfer said Contract and all my right, title and interest in and to the benefits payable to me under said Contract unto the beneficiary or beneficiaries absolutely and thereby terminate this trust; provided, however, that if any beneficiary hereunder shall not have attained the age of 21 years, the Successor Trustee shall hold such beneficiary's share of the trust assets in continuing trust until such beneficiary shall have attained the age of 21 years. During such period of continuing trust the Successor Trustee, in his absolute discretion, may retain the specific Contract herein described if he believes it to be in the best interests of the beneficiary so to do, or, subject to its terms, he may terminate it in whole or in part, investing and reinvesting the proceeds as he may deem appropriate. Prior to the date upon which such beneficiary attains the age of 21 years, the Successor Trustee may apply or expend any or all of the income or principal directly for the maintenance, education and support of the beneficiary without the intervention of any guardian and without application to any court. Such payments of income or principal may be made to the parents of such beneficiary or to the person with whom the beneficiary is living without any liability upon the Successor Trustee to see to the application thereof. If such beneficiary survives me but dies before attaining the age of 21 years, at his or her death the Successor Trustee shall transfer, pay over and deliver the trust property being held for such beneficiary to such beneficiary's personal representative, absolutely.

2. Each beneficiary hereunder shall be liable for his proportionate share of any taxes levied upon the Settlor's total taxable estate by reason of the Settlor's death.

3. All interests of a beneficiary hereunder shall be inalienable and free from anticipation, assignment, attachment, pledge or control by creditors or a present or former spouse of such beneficiary in any proceedings at law or in equity.

4. This trust is created with the express understanding that the other party to the Contract shall be under no liability whatsoever to see to its proper administration, and upon the transfer of the right, title and interest in and to such Contract by any trustee hereunder, said other party shall conclusively treat the transferee as the sole owner of all of my rights in the Contract. Until such other party shall receive from some person interested in this trust, written notice of any death or other event upon which the right to receive may depend, it shall incur no liability for payments made in good faith to persons whose interests shall have been affected by such event. Such other party shall be protected in acting upon any notice or other instrument or document believed by it to be genuine and to have been signed or presented by the proper party or parties.

5. I reserve unto myself the power and right to collect any royalties or other income which may accrue from the trust property and to pay such income to myself as an individual. I shall be exclusively entitled to all income accruing from the trust property during my lifetime, and no beneficiary named herein shall have any claim upon any such income distributed to me.

6. I reserve unto myself the power and right at any time during my lifetime to amend or revoke in whole or in part the trust hereby created without the necessity of obtaining the consent of the beneficiaries and without giving notice to the beneficiaries. The cancellation of the whole or any part of the Contract held hereunder shall constitute as to such whole or part a revocation of this trust.

7. The death during my lifetime, or in a common accident or disaster with me, of all of the beneficiaries designated hereunder shall revoke such designation, and in the former event, I reserve the right to designate a new beneficiary. Should I for any reason fail to designate such new beneficiary, this trust shall terminate upon my death and the trust property shall revert to my estate.

8. In the event of my physical or mental incapacity or my death, I hereby nominate and appoint as Successor Trustee hereunder the First Beneficiary, or if such First Beneficiary be not surviving or fails or ceases to act, I nominate and appoint

(Name) _____ , of

(Address) _____
          Number   *Street*   *City*   *State*   *Zip*

to be Successor Trustee. If such person fails or ceases to act or should I for any reason fail to designate the person above intended to be nominated, then I nominate and appoint as such Successor Trustee hereunder whosoever shall qualify as executor, administrator or guardian, as the case may be, of my estate.

9. This Declaration of Trust shall extend to and be binding upon the heirs, executors, administrators and assigns of the undersigned and upon the Successors to the Trustee.

10. The Trustee and his successors shall serve without bond.

11. This Declaration of Trust shall be construed and enforced in accordance with the laws of the State

of _____ .

IN WITNESS WHEREOF, I have hereunto set my hand and seal this _____

day of _____ , 19_____ .

(Settlor sign here) _____ L.S.

I, the undersigned legal spouse of the Settlor, hereby waive all community property rights which I may have in the hereinabove-described contract and give my assent to the provisions of the trust and to the inclusion in it of the said contract.

(Spouse sign here) _____ L.S.

Witness: (1) _____ Witness: (2) _____

STATE OF _____ City

COUNTY OF _____ or
                                              Town _____

On the _____ day of _____ , 19_____ , personally appeared

_____

known to me to be the individual(s) who executed the foregoing instrument, and acknowledged the same to be _____ free act and deed, before me.

(Notary Seal)

_____
Notary Public

CHAPTER 14

Avoiding Probate of Patent Rights and Royalties

The same estate planning problems which are applicable to a copyright on a literary work or musical composition are inherent in ownership of patent rights which are productive of royalties.

There are exceptions, of course, but it may fairly be said that literary works or musical compositions, if they are to find favor at all and thus be a source of income, generally do so without great delay. An inventor, on the other hand, may wait for a long time for a particular use to be found for his idea, or for a capitalist willing to finance its development. Indeed, many inventions have achieved commercial success only long after their creators have passed on.

Patent holders need to plan thoughtfully whom they wish to have enjoy such future benefits. Having selected the beneficiary, the simplest way for them to insure that the fruits of their imagination and ingenuity go to the person they choose is to place their patent rights and royalties in an inter vivos trust.

On the following pages will be found declarations of trust which will aid in achieving this objective.

CHAPTER 14

DECLARATION OF TRUST
For Naming
ONE BENEFICIARY
To Receive
A PATENT RIGHTS CONTRACT
HELD IN ONE NAME

INSTRUCTIONS:

On the following pages will be found a declaration of trust (DT-129) suitable for use in connection with the establishment of an inter vivos trust covering a patent rights contract held in one name only, where it is desired to name some one person to receive the contract upon the death of the owner.

Cross out *"city"* or *"town,"* leaving the appropriate designation of your community. Next, identify the patents by number, then enter the name and address of the individual or firm to whom the rights have been assigned, and the date of the contract.

Enter the name of the beneficiary in the appropriate place in Paragraph 1.

Note that Paragraph 8 designates as Successor Trustee *"whosoever shall at that time be beneficiary hereunder,"* which means that in most cases you don't need to fill anything in there. However, if there is any possibility of a beneficiary who has not attained the age of 21 years receiving the contract, make certain that you name an adult in this paragraph who can act as trustee for such beneficiary. Avoid naming as trustee a person not likely to survive until the beneficiary has attained age 21.

When completed in the manner shown on the reverse side hereof, make several photocopies. Hold the original in safekeeping and offer a copy to the Assignee with instructions to identify your account under the contract in this manner: *"(your name), Trustee u/d/t dated* (date you sign this declaration) _____." It is *not* necessary to include the "Trustee" designation on checks payable to you pursuant to the contract.

Important: Read carefully Note B on page 38, which applies to this declaration of trust.

Declaration of Trust

WHEREAS, I, __John J. Brown__, County of __Fairfax__, State of __Connecticut__, of the

Town of __Milton__ am the registrant under one or more design and/or utility patents numbered __29265689 and__

__D5643670__

which have been assigned to:

(Name) __Ajax Machinery Company__ __Chicago__ __Illinois 60411__ of
                                        City   State   Zip

(Address) __371__ __Broadway__
          Number   Street

(hereinafter referred to as "the Assignee"), under the terms of a contract (hereinafter called "the Contract"), entered into by

me and said Assignee under date of __January 20, 1980__,

pursuant to which certain royalty payments accrue to me from the exploitation of such patents;

NOW, THEREFORE, KNOW ALL MEN BY THESE PRESENTS, that I do hereby acknowledge and declare that I hold and will hold said patents and all my right, title and interest in and to the benefits payable to me under the said Contract IN TRUST

1. For the use and benefit of:

(Name) __Elizabeth A. Brown - my wife__ __Milton__ __Connecticut 06605__
                                       City   State   Zip

(Address) __525__ __Main Street__
          Number   Street

If because of my physical or mental incapacity certified in writing by a physician, the Successor Trustee hereinafter named shall assume active administration of this trust during my lifetime, such Successor Trustee shall be fully authorized to pay to me or disburse on my behalf such sums from income or principal as appear necessary or desirable for my comfort or welfare. Upon my death, unless the beneficiary shall predecease me or unless we both shall die as a result of a common accident, my Successor Trustee is hereby directed forthwith to transfer said patent rights and all right, title and interest in and to the benefits payable to me under said Contract unto the beneficiary absolutely and thereby terminate this trust; provided, however, that if the beneficiary hereunder shall not have attained the age of 21 years, the Successor Trustee shall hold the trust assets in continuing trust until such beneficiary shall have attained the age of 21 years. During such period of continuing trust the Successor Trustee, in his absolute discretion, may retain the specific Contract herein described if he believes it to be in the best interests of the beneficiary so to do, or, subject to its·terms, he may terminate it, investing and reinvesting the proceeds as he may deem appropriate. Prior to the date upon which such beneficiary attains the age of 21 years, the Successor Trustee may apply or expend any or all of the income or principal directly for the maintenance, education and support of the beneficiary without the intervention of any guardian and without application to any court. Such payments of income or principal may be made to the parents of such beneficiary or to the person with whom the beneficiary is living without any liability upon the Successor Trustee to see to the application thereof. If such beneficiary survives me but dies before attaining the age of 21 years, at his or her death the Successor Trustee shall transfer, pay over and deliver the trust property to such beneficiary's personal representative, absolutely.

2. The beneficiary hereunder shall be liable for his proportionate share of any taxes levied upon the Settlor's total taxable estate by reason of the Settlor's death.

3. All interests of the beneficiary hereunder shall be inalienable and free from anticipation, assignment, attachment, pledge or control by creditors or a present or former spouse of such beneficiary in any proceedings at law or in equity.

4. This trust is created with·the express understanding that the Assignee shall be under no liability whatsoever to see to its proper administration. On the contrary, upon the transfer of the right, title and interest in and to the Contract by any trustee hereunder, said Assignee shall conclusively treat the transferee as the sole owner of said Contract. The Assignee shall be fully authorized to pay all royalties due under the terms of the Contract direct to me individually. Until the Assignee shall receive from some person interested in this trust, written notice of any death or other event upon which the right to receive may depend, the Assignee shall incur no liability for payments made in good faith to persons whose interests shall have been affected by such event. The Assignee shall be protected in acting upon any notice or other instrument or document believed by it to be genuine and to have been signed or presented by the proper party or parties.

5. I reserve unto myself the power and right to collect all royalties or other income which may accrue under the terms of the Contract and to pay such royalties or other income to myself as an individual. I shall be exclusively entitled to all income accruing from the Contract during my lifetime and no beneficiary named herein shall have any claim upon any such income distributed to me.

6. I reserve unto myself the power and right at any time during my lifetime to amend or revoke in whole or in part the trust hereby created without the necessity of obtaining the consent of the beneficiary and without giving notice to the beneficiary. The termination of the whole or any part of the Contract held hereunder shall constitute as to such whole or part a revocation of this trust.

7. [text obscured] during my lifetime [text obscured] ___ such revoke such designation, and in the former event, I reserve the right to designate a new beneficiary. Should I for any reason fail to designate such new beneficiary, this trust shall terminate upon my death and the trust property shall revert to my estate.

8. In the event of my physical or mental incapacity or my death, I hereby nominate and appoint as Successor Trustee hereunder whosoever shall at that time be beneficiary hereunder, unless such beneficiary shall not have attained the age of 21 years or is otherwise legally incapacitated, in which event I hereby nominate and appoint

(Name) __Henry P. Adams__ __Milton__ __Connecticut 06605__
                                      City   State   Zip

(Address) __125__ __Barnum Street__
          Number   Street

to be Successor Trustee.

9. This Declaration of Trust shall extend to and be binding upon the heirs, executors, administrators and assigns of the undersigned and upon the Successors to the Trustee.

10. The Trustee and his successors shall serve without bond.

11. This Declaration of Trust shall be construed and enforced in accordance with the laws of the State of __Connecticut__

Declaration of Trust

WHEREAS, I, _____, of the

City/Town of _____, County of _____, State of _____,

am the registrant under one or more design and/or utility patents numbered _____

_____,

which have been assigned to:

(Name) _____, of

(Address) _____

            Number   *Street*   *City*   *State*   *Zip*

(hereinafter referred to as "the Assignee"), under the terms of a contract (hereinafter called "the Contract"), entered into by

me and said Assignee under date of _____,

pursuant to which certain royalty payments accrue to me from the exploitation of such patents;

NOW, THEREFORE, KNOW ALL MEN BY THESE PRESENTS, that I do hereby acknowledge and declare that I hold and will hold said patents and all my right, title and interest in and to the benefits payable to me under the said Contract IN TRUST

    1. For the use and benefit of:

(Name) _____, of

(Address) _____

            Number   *Street*   *City*   *State*   *Zip*

If because of my physical or mental incapacity certified in writing by a physician, the Successor Trustee hereinafter named shall assume active administration of this trust during my lifetime, such Successor Trustee shall be fully authorized to pay to me or disburse on my behalf such sums from income or principal as appear necessary or desirable for my comfort or welfare. Upon my death, unless the beneficiary shall predecease me or unless we both shall die as a result of a common accident, my Successor Trustee is hereby directed forthwith to transfer said patent rights and all right, title and interest in and to the benefits payable to me under said Contract unto the beneficiary absolutely and thereby terminate this trust; provided, however, that if the beneficiary hereunder shall not have attained the age of 21 years, the Successor Trustee shall hold the trust assets in continuing trust until such beneficiary shall have attained the age of 21 years. During such period of continuing trust the Successor Trustee, in his absolute discretion, may retain the specific Contract herein described if he believes it to be in the best interests of the beneficiary so to do, or, subject to its terms, he may terminate it, investing and reinvesting the proceeds as he may deem appropriate. Prior to the date upon which such beneficiary attains the age of 21 years, the Successor Trustee may apply or expend any or all of the income or principal directly for the maintenance, education and support of the beneficiary without the intervention of any guardian and without application to any court. Such payments of income or principal may be made to the parents of such beneficiary or to the person with whom the beneficiary is living without any liability upon the Successor Trustee to see to the application thereof. If such beneficiary survives me but dies before attaining the age of 21 years, at his or her death the Successor Trustee shall transfer, pay over and deliver the trust property to such beneficiary's personal representative, absolutely.

    2. The beneficiary hereunder shall be liable for his proportionate share of any taxes levied upon the Settlor's total taxable estate by reason of the Settlor's death.

    3. All interests of the beneficiary hereunder shall be inalienable and free from anticipation, assignment, attachment, pledge or control by creditors or a present or former spouse of such beneficiary in any proceedings at law or in equity.

    4. This trust is created with the express understanding that the Assignee shall be under no liability whatsoever to see to its proper administration. On the contrary, upon the transfer of the right, title and interest in and to the Contract by any trustee hereunder, said Assignee shall conclusively treat the transferee as the sole owner of said Contract. Until the Assignee shall receive from some person interested in this trust, written notice of any death or other event upon which the right to receive may depend, the Assignee shall incur no liability for payments made in good faith to persons whose interests shall have been affected by such event. The Assignee shall be protected in acting upon any notice or other instrument or document believed by it to be genuine and to have been signed or presented by the proper party or parties.

    5. I reserve unto myself the power and right to collect all royalties or other income which may accrue under the terms of the Contract and to pay such royalties or other income to myself as an individual. I shall be exclusively entitled to all income accruing from the Contract during my lifetime and no beneficiary named herein shall have any claim upon any such income distributed to me.

6. I reserve unto myself the power and right at any time during my lifetime to amend or revoke in whole or in part the trust hereby created without the necessity of obtaining the consent of the beneficiary and without giving notice to the beneficiary. The termination of the whole or any part of the Contract held hereunder shall constitute as to such whole or part a revocation of this trust.

7. The death during my lifetime, or in a common accident with me, of the beneficiary designated hereunder shall revoke such designation, and in the former event, I reserve the right to designate a new beneficiary. Should I for any reason fail to designate such new beneficiary, this trust shall terminate upon my death and the trust property shall revert to my estate.

8. In the event of my physical or mental incapacity or my death, I hereby nominate and appoint as Successor Trustee hereunder whosoever shall at that time be beneficiary hereunder, unless such beneficiary shall not have attained the age of 21 years or is otherwise legally incapacitated, in which event I hereby nominate and appoint

(Name) _____, of

(Address) _____
         Number   *Street*   *City*   *State*   *Zip*

to be Successor Trustee.

9. This Declaration of Trust shall extend to and be binding upon the heirs, executors, administrators and assigns of the undersigned and upon the Successors to the Trustee.

10. The Trustee and his successors shall serve without bond.

11. This Declaration of Trust shall be construed and enforced in accordance with the laws of the State of

_____.

IN WITNESS WHEREOF, I have hereunto set my hand and seal this _____

day of _____, 19_____.

        (Settlor sign here) _____ L.S.

I, the undersigned legal spouse of the above Settlor, hereby waive all community property rights which I may have in the hereinabove-described Contract and give my assent to the provisions of the trust and to the inclusion in it of the said Contract.

        (Spouse sign here) _____ L.S.

Witness: (1) _____   Witness: (2) _____

STATE OF _____ ⎫ City

COUNTY OF _____ ⎬ or

                            ⎭ Town _____

    On the _____ day of _____, 19_____, personally appeared

_____

known to me to be the individual(s) who executed the foregoing instrument, and acknowledged the same to be _____ free act and deed, before me.

(Notary Seal)   _____

                                                  Notary Public

CHAPTER 14

DECLARATION OF TRUST
For Naming
ONE PRIMARY BENEFICIARY
And
ONE CONTINGENT BENEFICIARY
To Receive
A PATENT RIGHTS CONTRACT HELD IN ONE NAME

INSTRUCTIONS:

On the following pages will be found a declaration of trust (DT-130) suitable for use in connection with the establishment of an inter vivos trust covering a patent rights contract held in one name, where it is desired to name some *one* person as primary beneficiary, with some *one* other person as contingent beneficiary to receive the contract if the primary beneficiary be not surviving upon the death of the owner.

Cross out *"city"* or *"town,"* leaving the appropriate designation of your community. Next, identify the patents by number, then enter the name and address of the individual or firm to whom the rights have been assigned, and the date of the contract.

Enter the names of the beneficiaries in the appropriate place in Paragraph 1.

Note that Paragraph 8 designates as Successor Trustee *"whosoever shall at that time be beneficiary hereunder,"* which means that in most cases you don't need to fill anything in there. However, if there is any possibility of a beneficiary who has not attained the age of 21 years receiving the contract, make certain that you name an adult in this paragraph who can act as trustee for such beneficiary. Avoid naming as trustee a person not likely to survive until the beneficiary has attained age 21.

When completed in the manner shown on the reverse side hereof, make several photocopies for reference purposes. Hold the original in safekeeping and offer a copy to the Assignee with instructions to identify your account under the contract in this manner: *"(your name), Trustee u/d/t dated _____."* It is *not* necessary to include the "Trustee" designation on checks payable to you pursuant to the contract.

Important: Read carefully Note B on page 38, which applies to this declaration of trust.

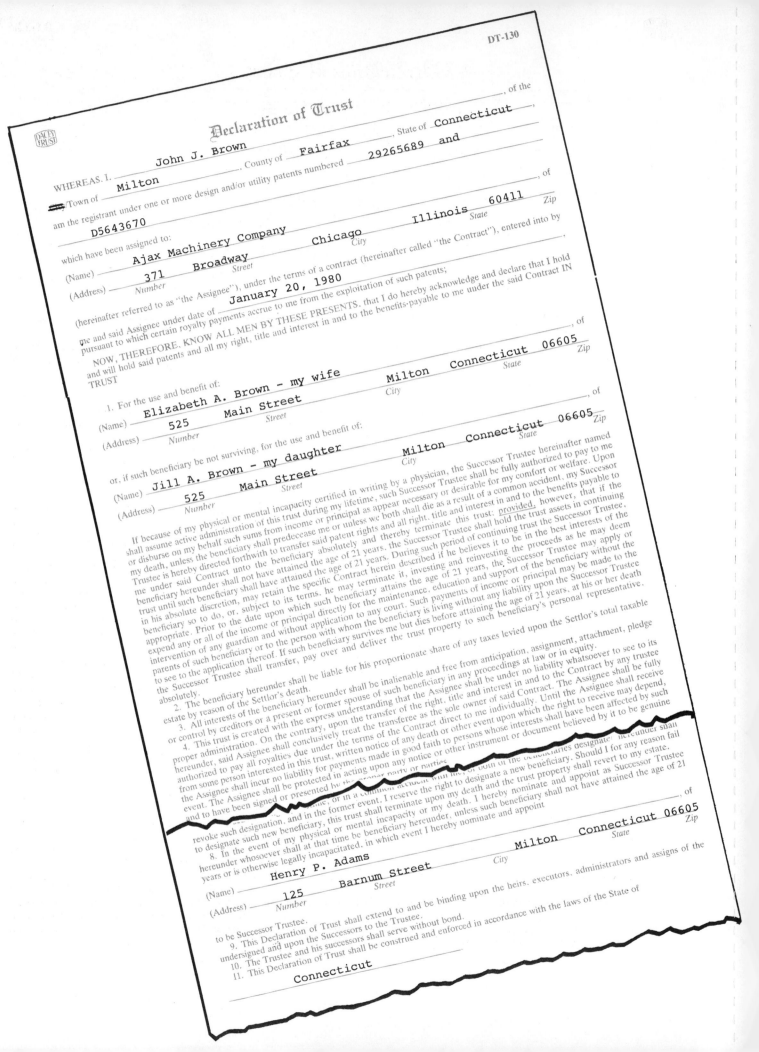

DT-130

Declaration of Trust

WHEREAS, I, __John J. Brown__, County of __Fairfax__, State of __Connecticut__, Town of __Milton__, am the registrant under one or more design and/or utility patents numbered __29265689__ and __D5643670__

which have been assigned to:

(Name) __Ajax Machinery Company__ __Chicago__ City __Illinois__ State __60411__ Zip

(Address) __371__ Number __Broadway__ Street

(hereinafter referred to as "the Assignee"), under the terms of a contract (hereinafter called "the Contract"), entered into by me and said Assignee under date of __January 20, 1980__, pursuant to which certain royalty payments accrue to me from the exploitation of such patents;

NOW, THEREFORE, KNOW ALL MEN BY THESE PRESENTS, that I do hereby acknowledge and declare that I hold and will hold said patents and all my right, title and interest in and to the benefits payable to me under the said Contract IN TRUST

1. For the use and benefit of:

(Name) __Elizabeth A. Brown - my wife__ __Milton__ City __Connecticut__ State __06605__ Zip

(Address) __525__ Number __Main Street__ Street

or, if such beneficiary be not surviving, for the use and benefit of:

(Name) __Jill A. Brown - my daughter__ __Milton__ City __Connecticut__ State __06605__ Zip

(Address) __525__ Number __Main Street__ Street

If because of my physical or mental incapacity certified in writing by a physician, the Successor Trustee hereinafter named shall assume active administration of this trust during my lifetime, such Successor Trustee shall be fully authorized to pay to me or disburse on my behalf such sums from income or principal as appear necessary or desirable for my comfort or welfare. Upon my death, unless the beneficiary shall predecease me or unless we both shall die as a result of a common accident, my Successor Trustee is hereby directed forthwith to transfer said patent rights and all right, title and interest in and to the benefits payable to me under said Contract unto the beneficiary absolutely and thereby terminate this trust; provided, however, that if the beneficiary hereunder shall not have attained the age of 21 years, the Successor Trustee shall hold the trust assets in continuing trust until such beneficiary shall have attained the age of 21 years. During such period of continuing trust the Successor Trustee, in his absolute discretion, may retain the specific Contract herein described if he believes it to be in the best interests of the beneficiary so to do, or, subject to its terms, he may terminate it, investing and reinvesting the proceeds as he may deem appropriate. Prior to the date upon which such beneficiary attains the age of 21 years, the Successor Trustee may apply or expend any or all of the income or principal directly for the maintenance, education and support of the beneficiary without the intervention of any guardian and without application to any court. Such payments of income or principal may be made to the parents of such beneficiary or to the person with whom the beneficiary is living without any liability upon the Successor Trustee to see to the application thereof. If such beneficiary survives me but dies before attaining the age of 21 years, at his or her death the Successor Trustee shall transfer, pay over and deliver the trust property to such beneficiary's personal representative, absolutely.

2. The beneficiary hereunder shall be liable for his proportionate share of any taxes levied upon the Settlor's total taxable estate by reason of the beneficiary's death.

3. All interests of the beneficiary hereunder shall be inalienable and free from anticipation, assignment, attachment, pledge or control by creditors or a present or former spouse of such beneficiary in any proceedings at law or in equity.

4. This trust is created with the express understanding that the Assignee shall be under no liability whatsoever to see to its proper administration. On the contrary, upon the transfer of the right, title and interest in and to the Contract by any trustee hereunder, said Assignee shall conclusively treat the transferee as the sole owner of said Contract. The Assignee shall receive authorized to pay all royalties due under the terms of the Contract direct to me individually. Until the Assignee shall be fully from some person interested in this trust, written notice of any death or other event upon which the right to receive may depend, the Assignee shall incur no liability for payments made in good faith to persons whose interests shall have been affected by such event. The Assignee shall be protected in acting upon any notice or other instrument or document believed by it to be genuine and to have been signed or presented by the proper party or parties.

~~...me, or in a common accident with me, or both of the beneficiaries designated hereunder shall~~
revoke such designation, and in the former event, I reserve the right to designate a new beneficiary. Should I for any reason fail to designate such new beneficiary, this trust shall terminate upon my death and the trust property shall revert to my estate.

8. In the event of my physical or mental incapacity or my death. I hereby nominate and appoint as Successor Trustee hereunder whosoever shall at that time be beneficiary hereunder, unless such beneficiary shall not have attained the age of 21 years or is otherwise legally incapacitated, in which event I hereby nominate and appoint

(Name) __Henry P. Adams__ __Milton__ City __Connecticut__ State __06605__ Zip

(Address) __125__ Number __Barnum Street__ Street

to be Successor Trustee.

9. This Declaration of Trust shall extend to and be binding upon the heirs, executors, administrators and assigns of the undersigned and upon the Successors to the Trustee.

10. The Trustee and his successors shall serve without bond.

11. This Declaration of Trust shall be construed and enforced in accordance with the laws of the State of __Connecticut__

Declaration of Trust

WHEREAS, I, _____, of the

City/Town of _____, County of _____, State of _____,

am the registrant under one or more design and/or utility patents numbered _____

_____,

which have been assigned to:

(Name) _____, of

(Address) _____

Number   Street   City   State   Zip

(hereinafter referred to as "the Assignee"), under the terms of a contract (hereinafter called "the Contract"), entered into by

me and said Assignee under date of _____,

pursuant to which certain royalty payments accrue to me from the exploitation of such patents;

NOW, THEREFORE, KNOW ALL MEN BY THESE PRESENTS, that I do hereby acknowledge and declare that I hold and will hold said patents and all my right, title and interest in and to the benefits payable to me under the said Contract IN TRUST

1. For the use and benefit of:

(Name) _____, of

(Address) _____

Number   Street   City   State   Zip

or, if such beneficiary be not surviving, for the use and benefit of:

(Name) _____, of

(Address) _____

Number   Street   City   State   Zip

If because of my physical or mental incapacity certified in writing by a physician, the Successor Trustee hereinafter named shall assume active administration of this trust during my lifetime, such Successor Trustee shall be fully authorized to pay to me or disburse on my behalf such sums from income or principal as appear necessary or desirable for my comfort or welfare. Upon my death, unless the beneficiary shall predecease me or unless we both shall die as a result of a common accident, my Successor Trustee is hereby directed forthwith to transfer said patent rights and all right, title and interest in and to the benefits payable to me under said Contract unto the beneficiary absolutely and thereby terminate this trust; provided, however, that if the beneficiary hereunder shall not have attained the age of 21 years, the Successor Trustee shall hold the trust assets in continuing trust until such beneficiary shall have attained the age of 21 years. During such period of continuing trust the Successor Trustee, in his absolute discretion, may retain the specific Contract herein described if he believes it to be in the best interests of the beneficiary so to do, or, subject to its terms, he may terminate it, investing and reinvesting the proceeds as he may deem appropriate. Prior to the date upon which such beneficiary attains the age of 21 years, the Successor Trustee may apply or expend any or all of the income or principal directly for the maintenance, education and support of the beneficiary without the intervention of any guardian and without application to any court. Such payments of income or principal may be made to the parents of such beneficiary or to the person with whom the beneficiary is living without any liability upon the Successor Trustee to see to the application thereof. If such beneficiary survives me but dies before attaining the age of 21 years, at his or her death the Successor Trustee shall transfer, pay over and deliver the trust property to such beneficiary's personal representative, absolutely.

2. The beneficiary hereunder shall be liable for his proportionate share of any taxes levied upon the Settlor's total taxable estate by reason of the Settlor's death.

3. All interests of the beneficiary hereunder shall be inalienable and free from anticipation, assignment, attachment, pledge or control by creditors or a present or former spouse of such beneficiary in any proceedings at law or in equity.

4. This trust is created with the express understanding that the Assignee shall be under no liability whatsoever to see to its proper administration. On the contrary, upon the transfer of the right, title and interest in and to the Contract by any trustee hereunder, said Assignee shall conclusively treat the transferee as the sole owner of said Contract. The Assignee shall be fully authorized to pay all royalties due under the terms of the Contract direct to me individually. Until the Assignee shall receive from some person interested in this trust, written notice of any death or other event upon which the right to receive may depend, the Assignee shall incur no liability for payments made in good faith to persons whose interests shall have been affected by such event. The Assignee shall be protected in acting upon any notice or other instrument or document believed by it to be genuine and to have been signed or presented by the proper party or parties.

5. I reserve unto myself the power and right to collect all royalties, or other income which may accrue under the terms of the Contract and to pay such royalties or other income to myself as an individual. I shall be exclusively entitled to all income accruing from the Contract during my lifetime and no beneficiary named herein shall have any claim upon any such income distributed to me.

6. I reserve unto myself the power and right at any time during my lifetime to amend or revoke in whole or in part the trust hereby created without the necessity of obtaining the consent of the beneficiaries and without giving notice to the beneficiaries. The termination of the whole or any part of the Contract held hereunder shall constitute as to such whole or part a revocation of this trust.

7. The death during my lifetime, or in a common accident with me, of both of the beneficiaries designated hereunder shall revoke such designation, and in the former event, I reserve the right to designate a new beneficiary. Should I for any reason fail to designate such new beneficiary, this trust shall terminate upon my death and the trust property shall revert to my estate.

8. In the event of my physical or mental incapacity or my death, I hereby nominate and appoint as Successor Trustee hereunder whosoever shall at that time be beneficiary hereunder, unless such beneficiary shall not have attained the age of 21 years or is otherwise legally incapacitated, in which event I hereby nominate and appoint

(Name) _____, of

(Address) _____

| Number | Street | City | State | Zip |

to be Successor Trustee.

9. This Declaration of Trust shall extend to and be binding upon the heirs, executors, administrators and assigns of the undersigned and upon the Successors to the Trustee.

10. The Trustee and his successors shall serve without bond.

11. This Declaration of Trust shall be construed and enforced in accordance with the laws of the State of

_____.

IN WITNESS WHEREOF, I have hereunto set my hand and seal this _____

day of _____, 19_____.

(Settlor sign here) _____ L.S.

I, the undersigned legal spouse of the above Settlor, hereby waive all community property rights which I may have in the hereinabove-described Contract and give my assent to the provisions of the trust and to the inclusion in it of the said Contract.

(Spouse sign here) _____ L.S.

Witness: (1) _____ Witness: (2) _____

STATE OF _____ City
                                   or
COUNTY OF _____ Town _____

On the _____ day of _____, 19_____, personally appeared

_____

known to me to be the individual(s) who executed the foregoing instrument, and acknowledged the same to be _____ free act and deed, before me.

_____

(Notary Seal)   Notary Public

CHAPTER 14

DECLARATION OF TRUST
For Naming
TWO OR MORE BENEFICIARIES, SHARING EQUALLY,
To Receive
A PATENT RIGHTS CONTRACT HELD IN ONE NAME

INSTRUCTIONS:

On the following pages will be found a declaration of trust (DT-131) suitable for use in connection with the establishment of an inter vivos trust covering a patent rights contract held in one name only, where it is desired to name two or more persons to receive the Contract upon the death of the owner.

Cross out *"city"* or *"town,"* leaving the appropriate designation of your community. Next, identify the patents by number, then enter the name and address of the individual or firm to whom the rights have been assigned, and the date of the contract.

In Paragraph 1, indicate the *number of persons* you are naming (to discourage unauthorized additions to the list) and then insert their names. The one whose name appears *first* will be the Successor Trustee responsible for seeing to the distribution of the trust property.

Note that the instrument specifies that the named beneficiaries are to receive *"in equal shares, or the survivor of them/per stirpes."* Now, think carefully: If you have named three persons with the understanding that if one of them predeceases you, *his* children will take *his* share, cross out *"or the survivor of them"* and *initial it.* If that is *not* what you want—if, for example, you prefer that the share of the deceased person be divided between the two surviving persons, cross out *"per stirpes"* and *initial it.* Remember, you <u>must</u> cross out *"or the survivor of them"* or *"per stirpes"*—one or the other.

Note that Paragraph 8 designates as Successor Trustee *"the beneficiary named first above,"* which means that in most cases you don't need to fill anything in there. However, if there is any possibility of a beneficiary who has not attained the age of 21 years receiving the Contract, make certain that you name an adult in this paragraph who can act as trustee for such beneficiary. Avoid naming as trustee a person not likely to survive until the beneficiary has attained age 21.

When completed in the manner shown on the reverse side hereof, make several photocopies for reference purposes. Hold the original in safekeeping and offer a copy to the Assignee with instructions to identify your account under the Contract in this manner: *"(your name), Trustee u/d/t dated _____."* It is *not* necessary to include the "Trustee" designation on checks payable to you pursuant to the Contract.

Important: Read carefully Note B on page 38, which applies to this declaration of trust.

DT-131

Declaration of Trust

WHEREAS, I, **John J. Brown**, County of **Fairfax**, State of **Connecticut**, of the Town of **Milton**, am the registrant under one or more design and/or utility patents numbered **29265689 and D5643670** which have been assigned to:

(Name) **Ajax Machinery Company** **Chicago** City **Illinois** State **60411** Zip

(Address) **371** Number **Broadway** Street

(hereinafter referred to as "the Assignee"), under the terms of a contract (hereinafter called "the Contract"), entered into by me and said Assignee under date of **January 20, 1980**, pursuant to which certain royalty payments accrue to me from the exploitation of such patents;

J.J.B.

NOW, THEREFORE, KNOW ALL MEN BY THESE PRESENTS, that I do hereby acknowledge and declare that I hold and will hold my rights under said patents and all my right, title and interest in and to the benefits payable to me under the said Contract IN TRUST

1. For the use and benefit of the following **three (3)** persons, in equal shares, or the survivor of them:

Thomas B. Brown - my brother
Helen A. Brown - my sister
Charles M. Brown - my brother

If because of my physical or mental incapacity certified in writing by a physician, the Successor Trustee hereinafter named shall assume active administration of this trust during my lifetime, such Successor Trustee shall be fully authorized to pay to me or disburse on my behalf such sums from income or principal as appear necessary or desirable for my comfort or welfare. Upon my death, unless the beneficiaries shall predecease me or unless we all shall die as a result of a common accident, my Successor Trustee is hereby directed forthwith to transfer said patent rights and all right, title and interest in and to the benefits payable to me under said Contract unto the beneficiaries absolutely and thereby terminate this trust; provided, however, that if any beneficiary hereunder shall not have attained the age of 21 years, the Successor Trustee shall hold such beneficiary's share of the trust assets in continuing trust until such beneficiary shall have attained the age of 21 years. During such period of continuing trust the Successor Trustee, in his absolute discretion, may retain the specific Contract herein described if he believes it to be in the best interests of the beneficiary so to do, or, subject to its terms, he may terminate it, investing and reinvesting the proceeds as he may deem appropriate. Prior to the date upon which such beneficiary attains the age of 21 years, the Successor Trustee may apply or expend any or all of the income or principal directly for the maintenance, education and support of the beneficiary without the intervention of any guardian and without application to any court. Such payments of income or principal may be made to the parents of such beneficiary or to the person with whom the beneficiary is living without any liability upon the Successor Trustee to see to the application thereof. If such beneficiary survives me but dies before attaining the age of 21 years, at his or her death the Successor Trustee shall transfer, pay over and deliver such beneficiary's share of the trust property to such beneficiary's personal representative, absolutely.

2. Each beneficiary hereunder shall be liable for his proportionate share of any taxes levied upon the Settlor's total taxable estate by reason of the Settlor's death.

3. All interests of a beneficiary hereunder shall be inalienable and free from anticipation, assignment, attachment, pledge or control by creditors or a present or former spouse of such beneficiary in any proceedings at law or in equity.

4. This trust is created with the express understanding that the Assignee shall be under no liability whatsoever to see to its proper administration. On the contrary, upon the transfer of the Contract direct to me individually. Until the Assignee shall receive hereunder, said Assignee shall conclusively treat the transferee as the sole owner of said Contract. The Assignee shall be fully authorized to pay all royalties due under the terms of the Contract to me individually. Until the Assignee shall be fully from some person interested in this trust, written notice of any death or other event upon which the right to receive may depend, the Assignee shall incur no liability for payments made in good faith to persons whose interests shall have been affected by such event. The Assignee shall be protected in acting upon any notice or other instrument or document believed by it to be genuine and to have been signed or presented by the proper party or parties.

5. I reserve unto myself the power and right to collect all royalties, or other income which may accrue under the terms of the Contract and to pay such royalties or other income to myself as an individual. I shall be exclusively entitled to all income accruing from the Contract during my lifetime and no beneficiary named herein shall construe as to such whole or part a revocation of Distributed to me.

The termination of the whole or any part of the Contract held hereunder shall construe as to such whole or part a revocation of this trust.

7. The death during my lifetime, or in a common accident or disaster with me, of all the beneficiaries designated hereunder shall revoke such designation, and in the former event, I reserve the right to designate a new beneficiary. Should I for any reason fail to designate such new beneficiary, this trust shall terminate upon my death and the trust property shall revert to my estate.

8. In the event of my physical or mental incapacity or my death, I hereby nominate and appoint as Successor Trustee the beneficiary named first above, unless such beneficiary shall not have attained the age of 21 years or is otherwise legally incapacitated, in which event I hereby nominate and appoint as Successor Trustee the beneficiary named second above, unless such beneficiary named second above shall not have attained the age of 21 years or is otherwise legally incapacitated, in which latter event I hereby nominate and appoint

(Name) **Henry P. Adams** **Milton** City **Connecticut** State **06605** Zip

(Address) **125** Number **Barnum Street** Street

to be Successor Trustee.

9. This Declaration of Trust shall extend to and be binding upon the heirs, executors, administrators and assigns of the undersigned and upon the Successors to the Trustee.

10. The Trustee and his successors shall serve without bond.

11. This Declaration of Trust shall be construed and enforced in accordance with the laws of the State of **Connecticut**

Declaration of Trust

WHEREAS, I, _____ , of the

City/Town of _____ , County of _____ , State of _____ ,

am the registrant under one or more design and/or utility patents numbered _____

_____ ,

which have been assigned to:

(Name) _____ , of

(Address) _____

       Number   *Street*   *City*   *State*   *Zip*

(hereinafter referred to as "the Assignee"), under the terms of a contract (hereinafter called "the Contract"), entered into by

me and said Assignee under date of _____ ,

pursuant to which certain royalty payments accrue to me from the exploitation of such patents;

NOW, THEREFORE, KNOW ALL MEN BY THESE PRESENTS, that I do hereby acknowledge and declare that I hold and will hold my rights under said patents and all my right, title and interest in and to the benefits payable to me under the said Contract IN TRUST

1. For the use and benefit of the following _____ persons, in equal shares, or the survivor of them/per stirpes:

If because of my physical or mental incapacity certified in writing by a physician, the Successor Trustee hereinafter named shall assume active administration of this trust during my lifetime, such Successor Trustee shall be fully authorized to pay to me or disburse on my behalf such sums from income or principal as appear necessary or desirable for my comfort or welfare. Upon my death, unless the beneficiaries shall predecease me or unless we all shall die as a result of a common accident, my Successor Trustee is hereby directed forthwith to transfer said patent rights and all right, title and interest in and to the benefits payable to me under said Contract unto the beneficiaries absolutely and thereby terminate this trust; provided, however, that if any beneficiary hereunder shall not have attained the age of 21 years, the Successor Trustee shall hold such beneficiary's share of the trust assets in continuing trust until such beneficiary shall have attained the age of 21 years. During such period of continuing trust the Successor Trustee, in his absolute discretion, may retain the specific Contract herein described if he believes it to be in the best interests of the beneficiary so to do, or, subject to its terms, he may terminate it, investing and reinvesting the proceeds as he may deem appropriate. Prior to the date upon which such beneficiary attains the age of 21 years, the Successor Trustee may apply or expend any or all of the income or principal directly for the maintenance, education and support of the beneficiary without the intervention of any guardian and without application to any court. Such payments of income or principal may be made to the parents of such beneficiary or to the person with whom the beneficiary is living without any liability upon the Successor Trustee to see to the application thereof. If such beneficiary survives me but dies before attaining the age of 21 years, at his or her death the Successor Trustee shall transfer, pay over and deliver such beneficiary's share of the trust property to such beneficiary's personal representative, absolutely.

2. Each beneficiary hereunder shall be liable for his proportionate share of any taxes levied upon the Settlor's total taxable estate by reason of the Settlor's death.

3. All interests of a beneficiary hereunder shall be inalienable and free from anticipation, assignment, attachment, pledge or control by creditors or a present or former spouse of such beneficiary in any proceedings at law or in equity.

4. This trust is created with the express understanding that the Assignee shall be under no liability whatsoever to see to its proper administration. On the contrary, upon the transfer of the right, title and interest in and to such Contract by any trustee hereunder, said Assignee shall conclusively treat the transferee as the sole owner of said Contract. Until the Assignee shall receive from some person interested in this trust, written notice of any death or other event upon which the right to receive may depend, the Assignee shall incur no liability for payments made in good faith to persons whose interests shall have been affected by such event. The Assignee shall be protected in acting upon any notice or other instrument or document believed by it to be genuine and to have been signed or presented by the proper party or parties.

5. I reserve unto myself the power and right to collect all royalties, or other income which may accrue under the terms of the Contract and to pay such royalties or other income to myself as an individual. I shall be exclusively entitled to all income accruing from the Contract during my lifetime and no beneficiary named herein shall have any claim upon any such income distributed to me.

6. I reserve unto myself the power and right at any time during my lifetime to amend or revoke in whole or in part the trust hereby created without the necessity of obtaining the consent of the beneficiaries and without giving notice to the beneficiaries. The termination of the whole or any part of the Contract held hereunder shall constitute as to such whole or part a revocation of this trust.

7. The death during my lifetime, or in a common accident or disaster with me, of all the beneficiaries designated hereunder shall revoke such designation, and in the former event, I reserve the right to designate a new beneficiary. Should I for any reason fail to designate such new beneficiary, this trust shall terminate upon my death and the trust property shall revert to my estate.

8. In the event of my physical or mental incapacity or my death, I hereby nominate and appoint as Successor Trustee the beneficiary named first above, unless such beneficiary shall not have attained the age of 21 years or is otherwise legally incapacitated, in which event I hereby nominate and appoint as Successor Trustee the beneficiary named second above, unless such beneficiary named second above shall not have attained the age of 21 years or is otherwise legally incapacitated, in which latter event I hereby nominate and appoint

(Name) _____, of

(Address) _____

         Number   *Street*   *City*   *State*   *Zip*

to be Successor Trustee.

9. This Declaration of Trust shall extend to and be binding upon the heirs, executors, administrators and assigns of the undersigned and upon the Successors to the Trustee.

10. The Trustee and his successors shall serve without bond.

11. This Declaration of Trust shall be construed and enforced in accordance with the laws of the State of

_____.

IN WITNESS WHEREOF, I have hereunto set my hand and seal this _____

day of _____, 19_____.

        (Settlor sign here) _____ L.S.

I, the undersigned legal spouse of the above Settlor, hereby waive all community property rights which I may have in the hereinabove-described Contract and give my assent to the provisions of the trust and to the inclusion in it of the said Contract.

        (Spouse sign here) _____ L.S.

Witness: (1) _____ Witness: (2) _____

STATE OF _____ City

COUNTY OF _____ or

                        Town _____

On the _____ day of _____, 19_____, personally appeared

_____

known to me to be the individual(s) who executed the foregoing instrument, and acknowledged the same to be _____ free act and deed, before me.

_____

(Notary Seal)   *Notary Public*

CHAPTER 14

DECLARATION OF TRUST

For Naming

**ONE PRIMARY BENEFICIARY WITH YOUR CHILDREN,
SHARING EQUALLY, AS CONTINGENT BENEFICIARIES**

To Receive

A PATENT RIGHTS CONTRACT HELD IN ONE NAME

INSTRUCTIONS:

On the following pages will be found a declaration of trust (DT-132) suitable for use in connection with the establishment of an inter vivos trust covering a patent rights contract held in one name only, where it is desired to name one person (ordinarily, but not necessarily, one's spouse) as primary beneficiary, with one's children as contingent beneficiaries to receive the contract if the primary beneficiary be not surviving.

Cross out *"city"* or *"town,"* leaving the appropriate designation of your community. Next, identify the patents by number, then enter the name of the individual or firm to whom the rights have been assigned.

Enter the name of the primary beneficiary (called the "First Beneficiary") in the appropriate place in Paragraph 1. Note that the instrument first refers to your children as *"natural not/or adopted."* Now, decide: If you have an adopted child and you wish to include him, cross out the word *"not"* in the phrase *"natural not/or adopted"* and *initial it.* If you wish to *exclude* your adopted child, cross out the word *"or"* in the same phrase and *initial it.* Remember, you <u>must</u> cross out *"not"* or *"or"*—one or the other. If you have no adopted child, simply cross out *"not."*

Note next that the instrument specifies that your children are to receive *"in equal shares, or the survivor of them/per stirpes."* Now, think carefully: If it is your wish that if one of your children does not survive you, *his* share will revert to *his* children in equal shares, cross out *"or the survivor of them"* and *initial it.* If that is *not* what you want—if, for example, you prefer that the share of any child of yours who predeceases you shall be divided between your other surviving children in equal shares, cross out *"per stirpes"* and *initial it.* Remember, you <u>must</u> cross out *"or the survivor of them"* or *"per stirpes"*—one or the other.

Note that in Paragraph 8, the First Beneficiary is designated as Successor Trustee, while a space is provided in which you should designate another person to so act if the named Successor Trustee is not surviving or otherwise fails or ceases to act. This could be one of your children, for example, but it must be an adult who can act as trustee for any beneficiary who comes into a share of the trust before attaining the age of 21. Avoid naming someone not likely to survive until the youngest such beneficiary has attained age 21.

When completed in the manner shown on the reverse side hereof, make several photocopies for reference purposes. Hold the original in safekeeping and offer a copy to the Assignee with instructions to identify your account under the Contract in this manner: *"(your name), Trustee u/d/t dated _____."* It is *not* necessary to include the "Trustee" designation on checks payable to you pursuant to the Contract.

Important: Read carefully Note B on page 38, which applies to this declaration of trust.

Declaration of Trust

WHEREAS, I, __John J. Brown__, County of __Fairfax__, State of __Connecticut__, of the City/Town of __Milton__, am the registrant under one or more design and/or utility patents numbered __29265689 and D5643670__

which have been assigned to:

(Name) __Ajax Machinery Company__ __Chicago__ __Illinois__ __60411__
City State Zip

(Address) __371__ __Broadway__
Number Street

(hereinafter referred to as "the Assignee"), under the terms of a contract (hereinafter called "the Contract"), entered into by me and said Assignee under date of __January 20, 1980__ pursuant to which certain royalty payments accrue to me from the exploitation of such patents;

NOW, THEREFORE, KNOW ALL MEN BY THESE PRESENTS, that I do hereby acknowledge and declare that I hold and will hold my rights under said patents and all my right, title and interest in and to the benefits payable to me under the said Contract IN TRUST

1. For the use and benefit of:

(Name) __Elizabeth A. Brown - my wife__ __Milton__ __Connecticut__ __06605__
City State Zip

(Address) __525 Main Street__
Number Street

(hereinafter referred to as the "First Beneficiary"), and upon his or her death prior to the termination of the trust, for the use and benefit of my children, natural or adopted, in equal shares, or the survivor of them, as follows:

If because of my physical or mental incapacity certified in writing by a physician, the Successor Trustee hereinafter named shall assume active administration of this trust during my lifetime, such Successor Trustee shall be fully authorized to pay to me or disburse on my behalf such sums from income or principal as appear necessary or desirable for my comfort or welfare. Upon my death, unless all of the beneficiaries shall predecease me or unless we all shall die as a result of a common accident, my Successor Trustee is hereby directed forthwith to transfer said Contract and all right, title and interest in and to said Contract unto the beneficiary or beneficiaries absolutely and thereby terminate this trust; provided, however, that if any beneficiary hereunder shall not have attained the age of 21 years, the Successor Trustee shall hold such beneficiary's share of the trust assets in continuing trust until such beneficiary shall have attained the age of 21 years. During such period of continuing trust the Successor Trustee, in his absolute discretion, may retain the specific Contract herein described if he believes it to be in the best interests of the beneficiary so to do, or, subject to its terms, he may terminate it, investing and reinvesting the proceeds as he may deem appropriate. Prior to the date upon which such beneficiary attains the age of 21 years, the Successor Trustee may apply or expend any or all of the income or principal directly for the maintenance, education and support of the beneficiary without the intervention of any guardian and without application to any court. Such payments of income or principal may be made to the parents of such beneficiary or to the person with whom the beneficiary is living without any liability upon the Successor Trustee to see to the application thereof. If such beneficiary survives me but dies before attaining the age of 21 years, at his or her death the Successor Trustee shall transfer, pay over and deliver the trust assets being held for such beneficiary to such beneficiary's personal representative, absolutely.

2. Each beneficiary hereunder shall be liable for his proportionate share of any taxes levied upon the Settlor's total taxable estate by reason of the Settlor's death.

3. All interests of a beneficiary hereunder shall be inalienable and free from anticipation, assignment, attachment, pledge or control by creditors or a present or former spouse of such beneficiary, in any proceedings at law or in equity.

4. This trust is created with the express understanding that the Assignee shall be under no liability whatsoever to see to its proper administration. On the contrary, upon the transfer of the right, title and interest in and to such Contract by any trustee hereunder, said Assignee shall conclusively treat the transferee as the sole owner of said Contract. The Assignee shall be fully authorized to pay all royalties due under the terms of the Contract direct to me individually. Until the Assignee shall receive from some person interested in this trust, written notice of any death or other event upon which the right to receive may depend, the Assignee shall incur no liability for payments made in good faith to persons whose interests shall have been affected by such event. The Assignee shall be protected in acting upon any notice or other instrument or document believed by it to be genuine and to have been signed or presented by the proper party or parties.

5. I reserve unto myself the power and right to collect all royalties or other income to myself as an individual. I shall be exclusively entitled to all income accruing from the Contract during my lifetime and no beneficiary named herein shall have any claim upon any such income distributed to me.

6. I reserve unto myself the power and right at any time during my lifetime to amend or revoke in whole or in part the trust hereby created without the necessity of obtaining the consent of the beneficiaries and without giving notice to the beneficiaries. The termination of the whole or any part of the Contract held hereunder shall constitute as to such whole or part a revocation of this trust.

7. This trust shall terminate upon my death and the trust property shall revert to my estate.

8. In the event of my physical or mental incapacity or my death, I hereby nominate and appoint as Successor Trustee hereunder the First Beneficiary, or if such First Beneficiary be not surviving or fails or ceases to act, I nominate and appoint

(Name) __Henry P. Adams__ __Milton__ __Connecticut__ __06605__
City State Zip

(Address) __125__ __Barnum Street__
Number Street

to be Successor Trustee.

9. This Declaration of Trust shall extend to and be binding upon the heirs, executors, administrators and assigns of the undersigned and upon the Successors to the Trustee.

10. The Trustee and his successors shall serve without bond.

11. This Declaration of Trust shall be construed and enforced in accordance with the laws of the State of __Connecticut__

Declaration of Trust

WHEREAS, I, _____, of the

City/Town of _____, County of _____, State of _____,

am the registrant under one or more design and/or utility patents numbered _____

_____,

which have been assigned to:

(Name) _____, of

(Address) _____

        Number   *Street*   *City*   *State*   *Zip*

(hereinafter referred to as "the Assignee"), under the terms of a contract (hereinafter called "the Contract"), entered into by

me and said Assignee under date of _____,

pursuant to which certain royalty payments accrue to me from the exploitation of such patents;

NOW, THEREFORE, KNOW ALL MEN BY THESE PRESENTS, that I do hereby acknowledge and declare that I hold and will hold my rights under said patents and all my right, title and interest in and to the benefits payable to me under the said Contract IN TRUST

1. For the use and benefit of:

(Name) _____, of

(Address) _____

        Number   *Street*   *City*   *State*   *Zip*

(hereinafter referred to as the "First Beneficiary"), and upon his or her death prior to the termination of the trust, for the use and benefit of my children, natural not/or adopted, in equal shares, or the survivor of them/per stirpes.

If because of my physical or mental incapacity certified in writing by a physician, the Successor Trustee hereinafter named shall assume active administration of this trust during my lifetime, such Successor Trustee shall be fully authorized to pay to me or disburse on my behalf such sums from income or principal as appear necessary or desirable for my comfort or welfare. Upon my death, unless all of the beneficiaries shall predecease me or unless we all shall die as a result of a common accident, my Successor Trustee is hereby directed forthwith to transfer said Contract and all right, title and interest in and to said Contract unto the beneficiary or beneficiaries absolutely and thereby terminate this trust; provided, however, that if any beneficiary hereunder shall not have attained the age of 21 years, the Successor Trustee shall hold such beneficiary's share of the trust assets in continuing trust until such beneficiary shall have attained the age of 21 years. During such period of continuing trust the Successor Trustee, in his absolute discretion, may retain the specific Contract herein described if he believes it to be in the best interests of the beneficiary so to do, or, subject to its terms, he may terminate it, investing and reinvesting the proceeds as he may deem appropriate. Prior to the date upon which such beneficiary attains the age of 21 years, the Successor Trustee may apply or expend any or all of the income or principal directly for the maintenance, education and support of the beneficiary without the intervention of any guardian and without application to any court. Such payments of income or principal may be made to the parents of such beneficiary or to the person with whom the beneficiary is living without any liability upon the Successor Trustee to see to the application thereof. If such beneficiary survives me but dies before attaining the age of 21 years, at his or her death the Successor Trustee shall transfer, pay over and deliver the trust assets being held for such beneficiary to such beneficiary's personal representative, absolutely.

2. Each beneficiary hereunder shall be liable for his proportionate share of any taxes levied upon the Settlor's total taxable estate by reason of the Settlor's death.

3. All interests of a beneficiary hereunder shall be inalienable and free from anticipation, assignment, attachment, pledge or control by creditors or a present or former spouse of such beneficiary in any proceedings at law or in equity.

4. This trust is created with the express understanding that the Assignee shall be under no liability whatsoever to see to . ; proper administration. On the contrary, upon the transfer of the right, title and interest in and to such Contract by any trustee hereunder, said Assignee shall conclusively treat the transferee as the sole owner of said Contract. The Assignee shall be fully authorized to pay all royalties due under the terms of the Contract direct to me individually. Until the Assignee shall receive from some person interested in this trust, written notice of any death or other event upon which the right to receive may depend, the Assignee shall incur no liability for payments made in good faith to persons whose interests shall have been affected by such event. The Assignee shall be protected in acting upon any notice or other instrument or document believed by it to be genuine and to have been signed or presented by the proper party or parties.

5. I reserve unto myself the power and right to collect all royalties or other income which may accrue under the terms of the Contract and to pay such royalties or other income to myself as an individual. I shall be exclusively entitled to all income accruing from the Contract during my lifetime and no beneficiary named herein shall have any claim upon any such income distributed to me.

6. I reserve unto myself the power and right at any time during my lifetime to amend or revoke in whole or in part the trust hereby created without the necessity of obtaining the consent of the beneficiaries and without giving notice to the beneficiaries. The termination of the whole or any part of the Contract held hereunder shall constitute as to such whole or part a revocation of this trust.

7. The death during my lifetime, or in a common accident or disaster with me, of all of the beneficiaries hereunder shall revoke such designation, and in the former event, I reserve the right to designate a new beneficiary. Should I for any reason fail to designate such new beneficiary, this trust shall terminate upon my death and the trust property shall revert to my estate.

8. In the event of my physical or mental incapacity or my death, I hereby nominate and appoint as Successor Trustee hereunder the First Beneficiary, or if such First Beneficiary be not surviving or fails or ceases to act, I nominate and appoint

(Name) _____ , of

(Address) _____

      Number   *Street*   *City*   *State*   *Zip*

to be Successor Trustee.

9. This Declaration of Trust shall extend to and be binding upon the heirs, executors, administrators and assigns of the undersigned and upon the Successors to the Trustee.

10. The Trustee and his successors shall serve without bond.

11. This Declaration of Trust shall be construed and enforced in accordance with the laws of the State of

_____.

IN WITNESS WHEREOF, I have hereunto set my hand and seal this _____

day of _____ , 19____.

                (Settlor sign here) _____ L.S.

I, the undersigned legal spouse of the above Settlor, hereby waive all community property rights which I may have in the hereinabove-described Contract and give my assent to the provisions of the trust and to the inclusion in it of the said Contract.

                (Spouse sign here) _____ L.S.

Witness: (1) _____   Witness: (2) _____

STATE OF _____ ⎫   City

COUNTY OF _____ ⎭   or
                                         Town _____

On the _____ day of _____ , 19____, personally appeared

_____

known to me to be the individual(s) who executed the foregoing instrument, and acknowledged the same to be _____ free act and deed, before me.

(Notary Seal)   _____

                                            Notary Public

CHAPTER 15

Avoiding Probate of a Partnership Interest

A partnership generally terminates upon the death of one of the partners, the value of his interest merging with the rest of his estate for distribution to his heirs along with his other assets in compliance with the instructions in his will or, if he has no will, in accordance with the laws of the state in which he lived.

The death of a partner can have a very disruptive effect upon the surviving partners and their business, particularly if there is no properly funded buy/sell agreement. These problems can be aggravated if the probate establishment sets to work making mountains out of legal molehills.

The surviving partners will need time to rearrange the business's affairs, to reassign the departed individual's duties and responsibilities among them or to find a replacement. So far as their late partner's interest is concerned, they need to have someone they can deal with immediately. If his interest in the business becomes a part of his general estate, it may be two or three years or longer before they learn who is slated to receive that interest. It is important that a partner's interest be promptly transferred to a specified beneficiary at his death.

The solution to these problems is a simple one: Place your partnership interest in a living trust of which you are trustee. The trust won't die, and thus there'll be no required dissolution of the partnership. At the instant of your death, your Successor Trustee will step into your shoes and the transition will be a smooth one. Remember, the beneficiary you name is also the Successor Trustee, which insures that your partnership interest will go to the individual you have chosen.

On the following pages will be found forms of declaration of trust which are specially designed for such use.

CHAPTER 15

DECLARATION OF TRUST

For Naming

ONE BENEFICIARY

To Receive

A PARTNERSHIP INTEREST HELD IN ONE NAME

INSTRUCTIONS:

On the following pages will be found a declaration of trust (DT-133) suitable for use in connection with the establishment of an inter vivos trust covering a partnership interest held in one name only, where it is desired to name some one person to receive the partnership interest upon the death of the owner.

Cross out *"city"* or *"town,"* leaving the appropriate designation of your community. Next, insert the fractional interest which you hold in the partnership (one-third, one-fifth, etc.). Then, insert the name and address of the partnership.

Finally, enter the name of the beneficiary in the appropriate place in Paragraph 1.

Note that Paragraph 8 designates as Successor Trustee *"whosoever shall at that time be beneficiary hereunder,"* which means that in most cases you don't need to fill anything in there. However, if there is any possibility of a beneficiary who has not attained the age of 21 years receiving the partnership interest, make certain that you name an adult in this paragraph who can act as trustee for such beneficiary. Avoid naming as trustee a person not likely to survive until the beneficiary has attained age 21.

When completed in the manner shown on the reverse side hereof, make several photocopies for reference purposes. Hold the original in safekeeping and offer a copy to the partnership, giving instructions that henceforth your interest should be identified in this manner: *"(your name), Trustee u/d/t dated _____."*

Important: Read carefully Note B on page 38, which applies to this declaration of trust.

Declaration of Trust

DACEY TRUST

WHEREAS, I, __John J. Brown__, County of __Fairfax__, State of __Connecticut__, of the

Town of __Milton__ am the owner of a __one-fourth__ partnership interest in the business or professional activity known as:
indicate fractional interest

__Ajax Tool Company__

(hereinafter referred to as "the Partnership"), located at: __371 Broadway__ __Chicago__ __Illinois__ __60411__
Number Street City State Zip

(Address)

NOW, THEREFORE, KNOW ALL MEN BY THESE PRESENTS, that I do hereby acknowledge and declare that I hold and will hold said partnership interest and all my right, title and interest in and to said partnership interest IN TRUST

1. For the use and benefit of:

(Name) __Elizabeth A. Brown - my wife__ __Milton__ __Connecticut 06605__
City State Zip

(Address) __525 Main Street__
Number Street

If because of my physical or mental incapacity certified in writing by a physician, the Successor Trustee hereinafter named shall assume active administration of this trust during my lifetime, such Successor Trustee shall be fully authorized to pay to me or disburse on my behalf such sums from income or principal as appear necessary or desirable for my comfort or welfare. Upon my death, unless the beneficiary shall predecease me or unless we both shall die as a result of a common accident or disaster, my Successor Trustee is hereby directed forthwith to transfer said partnership interest and all right, title and interest in and to said partnership interest unto the beneficiary absolutely and thereby terminate this trust; provided, however, that if the beneficiary hereunder shall not have attained the age of 21 years, the Successor Trustee shall hold the trust assets in continuing trust until such beneficiary shall have attained the age of 21 years. During such period of continuing trust the Successor Trustee, in his absolute discretion, may retain the partnership interest herein described if he believes it to be in the best interests of the beneficiary so to do, or, subject to any restrictions placed upon such action by the Partnership, he may terminate it, investing and reinvesting the proceeds of such termination as he may deem appropriate. Prior to the date upon which such beneficiary attains the age of 21 years, the Successor Trustee may apply or expend any or all of the income or principal directly for the maintenance, education and support of the beneficiary without the intervention of any guardian and without application to any court. Such payments of income or principal may be made to the parents of such beneficiary or to the person with whom the beneficiary is living without any liability upon the Successor Trustee to see to the application thereof. If such beneficiary survives me but dies before attaining the age of 21 years, at his or her death the Successor Trustee shall transfer, pay over and deliver the trust property to such beneficiary's personal representative, absolutely.

2. The beneficiary hereunder shall be liable for his proportionate share of any taxes levied upon the Settlor's total taxable estate by reason of the Settlor's death.

3. All interests of a beneficiary hereunder shall be inalienable and free from anticipation, assignment, attachment, pledge or control by creditors or a present or former spouse of such beneficiary in any proceedings at law or in equity.

4. This trust is created with the express understanding that the Partnership shall be under no liability whatsoever to see to its proper administration. On the contrary, upon the transfer of the right, title and interest in and to such partnership interest by any trustee hereunder, the Partnership shall conclusively treat the transferee as the sole owner of said interest. The Partnership shall [...] written notice of any death or other event upon which the right to receive may depend, it shall incur no liability for payments made in good faith to persons whose interests shall have been affected by such event. The Partnership shall be protected in acting upon any notice or other instrument or document believed by it to be genuine and to have been signed or presented by the proper party or parties.

5. I reserve unto myself as an individual, I shall be exclusively entitled to all income accruing from the trust property during my lifetime, and no beneficiary named herein shall have any claim upon any such income distributed to me.

6. I reserve unto myself the power and right at any time during my lifetime to amend or revoke in whole or in part the trust hereby created without the necessity of obtaining the consent of the beneficiary and without giving notice to the beneficiary. The dissolution of the Partnership or the sale by me of the whole or any part of the partnership interest held hereunder shall constitute as to such whole or part a revocation of this trust.

7. The death during my lifetime, or in a common accident or disaster with me, of the beneficiary designated hereunder shall revoke such designation, and in the former event, I reserve the right to designate a new beneficiary. Should I for any reason fail to designate such new beneficiary, this trust shall terminate upon my death and the trust property shall revert to my estate.

8. In the event of my physical or mental incapacity or my death, I hereby nominate and appoint as Successor Trustee hereunder whosoever shall at that time be beneficiary hereunder, unless such beneficiary shall not have attained the age of 21 years or is otherwise legally incapacitated, in which event I hereby nominate and appoint

(Name) __Henry P. Adams__ __Milton__ __Connecticut__ __06605__, of
City State Zip

(Address) __125 Barnum Street__
Number Street

to be Successor Trustee.

9. This Declaration of Trust shall extend to and be binding upon the heirs, executors, administrators and assigns of the undersigned and upon the Successors to the Trustee.

10. The Trustee and his successors shall serve without bond.

11. This Declaration of Trust shall be construed and enforced in accordance with the laws of the State of

__Connecticut__

Declaration of Trust

WHEREAS, I, _____, of the

City/Town of _____, County of _____, State of _____,

am the owner of a _____ partnership interest in the business or professional activity known as:

indicate fractional interest

_____

(hereinafter referred to as "the Partnership"), located at:

(Address) _____

    Number   Street   City   State   Zip

NOW, THEREFORE, KNOW ALL MEN BY THESE PRESENTS, that I do hereby acknowledge and declare that I hold and will hold said partnership interest and all my right, title and interest in and to said partnership interest IN TRUST

1. For the use and benefit of:

(Name) _____, of

(Address) _____

    Number   Street   City   State   Zip

If because of my physical or mental incapacity certified in writing by a physician, the Successor Trustee hereinafter named shall assume active administration of this trust during my lifetime, such Successor Trustee shall be fully authorized to pay to me or disburse on my behalf such sums from income or principal as appear necessary or desirable for my comfort or welfare. Upon my death, unless the beneficiary shall predecease me or unless we both shall die as a result of a common accident or disaster, my Successor Trustee is hereby directed forthwith to transfer said partnership interest and all right, title and interest in and to said partnership interest unto the beneficiary absolutely and thereby terminate this trust; provided, however, that if the beneficiary hereunder shall not have attained the age of 21 years, the Successor Trustee shall hold the trust assets in continuing trust until such beneficiary shall have attained the age of 21 years. During such period of continuing trust the Successor Trustee, in his absolute discretion, may retain the partnership interest herein described if he believes it to be in the best interests of the beneficiary so to do, or, subject to any restrictions placed upon such action by the Partnership, he may terminate it, investing and reinvesting the proceeds of such termination as he may deem appropriate. Prior to the date upon which such beneficiary attains the age of 21 years, the Successor Trustee may apply or expend any or all of the income or principal directly for the maintenance, education and support of the beneficiary without the intervention of any guardian and without application to any court. Such payments of income or principal may be made to the parents of such beneficiary or to the person with whom the beneficiary is living without any liability upon the Successor Trustee to see to the application thereof. If such beneficiary survives me but dies before attaining the age of 21 years, at his or her death the Successor Trustee shall transfer, pay over and deliver the trust property to such beneficiary's personal representative, absolutely.

2. The beneficiary hereunder shall be liable for his proportionate share of any taxes levied upon the Settlor's total taxable estate by reason of the Settlor's death.

3. All interests of a beneficiary hereunder shall be inalienable and free from anticipation, assignment, attachment, pledge or control by creditors or a present or former spouse of such beneficiary in any proceedings at law or in equity.

4. This trust is created with the express understanding that the Partnership shall be under no liability whatsoever to see to its proper administration. On the contrary, upon the transfer of the right, title and interest in and to such partnership interest by any trustee hereunder, the Partnership shall conclusively treat the transferee as the sole owner of said interest. The Partnership shall be fully authorized to make all payments due me direct to me individually. Until the Partnership shall receive from some person interested in this trust, written notice of any death or other event upon which the right to receive may depend, it shall incur no liability for payments made in good faith to persons whose interests shall have been affected by such event. The Partnership shall be protected in acting upon any notice or other instrument or document believed by it to be genuine and to have been signed or presented by the proper party or parties.

5. I reserve unto myself the power and right to collect any income which may accrue from the trust property and to pay such income to myself as an individual. I shall be exclusively entitled to all income accruing from the trust property during my lifetime, and no beneficiary named herein shall have any claim upon any such income distributed to me.

6. I reserve unto myself the power and right at any time during my lifetime to amend or revoke in whole or in part the trust hereby created without the necessity of obtaining the consent of the beneficiary and without giving notice to the beneficiary. The dissolution of the Partnership or the sale by me of the whole or any part of the partnership interest held hereunder shall constitute as to such whole or part a revocation of this trust.

7. The death during my lifetime, or in a common accident or disaster with me, of the beneficiary designated hereunder shall revoke such designation, and in the former event, I reserve the right to designate a new beneficiary. Should I for any reason fail to designate such new beneficiary, this trust shall terminate upon my death and the trust property shall revert to my estate.

8. In the event of my physical or mental incapacity or my death, I hereby nominate and appoint as Successor Trustee hereunder whosoever shall at that time be beneficiary hereunder, unless such beneficiary shall not have attained the age of 21 years or is otherwise legally incapacitated, in which event I hereby nominate and appoint

(Name) _____ , of

(Address) _____

          Number   *Street*   *City*   *State*   *Zip*

to be Successor Trustee.

9. This Declaration of Trust shall extend to and be binding upon the heirs, executors, administrators and assigns of the undersigned and upon the Successors to the Trustee.

10. The Trustee and his successors shall serve without bond.

11. This Declaration of Trust shall be construed and enforced in accordance with the laws of the State of

_____ .

IN WITNESS WHEREOF, I have hereunto set my hand and seal this _____

day of _____ , 19_____ .

          (Settlor sign here) _____ L.S.

I, the undersigned legal spouse of the above Settlor, hereby waive all community property rights which I may have in the hereinabove-described partnership interest and give my assent to the provisions of the trust and to the inclusion in it of the said partnership interest.

          (Spouse sign here) _____ L.S.

Witness: (1) _____   Witness: (2) _____

STATE OF _____   City

COUNTY OF _____   or

                                           Town _____

On the _____ day of _____ , 19_____ , personally appeared

_____

known to me to be the individual(s) who executed the foregoing instrument, and acknowledged the same to be _____ free act and deed, before me.

(Notary Seal)   _____

                                               Notary Public

CHAPTER 15

DECLARATION OF TRUST
For Naming
ONE PRIMARY BENEFICIARY
And
ONE CONTINGENT BENEFICIARY
To Receive
A PARTNERSHIP INTEREST HELD IN ONE NAME

INSTRUCTIONS:

On the following pages will be found a declaration of trust (DT-134) suitable for use in connection with the establishment of an inter vivos trust covering a partnership interest held in one name only, where it is desired to name some *one* person as primary beneficiary, with some *one* other person as contingent beneficiary to receive the partnership interest if the primary beneficiary be not surviving upon the death of the owner.

Cross out *"city"* or *"town,"* leaving the appropriate designation of your community. Next, insert the fractional interest which you hold in the partnership (one-third, one-fifth, etc.). Then, insert the name and address of the partnership.

Finally, enter the names of the beneficiaries in the appropriate place in Paragraph 1.

Note that Paragraph 8 designates as Successor Trustee *"whosoever shall at that time be beneficiary hereunder,"* which means that in most cases you don't need to fill anything in there. However, if there is any possibility of a beneficiary who has not attained the age of 21 years receiving the partnership interest, make certain that you name an adult in this paragraph who can act as trustee for such beneficiary. Avoid naming as trustee a person not likely to survive until the beneficiary has attained age 21.

When completed in the manner shown on the reverse side hereof, make several photocopies for reference purposes. Hold the original in safekeeping and offer a copy to the partnership, giving instructions that henceforth your interest should be identified in this manner: *"(your name), Trustee u/d/t dated _____."*

Important: Read carefully Note B on page 38, which applies to this declaration of trust.

Declaration of Trust

WHEREAS, I, _____ **John J. Brown** _____, County of _____ **Fairfax** _____, State of _____ **Connecticut** _____, of the

Town of _____ **Milton** _____ am the owner of a **one-fourth** *indicate fractional interest* partnership interest in the business or professional activity known as:

Ajax Tool Company

(hereinafter referred to as "the Partnership"), located at: _____ **Chicago** _____ **Illinois** _____ **60411** _____
                                                                        City   *State*   *Zip*

(Address) _____ **371** _____ **Broadway** _____
                  Number   *Street*

NOW, THEREFORE, KNOW ALL MEN BY THESE PRESENTS, that I do hereby acknowledge and declare that I hold and will hold said partnership interest and all my right, title and interest in and to said partnership interest IN TRUST

1. For the use and benefit of:

(Name) _____ **Elizabeth A. Brown – my wife** _____ **Milton** _____ **Connecticut** _____ **06605** _____, of
                                                          City   *State*   *Zip*

(Address) _____ **525 Main Street** _____
                  Number   *Street*

or, if such beneficiary be not surviving, for the use and benefit of:

(Name) _____ **Jill A. Brown – my daughter** _____ **Milton** _____ **Connecticut** _____ **06605** _____, of
                                                        City   *State*   *Zip*

(Address) _____ **525 Main Street** _____
                  Number   *Street*

If because of my physical or mental incapacity certified in writing by a physician, the Successor Trustee shall be fully authorized to pay to me or disburse on my behalf such sums from income or principal as appear necessary or desirable for my comfort or welfare. Upon my death, unless both beneficiaries shall predecease me or unless we all shall die as a result of a common accident or disaster, my Successor Trustee is hereby directed forthwith to transfer said partnership interest and all right, title and interest in and to said partnership interest unto the beneficiary absolutely and thereby terminate this trust: *provided*, however, that if the beneficiary hereunder shall not have attained the age of 21 years, the Successor Trustee shall hold the trust assets in continuing trust until such beneficiary shall have attained the age of 21 years. During such period of continuing trust the Successor Trustee, in his absolute discretion, may retain the partnership interest herein described if he believes it to be in the best interests of the beneficiary so to do, or, subject to any restrictions placed upon such action by the Partnership, he may terminate it, investing and reinvesting the proceeds of such termination as he may deem appropriate. Prior to the date upon which such beneficiary attains the age of 21 years, the Successor Trustee may apply or expend any or all of the income or principal directly for the maintenance, education and support of the beneficiary without the intervention of any guardian and without application to any court. Such payments of income or principal may be made to the parents of such beneficiary or to the person with whom the beneficiary is living without any liability upon the Successor Trustee to see to the application thereof. If such beneficiary survives me but dies before attaining the age of 21 years, at his or her death the Successor Trustee shall transfer, pay over and deliver the trust property being held for such beneficiary to such beneficiary's personal representative, absolutely.

2. The beneficiary hereunder shall be liable for his proportionate share of any taxes levied upon the Settlor's total taxable estate by reason of the Settlor's death.

3. All interests of a beneficiary hereunder shall be inalienable and free from anticipation, assignment, attachment, pledge or control by creditors or a present or former spouse of such beneficiary in any proceedings at law or in equity.

4. This trust is created with the express understanding that the Partnership shall be under no liability whatsoever to see to its proper administration. On the contrary, upon the transfer of the right, title and interest in and to such partnership interest by any trustee hereunder, said Partnership shall conclusively treat the transferee as the sole owner of said interest. The Partnership shall be fully authorized to make all payments due me direct to me individually. Until the Partnership shall receive from some person interested in this trust, written notice of any death or other event upon which the right to receive may depend, it shall incur no liability for payments made in good faith to persons whose interests shall have been affected by it to be genuine and to have been signed or presented by the proper party or parties.

5. I reserve unto myself as an individual, I shall be exclusively entitled to all income which may accrue from the trust property and to pay such income to myself during my lifetime, and no beneficiary named herein shall have any claim upon any such income accruing from the trust property during my lifetime, and no beneficiary named herein shall have any claim upon any such income accruing from the trust property during my lifetime.

6. I reserve unto myself the power and right at any time during my lifetime to amend or revoke in whole or in part the trust hereby created without the necessity of obtaining the consent of any beneficiary and without giving notice to any beneficiary. The dissolution of the Partnership or the sale by me of the whole or any part of the partnership interest held hereunder shall constitute as to such whole or part a revocation of this trust.

7. The death during my lifetime, or in a common accident or disaster with me, of both of the beneficiaries designated hereby shall revoke such designation, and in the former event, I reserve the right to designate a new beneficiary. Should I for any reason fail to designate such new beneficiary, this trust shall terminate upon my death and the trust property shall revert to my estate.

8. In the event of my physical or mental incapacity or my death, I hereby nominate and appoint as Successor Trustee hereunder whosoever shall at that time be beneficiary hereunder, unless such beneficiary shall not have attained the age of 21 years or is otherwise legally incapacitated, in which event I hereby nominate and appoint

(Name) _____ **Henry P. Adams** _____ **Milton** _____ **Connecticut** _____ **06605** _____, of
                                          City   *State*   *Zip*

(Address) _____ **125** _____ **Barnum Street** _____
                  Number   *Street*

to be Successor Trustee.

9. This Declaration of Trust shall extend to and be binding upon the heirs, executors, administrators and assigns of the undersigned and upon the Successors to the Trustee.

10. The Trustee and his successors shall serve without bond.

11. This Declaration of Trust shall be construed and enforced in accordance with the laws of the State of

_____ **Connecticut** _____

Declaration of Trust

WHEREAS, I, _____, of the

City/Town of _____, County of _____, State of _____,

am the owner of a _____ partnership interest in the business or professional activity known as:
indicate fractional interest

_____

(hereinafter referred to as "the Partnership"), located at:

(Address) _____,
        Number   *Street*   *City*   *State*   *Zip*

    NOW, THEREFORE, KNOW ALL MEN BY THESE PRESENTS, that I do hereby acknowledge and declare that I hold and will hold said partnership interest and all my right, title and interest in and to said partnership interest IN TRUST

    1. For the use and benefit of:

(Name) _____, of

(Address) _____
        Number   *Street*   *City*   *State*   *Zip*

or, if such beneficiary be not surviving, for the use and benefit of:

(Name) _____, of

(Address) _____
        Number   *Street*   *City*   *State*   *Zip*

    If because of my physical or mental incapacity certified in writing by a physician, the Successor Trustee hereinafter named shall assume active administration of this trust during my lifetime, such Successor Trustee shall be fully authorized to pay to me or disburse on my behalf such sums from income or principal as appear necessary or desirable for my comfort or welfare. Upon my death, unless both beneficiaries shall predecease me or unless we all shall die as a result of a common accident or disaster, my Successor Trustee is hereby directed forthwith to transfer said partnership interest and all right, title and interest in and to said partnership interest unto the beneficiary absolutely and thereby terminate this trust; provided, however, that if the beneficiary hereunder shall not have attained the age of 21 years, the Successor Trustee shall hold the trust assets in continuing trust until such beneficiary shall have attained the age of 21 years. During such period of continuing trust the Successor Trustee, in his absolute discretion, may retain the partnership interest herein described if he believes it to be in the best interests of the beneficiary so to do, or, subject to any restrictions placed upon such action by the Partnership, he may terminate it, investing and reinvesting the proceeds of such termination as he may deem appropriate. Prior to the date upon which such beneficiary attains the age of 21 years, the Successor Trustee may apply or expend any or all of the income or principal directly for the maintenance, education and support of the beneficiary without the intervention of any guardian and without application to any court. Such payments of income or principal may be made to the parents of such beneficiary or to the person with whom the beneficiary is living without any liability upon the Successor Trustee to see to the application thereof. If such beneficiary survives me but dies before attaining the age of 21 years, at his or her death the Successor Trustee shall transfer, pay over and deliver the trust property being held for such beneficiary to such beneficiary's personal representative, absolutely.

    2. The beneficiary hereunder shall be liable for his proportionate share of any taxes levied upon the Settlor's total taxable estate by reason of the Settlor's death.

    3. All interests of a beneficiary hereunder shall be inalienable and free from anticipation, assignment, attachment, pledge or control by creditors or a present or former spouse of such beneficiary in any proceedings at law or in equity.

    4. This trust is created with the express understanding that the Partnership shall be under no liability whatsoever to see to its proper administration. On the contrary, upon the transfer of the right, title and interest in and to such partnership interest by any trustee hereunder, said Partnership shall conclusively treat the transferee as the sole owner of said interest. The Partnership shall be fully authorized to make all payments due me direct to me individually. Until the Partnership shall receive from some person interested in this trust, written notice of any death or other event upon which the right to receive may depend, it shall incur no liability for payments made in good faith to persons whose interests shall have been affected by such event. The Partnership shall be protected in acting upon any notice or other instrument or document believed by it to be genuine and to have been signed or presented by the proper party or parties.

    5. I reserve unto myself the power and right to collect any income which may accrue from the trust property and to pay such income to myself as an individual. I shall be exclusively entitled to all income accruing from the trust property during my lifetime, and no beneficiary named herein shall have any claim upon any such income distributed to me.

    6. I reserve unto myself the power and right at any time during my lifetime to amend or revoke in whole or in part the trust hereby created without the necessity of obtaining the consent of any beneficiary and without giving notice to any beneficiary. The dissolution of the Partnership or the sale by me of the whole or any part of the partnership interest held hereunder shall constitute as to such whole or part a revocation of this trust.

    7. The death during my lifetime, or in a common accident or disaster with me, of both of the beneficiaries designated hereunder shall revoke such designation, and in the former event, I reserve the right to designate a new beneficiary. Should I for

any reason fail to designate such new beneficiary, this trust shall terminate upon my death and the trust property shall revert to my estate.

8. In the event of my physical or mental incapacity or my death, I hereby nominate and appoint as Successor Trustee hereunder whosoever shall at that time be beneficiary hereunder, unless such beneficiary shall not have attained the age of 21 years or is otherwise legally incapacitated, in which event I hereby nominate and appoint

(Name) _____, of

(Address) _____
         Number   *Street*   *City*   *State*   *Zip*

to be Successor Trustee.

9. This Declaration of Trust shall extend to and be binding upon the heirs, executors, administrators and assigns of the undersigned and upon the Successors to the Trustee.

10. The Trustee and his successors shall serve without bond.

11. This Declaration of Trust shall be construed and enforced in accordance with the laws of the State of

_____.

IN WITNESS WHEREOF, I have hereunto set my hand and seal this _____

day of _____, 19_____.

(Settlor sign here) _____ L.S.

I, the undersigned legal spouse of the above Settlor, hereby waive all community property rights which I may have in the hereinabove-described partnership interest and give my assent to the provisions of the trust and to the inclusion in it of the said partnership interest.

(Spouse sign here) _____ L.S.

Witness: (1) _____   Witness: (2) _____

STATE OF _____ ⎫ City

COUNTY OF _____ ⎬ or

                    ⎭ Town _____

On the _____ day of _____, 19_____, personally appeared

_____

known to me to be the individual(s) who executed the foregoing instrument, and acknowledged the same to be _____ free act and deed, before me.

(Notary Seal)

_____
                    Notary Public

CHAPTER 15

DECLARATION OF TRUST
For Naming
TWO OR MORE BENEFICIARIES, SHARING EQUALLY,
To Receive
A PARTNERSHIP INTEREST HELD IN ONE NAME

INSTRUCTIONS:

On the following pages will be found a declaration of trust (DT-135) suitable for use in connection with the establishment of an inter vivos trust covering a partnership interest held in one name only, where it is desired to name two or more persons to share the partnership interest equally upon the death of the owner.

Cross out *"city"* or *"town,"* leaving the appropriate designation of your community. Next, insert the fractional interest which you hold in the partnership (one-third, one-fifth, etc.). Then, insert the name and address of the partnership.

In Paragraph 1, indicate the *number of persons* you are naming (to discourage unauthorized additions to the list) and then insert their names. The one whose name appears *first* will be the Successor Trustee responsible for seeing to the distribution of the trust property.

Note that the instrument specifies that the named beneficiaries are to receive *"in equal shares, or the survivor of them/per stirpes."* Now, think carefully: If you have named three persons with the understanding that if one of them predeceases you, *his* children will take *his* share, cross out *"or the survivor of them"* and *initial it.* If that is *not* what you want—if, for example, you prefer that the share of the deceased person be divided between the two surviving persons, cross out *"per stirpes"* and *initial it.* Remember, you <u>must</u> cross out *"or the survivor of them"* or *"per stirpes"*—one or the other.

Note that Paragraph 8 designates as Successor Trustee *"the beneficiary first above named."* Whenever there is any possibility of a beneficiary who has not attained the age of 21 years receiving the partnership interest, make certain that you name an adult in this paragraph who can act as trustee for such beneficiary. Avoid naming as trustee a person not likely to survive until the beneficiary has attained age 21.

When completed in the manner shown on the reverse side hereof, make several photocopies for reference purposes. Hold the original in safekeeping and offer a copy to the partnership with instructions that henceforth your interest should be identified in this manner: *"(your name), Trustee u/d/t dated _____."*

Important: Read carefully Note B on page 38, which applies to this declaration of trust.

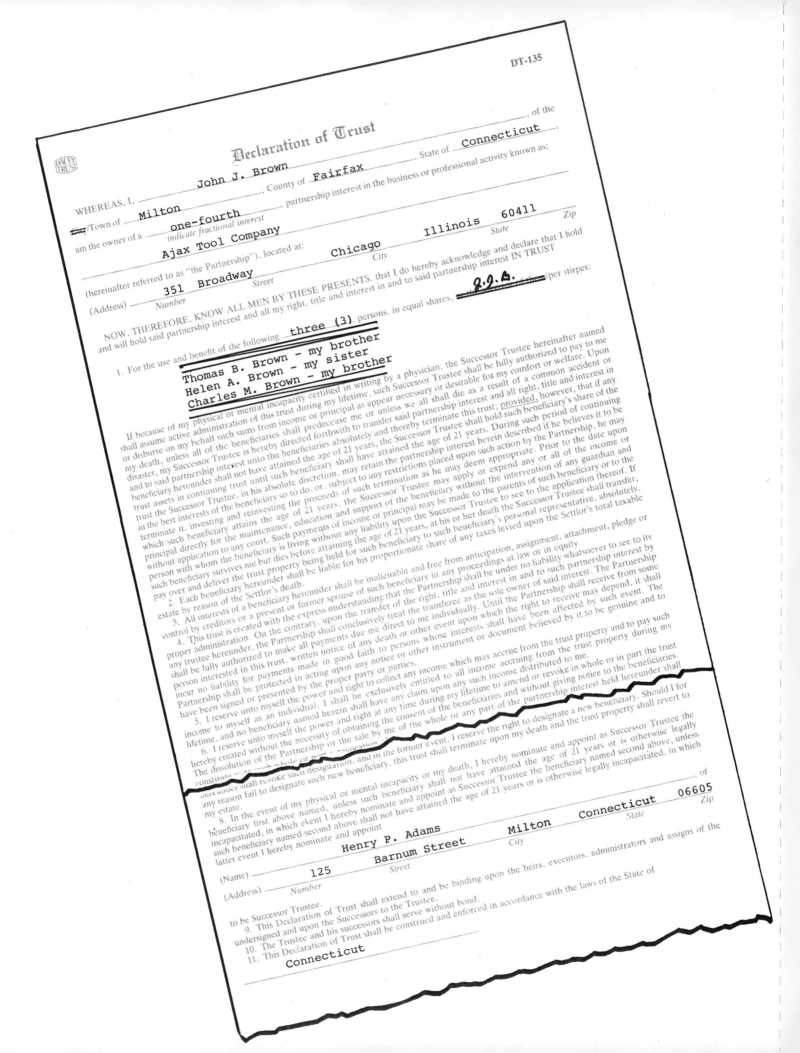

DT-135

Declaration of Trust

WHEREAS, I, _____**John J. Brown**_____, County of _**Fairfax**_, State of _**Connecticut**_, of the

~~City~~/Town of _**Milton**_ am the owner of a _**one-fourth**_ partnership interest in the business or professional activity known as:
indicate fractional interest

**Ajax Tool Company** located at: _**Chicago**_ _**Illinois**_ _**60411**_
City State Zip

(hereinafter referred to as "the Partnership"), located at:

**351 Broadway**
(Address) Number Street

NOW, THEREFORE, KNOW ALL MEN BY THESE PRESENTS, that I do hereby acknowledge and declare that I hold and will hold said partnership interest and all my right, title and interest in and to said partnership interest IN TRUST

1. For the use and benefit of the following _**three (3)**_ persons, in equal shares, ~~or the survivor of them~~ *per stirpes:*

Thomas B. Brown — my brother
Helen A. Brown — my sister
Charles M. Brown — my brother

If because of my physical or mental incapacity certified in writing by a physician, the Successor Trustee hereinafter named shall assume active administration of this trust during my lifetime, such Successor Trustee shall be fully authorized to pay to me or disburse on my behalf such sums from income or principal as appear necessary or desirable for my comfort or welfare. Upon my death, unless all of the beneficiaries shall predecease me or unless we all shall die as a result of a common accident or disaster, my Successor Trustee is hereby directed forthwith to transfer said partnership interest and all right, title and interest in and to said partnership interest unto the beneficiaries absolutely and thereby terminate this trust; *provided,* however, that if any beneficiary hereunder shall not have attained the age of 21 years, the Successor Trustee shall hold such beneficiary's share of the trust assets in continuing trust until such beneficiary shall have attained the age of 21 years. During such period of continuing trust the Successor Trustee, in his absolute discretion, may retain the partnership interest herein described if he believes it to be in the best interests of the beneficiary so to do, or, subject to any restrictions placed upon such action by the Partnership, he may terminate it, investing and reinvesting the proceeds of such termination as he may deem appropriate. Prior to the date upon which such beneficiary attains the age of 21 years, the Successor Trustee may apply or expend any or all of the income or principal directly for the maintenance, education and support of the beneficiary without the intervention of any guardian and without application to any court. Such payments of income or principal may be made to the parents of such beneficiary or to the person with whom the beneficiary is living without any liability upon the Successor Trustee to see to the application thereof. If such beneficiary survives me but dies before attaining the age of 21 years, at his or her death the Successor Trustee shall transfer, pay over and deliver the trust property being held for such beneficiary to such beneficiary's personal representative, absolutely.

2. Each beneficiary hereunder shall be liable for his proportionate share of any taxes levied upon the Settlor's total taxable estate by reason of the Settlor's death.

3. All interests of a beneficiary hereunder shall be inalienable and free from anticipation, assignment, attachment, pledge or control by creditors or a present or former spouse of such beneficiary in any proceedings at law or in equity.

4. This trust is created on the contrary, upon the transfer of the right, title and interest in and to such partnership interest by any trustee hereunder, the Partnership shall conclusively treat the transferee as the sole owner of said interest. The Partnership shall be fully authorized to make all payments due me direct to me individually. Until the Partnership shall receive from some person interested in this trust, written notice of any death or other event upon which the right to receive may depend, it shall incur no liability for payments made in good faith to persons whose interests shall have been affected by such event. The Partnership shall be protected in acting upon any notice or other instrument or document believed by it to be genuine and to have been signed or presented by the proper party or parties.

5. I reserve unto myself the power and right to collect any income which may accrue from the trust property and to pay such income to myself as an individual. I shall be exclusively entitled to all income accruing from the trust property during my lifetime, and no beneficiary named herein shall have any claim upon any such income distributed to me.

6. I reserve unto myself the power and right at any time during my lifetime to amend or revoke in whole or in part the trust hereby created without the necessity of obtaining the consent of the beneficiaries and without giving notice to the beneficiaries. The dissolution of the Partnership or the sale by me of the whole or any part of the partnership interest held hereunder shall constitute ~~as to~~ such whole or ~~part, a revocation~~ ...

~~hereunder shall revoke such designation, and in the former event, I reserve the right to designate a new beneficiary. Should I for~~ any reason fail to designate such new beneficiary, this trust shall terminate upon my death and the trust property shall revert to my estate.

8. In the event of my physical or mental incapacity or my death, I hereby nominate and appoint as Successor Trustee the beneficiary first above named, unless such beneficiary shall not have attained the age of 21 years or is otherwise legally incapacitated, in which event I hereby nominate and appoint as Successor Trustee the beneficiary named second above, unless such beneficiary named second above shall not have attained the age of 21 years or is otherwise legally incapacitated, in which latter event I hereby nominate and appoint

**Henry P. Adams** _**Milton**_ _**Connecticut**_ _**06605**_, of
(Name) City State Zip

_**125**_ _**Barnum Street**_
(Address) Number Street

to be Successor Trustee.

9. This Declaration of Trust shall extend to and be binding upon the heirs, executors, administrators and assigns of the undersigned and upon the Successors to the Trustee.

10. The Trustee and his successors shall serve without bond.

11. This Declaration of Trust shall be construed and enforced in accordance with the laws of the State of

**Connecticut**

Declaration of Trust

WHEREAS, I, _____, of the

City/Town of _____, County of _____, State of _____,

am the owner of a _____ partnership interest in the business or professional activity known as:
indicate fractional interest

_____

(hereinafter referred to as "the Partnership"), located at:

(Address) _____
      Number   *Street*   *City*   *State*   *Zip*

NOW, THEREFORE, KNOW ALL MEN BY THESE PRESENTS, that I do hereby acknowledge and declare that I hold and will hold said partnership interest and all my right, title and interest in and to said partnership interest IN TRUST

1. For the use and benefit of the following _____ persons, in equal shares, or the survivor of them/per stirpes:

If because of my physical or mental incapacity certified in writing by a physician, the Successor Trustee hereinafter named shall assume active administration of this trust during my lifetime, such Successor Trustee shall be fully authorized to pay to me or disburse on my behalf such sums from income or principal as appear necessary or desirable for my comfort or welfare. Upon my death, unless all of the beneficiaries shall predecease me or unless we all shall die as a result of a common accident or disaster, my Successor Trustee is hereby directed forthwith to transfer said partnership interest and all right, title and interest in and to said partnership interest unto the beneficiaries absolutely and thereby terminate this trust; provided, however, that if any beneficiary hereunder shall not have attained the age of 21 years, the Successor Trustee shall hold such beneficiary's share of the trust assets in continuing trust until such beneficiary shall have attained the age of 21 years. During such period of continuing trust the Successor Trustee, in his absolute discretion, may retain the partnership interest herein described if he believes it to be in the best interests of the beneficiary so to do, or, subject to any restrictions placed upon such action by the Partnership, he may terminate it, investing and reinvesting the proceeds of such termination as he may deem appropriate. Prior to the date upon which such beneficiary attains the age of 21 years, the Successor Trustee may apply or expend any or all of the income or principal directly for the maintenance, education and support of the beneficiary without the intervention of any guardian and without application to any court. Such payments of income or principal may be made to the parents of such beneficiary or to the person with whom the beneficiary is living without any liability upon the Successor Trustee to see to the application thereof. If such beneficiary survives me but dies before attaining the age of 21 years, at his or her death the Successor Trustee shall transfer, pay over and deliver the trust property being held for such beneficiary to such beneficiary's personal representative, absolutely.

2. Each beneficiary hereunder shall be liable for his proportionate share of any taxes levied upon the Settlor's total taxable estate by reason of the Settlor's death.

3. All interests of a beneficiary hereunder shall be inalienable and free from anticipation, assignment, attachment, pledge or control by creditors or a present or former spouse of such beneficiary in any proceedings at law or in equity.

4. This trust is created with the express understanding that the Partnership shall be under no liability whatsoever to see to its proper administration. On the contrary, upon the transfer of the right, title and interest in and to such partnership interest by any trustee hereunder, the Partnership shall conclusively treat the transferee as the sole owner of said interest. The Partnership shall be fully authorized to make all payments due me direct to me individually. Until the Partnership shall receive from some person interested in this trust, written notice of any death or other event upon which the right to receive may depend, it shall incur no liability for payments made in good faith to persons whose interests shall have been affected by such event. The Partnership shall be protected in acting upon any notice or other instrument or document believed by it to be genuine and to have been signed or presented by the proper party or parties.

5. I reserve unto myself the power and right to collect any income which may accrue from the trust property and to pay such income to myself as an individual. I shall be exclusively entitled to all income accruing from the trust property during my lifetime, and no beneficiary named herein shall have any claim upon any such income distributed to me.

6. I reserve unto myself the power and right at any time during my lifetime to amend or revoke in whole or in part the trust hereby created without the necessity of obtaining the consent of the beneficiaries and without giving notice to the beneficiaries. The dissolution of the Partnership or the sale by me of the whole or any part of the partnership interest held hereunder shall constitute as to such whole or part a revocation of this trust.

7. The death during my lifetime, or in a common accident or disaster with me, of all of the beneficiaries designated hereunder shall revoke such designation, and in the former event, I reserve the right to designate a new beneficiary. Should I for any reason fail to designate such new beneficiary, this trust shall terminate upon my death and the trust property shall revert to my estate.

8. In the event of my physical or mental incapacity or my death, I hereby nominate and appoint as Successor Trustee the beneficiary first above named, unless such beneficiary shall not have attained the age of 21 years or is otherwise legally incapacitated, in which event I hereby nominate and appoint as Successor Trustee the beneficiary named second above, unless such beneficiary named second above shall not have attained the age of 21 years or is otherwise legally incapacitated, in which latter event I hereby nominate and appoint

(Name) _____ , of

(Address) _____
          Number   Street   City   State   Zip

to be Successor Trustee.

9. This Declaration of Trust shall extend to and be binding upon the heirs, executors, administrators and assigns of the undersigned and upon the Successors to the Trustee.

10. The Trustee and his successors shall serve without bond.

11. This Declaration of Trust shall be construed and enforced in accordance with the laws of the State of

_____ .

IN WITNESS WHEREOF, I have hereunto set my hand and seal this _____

day of _____ , 19_____ .

(Settlor sign here) _____ L.S.

I, the undersigned legal spouse of the above Settlor, hereby waive all community property rights which I may have in the hereinabove-described partnership interest and give my assent to the provisions of the trust and to the inclusion in it of the said partnership interest.

(Spouse sign here) _____ L.S.

Witness: (1) _____   Witness: (2) _____

STATE OF _____ ⎫   City
                                        ⎬   or
COUNTY OF _____ ⎭   Town _____

On the _____ day of _____ , 19_____ , personally appeared

_____

known to me to be the individual(s) who executed the foregoing instrument, and acknowledged the same to be _____ free act and deed, before me.

(Notary Seal)

_____
Notary Public

CHAPTER 15

DECLARATION OF TRUST

For Naming

**ONE PRIMARY BENEFICIARY WITH YOUR CHILDREN,
SHARING EQUALLY, AS CONTINGENT BENEFICIARIES**

To Receive

A PARTNERSHIP INTEREST HELD IN ONE NAME

INSTRUCTIONS:

On the following pages will be found a declaration of trust (DT-136) suitable for use in connection with the establishment of an inter vivos trust covering a partnership interest held in one name only, where it is desired to name one person (ordinarily, but not necessarily, one's spouse) as primary beneficiary, with one's children, sharing equally, as contingent beneficiaries to receive the partnership interest if the primary beneficiary be not surviving.

Cross out *"city"* or *"town,"* leaving the appropriate designation of your community. Next, insert the fractional interest which you hold in the partnership (one-third, one-fifth, etc.). Then, insert the name and address of the partnership.

Enter the name of the primary beneficiary (called the "First Beneficiary") in the appropriate place in Paragraph 1. Note that the instrument first refers to your children as *"natural not/or adopted."* Now, decide: If you have an adopted child and you wish to include him, cross out the word *"not"* in the phrase *"natural not/or adopted"* and *initial it.* If you wish to *exclude* your adopted child, cross out the word *"or"* in the same phrase and *initial it.* Remember, you <u>must</u> cross out *"not"* or *"or"*—one or the other. If you have no adopted child, simply cross out *"not."*

Note next that the instrument specifies that your children are to receive *"in equal shares, or the survivor of them/per stirpes."* Now, think carefully: If it is your wish that if one of your children does not survive you, *his* share will revert to *his* children in equal shares, cross out *"or the survivor of them"* and *initial it.* If that is *not* what you want—if, for example, you prefer that the share of any child of yours who predeceases you shall be divided between your other surviving children in equal shares, cross out *"per stirpes"* and *initial it.* Remember, you <u>must</u> cross out *"or the survivor of them"* or *"per stirpes"*—one or the other.

Note that in Paragraph 8, the First Beneficiary is designated as Successor Trustee, while a space is provided in which you should designate another person to so act if the named Successor Trustee is not surviving or otherwise fails or ceases to act. This could be one of your children, for example, but it must be an adult who can act as trustee for any beneficiary who comes into a share of the trust before attaining the age of 21. Avoid naming someone not likely to survive until the youngest such beneficiary has attained age 21.

When completed in the manner shown on the reverse side hereof, make several photocopies for reference purposes. Hold the original in safekeeping and offer a copy to the partnership with instructions that henceforth your interest should be identified in this manner: *"(your name), Trustee u/d/t dated _____."*

Important: Read carefully Note B on page 38, which applies to this declaration of trust.

DT-136

Declaration of Trust

WHEREAS, I, __John J. Brown__, County of __Fairfax__, State of __Connecticut__, of the

Town of __Milton__ am the owner of a __one-fourth__ partnership interest in the business or professional activity known as:
indicate fractional interest

__Ajax Tool Company__

(hereinafter referred to as "the Partnership"), located at: __Chicago__ City __Illinois__ State __60411__ Zip

(Address) __351 Broadway__
Number _Street_

NOW, THEREFORE, KNOW ALL MEN BY THESE PRESENTS, that I do hereby acknowledge and declare that I hold and will hold said partnership interest and all my right, title and interest in and to said partnership interest IN TRUST

1. For the use and benefit of:

(Name) __Elizabeth A. Brown - my wife__ __Milton__ City __Connecticut 06605__ State Zip

(Address) __525 Main Street__
Number _Street_

(hereinafter referred to as the "First Beneficiary"), and upon his or her death prior to the termination of the trust, for the use and benefit of my children, natural or adopted, in equal shares, or the survivor of them, as follows:

If because of my physical or mental incapacity certified in writing by a physician, such Successor Trustee hereinafter named shall assume active administration of this trust during my lifetime, such Successor Trustee shall be fully authorized to pay to me or disburse on my behalf such sums from income or principal as appear necessary or desirable for my comfort or welfare. Upon my death, unless all of the beneficiaries shall predecease me or unless we all shall die as a result of a common accident or disaster, my Successor Trustee is hereby directed forthwith to transfer said partnership interest and all right, title and interest in and to said partnership interest hereunder ... such beneficiary ... attained the age of 21 years. During

such period of continuing trust the Successor Trustee, in his absolute discretion, may retain the partnership interest herein described if he believes it to be in the best interests of the beneficiary so to do, or, subject to any restrictions placed upon such action by the Partnership, he may terminate it, investing and reinvesting the proceeds of such termination as he may deem appropriate. Prior to the date upon which such beneficiary attains the age of 21 years, the Successor Trustee may apply or expend any or all of the income or principal directly for the maintenance, education and support of the beneficiary without the intervention of any guardian and without application to any court. Such payments of income or principal upon the Successor Trustee to see to the application thereof. If such beneficiary survives me but dies before attaining the age of 21 years, at his or her death the Successor Trustee shall transfer, pay over and deliver the trust property being held for such beneficiary to such beneficiary's personal representative, absolutely.

2. Each beneficiary hereunder shall be liable for his proportionate share of any taxes levied upon the Settlor's total taxable estate by reason of the Settlor's death.

3. All interests of a beneficiary hereunder shall be inalienable and free from anticipation, assignment, attachment, pledge or control by creditors or a present or former spouse of such beneficiary in any proceedings at law or in equity.

4. This trust is created with the express understanding that the Partnership shall be under no liability whatsoever to see to its proper administration. On the contrary, upon the transfer of the right, title and interest in and to such partnership interest by any trustee hereunder, the Partnership shall conclusively treat the transferee as the sole owner of said interest. The Partnership shall be fully authorized to make all payments due me direct to me individually. Until the Partnership shall receive from some person interested in this trust, written notice of any death or other event upon which the right to receive may depend, it shall incur no liability for payments made in good faith to persons whose interests shall have been affected by such event. The Partnership shall be protected in acting upon any notice or other instrument or document believed by it to be genuine and to have been signed or presented by the proper party or parties.

5. I reserve unto myself the power and right to collect any income which may accrue from the trust property and to pay such ... lifetime, and no beneficiary named herein shall have any claim upon any such income distributed to me.

6. I reserve unto myself the power and right at any time during my lifetime to amend or revoke in whole or in part the trust hereby created without the necessity of obtaining the consent of the beneficiaries and without giving notice to the beneficiaries. The dissolution of the Partnership or the sale by me of the whole or any part of the partnership interest held hereunder shall constitute as to such whole or part a revocation of this trust.

7. The death during my lifetime, or in a common accident or disaster with me, of all of the beneficiaries designated hereunder shall revoke such designation, and in the former event, I reserve the right to designate a new beneficiary. Should I for any reason fail to designate such new beneficiary, this trust shall terminate upon my death and the trust property shall revert to my estate.

8. In the event of my physical or mental incapacity or my death, I hereby nominate and appoint as Successor Trustee hereunder the First Beneficiary, or if such First Beneficiary be not surviving or fails or ceases to act, I nominate and appoint

(Name) __Henry P. Adams__ __Milton__ City __Connecticut 06605__ State Zip

(Address) __125 Barnum Street__
Number _Street_

to be Successor Trustee. If such person fails or ceases to act or should I for any reason fail to designate the person above intended to be nominated, then I nominate and appoint as such Successor Trustee hereunder whosoever shall qualify as executor, administrator or guardian, as the case may be, of my estate.

9. This Declaration of Trust shall extend to and be binding upon the heirs, executors, administrators and assigns of the undersigned and upon the Successors to the Trustee.

10. The Trustee and his successors shall serve without bond.

11. This Declaration of Trust shall be construed and enforced in accordance with the laws of the State of

__Connecticut__

Declaration of Trust

WHEREAS, I, ‾‾‾ , of the

City/Town of ‾‾‾‾‾‾‾‾‾‾‾‾‾‾‾‾‾‾‾‾‾‾‾ , County of ‾‾‾‾‾‾‾‾‾‾‾‾‾‾‾‾ , State of ‾‾‾‾‾‾‾‾‾‾‾ ,

am the owner of a ‾‾‾‾‾‾‾‾‾‾‾‾‾‾‾‾‾‾‾‾‾‾‾ partnership interest in the business or professional activity known as:
indicate fractional interest

‾‾

(hereinafter referred to as "the Partnership"), located at:

(Address) ‾‾‾
      Number   *Street*   *City*   *State*   *Zip*

NOW, THEREFORE, KNOW ALL MEN BY THESE PRESENTS, that I do hereby acknowledge and declare that I hold and will hold said partnership interest and all my right, title and interest in and to said partnership interest IN TRUST

    1. For the use and benefit of:

(Name) ‾‾‾ , of

(Address) ‾‾‾
      Number   *Street*   *City*   *State*   *Zip*

(hereinafter referred to as the "First Beneficiary"), and upon his or her death prior to the termination of the trust, for the use and benefit of my children, natural not/or adopted, in equal shares, or the survivor of them/per stirpes.

    If because of my physical or mental incapacity certified in writing by a physician, the Successor Trustee hereinafter named shall assume active administration of this trust during my lifetime, such Successor Trustee shall be fully authorized to pay to me or disburse on my behalf such sums from income or principal as appear necessary or desirable for my comfort or welfare. Upon my death, unless all of the beneficiaries shall predecease me or unless we all shall die as a result of a common accident or disaster, my Successor Trustee is hereby directed forthwith to transfer said partnership interest and all right, title and interest in and to said partnership interest unto the beneficiary or beneficiaries absolutely and thereby terminate this trust; provided, however, that if any beneficiary hereunder shall not have attained the age of 21 years, the Successor Trustee shall hold such beneficiary's share of the trust assets in continuing trust until such beneficiary shall have attained the age of 21 years. During such period of continuing trust the Successor Trustee, in his absolute discretion, may retain the partnership interest herein described if he believes it to be in the best interests of the beneficiary so to do, or, subject to any restrictions placed upon such action by the Partnership, he may terminate it, investing and reinvesting the proceeds of such termination as he may deem appropriate. Prior to the date upon which such beneficiary attains the age of 21 years, the Successor Trustee may apply or expend any or all of the income or principal directly for the maintenance, education and support of the beneficiary without the intervention of any guardian and without application to any court. Such payments of income or principal may be made to the parents of such beneficiary or to the person with whom the beneficiary is living without any liability upon the Successor Trustee to see to the application thereof. If such beneficiary survives me but dies before attaining the age of 21 years, at his or her death the Successor Trustee shall transfer, pay over and deliver the trust property being held for such beneficiary to such beneficiary's personal representative, absolutely.

    2. Each beneficiary hereunder shall be liable for his proportionate share of any taxes levied upon the Settlor's total taxable estate by reason of the Settlor's death.

    3. All interests of a beneficiary hereunder shall be inalienable and free from anticipation, assignment, attachment, pledge or control by creditors or a present or former spouse of such beneficiary in any proceedings at law or in equity.

    4. This trust is created with the express understanding that the Partnership shall be under no liability whatsoever to see to its proper administration. On the contrary, upon the transfer of the right, title and interest in and to such partnership interest by any trustee hereunder, the Partnership shall conclusively treat the transferee as the sole owner of said interest. The Partnership shall be fully authorized to make all payments due me direct to me individually. Until the Partnership shall receive from some person interested in this trust, written notice of any death or other event upon which the right to receive may depend, it shall incur no liability for payments made in good faith to persons whose interests shall have been affected by such event. The Partnership shall be protected in acting upon any notice or other instrument or document believed by it to be genuine and to have been signed or presented by the proper party or parties.

    5. I reserve unto myself the power and right to collect any income which may accrue from the trust property and to pay such income to myself as an individual. I shall be exclusively entitled to all income accruing from the trust property during my lifetime, and no beneficiary named herein shall have any claim upon any such income distributed to me.

    6. I reserve unto myself the power and right at any time during my lifetime to amend or revoke in whole or in part the trust hereby created without the necessity of obtaining the consent of the beneficiaries and without giving notice to the beneficiaries. The dissolution of the Partnership or the sale by me of the whole or any part of the partnership interest held hereunder shall constitute as to such whole or part a revocation of this trust.

    7. The death during my lifetime, or in a common accident or disaster with me, of all of the beneficiaries designated hereunder shall revoke such designation, and in the former event, I reserve the right to designate a new beneficiary. Should I for any reason fail to designate such new beneficiary, this trust shall terminate upon my death and the trust property shall revert to my estate.

8. In the event of my physical or mental incapacity or my death, I hereby nominate and appoint as Successor Trustee hereunder the First Beneficiary, or if such First Beneficiary be not surviving or fails or ceases to act, I nominate and appoint

(Name) _____, of

(Address) _____

       Number   *Street*   *City*   *State*   *Zip*

to be Successor Trustee. If such person fails or ceases to act or should I for any reason fail to designate the person above intended to be nominated, then I nominate and appoint as such Successor Trustee hereunder whosoever shall qualify as executor, administrator or guardian, as the case may be, of my estate.

9. This Declaration of Trust shall extend to and be binding upon the heirs, executors, administrators and assigns of the undersigned and upon the Successors to the Trustee.

10. The Trustee and his successors shall serve without bond.

11. This Declaration of Trust shall be construed and enforced in accordance with the laws of the State of

_____.

IN WITNESS WHEREOF, I have hereunto set my hand and seal this _____

day of _____, 19_____.

        (Settlor sign here) _____ L.S.

I, the undersigned legal spouse of the above Settlor, hereby waive all community property rights which I may have in the hereinabove-described partnership interest and give my assent to the provisions of the trust and to the inclusion in it of the said partnership interest.

        (Spouse sign here) _____ L.S.

Witness: (1) _____   Witness: (2) _____

STATE OF _____   City

COUNTY OF _____   or
                                Town _____

On the _____ day of _____, 19_____, personally appeared

_____

known to me to be the individual(s) who executed the foregoing instrument, and acknowledged the same to be _____ free act and deed, before me.

(Notary Seal)

                                _____

                                       Notary Public

CHAPTER 16

Avoiding Probate of a Motor Vehicle or Trailer

By now, you've probably concluded that you've taken care of everything and there'll be nothing left to probate. You may have forgotten something, however—your automobile or the family trailer.

Through joint ownership of their home, their bank accounts, and their securities, many persons have avoided probate, only to have the wife discover after the death of her husband that she must either sign her deceased husband's name illegally on the back of the automobile registration certificate if she wishes to sell the car or simply transfer it into her name, or apply to the probate court for appointment as executor or administrator which will legally entitle her to transfer title to the vehicle.

A used car frequently has a very limited sale value, and the trouble and expense of going through the probate process in order to dispose of it is way out of proportion to that value. Be careful, then, that you don't force your estate into probate just because of your automobile.

A few rare souls seek to avoid probate of their automobile by registering it in joint tenancy. Considering that the amount involved is relatively small, this rather extreme manifestation of togetherness seems unnecessarily complicated, considering that whenever the car is to be sold or turned in on a new one, or simply reregistered, it will take two to tango.

As for trailers, in the last two decades they have come to play an important role in American life. House trailers, once little boxes, have given way to long, gleaming, handsomely appointed "mobile homes" parked more or less permanently on leased concrete slabs, with water, electricity, and even piped gas laid on conveniently beside them. Rising land prices, forcing upward the price of new homes, have caused many to seek the comforts of life in a spacious trailer in preference to the struggle to pay off a mortgage and to contend with skyrocketing real estate taxes. Retirees have tended to be more affluent in recent years, and many have opted for mobile-home life in a warmer climate in well-landscaped retirement colonies which bear no resemblance whatever to the sometimes squalid trailer parks of a generation ago.

With the improved facilities in our national parks and in the many attractive, privately operated transient sites across the land, millions of Americans now regularly take to the road in travel trailers, a scaled-down version of the house trailer, small enough to tow behind the family car.

Finally, there are the camping trailers, "tents on wheels," which our sybaritic generation prefers to the rigors of actually pitching a tent and sleeping on the ground.

Trailers in all of these classifications used to represent a comparatively small investment. Today, however, camping trailers cost upward of a thousand dollars, while mobile homes sell as high as $50,000 or more, and represent an asset which in size and importance is the equivalent of a modest traditional dwelling.

Motor vehicles (including motorcycles and privately owned trucks) and trailers, be they modest or elaborate, should be protected from the ravages of probate. On the following pages will be found declarations of trust to accomplish that desirable end. Recognizing that many house trailers are jointly owned, I have provided instruments for putting these into joint trust.

CHAPTER 16

DECLARATION OF TRUST
For Naming
ONE BENEFICIARY
To Receive
A MOTOR VEHICLE OR TRAILER
HELD IN ONE NAME

INSTRUCTIONS:

On the following pages will be found a declaration of trust (DT-137) suitable for use in connection with the establishment of an inter vivos trust covering a motor vehicle or trailer held in one name where it is desired to name some one person to receive the vehicle upon the death of the owner.

Cross out *"city"* or *"town,"* leaving the appropriate designation of your community. Next, identify the vehicle (make, model, year, color, registration number).

Enter the name of the beneficiary in the appropriate place in Paragraph 1.

Note that Paragraph 6 designates as Successor Trustee *"whosoever shall at that time be beneficiary hereunder,"* which means that in most cases you don't need to fill anything in there. However, if there is any possibility of a beneficiary who has not attained the age of 21 years receiving the vehicle, make certain that you name an adult in this paragraph who can act as trustee for such beneficiary. Avoid naming as trustee a person not likely to survive until the beneficiary has attained age 21.

When completed in the manner shown on the reverse side hereof, make one or two photocopies for reference purposes. Hold the original in safekeeping and display a copy to the Motor Vehicle Department or other agency with whom the vehicle is registered when you go there to change the registration to read: *"(your name), Trustee u/d/t dated _____."*

Important: Read carefully Note B on page 38, which applies to this declaration of trust.

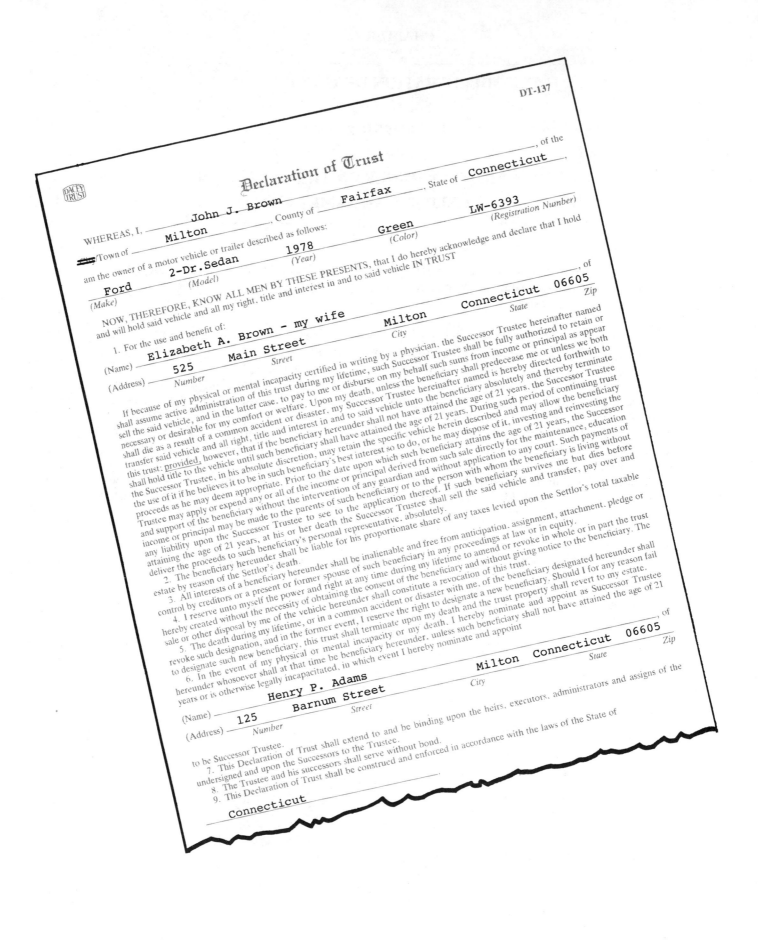

DT-137

Declaration of Trust

WHEREAS, I, **John J. Brown**, County of **Fairfax**, State of **Connecticut**, of the Town of **Milton**, am the owner of a motor vehicle or trailer described as follows:

Green (Color)　**LW-6393** (Registration Number)

Ford (Make)　**2-Dr.Sedan** (Model)　**1978** (Year)

NOW, THEREFORE, KNOW ALL MEN BY THESE PRESENTS, that I do hereby acknowledge and declare that I hold and will hold said vehicle and all my right, title and interest in and to said vehicle IN TRUST

1. For the use and benefit of:

(Name) **Elizabeth A. Brown - my wife**　**Milton** (City)　**Connecticut** (State)　**06605** (Zip)

(Address) **525** (Number)　**Main Street** (Street)

If because of my physical or mental incapacity certified in writing by a physician, the Successor Trustee hereinafter named shall assume active administration of this trust during my lifetime, such Successor Trustee shall be fully authorized to retain or sell the said vehicle, and in the latter case, to pay to me or disburse on my behalf such sums from income or principal as appear necessary or desirable for my comfort or welfare. Upon my death, unless the beneficiary shall predecease me or unless we both shall die as a result of a common accident or disaster, my Successor Trustee hereinafter named is hereby directed forthwith to transfer said vehicle and all right, title and interest in and to said vehicle unto the beneficiary absolutely and thereby terminate this trust: provided, however, that if the beneficiary hereunder shall have attained the age of 21 years. During such period of continuing trust the Successor Trustee, in his absolute discretion, may retain the specific vehicle herein described and may allow the beneficiary the use of it if he believes it to be in such beneficiary's best interest so to do, or he may dispose of it. investing and reinvesting the proceeds as he may deem appropriate. Prior to the date upon which such beneficiary attains the age of 21 years, the Successor Trustee may apply or expend any or all of the income or principal derived from such sale directly for the maintenance, education and support of the beneficiary without the intervention of any guardian and without application to any court. Such payments of income or principal may be made to the parents of such beneficiary or to the person with whom the beneficiary is living without any liability upon the Successor Trustee to see to the application thereof. If such beneficiary survives me but dies before attaining the age of 21 years, at his or her death the Successor Trustee shall sell the said vehicle and transfer, pay over and deliver the proceeds to such beneficiary's personal representative, absolutely.

2. The beneficiary hereunder shall be liable for his proportionate share of any taxes levied upon the Settlor's total taxable estate by reason of the Settlor's death.

3. All interests of a beneficiary hereunder shall be inalienable and free from anticipation, assignment, attachment, pledge or control by creditors or a present or former spouse of such beneficiary in any proceedings at law or in equity.

4. I reserve unto myself the power and right at any time during my lifetime to amend or revoke in whole or in part the trust hereby created without the necessity of obtaining the consent of the beneficiary and without giving notice to the beneficiary. The sale or other disposal by me of the vehicle hereunder shall constitute a revocation of this trust.

5. The death during my lifetime, or in a common accident or disaster with me, of the beneficiary designated hereunder shall revoke such designation, and in the former event, I reserve the right to designate a new beneficiary. Should I for any reason fail to designate such new beneficiary, this trust shall terminate upon my death and the trust property shall revert to my estate.

6. In the event of my physical or mental incapacity or my death. I hereby nominate and appoint as Successor Trustee hereunder whosoever shall at that time be beneficiary hereunder, unless such beneficiary shall not have attained the age of 21 years or is otherwise legally incapacitated, in which event I hereby nominate and appoint

(Name) **Henry P. Adams**　**Milton** (City)　**Connecticut** (State)　**06605** (Zip), of

(Address) **125** (Number)　**Barnum Street** (Street)

to be Successor Trustee.

7. This Declaration of Trust shall extend to and be binding upon the heirs, executors, administrators and assigns of the undersigned and upon the Successors to the Trustee.

8. The Trustee and his successors shall serve without bond.

9. This Declaration of Trust shall be construed and enforced in accordance with the laws of the State of

Connecticut

Declaration of Trust

WHEREAS, I, _____, of the

City/Town of _____, County of _____, State of _____,

am the owner of a motor vehicle or trailer described as follows:

_____ ;

(Make)   (Model)   (Year)   (Color)   (Registration Number)

NOW, THEREFORE, KNOW ALL MEN BY THESE PRESENTS, that I do hereby acknowledge and declare that I hold and will hold said vehicle and all my right, title and interest in and to said vehicle IN TRUST

   1. For the use and benefit of:

(Name) _____, of

(Address) _____
          Number   Street   City   State   Zip

If because of my physical or mental incapacity certified in writing by a physician, the Successor Trustee hereinafter named shall assume active administration of this trust during my lifetime, such Successor Trustee shall be fully authorized to retain or sell the said vehicle, and in the latter case, to pay to me or disburse on my behalf such sums from income or principal as appear necessary or desirable for my comfort or welfare. Upon my death, unless the beneficiary shall predecease me or unless we both shall die as a result of a common accident or disaster, my Successor Trustee hereinafter named is hereby directed forthwith to transfer said vehicle and all right, title and interest in and to said vehicle unto the beneficiary absolutely and thereby terminate this trust; provided, however, that if the beneficiary hereunder shall not have attained the age of 21 years, the Successor Trustee shall hold title to the vehicle until such beneficiary shall have attained the age of 21 years. During such period of continuing trust the Successor Trustee, in his absolute discretion, may retain the specific vehicle herein described and may allow the beneficiary the use of it if he believes it to be in such beneficiary's best interest so to do, or he may dispose of it, investing and reinvesting the proceeds as he may deem appropriate. Prior to the date upon which such beneficiary attains the age of 21 years, the Successor Trustee may apply or expend any or all of the income or principal derived from such sale directly for the maintenance, education and support of the beneficiary without the intervention of any guardian and without application to any court. Such payments of income or principal may be made to the parents of such beneficiary or to the person with whom the beneficiary is living without any liability upon the Successor Trustee to see to the application thereof. If such beneficiary survives me but dies before attaining the age of 21 years, at his or her death the Successor Trustee shall sell the said vehicle and transfer, pay over and deliver the proceeds to such beneficiary's personal representative, absolutely.

   2. The beneficiary hereunder shall be liable for his proportionate share of any taxes levied upon the Settlor's total taxable estate by reason of the Settlor's death.

   3. All interests of a beneficiary hereunder shall be inalienable and free from anticipation, assignment, attachment, pledge or control by creditors or a present or former spouse of such beneficiary in any proceedings at law or in equity.

   4. I reserve unto myself the power and right at any time during my lifetime to amend or revoke in whole or in part the trust hereby created without the necessity of obtaining the consent of the beneficiary and without giving notice to the beneficiary. The sale or other disposal by me of the vehicle hereunder shall constitute a revocation of this trust.

   5. The death during my lifetime, or in a common accident or disaster with me, of the beneficiary designated hereunder shall revoke such designation, and in the former event, I reserve the right to designate a new beneficiary. Should I for any reason fail to designate such new beneficiary, this trust shall terminate upon my death and the trust property shall revert to my estate.

   6. In the event of my physical or mental incapacity or my death, I hereby nominate and appoint as Successor Trustee hereunder whosoever shall at that time be beneficiary hereunder, unless such beneficiary shall not have attained the age of 21 years or is otherwise legally incapacitated, in which event I hereby nominate and appoint

(Name) _____, of

(Address) _____
          Number   Street   City   State   Zip

to be Successor Trustee.

   7. This Declaration of Trust shall extend to and be binding upon the heirs, executors, administrators and assigns of the undersigned and upon the Successors to the Trustee.

   8. The Trustee and his successors shall serve without bond.

   9. This Declaration of Trust shall be construed and enforced in accordance with the laws of the State of

_____ .

   IN WITNESS WHEREOF, I have hereunto set my hand and seal this _____

day of _____, 19_____ .

   •   (Settlor sign here) _____ L.S.

I, the undersigned legal spouse of the above Settlor, hereby waive all community property rights which I may have in the hereinabove-described vehicle and give my assent to the provisions of the trust and to the inclusion in it of the said vehicle.

(Spouse sign here) _____ L.S.

Witness: (1) _____ Witness: (2) _____

STATE OF _____ City

or

COUNTY OF _____ Town _____

On the _____ day of _____, 19_____, personally appeared

_____

known to me to be the individual(s) who executed the foregoing instrument, and acknowledged the same to be _____ free act and deed, before me.

(Notary Seal)

_____

Notary Public

CHAPTER 16

DECLARATION OF TRUST
For Naming
ONE PRIMARY BENEFICIARY
And
ONE CONTINGENT BENEFICIARY
To Receive
A MOTOR VEHICLE OR TRAILER HELD IN ONE NAME

INSTRUCTIONS:

On the following pages will be found a declaration of trust (DT-138) suitable for use in connection with the establishment of an inter vivos trust covering a motor vehicle or trailer held in one name where it is desired to name some *one* person as primary beneficiary with some *one* other person as contingent beneficiary to receive the vehicle if the primary beneficiary be not surviving upon the death of the owner.

Cross out *"city"* or *"town,"* leaving the appropriate designation of your community. Next, identify the vehicle (make, model, year, color and registration number).

Enter the names of the beneficiaries in the appropriate place in Paragraph 1.

Note that Paragraph 6 designates as Successor Trustee *"whosoever shall at that time be beneficiary hereunder,"* which means that in most cases you don't need to fill anything in there. However, if there is any possibility of a beneficiary who has not attained the age of 21 years receiving the vehicle, make certain that you name an adult in this paragraph who can act as trustee for such beneficiary. Avoid naming as trustee a person not likely to survive until the beneficiary has attained age 21.

When completed in the manner shown on the reverse side hereof, make one or two photocopies for reference purposes. Hold the original in safekeeping and display a copy to the Motor Vehicle Department or other agency with whom the vehicle is registered when you go there to change the registration to read: *"(your name), Trustee u/d/t dated _____."*

Important: Read carefully Note B on page 38, which applies to this declaration of trust.

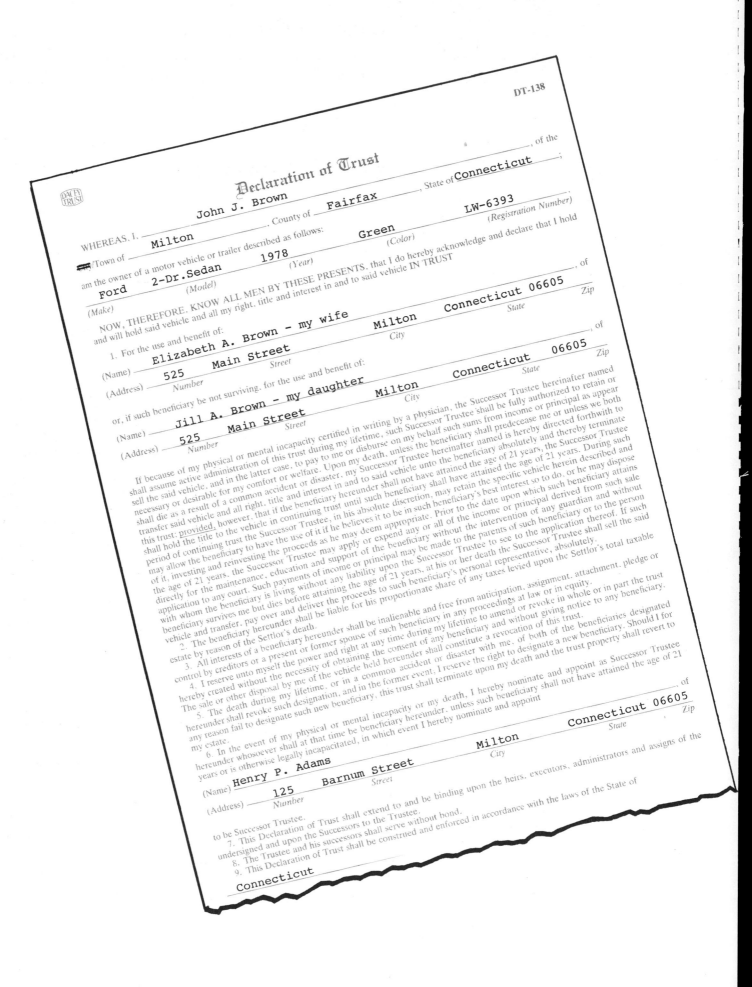

DT-138

Declaration of Trust

WHEREAS, I, __John J. Brown__, County of __Fairfax__, State of __Connecticut__, of the
Town of __Milton__

am the owner of a motor vehicle or trailer described as follows: __Green__ (Color) __LW-6393__ (Registration Number)

__Ford__ __2-Dr.Sedan__ __1978__ (Year)
(Make) (Model)

NOW, THEREFORE, KNOW ALL MEN BY THESE PRESENTS, that I do hereby acknowledge and declare that I hold and will hold said vehicle and all my right, title and interest in and to said vehicle IN TRUST

1. For the use and benefit of:

__Elizabeth A. Brown - my wife__ __Milton__ __Connecticut__ __06605__
(Name) City State Zip

__525__ __Main Street__ of
(Address) Number Street

or, if such beneficiary be not surviving, for the use and benefit of:

__Jill A. Brown - my daughter__ __Milton__ __Connecticut__ __06605__
(Name) City State Zip

__525__ __Main Street__
(Address) Number Street

If because of my physical or mental incapacity certified in writing by a physician, the Successor Trustee hereinafter named shall assume active administration of this trust during my lifetime, such Successor Trustee shall be fully authorized to retain or sell the said vehicle, and in the latter case, to pay to me or disburse on my behalf such sums from income or principal as appear necessary or desirable for my comfort or welfare. Upon my death, unless the beneficiary shall predecease me or unless we both shall die as a result of a common accident or disaster, my Successor Trustee hereinafter named is hereby directed forthwith to transfer said vehicle and all right, title and interest in and to said vehicle unto the beneficiary absolutely and thereby terminate this trust; provided, however, that if the beneficiary hereunder shall not have attained the age of 21 years, the Successor Trustee shall hold the title to the vehicle in continuing trust until such beneficiary shall have attained the age of 21 years. During such period of continuing trust the Successor Trustee, in his absolute discretion, may retain the specific vehicle herein described and may allow the beneficiary to have the use of it if he believes it to be in such beneficiary's best interest so to do, or he may dispose of it, investing and reinvesting the proceeds as he may deem appropriate. Prior to the date upon which such beneficiary attains the age of 21 years, the Successor Trustee may apply or expend any or all of the income or principal derived from such sale directly for the maintenance, education and support of the beneficiary without the intervention of any guardian and without application to any court. Such payments of income or principal may be made to the parents of such beneficiary or to the person with whom the beneficiary is living without any liability upon the Successor Trustee to see to the application thereof. If such beneficiary survives me but dies before attaining the age of 21 years, at his or her death the Successor Trustee shall sell the said vehicle and transfer, pay over and deliver the proceeds to such beneficiary's personal representative, absolutely.

2. The beneficiary hereunder shall be inalienable and free from anticipation, assignment, attachment, pledge or estate by reason of the Settlor's death.

3. All interests of a beneficiary hereunder shall be inalienable and free from anticipation, assignment, attachment, pledge or control by creditors or a present or former spouse of such beneficiary in any proceedings at law or in equity.

4. I reserve unto myself the power and right at any time during my lifetime to amend or revoke in whole or in part the trust hereby created without the necessity of obtaining the consent of any beneficiary and without giving notice to any beneficiary. The sale or other disposal by me of the vehicle held hereunder shall constitute a revocation of this trust.

5. The death during my lifetime, or in a common accident or disaster with me, of both of the beneficiaries designated hereunder shall revoke such designation, and in the former event, I reserve the right to designate a new beneficiary. Should I for any reason fail to designate such new beneficiary, this trust shall terminate upon my death and the trust property shall revert to my estate.

6. In the event of my physical or mental incapacity or my death, I hereby nominate and appoint as Successor Trustee hereunder whosoever shall at that time be beneficiary hereunder, unless such beneficiary shall not have attained the age of 21 years or is otherwise legally incapacitated, in which event I hereby nominate and appoint

__Henry P. Adams__ __Milton__ __Connecticut__ __06605__ of
(Name) City State Zip

__125__ __Barnum Street__
(Address) Number Street

to be Successor Trustee.

7. This Declaration of Trust shall extend to and be binding upon the heirs, executors, administrators and assigns of the undersigned and upon the Successors to the Trustee.

8. The Trustee and his successors shall serve without bond.

9. This Declaration of Trust shall be construed and enforced in accordance with the laws of the State of __Connecticut__

Declaration of Trust

WHEREAS, I, _____, of the

City/Town of _____, County of _____, State of _____,

am the owner of a motor vehicle or trailer described as follows:

_____;
(Make)   (Model)   (Year)   (Color)   (Registration Number)

NOW, THEREFORE, KNOW ALL MEN BY THESE PRESENTS, that I do hereby acknowledge and declare that I hold and will hold said vehicle and all my right, title and interest in and to said vehicle IN TRUST

1. For the use and benefit of:

(Name) _____, of

(Address) _____
      Number   Street   City   State   Zip

or, if such beneficiary be not surviving, for the use and benefit of:

(Name) _____, of

(Address) _____
      Number   Street   City   State   Zip

If because of my physical or mental incapacity certified in writing by a physician, the Successor Trustee hereinafter named shall assume active administration of this trust during my lifetime, such Successor Trustee shall be fully authorized to retain or sell the said vehicle, and in the latter case, to pay to me or disburse on my behalf such sums from income or principal as appear necessary or desirable for my comfort or welfare. Upon my death, unless the beneficiary shall predecease me or unless we both shall die as a result of a common accident or disaster, my Successor Trustee hereinafter named is hereby directed forthwith to transfer said vehicle and all right, title and interest in and to said vehicle unto the beneficiary absolutely and thereby terminate this trust; provided, however, that if the beneficiary hereunder shall not have attained the age of 21 years, the Successor Trustee shall hold the title to the vehicle in continuing trust until such beneficiary shall have attained the age of 21 years. During such period of continuing trust the Successor Trustee, in his absolute discretion, may retain the specific vehicle herein described and may allow the beneficiary to have the use of it if he believes it to be in such beneficiary's best interest so to do, or he may dispose of it, investing and reinvesting the proceeds as he may deem appropriate. Prior to the date upon which such beneficiary attains the age of 21 years, the Successor Trustee may apply or expend any or all of the income or principal derived from such sale directly for the maintenance, education and support of the beneficiary without the intervention of any guardian and without application to any court. Such payments of income or principal may be made to the parents of such beneficiary or to the person with whom the beneficiary is living without any liability upon the Successor Trustee to see to the application thereof. If such beneficiary survives me but dies before attaining the age of 21 years, at his or her death the Successor Trustee shall sell the said vehicle and transfer, pay over and deliver the proceeds to such beneficiary's personal representative, absolutely.

2. The beneficiary hereunder shall be liable for his proportionate share of any taxes levied upon the Settlor's total taxable estate by reason of the Settlor's death.

3. All interests of a beneficiary hereunder shall be inalienable and free from anticipation, assignment, attachment, pledge or control by creditors or a present or former spouse of such beneficiary in any proceedings at law or in equity.

4. I reserve unto myself the power and right at any time during my lifetime to amend or revoke in whole or in part the trust hereby created without the necessity of obtaining the consent of any beneficiary and without giving notice to any beneficiary. The sale or other disposal by me of the vehicle held hereunder shall constitute a revocation of this trust.

5. The death during my lifetime, or in a common accident or disaster with me, of both of the beneficiaries designated hereunder shall revoke such designation, and in the former event, I reserve the right to designate a new beneficiary. Should I for any reason fail to designate such new beneficiary, this trust shall terminate upon my death and the trust property shall revert to my estate.

6. In the event of my physical or mental incapacity or my death, I hereby nominate and appoint as Successor Trustee hereunder whosoever shall at that time be beneficiary hereunder, unless such beneficiary shall not have attained the age of 21 years or is otherwise legally incapacitated, in which event I hereby nominate and appoint

(Name) _____, of

(Address) _____
      Number   Street   City   State   Zip

to be Successor Trustee.

7. This Declaration of Trust shall extend to and be binding upon the heirs, executors, administrators and assigns of the undersigned and upon the Successors to the Trustee.

8. The Trustee and his successors shall serve without bond.
9. This Declaration of Trust shall be construed and enforced in accordance with the laws of the State of

_____.

IN WITNESS WHEREOF, I have hereunto set my hand and seal this _____

day of _____, 19_____.

(Settlor sign here) _____ L.S.

I, the undersigned legal spouse of the above Settlor, hereby waive all community property rights which I may have in the hereinabove-described vehicle and give my assent to the provisions of the trust and to the inclusion in it of the said vehicle.

(Spouse sign here) _____ L.S.

Witness: (1) _____ Witness: (2) _____

STATE OF _____ } City
                                        or
COUNTY OF _____ } Town _____

On the _____ day of _____, 19_____, personally appeared

_____

known to me to be the individual(s) who executed the foregoing instrument, and acknowledged the same to be _____ free act and deed, before me.

(Notary Seal)

_____
Notary Public

CHAPTER 16

DECLARATION OF TRUST
For Naming
TWO OR MORE BENEFICIARIES, SHARING EQUALLY,
To Receive
A MOTOR VEHICLE OR TRAILER HELD IN ONE NAME

INSTRUCTIONS:

On the following pages will be found a declaration of trust (DT-139) suitable for use in connection with the establishment of an inter vivos trust covering a motor vehicle or trailer held in one name where it is desired to name two or more persons to share equally the ownership of the vehicle upon the death of the present owner.

Cross out *"city"* or *"town,"* leaving the appropriate designation of your community. Next, identify the vehicle (make, model, year, color and registration number).

In Paragraph 1, indicate the *number of persons* you are naming (to discourage unauthorized additions to the list) and then insert their names. The one whose name appears *first* will be the Successor Trustee responsible for seeing to the transfer or sale of the vehicle.

Note that the instrument specifies that the named beneficiaries are to receive *"in equal shares, or the survivor of them/per stirpes."* Now, think carefully: If you have named three persons with the understanding that if one of them predeceases you, *his* children will take *his* share, cross out *"or the survivor of them"* and *initial it.* If that is *not* what you want—if, for example, you prefer that the share of the deceased person be divided between the two surviving persons, cross out *"per stirpes"* and *initial it.* Remember, you <u>must</u> cross out either *"or the survivor of them"* or *"per stirpes"*—one or the other.

Note that Paragraph 6 designates as Successor Trustee *"the beneficiary named first above."* However, if there is any possibility of a beneficiary who has not attained the age of 21 years receiving a share in the trust, make certain that you name an adult in this paragraph who can act as trustee for such beneficiary. Avoid naming as trustee a person not likely to survive until the beneficiary has attained age 21.

When completed in the manner shown on the reverse side hereof, make one or two photocopies for reference purposes. Hold the original in safekeeping and display a copy to the Motor Vehicle Department or other agency with whom the vehicle is registered when you go there to change the name on the registration to read: *"(your name), Trustee u/d/t dated _____."*

Important: Read carefully Note B on page 38, which applies to this declaration of trust.

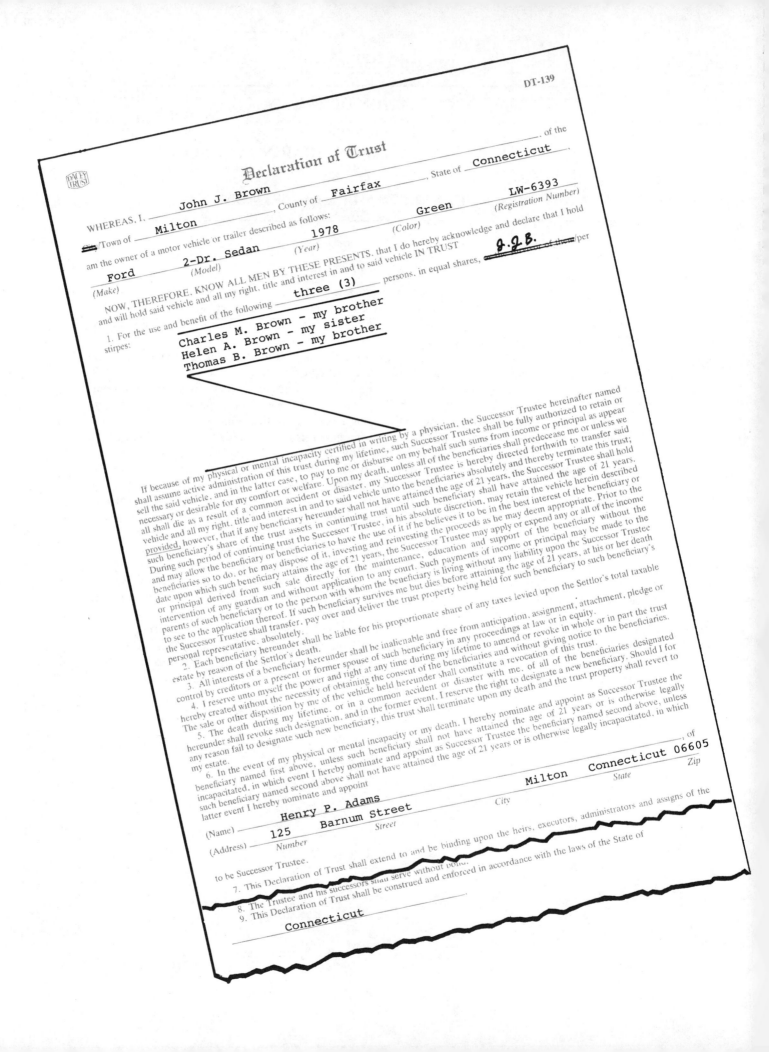

DT-139

Declaration of Trust

WHEREAS, I, __John J. Brown__, County of __Fairfax__, State of __Connecticut__, of the Town of __Milton__

am the owner of a motor vehicle or trailer described as follows:

__Green__   __LW-6393__
(Color)   (Registration Number)

__1978__
(Year)

__Ford__   __2-Dr. Sedan__
(Make)   (Model)

NOW, THEREFORE, KNOW ALL MEN BY THESE PRESENTS, that I do hereby acknowledge and declare that I hold and will hold said vehicle and all my right, title and interest in and to said vehicle IN TRUST   __J.J.B.__

1. For the use and benefit of the following __three (3)__ persons, in equal shares, ~~the amount of them~~/per stirpes:

Charles M. Brown - my brother
Helen A. Brown - my sister
Thomas B. Brown - my brother

If because of my physical or mental incapacity certified in writing by a physician, the Successor Trustee hereinafter named shall assume active administration of this trust during my lifetime, such Successor Trustee shall be fully authorized to retain or sell the said vehicle, and in the latter case, to pay to me or disburse on my behalf such sums from income or principal as appear necessary or desirable for my comfort or welfare. Upon my death, unless all of the beneficiaries shall predecease me or unless we all shall die as a result of a common accident or disaster, my Successor Trustee is hereby directed forthwith to transfer said vehicle and all my right, title and interest in and to said vehicle unto the beneficiaries absolutely and thereby terminate this trust; provided, however, that if any beneficiary hereunder shall not have attained the age of 21 years, the Successor Trustee shall hold such beneficiary's share of the trust assets in continuing trust until such beneficiary shall have attained the age of 21 years. During such period of continuing trust the Successor Trustee, in his absolute discretion, may retain the vehicle herein described and may allow the beneficiary or beneficiaries to have the use of it if he believes it to be in the best interest of the beneficiary or beneficiaries so to do, or he may dispose of it, investing and reinvesting the proceeds as he may deem appropriate. Prior to the date upon which such beneficiary attains the age of 21 years, the Successor Trustee may apply or expend any or all of the income or principal derived from such sale directly for the maintenance, education and support of the beneficiary without the intervention of any guardian and without application to any court. Such payments of income or principal may be made to the parents of such beneficiary or to the person with whom the beneficiary is living without any liability upon the Successor Trustee to see to the application thereof. If such beneficiary survives me but dies before attaining the age of 21 years, at his or her death the Successor Trustee shall transfer, pay over and deliver the trust property being held for such beneficiary to such beneficiary's personal representative, absolutely.

2. Each beneficiary hereunder shall be liable for his proportionate share of any taxes levied upon the Settlor's total taxable estate by reason of the Settlor's death.

3. All interests of a beneficiary hereunder shall be inalienable and free from anticipation, assignment, attachment, pledge or control by creditors or a present or former spouse of such beneficiary in any proceedings at law or in equity.

4. I reserve unto myself the power and right at any time during my lifetime to amend or revoke in whole or in part the trust hereby created without the necessity of obtaining the consent of the beneficiaries and without giving notice to the beneficiaries. The sale or other disposition by me of the vehicle held hereunder shall constitute a revocation of this trust.

5. The death during my lifetime, or in a common accident or disaster with me, of all of the beneficiaries designated hereunder shall revoke such designation, and in the former event, I reserve the right to designate a new beneficiary. Should I for any reason fail to designate such new beneficiary, this trust shall terminate upon my death and the trust property shall revert to my estate.

6. In the event of my physical or mental incapacity or my death, I hereby nominate and appoint as Successor Trustee the beneficiary named first above, unless such beneficiary shall not have attained the age of 21 years or is otherwise legally incapacitated, in which event I hereby nominate and appoint as Successor Trustee the beneficiary named second above, unless such beneficiary named second above shall not have attained the age of 21 years or is otherwise legally incapacitated, in which latter event I hereby nominate and appoint

__Henry P. Adams__, of __Milton__   __Connecticut__   __06605__
(Name)   City   State   Zip

__125__   __Barnum Street__
(Address)   Number   Street

to be Successor Trustee.

7. This Declaration of Trust shall extend to and be binding upon the heirs, executors, administrators and assigns of the

8. The Trustee and his successors shall serve without bond.

9. This Declaration of Trust shall be construed and enforced in accordance with the laws of the State of __Connecticut__

Declaration of Trust

WHEREAS, I, _____ , of the

City/Town of _____ , County of _____ , State of _____ ,

am the owner of a motor vehicle or trailer described as follows:

_____ ;

(Make)   *(Model)*   *(Year)*   *(Color)*   *(Registration Number)*

NOW, THEREFORE, KNOW ALL MEN BY THESE PRESENTS, that I do hereby acknowledge and declare that I hold and will hold said vehicle and all my right, title and interest in and to said vehicle IN TRUST

1. For the use and benefit of the following _____ persons, in equal shares, or the survivor of them/per stirpes:

If because of my physical or mental incapacity certified in writing by a physician, the Successor Trustee hereinafter named shall assume active administration of this trust during my lifetime, such Successor Trustee shall be fully authorized to retain or sell the said vehicle, and in the latter case, to pay to me or disburse on my behalf such sums from income or principal as appear necessary or desirable for my comfort or welfare. Upon my death, unless all of the beneficiaries shall predecease me or unless we all shall die as a result of a common accident or disaster, my Successor Trustee is hereby directed forthwith to transfer said vehicle and all my right, title and interest in and to said vehicle unto the beneficiaries absolutely and thereby terminate this trust; provided, however, that if any beneficiary hereunder shall not have attained the age of 21 years, the Successor Trustee shall hold such beneficiary's share of the trust assets in continuing trust until such beneficiary shall have attained the age of 21 years. During such period of continuing trust the Successor Trustee, in his absolute discretion, may retain the vehicle herein described and may allow the beneficiary or beneficiaries to have the use of it if he believes it to be in the best interest of the beneficiary or beneficiaries so to do, or he may dispose of it, investing and reinvesting the proceeds as he may deem appropriate. Prior to the date upon which such beneficiary attains the age of 21 years, the Successor Trustee may apply or expend any or all of the income or principal derived from such sale directly for the maintenance, education and support of the beneficiary without the intervention of any guardian and without application to any court. Such payments of income or principal may be made to the parents of such beneficiary or to the person with whom the beneficiary is living without any liability upon the Successor Trustee to see to the application thereof. If such beneficiary survives me but dies before attaining the age of 21 years, at his or her death the Successor Trustee shall transfer, pay over and deliver the trust property being held for such beneficiary to such beneficiary's personal representative, absolutely.

2. Each beneficiary hereunder shall be liable for his proportionate share of any taxes levied upon the Settlor's total taxable estate by reason of the Settlor's death.

3. All interests of a beneficiary hereunder shall be inalienable and free from anticipation, assignment, attachment, pledge or control by creditors or a present or former spouse of such beneficiary in any proceedings at law or in equity.

4. I reserve unto myself the power and right at any time during my lifetime to amend or revoke in whole or in part the trust hereby created without the necessity of obtaining the consent of the beneficiaries and without giving notice to the beneficiaries. The sale or other disposition by me of the vehicle held hereunder shall constitute a revocation of this trust.

5. The death during my lifetime, or in a common accident or disaster with me, of all of the beneficiaries designated hereunder shall revoke such designation, and in the former event, I reserve the right to designate a new beneficiary. Should I for any reason fail to designate such new beneficiary, this trust shall terminate upon my death and the trust property shall revert to my estate.

6. In the event of my physical or mental incapacity or my death, I hereby nominate and appoint as Successor Trustee the beneficiary named first above, unless such beneficiary shall not have attained the age of 21 years or is otherwise legally incapacitated, in which event I hereby nominate and appoint as Successor Trustee the beneficiary named second above, unless such beneficiary named second above shall not have attained the age of 21 years or is otherwise legally incapacitated, in which latter event I hereby nominate and appoint

(Name) _____ , of

(Address) _____

     Number   *Street*   *City*   *State*   *Zip*

to be Successor Trustee.

7. This Declaration of Trust shall extend to and be binding upon the heirs, executors, administrators and assigns of the undersigned and upon the Successors to the Trustee.

8. The Trustee and his successors shall serve without bond.

9. This Declaration of Trust shall be construed and enforced in accordance with the laws of the State of

_____.

IN WITNESS WHEREOF, I have hereunto set my hand and seal this _____

day of _____, 19_____.

(Settlor sign here) _____ L.S.

I, the undersigned legal spouse of the above Settlor, hereby waive all community property rights which I may have in the hereinabove-described vehicle and give my assent to the provisions of the trust and to the inclusion in it of the said vehicle.

(Spouse sign here) _____ L.S.

Witness: (1) _____   Witness: (2) _____

STATE OF _____   City
                                                                          or
COUNTY OF _____   Town _____

On the _____ day of _____, 19_____, personally appeared

_____

known to me to be the individual(s) who executed the foregoing instrument, and acknowledged the same to be _____ free act and deed, before me.

(Notary Seal)

_____
Notary Public

CHAPTER 16

DECLARATION OF TRUST
For Naming
ONE PRIMARY BENEFICIARY WITH YOUR CHILDREN,
SHARING EQUALLY, AS CONTINGENT BENEFICIARIES
To Receive
A MOTOR VEHICLE OR TRAILER HELD IN ONE NAME

INSTRUCTIONS:

On the following pages will be found a declaration of trust (DT-140) suitable for use in connection with the establishment of an inter vivos trust covering a motor vehicle or trailer held in one name where it is desired to name one person (ordinarily, but not necessarily, one's spouse) as primary beneficiary, with one's children as contingent beneficiaries to receive the vehicle if the primary beneficiary be not surviving.

Cross out *"city"* or *"town,"* leaving the appropriate designation of your community. Next, identify the vehicle (make, model, year, color, registration number).

Enter the name of the primary beneficiary (called the "First Beneficiary") in the appropriate place in Paragraph 1. Note that the instrument first refers to your children as *"natural not/or adopted."* Now, decide: If you have an adopted child and you wish to include him, cross out the word *"not"* in the phrase *"natural not/or adopted"* and *initial it.* If you wish to exclude your adopted child, cross out the word *"or"* in the same phrase and *initial it.* Remember, you <u>must</u> cross out *"not"* or *"or"*—one or the other. If you have no adopted child, simply cross out *"not."*

Note next that the instrument specifies that your children are to receive *"in equal shares, or the survivor of them/per stirpes."* Now, think carefully: If it is your wish that if one of your children does not survive you, *his* share will revert to *his* children in equal shares, cross out *"or the survivor of them"* and *initial it.* If that is *not* what you want—if, for example, you prefer that the share of any child of yours who predeceases you shall be divided between your other surviving children in equal shares, cross out *"per stirpes"* and *initial it.* Remember, you <u>must</u> cross out *"or the survivor of them"* or *"per stirpes"*—one or the other.

Note that in Paragraph 6, the First Beneficiary is designated as Successor Trustee, while a space is provided in which you should designate another person to so act if the named Successor Trustee is not surviving or otherwise fails or ceases to act. This could be one of your children, for example, but it must be an adult who can act as trustee for any beneficiary who comes into a share of the trust before attaining the age of 21. Avoid naming someone not likely to survive until the youngest such beneficiary has attained age 21.

When completed in the manner shown on the reverse side hereof, make one or two photocopies for reference purposes. Hold the original in safekeeping and display a copy to the Motor Vehicle Department or other agency with whom the vehicle is registered when you go there to change the registration to read: *"(your name), Trustee u/d/t dated _____."*

Important: Read carefully Note B on page 38, which applies to this declaration of trust.

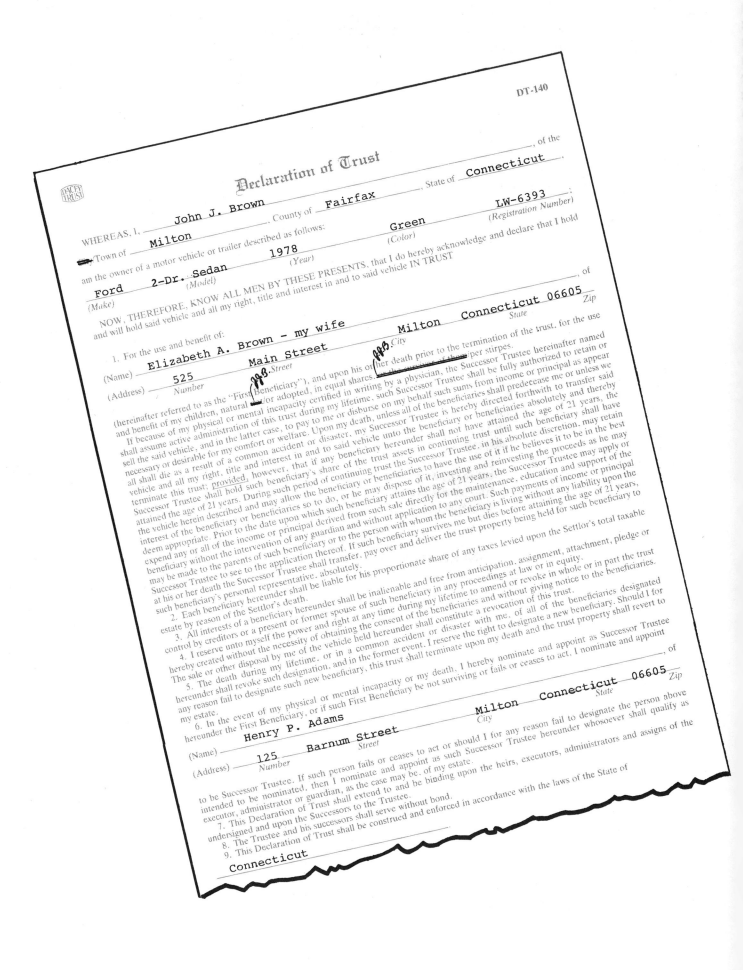

DT-140

Declaration of Trust

WHEREAS, I, ___John J. Brown___, County of ___Fairfax___, State of ___Connecticut___, of the

Town of ___Milton___ ___LW-6393___ *(Registration Number)*

am the owner of a motor vehicle or trailer described as follows:

___Ford___ ___2-Dr. Sedan___ ___1978___ ___Green___
(Make) *(Model)* *(Year)* *(Color)*

NOW, THEREFORE, KNOW ALL MEN BY THESE PRESENTS, that I do hereby acknowledge and declare that I hold and will hold said vehicle and all my right, title and interest in and to said vehicle IN TRUST

1. For the use and benefit of:

___Elizabeth A. Brown — my wife___ ___Milton___ ___Connecticut___ ___06605___
(Name) *City* *State* *Zip*

___525___ ___Main Street___
(Address) *Number* *Street*

(hereinafter referred to as the "First Beneficiary"), and upon his or her death prior to the termination of the trust, for the use and benefit of my children, natural or adopted, in equal shares, the survivor of them per stirpes.

If because of my physical or mental incapacity certified in writing by a physician, the Successor Trustee hereinafter named shall assume active administration of this trust during my lifetime, such Successor Trustee shall be fully authorized to retain or sell the said vehicle, and in the latter case, to pay to me or disburse on my behalf such sums from income or principal as appear necessary or desirable for my comfort or welfare. Upon my death, unless all of the beneficiaries shall predecease me or unless we all shall die as a result of a common accident or disaster, my Successor Trustee is hereby directed forthwith to transfer said vehicle and all my right, title and interest in and to said vehicle unto the beneficiary or beneficiaries absolutely and thereby terminate this trust; provided, however, that if any beneficiary hereunder shall not have attained the age of 21 years, the Successor Trustee shall hold such beneficiary's share of the trust assets in continuing trust until such beneficiary shall have attained the age of 21 years. During such period of continuing trust the Successor Trustee, in his absolute discretion, may retain the vehicle herein described and may allow the beneficiary or beneficiaries to have the use of it if he believes it to be in the best interest of the beneficiary or beneficiaries so to do, or he may dispose of it, investing and reinvesting the proceeds as he may deem appropriate. Prior to the date upon which such beneficiary attains the age of 21 years, the Successor Trustee may apply or expend any or all of the income or principal derived from such sale directly for the maintenance, education and support of the beneficiary without the intervention of any guardian and without application to any court. Such payments of income or principal may be made to the parents of such beneficiary or to the person with whom the beneficiary is living without any liability upon the Successor Trustee to see to the application thereof. If such beneficiary survives me but dies before attaining the age of 21 years, at his or her death the Successor Trustee shall transfer, pay over and deliver the trust property being held for such beneficiary to such beneficiary's personal representative, absolutely.

2. Each beneficiary hereunder shall be liable for his proportionate share of any taxes levied upon the Settlor's total taxable estate by reason of the Settlor's death.

3. All interests of a beneficiary hereunder shall be inalienable and free from anticipation, assignment, attachment, pledge or control by creditors or a present or former spouse of such beneficiary in any proceedings at law or in equity.

4. I reserve unto myself the power and right at any time during my lifetime to amend or revoke in whole or in part the trust hereby created without the necessity of obtaining the consent of the beneficiaries and without giving notice to the beneficiaries. The sale or other disposal by me of the vehicle held hereunder shall constitute a revocation of this trust.

5. The death during my lifetime, or in a common accident or disaster with me, of all of the beneficiaries designated hereunder shall revoke such designation, and in the former event. I reserve the right to designate a new beneficiary. Should I for any reason fail to designate such new beneficiary, this trust shall terminate upon my death and the trust property shall revert to my estate.

6. In the event of my physical or mental incapacity or my death, I hereby nominate and appoint as Successor Trustee hereunder the First Beneficiary, or if such First Beneficiary be not surviving or fails or ceases to act. I nominate and appoint

___Henry P. Adams___ ___Milton___ ___Connecticut___ ___06605___, of
(Name) *City* *State* *Zip*

___125___ ___Barnum Street___
(Address) *Number* *Street*

to be Successor Trustee. If such person fails or ceases to act or should I for any reason fail to designate the person above intended to be nominated, then I nominate and appoint as such Successor Trustee hereunder whosoever shall qualify as executor, administrator or guardian, as the case may be, of my estate.

7. This Declaration of Trust shall extend to and be binding upon the heirs, executors, administrators and assigns of the undersigned and upon the Successors to the Trustee.

8. The Trustee and his successors shall serve without bond.

9. This Declaration of Trust shall be construed and enforced in accordance with the laws of the State of

___Connecticut___

Declaration of Trust

WHEREAS, I, _____, of the

City/Town of _____, County of _____, State of _____,

am the owner of a motor vehicle or trailer described as follows:

_____ ;

  (Make)   *(Model)*   *(Year)*   *(Color)*   *(Registration Number)*

    NOW, THEREFORE, KNOW ALL MEN BY THESE PRESENTS, that I do hereby acknowledge and declare that I hold and will hold said vehicle and all my right, title and interest in and to said vehicle IN TRUST

    1. For the use and benefit of:

(Name) _____, of

(Address) _____

    Number   *Street*   *City*   *State*   *Zip*

(hereinafter referred to as the "First Beneficiary"), and upon his or her death prior to the termination of the trust, for the use and benefit of my children, natural not/or adopted, in equal shares, or the survivor of them/per stirpes.

    If because of my physical or mental incapacity certified in writing by a physician, the Successor Trustee hereinafter named shall assume active administration of this trust during my lifetime, such Successor Trustee shall be fully authorized to retain or sell the said vehicle, and in the latter case, to pay to me or disburse on my behalf such sums from income or principal as appear necessary or desirable for my comfort or welfare. Upon my death, unless all of the beneficiaries shall predecease me or unless we all shall die as a result of a common accident or disaster, my Successor Trustee is hereby directed forthwith to transfer said vehicle and all my right, title and interest in and to said vehicle unto the beneficiary or beneficiaries absolutely and thereby terminate this trust; provided, however, that if any beneficiary hereunder shall not have attained the age of 21 years, the Successor Trustee shall hold such beneficiary's share of the trust assets in continuing trust until such beneficiary shall have attained the age of 21 years. During such period of continuing trust the Successor Trustee, in his absolute discretion, may retain the vehicle herein described and may allow the beneficiary or beneficiaries to have the use of it if he believes it to be in the best interest of the beneficiary or beneficiaries so to do, or he may dispose of it, investing and reinvesting the proceeds as he may deem appropriate. Prior to the date upon which such beneficiary attains the age of 21 years, the Successor Trustee may apply or expend any or all of the income or principal derived from such sale directly for the maintenance, education and support of the beneficiary without the intervention of any guardian and without application to any court. Such payments of income or principal may be made to the parents of such beneficiary or to the person with whom the beneficiary is living without any liability upon the Successor Trustee to see to the application thereof. If such beneficiary survives me but dies before attaining the age of 21 years, at his or her death the Successor Trustee shall transfer, pay over and deliver the trust property being held for such beneficiary to such beneficiary's personal representative, absolutely.

    2. Each beneficiary hereunder shall be liable for his proportionate share of any taxes levied upon the Settlor's total taxable estate by reason of the Settlor's death.

    3. All interests of a beneficiary hereunder shall be inalienable and free from anticipation, assignment, attachment, pledge or control by creditors or a present or former spouse of such beneficiary in any proceedings at law or in equity.

    4. I reserve unto myself the power and right at any time during my lifetime to amend or revoke in whole or in part the trust hereby created without the necessity of obtaining the consent of the beneficiaries and without giving notice to the beneficiaries. The sale or other disposal by me of the vehicle held hereunder shall constitute a revocation of this trust.

    5. The death during my lifetime, or in a common accident or disaster with me, of all of the beneficiaries designated hereunder shall revoke such designation, and in the former event, I reserve the right to designate a new beneficiary. Should I for any reason fail to designate such new beneficiary, this trust shall terminate upon my death and the trust property shall revert to my estate.

    6. In the event of my physical or mental incapacity or my death, I hereby nominate and appoint as Successor Trustee hereunder the First Beneficiary, or if such First Beneficiary be not surviving or fails or ceases to act, I nominate and appoint

(Name) _____, of

(Address) _____

    Number   *Street*   *City*   *State*   *Zip*

to be Successor Trustee. If such person fails or ceases to act or should I for any reason fail to designate the person above intended to be nominated, then I nominate and appoint as such Successor Trustee hereunder whosoever shall qualify as executor, administrator or guardian, as the case may be, of my estate.

    7. This Declaration of Trust shall extend to and be binding upon the heirs, executors, administrators and assigns of the undersigned and upon the Successors to the Trustee.

    8. The Trustee and his successors shall serve without bond.

    9. This Declaration of Trust shall be construed and enforced in accordance with the laws of the State of

_____.

IN WITNESS WHEREOF, I have hereunto set my hand and seal this _____

day of _____, 19_____.

(Settlor sign here) _____ L.S.

I, the undersigned legal spouse of the above Settlor, hereby waive all community property rights which I may have in the hereinabove-described vehicle and give my assent to the provisions of the trust and to the inclusion in it of the said vehicle.

(Spouse sign here) _____ L.S.

Witness: (1) _____   Witness: (2) _____

STATE OF _____ ⎫   City
                                          ⎬   or
COUNTY OF _____ ⎭   Town _____

On the _____ day of _____, 19_____, personally appeared

_____

known to me to be the individual(s) who executed the foregoing instrument, and acknowledged the same to be _____ free act and deed, before me.

(Notary Seal)

_____
Notary Public

CHAPTER 16

DECLARATION OF TRUST
For Naming
ONE BENEFICIARY
To Receive
A MOTOR VEHICLE OR TRAILER HELD IN JOINT NAMES

INSTRUCTIONS:

On the following pages will be found a declaration of trust (DT-137-J) suitable for use in connection with the establishment of an inter vivos trust covering a motor vehicle or trailer held in joint names where it is desired to name some one person to receive the vehicle upon the death of the survivor of the two joint owners.

Enter the names of the two co-owners on the first line.

Cross out *"city"* or *"town,"* leaving the appropriate designation of your community. Next, identify the vehicle (make, model, year, color, registration number).

Enter the name of the beneficiary in the appropriate place in Paragraph 1.

Note that Paragraph 6 designates as Successor Trustee *"whosoever shall at that time be beneficiary hereunder,"* which means that in most cases you don't need to fill anything in there. However, if there is any possibility of a beneficiary who has not attained the age of 21 years receiving the vehicle, make certain that you name an adult in this paragraph who can act as trustee for such beneficiary. Avoid naming as trustee a person not likely to survive until the beneficiary has attained age 21.

When completed in the manner shown on the reverse side hereof, make one or two photocopies for reference purposes. Hold the original in safekeeping and display a copy to the Motor Vehicle Department or other agency with whom the vehicle is registered when you go there to change the registration to read: *"(your name) and (your co-owner's name), Trustees u/d/t dated _____."*

Important: Read carefully Note B on page 38, which applies to this declaration of trust.

DT-137-J

Declaration of Trust

WHEREAS, WE, __John J. Brown__ and __Elizabeth A. Brown__, of the Town of __Milton__, County of __Fairfax__, State of __Connecticut__,

are the joint owners of a motor vehicle or trailer described as follows:

| __LW-6393__ (Registration Number) |
| __Green__ (Color) |
| __1978__ (Year) |
| __Ford__ (Make) __2-Dr. Sedan__ (Model) |

NOW, THEREFORE, KNOW ALL MEN BY THESE PRESENTS, that we do hereby acknowledge and declare that we hold and will hold said vehicle and all our right, title and interest in and to said vehicle IN TRUST

1. For the use and benefit of:

(Name) __Jill A. Brown – our daughter__

(Address) __525__ __Main Street__ __Milton__ __Connecticut 06605__
Number   Street   City   State   Zip

If because of the physical or mental incapacity of both of us certified in writing by a physician, the Successor Trustee hereinafter named shall assume active administration of this trust during our lifetime, such Successor Trustee shall be fully authorized to retain or sell the said vehicle, and in the latter case, to pay to us or disburse on our behalf such sums from income or principal as appear necessary or desirable for our comfort or welfare. Upon the death of the survivor of us, unless the beneficiary shall predecease us or unless we all shall die as a result of a common accident or disaster, our Successor Trustee is hereby directed forthwith to transfer said vehicle and all right, title and interest in and to said vehicle unto the beneficiary absolutely and thereby terminate this trust; provided, however, that if the beneficiary hereunder shall not have attained the age of 21 years, the Successor Trustee shall hold the trust assets in continuing trust until such beneficiary shall have attained the age herein described and may allow the beneficiary to have the use of it if he believes it in the best interest of the beneficiary so to do, or he may dispose of it, investing and reinvesting the proceeds as he may deem appropriate. Prior to the date upon which such beneficiary attains the age of 21 years, the Successor Trustee may apply or expend any or all of the income or principal derived from such sale directly for the maintenance, education and support of the beneficiary without the intervention of any guardian and without application to any court. Such payments of income or principal may be made to the parents of such beneficiary or to the person with whom the beneficiary is living without any liability upon the Successor Trustee to see to the application thereof. If such beneficiary survives us but dies before attaining the age of 21 years, at his or death the Successor Trustee shall transfer, pay over and deliver the trust property to such beneficiary's personal representative, absolutely.

2. The beneficiary hereunder shall be liable for his proportionate share of any taxes levied upon the total taxable estate of the survivor of us by reason of the death of such survivor.

3. All interests of the beneficiary hereunder shall be inalienable and free from anticipation, assignment, attachment, pledge or control by creditors or a present or former spouse of such beneficiary in any proceedings at law or in equity.

4. We reserve unto ourselves the power and right at any time during our lifetime to amend or revoke in whole or in part the trust hereby created without the necessity of obtaining the consent of the beneficiary and without giving notice to the beneficiary. The sale or other disposition by us of the vehicle held hereunder shall constitute a revocation of this trust.

5. The death during our lifetime, or in a common accident or disaster with us, of the beneficiary designated hereunder shall revoke such designation, and in the former event, we reserve the right to designate a new beneficiary. Should we for any reason fail to designate such new beneficiary, this trust shall terminate upon the death of the survivor of us and the trust property shall revert to the estate of such survivor.

6. In the event of the physical or mental incapacity or death of one of us, the survivor shall continue as sole Trustee. In the event of the physical or mental incapacity or death of the survivor of us, or if we both shall die in a common accident, we hereby nominate and appoint as Successor Trustee hereunder whosoever shall at that time be beneficiary hereunder, unless such beneficiary shall not have attained the age of 21 years or is otherwise legally incapacitated, in which event we hereby nominate and appoint

(Name) __Henry P. Adams__ __Barnum Street__ __Milton__ __Connecticut 06605__, of the
(Address) __125__   Street   City   Connecticut   State   Zip
Number

to be Successor Trustee.

7. This Declaration of Trust shall extend to and be binding upon the heirs, executors, administrators and assigns of the undersigned and upon the Successors to the Trustees.

8. We as Trustees and our Successor Trustee shall serve without bond.

9. This Declaration of Trust shall be construed and enforced in accordance with the laws of the State of __Connecticut__

Declaration of Trust

WHEREAS, WE, _____ and _____, of the

City/Town of _____, County of _____, State of _____,

are the joint owners of a motor vehicle or trailer described as follows:

_____ ;

(Make)   (Model)   (Year)   (Color)   (Registration Number)

   NOW, THEREFORE, KNOW ALL MEN BY THESE PRESENTS, that we do hereby acknowledge and declare that we hold and will hold said vehicle and all our right, title and interest in and to said vehicle IN TRUST

   1. For the use and benefit of:

(Name) _____, of

(Address) _____

      Number   Street   City   State   Zip

   If because of the physical or mental incapacity of both of us certified in writing by a physician, the Successor Trustee hereinafter named shall assume active administration of this trust during our lifetime, such Successor Trustee shall be fully authorized to retain or sell the said vehicle, and in the latter case, to pay to us or disburse on our behalf such sums from income or principal as appear necessary or desirable for our comfort or welfare. Upon the death of the survivor of us, unless the beneficiary shall predecease us or unless we all shall die as a result of a common accident or disaster, our Successor Trustee is hereby directed forthwith to transfer said vehicle and all right, title and interest in and to said vehicle unto the beneficiary absolutely and thereby terminate this trust; <u>provided</u>, however, that if the beneficiary hereunder shall not have attained the age of 21 years, the Successor Trustee shall hold the trust assets in continuing trust until such beneficiary shall have attained the age of 21 years. During such period of continuing trust the Successor Trustee, in his absolute discretion, may retain the vehicle herein described and may allow the beneficiary to have the use of it if he believes it in the best interest of the beneficiary so to do, or he may dispose of it, investing and reinvesting the proceeds as he may deem appropriate. Prior to the date upon which such beneficiary attains the age of 21 years, the Successor Trustee may apply or expend any or all of the income or principal derived from such sale directly for the maintenance, education and support of the beneficiary without the intervention of any guardian and without application to any court. Such payments of income or principal may be made to the parents of such beneficiary or to the person with whom the beneficiary is living without any liability upon the Successor Trustee to see to the application thereof. If such beneficiary survives us but dies before attaining the age of 21 years, at his or her death the Successor Trustee shall transfer, pay over and deliver the trust property to such beneficiary's personal representative, absolutely.

   2. The beneficiary hereunder shall be liable for his proportionate share of any taxes levied upon the total taxable estate of the survivor of us by reason of the death of such survivor.

   3. All interests of the beneficiary hereunder shall be inalienable and free from anticipation, assignment, attachment, pledge or control by creditors or a present or former spouse of such beneficiary in any proceedings at law or in equity.

   4. We reserve unto ourselves the power and right at any time during our lifetime to amend or revoke in whole or in part the trust hereby created without the necessity of obtaining the consent of the beneficiary and without giving notice to the beneficiary. The sale or other disposition by us of the vehicle held hereunder shall constitute a revocation of this trust.

   5. The death during our lifetime, or in a common accident or disaster with us, of the beneficiary designated hereunder shall revoke such designation, and in the former event, we reserve the right to designate a new beneficiary. Should we for any reason fail to designate such new beneficiary, this trust shall terminate upon the death of the survivor of us and the trust property shall revert to the estate of such survivor.

   6. In the event of the physical or mental incapacity or death of one of us, the survivor shall continue as sole Trustee. In the event of the physical or mental incapacity or death of the survivor of us, or if we both shall die in a common accident, we hereby nominate and appoint as Successor Trustee hereunder whosoever shall at that time be beneficiary hereunder, unless such beneficiary shall not have attained the age of 21 years or is otherwise legally incapacitated, in which event we hereby nominate and appoint

(Name) _____, of

(Address) _____

      Number   Street   City   State   Zip

to be Successor Trustee.

   7. This Declaration of Trust shall extend to and be binding upon the heirs, executors, administrators and assigns of the undersigned and upon the Successors to the Trustees.

   8. We as Trustees and our Successor Trustee shall serve without bond.

   9. This Declaration of Trust shall be construed and enforced in accordance with the laws of the State of

_____.

IN WITNESS WHEREOF, we have hereunto set our hands and seals this _____

day of _____, 19_____.

(First Settlor sign here) _____ L.S.

(Second Settlor sign here) _____ L.S.

I, the undersigned legal spouse of one of the above Settlors, hereby waive all community property rights which I may have in the hereinabove-described vehicle and give my assent to the provisions of the trust and to the inclusion in it of the said vehicle.

(Spouse sign here) _____ L.S.

Witness: (1) _____   Witness: (2) _____

STATE OF _____ ⎫   City

COUNTY OF _____ ⎬   or

⎭   Town _____

On the _____ day of _____, 19_____, personally appeared

_____ and _____

known to me to be the individuals who executed the foregoing instrument, and acknowledged the same to be their free act and deed, before me.

(Notary Seal)

_____

Notary Public

CHAPTER 16

DECLARATION OF TRUST
For Naming
ONE PRIMARY BENEFICIARY
And
ONE CONTINGENT BENEFICIARY
To Receive
A MOTOR VEHICLE OR TRAILER HELD IN JOINT NAMES

INSTRUCTIONS:

On the following pages will be found a declaration of trust (DT-138-J) suitable for use in connection with the establishment of an inter vivos trust covering a vehicle held in joint names, where it is desired to name some *one* person as primary beneficiary with some *one* other person as contingent beneficiary to receive the vehicle if the primary beneficiary be not living upon the death of the survivor of the two joint owners.

Enter the names of the two co-owners on the first line.

Cross out *"city"* or *"town,"* leaving the appropriate designation of your community. Next, identify the vehicle (make, model, year, color, registration number).

Enter the names of the beneficiaries in the appropriate place in Paragraph 1.

Note that Paragraph 6 designates as Successor Trustee *"whosoever shall at that time be beneficiary hereunder,"* which means that in most cases you don't need to fill anything in there. However, if there is any possibility of a beneficiary who has not attained the age of 21 years receiving the property, make certain that you name an adult in this paragraph who can act as trustee for such beneficiary. Avoid naming as trustee a person not likely to survive until the beneficiary has attained age 21.

When completed in the manner shown on the reverse side hereof, make one or two photocopies for reference purposes. Hold the original in safekeeping and display a copy to the Motor Vehicle Department or other agency with whom the vehicle is registered when you go there to change the name on the registration to read: *"(your name) and (your co-owner's name), Trustees u/d/t dated _____."*

Important: Read carefully Note B on page 38, which applies to this declaration of trust.

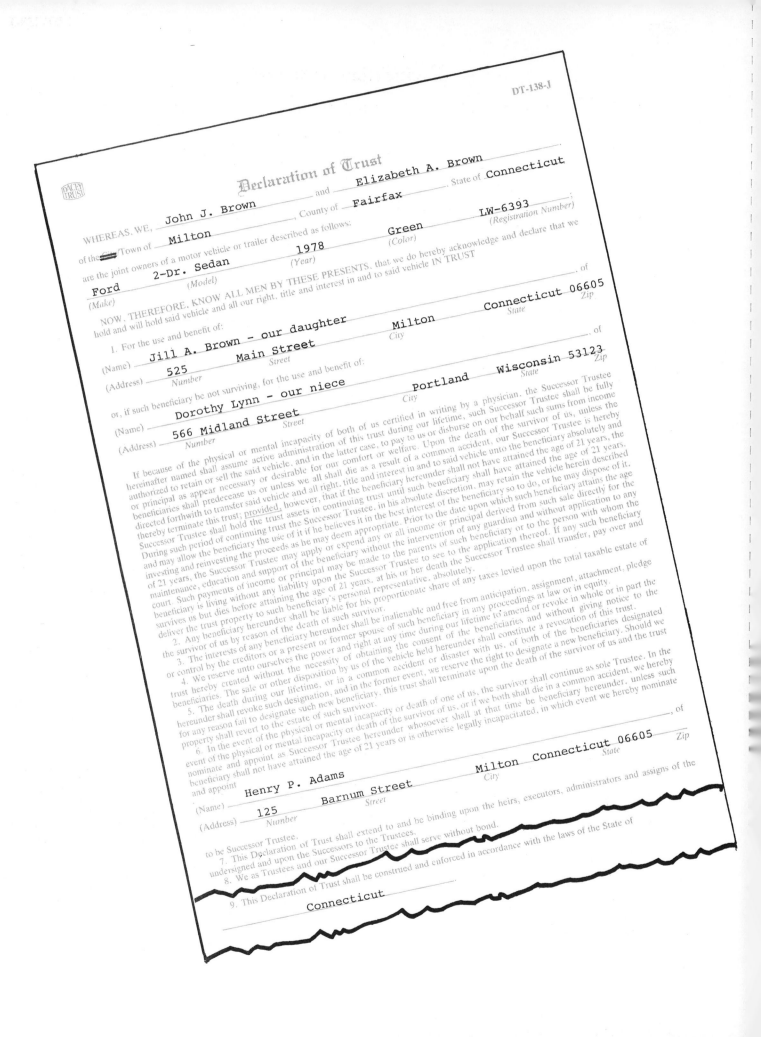

DT-138-J

Declaration of Trust

WHEREAS, WE, __John J. Brown__ and __Elizabeth A. Brown__, State of __Connecticut__, County of __Fairfax__

of the City/Town of __Milton__ are the joint owners of a motor vehicle or trailer described as follows:

__Green__ (Color) __LW-6393__ (Registration Number)

__1978__ (Year)

__2-Dr. Sedan__ (Model)

__Ford__ (Make)

NOW, THEREFORE, KNOW ALL MEN BY THESE PRESENTS, that we do hereby acknowledge and declare that we hold and will hold said vehicle and all our right, title and interest in and to said vehicle IN TRUST

1. For the use and benefit of:

(Name) __Jill A. Brown - our daughter__

(Address) __525__ __Main Street__ __Milton__ __Connecticut 06605__
Number   Street   City   State   Zip

or, if such beneficiary be not surviving, for the use and benefit of:

(Name) __Dorothy Lynn - our niece__ __Portland__ __Wisconsin 53123__
                                     City   State   Zip

(Address) __566 Midland Street__
Number   Street

If because of the physical or mental incapacity of both of us certified in writing by a physician, the Successor Trustee hereinafter named shall assume active administration of this trust during our lifetime, such Successor Trustee shall be fully authorized to retain or sell the said vehicle, and in the latter case, to pay to us or disburse on our behalf such sums from income or principal as appear necessary or desirable for our comfort or welfare. Upon the death of the survivor of us, unless the beneficiaries shall predecease us or unless we all shall die as a result of a common accident, our Successor Trustee is hereby directed forthwith to transfer said vehicle and all right, title and interest in and to said vehicle unto the beneficiary absolutely and thereby terminate this trust; provided, however, that if the beneficiary hereunder shall not have attained the age of 21 years, the Successor Trustee shall hold the trust assets in continuing trust until such beneficiary shall have attained the age of 21 years. During such period of continuing trust the Successor Trustee, in his absolute discretion, may retain the vehicle herein described and may allow the beneficiary the use of it if he believes it in the best interest of the beneficiary so to do, or he may dispose of it, investing and reinvesting the proceeds as he may deem appropriate. Prior to the date upon which such beneficiary attains the age of 21 years, the Successor Trustee may apply or expend any or all income or principal derived from such sale directly for the maintenance, education and support of the beneficiary without the intervention of any guardian and without application to any court. Such payments of income or principal may be made to the parents of such beneficiary or to the person with whom the beneficiary is living without any liability upon the Successor Trustee to see to the application thereof. If any such beneficiary survives us but dies before attaining the age of 21 years, at his or her death the Successor Trustee shall transfer, pay over and deliver the trust property to such beneficiary's personal representative, absolutely.

2. Any beneficiary hereunder shall be liable for his proportionate share of any taxes levied upon the total taxable estate of the survivor of us by reason of the death of such survivor.

3. The interests of any beneficiary hereunder shall be inalienable and free from anticipation, assignment, attachment, pledge or control by the creditors or a present or former spouse of such beneficiary in any proceedings at law or in equity.

4. We reserve unto ourselves the power and right at any time during our lifetime to amend or revoke in whole or in part the trust hereby created without the necessity of obtaining the consent of the beneficiaries and without giving notice to the beneficiaries. The sale or other disposition by us of the vehicle held hereunder shall constitute a revocation of this trust. Should we for any reason fail to designate such new beneficiary, this trust shall terminate upon the death of the survivor of us and the trust property shall revert to the estate of such survivor.

5. The death during our lifetime, or in a common accident or disaster with us, of both of the beneficiaries designated hereunder shall revoke such designation, and in the former event, we reserve the right to designate a new beneficiary.

6. In the event of the physical or mental incapacity or death of one of us, the survivor shall continue as sole Trustee. In the event of the physical or mental incapacity or death of the survivor of us, or if we both shall die in a common accident, we hereby nominate and appoint as Successor Trustee hereunder whosoever shall at that time be beneficiary hereunder, unless such beneficiary shall not have attained the age of 21 years or is otherwise legally incapacitated, in which event we hereby nominate and appoint __Henry P. Adams__ __Milton__ __Connecticut 06605__, of
                                                          City   State   Zip

(Name) __Henry P. Adams__

(Address) __125__ __Barnum Street__
Number   Street

to be Successor Trustee.

7. This Declaration of Trust shall extend to and be binding upon the heirs, executors, administrators and assigns of the undersigned and upon the Successors to the Trustees.

8. We as Trustees and our Successor Trustee shall serve without bond.

9. This Declaration of Trust shall be construed and enforced in accordance with the laws of the State of

__Connecticut__

Declaration of Trust

WHEREAS, WE, _____ and _____,

of the City/Town of _____, County of _____, State of _____,

are the joint owners of a motor vehicle or trailer described as follows:

_____ ;

| *(Make)* | *(Model)* | *(Year)* | *(Color)* | *(Registration Number)* |

NOW, THEREFORE, KNOW ALL MEN BY THESE PRESENTS, that we do hereby acknowledge and declare that we hold and will hold said vehicle and all our right, title and interest in and to said vehicle IN TRUST

 1. For the use and benefit of:

(Name) _____, of

(Address) _____

         Number   *Street*   *City*   *State*   *Zip*

or, if such beneficiary be not surviving, for the use and benefit of:

(Name) _____, of

(Address) _____

         Number   *Street*   *City*   *State*   *Zip*

If because of the physical or mental incapacity of both of us certified in writing by a physician, the Successor Trustee hereinafter named shall assume active administration of this trust during our lifetime, such Successor Trustee shall be fully authorized to retain or sell the said vehicle, and in the latter case, to pay to us or disburse on our behalf such sums from income or principal as appear necessary or desirable for our comfort or welfare. Upon the death of the survivor of us, unless the beneficiaries shall predecease us or unless we all shall die as a result of a common accident, our Successor Trustee is hereby directed forthwith to transfer said vehicle and all right, title and interest in and to said vehicle unto the beneficiary absolutely and thereby terminate this trust; provided, however, that if the beneficiary hereunder shall not have attained the age of 21 years, the Successor Trustee shall hold the trust assets in continuing trust until such beneficiary shall have attained the age of 21 years. During such period of continuing trust the Successor Trustee, in his absolute discretion, may retain the vehicle herein described and may allow the beneficiary the use of it if he believes it in the best interest of the beneficiary so to do, or he may dispose of it, investing and reinvesting the proceeds as he may deem appropriate. Prior to the date upon which such beneficiary attains the age of 21 years, the Successor Trustee may apply or expend any or all income or principal derived from such sale directly for the maintenance, education and support of the beneficiary without the intervention of any guardian and without application to any court. Such payments of income or principal may be made to the parents of such beneficiary or to the person with whom the beneficiary is living without any liability upon the Successor Trustee to see to the application thereof. If any such beneficiary survives us but dies before attaining the age of 21 years, at his or her death the Successor Trustee shall transfer, pay over and deliver the trust property to such beneficiary's personal representative, absolutely.

 2. Any beneficiary hereunder shall be liable for his proportionate share of any taxes levied upon the total taxable estate of the survivor of us by reason of the death of such survivor.

 3. The interests of any beneficiary hereunder shall be inalienable and free from anticipation, assignment, attachment, pledge or control by creditors or a present or former spouse of such beneficiary in any proceedings at law or in equity.

 4. We reserve unto ourselves the power and right at any time during our lifetime to amend or revoke in whole or in part the trust hereby created without the necessity of obtaining the consent of the beneficiaries and without giving notice to the beneficiaries. The sale or other disposition by us of the vehicle held hereunder shall constitute a revocation of this trust.

 5. The death during our lifetime, or in a common accident or disaster with us, of both of the beneficiaries designated hereunder shall revoke such designation, and in the former event, we reserve the right to designate a new beneficiary. Should we for any reason fail to designate such new beneficiary, this trust shall terminate upon the death of the survivor of us and the trust property shall revert to the estate of such survivor.

 6. In the event of the physical or mental incapacity or death of one of us, the survivor shall continue as sole Trustee. In the event of the physical or mental incapacity or death of the survivor of us, or if we both shall die in a common accident, we hereby nominate and appoint as Successor Trustee hereunder whosoever shall at that time be beneficiary hereunder, unless such beneficiary shall not have attained the age of 21 years or is otherwise legally incapacitated, in which event we hereby nominate and appoint

(Name) _____, of

(Address) _____

         Number   *Street*   *City*   *State*   *Zip*

to be Successor Trustee.

7. This Declaration of Trust shall extend to and be binding upon the heirs, executors, administrators and assigns of the undersigned and upon the Successors to the Trustees.

8. We as Trustees and our Successor Trustee shall serve without bond.

9. This Declaration of Trust shall be construed and enforced in accordance with the laws of the State of

_____ .

IN WITNESS WHEREOF, we have hereunto set our hands and seals this _____

day of _____ , 19_____ .

(First Settlor sign here) _____ L.S.

(Second Settlor sign here) _____ L.S.

I, the undersigned legal spouse of one of the above Settlors, hereby waive all community property rights which I may have in the hereinabove-described vehicle and give my assent to the provisions of the trust and to the inclusion in it of the said vehicle.

(Spouse sign here) _____ L.S.

Witness: (1) _____   Witness: (2) _____

STATE OF _____   City

COUNTY OF _____   or
Town _____

On the _____ day of _____ , 19_____ , personally appeared

_____ and _____

known to me to be the individuals who executed the foregoing instrument, and acknowledged the same to be their free act and deed, before me.

(Notary Seal)

_____
Notary Public

CHAPTER 16

DECLARATION OF TRUST
For Naming
TWO OR MORE BENEFICIARIES, SHARING EQUALLY,
To Receive
A MOTOR VEHICLE OR TRAILER HELD IN JOINT NAMES

INSTRUCTIONS:

On the following pages will be found a declaration of trust (DT-139-J) suitable for use in connection with the establishment of an inter vivos trust covering a motor vehicle or trailer held in joint names where it is desired to name two or more persons, sharing equally, to receive the vehicle upon the death of the survivor of the two owners.

Enter the names of the two co-owners on the first line.

Cross out *"city"* or *"town,"* leaving the appropriate designation of your community. Next, identify the vehicle (make, model, year, color, registration number).

In Paragraph 1, indicate the *number of persons* you are naming (to discourage unauthorized additions to the list) and then insert their names. The one whose name appears *first* will be the Successor Trustee responsible for seeing to the distribution of the trust property.

Note that the instrument specifies that the named beneficiaries are to receive *"in equal shares, or the survivor of them/per stirpes."* Now, think carefully: If you have named three persons with the intention that if one of them predeceases you, *his* children will take *his* share, cross out *"or the survivor of them"* and *initial it.* If that is *not* what you want—if, for example, you prefer that the share of the deceased person be divided between the two surviving persons, cross out *"per stirpes"* and *initial it.* Remember, you <u>must</u> cross out either *"or the survivor of them"* or *"per stirpes"*—one or the other.

Note that Paragraph 6 designates as Successor Trustee *"the beneficiary named first above."* Whenever there is a possibility of a beneficiary who has not attained the age of 21 years receiving a share of the trust property, make certain that you name an adult in this paragraph who can act as trustee for such beneficiary. Avoid naming as trustee a person not likely to survive until the beneficiary has attained age 21.

When completed in the manner shown on the reverse side hereof, make one or two photocopies for reference purposes. Hold the original in safekeeping and display a copy to the Motor Vehicle Department or other agency with whom the vehicle is registered when you go there to change the name on the registration to read: *"(your name) and (your co-owner's name), Trustees u/d/t dated _____."*

Important: Read carefully Note B on page 38, which applies to this declaration of trust.

WHEREVER THE INSTRUCTION "INITIAL IT" APPEARS ABOVE,
IT MEANS THAT *BOTH* CO-OWNERS SHOULD INITIAL IT.

DT-139-J

Declaration of Trust

WHEREAS, WE, __John J. Brown__ and __Elizabeth A. Brown__, of the City/Town of __Milton__, County of __Fairfax__, State of __Connecticut__ are the joint owners of a motor vehicle or trailer described as follows:

__Ford__ __2-Dr. Sedan__ __1978__ __Green__ __LW-6393__
(Make)   (Model)   (Year)   (Color)   (Registration Number)

NOW, THEREFORE, KNOW ALL MEN BY THESE PRESENTS, that we do hereby acknowledge and declare that we hold and will hold said vehicle and all our right, title and interest in and to said vehicle IN TRUST   _J.J.B._ _E.A.B_

1. For the use and benefit of the following __three (3)__ persons, in equal shares, /or the survivor of them/ per stirpes:

Thomas B. Brown - our brother
Helen A. Brown - our sister
Charles M. Brown - our brother

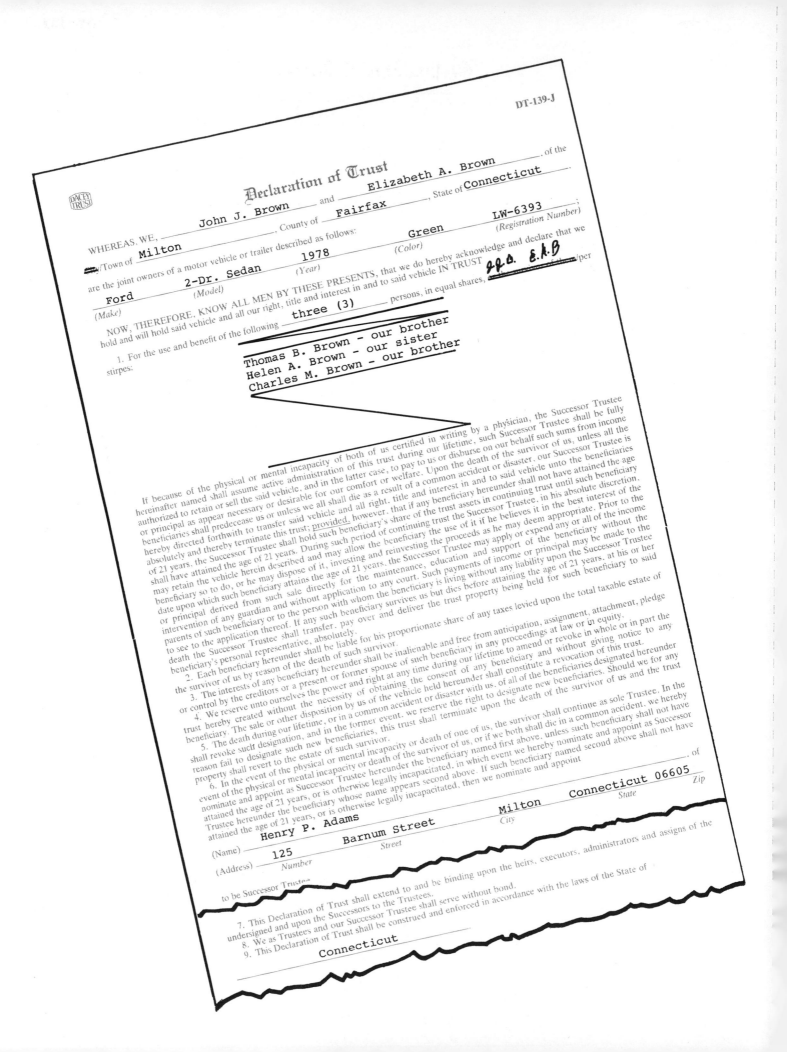

If because of the physical or mental incapacity of both of us certified in writing by a physician, the Successor Trustee hereinafter named shall assume active administration of this trust during our lifetime, such Successor Trustee shall be fully authorized to retain or sell the said vehicle, and in the latter case, to pay to us or disburse on our behalf such sums from income or principal as appear necessary or desirable for our comfort or welfare. Upon the death of the survivor of us, unless all the beneficiaries shall predecease us or unless we all shall die as a result of a common accident or disaster, our Successor Trustee is hereby directed forthwith to transfer said vehicle and all right, title and interest in and to said vehicle unto the beneficiaries absolutely and thereby terminate this trust; provided, however, that if any beneficiary hereunder shall not have attained the age of 21 years, the Successor Trustee shall hold such beneficiary's share of the trust assets in continuing trust until such beneficiary shall have attained the age of 21 years. During such period of continuing trust the Successor Trustee, in his absolute discretion, may retain the vehicle herein described and may allow the beneficiary the use of it if he believes it in the best interest of the beneficiary so to do, or he may dispose of it, investing and reinvesting the proceeds as he may deem appropriate. Prior to the date upon which such beneficiary attains the age of 21 years, the Successor Trustee may apply or expend any or all of the income or principal derived from such sale directly for the maintenance, education and support of the beneficiary without the intervention of any guardian and without application to any court. Such payments of income or principal may be made to the parents of such beneficiary or to the person with whom the beneficiary is living without any liability upon the Successor Trustee to see to the application thereof. If any such beneficiary survives us but dies before attaining the age of 21 years, at his or her death the Successor Trustee shall transfer, pay over and deliver the trust property being held for such beneficiary to said beneficiary's personal representative, absolutely.

2. Each beneficiary hereunder shall be liable for his proportionate share of any taxes levied upon the total taxable estate of the survivor of us by reason of the death of such survivor.

3. The interests of any beneficiary hereunder shall be inalienable and free from anticipation, assignment, attachment, pledge or control by the creditors or a present or former spouse of such beneficiary in any proceedings at law or in equity.

4. We reserve unto ourselves the power and right at any time during our lifetime to amend or revoke in whole or in part the trust hereby created without the necessity of obtaining the consent of any beneficiary and without giving notice to any beneficiary. The sale or other disposition by us of the vehicle held hereunder shall constitute a revocation of this trust.

5. The death during our lifetime, or in a common accident or disaster with us, of all of the beneficiaries designated hereunder shall revoke such designation, and in the former event, we reserve the right to designate new beneficiaries. Should we for any reason fail to designate such new beneficiaries, this trust shall terminate upon the death of the survivor of us and the trust property shall revert to the estate of such survivor.

6. In the event of the physical or mental incapacity or death of one of us, the survivor shall continue as sole Trustee. In the event of the physical or mental incapacity or death of the survivor of us, or if we both shall die in a common accident, we hereby nominate and appoint as Successor Trustee hereunder the beneficiary named first above, unless such beneficiary shall not have attained the age of 21 years, or is otherwise legally incapacitated, in which event we hereby nominate and appoint as Successor Trustee hereunder the beneficiary whose name appears second above. If such beneficiary named second above shall not have attained the age of 21 years, or is otherwise legally incapacitated, then we nominate and appoint

__Henry P. Adams__ , of
(Name)

__125__ __Barnum Street__ __Milton__ __Connecticut__ __06605__
(Address) Number   Street   City   State   Zip

to be Successor Trustee.

This Declaration of Trust shall extend to and be binding upon the heirs, executors, administrators and assigns of the undersigned and upon the Successors to the Trustees.

7. This Declaration of Trust shall extend to and be binding upon the heirs, executors, administrators and assigns of the undersigned and upon the Successors to the Trustees.
8. We as Trustees and our Successor Trustee shall serve without bond.
9. This Declaration of Trust shall be construed and enforced in accordance with the laws of the State of __Connecticut__

Declaration of Trust

WHEREAS, WE, _____ and _____, of the

City/Town of _____, County of _____, State of _____,

are the joint owners of a motor vehicle or trailer described as follows:

_____;

(Make)   (Model)   (Year)   (Color)   (Registration Number)

NOW, THEREFORE, KNOW ALL MEN BY THESE PRESENTS, that we do hereby acknowledge and declare that we hold and will hold said vehicle and all our right, title and interest in and to said vehicle IN TRUST

1. For the use and benefit of the following _____ persons, in equal shares, or the survivor of them/per stirpes:

If because of the physical or mental incapacity of both of us certified in writing by a physician, the Successor Trustee hereinafter named shall assume active administration of this trust during our lifetime, such Successor Trustee shall be fully authorized to retain or sell the said vehicle, and in the latter case, to pay to us or disburse on our behalf such sums from income or principal as appear necessary or desirable for our comfort or welfare. Upon the death of the survivor of us, unless all the beneficiaries shall predecease us or unless we all shall die as a result of a common accident or disaster, our Successor Trustee is hereby directed forthwith to transfer said vehicle and all right, title and interest in and to said vehicle unto the beneficiaries absolutely and thereby terminate this trust; provided, however, that if any beneficiary hereunder shall not have attained the age of 21 years, the Successor Trustee shall hold such beneficiary's share of the trust assets in continuing trust until such beneficiary shall have attained the age of 21 years. During such period of continuing trust the Successor Trustee, in his absolute discretion, may retain the vehicle herein described and may allow the beneficiary the use of it if he believes it in the best interest of the beneficiary so to do, or he may dispose of it, investing and reinvesting the proceeds as he may deem appropriate. Prior to the date upon which such beneficiary attains the age of 21 years, the Successor Trustee may apply or expend any or all of the income or principal derived from such sale directly for the maintenance, education and support of the beneficiary without the intervention of any guardian and without application to any court. Such payments of income or principal may be made to the parents of such beneficiary or to the person with whom the beneficiary is living without any liability upon the Successor Trustee to see to the application thereof. If any such beneficiary survives us but dies before attaining the age of 21 years, at his or her death the Successor Trustee shall transfer, pay over and deliver the trust property being held for such beneficiary to said beneficiary's personal representative, absolutely.

2. Each beneficiary hereunder shall be liable for his proportionate share of any taxes levied upon the total taxable estate of the survivor of us by reason of the death of such survivor.

3. The interests of any beneficiary hereunder shall be inalienable and free from anticipation, assignment, attachment, pledge or control by creditors or a present or former spouse of such beneficiary in any proceedings at law or in equity.

4. We reserve unto ourselves the power and right at any time during our lifetime to amend or revoke in whole or in part the trust hereby created without the necessity of obtaining the consent of any beneficiary and without giving notice to any beneficiary. The sale or other disposition by us of the vehicle held hereunder shall constitute a revocation of this trust.

5. The death during our lifetime, or in a common accident or disaster with us, of all of the beneficiaries designated hereunder shall revoke such designation, and in the former event, we reserve the right to designate new beneficiaries. Should we for any reason fail to designate such new beneficiaries, this trust shall terminate upon the death of the survivor of us and the trust property shall revert to the estate of such survivor.

6. In the event of the physical or mental incapacity or death of one of us, the survivor shall continue as sole Trustee. In the event of the physical or mental incapacity or death of the survivor of us, or if we both shall die in a common accident, we hereby nominate and appoint as Successor Trustee hereunder the beneficiary named first above, unless such beneficiary shall not have attained the age of 21 years, or is otherwise legally incapacitated, in which event we hereby nominate and appoint as Successor Trustee hereunder the beneficiary whose name appears second above. If such beneficiary named second above shall not have attained the age of 21 years, or is otherwise legally incapacitated, then we nominate and appoint

(Name) _____, of

(Address) _____
     Number   Street   City   State   Zip

to be Successor Trustee.

7. This Declaration of Trust shall extend to and be binding upon the heirs, executors, administrators and assigns of the undersigned and upon the Successors to the Trustees.

8. We as Trustees and our Successor Trustee shall serve without bond.

9. This Declaration of Trust shall be construed and enforced in accordance with the laws of the State of

_____.

IN WITNESS WHEREOF, we have hereunto set our hands and seals this _____

day of _____, 19_____.

               (First Settlor sign here) _____ L.S.

           (Second Settlor sign here) _____ L.S.

I, the undersigned legal spouse of one of the above Settlors, hereby waive all community property rights which I may have in the hereinabove-described vehicle, and give my assent to the provisions of the trust and to the inclusion in it of the said vehicle.

              (Spouse sign here) _____ L.S.

Witness: (1) _____   Witness: (2) _____

STATE OF _____   City

COUNTY OF _____   or

                                    Town _____

On the _____ day of _____, 19_____, personally appeared

_____ and _____

known to me to be the individuals who executed the foregoing instrument, and acknowledged the same to be their free act and deed, before me.

(Notary Seal)

_____

Notary Public

Avoiding Probate
of Personal Effects

Many a pitched battle has been fought over who is to inherit Granny's quaint little lace hat—and who is to get her diamond ring. Many families have suffered lasting disaffection among their members because those members could not agree upon a division of the personal effects of someone who had gone. The one best qualified to allocate personal effects, be their value great or small, is the owner. Decide for yourself to whom you wish to leave each significant article of personal property, bearing in mind that the recipient may not attach the same sentimental value to it which you feel for it. If you make the division, no family member will feel that another member has taken unfair advantage but will simply resign himself to the fact that "that's the way Mother (or Dad) wanted it." You may take the blame, but you will have reduced the chances of leaving a disunited family.

On the pages which follow will be found declarations of trust which will serve the dual purpose of (a) providing a means for you to designate the person or persons to receive the articles of personal property, and (b) insuring that such property passes to the named beneficiaries without becoming subject to probate.

You may list any number of articles in one declaration of trust, but if you wish to leave some articles to one particular beneficiary and other articles to some other beneficiary, you will need to use two different forms.

Note: The declarations of trust covering real estate which are to be found in Chapter 7 provide for all personal effects in a house to pass with the house. If your fur coat is not in the house but in cold storage, cover it with one of the declarations in this chapter. If you want most of your things to pass to the beneficiary who is named to receive the house but have certain articles which you wish to leave to some other beneficiary, use one of the forms in this chapter to accomplish this latter purpose.

To eliminate any misunderstandings among beneficiaries, it would be well to supply them with copies of the declarations which apply to them.

CHAPTER 17

DECLARATION OF TRUST

For Naming

ONE BENEFICIARY

To Receive

PERSONAL EFFECTS HELD IN ONE NAME

INSTRUCTIONS:

On the following pages will be found a declaration of trust (DT-141) suitable for use in connection with the establishment of an inter vivos trust covering personal effects where it is desired to name some one person to receive such personal effects upon the death of the owner.

Cross out *"city"* or *"town,"* leaving the appropriate designation of your community. Next, insert a description of the property which is sufficiently detailed to insure its accurate identification. Don't just say "my diamond ring"; if you cannot describe it completely and accurately, take it to a jeweler and ask him to dictate a description of it. Don't just leave someone "a sofa"—it's the "antique Empire sofa upholstered in green velvet which I inherited from my Aunt Elizabeth and which stands in the living room of my home." If it's a painting, identify the artist and describe the subject and the frame and indicate the room in your home where it is to be found. If it is jewelry you're leaving, always indicate where it is to be found.

Enter the name of the beneficiary in the appropriate place in Paragraph 1.

Note that Paragraph 5 designates as Successor Trustee *"whosoever shall at that time be beneficiary hereunder,"* which means that in most cases you don't need to fill anything in there. However, if there is any possibility of a beneficiary who has not attained the age of 21 years receiving the trust property, make certain that you name an adult in this paragraph who can act as trustee for such beneficiary. Avoid naming as trustee a person not likely to survive until the beneficiary has attained age 21.

When completed in the manner shown on the reverse side hereof, make one or two photocopies for reference purposes and give one to the beneficiary. Hold the original in safekeeping.

Important: Read carefully Note B on page 38, which applies to this declaration of trust.

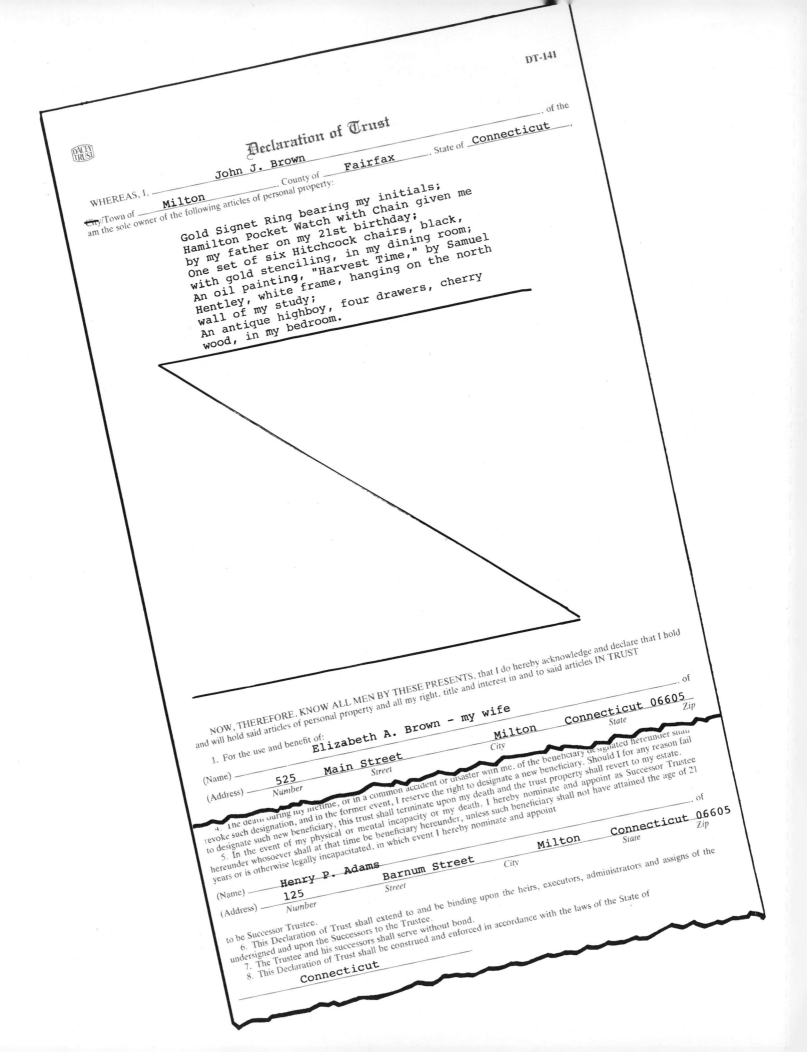

DT-141

Declaration of Trust

WHEREAS, I, **John J. Brown**, County of **Fairfax**, State of **Connecticut**,

City/Town of **Milton**, am the sole owner of the following articles of personal property:

Gold Signet Ring bearing my initials;
Hamilton Pocket Watch with Chain given me
by my father on my 21st birthday;
One set of six Hitchcock chairs, black,
with gold stenciling, in my dining room;
An oil painting, "Harvest Time," by Samuel
Hentley, white frame, hanging on the north
wall of my study;
An antique highboy, four drawers, cherry
wood, in my bedroom.

NOW, THEREFORE, KNOW ALL MEN BY THESE PRESENTS, that I do hereby acknowledge and declare that I hold and will hold said articles of personal property and all my right, title and interest in and to said articles IN TRUST

1. For the use and benefit of: **Elizabeth A. Brown - my wife**, of the

(Name) **Milton**, **Connecticut 06605**
City State Zip

(Address) **525** **Main Street**
Number Street

4. The death during my lifetime, or in a common accident or disaster with me, of the beneficiary designated hereunder shall revoke such designation, and in the former event, I reserve the right to designate a new beneficiary. Should I for any reason fail to designate such new beneficiary, this trust shall terminate upon my death and the trust property shall revert to my estate.

5. In the event of my physical or mental incapacity or my death, I hereby nominate and appoint as Successor Trustee hereunder whosoever shall at that time be beneficiary hereunder, unless such beneficiary shall not have attained the age of 21 years or is otherwise legally incapacitated, in which event I hereby nominate and appoint **Henry P. Adams**, of

(Name) **Milton**, **Connecticut 06605**
City State Zip

(Address) **125** **Barnum Street**
Number Street

to be Successor Trustee.

6. This Declaration of Trust shall extend to and be binding upon the heirs, executors, administrators and assigns of the undersigned and upon the Successors to the Trustee.

7. The Trustee and his successors shall serve without bond.

8. This Declaration of Trust shall be construed and enforced in accordance with the laws of the State of **Connecticut**.

Declaration of Trust

WHEREAS, I, _____, of the

City/Town of _____, County of _____, State of _____,

am the sole owner of the following articles of personal property:

NOW, THEREFORE, KNOW ALL MEN BY THESE PRESENTS, that I do hereby acknowledge and declare that I hold and will hold said articles of personal property and all my right, title and interest in and to said articles IN TRUST

    1. For the use and benefit of:

(Name) _____, of

(Address) _____

| Number | Street | City | State | Zip |

    If because of my physical or mental incapacity certified in writing by a physician, the Successor Trustee hereinafter named shall assume active administration of this trust during my lifetime, such Successor Trustee shall be fully authorized, if the need should arise, to dispose of all or any part of the trust property and to pay to me or disburse on my behalf from the proceeds such sums from income or principal as appear necessary or desirable for my comfort or welfare. Upon my death, unless the beneficiary shall predecease me or unless we both shall die as a result of a common accident, my Successor Trustee is hereby directed forthwith to transfer the trust property and all my right, title and interest in and to said trust property unto the beneficiary absolutely and thereby terminate this trust.

2. All interests of a beneficiary hereunder shall be inalienable and free from anticipation, assignment, attachment, pledge or control by creditors or a present or former spouse of such beneficiary in any proceedings at law or in equity.

3. I reserve unto myself the power and right at any time during my lifetime to amend or revoke in whole or in part the trust hereby created without the necessity of obtaining the consent of the beneficiary and without giving notice to the beneficiary. The sale or other disposition by me of the whole or any part of the trust property held hereunder shall constitute as to such whole or part a revocation of this trust.

4. The death during my lifetime, or in a common accident or disaster with me, of the beneficiary designated hereunder shall revoke such designation, and in the former event, I reserve the right to designate a new beneficiary. Should I for any reason fail to designate such new beneficiary, this trust shall terminate upon my death and the trust property shall revert to my estate.

5. In the event of my physical or mental incapacity or my death, I hereby nominate and appoint as Successor Trustee hereunder whosoever shall at that time be beneficiary hereunder, unless such beneficiary shall not have attained the age of 21 years or is otherwise legally incapacitated, in which event I hereby nominate and appoint

(Name) _____ , of

(Address) _____
　　　　　　　　Number　　　　　　Street　　　　　　　City　　　　　　　State　　　　Zip

to be Successor Trustee.

6. This Declaration of Trust shall extend to and be binding upon the heirs, executors, administrators and assigns of the undersigned and upon the Successors to the Trustee.

7. The Trustee and his successors shall serve without bond.

8. This Declaration of Trust shall be construed and enforced in accordance with the laws of the State of

_____ .

IN WITNESS WHEREOF, I have hereunto set my hand and seal this _____

day of _____ , 19_____ .

(Settlor sign here) _____ L.S.

I, the undersigned legal spouse of the above Settlor, hereby waive all community property rights which I may have in the hereinabove-described personal effects and give my assent to the provisions of the trust and to the inclusion in it of the said personal effects.

(Spouse sign here) _____ L.S.

Witness: (1) _____　　Witness: (2) _____

STATE OF _____　　City

COUNTY OF _____　　or
　　　　　　　　　　　　　　　　　　　　　　Town _____

On the _____ day of _____ , 19_____ , personally appeared

_____

known to me to be the individual(s) who executed the foregoing instrument, and acknowledged the same to be _____ free act and deed, before me.

_____

(Notary Seal)　　　　　　　　　　　　　　　　Notary Public

CHAPTER 17

DECLARATION OF TRUST
For Naming
ONE PRIMARY BENEFICIARY
And
ONE CONTINGENT BENEFICIARY
To Receive
PERSONAL EFFECTS HELD IN ONE NAME

INSTRUCTIONS:

On the following pages will be found a declaration of trust (DT-142) suitable for use in connection with the establishment of an inter vivos trust covering personal effects, where it is desired to name some *one* person as primary beneficiary, with some *one* other person as contingent beneficiary to receive such personal effects if the primary beneficiary be not surviving upon the death of the owner.

Cross out *"city"* or *"town,"* leaving the appropriate designation of your community. Next, insert a description of the property which is sufficiently detailed to insure its accurate identification. Don't just say "my diamond ring"; if you cannot describe it completely and accurately, take it to a jeweler and ask him to dictate a description of it. Don't just leave someone "a sofa"—it's the "antique Empire sofa upholstered in green velvet which I inherited from my Aunt Elizabeth and which stands in the living room of my home." If it's a painting, identify the artist and describe the subject and the frame and indicate the room in your home where it is to be found. If it is jewelry you're leaving, always indicate where it is to be found.

Enter the names of the beneficiaries in the appropriate place in Paragraph 1.

Note that Paragraph 5 designates as Successor Trustee *"whosoever shall at that time be beneficiary hereunder,"* which means that in most cases you don't need to fill anything in there. However, if there is any possibility of a beneficiary who has not attained the age of 21 years receiving the trust property, make certain that you name an adult in this paragraph who can act as trustee for such beneficiary. Avoid naming as trustee a person not likely to survive until the beneficiary has attained age 21.

When completed in the manner shown on the reverse side hereof, make one or two photocopies for reference purposes and to give to the beneficiaries.

Important: Read carefully Note B on page 38, which applies to this declaration of trust.

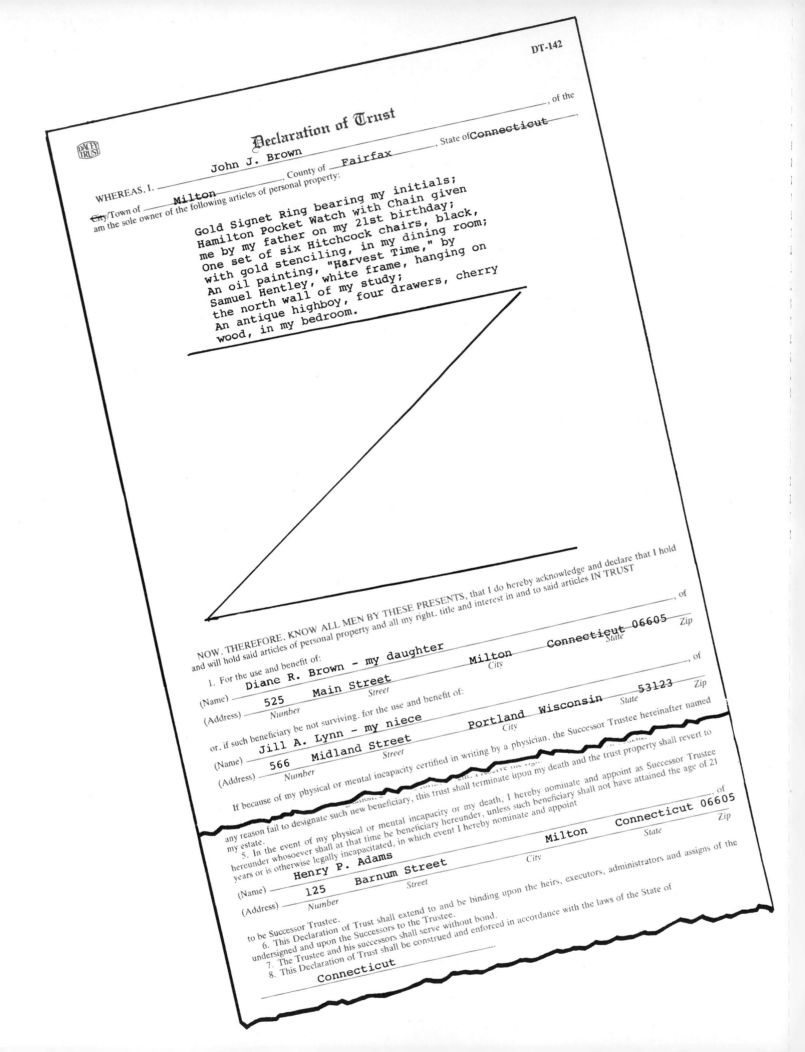

DT-142

Declaration of Trust

WHEREAS. I, **John J. Brown**, of the City/Town of **Milton**, County of **Fairfax**, State of **Connecticut** am the sole owner of the following articles of personal property:

Gold Signet Ring bearing my initials;
Hamilton Pocket Watch with Chain given me by my father on my 21st birthday;
One set of six Hitchcock chairs, black, with gold stenciling, in my dining room;
An oil painting, "Harvest Time," by Samuel Hentley, white frame, hanging on the north wall of my study;
An antique highboy, four drawers, cherry wood, in my bedroom.

NOW. THEREFORE. KNOW ALL MEN BY THESE PRESENTS, that I do hereby acknowledge and declare that I hold and will hold said articles of personal property and all my right. title and interest in and to said articles IN TRUST

1. For the use and benefit of:

(Name) **Diane R. Brown - my daughter**, of **Milton** City **Connecticut** State **06605** Zip

(Address) **525** Number **Main Street** Street

or. if such beneficiary be not surviving. for the use and benefit of:

(Name) **Jill A. Lynn - my niece**, of **Portland** City **Wisconsin** State **53123** Zip

(Address) **566** Number **Midland Street** Street

If because of my physical or mental incapacity certified in writing by a physician. the Successor Trustee hereinafter named

any reason fail to designate such new beneficiary, this trust shall terminate upon my death and the trust property shall revert to my estate.

5. In the event of my physical or mental incapacity or my death; I hereby nominate and appoint as Successor Trustee hereunder whosoever shall at that time be beneficiary hereunder, unless such beneficiary shall not have attained the age of 21 years or is otherwise legally incapacitated, in which event I hereby nominate and appoint

(Name) **Henry P. Adams**, of **Milton** City **Connecticut** State **06605** Zip

(Address) **125** Number **Barnum Street** Street

to be Successor Trustee.

6. This Declaration of Trust shall extend to and be binding upon the heirs, executors, administrators and assigns of the undersigned and upon the Successors to the Trustee.

7. The Trustee and his successors shall serve without bond.

8. This Declaration of Trust shall be construed and enforced in accordance with the laws of the State of

Connecticut

Declaration of Trust

WHEREAS, I, _____, of the

City/Town of _____, County of _____, State of _____,

am the sole owner of the following articles of personal property:

NOW, THEREFORE, KNOW ALL MEN BY THESE PRESENTS, that I do hereby acknowledge and declare that I hold and will hold said articles of personal property and all my right, title and interest in and to said articles IN TRUST

1. For the use and benefit of:

(Name) _____, of

(Address) _____
                 Number   *Street*   *City*   *State*   *Zip*

or, if such beneficiary be not surviving, for the use and benefit of:

(Name) _____, of

(Address) _____
                 Number   *Street*   *City*   *State*   *Zip*

If because of my physical or mental incapacity certified in writing by a physician, the Successor Trustee hereinafter named shall assume active administration of this trust during my lifetime, such Successor Trustee shall be fully authorized, if the need should arise, to dispose of all or any part of the trust property and to pay to me or disburse on my behalf from the proceeds such sums from income or principal as appear necessary or desirable for my comfort or welfare. Upon my death, unless both beneficiaries shall predecease me or unless we all shall die as a result of a common accident, my Successor Trustee is hereby directed forthwith to transfer said trust property and all my right, title and interest in and to said trust property unto the beneficiary absolutely and thereby terminate this trust.

2. All interests of a beneficiary hereunder shall be inalienable and free from anticipation, assignment, attachment, pledge or control by creditors or a present or former spouse of such beneficiary in any proceedings at law or in equity.

3. I reserve unto myself the power and right at any time during my lifetime to amend or revoke in whole or in part the trust hereby created without the necessity of obtaining the consent of any beneficiary and without giving notice to any beneficiary. The sale or other disposition by me of the whole or any part of the trust property held hereunder shall constitute as to such whole or part a revocation of this trust.

4. The death during my lifetime, or in a common accident or disaster with me, of both of the beneficiaries designated hereunder shall revoke such designation, and in the former event, I reserve the right to designate a new beneficiary. Should I for any reason fail to designate such new beneficiary, this trust shall terminate upon my death and the trust property shall revert to my estate.

5. In the event of my physical or mental incapacity or my death, I hereby nominate and appoint as Successor Trustee hereunder whosoever shall at that time be beneficiary hereunder, unless such beneficiary shall not have attained the age of 21 years or is otherwise legally incapacitated, in which event I hereby nominate and appoint

(Name) _____ , of

(Address) _____
  Number   Street   City   State   Zip

to be Successor Trustee.

6. This Declaration of Trust shall extend to and be binding upon the heirs, executors, administrators and assigns of the undersigned and upon the Successors to the Trustee.

7. The Trustee and his successors shall serve without bond.

8. This Declaration of Trust shall be construed and enforced in accordance with the laws of the State of

_____ .

IN WITNESS WHEREOF, I have hereunto set my hand and seal this _____

day of _____ , 19_____ .

(Settlor sign here) _____ L.S.

I, the undersigned legal spouse of the above Settlor, hereby waive all community property rights which I may have in the hereinabove-described personal effects and give my assent to the provisions of the trust and to the inclusion in it of the said personal effects.

(Spouse sign here) _____ L.S.

Witness: (1) _____   Witness: (2) _____

STATE OF _____ ⎫ City
                                                                       ⎬ or
COUNTY OF _____ ⎭ Town _____

On the _____ day of _____ , 19_____ , personally appeared

_____

known to me to be the individual(s) who executed the foregoing instrument, and acknowledged the same to be _____ free act and deed, before me.

_____
(Notary Seal)   Notary Public

CHAPTER 17

DECLARATION OF TRUST
For Naming
TWO OR MORE BENEFICIARIES, SHARING EQUALLY,
To Receive
PERSONAL EFFECTS HELD IN ONE NAME

INSTRUCTIONS:

On the following pages will be found a declaration of trust (DT-143) suitable for use in connection with the establishment of an inter vivos trust covering personal effects where it is desired to name two or more persons to share such personal effects equally upon the death of the owner.

Cross out *"city"* or *"town,"* leaving the appropriate designation of your community. Next, insert a description of the property which is sufficiently detailed to insure its accurate identification. Don't just say "my diamond ring"; if you cannot describe it completely and accurately, take it to a jeweler and ask him to dictate a description of it. Don't just leave someone "a sofa"—it's the "antique Empire sofa upholstered in green velvet which I inherited from my Aunt Elizabeth and which stands in the living room of my home." If it's a painting, identify the artist and describe the subject and the frame and indicate the room in your home where it is to be found. If it is jewelry you're leaving, always indicate where it is to be found.

In Paragraph 1, indicate the *number of persons* you are naming (to discourage unauthorized additions to the list) and then insert their names. The one whose name appears *first* will be the Successor Trustee responsible for seeing to the distribution of the trust property.

Note that the instrument specifies that the named beneficiaries are to receive *"in equal shares, or the survivor of them/per stirpes."* Now, think carefully: If you have named three persons with the understanding that if one of them predeceases you, *his* children will take *his* share, cross out *"or the survivor of them"* and *initial it.* If that is *not* what you want—if, for example, you prefer that the share of the deceased person be divided between the surviving persons, cross out *"per stirpes"* and *initial it.* Remember, you <u>must</u> cross out either *"or the survivor of them"* or *"per stirpes"*—one or the other.

Note that Paragraph 5 designates as Successor Trustee *"the beneficiary named first above."* Whenever there is any possibility of a beneficiary who has not attained the age of 21 years receiving the trust property, make certain that you name an adult in this paragraph who can act as trustee for such beneficiary. Avoid naming as trustee a person not likely to survive until the beneficiary has attained age 21.

When completed in the manner shown on the reverse side hereof, make several photocopies for reference purposes and to give to the beneficiaries. Hold the original in safekeeping.

Important: Read carefully Note B on page 38, which applies to this declaration of trust.

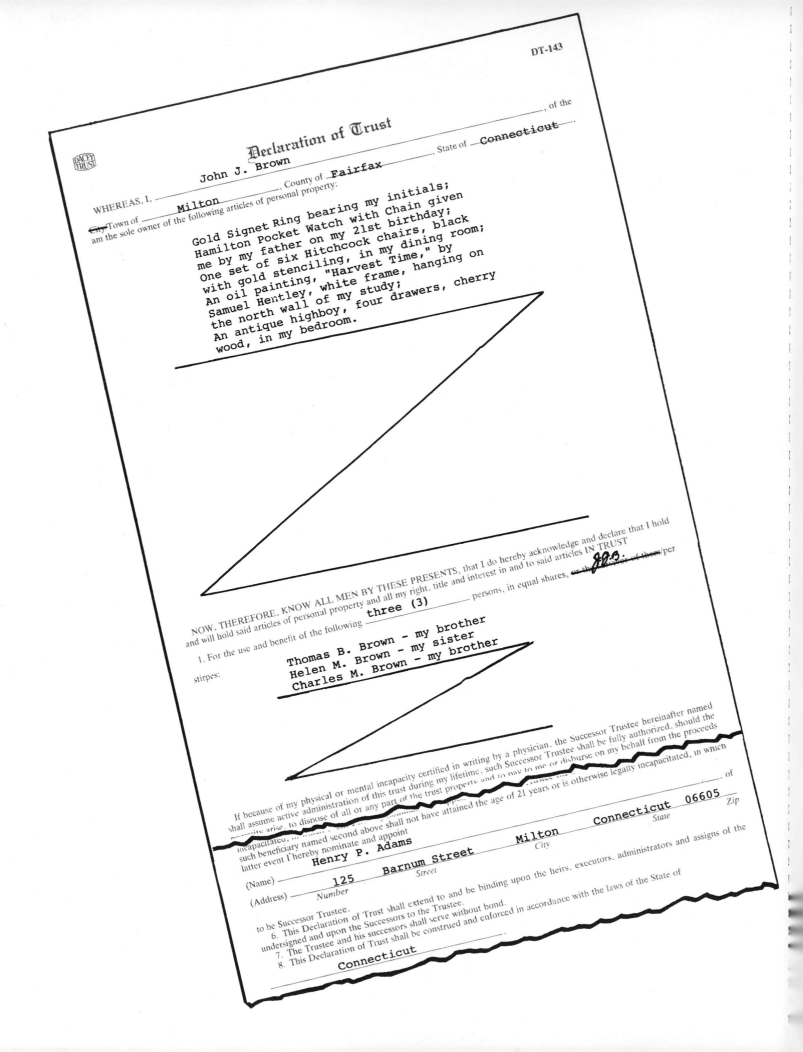

Declaration of Trust

State of **Connecticut**

WHEREAS, I, **John J. Brown**, County of **Fairfax**

City/Town of **Milton**, of the

am the sole owner of the following articles of personal property:

Gold Signet Ring bearing my initials;
Hamilton Pocket Watch with Chain given
me by my father on my 21st birthday;
One set of six Hitchcock chairs, black
with gold stenciling, in my dining room;
An oil painting, "Harvest Time," by
Samuel Hentley, white frame, hanging on
the north wall of my study;
An antique highboy, four drawers, cherry
wood, in my bedroom.

NOW, THEREFORE, KNOW ALL MEN BY THESE PRESENTS, that I do hereby acknowledge and declare that I hold and will hold said articles of personal property and all my right, title and interest in and to said articles IN TRUST

1. For the use and benefit of the following **three (3)** persons, in equal shares, or the survivor of them/per stirpes:

Thomas B. Brown - my brother
Helen M. Brown - my sister
Charles M. Brown - my brother

If because of my physical or mental incapacity certified in writing by a physician, the Successor Trustee hereinafter named shall assume active administration of this trust during my lifetime, such Successor Trustee shall be fully authorized, should the necessity arise, to dispose of all or any part of the trust property and to pay to me or disburse on my behalf from the proceeds incapacitated, ...Trustee the... such beneficiary named second above shall not have attained the age of 21 years or is otherwise legally incapacitated, in which latter event I hereby nominate and appoint

(Name) **Henry P. Adams**

(Address) **125** **Barnum Street** **Milton** **Connecticut** **06605**
Number   Street   City   State   Zip

to be Successor Trustee.

6. This Declaration of Trust shall extend to and be binding upon the heirs, executors, administrators and assigns of the undersigned and upon the Successors to the Trustee.

7. The Trustee and his successors shall serve without bond.

8. This Declaration of Trust shall be construed and enforced in accordance with the laws of the State of **Connecticut**.

Declaration of Trust

WHEREAS, I, _____ , of the

City/Town of _____ , County of _____ , State of _____ ,

am the sole owner of the following articles of personal property:

NOW, THEREFORE, KNOW ALL MEN BY THESE PRESENTS, that I do hereby acknowledge and declare that I hold and will hold said articles of personal property and all my right, title and interest in and to said articles IN TRUST

1. For the use and benefit of the following _____ persons, in equal shares, or the survivor of them/per stirpes:

If because of my physical or mental incapacity certified in writing by a physician, the Successor Trustee hereinafter named shall assume active administration of this trust during my lifetime, such Successor Trustee shall be fully authorized, should the necessity arise, to dispose of all or any part of the trust property and to pay to me or disburse on my behalf from the proceeds such sums from income or principal as appear necessary or desirable for my comfort or welfare. Upon my death, unless all of the beneficiaries shall predecease me or unless we all shall die as a result of a common accident or disaster, my Successor Trustee is hereby directed forthwith to transfer said trust property and all right, title and interest in and to said trust property unto the beneficiaries absolutely and thereby terminate this trust.

2. All interests of a beneficiary hereunder shall be inalienable and free from anticipation, assignment, attachment, pledge or control by creditors or a present or former spouse of such beneficiary in any proceedings at law or in equity.

3. I reserve unto myself the power and right at any time during my lifetime to amend or revoke in whole or in part the trust hereby created without the necessity of obtaining the consent of the beneficiaries and without giving notice to the beneficiaries. The sale or other disposition by me of the whole or any part of the trust property held hereunder shall constitute as to such whole or part a revocation of this trust.

4. The death during my lifetime, or in a common accident or disaster with me, of all of the beneficiaries designated hereunder shall revoke such designation, and in the former event, I reserve the right to designate a new beneficiary. Should I for any reason fail to designate such new beneficiary, this trust shall terminate upon my death and the trust property shall revert to my estate.

5. In the event of my physical or mental incapacity or my death, I hereby nominate and appoint as Successor Trustee the beneficiary named first above, unless such beneficiary shall not have attained the age of 21 years or is otherwise legally incapacitated, in which event I hereby nominate and appoint as Successor Trustee the beneficiary named second above, unless such beneficiary named second above shall not have attained the age of 21 years or is otherwise legally incapacitated, in which latter event I hereby nominate and appoint

(Name) _____, of

(Address) _____
        Number   *Street*   *City*   *State*   *Zip*

to be Successor Trustee.

6. This Declaration of Trust shall extend to and be binding upon the heirs, executors, administrators and assigns of the undersigned and upon the Successors to the Trustee.

7. The Trustee and his successors shall serve without bond.

8. This Declaration of Trust shall be construed and enforced in accordance with the laws of the State of

_____.

IN WITNESS WHEREOF, I have hereunto set my hand and seal this _____

day of _____, 19_____.

        (Settlor sign here) _____ L.S.

I, the undersigned legal spouse of the above Settlor, hereby waive all community property rights which I may have in the hereinabove-described personal effects and give my assent to the provisions of the trust and to the inclusion in it of the said personal effects.

        (Spouse sign here) _____ L.S.

Witness: (1) _____   Witness: (2) _____

STATE OF _____   City

COUNTY OF _____   or Town _____

On the _____ day of _____, 19_____, personally appeared

_____

known to me to be the individual(s) who executed the foregoing instrument, and acknowledged the same to be _____ free act and deed, before me.

_____

(Notary Seal)   *Notary Public*

CHAPTER 17

DECLARATION OF TRUST

For Naming

ONE PRIMARY BENEFICIARY WITH YOUR CHILDREN,

SHARING EQUALLY, AS CONTINGENT BENEFICIARIES

To Receive

PERSONAL EFFECTS HELD IN ONE NAME

INSTRUCTIONS:

On the following pages will be found a declaration of trust (DT-144) suitable for use in connection with the establishment of an inter vivos trust covering personal effects where it is desired to name two or more persons to share such personal effects equally upon the death of the owner.

Cross out *"city"* or *"town,"* leaving the appropriate designation of your community. Next, insert a description of the property which is sufficiently detailed to insure its accurate identification. Don't just say "my diamond ring"; if you cannot describe it completely and accurately, take it to a jeweler and ask him to dictate a description of it. Don't just leave someone "a sofa"—it's the "antique Empire sofa upholstered in green velvet which I inherited from my Aunt Elizabeth and which stands in the living room of my home." If it's a painting, identify the artist and describe the subject and the frame and indicate the room in your home where it is to be found. If it is jewelry you're leaving, always indicate where it is to be found.

In Paragraph 1, indicate the *number of persons* you are naming (to discourage unauthorized additions to the list) and then insert their names. The one whose name appears *first* will be the Successor Trustee responsible for seeing to the distribution of the trust property.

Note that the instrument specifies that the named beneficiaries are to receive *"in equal shares, or the survivor of them/per stirpes."* Now, think carefully: If you have named three persons with the understanding that if one of them predeceases you, *his* children will take *his* share, cross out *"or the survivor of them"* and *initial it.* If that is *not* what you want—if, for example, you prefer that the share of the deceased person be divided between the surviving persons, cross out *"per stirpes"* and *initial it.* Remember, you <u>must</u> cross out either *"or the survivor of them"* or *"per stirpes"*—one or the other.

Note that Paragraph 5 designates as Successor Trustee *"the beneficiary named first above."* Whenever there is any possibility of a beneficiary who has not attained the age of 21 years receiving the trust property, make certain that you name an adult in this paragraph who can act as trustee for such beneficiary. Avoid naming as trustee a person not likely to survive until the beneficiary has attained age 21.

When completed in the manner shown on the reverse side hereof, make several photocopies for reference purposes and to give to the beneficiaries. Hold the original in safekeeping.

Important: Read carefully Note B on page 38, which applies to this declaration of trust.

DT-144

Declaration of Trust

WHEREAS, I, __John J. Brown__, County of __Fairfax__, State of __Connecticut__, of the City/Town of __Milton__

am the sole owner of the following articles of personal property:

Gold Signet Ring bearing my initials;
Hamilton Pocket Watch with Chain given
me by my father on my 21st birthday;
One set of six Hitchcock chairs, black,
with gold stenciling, in my dining room;
An oil painting, "Harvest Time," by
Samuel Hentley, white frame, hanging on
the north wall of my study;
An antique highboy, four drawers, cherry
wood, in my bedroom.

NOW, THEREFORE, KNOW ALL MEN BY THESE PRESENTS, that I do hereby acknowledge and declare that I hold and will hold said articles of personal property and all my right, title and interest in and to said articles IN TRUST

1. For the use and benefit of:

(Name) __Elizabeth M. Brown - my wife__ __Milton__ __Connecticut__ __06605__
City State Zip

(Address) __525__ __Main Street__
Number Street

(hereinafter referred to as the "First Beneficiary"), and upon his or her death prior to the termination of the trust, for the use and benefit of my children, natural and/or adopted, in equal shares, or the survivor of them/per stirpes.

If because of my physical or mental incapacity certified in writing by a physician, the Successor Trustee hereinafter named

5. In the event of my physical or mental incapacity or my death, I hereby nominate and appoint as Successor Trustee hereunder the First Beneficiary, or if such First Beneficiary be not surviving or fails or ceases to act, I nominate and appoint

(Name) __Henry P.Adams__ __Milton__ __Connecticut__ __06605__
City State Zip

(Address) __125__ __Barnum Street__
Number Street

to be Successor Trustee. If such person fails or ceases to act or should I for any reason fail to designate the person above intended to be nominated, then I nominate and appoint as such Successor Trustee hereunder whosoever shall qualify as executor, administrator or guardian, as the case may be, of my estate.

6. This Declaration of Trust shall extend to and be binding upon the heirs, executors, administrators and assigns of the undersigned and upon the Successors to the Trustee.

7. The Trustee and his successors shall serve without bond.

8. This Declaration of Trust shall be construed and enforced in accordance with the laws of the State of __Connecticut__

Declaration of Trust

WHEREAS, I, _____, of the

City/Town of _____, County of _____, State of _____,

am the sole owner of the following articles of personal property:

NOW, THEREFORE, KNOW ALL MEN BY THESE PRESENTS, that I do hereby acknowledge and declare that I hold and will hold said articles of personal property and all my right, title and interest in and to said articles IN TRUST

1. For the use and benefit of:

(Name) _____, of

(Address) _____

| Number | Street | City | State | Zip |

(hereinafter referred to as the "First Beneficiary"), and upon his or her death prior to the termination of the trust, for the use and benefit of my children, natural not/or adopted, in equal shares, or the survivor of them/per stirpes.

If because of my physical or mental incapacity certified in writing by a physician, the Successor Trustee hereinafter named shall assume active administration of this trust during my lifetime, such Successor Trustee shall be fully authorized, if the need arises, to dispose of all or any part of the trust property and to pay to me or disburse on my behalf from the proceeds such sums

sums from income or principal as appear necessary or desirable for my comfort or welfare. Upon my death, unless all of the beneficiaries shall predecease me or unless we all shall die as a result of a common accident or disaster, my Successor Trustee is hereby directed forthwith to transfer said trust property and all my right, title and interest in and to said trust property unto the beneficiary or beneficiaries absolutely and thereby terminate this trust.

2. All interests of a beneficiary hereunder shall be inalienable and free from anticipation, assignment, attachment, pledge or control by creditors or a present or former spouse of such beneficiary in any proceedings at law or in equity.

3. I reserve unto myself the power and right at any time during my lifetime to amend or revoke in whole or in part the trust hereby created without the necessity of obtaining the consent of the beneficiaries and without giving notice to the beneficiaries. The sale or other disposition by me of the whole or any part of the trust property held hereunder shall constitute as to such whole or part a revocation of this trust.

4. The death during my lifetime, or in a common accident or disaster with me, of all of the beneficiaries designated hereunder shall revoke such designation, and in the former event, I reserve the right to designate a new beneficiary. Should I for any reason fail to designate such new beneficiary, this trust shall terminate upon my death and the trust property shall revert to my estate.

5. In the event of my physical or mental incapacity or my death, I hereby nominate and appoint as Successor Trustee hereunder the First Beneficiary, or if such First Beneficiary be not surviving or fails or ceases to act, I nominate and appoint

(Name) _____ , of

(Address) _____
          Number   *Street*   *City*   *State*   *Zip*

to be Successor Trustee. If such person fails or ceases to act or should I for any reason fail to designate the person above intended to be nominated, then I nominate and appoint as such Successor Trustee hereunder whosoever shall qualify as executor, administrator or guardian, as the case may be, of my estate.

6. This Declaration of Trust shall extend to and be binding upon the heirs, executors, administrators and assigns of the undersigned and upon the Successors to the Trustee.

7. The Trustee and his successors shall serve without bond.

8. This Declaration of Trust shall be construed and enforced in accordance with the laws of the State of

_____ .

IN WITNESS WHEREOF, I have hereunto set my hand and seal this _____

day of _____ , 19_____.

(Settlor sign here) _____ L.S.

I, the undersigned legal spouse of the above Settlor, hereby waive all community property rights which I may have in the hereinabove-described personal effects and give my assent to the provisions of the trust and to the inclusion in it of the said personal effects.

(Spouse sign here) _____ L.S.

Witness: (1) _____   Witness: (2) _____

STATE OF _____   City

COUNTY OF _____   or
                                       Town _____

On the _____ day of _____ , 19_____, personally appeared

_____

known to me to be the individual(s) who executed the foregoing instrument, and acknowledged the same to be _____ free act and deed, before me.

_____

(Notary Seal)   *Notary Public*

Avoiding Probate of
an Unincorporated Business

Helen Woodruff, a widow, is the owner of a small but successful shop selling greeting cards and giftwares.

Although her friend, Martha McEwan, owns no part of the business, she has been a faithful assistant to Mrs. Woodruff in its operation over the years, carrying on efficiently when the proprietress was hospitalized once or twice and during her annual vacations. By any standards, the business is a modest one but it has provided the two ladies with a dignified, comfortable living for more than a decade.

Such an enterprise has very little sale value upon the death of the owner, a fact which Helen Woodruff well recognizes. Liquidation of the business as a part of her estate would be a sad affair, with the stock going for ten cents on the dollar. Besides not wanting to see her little business come to such a dreary end, she feels a certain obligation to her loyal employee, Miss McEwan, whose age would probably preclude her finding other work.

In a word, Helen Woodruff wants to retain complete ownership and control of the business during her lifetime, but upon her death she wants it to go to Martha McEwan with no strings attached, for she realizes that her friend could never raise any appreciable sum of money to buy it from the estate.

If she leaves it to Miss McEwan in her will, the inevitable delays of the probate procedure may dry up the flow of funds needed for everyday operation of the shop, thus interfering with the successful transition of the business to the new owner.

The answer, of course, is for Helen Woodruff to create an inter vivos trust for the benefit of Martha McEwan. The trust is revocable—if Miss McEwan should predecease her friend, or in the unlikely circumstance of their having an irreparable falling out, Mrs. Woodruff can name a different beneficiary or cancel the trust entirely.

Heinz Hersholt and his wife, Hilda, operate a thriving delicatessen in a midwest city. It's a family business; a son and daughter help them in the store. Heinz and Hilda will operate the store as long as either or both of them live, then they want it to go to the children. Here the answer is a joint inter vivos trust with the children named as beneficiaries to share equally.

All over America there are to be found endless variations of these situations involving the fate of small businesses operated as proprietorships or co-proprietorships. In some instances, a loyal employee or co-worker is the likely beneficiary. In other cases, the owner may simply choose to pass the business on to a relative. These suggested situations are intended merely to be illustrative of the point that through the use of an inter vivos trust, an unincorporated business or proprietorship may be passed on to another person without the delay, expense, and publicity of probate.

On the following pages will be found declarations of trust which will provide for a variety of such situations.

Note: Where a bank account is maintained in the name of the business, it is not necessary to cover it with a separate trust instrument. The business owns the bank account and "whoever owns the cow, owns the milk."

CHAPTER 18

DECLARATION OF TRUST
For Naming
ONE BENEFICIARY
To Receive
AN UNINCORPORATED BUSINESS HELD IN ONE NAME

INSTRUCTIONS:

On the following pages will be found a declaration of trust (DT-145) suitable for use in connection with the establishment of an inter vivos trust covering an unincorporated business held in one name only, where it is desired to name some one person to receive the business upon the death of the owner.

Cross out *"city"* or *"town,"* leaving the appropriate designation of your community. Next, give the name and location and explain exactly what kind of business it is.

Enter the name of the beneficiary in the appropriate place in Paragraph 1.

Note that Paragraph 8 designates as Successor Trustee *"whosoever shall at that time be beneficiary hereunder,"* which means that in most cases you don't need to fill anything in there. However, if there is any possibility of a beneficiary who has not attained the age of 21 years receiving the trust property, make certain that you name an adult in this paragraph who can act as trustee for such beneficiary. Avoid naming as trustee a person not likely to survive until the beneficiary has attained age 21.

When completed in the manner shown on the reverse side hereof, make several photocopies for reference purposes. Hold the original in safekeeping and offer a copy to the bank where your business account is maintained.

Important: Read carefully Note B on page 38, which applies to this declaration of trust.

Declaration of Trust

DACEY TRUST

DT-145

WHEREAS, I, __Elizabeth A. Brown__, County of __Fairfax__, State of __Connecticut__, of the

City/Town of __Milton__

am the sole owner of the unincorporated business known as __The Fairport Gift Shoppe__,
(Name of Business)

located at __120 Main Street__, in the City/Town of __Milton__; and

County of __Fairfax__, and State of __Connecticut__

WHEREAS, the principal business of the said __The Fairport Gift Shoppe__
(Name of Business)

is __the retail sale of greeting cards and giftware.__

NOW, THEREFORE, KNOW ALL MEN BY THESE PRESENTS, that I do hereby acknowledge and declare that I hold and will hold said business and all my right, title and interest in and to said business and all furniture, fixtures, stock in trade, inventory, machinery, vehicles, accounts receivable, prepaid insurance and all other assets of such business IN TRUST

1. For the use and benefit of:

__Diane R. Brown — my daughter__

(Name)

__525   Main Street   Milton   Connecticut   06605__
(Address)   Number   Street   City   State   Zip

If because of my physical or mental incapacity certified in writing by a physician, the Successor Trustee hereinafter named shall assume active administration of this trust during my lifetime, such Successor Trustee shall be fully authorized to pay to me or disburse on my behalf such sums from income or principal as appear necessary or desirable for my comfort or welfare. Upon my death, unless the beneficiary shall predecease me or unless we both shall die as a result of a common accident or disaster, my Successor Trustee is hereby directed forthwith to transfer said business and all my right, title and interest in and to said business unto the beneficiary absolutely and thereby terminate this trust; provided, however, that if the beneficiary hereunder shall not have attained the age of 21 years, the Successor Trustee shall hold the trust assets in continuing trust until such beneficiary shall have attained the age of 21 years. During such period of continuing trust the Successor Trustee, in his absolute discretion, may retain the business herein described if he believes it to be in the best interests of the beneficiary so to do, or he may dispose of it, investing and reinvesting the proceeds as he may deem appropriate. Prior to the date upon which such beneficiary attains the age of 21 years, the Successor Trustee may apply or expend any or all of the income or principal directly for the maintenance, education and support of the beneficiary without the intervention of any guardian and without application to any court. Such payments of income or principal may be made to the parents of such beneficiary or to the person with whom the beneficiary is living without any liability upon the Successor Trustee to see to the application thereof. If such beneficiary survives me but dies before attaining the age of 21 years, at his or her death the Successor Trustee shall transfer, pay over and deliver the trust property to such beneficiary's personal representative, absolutely.

2. The beneficiary hereunder shall be liable for his proportionate share of any taxes levied upon the Settlor's total taxable estate by reason of the Settlor's death.

3. All interests of a beneficiary hereunder shall be inalienable and free from anticipation, assignment, attachment, pledge or control by creditors or a present or former spouse of such beneficiary in any proceedings at law or in equity.

4. This trust is created with the express understanding that the bank at which an account is maintained in the name of the business shall be under no liability whatsoever to see to such trust's proper administration. On the contrary, upon the transfer of the right, title and interest in and to the business by any trustee hereunder, said bank shall conclusively treat the transferee as the sole owner of said account. Until the bank shall receive from some person interested in this trust, written notice of any death or other event upon which the right to receive may depend, the bank shall incur no liability for payments made in good faith to persons whose interests shall have been affected by such event. The bank shall be protected in acting upon any notice or other instrument or document believed by it to be genuine and to have been signed or presented by the proper party or parties.

5. I reserve unto myself as an individual, I shall be exclusively entitled to all such income accruing from the trust property and to pay such income to myself as an individual. I shall be exclusively entitled to all such income which may accrue from the trust property during my lifetime, and no beneficiary named herein shall have any claim upon any such income distributed to me.

6. I reserve unto myself the power and right at any time during my lifetime to amend or revoke in whole or in part the trust hereby created without the necessity of obtaining the consent of the beneficiary and without giving notice to the beneficiary. The sale or other disposition by me of the whole or any part of the assets of the business held hereunder shall constitute as to such whole or part a revocation of this trust.

8. In the event of my physical or mental incapacity or my death, I hereby nominate and appoint as Successor Trustee hereunder whosoever shall at that time be beneficiary hereunder, unless such beneficiary shall not have attained the age of 21 years or is otherwise legally incapacitated, in which event I hereby nominate and appoint

__Henry P. Adams__

(Name)

__125   Barnum Street   Milton   Connecticut   06605__
(Address)   Number   Street   City   State   Zip
, of

to be Successor Trustee.

9. This Declaration of Trust shall extend to and be binding upon the heirs, executors, administrators and assigns of the undersigned and upon the Successors to the Trustee.

10. The Trustee and his successors shall serve without bond.

11. This Declaration of Trust shall be construed and enforced in accordance with the laws of the State of __Connecticut__

Declaration of Trust

WHEREAS, I, _____, of the

City/Town of _____, County of _____, State of _____,

am the sole owner of the unincorporated business known as _____

_____
(Name of Business)

located at _____, in the City/Town of _____,

County of _____ and State of _____; and

WHEREAS, the principal business of the said _____
(Name of Business)

is _____

_____

_____ ;

NOW, THEREFORE, KNOW ALL MEN BY THESE PRESENTS, that I do hereby acknowledge and declare that I hold and will hold said business and all my right, title and interest in and to said business and all furniture, fixtures, stock in trade, inventory, machinery, vehicles, accounts receivable, prepaid insurance and all other assets of such business IN TRUST

1. For the use and benefit of:

(Name) _____, of

(Address) _____
        Number   Street   City   State   Zip

If because of my physical or mental incapacity certified in writing by a physician, the Successor Trustee hereinafter named shall assume active administration of this trust during my lifetime, such Successor Trustee shall be fully authorized to pay to me or disburse on my behalf such sums from income or principal as appear necessary or desirable for my comfort or welfare. Upon my death, unless the beneficiary shall predecease me or unless we both shall die as a result of a common accident or disaster, my Successor Trustee is hereby directed forthwith to transfer said business and all my right, title and interest in and to said business unto the beneficiary absolutely and thereby terminate this trust; provided, however, that if the beneficiary hereunder shall not have attained the age of 21 years, the Successor Trustee shall hold the trust assets in continuing trust until such beneficiary shall have attained the age of 21 years. During such period of continuing trust the Successor Trustee, in his absolute discretion, may retain the business herein described if he believes it to be in the best interests of the beneficiary so to do, or he may dispose of it, investing and reinvesting the proceeds as he may deem appropriate. Prior to the date upon which such beneficiary attains the age of 21 years, the Successor Trustee may apply or expend any or all of the income or principal directly for the maintenance, education and support of the beneficiary without the intervention of any guardian and without application to any court. Such payments of income or principal may be made to the parents of such beneficiary or to the person with whom the beneficiary is living without any liability upon the Successor Trustee to see to the application thereof. If such beneficiary survives me but dies before attaining the age of 21 years, at his or her death the Successor Trustee shall transfer, pay over and deliver the trust property to such beneficiary's personal representative, absolutely.

2. The beneficiary hereunder shall be liable for his proportionate share of any taxes levied upon the Settlor's total taxable estate by reason of the Settlor's death.

3. All interests of a beneficiary hereunder shall be inalienable and free from anticipation, assignment, attachment, pledge or control by creditors or a present or former spouse of such beneficiary in any proceedings at law or in equity.

4. This trust is created with the express understanding that the bank at which an account is maintained in the name of the business shall be under no liability whatsoever to see to such trust's proper administration. On the contrary, upon the transfer of the right, title and interest in and to the business by any trustee hereunder, said bank shall conclusively treat the transferee as the sole owner of said account. Until the bank shall receive from some person interested in this trust, written notice of any death or other event upon which the right to receive may depend, the bank shall incur no liability for payments made in good faith to persons whose interests shall have been affected by such event. The bank shall be protected in acting upon any notice or other instrument or document believed by it to be genuine and to have been signed or presented by the proper party or parties.

5. I reserve unto myself the power and right to collect all income which may accrue from the trust property and to pay such income to myself as an individual. I shall be exclusively entitled to all such income accruing from the trust property during my lifetime, and no beneficiary named herein shall have any claim upon any such income distributed to me.

6. I reserve unto myself the power and right at any time during my lifetime to amend or revoke in whole or in part the trust hereby created without the necessity of obtaining the consent of the beneficiary and without giving notice to the beneficiary. The sale or other disposition by me of the whole or any part of the assets of the business held hereunder shall constitute as to such whole or part a revocation of this trust.

7. The death during my lifetime, or in a common accident with me, of the beneficiary designated hereunder shall revoke such designation, and in the former event, I reserve the right to designate a new beneficiary. Should I for any reason fail to designate such new beneficiary, this trust shall terminate upon my death and the trust property shall revert to my estate.

8. In the event of my physical or mental incapacity or my death, I hereby nominate and appoint as Successor Trustee hereunder whosoever shall at that time be beneficiary hereunder, unless such beneficiary shall not have attained the age of 21 years or is otherwise legally incapacitated, in which event I hereby nominate and appoint

(Name) _____ , of

(Address) _____
              Number   *Street*   *City*   *State*   *Zip*

to be Successor Trustee.

9. This Declaration of Trust shall extend to and be binding upon the heirs, executors, administrators and assigns of the undersigned and upon the Successors to the Trustee.

10. The Trustee and his successors shall serve without bond.

11. This Declaration of Trust shall be construed and enforced in accordance with the laws of the State of

_____ .

IN WITNESS WHEREOF, I have hereunto set my hand and seal this _____

day of _____ , 19_____ .

          (Settlor sign here) _____ L.S.

I, the undersigned legal spouse of the above Settlor, hereby waive all community property rights which I may have in the hereinabove-described business and give my assent to the provisions of the trust and to the inclusion in it of the said business.

          (Spouse sign here) _____ L.S.

Witness: (1) _____   Witness: (2) _____

STATE OF _____ }   City

COUNTY OF _____ }   or Town _____

On the _____ day of _____ , 19_____ , personally appeared

_____

known to me to be the individual(s) who executed the foregoing instrument, and acknowledged the same to be _____ free act and deed, before me.

_____

  (Notary Seal)   *Notary Public*

CHAPTER 18

DECLARATION OF TRUST

For Naming

ONE PRIMARY BENEFICIARY

And

ONE CONTINGENT BENEFICIARY

To Receive

AN UNINCORPORATED BUSINESS HELD IN ONE NAME

INSTRUCTIONS:

On the following pages will be found a declaration of trust (DT-146) suitable for use in connection with the establishment of an inter vivos trust covering an unincorporated business held in one name only, where it is desired to name some *one* person as primary beneficiary, with some *one* other person as contingent beneficiary to receive the business if the primary beneficiary be not surviving upon the death of the owner.

Cross out *"city"* or *"town,"* leaving the appropriate designation of your community. Next, give the name and location and explain exactly what kind of business it is.

Enter the names of the beneficiaries in the appropriate place in Paragraph 1.

Note that Paragraph 8 designates as Successor Trustee *"whosoever shall at that time be beneficiary hereunder,"* which means that in most cases you don't need to fill anything in there. However, if there is any possibility of a beneficiary who has not attained the age of 21 years receiving the trust property, make certain that you name an adult in this paragraph who can act as trustee for such beneficiary. Avoid naming as trustee a person not likely to survive until the beneficiary has attained age 21.

When completed in the manner shown on the reverse side hereof, make several photocopies for reference purposes. Hold the original in safekeeping and offer a copy to the bank where your business account is maintained.

Important: Read carefully Note B on page 38, which applies to this declaration of trust.

Declaration of Trust

WHEREAS, I, __Elizabeth A. Brown__, County of __Fairfax__, State of __Connecticut__, of the
City/Town of __Milton__ am the sole owner of the unincorporated business known as __The Fairport Gift Shoppe__

(Name of Business)

located at __120 Main Street__, in the City/Town of __Milton__; and

County of __Fairfax__ and State of __Connecticut__

WHEREAS, the principal business of the said __The Fairport Gift Shoppe__

(Name of Business)

is __the retail sale of greeting cards and giftware.__

NOW, THEREFORE, KNOW ALL MEN BY THESE PRESENTS, that I do hereby acknowledge and declare that I hold and will hold said business and all my right, title and interest in and to said business and all furniture, fixtures, stock in trade, inventory, machinery, vehicles, accounts receivable, prepaid insurance and all other assets of such business IN TRUST

1. For the use and benefit of:

(Name) __Diane R. Brown - my daughter__, of __Milton__ __Connecticut__ __06605__
City _State_ _Zip_

(Address) __525__ __Main Street__
Number _Street_

or, if such beneficiary be not surviving, for the use and benefit of:

(Name) __Jill A. Lynn - my niece__, of __Portland__ __Wisconsin__ __53123__
City _State_ _Zip_

(Address) __566__ __Midland Street__
Number _Street_

If because of my physical or mental incapacity certified in writing by a physician, the Successor Trustee hereinafter named shall assume active administration of this trust during my lifetime, such Successor Trustee shall be fully authorized to pay to me or disburse on my behalf such sums from income or principal as appear necessary or desirable for my comfort or welfare. Upon my death, unless both beneficiaries shall predecease me or unless we all shall die as a result of a common accident or disaster, my Successor Trustee is hereby directed forthwith to transfer said business and all my right, title and interest in and to said business unto the beneficiary absolutely and thereby terminate this trust; _provided_, however, that if the beneficiary hereunder shall not have attained the age of 21 years, the Successor Trustee shall hold the trust assets in continuing trust until such beneficiary shall have attained the age of 21 years. During such period of continuing trust the Successor Trustee, in his absolute discretion, may retain the business herein described if he believes it to be in the best interests of the beneficiary so to do, or he may dispose of it, investing and reinvesting the proceeds as he may deem appropriate. Prior to the date upon which such beneficiary attains the age of 21 years, the Successor Trustee may apply or expend any or all of the income or principal directly for the maintenance, education and support of the beneficiary without the intervention of any guardian and without application to any court. Such payments of income or principal may be made to the parents of such beneficiary or to the person with whom the beneficiary is living without any liability upon the Successor Trustee to see to the application thereof. If such beneficiary survives me but dies before attaining the age of 21 years, at his or her death the Successor Trustee shall transfer, pay over and deliver the trust property being held for such beneficiary to such beneficiary's personal representative, absolutely.

2. The beneficiary hereunder shall be inalienable and free from anticipation, assignment, attachment, pledge or control by creditors or a present or former spouse of such beneficiary in any proceedings at law or in equity.

3. All interests of a beneficiary hereunder shall be the Settlor's total taxable estate by reason of the Settlor's death.

4. This trust is created with the express understanding that the bank at which an account is maintained in the name of the

hereby created without the necessity of obtaining the consent of any beneficiary and without giving notice to any beneficiary. The sale or other disposition by me of the whole or any part of the assets of the business held hereunder shall constitute as to such whole or part a revocation of this trust.

7. The death during my lifetime, or in a common accident or disaster with me, of both of the beneficiaries designated hereunder shall revoke such designation, and in the former event, I reserve the right to designate a new beneficiary. Should I for any reason fail to designate such new beneficiary, this trust shall terminate upon my death and the trust property shall revert to my estate.

8. In the event of my physical or mental incapacity or my death, I hereby nominate and appoint as Successor Trustee hereunder whosoever shall at that time be beneficiary hereunder, unless such beneficiary shall not have attained the age of 21 years or is otherwise legally incapacitated, in which event I hereby nominate and appoint

(Name) __Henry P. Adams__, of __Milton__ __Connecticut__ __06605__
City _State_ _Zip_

(Address) __125__ __Barnum Street__
Number _Street_

to be Successor Trustee.

9. This Declaration of Trust shall extend to and be binding upon the heirs, executors, administrators and assigns of the undersigned and upon the Successors to the Trustee.

10. The Trustee and his successors shall serve without bond.

11. This Declaration of Trust shall be construed and enforced in accordance with the laws of the State of __Connecticut__

Declaration of Trust

WHEREAS, I, _____, of the

City/Town of _____, County of _____, State of _____,

am the sole owner of the unincorporated business known as _____

_____
(Name of Business)

located at _____, in the City/Town of _____,

County of _____ and State of _____; and

WHEREAS, the principal business of the said _____
(Name of Business)

is _____

_____

_____;

NOW, THEREFORE, KNOW ALL MEN BY THESE PRESENTS, that I do hereby acknowledge and declare that I hold and will hold said business and all my right, title and interest in and to said business and all furniture, fixtures, stock in trade, inventory, machinery, vehicles, accounts receivable, prepaid insurance and all other assets of such business IN TRUST

1. For the use and benefit of:

(Name) _____, of

(Address) _____

| Number | Street | City | State | Zip |

or, if such beneficiary be not surviving, for the use and benefit of:

(Name) _____, of

(Address) _____

| Number | Street | City | State | Zip |

If because of my physical or mental incapacity certified in writing by a physician, the Successor Trustee hereinafter named shall assume active administration of this trust during my lifetime, such Successor Trustee shall be fully authorized to pay to me or disburse on my behalf such sums from income or principal as appear necessary or desirable for my comfort or welfare. Upon my death, unless both beneficiaries shall predecease me or unless we all shall die as a result of a common accident or disaster, my Successor Trustee is hereby directed forthwith to transfer said business and all my right, title and interest in and to said business unto the beneficiary absolutely and thereby terminate this trust; provided, however, that if the beneficiary hereunder shall not have attained the age of 21 years, the Successor Trustee shall hold the trust assets in continuing trust until such beneficiary shall have attained the age of 21 years. During such period of continuing trust the Successor Trustee, in his absolute discretion, may retain the business herein described if he believes it to be in the best interests of the beneficiary so to do, or he may dispose of it, investing and reinvesting the proceeds as he may deem appropriate. Prior to the date upon which such beneficiary attains the age of 21 years, the Successor Trustee may apply or expend any or all of the income or principal directly for the maintenance, education and support of the beneficiary without the intervention of any guardian and without application to any court. Such payments of income or principal may be made to the parents of such beneficiary or to the person with whom the beneficiary is living without any liability upon the Successor Trustee to see to the application thereof. If such beneficiary survives me but dies before attaining the age of 21 years, at his or her death the Successor Trustee shall transfer, pay over and deliver the trust property being held for such beneficiary to such beneficiary's personal representative, absolutely.

2. The beneficiary hereunder shall be liable for his proportionate share of any taxes levied upon the Settlor's total taxable estate by reason of the Settlor's death.

3. All interests of a beneficiary hereunder shall be inalienable and free from anticipation, assignment, attachment, pledge or control by creditors or a present or former spouse of such beneficiary in any proceedings at law or in equity.

4. This trust is created with the express understanding that the bank at which an account is maintained in the name of the business shall be under no liability whatsoever to see to such trust's proper administration. On the contrary, upon the transfer of the right, title and interest in and to such business by any trustee hereunder, said bank shall conclusively treat the transferee as the sole owner of said account. Until the bank shall receive from some person interested in this trust, written notice of any death or other event upon which the right to receive may depend, the bank shall incur no liability for payments made in good faith to persons whose interests shall have been affected by such event. The bank shall be protected in acting upon any notice or other instrument or document believed by it to be genuine and to have been signed or presented by the proper party or parties.

5. I reserve unto myself the power and right to collect all income which may accrue from the trust property and to pay such income to myself as an individual. I shall be exclusively entitled to all such income accruing from the trust property during my lifetime and no beneficiary named herein shall have any claim upon any such income distributed to me.

6. I reserve unto myself the power and right at any time during my lifetime to amend or revoke in whole or in part the trust hereby created without the necessity of obtaining the consent of any beneficiary and without giving notice to any beneficiary. The sale or other disposition by me of the whole or any part of the assets of the business held hereunder shall constitute as to such whole or part a revocation of this trust.

7. The death during my lifetime, or in a common accident or disaster with me, of both of the beneficiaries designated hereunder shall revoke such designation, and in the former event, I reserve the right to designate a new beneficiary. Should I for any reason fail to designate such new beneficiary, this trust shall terminate upon my death and the trust property shall revert to my estate.

8. In the event of my physical or mental incapacity or my death, I hereby nominate and appoint as Successor Trustee hereunder whosoever shall at that time be beneficiary hereunder, unless such beneficiary shall not have attained the age of 21 years or is otherwise legally incapacitated, in which event I hereby nominate and appoint

(Name) _____, of

(Address) _____

      Number   *Street*   *City*   *State*   *Zip*

to be Successor Trustee.

9. This Declaration of Trust shall extend to and be binding upon the heirs, executors, administrators and assigns of the undersigned and upon the Successors to the Trustee.

10. The Trustee and his successors shall serve without bond.

11. This Declaration of Trust shall be construed and enforced in accordance with the laws of the State of

_____.

IN WITNESS WHEREOF, I have hereunto set my hand and seal this _____

day of _____, 19_____.

           (Settlor sign here) _____ L.S.

I, the undersigned legal spouse of the above Settlor, hereby waive all community property rights which I may have in the hereinabove-described business and give my assent to the provisions of the trust and to the inclusion in it of the said business.

           (Spouse sign here) _____ L.S.

Witness: (1) _____   Witness: (2) _____

STATE OF _____   } City

COUNTY OF _____   } or

                                   Town _____

On the _____ day of _____, 19_____, personally appeared

_____

known to me to be the individual(s) who executed the foregoing instrument, and acknowledged the same to be _____ free act and deed, before me.

(Notary Seal)   _____

                                                              Notary Public

CHAPTER 18

DECLARATION OF TRUST
For Naming
TWO OR MORE BENEFICIARIES, SHARING EQUALLY,
To Receive
AN UNINCORPORATED BUSINESS HELD IN ONE NAME

INSTRUCTIONS:

On the following pages will be found a declaration of trust (DT-147) suitable for use in connection with the establishment of an inter vivos trust covering an unincorporated business held in one name only, where it is desired to name two or more persons to share the business equally upon the death of the owner.

Cross out *"city"* or *"town,"* leaving the appropriate designation of your community. Next, give the name and location and explain exactly what kind of business it is.

In Paragraph 1, indicate the *number of persons* you are naming (to discourage unauthorized additions to the list) and then insert their names. The one whose name appears *first* will be the Successor Trustee responsible for seeing to the distribution of the trust property.

Note that the instrument specifies that the named beneficiaries are to receive *"in equal shares, or the survivor of them/per stirpes."* Now, think carefully: If you have named three persons with the understanding that if one of them predeceases you, *his* children will take *his* share, cross out *"or the survivor of them"* and *initial it.* If that is *not* what you want—if, for example, you prefer that the share of the deceased person be divided between the two surviving persons, cross out *"per stirpes"* and *initial it.* Remember, you <u>must</u> cross out either *"or the survivor of them"* or *"per stirpes"*—one or the other.

Note that Paragraph 8 designates as Successor Trustee *"the beneficiary named first above."* Whenever there is any possibility of a beneficiary who has not attained the age of 21 years receiving the trust property, make certain that you name an adult in this paragraph who can act as trustee for such beneficiary. Avoid naming as trustee a person not likely to survive until the beneficiary has attained age 21.

When completed in the manner shown on the reverse side hereof, make several photocopies. Hold the original in safekeeping and offer a copy to each beneficiary and to the bank where your business account is maintained.

Important: Read carefully Note B on page 38, which applies to this declaration of trust.

Declaration of Trust

WHEREAS, I, __Elizabeth A. Brown__, County of __Fairfax__, State of __Connecticut__, of the

City/Town of __Milton__ am the sole owner of the unincorporated business known as __The Fairport Gift Shoppe__; and

(Name of Business)

located at __120 Main Street__, in the City/Town of __Milton__

County of __Fairfax__ and State of __Connecticut__

WHEREAS, the principal business of the said __The Fairport Gift Shoppe__

(Name of Business)

is __the retail sale of greeting cards and giftware.__

NOW, THEREFORE, KNOW ALL MEN BY THESE PRESENTS, that I do hereby acknowledge and declare that I hold and will hold said business, and all my right, title and interest in and to said business and all furniture, fixtures, stock in trade, inventory, machinery, vehicles, accounts receivable, prepaid insurance and all other assets of such business IN TRUST _E.A.B._

1. For the use and benefit of the following __three (3)__ persons, in equal shares, ~~the survivor or survivor per~~ stirpes:

Diane R. Brown - my sister
Charles L. Brown - my brother
Jill A. Lynn - my niece

If because of my physical or mental incapacity certified in writing by a physician, the Successor Trustee hereinafter named shall assume active administration of this trust during my lifetime, such Successor Trustee shall be fully authorized to pay to me or disburse on my behalf such sums from income or principal as appear necessary or desirable for my comfort or welfare. Upon my death, unless all of the beneficiaries shall predecease me or unless we all shall die as a result of a common accident, my Successor Trustee is hereby directed forthwith to transfer said business and all my right, title and interest in and to said business unto the beneficiaries absolutely and thereby terminate this trust; provided, however, that if any beneficiary hereunder shall not have attained the age of 21 years, the Successor Trustee shall hold such beneficiary's share of the trust assets in continuing trust until such beneficiary shall have attained the age of 21 years. During such period of continuing trust the Successor Trustee, in his absolute discretion, may retain the business herein described if he believes it to be in the best interests of the beneficiary so to do, or he may dispose of it, investing and reinvesting the proceeds as he may deem appropriate. Prior to the date upon which such beneficiary attains the age of 21 years, the Successor Trustee may apply or expend any or all of the income or principal directly to or for the maintenance, education and support of the beneficiary without the intervention of any guardian and without application to any court. Such payments of income or principal may be made to the parents of such beneficiary or to the person with whom the beneficiary is living without any liability upon the Successor Trustee to see to the application thereof. If such beneficiary survives me but dies before attaining the age of 21 years, at his or her death the Successor Trustee shall transfer, pay

hereby created without the necessity of obtaining the consent of the beneficiaries and without giving notice to the beneficiaries. The sale or other disposition by me of the whole or any part of the assets of the business held hereunder shall constitute as to such whole or part a revocation of this trust.

7. The death during my lifetime, or in a common accident or disaster with me, of all of the beneficiaries designated hereunder shall revoke such designation, and in the former event, I reserve the right to designate a new beneficiary. Should I for any reason fail to designate such new beneficiary, this trust shall terminate upon my death and the trust property shall revert to my estate.

8. In the event of my physical or mental incapacity or my death, I hereby nominate and appoint as Successor Trustee the beneficiary named first above, unless such beneficiary shall not have attained the age of 21 years or is otherwise legally incapacitated, in which event I hereby nominate and appoint as Successor Trustee the beneficiary named second above, unless such beneficiary named second above shall not have attained the age of 21 years or is otherwise legally incapacitated, in which latter event I hereby nominate and appoint

__Henry P. Adams__, of

(Name)

__125 Barnum Street__ __Milton__ __Connecticut 06605__

(Address) _Number_ _Street_ _City_ _State_ _Zip_

to be Successor Trustee.

9. This Declaration of Trust shall extend to and be binding upon the heirs, executors, administrators and assigns of the undersigned and upon the Successors to the Trustee.

10. The Trustee and his successors shall serve without bond.

11. This Declaration of Trust shall be construed and enforced in accordance with the laws of the State of __Connecticut__

Declaration of Trust

WHEREAS, I, _____, of the

City/Town of _____, County of _____, State of _____,

am the sole owner of the unincorporated business known as _____

_____
(Name of Business)

located at _____, in the City/Town of _____,

County of _____ and State of _____; and

WHEREAS, the principal business of the said _____
(Name of Business)

is _____

_____

_____;

NOW, THEREFORE, KNOW ALL MEN BY THESE PRESENTS, that I do hereby acknowledge and declare that I hold and will hold said business, and all my right, title and interest in and to said business, and all furniture, fixtures, stock in trade, inventory, machinery, vehicles, accounts receivable, prepaid insurance and all other assets of such business IN TRUST

1. For the use and benefit of the following _____ persons, in equal shares, or the survivor of them/per stirpes:

If because of my physical or mental incapacity certified in writing by a physician, the Successor Trustee hereinafter named shall assume active administration of this trust during my lifetime, such Successor Trustee shall be fully authorized to pay to me or disburse on my behalf such sums from income or principal as appear necessary or desirable for my comfort or welfare. Upon my death, unless all of the beneficiaries shall predecease me or unless we all shall die as a result of a common accident, my Successor Trustee is hereby directed forthwith to transfer said business and all my right, title and interest in and to said business unto the beneficiaries absolutely and thereby terminate this trust; provided, however, that if any beneficiary hereunder shall not have attained the age of 21 years, the Successor Trustee shall hold such beneficiary's share of the trust assets in continuing trust until such beneficiary shall have attained the age of 21 years. During such period of continuing trust the Successor Trustee, in his absolute discretion, may retain the business herein described if he believes it to be in the best interests of the beneficiary so to do, or he may dispose of it, investing and reinvesting the proceeds as he may deem appropriate. Prior to the date upon which such beneficiary attains the age of 21 years, the Successor Trustee may apply or expend any or all of the income or principal directly for the maintenance, education and support of the beneficiary without the intervention of any guardian and without application to any court. Such payments of income or principal may be made to the parents of such beneficiary or to the person with whom the beneficiary is living without any liability upon the Successor Trustee to see to the application thereof. If such beneficiary survives me but dies before attaining the age of 21 years, at his or her death the Successor Trustee shall transfer, pay over and deliver such beneficiary's share of the trust property to such beneficiary's personal representative, absolutely.

2. Each beneficiary hereunder shall be liable for his proportionate share of any taxes levied upon the Settlor's total taxable estate by reason of the Settlor's death.

3. All interests of a beneficiary hereunder shall be inalienable and free from anticipation, assignment, attachment, pledge or control by creditors or a present or former spouse of such beneficiary in any proceedings at law or in equity.

4. This trust is created with the express understanding that the bank at which an account is maintained in the name of the business shall be under no liability whatsoever to see to such trust's proper administration. On the contrary, upon the transfer of the right, title and interest in and to the business by any trustee hereunder, said bank shall conclusively treat the transferee as the sole owner of said account. Until the bank shall receive from some person interested in this trust, written notice of any death or other event upon which the right to receive may depend, the bank shall incur no liability for payments made in good faith to persons whose interests shall have been affected by such event. The bank shall be protected in acting upon any notice or other instrument or document believed by it to be genuine and to have been signed or presented by the proper party or parties.

5. I reserve unto myself the power and right to collect all income which may accrue from the trust property and to pay such income to myself as an individual. I shall be exclusively entitled to all such income accruing from the trust property during my lifetime, and no beneficiary named herein shall have any claim upon any such income distributed to me.

6. I reserve unto myself the power and right at any time during my lifetime to amend or revoke in whole or in part the trust hereby created without the necessity of obtaining the consent of the beneficiaries and without giving notice to the beneficiaries. The sale or other disposition by me of the whole or any part of the assets of the business held hereunder shall constitute as to such whole or part a revocation of this trust.

7. The death during my lifetime, or in a common accident or disaster with me, of all of the beneficiaries designated hereunder shall revoke such designation, and in the former event, I reserve the right to designate a new beneficiary. Should I for any reason fail to designate such new beneficiary, this trust shall terminate upon my death and the trust property shall revert to my estate.

8. In the event of my physical or mental incapacity or my death, I hereby nominate and appoint as Successor Trustee the beneficiary named first above, unless such beneficiary shall not have attained the age of 21 years or is otherwise legally incapacitated, in which event I hereby nominate and appoint as Successor Trustee the beneficiary named second above, unless such beneficiary named second above shall not have attained the age of 21 years or is otherwise legally incapacitated, in which latter event I hereby nominate and appoint

(Name) _____ , of

(Address) _____

       Number   *Street*   *City*   *State*   *Zip*

to be Successor Trustee.

9. This Declaration of Trust shall extend to and be binding upon the heirs, executors, administrators and assigns of the undersigned and upon the Successors to the Trustee.

10. The Trustee and his successors shall serve without bond.

11. This Declaration of Trust shall be construed and enforced in accordance with the laws of the State of

_____ .

IN WITNESS WHEREOF, I have hereunto set my hand and seal this _____

day of _____ , 19_____ .

       (Settlor sign here) _____ L.S.

I, the undersigned legal spouse of the above Settlor, hereby waive all community property rights which I may have in the hereinabove-described business and give my assent to the provisions of the trust and to the inclusion in it of the said business.

       (Spouse sign here) _____ L.S.

Witness: (1) _____   Witness: (2) _____

STATE OF _____   City

COUNTY OF _____   or

                                Town _____

On the _____ day of _____ , 19_____ , personally appeared

_____

known to me to be the individual(s) who executed the foregoing instrument, and acknowledged the same to be _____ free act and deed, before me.

(Notary Seal)

                            _____

                                       Notary Public

CHAPTER 18

DECLARATION OF TRUST

For Naming

ONE PRIMARY BENEFICIARY WITH YOUR CHILDREN, SHARING EQUALLY, AS CONTINGENT BENEFICIARIES

To Receive

AN UNINCORPORATED BUSINESS HELD IN ONE NAME

INSTRUCTIONS:

On the following pages will be found a declaration of trust (DT-148) suitable for use in connection with the establishment of an inter vivos trust covering an unincorporated business held in one name where it is desired to name one person (ordinarily, but not necessarily, one's spouse) as primary beneficiary, with one's children as contingent beneficiaries to receive the business upon the death of the owner.

Cross out *"city"* or *"town,"* leaving the appropriate designation of your community. Next, give the name and location and explain exactly what kind of business it is.

Enter the name of the primary beneficiary (called the "First Beneficiary") in the appropriate place in Paragraph 1. Note that the instrument first refers to your children as *"natural not/or adopted."* Now, decide: If you have an adopted child and you wish to include him, cross out the word *"not"* in the phrase *"natural not/or adopted"* and *initial it*. If you wish to *exclude* your adopted child, cross out the word *"or"* in the same phrase and *initial it*. Remember, you <u>must</u> cross out *"not"* or *"or"*—one or the other. If you have no adopted child, simply cross out *"not."*

Note next that the instrument specifies that your children are to receive *"in equal shares, or the survivor of them/per stirpes."* Now, think carefully: If it is your wish that if one of your children does not survive you, *his* share will revert to *his* children in equal shares, cross out *"or the survivor of them"* and *initial it*. If that is *not* what you want—if, for example, you prefer that the share of any child of yours who predeceases you shall be divided between your other surviving children in equal shares, cross out *"per stirpes"* and *initial it*. Remember, you <u>must</u> cross out *"or the survivor of them"* or *"per stirpes"*—one or the other.

Note that in Paragraph 8, the First Beneficiary is designated as Successor Trustee, while a space is provided in which you should designate another person to so act if the named Successor Trustee is not surviving or otherwise fails or ceases to act. This could be one of your children, for example, but it must be an adult who can act as trustee for any beneficiary who comes into a share of the trust before attaining the age of 21. Avoid naming someone not likely to survive until the youngest such beneficiary has attained age 21.

When completed in the manner shown on the reverse side hereof, make several photocopies for reference purposes. Hold the original in safekeeping and offer a copy to each beneficiary and to the bank where your business account is maintained.

Important: Read carefully Note B on page 38, which applies to this declaration of trust.

Declaration of Trust

WHEREAS, I, _____ Elizabeth A. Brown _____, County of _____ Fairfax _____, State of _____ Connecticut _____; of the City/Town of _____ Milton _____

am the sole owner of the unincorporated business known as _____ The Fairport Gift Shoppe _____; and

(Name of Business)

located at _____ 120 Main Street _____ in the City/Town of _____ Milton _____; and

County of _____ Fairfax _____ and State of _____ Connecticut _____

WHEREAS, the principal business of the said _____ The Fairport Gift Shoppe _____

(Name of Business)

is _____ the retail sale of greeting cards and giftware. _____

NOW, THEREFORE, KNOW ALL MEN BY THESE PRESENTS, that I do hereby acknowledge and declare that I hold and will hold said business, and all my right, title and interest in and to said business and all furniture, fixtures, stock in trade, inventory, machinery, vehicles, accounts receivable, prepaid insurance and all other assets of such business IN TRUST, of

1. For the use and benefit of:

(Name) _____ John J. Brown – my husband _____ Milton _____ City _____ Connecticut _____ State _____ 06605 _____ Zip

(Address) _____ 525 _____ Main _____ Street _____ *E.a.B.*
Number   Street

E.a.B.

(hereinafter referred to as the "First Beneficiary"), and upon his or her death prior to the termination of the trust, for the use and benefit of my children, natural or adopted, in equal shares, _____ per stirpes.

If because of my physical or mental incapacity certified in writing by a physician, such Successor Trustee shall be fully authorized to pay to me or disburse on my behalf such sums from income or principal as appear necessary or desirable for my comfort or welfare. Upon my death, unless all of the beneficiaries shall predecease me or unless we all shall die as a result of a common accident, my Successor Trustee is hereby directed forthwith to transfer said business and all my right, title and interest in and to said business unto the beneficiary or beneficiaries absolutely and thereby terminate this trust; provided, however, that if any beneficiary hereunder shall not have attained the age of 21 years, the Successor Trustee shall hold such beneficiary's share of the trust assets in continuing trust until such beneficiary shall have attained the age of 21 years. During such period of continuing trust the Successor Trustee, in his absolute discretion, may retain the business herein described if he believes it to be in the best interests of the beneficiary so to do, or he may dispose of it, investing and reinvesting the proceeds as he may deem appropriate. Prior to the date upon which such beneficiary attains the age of 21 years, the Successor Trustee may apply or expend any or all of the income or principal directly for the maintenance, education and support of the beneficiary without the intervention of any guardian and without application to any court. Such payments of income or principal may be made to the parents of such beneficiary or to the person with whom the beneficiary is living without any liability upon the Successor Trustee to see to the application thereof. If such beneficiary survives me but dies before attaining the age of 21 years, at his or her death the Successor Trustee shall transfer, pay over and deliver such beneficiary's share of the trust property to such beneficiary's personal representative, absolutely.

2. Each beneficiary hereunder shall be liable for his proportionate share of any taxes levied upon the Settlor's total taxable estate by reason of the Settlor's death.

3. All interests of a beneficiary hereunder shall be inalienable and free from anticipation, assignment, attachment, pledge or control by creditors or a present or former spouse of such beneficiary in any proceedings at law or in equity.

4. This trust is created with the express understanding that the bank at which an account is maintained in the name of the business shall be under no liability whatsoever to see to such trust's proper administration. On the contrary, upon the transfer of the right, title and interest in and to such business by any trustee hereunder, said bank shall conclusively treat the transferee as the sole owner of said account. Until the bank shall receive from some person interested in this trust, written notice of any death or other event upon which the right to receive may depend, the bank shall incur no liability for payments made in good faith to persons whose interests shall have been affected by such event. The bank shall be protected in acting upon any notice or other _____ assets of the business _____ shall constitute as to such whole or part a revocation of this trust.

7. The death during my lifetime, or in a common accident with me, of all of the beneficiaries designated hereunder shall revoke such designation, and in the former event, this trust shall terminate upon my death and the trust property shall revert to my estate.

8. In the event of my physical or mental incapacity or my death, I hereby nominate and appoint as Successor Trustee hereunder the First Beneficiary, or if such First Beneficiary be not surviving or fails or ceases to act, I nominate and appoint _____, of

(Name) _____ Henry P. Adams _____ Milton _____ City _____ Connecticut _____ State _____ 06605 _____ Zip

(Address) _____ 125 _____ Barnum _____ Street
Number   Street

to be Successor Trustee. If such person fails or ceases to act or should I for any reason fail to designate the person above intended to be nominated, then I nominate and appoint as such Successor Trustee hereunder whosoever shall qualify as executor, administrator or guardian, as the case may be, of my estate.

9. This Declaration of Trust shall extend to and be binding upon the heirs, executors, administrators and assigns of the undersigned and upon the Successors to the Trustee.

10. The Trustee and his successors shall serve without bond.

11. This Declaration of Trust shall be construed and enforced in accordance with the laws of the State of _____ Connecticut

Declaration of Trust

WHEREAS, I, _____, of the

City/Town of _____, County of _____, State of _____,

am the sole owner of the unincorporated business known as _____

_____

(Name of Business)

located at _____, in the City/Town of _____,

County of _____ and State of _____; and

WHEREAS, the principal business of the said _____

(Name of Business)

is _____

_____

_____;

NOW, THEREFORE, KNOW ALL MEN BY THESE PRESENTS, that I do hereby acknowledge and declare that I hold and will hold said business, and all my right, title and interest in and to said business, and all furniture, fixtures, stock in trade, inventory, machinery, vehicles, accounts receivable, prepaid insurance and all other assets of such business IN TRUST

1. For the use and benefit of:

(Name) _____, of

(Address) _____
Number   Street   City   State   Zip

(hereinafter referred to as the "First Beneficiary"), and upon his or her death prior to the termination of the trust, for the use and benefit of my children, natural not/or adopted, in equal shares, or the survivor of them/per stirpes.

If because of my physical or mental incapacity certified in writing by a physician, the Successor Trustee hereinafter named shall assume active administration of this trust during my lifetime, such Successor Trustee shall be fully authorized to pay to me or disburse on my behalf such sums from income or principal as appear necessary or desirable for my comfort or welfare. Upon my death, unless all of the beneficiaries shall predecease me or unless we all shall die as a result of a common accident, my Successor Trustee is hereby directed forthwith to transfer said business and all my right, title and interest in and to said business unto the beneficiary or beneficiaries absolutely and thereby terminate this trust; provided, however, that if any beneficiary hereunder shall not have attained the age of 21 years, the Successor Trustee shall hold such beneficiary's share of the trust assets in continuing trust until such beneficiary shall have attained the age of 21 years. During such period of continuing trust the Successor Trustee, in his absolute discretion, may retain the business herein described if he believes it to be in the best interests of the beneficiary so to do, or he may dispose of it, investing and reinvesting the proceeds as he may deem appropriate. Prior to the date upon which such beneficiary attains the age of 21 years, the Successor Trustee may apply or expend any or all of the income or principal directly for the maintenance, education and support of the beneficiary without the intervention of any guardian and without application to any court. Such payments of income or principal may be made to the parents of such beneficiary or to the person with whom the beneficiary is living without any liability upon the Successor Trustee to see to the application thereof. If such beneficiary survives me but dies before attaining the age of 21 years, at his or her death the Successor Trustee shall transfer, pay over and deliver such beneficiary's share of the trust property to such beneficiary's personal representative, absolutely.

2. Each beneficiary hereunder shall be liable for his proportionate share of any taxes levied upon the Settlor's total taxable estate by reason of the Settlor's death.

3. All interests of a beneficiary hereunder shall be inalienable and free from anticipation, assignment, attachment, pledge or control by creditors or a present or former spouse of such beneficiary in any proceedings at law or in equity.

4. This trust is created with the express understanding that the bank at which an account is maintained in the name of the business shall be under no liability whatsoever to see to such trust's proper administration. On the contrary, upon the transfer of the right, title and interest in and to such business by any trustee hereunder, said bank shall conclusively treat the transferee as the sole owner of said account. Until the bank shall receive from some person interested in this trust, written notice of any death or other event upon which the right to receive may depend, the bank shall incur no liability for payments made in good faith to persons whose interests shall have been affected by such event. The bank shall be protected in acting upon any notice or other instrument or document believed by it to be genuine and to have been signed or presented by the proper party or parties.

5. I reserve unto myself the power and right to collect all income which may accrue from the trust property and to pay such income to myself as an individual. I shall be exclusively entitled to all such income accruing from the trust property during my lifetime, and no beneficiary named herein shall have any claim upon any such income distributed to me.

6. I reserve unto myself the power and right at any time during my lifetime to amend or revoke in whole or in part the trust hereby created without the necessity of obtaining the consent of any beneficiary and without giving notice to any beneficiary.

The sale or other disposition by me of the whole or any part of the assets of the business held hereunder shall constitute as to such whole or part a revocation of this trust.

7. The death during my lifetime, or in a common accident with me, of all of the beneficiaries designated hereunder shall revoke such designation, and in the former event, I reserve the right to designate a new beneficiary. Should I for any reason fail to designate such new beneficiary, this trust shall terminate upon my death and the trust property shall revert to my estate.

8. In the event of my physical or mental incapacity or my death, I hereby nominate and appoint as Successor Trustee hereunder the First Beneficiary, or if such First Beneficiary be not surviving or fails or ceases to act, I nominate and appoint

(Name) _____ , of

(Address) _____

| *Number* | *Street* | *City* | *State* | *Zip* |

to be Successor Trustee. If such person fails or ceases to act or should I for any reason fail to designate the person above intended to be nominated, then I nominate and appoint as such Successor Trustee hereunder whosoever shall qualify as executor, administrator or guardian, as the case may be, of my estate.

9. This Declaration of Trust shall extend to and be binding upon the heirs, executors, administrators and assigns of the undersigned and upon the Successors to the Trustee.

10. The Trustee and his successors shall serve without bond.

11. This Declaration of Trust shall be construed and enforced in accordance with the laws of the State of

_____ .

IN WITNESS WHEREOF, I have hereunto set my hand and seal this _____

day of _____ , 19_____ .

(Settlor sign here) _____ L.S.

I, the undersigned legal spouse of the above Settlor, hereby waive all community property rights which I may have in the hereinabove-described business and give my assent to the provisions of the trust and to the inclusion in it of the said business.

(Spouse sign here) _____ L.S.

Witness: (1) _____ Witness: (2) _____

STATE OF _____ City

COUNTY OF _____ or
Town _____

On the _____ day of _____ , 19_____ , personally appeared

_____

known to me to be the individual(s) who executed the foregoing instrument, and acknowledged the same to be _____ free act and deed, before me.

(Notary Seal)

_____
Notary Public

CHAPTER 18

DECLARATION OF TRUST

For Naming

ONE BENEFICIARY

To Receive

AN UNINCORPORATED BUSINESS HELD IN JOINT NAMES

INSTRUCTIONS:

On the following pages will be found a declaration of trust (DT-145-J) suitable for use in connection with the establishment of an inter vivos trust covering an unincorporated business held in two names where it is desired to name some *one* person to receive the business upon the death of the survivor of the two joint owners.

Enter the names of the two co-owners on the first line.

Cross out *"city"* or *"town,"* leaving the appropriate designation of your community. Next, give the name and location, and explain exactly what kind of business it is.

Enter the name of the beneficiary in the appropriate place in Paragraph 1.

Note that Paragraph 8 designates as Successor Trustee *"whosoever shall at that time be beneficiary hereunder,"* which means that in most cases you don't need to fill anything in there. However, if there is any possibility of a beneficiary who has not attained the age of 21 years receiving the trust property, make certain that you name an adult in this paragraph who can act as trustee for such beneficiary. Avoid naming as trustee a person not likely to survive until the beneficiary has attained age 21.

When completed in the manner shown on the reverse side hereof, make several photocopies for reference purposes. Hold the original in safekeeping and offer a copy to the beneficiary and to the bank where your business account is maintained.

Important: Read carefully Note B on page 38, which applies to this declaration of trust.

DT-145-J

Declaration of Trust

WHEREAS, WE, __John J. Brown__ and __Elizabeth A. Brown__, of the City/Town of __Milton__, County of __Fairfax__, State of __Connecticut__

are joint owners of the unincorporated business known as __The Fairport Gift Shoppe__
(Name of Business)

located at __120 Main Street__, in the City/Town of __Milton__; and

County of __Fairfax__ and State of __Connecticut__

WHEREAS the principal business of the said __The Fairport Gift Shoppe__
(Name of Business)

is __the retail sale of greeting cards and giftware.__

NOW, THEREFORE, KNOW ALL MEN BY THESE PRESENTS, that we do hereby acknowledge and declare that we hold and will hold said business, and all our right, title and interest in and to said business and all furniture, fixtures, stock in trade, inventory, machinery, vehicles, accounts receivable, prepaid insurance and all other assets of such business IN TRUST

1. For the use and benefit of:

(Name) __Diane R. Brown — our daughter__ City __Milton__ State __Connecticut__ Zip __06605__

(Address) __525__ __Main Street__
       Number   Street

If because of the physical or mental incapacity of both of us certified in writing by a physician, the Successor Trustee hereinafter named shall assume active administration of this trust during our lifetime, such Successor Trustee shall be fully authorized to pay to us or disburse on our behalf such sums from income or principal as appear necessary or desirable for our comfort or welfare. Upon the death of the survivor of us, unless the beneficiary shall predecease us or unless we all shall die as a result of a common accident, our Successor Trustee is hereby directed to transfer said business and all our right, title and interest in and to said business unto the beneficiary absolutely and thereby terminate this trust; provided, however, that if the beneficiary hereunder shall not have attained the age of 21 years, the Successor Trustee shall hold the trust assets in continuing trust until such beneficiary shall have attained the age of 21 years. During such period of continuing trust the Successor Trustee, in his absolute discretion, may retain the business herein described if he believes it in the best interests of the beneficiary so to do, or he may dispose of it, investing and reinvesting the proceeds as he may deem appropriate. Prior to the date upon which such beneficiary attains the age of 21 years, the Successor Trustee may apply or expend any or all of the income or principal directly for the maintenance, education and support of the beneficiary without the intervention of any guardian and without application to any court. Such payments of income or principal may be made to the parents of such beneficiary or to the person with whom the beneficiary is living without any liability upon the Successor Trustee to see to the application thereof. If such beneficiary survives us but dies before attaining the age of 21 years, at his or her death the Successor Trustee shall transfer, pay over and deliver the trust property to such beneficiary's personal representative, absolutely.

2. The beneficiary hereunder shall be liable for his proportionate share of any taxes levied upon the total taxable estate of the survivor of us by reason of the death of such survivor.

3. All interests of the beneficiary hereunder shall be inalienable and free from anticipation, assignment, attachment, pledge or control by creditors or a present or former spouse of such beneficiary in any proceedings at law or in equity.

4. This trust is created with the express understanding that the bank at which an account is maintained in the name of the business shall be under no liability whatsoever to see to such trust's proper administration. On the contrary, upon the transfer of the right, title and interest in and to the business by any trustee hereunder, said bank shall conclusively treat the transferee as the sole owner of said account. Until the bank shall receive from some person interested in this trust, written notice of any death or other event upon which the right to receive may depend, the bank shall incur no liability for payments made in good faith to persons whose interest shall have been affected by it to be genuine and to have been signed or presented by the proper party or parties. The bank shall be protected in acting upon any notice or other instrument or document believed by it to be genuine and to have been signed or presented by the proper party or parties.

5. We reserve unto ourselves the power and right to collect all income which may accrue from the trust property and to pay such income to ourselves as individuals. We shall be exclusively entitled to all such income accruing from the trust property to the estate of such survivor.

8. In the event of the physical or mental incapacity or death of one of us, the survivor shall continue as sole Trustee. In the event of the physical or mental incapacity or death of the survivor of us, or if we both shall die in a common accident, we hereby nominate and appoint as Successor Trustee hereunder the beneficiary named first above, unless such beneficiary named first above shall not have attained the age of 21 years or is otherwise legally incapacitated, in which event we hereby nominate and appoint as Successor Trustee the beneficiary named second above, unless such beneficiary shall not have attained the age of 21 years or is otherwise legally incapacitated, in which event we hereby nominate and appoint

(Name) __Henry P. Adams__ City __Milton__ State __Connecticut__ Zip __06605__

(Address) __125__ __Barnum Street__
       Number   Street

to be Successor Trustee.

9. This Declaration of Trust shall extend to and be binding upon the heirs, executors, administrators and assigns of the undersigned and upon the Successors to the Trustees.

10. We as Trustees and our Successor Trustee shall serve without bond.

11. This Declaration of Trust shall be construed and enforced in accordance with the laws of the State of __Connecticut__

Declaration of Trust

WHEREAS, WE, _____ and _____, of the

City/Town of _____, County of _____, State of _____,

are joint owners of the unincorporated business known as _____

_____

(Name of Business)

located at _____, in the City/Town of _____,

County of _____ and State of _____; and

WHEREAS the principal business of the said _____

(Name of Business)

is _____

_____

_____ ;

NOW, THEREFORE, KNOW ALL MEN BY THESE PRESENTS, that we do hereby acknowledge and declare that we hold and will hold said business, and all our right, title and interest in and to said business, and all furniture, fixtures, stock in trade, inventory, machinery, vehicles, accounts receivable, prepaid insurance and all other assets of such business IN TRUST

1. For the use and benefit of:

(Name) _____ , of

(Address) _____

| Number | Street | City | State | Zip |

If because of the physical or mental incapacity of both of us certified in writing by a physician, the Successor Trustee hereinafter named shall assume active administration of this trust during our lifetime, such Successor Trustee shall be fully authorized to pay to us or disburse on our behalf such sums from income or principal as appear necessary or desirable for our comfort or welfare. Upon the death of the survivor of us, unless the beneficiary shall predecease us or unless we all shall die as a result of a common accident, our Successor Trustee is hereby directed to transfer said business and all our right, title and interest in and to said business unto the beneficiary absolutely and thereby terminate this trust; provided, however, that if the beneficiary hereunder shall not have attained the age of 21 years, the Successor Trustee shall hold the trust assets in continuing trust until such beneficiary shall have attained the age of 21 years. During such period of continuing trust the Successor Trustee, in his absolute discretion, may retain the business herein described if he believes it in the best interests of the beneficiary so to do, or he may dispose of it, investing and reinvesting the proceeds as he may deem appropriate. Prior to the date upon which such beneficiary attains the age of 21 years, the Successor Trustee may apply or expend any or all of the income or principal directly for the maintenance, education and support of the beneficiary without the intervention of any guardian and without application to any court. Such payments of income or principal may be made to the parents of such beneficiary or to the person with whom the beneficiary is living without any liability upon the Successor Trustee to see to the application thereof. If such beneficiary survives us but dies before attaining the age of 21 years, at his or her death the Successor Trustee shall transfer, pay over and deliver the trust property to such beneficiary's personal representative, absolutely.

2. The beneficiary hereunder shall be liable for his proportionate share of any taxes levied upon the total taxable estate of the survivor of us by reason of the death of such survivor.

3. All interests of the beneficiary hereunder shall be inalienable and free from anticipation, assignment, attachment, pledge or control by creditors or a present or former spouse of such beneficiary in any proceedings at law or in equity.

4. This trust is created with the express understanding that the bank at which an account is maintained in the name of the business shall be under no liability whatsoever to see to such trust's proper administration. On the contrary, upon the transfer of the right, title and interest in and to the business by any trustee hereunder, said bank shall conclusively treat the transferee as the sole owner of said account. Until the bank shall receive from some person interested in this trust, written notice of any death or other event upon which the right to receive may depend, the bank shall incur no liability for payments made in good faith to persons whose interest shall have been affected by such event. The bank shall be protected in acting upon any notice or other instrument or document believed by it to be genuine and to have been signed or presented by the proper party or parties.

5. We reserve unto ourselves the power and right to collect all income which may accrue from the trust property and to pay such income to ourselves as individuals. We shall be exclusively entitled to all such income accruing from the trust property during our lifetime, and no beneficiary named herein shall have any claim upon any such income distributed to us.

6. We reserve unto ourselves the power and right at any time during our lifetime to amend or revoke in whole or in part the trust hereby created without the necessity of obtaining the consent of the beneficiary and without giving notice to the beneficiary. The sale or other disposition by us of the whole or any part of the assets of the business held hereunder shall constitute as to such whole or part a revocation of this trust.

7. The death during our lifetime, or in a common accident with us, of the beneficiary designated hereunder shall revoke such designation, and in the former event, we reserve the right to designate a new beneficiary. Should we for any reason fail to designate such new beneficiary, this trust shall terminate upon the death of the survivor of us and the trust property shall revert to the estate of such survivor.

8. In the event of the physical or mental incapacity or death of one of us, the survivor shall continue as sole Trustee. In the event of the physical or mental incapacity or death of the survivor of us, or if we both shall die in a common accident, we hereby nominate and appoint as Successor Trustee hereunder the beneficiary named first above, unless such beneficiary shall not have attained the age of 21 years or is otherwise legally incapacitated, in which event we hereby nominate and appoint as Successor Trustee the beneficiary named second above, unless such beneficiary named second above shall not have attained the age of 21 years or is otherwise legally incapacitated, in which event we hereby nominate and appoint

(Name) _____ , of

(Address) _____
          Number   Street   City   State   Zip

to be Successor Trustee.

9. This Declaration of Trust shall extend to and be binding upon the heirs, executors, administrators and assigns of the undersigned and upon the Successors to the Trustees.

10. We as Trustees and our Successor Trustee shall serve without bond.

11. This Declaration of Trust shall be construed and enforced in accordance with the laws of the State of

_____ .

IN WITNESS WHEREOF, we have hereunto set our hands and seals this _____

day of _____ , 19_____ .

(First Settlor sign here) _____ L.S.

(Second Settlor sign here) _____ L.S.

I, the undersigned legal spouse of one of the above Settlors, hereby waive all community property rights which I may have in the hereinabove-described business and give my assent to the provisions of the trust and to the inclusion in it of the said business.

(Spouse sign here) _____ L.S.

Witness: (1) _____   Witness: (2) _____

STATE OF _____ ⎫   City
                                    ⎬   or
COUNTY OF _____ ⎭   Town _____

On the _____ day of_____ , 19_____ , personally appeared

_____ and _____

known to me to be the individuals who executed the foregoing instrument, and acknowledged the same to be their free act and deed, before me.

(Notary Seal)   _____
                                                                      Notary Public

CHAPTER 18

DECLARATION OF TRUST
For Naming
ONE PRIMARY BENEFICIARY
And
ONE CONTINGENT BENEFICIARY
To Receive
AN UNINCORPORATED BUSINESS HELD IN JOINT NAMES

INSTRUCTIONS:

On the following pages will be found a declaration of trust (DT-146-J) suitable for use in connection with the establishment of an inter vivos trust covering an unincorporated business held in two names, where it is desired to name some *one* person as primary beneficiary with some *one* other person as contingent beneficiary to receive the business upon the death of the survivor of the two joint owners.

Enter the names of the two co-owners on the first line.

Cross out *"city"* or *"town,"* leaving the appropriate designation of your community. Next, give the name and location and explain exactly what kind of business it is.

Enter the names of the beneficiaries in the appropriate place in Paragraph 1.

Note that Paragraph 8 designates as Successor Trustee *"whosoever shall at that time be beneficiary hereunder,"* which means that in most cases you don't need to fill anything in there. However, if there is any possibility of a beneficiary who has not attained the age of 21 years receiving the property, make certain that you name an adult in this paragraph who can act as trustee for such beneficiary. Avoid naming as trustee a person not likely to survive until the beneficiary has attained age 21.

When completed in the manner shown on the reverse side hereof, make several photocopies for reference purposes. Hold the original in safekeeping and offer a copy to the beneficiaries and to the bank where your business account is maintained.

Important: Read carefully Note B on page 38, which applies to this declaration of trust.

DT-146-J

Declaration of Trust

DACEY TRUST

WHEREAS, WE, __John J. Brown__ and __Elizabeth A. Brown__, of the City/Town of __Milton__, County of __Fairfax__, State of __Connecticut__, are joint owners of the unincorporated business known as __The Fairport Gift Shoppe__

(Name of Business)

located at __120 Main Street__, in the City/Town of __Milton__; and

County of __Fairfax__ and State of __Connecticut__

WHEREAS the principal business of the said __The Fairport Gift Shoppe__

(Name of Business)

is __the retail sale of greeting cards and giftware.__

NOW, THEREFORE, KNOW ALL MEN BY THESE PRESENTS, that we do hereby acknowledge and declare that we hold and will hold said business and all our right, title and interest in and to said business, and all furniture, fixtures, stock in trade, inventory, machinery, vehicles, accounts receivable, prepaid insurance and all other assets of such business IN TRUST

1. For the use and benefit of:

(Name) __Diane R. Brown – our daughter__ __Milton__ __Connecticut__ __06605__, of
City / State / Zip

(Address) __525__ __Main Street__
Number / Street

or, if such beneficiary be not surviving, for the use and benefit of:

(Name) __Jill A. Lynn – our niece__ __Portland__ __Wisconsin__ __53123__, of
City / State / Zip

(Address) __566__ __Midland Street__
Number / Street

If because of the physical or mental incapacity of both of us certified in writing by a physician, the Successor Trustee hereinafter named shall assume active administration of this trust during our lifetime, such Successor Trustee shall be fully authorized to pay to us or disburse on our behalf such sums from income or principal as appear necessary or desirable for our comfort or welfare. Upon the death of the survivor of us, unless the beneficiaries shall predecease us or unless we all shall die as a result of a common accident, our Successor Trustee is hereby directed forthwith to transfer said business and all our right, title and interest in and to said business unto the beneficiary absolutely and thereby terminate this trust; provided, however, that if the beneficiary hereunder shall not have attained the age of 21 years, the Successor Trustee shall hold the trust assets in continuing trust until such beneficiary attains the age of 21 years. During such period of continuing trust the Successor Trustee, in his absolute discretion, may retain the business herein described if he believes it to be in the best interests of the beneficiary so to do, or he may dispose of it, investing and reinvesting the proceeds as he may deem appropriate. Prior to the date upon which such beneficiary attains the age of 21 years, the Successor Trustee may apply or expend any or all of the income or principal directly for the maintenance, education and support of the beneficiary without the intervention of any guardian and without application to any court. Such payments of income or principal may be made to the parents of such beneficiary or to the person with whom the beneficiary is living without any liability upon the Successor Trustee to see to the application thereof. If any such beneficiary survives us but dies before attaining the age of 21 years, at his or her death the Successor Trustee shall transfer, pay over and deliver the trust property to such beneficiary's personal representative, absolutely.

2. Any beneficiary hereunder shall be liable for his proportionate share of any taxes levied upon the total taxable estate of the survivor of us by reason of the death of such survivor.

3. The interests of any beneficiary hereunder shall be inalienable and free from anticipation, assignment, attachment, pledge

constitute as to such whole or part a revocation of this trust.

7. The death during our lifetime, or in a common accident or disaster with us, of both of the beneficiaries designated hereunder shall revoke such designation, and in the former event, we reserve the right to designate a new beneficiary. Should we for any reason fail to designate such new beneficiary, this trust shall terminate upon the death of the survivor of us and the trust property shall revert to the estate of such survivor.

8. In the event of the physical or mental incapacity or death of one of us, or if we both shall die in a common accident, we hereby nominate and appoint as Successor Trustee hereunder the beneficiary named first above, unless such beneficiary named first above shall not have attained the age of 21 years or is otherwise legally incapacitated, in which event we hereby nominate and appoint the beneficiary named second above, unless such beneficiary shall not have attained the age of 21 years or is otherwise legally incapacitated, in which event we hereby nominate and appoint

(Name) __Henry P. Adams__ __Milton__ __Connecticut__ __06605__, of
City / State / Zip

(Address) __125__ __Barnum Street__
Number / Street

to be Successor Trustee.

9. This Declaration of Trust shall extend to and be binding upon the heirs, executors, administrators and assigns of the undersigned and upon the Successors to the Trustees.

10. We as Trustees and our Successor Trustee shall serve without bond.

11. This Declaration of Trust shall be construed and enforced in accordance with the laws of the State of __Connecticut__

Declaration of Trust

WHEREAS, WE, _____ and _____, of the

City/Town of _____, County of _____, State of _____,

are joint owners of the unincorporated business known as _____

_____

(Name of Business)

located at _____, in the City/Town of _____,

County of _____ and State of _____; and

WHEREAS the principal business of the said _____

(Name of Business)

is _____

_____

_____;

NOW, THEREFORE, KNOW ALL MEN BY THESE PRESENTS, that we do hereby acknowledge and declare that we hold and will hold said business and all our right, title and interest in and to said business, and all furniture, fixtures, stock in trade, inventory, machinery, vehicles, accounts receivable, prepaid insurance and all other assets of such business IN TRUST

   1. For the use and benefit of:

(Name) _____, of

(Address) _____

          Number   *Street*   *City*   *State*   *Zip*

or, if such beneficiary be not surviving, for the use and benefit of:

(Name) _____, of

(Address) _____

          Number   *Street*   *City*   *State*   *Zip*

    If because of the physical or mental incapacity of both of us certified in writing by a physician, the Successor Trustee hereinafter named shall assume active administration of this trust during our lifetime, such Successor Trustee shall be fully authorized to pay to us or disburse on our behalf such sums from income or principal as appear necessary or desirable for our comfort or welfare. Upon the death of the survivor of us, unless the beneficiaries shall predecease us or unless we all shall die as a result of a common accident, our Successor Trustee is hereby directed forthwith to transfer said business and all our right, title and interest in and to said business unto the beneficiary absolutely and thereby terminate this trust; provided, however, that if the beneficiary hereunder shall not have attained the age of 21 years, the Successor Trustee shall hold the trust assets in continuing trust until such beneficiary shall have attained the age of 21 years. During such period of continuing trust the Successor Trustee, in his absolute discretion, may retain the business herein described if he believes it to be in the best interests of the beneficiary so to do, or he may dispose of it, investing and reinvesting the proceeds as he may deem appropriate. Prior to the date upon which such beneficiary attains the age of 21 years, the Successor Trustee may apply or expend any or all of the income or principal directly for the maintenance, education and support of the beneficiary without the intervention of any guardian and without application to any court. Such payments of income or principal may be made to the parents of such beneficiary or to the person with whom the beneficiary is living without any liability upon the Successor Trustee to see to the application thereof. If any such beneficiary survives us but dies before attaining the age of 21 years, at his or her death the Successor Trustee shall transfer, pay over and deliver the trust property to such beneficiary's personal representative, absolutely.

    2. Any beneficiary hereunder shall be liable for his proportionate share of any taxes levied upon the total taxable estate of the survivor of us by reason of the death of such survivor.

    3. The interests of any beneficiary hereunder shall be inalienable and free from anticipation, assignment, attachment, pledge or control by creditors or a present or former spouse of such beneficiary in any proceedings at law or in equity.

    4. This trust is created with the express understanding that the bank at which an account is maintained in the name of the business shall be under no liability whatsoever to see to its proper administration. On the contrary, upon the transfer of the right, title and interest in and to the business by any trustee hereunder, said bank shall conclusively treat the transferee as the sole owner of said account. Until the bank shall receive from some person interested in this trust, written notice of any death or other event upon which the right to receive may depend, the bank shall incur no liability for payments made in good faith to persons whose interests shall have been affected by such event. The bank shall be protected in acting upon any notice or other instrument or document believed by it to be genuine and to have been signed or presented by the proper party or parties.

    5. We reserve unto ourselves the power and right to collect all income which may accrue from the trust property and to pay such income to ourselves as individuals. We shall be exclusively entitled to all such income accruing from the trust property during our lifetime, and no beneficiary named herein shall have any claim upon any such income distributed to us.

6. We reserve unto ourselves the power and right at any time during our lifetime to amend or revoke in whole or in part the trust hereby created without the necessity of obtaining the consent of the beneficiaries and without giving notice to the beneficiaries. The sale or other disposition by us of the whole or any part of the assets of the business held hereunder shall constitute as to such whole or part a revocation of this trust.

7. The death during our lifetime, or in a common accident or disaster with us, of both of the beneficiaries designated hereunder shall revoke such designation, and in the former event, we reserve the right to designate a new beneficiary. Should we for any reason fail to designate such new beneficiary, this trust shall terminate upon the death of the survivor of us and the trust property shall revert to the estate of such survivor.

8. In the event of the physical or mental incapacity or death of one of us, the survivor shall continue as sole Trustee. In the event of the physical or mental incapacity or death of the survivor of us, or if we both shall die in a common accident, we hereby nominate and appoint as Successor Trustee hereunder the beneficiary named first above, unless such beneficiary shall not have attained the age of 21 years or is otherwise legally incapacitated, in which event we hereby nominate and appoint the beneficiary named second above, unless such beneficiary named second above shall not have attained the age of 21 years or is otherwise legally incapacitated, in which event we hereby nominate and appoint

(Name) _____ , of

(Address) _____

Number   Street   City   State   Zip

to be Successor Trustee.

9. This Declaration of Trust shall extend to and be binding upon the heirs, executors, administrators and assigns of the undersigned and upon the Successors to the Trustees.

10. We as Trustees and our Successor Trustee shall serve without bond.

11. This Declaration of Trust shall be construed and enforced in accordance with the laws of the State of

_____ .

IN WITNESS WHEREOF, we have hereunto set our hands and seals this _____

day of _____ , 19_____ .

(First Settlor sign here) _____ L.S.

(Second Settlor sign here) _____ L.S.

I, the undersigned legal spouse of one of the above Settlors, hereby waive all community property rights which I may have in the hereinabove-described business and give my assent to the provisions of the trust and to the inclusion in it of the said business.

(Spouse sign here) _____ L.S.

Witness: (1) _____   Witness: (2) _____

STATE OF _____   City
                                     or
COUNTY OF _____   Town _____

On the _____ day of_____ , 19_____ , personally appeared

_____ and _____

known to me to be the individuals who executed the foregoing instrument, and acknowledged the same to be their free act and deed, before me.

_____

(Notary Seal)   Notary Public

CHAPTER 18

DECLARATION OF TRUST
For Naming
TWO OR MORE BENEFICIARIES, SHARING EQUALLY,
To Receive
AN UNINCORPORATED BUSINESS HELD IN JOINT NAMES

INSTRUCTIONS:

On the following pages will be found a declaration of trust (DT-147-J) suitable for use in connection with the establishment of an inter vivos trust covering an unincorporated business held in joint names where it is desired to name two or more persons, sharing equally, to receive the business upon the death of the survivor of the two owners.

Enter the names of the two co-owners on the first line.

Cross out *"city"* or *"town,"* leaving the appropriate designation of your community. Next, give the name and location and explain exactly what kind of business it is.

In Paragraph 1, indicate the *number of persons* you are naming (to discourage unauthorized additions to the list) and then insert their names. The one whose name appears *first* will be the Successor Trustee responsible for seeing to the distribution of the trust property.

Note that the instrument specifies that the named beneficiaries are to receive *"in equal shares, or the survivor of them/per stirpes."* Now, think carefully: If you have named three persons with the intention that if one of them predeceases you, *his* children will take *his* share, cross out *"or the survivor of them"* and *initial it.* If that is *not* what you want—if, for example, you prefer that the share of the deceased person be divided between the two surviving persons, cross out *"per stirpes"* and *initial it.* Remember, you <u>must</u> cross out either *"or the survivor of them"* or *"per stirpes"*—one or the other.

Note that Paragraph 8 designates as Successor Trustee *"the beneficiary named first above,"* which means that in most cases you don't need to fill anything in there. However, if there is a possibility of a beneficiary who has not attained the age of 21 years receiving a share of the trust property, make certain that you name an adult in this paragraph who can act as trustee for such beneficiary. Avoid naming as trustee a person not likely to survive until the beneficiary has attained age 21.

When completed in the manner shown on the reverse side hereof, make several photocopies for reference purposes. Hold the original in safekeeping and offer a copy to the beneficiaries and to the bank where your business account is maintained.

Important: Read carefully Note B on page 38, which applies to this declaration of trust.

WHEREVER THE INSTRUCTION "INITIAL IT" APPEARS ABOVE,
IT MEANS THAT *BOTH* CO-OWNERS SHOULD INITIAL IT.

Declaration of Trust

WHEREAS, WE, __John J. Brown__ and __Elizabeth A. Brown__ , of the

City/Town of __Milton__ , County of __Fairfax__ , State of __Connecticut__ ,

are joint owners of the unincorporated business known as __The Fairport Gift Shoppe__ ;

(Name of Business)

located at __120 Main Street__ , in the City/Town of __Milton__ ; and

County of __Fairfax__ and State of __Connecticut__ __The Fairport Gift Shoppe__

(Name of Business)

WHEREAS the principal business of the said

is __the retail sale of greeting cards and giftware.__

NOW, THEREFORE, KNOW ALL MEN BY THESE PRESENTS, that we do hereby acknowledge and declare that we hold and will hold said business and all our right, title and interest in and to said business, and all furniture, fixtures, stock in trade, inventory, machinery, vehicles, accounts receivable, prepaid insurance and all other assets of such business IN TRUST

1. For the use and benefit of the following __three (3)__ persons, in equal shares of the survivor of them/per stirpes:

Diane R. Brown - our daughter
Jill A. Lynn - our niece
Charles A. Brown - our son

If because of the physical or mental incapacity of both of us certified in writing by a physician, the Successor Trustee hereinafter named shall assume active administration of this trust during our lifetime, such Successor Trustee shall be fully authorized to pay to us or disburse on our behalf such sums from income or principal as appear necessary or desirable for our comfort or welfare. Upon the death of the survivor of us, unless all the beneficiaries shall predecease us or unless we all shall die as a result of a common accident or disaster, our Successor Trustee is hereby directed forthwith to transfer said business and all our right, title and interest in and to said business unto the beneficiaries absolutely and thereby terminate this trust; provided, however, that if any beneficiary hereunder shall not have attained the age of 21 years, the Successor Trustee shall hold such beneficiary's share of the trust assets in continuing trust until such beneficiary shall have attained the age of 21 years. During such period of continuing trust the Successor Trustee, in his absolute discretion, may retain the business herein described if he believes it to be in the best interests of the beneficiary so to do, or he may dispose of it, investing and reinvesting the proceeds as he may deem appropriate. Prior to the date upon which such beneficiary attains the age of 21 years, the Successor Trustee may apply or expend any or all of the income or principal directly for the maintenance, education and support of the beneficiary without the intervention of any guardian and without application to any court. Such payments of income or principal may be made to the parents of such beneficiary or to the person with whom the beneficiary is living without any liability upon the Successor Trustee to see to the application thereof. If any such beneficiary survives us but dies before the age of 21 years, at his or her death the Successor Trustee shall transfer, pay over and deliver such beneficiary's share of the trust property to such beneficiary's personal representative, absolutely.

2. Each beneficiary hereunder shall be liable for his proportionate share of any taxes levied upon the total taxable estate of the survivor of us by reason of the death of such survivor.

3. The interests of any beneficiary hereunder shall be inalienable and free from anticipation, assignment, attachment, pledge

shall revoke such designation, and in the former event, we reserve the right to designate new beneficiaries. Should we for any reason fail to designate such new beneficiaries, this trust shall terminate upon the death of the survivor of us and the trust property shall revert to the estate of such survivor.

8. In the event of the physical or mental incapacity or death of one of us, the survivor shall continue as sole Trustee. In the event of the physical or mental incapacity or death of the survivor of us, or if we both shall die in a common accident or disaster, we hereby nominate and appoint as Successor Trustee hereunder the beneficiary named first above, unless such beneficiary named second above shall not have attained the age of 21 years or is otherwise legally incapacitated, in which event we hereby nominate and appoint the beneficiary named second above, unless such beneficiary shall not have attained the age of 21 years or is otherwise legally incapacitated, in which event we hereby nominate and appoint

__Henry P. Adams__ __Milton__ , __Connecticut__ __06605__
(Name) *City* *State* *Zip*

(Address) __125 Barnum Street__
Number *Street*

to be Successor Trustee.

9. This Declaration of Trust shall extend to and be binding upon the heirs, executors, administrators and assigns of the undersigned and upon the Successors to the Trustees.

10. We as Trustees and our Successor Trustee shall serve without bond.

11. This Declaration of Trust shall be construed and enforced in accordance with the laws of the State of __Connecticut__

Declaration of Trust

WHEREAS, WE, _____ and _____, of the

City/Town of _____, County of _____, State of _____,

are joint owners of the unincorporated business known as _____

_____

(Name of Business)

located at _____, in the City/Town of _____,

County of _____ and State of _____; and

WHEREAS the principal business of the said _____

(Name of Business)

is _____

_____

_____;

NOW, THEREFORE, KNOW ALL MEN BY THESE PRESENTS, that we do hereby acknowledge and declare that we hold and will hold said business and all our right, title and interest in and to said business, and all furniture, fixtures, stock in trade, inventory, machinery, vehicles, accounts receivable, prepaid insurance and all other assets of such business IN TRUST

1. For the use and benefit of the following _____ persons, in equal shares, or the survivor of them/per stirpes:

If because of the physical or mental incapacity of both of us certified in writing by a physician, the Successor Trustee hereinafter named shall assume active administration of this trust during our lifetime, such Successor Trustee shall be fully authorized to pay to us or disburse on our behalf such sums from income or principal as appear necessary or desirable for our comfort or welfare. Upon the death of the survivor of us, unless all the beneficiaries shall predecease us or unless we all shall die as a result of a common accident or disaster, our Successor Trustee is hereby directed forthwith to transfer said business and all our right, title and interest in and to said business unto the beneficiaries absolutely and thereby terminate this trust; provided, however, that if any beneficiary hereunder shall not have attained the age of 21 years, the Successor Trustee shall hold such beneficiary's share of the trust assets in continuing trust until such beneficiary shall have attained the age of 21 years. During such period of continuing trust the Successor Trustee, in his absolute discretion, may retain the business herein described if he believes it to be in the best interests of the beneficiary so to do, or he may dispose of it, investing and reinvesting the proceeds as he may deem appropriate. Prior to the date upon which such beneficiary attains the age of 21 years, the Successor Trustee may apply or expend any or all of the income or principal directly for the maintenance, education and support of the beneficiary without the intervention of any guardian and without application to any court. Such payments of income or principal may be made to the parents of such beneficiary or to the person with whom the beneficiary is living without any liability upon the Successor Trustee to see to the application thereof. If any such beneficiary survives us but dies before the age of 21 years, at his or her death the Successor Trustee shall transfer, pay over and deliver such beneficiary's share of the trust property to such beneficiary's personal representative, absolutely.

2. Each beneficiary hereunder shall be liable for his proportionate share of any taxes levied upon the total taxable estate of the survivor of us by reason of the death of such survivor.

3. The interests of any beneficiary hereunder shall be inalienable and free from anticipation, assignment, attachment, pledge or control by creditors or a present or former spouse of such beneficiary in any proceedings at law or in equity.

4. This trust is created with the express understanding that the bank at which an account is maintained in the name of the business shall be under no liability whatsoever to see to such trust's proper administration. On the contrary, upon the transfer of the right, title and interest in and to the business by any trustee hereunder, said bank shall conclusively treat the transferee as the

sole owner of said account. Until the bank shall receive from some person interested in this trust, written notice of any death or other event upon which the right to receive may depend, the bank shall incur no liability for payments made in good faith to persons whose interest shall have been affected by such event. The bank shall be protected in acting upon any notice or other instrument or document believed by it to be genuine and to have been signed or presented by the proper party or parties.

5. We reserve unto ourselves the power and right to collect all income which may accrue from the trust property and to pay such income to ourselves as individuals. We shall be exclusively entitled to all such income accruing from the trust property during our lifetime and no beneficiary named herein shall have any claim upon any such income distributed to us.

6. We reserve unto ourselves the power and right at any time during our lifetime to amend or revoke in whole or in part the trust hereby created without the necessity of obtaining the consent of any beneficiary and without giving notice to any beneficiary. The sale or other disposition by us of the whole or any part of the assets of the business held hereunder shall constitute as to such whole or part a revocation of this trust.

7. The death during our lifetime, or in a common accident or disaster with us, of all of the beneficiaries designated hereunder shall revoke such designation, and in the former event, we reserve the right to designate new beneficiaries. Should we for any reason fail to designate such new beneficiaries, this trust shall terminate upon the death of the survivor of us and the trust property shall revert to the estate of such survivor.

8. In the event of the physical or mental incapacity or death of one of us, the survivor shall continue as sole Trustee. In the event of the physical or mental incapacity or death of the survivor of us, or if we both shall die in a common accident or disaster, we hereby nominate and appoint as Successor Trustee hereunder the beneficiary named first above, unless such beneficiary shall not have attained the age of 21 years or is otherwise legally incapacitated, in which event we hereby nominate and appoint the beneficiary named second above, unless such beneficiary named second above shall not have attained the age of 21 years or is otherwise legally incapacitated, in which event we hereby nominate and appoint

(Name) _____ _____ , of

(Address) _____ ,
$\quad\quad\quad\quad\quad$ *Number* $\quad\quad\quad\quad$ *Street* $\quad\quad\quad\quad\quad$ *City* $\quad\quad\quad\quad\quad$ *State* $\quad\quad\quad$ *Zip*

to be Successor Trustee.

9. This Declaration of Trust shall extend to and be binding upon the heirs, executors, administrators and assigns of the undersigned and upon the Successors to the Trustees.

10. We as Trustees and our Successor Trustee shall serve without bond.

11. This Declaration of Trust shall be construed and enforced in accordance with the laws of the State of

_____ .

IN WITNESS WHEREOF, we have hereunto set our hands and seals this _____

day of _____ , 19_____ .

$\quad\quad\quad\quad\quad\quad\quad$ *(First Settlor sign here)* _____ L.S.

$\quad\quad\quad\quad\quad$ *(Second Settlor sign here)* _____ L.S.

I, the undersigned legal spouse of one of the above Settlors, hereby waive all community property rights which I may have in the hereinabove-described business and give my assent to the provisions of the trust and to the inclusion in it of the said business.

$\quad\quad\quad\quad\quad\quad\quad\quad$ *(Spouse sign here)* _____ L.S.

Witness: (1) _____ $\quad$ Witness: (2) _____

STATE OF _____ ⎱ City
$\quad\quad\quad\quad\quad\quad\quad\quad\quad\quad\quad\quad\quad\quad\quad\quad$ ⎰ or
COUNTY OF _____ ⎰ Town _____

On the _____ day of _____ , 19_____ , personally appeared

_____ and _____

known to me to be the individuals who executed the foregoing instrument, and acknowledged the same to be their free act and deed, before me.

(Notary Seal) $\quad\quad\quad\quad\quad\quad\quad\quad\quad\quad\quad\quad\quad\quad$ _____
$\quad\quad\quad\quad\quad\quad\quad\quad\quad\quad\quad\quad\quad\quad\quad\quad\quad\quad\quad\quad\quad\quad$ *Notary Public*

CHAPTER 19

Avoiding Probate of the Contents of a Rented House or Apartment

In earlier chapters, trust forms have been provided for use by individuals who desired to avoid probate of a home they owned. These forms were designed to pass all furniture, fixtures, and personal property on the premises along with the house to the beneficiary named.

But millions of Americans live in rented or leased houses or apartments, and it is equally important to them that the contents of these premises pass to heirs of their choice without having to go through the probate wringer.

Accordingly, in the pages which follow will be found a variety of trust forms which may be used to place these articles of personal property in an inter vivos trust without the necessity of itemizing such contents.

CHAPTER 19

DECLARATION OF TRUST
For Naming
ONE BENEFICIARY
To Receive
THE CONTENTS OF A RENTED HOUSE
OR APARTMENT HELD IN ONE NAME

INSTRUCTIONS:

On the following pages will be found a declaration of trust (DT-149) suitable for use in connection with the establishment of an inter vivos trust covering the contents of a rented house or apartment held in one name only, where it is desired to name some one person to receive such contents upon the death of the owner.

Cross out *"city"* or *"town,"* leaving the appropriate designation of your community. Next, give the exact location (apartment number and street number) of the premises the contents of which you are placing in trust.

Enter the name of the beneficiary in the appropriate place in Paragraph 1.

Note that Paragraph 6 designates as Successor Trustee *"whosoever shall at that time be beneficiary hereunder,"* which means that in most cases you don't need to fill anything in there. However, if there is any possibility of a beneficiary who has not attained the age of 21 years receiving the trust property, make certain that you name an adult in this paragraph who can act as trustee for such beneficiary. Avoid naming as trustee a person not likely to survive until the beneficiary has attained age 21.

When completed in the manner shown on the reverse side hereof, make one or two photocopies for reference purposes and to give to the beneficiary. Hold the original in safekeeping.

Important: Read carefully Note B on page 38, which applies to this declaration of trust.

Declaration of Trust

DACEY TRUST

WHEREAS, I, _____ John J. Brown _____, County of _____ Fairfax _____, State of _____ Connecticut _____;

City/Town of _____ Milton _____

am the owner of the contents of a rented house or apartment located at (and known as) _____, in the said City/Town of _____ Milton _____

6A   525 Main Street
(Apartment Number)   (Street Number)

State of _____ Connecticut _____.

NOW, THEREFORE, KNOW ALL MEN BY THESE PRESENTS, that I do hereby acknowledge and declare that I hold and will hold said contents and all my right, title and interest in and to said contents IN TRUST

1. For the use and benefit of:

(Name) _____ Charles M. Brown - my brother _____ Milton _____ Connecticut 06605 _____
                                                    City   State   Zip

(Address) _____ 80 _____ College Street _____
                 Number   Street

If because of my physical or mental incapacity certified in writing by a physician, the Successor Trustee hereinafter named shall assume active administration of this trust during my lifetime, such Successor Trustee shall be fully authorized, if the need arises, to dispose of all or any part of such contents and to pay to me or disburse on my behalf from the proceeds such sums from income or principal as appear necessary or desirable for my comfort or welfare. Upon my death, unless the beneficiary shall predecease me or unless we both shall die as a result of a common accident or disaster, my Successor Trustee is hereby directed forthwith to transfer said contents and all my right, title and interest in and to said contents unto the beneficiary absolutely and thereby terminate this trust; provided, however, that if the beneficiary hereunder shall not have attained the age of 21 years, the Successor Trustee shall hold the trust assets in continuing trust until such beneficiary shall have attained the age of 21 years. During such period of continuing trust the Successor Trustee, in his absolute discretion, may retain the trust property herein described if he believes it to be in the best interests of the beneficiary so to do, or he may dispose of it, investing and reinvesting the proceeds as he may deem appropriate. Prior to the date upon which such beneficiary attains the age of 21 years, the Successor Trustee may apply or expend any or all of the income or principal directly for the maintenance, education and support of the beneficiary without the intervention of any guardian and without application to any court. Such payments of income or principal may be made to the parents of such beneficiary or to the person with whom the beneficiary is living without any liability upon the Successor Trustee to see to the application thereof. If such beneficiary survives me but dies before attaining the age of 21 years, at his or her death the Successor Trustee shall transfer, pay over and deliver the trust property to such beneficiary's personal representative, absolutely.

If among the contents of the house of apartment held hereunder there be any asset identifiable as having been covered by a separate declaration of trust in connection with which a beneficiary other than the one named in this trust has been designated, the Successor Trustee of this trust shall assert no claim to such asset but shall promptly deliver up the same to the individual named as Successor Trustee of such other trust.

2. The beneficiary hereunder shall be liable for his proportionate share of any taxes levied upon the Settlor's total taxable estate by reason of the Settlor's death.

3. All interests of a beneficiary hereunder shall be inalienable and free from anticipation, assignment, attachment, pledge or control by creditors or a present or former spouse of such beneficiary in any proceedings at law or in equity.

4. I reserve unto myself the power and right at any time during my lifetime to amend or revoke in whole or in part the trust hereby created without the necessity of obtaining the consent of the beneficiary and without giving notice to the beneficiary. The sale or other disposition by me of the whole or any part of the trust property held hereunder shall constitute as to such whole or part a revocation of this trust.

5. The death during my lifetime, or in a common accident with me, of the beneficiary designated hereunder shall revoke such designation, and in the former event, I reserve the right to designate a new beneficiary. Should I for any reason fail to designate such new beneficiary, this trust shall terminate upon my death and the trust property shall revert to my estate.

6. In the event of my physical or mental incapacity or my death, I hereby nominate and appoint as Successor Trustee hereunder whosoever shall at that time be beneficiary hereunder, unless such beneficiary shall not have attained the age of 21 years or is otherwise legally incapacitated, in which event I hereby nominate and appoint

(Name) _____ Henry P. Adams _____ Milton _____ Connecticut _____ 06605 _____
                                          City   State   Zip

(Address) _____ 125 _____ Barnum Street _____
                 Number   Street

to be Successor Trustee.

7. This Declaration of Trust shall extend to and be binding upon the heirs, executors, administrators and assigns of the undersigned and upon the Successors to the Trustee.

8. The Trustee and his successors shall serve without bond.

9. This Declaration of Trust shall be construed and enforced in accordance with the laws of the State of _____ Connecticut _____

Declaration of Trust

WHEREAS, I, _____, of the

City/Town of _____, County of _____, State of _____,

am the owner of the contents of a rented house or apartment located at (and known as)

_____, in the said City/Town of _____,

(Apartment Number)   (Street Number)

State of _____;

NOW, THEREFORE, KNOW ALL MEN BY THESE PRESENTS, that I do hereby acknowledge and declare that I hold and will hold said contents and all my right, title and interest in and to said contents IN TRUST

1. For the use and benefit of:

(Name) _____, of

(Address) _____

       Number   Street   City   State   Zip

If because of my physical or mental incapacity certified in writing by a physician, the Successor Trustee hereinafter named shall assume active administration of this trust during my lifetime, such Successor Trustee shall be fully authorized, if the need arises, to dispose of all or any part of such contents and to pay to me or disburse on my behalf from the proceeds such sums from income or principal as appear necessary or desirable for my comfort or welfare. Upon my death, unless the beneficiary shall predecease me or unless we both shall die as a result of a common accident or disaster, my Successor Trustee is hereby directed forthwith to transfer said contents and all my right, title and interest in and to said contents unto the beneficiary absolutely and thereby terminate this trust; provided, however, that if the beneficiary hereunder shall not have attained the age of 21 years, the Successor Trustee shall hold the trust assets in continuing trust until such beneficiary shall have attained the age of 21 years. During such period of continuing trust the Successor Trustee, in his absolute discretion, may retain the trust property herein described if he believes it to be in the best interests of the beneficiary so to do, or he may dispose of it, investing and reinvesting the proceeds as he may deem appropriate. Prior to the date upon which such beneficiary attains the age of 21 years, the Successor Trustee may apply or expend any or all of the income or principal directly for the maintenance, education and support of the beneficiary without the intervention of any guardian and without application to any court. Such payments of income or principal may be made to the parents of such beneficiary or to the person with whom the beneficiary is living without any liability upon the Successor Trustee to see to the application thereof. If such beneficiary survives me but dies before attaining the age of 21 years, at his or her death the Successor Trustee shall transfer, pay over and deliver the trust property to such beneficiary's personal representative, absolutely.

If among the contents of the house or apartment held hereunder there be any asset identifiable as having been covered by a separate declaration of trust in connection with which a beneficiary other than the one named in this trust has been designated, the Successor Trustee of this trust shall assert no claim to such asset but shall promptly deliver up the same to the individual named as Successor Trustee of such other trust.

2. The beneficiary hereunder shall be liable for his proportionate share of any taxes levied upon the Settlor's total taxable estate by reason of the Settlor's death.

3. All interests of a beneficiary hereunder shall be inalienable and free from anticipation, assignment, attachment, pledge or control by creditors or a present or former spouse of such beneficiary in any proceedings at law or in equity.

4. I reserve unto myself the power and right at any time during my lifetime to amend or revoke in whole or in part the trust hereby created without the necessity of obtaining the consent of the beneficiary and without giving notice to the beneficiary. The sale or other disposition by me of the whole or any part of the trust property held hereunder shall constitute as to such whole or part a revocation of this trust.

5. The death during my lifetime, or in a common accident with me, of the beneficiary designated hereunder shall revoke such designation, and in the former event, I reserve the right to designate a new beneficiary. Should I for any reason fail to designate such new beneficiary, this trust shall terminate upon my death and the trust property shall revert to my estate.

6. In the event of my physical or mental incapacity or my death, I hereby nominate and appoint as Successor Trustee hereunder whosoever shall at that time be beneficiary hereunder, unless such beneficiary shall not have attained the age of 21 years or is otherwise legally incapacitated, in which event I hereby nominate and appoint

(Name) _____, of

(Address) _____

       Number   Street   City   State   Zip

to be Successor Trustee.

7. This Declaration of Trust shall extend to and be binding upon the heirs, executors, administrators and assigns of the undersigned and upon the Successors to the Trustee.

8. The Trustee and his successors shall serve without bond.

9. This Declaration of Trust shall be construed and enforced in accordance with the laws of the State of

_____.

IN WITNESS WHEREOF, I have hereunto set my hand and seal this _____

day of _____, 19_____.

(Settlor sign here) _____ L.S.

I, the undersigned legal spouse of the above Settlor, hereby waive all community property rights which I may have in the hereinabove-described trust property and give my assent to the provisions of the trust and to the inclusion in it of the said property.

(Spouse sign here) _____ L.S.

Witness: (1) _____   Witness: (2) _____

STATE OF _____⎫   City

COUNTY OF _____⎬   or

                                          ⎭   Town _____

On the _____ day of _____, 19_____, personally appeared

_____

known to me to be the individual(s) who executed the foregoing instrument, and acknowledged the same to be _____ free act and deed, before me.

(Notary Seal)

_____

Notary Public

CHAPTER 19

DECLARATION OF TRUST
For Naming
ONE PRIMARY BENEFICIARY
And
ONE CONTINGENT BENEFICIARY
To Receive
THE CONTENTS OF A RENTED HOUSE
OR APARTMENT HELD IN ONE NAME

INSTRUCTIONS:

On the following pages will be found a declaration of trust (DT-150) suitable for use in connection with the establishment of an inter vivos trust covering the contents of a rented house or apartment held in one name only, where it is desired to name some *one* person as primary beneficiary, with some *one* other person as contingent beneficiary to receive such contents if the primary beneficiary be not surviving upon the death of the owner.

Cross out *"city"* or *"town,"* leaving the appropriate designation of your community. Next, give the exact location (apartment number and street number) of the premises the contents of which you are placing in trust.

Enter the names of the beneficiaries in the appropriate place in Paragraph 1.

Note that Paragraph 6 designates as Successor Trustee *"whosoever shall at that time be beneficiary hereunder,"* which means that in most cases you don't need to fill anything in there. However, if there is any possibility of a beneficiary who has not attained the age of 21 years receiving the trust property, make certain that you name an adult in this paragraph who can act as trustee for such beneficiary. Avoid naming as trustee a person not likely to survive until the beneficiary has attained age 21.

When completed in the manner shown on the reverse side hereof, make several photocopies for reference purposes and to give to the beneficiaries. Hold the original in safekeeping.

Important: Read carefully Note B on page 38, which applies to this declaration of trust.

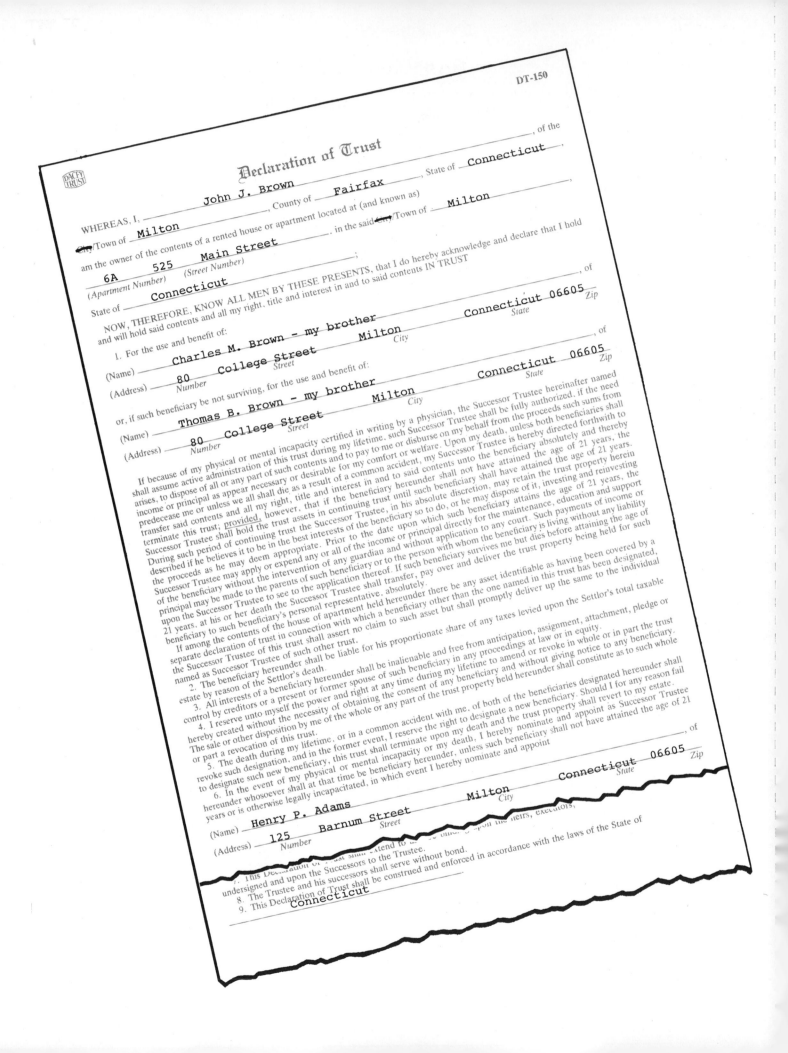

DT-150

Declaration of Trust

WHEREAS, I, __John J. Brown__, County of __Fairfax__, State of __Connecticut__, of the City/Town of __Milton__

am the owner of the contents of a rented house or apartment located at (and known as) __Milton__, in the said City/Town of __Milton__

__6A__ __525__ __Main Street__
(Apartment Number) (Street Number)

State of __Connecticut__;

NOW, THEREFORE, KNOW ALL MEN BY THESE PRESENTS, that I do hereby acknowledge and declare that I hold and will hold said contents and all my right, title and interest in and to said contents IN TRUST

1. For the use and benefit of:

__Charles M. Brown – my brother__ __Milton__ __Connecticut__ __06605__
(Name) City State Zip

__80__ __College Street__
(Address) Number Street

or, if such beneficiary be not surviving, for the use and benefit of:

__Thomas B. Brown – my brother__ __Milton__ __Connecticut__ __06605__
(Name) City State Zip

__80__ __College Street__
(Address) Number Street

If because of my physical or mental incapacity certified in writing by a physician, the Successor Trustee hereinafter named shall assume active administration of this trust during my lifetime, such Successor Trustee shall be fully authorized, if the need arises, to dispose of all or any part of such contents and to pay to me or disburse on my behalf from the proceeds such sums from income or principal as appear necessary or desirable for my comfort or welfare. Upon my death, unless both beneficiaries shall predecease me or unless we all shall die as a result of a common accident and to said contents unto the beneficiary absolutely and thereby transfer said contents and all my right, title and interest in and to said contents unto the beneficiary absolutely and thereby terminate this trust; provided, however, that if the beneficiary hereunder shall not have attained the age of 21 years, the Successor Trustee shall hold the trust assets in continuing trust until such beneficiary shall have attained the age of 21 years, the Successor Trustee shall hold the trust assets in continuing trust until such beneficiary attains the age of 21 years, the During such period of continuing trust the Successor Trustee, in his absolute discretion, may retain the trust property herein described if he believes it to be in the best interests of the beneficiary so to do, or he may dispose of it, investing and reinvesting the proceeds as he may deem appropriate. Prior to the date upon which such beneficiary attains the age of 21 years, the Successor Trustee may apply or expend any or all of the income or principal directly for the maintenance, education and support of the beneficiary without the intervention of any guardian and without application to any court. Such payments of income or principal may be made to the parents of such beneficiary or to the person with whom the beneficiary is living without any liability upon the Successor Trustee to see to the application thereof. If such beneficiary survives me but dies before attaining the age of 21 years, at his or her death the Successor Trustee shall transfer, pay over and deliver the trust property being held for such beneficiary to such beneficiary's personal representative, absolutely.

If among the contents of the house of apartment held hereunder there be any asset identifiable as having been covered by a separate declaration of trust in connection with which a beneficiary other than the one named in this trust has been designated, the Successor Trustee of this trust shall assert no claim to such asset but shall promptly deliver up the same to the individual named as Successor Trustee of such other trust.

2. The beneficiary hereunder shall be liable for his proportionate share of any taxes levied upon the Settlor's total taxable estate by reason of the Settlor's death.

3. All interests of a beneficiary hereunder shall be inalienable and free from anticipation, assignment, attachment, pledge or control by creditors or a present or former spouse of such beneficiary in any proceedings at law or in equity.

4. I reserve unto myself the power and right at any time during my lifetime to amend or revoke in whole or in part the trust hereby created without the necessity of obtaining the consent of any beneficiary and without giving notice to any beneficiary. The sale or other disposition by me of the whole or any part of the trust property held hereunder shall constitute as to such whole or part a revocation of this trust.

5. The death during my lifetime, or in a common accident with me, of both of the beneficiaries designated hereunder shall revoke such designation, and in the former event, I reserve the right to designate a new beneficiary. Should I for any reason fail to designate such new beneficiary, this trust shall terminate upon my death and the trust property shall revert to my estate.

6. In the event of my physical or mental incapacity or my death, I hereby nominate and appoint as Successor Trustee hereunder whosoever shall at that time be beneficiary hereunder, unless such beneficiary shall not have attained the age of 21 years or is otherwise legally incapacitated, in which event I hereby nominate and appoint

__Henry P. Adams__ __Milton__ __Connecticut__ __06605__, of
(Name) City State Zip

__125__ __Barnum Street__
(Address) Number Street

7. This Declaration of Trust shall extend to and be binding upon the heirs, executors, undersigned and upon the Successors to the Trustee.

8. The Trustee and his successors shall serve without bond.

9. This Declaration of Trust shall be construed and enforced in accordance with the laws of the State of __Connecticut__

Declaration of Trust

WHEREAS, I, _____, of the

City/Town of _____, County of _____, State of _____,

am the owner of the contents of a rented house or apartment located at (and known as)

_____, in the said City/Town of _____,

(Apartment Number)   (Street Number)

State of _____;

NOW, THEREFORE, KNOW ALL MEN BY THESE PRESENTS, that I do hereby acknowledge and declare that I hold and will hold said contents and all my right, title and interest in and to said contents IN TRUST

1. For the use and benefit of:

(Name) _____, of

(Address) _____
　　　　　　　Number　　　　　　Street　　　　　　City　　　　　　State　　　　Zip

or, if such beneficiary be not surviving, for the use and benefit of:

(Name) _____, of

(Address) _____
　　　　　　　Number　　　　　　Street　　　　　　City　　　　　　State　　　　Zip

If because of my physical or mental incapacity certified in writing by a physician, the Successor Trustee hereinafter named shall assume active administration of this trust during my lifetime, such Successor Trustee shall be fully authorized, if the need arises, to dispose of all or any part of such contents and to pay to me or disburse on my behalf from the proceeds such sums from income or principal as appear necessary or desirable for my comfort or welfare. Upon my death, unless both beneficiaries shall predecease me or unless we all shall die as a result of a common accident, my Successor Trustee is hereby directed forthwith to transfer said contents and all my right, title and interest in and to said contents unto the beneficiary absolutely and thereby terminate this trust; provided, however, that if the beneficiary hereunder shall not have attained the age of 21 years, the Successor Trustee shall hold the trust assets in continuing trust until such beneficiary shall have attained the age of 21 years. During such period of continuing trust the Successor Trustee, in his absolute discretion, may retain the trust property herein described if he believes it to be in the best interests of the beneficiary so to do, or he may dispose of it, investing and reinvesting the proceeds as he may deem appropriate. Prior to the date upon which such beneficiary attains the age of 21 years, the Successor Trustee may apply or expend any or all of the income or principal directly for the maintenance, education and support of the beneficiary without the intervention of any guardian and without application to any court. Such payments of income or principal may be made to the parents of such beneficiary or to the person with whom the beneficiary is living without any liability upon the Successor Trustee to see to the application thereof. If such beneficiary survives me but dies before attaining the age of 21 years, at his or her death the Successor Trustee shall transfer, pay over and deliver the trust property being held for such beneficiary to such beneficiary's personal representative, absolutely.

If among the contents of the house or apartment held hereunder there be any asset identifiable as having been covered by a separate declaration of trust in connection with which beneficiaries other than those named in this trust have been designated, the Successor Trustee of this trust shall assert no claim to such asset but shall promptly deliver up the same to the individual named as Successor Trustee of such other trust.

2. The beneficiary hereunder shall be liable for his proportionate share of any taxes levied upon the Settlor's total taxable estate by reason of the Settlor's death.

3. All interests of a beneficiary hereunder shall be inalienable and free from anticipation, assignment, attachment, pledge or control by creditors or a present or former spouse of such beneficiary in any proceedings at law or in equity.

4. I reserve unto myself the power and right at any time during my lifetime to amend or revoke in whole or in part the trust hereby created without the necessity of obtaining the consent of any beneficiary and without giving notice to any beneficiary. The sale or other disposition by me of the whole or any part of the trust property held hereunder shall constitute as to such whole or part a revocation of this trust.

5. The death during my lifetime, or in a common accident with me, of both of the beneficiaries designated hereunder shall revoke such designation, and in the former event, I reserve the right to designate a new beneficiary. Should I for any reason fail to designate such new beneficiary, this trust shall terminate upon my death and the trust property shall revert to my estate.

6. In the event of my physical or mental incapacity or my death, I hereby nominate and appoint as Successor Trustee hereunder whosoever shall at that time be beneficiary hereunder, unless such beneficiary shall not have attained the age of 21

years or is otherwise legally incapacitated, in which event I hereby nominate and appoint

(Name) _____ , of

(Address) _____

      Number   *Street*   *City*   *State*   *Zip*

to be Successor Trustee.

    7. This Declaration of Trust shall extend to and be binding upon the heirs, executors, administrators and assigns of the undersigned and upon the Successors to the Trustee.

    8. The Trustee and his successors shall serve without bond.

    9. This Declaration of Trust shall be construed and enforced in accordance with the laws of the State of

_____ .

    IN WITNESS WHEREOF, I have hereunto set my hand and seal this _____

day of _____ , 19_____ .

                 (Settlor sign here) _____ L.S.

I, the undersigned legal spouse of the above Settlor, hereby waive all community property rights which I may have in the hereinabove-described trust property and give my assent to the provisions of the trust and to the inclusion in it of the said property.

                 (Spouse sign here) _____ L.S.

Witness: (1) _____ Witness: (2) _____

STATE OF _____ ⎫ City

COUNTY OF _____ ⎬ or Town _____

    On the _____ day of _____ , 19_____ , personally appeared

_____

known to me to be the individual(s) who executed the foregoing instrument, and acknowledged the same to be _____ free act and deed, before me.

(Notary Seal)

_____
                    Notary Public

DECLARATION OF TRUST

For Naming

TWO OR MORE BENEFICIARIES, SHARING EQUALLY,

To Receive

THE CONTENTS OF A RENTED HOUSE

OR APARTMENT HELD IN ONE NAME

INSTRUCTIONS:

On the following pages will be found a declaration of trust (DT-151) suitable for use in connection with the establishment of an inter vivos trust covering the contents of a rented house or apartment held in one name only, where it is desired to name two or more persons to share such contents upon the death of the owner.

Cross out *"city"* or *"town,"* leaving the appropriate designation of your community. Next, give the exact location (apartment number and street number) of the premises the contents of which you are placing in trust.

In Paragraph 1, indicate the *number of persons* you are naming (to discourage unauthorized additions to the list) and then insert their names. The one whose name appears *first* will be the Successor Trustee responsible for seeing to the distribution of the trust property.

Note that the instrument specifies that the named beneficiaries are to receive *"in equal shares, or the survivor of them/per stirpes."* Now, think carefully: If you have named three persons with the understanding that if one of them predeceases you, *his* children will take *his* share, cross out *"or the survivor of them"* and *initial it.* If that is *not* what you want—if, for example, you prefer that the share of the deceased person be divided between the two surviving persons, cross out *"per stirpes"* and *initial it.* Remember, you <u>must</u> cross out either *"or the survivor of them"* or *"per stirpes"*—one or the other.

Note that Paragraph 6 designates as Successor Trustee *"the beneficiary named first above."* Whenever there is any possibility of a beneficiary who has not attained the age of 21 years receiving the trust property, make certain that you name an adult in this paragraph who can act as trustee for such beneficiary. Avoid naming as trustee a person not likely to survive until the beneficiary has attained age 21.

When completed in the manner shown on the reverse side hereof, make several photocopies for reference purposes and to give to the beneficiaries. Hold the original in safekeeping.

Important: Read carefully Note B on page 38, which applies to this declaration of trust.

Declaration of Trust

WHEREAS, I, _____ John J. Brown _____, _____, of the

City/Town of _____ Milton _____ County of _____ Fairfax _____

am the owner of the contents of a rented house or apartment located at (and known as) _____ , in the said City/Town of _____ Milton _____

6A _____ 525 Main Street _____
(Apartment Number) _____ (Street Number) _____

State of _____ Connecticut _____ :

NOW, THEREFORE, KNOW ALL MEN BY THESE PRESENTS, that I do hereby acknowledge and declare that I hold and will hold said contents and all my right, title and interest in and to said contents IN TRUST

1. For the use and benefit of the following _____ three (3) _____ persons, in equal shares, or the survivor of them/per stirpes:

    Charles M. Brown - my brother
    Helen A. Brown - my sister
    Thomas B. Brown - my brother

If because of my physical or mental incapacity certified in writing by a physician, the Successor Trustee hereinafter named shall assume active administration of this trust during my lifetime, such Successor Trustee shall be fully authorized, if the need arises, to dispose of all or any part of such contents and to pay to me or disburse on my behalf from the proceeds such sums from income or principal as appear necessary or desirable for my comfort or welfare. Upon my death, unless all of the beneficiaries shall predecease me or unless we all shall die as a result of a common accident, my Successor Trustee is hereby directed forthwith to transfer said contents and all my right, title and interest in and to said contents unto the beneficiaries absolutely and thereby terminate this trust; provided, however, that if any beneficiary hereunder shall not have attained the age of 21 years, the Successor Trustee shall hold such beneficiary's share of the trust assets in continuing trust until such beneficiary shall have attained the age of 21 years. During such period of continuing trust the Successor Trustee, in his absolute discretion, may retain the specific trust property herein described if he believes it to be in the best interests of the beneficiary so to do, or he may dispose of it, investing and reinvesting the proceeds as he may deem appropriate. Prior to the date upon which such beneficiary attains the age of 21 years, the Successor Trustee may apply or expend any or all of the income or principal directly for the maintenance, education and support of the beneficiary without the intervention of any guardian and without application to any court. Such payments of income or principal may be made to the parents of such beneficiary or to the person with whom the beneficiary is living without any liability upon the Successor Trustee to see to the application thereof. If such beneficiary survives me but dies before attaining the age of 21 years, at his or her death the Successor Trustee shall transfer, pay over and deliver the trust property being held for such beneficiary to such beneficiary's personal representative, absolutely.

If among the contents of the house or apartment held hereunder there be any asset identifiable as having been covered by a separate declaration of trust in connection with which a beneficiary other than the one named in this trust has been designated, the Successor Trustee of this trust shall assert no claim to such asset but shall promptly deliver up the same to the individual named as Successor Trustee of such other trust.

2. Each beneficiary hereunder shall be liable for his proportionate share of any taxes levied upon the Settlor's total taxable estate by reason of the Settlor's death.

3. All interests of a beneficiary hereunder shall be inalienable and free from anticipation, assignment, attachment, pledge or control by creditors or a present or former spouse of such beneficiary in any proceedings at law or in equity.

4. I reserve unto myself the power and right at any time during my lifetime to amend or revoke in whole or in part the trust hereby created without the necessity of obtaining the consent of the beneficiaries and without giving notice to the beneficiaries. The sale or other disposition by me of the whole or any part of the trust property held hereunder shall constitute as to such whole or part a revocation of this trust.

5. The death during my lifetime, or in a common accident or disaster with me, of all of the beneficiaries designated hereunder shall revoke such designation, and in the former event, I reserve the right to designate a new beneficiary. Should I for any reason fail to designate such new beneficiary, this trust shall terminate upon my death and the trust property shall revert to my estate.

6. In the event of my physical or mental incapacity or my death, I hereby nominate and appoint as Successor Trustee the beneficiary named first above, unless such beneficiary shall not have attained the age of 21 years or is otherwise legally incapacitated, in which event I hereby nominate and appoint as Successor Trustee the beneficiary named second above, unless

_____ Henry P. Adams _____ Milton _____ Connecticut 06605 _____
(Name) _____ City _____ State _____ Zip

(Address) _____ 125 _____ Barnum Street _____
Number _____ Street _____

to be Successor Trustee.

7. This Declaration of Trust shall extend to and be binding upon the heirs, executors, administrators and assigns of the undersigned and upon the Successors to the Trustee.

8. The Trustee and his successors shall serve without bond.

9. This Declaration of Trust shall be construed and enforced in accordance with the laws of the State of _____ Connecticut _____

Declaration of Trust

WHEREAS, I, _____, of the

City/Town of _____, County of _____, State of _____,

am the owner of the contents of a rented house or apartment located at (and known as)

_____, in the said City/Town of _____,

(Apartment Number)   (Street Number)

State of _____;

NOW, THEREFORE, KNOW ALL MEN BY THESE PRESENTS, that I do hereby acknowledge and declare that I hold and will hold said contents and all my right, title and interest in and to said contents IN TRUST

　　1. For the use and benefit of the following _____ persons, in equal shares, or the survivor of them/per stirpes:

　　If because of my physical or mental incapacity certified in writing by a physician, the Successor Trustee hereinafter named shall assume active administration of this trust during my lifetime, such Successor Trustee shall be fully authorized, if the need arises, to dispose of all or any part of such contents and to pay to me or disburse on my behalf from the proceeds such sums from income or principal as appear necessary or desirable for my comfort or welfare. Upon my death, unless all of the beneficiaries shall predecease me or unless we all shall die as a result of a common accident, my Successor Trustee is hereby directed forthwith to transfer said contents and all my right, title and interest in and to said contents unto the beneficiaries absolutely and thereby terminate this trust; provided, however, that if any beneficiary hereunder shall not have attained the age of 21 years, the Successor Trustee shall hold such beneficiary's share of the trust assets in continuing trust until such beneficiary shall have attained the age of 21 years. During such period of continuing trust the Successor Trustee, in his absolute discretion, may retain the specific trust property herein described if he believes it to be in the best interests of the beneficiary so to do, or he may dispose of it, investing and reinvesting the proceeds as he may deem appropriate. Prior to the date upon which such beneficiary attains the age of 21 years, the Successor Trustee may apply or expend any or all of the income or principal directly for the maintenance, education and support of the beneficiary without the intervention of any guardian and without application to any court. Such payments of income or principal may be made to the parents of such beneficiary or to the person with whom the beneficiary is living without any liability upon the Successor Trustee to see to the application thereof. If such beneficiary survives me but dies before attaining the age of 21 years, at his or her death the Successor Trustee shall transfer, pay over and deliver the trust property being held for such beneficiary to such beneficiary's personal representative, absolutely.

　　If among the contents of the house or apartment held hereunder there be any asset identifiable as having been covered by a separate declaration of trust in connection with which beneficiaries other than those named in this trust have been designated, the Successor Trustee of this trust shall assert no claim to such asset but shall promptly deliver up the same to the individual named as Successor Trustee of such other trust.

　　2. Each beneficiary hereunder shall be liable for his proportionate share of any taxes levied upon the Settlor's total taxable estate by reason of the Settlor's death.

　　3. All interests of a beneficiary hereunder shall be inalienable and free from anticipation, assignment, attachment, pledge or control by creditors or a present or former spouse of such beneficiary in any proceedings at law or in equity.

　　4. I reserve unto myself the power and right at any time during my lifetime to amend or revoke in whole or in part the trust hereby created without the necessity of obtaining the consent of the beneficiaries and without giving notice to the beneficiaries. The sale or other disposition by me of the whole or any part of the trust property held hereunder shall constitute as to such whole or part a revocation of this trust.

　　5. The death during my lifetime, or in a common accident or disaster with me, of all of the beneficiaries designated hereunder shall revoke such designation, and in the former event, I reserve the right to designate a new beneficiary. Should I for any reason fail to designate such new beneficiary, this trust shall terminate upon my death and the trust property shall revert to my estate.

　　6. In the event of my physical or mental incapacity or my death, I hereby nominate and appoint as Successor Trustee the beneficiary named first above, unless such beneficiary shall not have attained the age of 21 years or is otherwise legally incapacitated, in which event I hereby nominate and appoint as Successor Trustee the beneficiary named second above, unless such beneficiary named second above shall not have attained the age of 21 years or is otherwise legally incapacitated, in which latter event I hereby nominate and appoint

(Name) _____, of

(Address) _____

        Number   *Street*   *City*   *State*   *Zip*

to be Successor Trustee.

    7. This Declaration of Trust shall extend to and be binding upon the heirs, executors, administrators and assigns of the undersigned and upon the Successors to the Trustee.

    8. The Trustee and his successors shall serve without bond.

    9. This Declaration of Trust shall be construed and enforced in accordance with the laws of the State of

_____.

    IN WITNESS WHEREOF, I have hereunto set my hand and seal this _____

day of _____, 19_____.

               (Settlor sign here) _____ L.S.

I, the undersigned legal spouse of the above Settlor, hereby waive all community property rights which I may have in the hereinabove-described trust property and give my assent to the provisions of the trust and to the inclusion in it of the said property.

              (Spouse sign here) _____ L.S.

Witness: (1) _____   Witness: (2) _____

STATE OF _____ ⎱ City

COUNTY OF _____ ⎰ or

                         Town _____

    On the _____ day of _____, 19_____, personally appeared

_____

known to me to be the individual(s) who executed the foregoing instrument, and acknowledged the same to be _____ free act and deed, before me.

(Notary Seal)

                              _____

                                   Notary Public

CHAPTER 19

DECLARATION OF TRUST

For Naming

**ONE PRIMARY BENEFICIARY WITH YOUR CHILDREN,
SHARING EQUALLY, AS CONTINGENT BENEFICIARIES**

To Receive

**THE CONTENTS OF A RENTED HOUSE
OR APARTMENT HELD IN ONE NAME**

INSTRUCTIONS:

On the following pages will be found a declaration of trust (DT-152) suitable for use in connection with the establishment of an inter vivos trust covering the contents of a rented house or apartment held in one name, where it is desired to name one person (ordinarily, but not necessarily, one's spouse) as primary beneficiary, with one's children as contingent beneficiaries to receive such contents if the primary beneficiary be not surviving.

Cross out *"city"* or *"town,"* leaving the appropriate designation of your community. Next, give the exact location (apartment number and street number) of the premises the contents of which you are placing in trust.

Enter the name of the primary beneficiary (called the "First Beneficiary") in the appropriate place in Paragraph 1. Note that the instrument first refers to your children as *"natural not/or adopted."* Now, decide: If you have an adopted child and you wish to include him, cross out the word *"not"* in the phrase *"natural not/or adopted"* and *initial it.* If you wish to *exclude* your adopted child, cross out the word *"or"* in the same phrase and *initial it.* Remember, you <u>must</u> cross out *"not"* or *"or"*—one or the other. If you have no adopted child, simply cross out *"not."*

Note next that the instrument specifies that your children are to receive *"in equal shares, or the survivor of them/per stirpes."* Now, think carefully: If it is your wish that if one of your children does not survive you, *his* share will revert to *his* children in equal shares, cross out *"or the survivor of them"* and *initial it.* If that is *not* what you want—if, for example, you prefer that the share of any child of yours who predeceases you shall be divided between your other surviving children in equal shares, cross out *"per stirpes"* and *initial it.* Remember, you <u>must</u> cross out *"or the survivor of them"* or *"per stirpes"*—one or the other.

Note that in Paragraph 6, the First Beneficiary is designated as Successor Trustee, while a space is provided in which you should designate another person to so act if the named Successor Trustee is not surviving or otherwise fails or ceases to act. This could be one of your children, for example, but it must be an adult who can act as trustee for any beneficiary who comes into a share of the trust before attaining the age of 21. Avoid naming someone not likely to survive until the youngest such beneficiary has attained age 21.

When completed in the manner shown on the reverse side hereof, make several photocopies for reference purposes and to give to the beneficiaries. Hold the original in safekeeping.

Important: Read carefully Note B on page 38, which applies to this declaration of trust.

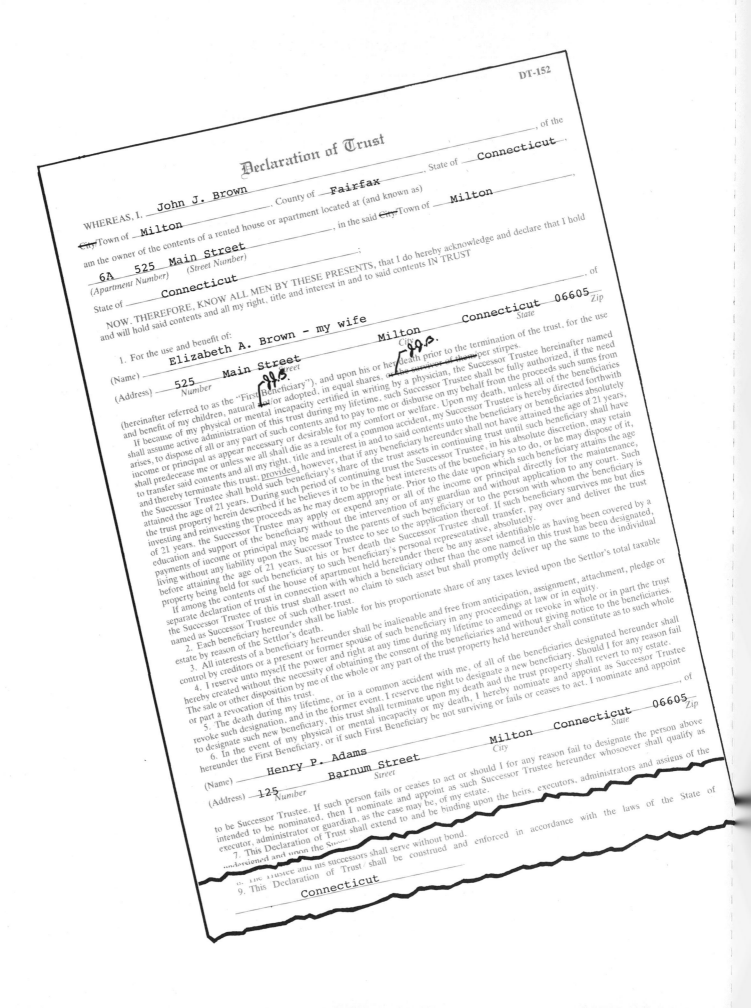

DT-152

Declaration of Trust

WHEREAS, I, __John J. Brown__, County of __Fairfax__ , State of __Connecticut__ , of the

City/Town of __Milton__ , in the said City/Town of __Milton__

an the owner of the contents of a rented house or apartment located at (and known as)

__6A__   __525   Main Street__
(Apartment Number)   (Street Number)

State of __Connecticut__ ,

NOW, THEREFORE, KNOW ALL MEN BY THESE PRESENTS, that I do hereby acknowledge and declare that I hold
and will hold said contents and all my right, title and interest in and to said contents IN TRUST

1. For the use and benefit of:

__Elizabeth A. Brown - my wife__   __Milton__   __Connecticut   06605__
(Name)   City   State   Zip

(Address) __525__   __Main Street__
           Number   Street

(hereinafter referred to as the "First Beneficiary"), and upon his or her death prior to the termination of the trust, for the use
and benefit of my children, natural and/or adopted, in equal shares, or the survivor of them, per stirpes.

If because of my physical or mental incapacity certified in writing by a physician, the Successor Trustee hereinafter named
shall assume active administration of this trust during my lifetime, such Successor Trustee shall be fully authorized, if the need
arises, to dispose of all or any part of such contents and to pay to me or disburse on my behalf from the proceeds such sums from
income or principal as appear necessary or desirable for my comfort or welfare. Upon my death, unless all of the beneficiaries
shall predecease me or unless we all shall die as a result of a common accident, my Successor Trustee is hereby directed forthwith
to transfer said contents and all my right, title and interest in and to said contents unto the beneficiary or beneficiaries absolutely
and thereby terminate this trust; provided, however, that if any beneficiary hereunder shall not have attained the age of 21 years,
the Successor Trustee shall hold such beneficiary's share of the trust assets in continuing trust until such beneficiary shall have
attained the age of 21 years. During such period of continuing trust the Successor Trustee, in his absolute discretion, may retain
the trust property herein described if he believes it to be in the best interests of the beneficiary so to do, or he may dispose of it,
investing and reinvesting the proceeds as he may deem appropriate. Prior to the date upon which such beneficiary attains the age
of 21 years, the Successor Trustee may apply or expend any or all of the income or principal directly for the maintenance,
education and support of the beneficiary without the intervention of any guardian and without application to any court. Such
payments of income or principal may be made to the parents of such beneficiary or to the person with whom the beneficiary is
living without any liability upon the Successor Trustee to see to the application thereof. If such beneficiary survives me but dies
before attaining the age of 21 years, at his or her death the Successor Trustee shall transfer, pay over and deliver the trust
property being held for such beneficiary to such beneficiary's personal representative, absolutely.

If among the contents of the house of apartment held hereunder there be any asset identifiable as having been covered by a
separate declaration of trust in connection with which a beneficiary other than the one named in this trust has been designated,
the Successor Trustee of this trust shall assert no claim to such asset but shall promptly deliver up the same to the individual
named as Successor Trustee of such other trust.

2. Each beneficiary hereunder shall be liable for his proportionate share of any taxes levied upon the Settlor's total taxable
estate by reason of the Settlor's death.

3. All interests of a beneficiary hereunder shall be inalienable and free from anticipation, assignment, attachment, pledge or
control by creditors or a present or former spouse of such beneficiary in any proceedings at law or in equity.

4. I reserve unto myself the power and right at any time during my lifetime to amend or revoke in whole or in part the trust
hereby created without the necessity of obtaining the consent of the beneficiaries and without giving notice to the beneficiaries.
The sale or other disposition by me of the whole or any part of the trust property held hereunder shall constitute as to such whole
or part a revocation of this trust.

5. The death during my lifetime, or in a common accident with me, of all of the beneficiaries designated hereunder shall
revoke such designation, and in the former event. I reserve the right to designate a new beneficiary. Should I for any reason fail
to designate such new beneficiary, this trust shall terminate upon my death and the trust property shall revert to my estate.

6. In the event of my physical or mental incapacity or my death, I hereby nominate and appoint as Successor Trustee
hereunder the First Beneficiary, or if such First Beneficiary be not surviving or fails or ceases to act. I nominate and appoint

__Henry P. Adams__   __Milton__   __Connecticut__   __06605__
(Name)   City   State   Zip

(Address) __125__   __Barnum Street__
           Number   Street

to be Successor Trustee. If such person fails or ceases to act or should I for any reason fail to designate the person above
intended to be nominated, then I nominate and appoint as such Successor Trustee hereunder whosoever shall qualify as
executor, administrator or guardian, as the case may be, of my estate.

7. This Declaration of Trust shall extend to and be binding upon the heirs, executors, administrators and assigns of the
undersigned and upon the Successor...

8. The Trustee and his successors shall serve without bond.

9. This Declaration of Trust shall be construed and enforced in accordance with the laws of the State of
__Connecticut__

Declaration of Trust

WHEREAS, I, _____, of the

City/Town of _____, County of _____, State of _____,

am the owner of the contents of a rented house or apartment located at (and known as)

_____, in the said City/Town of _____,

(Apartment Number)   *(Street Number)*

State of _____;

NOW, THEREFORE, KNOW ALL MEN BY THESE PRESENTS, that I do hereby acknowledge and declare that I hold and will hold said contents and all my right, title and interest in and to said contents IN TRUST

1. For the use and benefit of:

(Name) _____, of

(Address) _____
   Number   *Street*   *City*   *State*   *Zip*

(hereinafter referred to as the "First Beneficiary"), and upon his or her death prior to the termination of the trust, for the use and benefit of my children, natural not/or adopted, in equal shares, or the survivor of them/per stirpes.

If because of my physical or mental incapacity certified in writing by a physician, the Successor Trustee hereinafter named shall assume active administration of this trust during my lifetime, such Successor Trustee shall be fully authorized, if the need arises, to dispose of all or any part of such contents and to pay to me or disburse on my behalf from the proceeds such sums from income or principal as appear necessary or desirable for my comfort or welfare. Upon my death, unless all of the beneficiaries shall predecease me or unless we all shall die as a result of a common accident, my Successor Trustee is hereby directed forthwith to transfer said contents and all my right, title and interest in and to said contents unto the beneficiary or beneficiaries absolutely and thereby terminate this trust; provided, however, that if any beneficiary hereunder shall not have attained the age of 21 years, the Successor Trustee shall hold such beneficiary's share of the trust assets in continuing trust until such beneficiary shall have attained the age of 21 years. During such period of continuing trust the Successor Trustee, in his absolute discretion, may retain the trust property herein described if he believes it to be in the best interests of the beneficiary so to do, or he may dispose of it, investing and reinvesting the proceeds as he may deem appropriate. Prior to the date upon which such beneficiary attains the age of 21 years, the Successor Trustee may apply or expend any or all of the income or principal directly for the maintenance, education and support of the beneficiary without the intervention of any guardian and without application to any court. Such payments of income or principal may be made to the parents of such beneficiary or to the person with whom the beneficiary is living without any liability upon the Successor Trustee to see to the application thereof. If such beneficiary survives me but dies before attaining the age of 21 years, at his or her death the Successor Trustee shall transfer, pay over and deliver the trust property being held for such beneficiary to such beneficiary's personal representative, absolutely.

If among the contents of the house or apartment held hereunder there be any asset identifiable as having been covered by a separate declaration of trust in connection with which beneficiaries other than those named in this trust have been designated, the Successor Trustee of this trust shall assert no claim to such asset but shall promptly deliver up the same to the individual named as Successor Trustee of such other trust.

2. Each beneficiary hereunder shall be liable for his proportionate share of any taxes levied upon the Settlor's total taxable estate by reason of the Settlor's death.

3. All interests of a beneficiary hereunder shall be inalienable and free from anticipation, assignment, attachment, pledge or control by creditors or a present or former spouse of such beneficiary in any proceedings at law or in equity.

4. I reserve unto myself the power and right at any time during my lifetime to amend or revoke in whole or in part the trust hereby created without the necessity of obtaining the consent of the beneficiaries and without giving notice to the beneficiaries. The sale or other disposition by me of the whole or any part of the trust property held hereunder shall constitute as to such whole or part a revocation of this trust.

5. The death during my lifetime, or in a common accident with me, of all of the beneficiaries designated hereunder shall revoke such designation, and in the former event, I reserve the right to designate a new beneficiary. Should I for any reason fail to designate such new beneficiary, this trust shall terminate upon my death and the trust property shall revert to my estate.

6. In the event of my physical or mental incapacity or my death, I hereby nominate and appoint as Successor Trustee hereunder the First Beneficiary, or if such First Beneficiary be not surviving or fails or ceases to act, I nominate and appoint

(Name) _____, of

(Address) _____
   Number   *Street*   *City*   *State*   *Zip*

to be Successor Trustee. If such person fails or ceases to act or should I for any reason fail to designate the person above intended to be nominated, then I nominate and appoint as such Successor Trustee hereunder whosoever shall qualify as executor, administrator or guardian, as the case may be, of my estate.

7. This Declaration of Trust shall extend to and be binding upon the heirs, executors, administrators and assigns of the undersigned and upon the Successors to the Trustee.

8. The Trustee and his successors shall serve without bond.

9. This Declaration of Trust shall be construed and enforced in accordance with the laws of the State of

_____.

IN WITNESS WHEREOF, I have hereunto set my hand and seal this _____

day of _____, 19_____.

(Settlor sign here) _____ L.S.

I, the undersigned legal spouse of the above Settlor, hereby waive all community property rights which I may have in the hereinabove-described trust property and give my assent to the provisions of the trust and to the inclusion in it of the said property.

(Spouse sign here) _____ L.S.

Witness: (1) _____   Witness: (2) _____

STATE OF _____   City

COUNTY OF _____   or
                                                 Town _____

On the _____ day of _____, 19_____, personally appeared

_____

known to me to be the individual(s) who executed the foregoing instrument, and acknowledged the same to be _____ free act and deed, before me.

(Notary Seal)

                                                 Notary Public

CHAPTER 19

DECLARATION OF TRUST
For Naming
ONE BENEFICIARY
To Receive
**THE CONTENTS OF A RENTED HOUSE
OR APARTMENT HELD IN JOINT NAMES**

INSTRUCTIONS:

On the following pages will be found a declaration of trust (DT-149-J) suitable for use in connection with the establishment of an inter vivos trust covering the contents of a rented house or apartment held in joint names where it is desired to name one person to receive such contents upon the death of the survivor of the two joint owners.

Enter the names of the two co-owners on the first line.

Cross out *"city"* or *"town,"* leaving the appropriate designation of your community. Next, give the exact location (apartment number and street number) of the premises the contents of which you are placing in trust.

Enter the name of the beneficiary in the appropriate place in Paragraph 1.

Note that Paragraph 6 designates as Successor Trustee *"whosoever shall at that time be beneficiary hereunder,"* which means that in most cases you don't need to fill anything in there. However, if there is any possibility of a beneficiary who has not attained the age of 21 years receiving the property, make certain that you name an adult in this paragraph who can act as trustee for such beneficiary. Avoid naming as trustee a person not likely to survive until the beneficiary has attained age 21.

When completed in the manner shown on the reverse side hereof, make one or two photocopies for reference purposes and to give to the beneficiary. Hold the original in safekeeping.

Important: Read carefully Note B on page 38, which applies to this declaration of trust.

DT-149-J

Declaration of Trust

WHEREAS, WE, __John J. Brown__ and __Elizabeth A. Brown__, State of __Connecticut__
of the City/Town of __Milton__, County of __Fairfax__, in the said City/Town of __Milton__
are the owners of the contents of a rented house or apartment located at (and known as)

__6A__ __525__ __Main Street__
(Apartment Number) (Street Number)

State of __Connecticut__

NOW, THEREFORE, KNOW ALL MEN BY THESE PRESENTS, that we do hereby acknowledge and declare that we
hold and will hold said contents and all our right, title and interest in and to said contents IN TRUST

1. For the use and benefit of:

(Name) __Diane R. Brown - our daughter__ __Milton__ __Connecticut__ __06605__
City State Zip

(Address) __525__ __Main Street__ __Milton__
Number Street City

If because of the physical or mental incapacity of both of us certified in writing by a physician, the Successor Trustee
hereinafter named shall assume active administration of this trust during our lifetime, such Successor Trustee shall be fully
authorized, if the need arises, to dispose of all or any part of such contents and to pay to us or disburse on our behalf from the
proceeds such sums from income or principal as appear necessary or desirable for our comfort or welfare. Upon the death of the
survivor of us, unless the beneficiary shall predecease us or unless we all shall die as a result of a common accident, our Successor
Trustee is hereby directed forthwith to transfer said contents and all our right, title and interest in and to said contents unto the
beneficiary absolutely and thereby terminate this trust: provided, however, that if the beneficiary hereunder shall not have
attained the age of 21 years, the Successor Trustee shall hold the trust assets in continuing trust until such beneficiary shall have
attained the age of 21 years. During such period of continuing trust the Successor Trustee, in his absolute discretion, may retain

It among the contents of the house of apartment held hereunder there be any asset identifiable as having been covered by a
separate declaration of trust in connection with which a beneficiary other than the one named in this trust has been designated,
the Successor Trustee of this trust shall assert no claim to such asset but shall promptly deliver up the same to the individual
named as Successor Trustee of such other trust.

2. The beneficiary hereunder shall be liable for his proportionate share of any taxes levied upon the total taxable estate of
the survivor of us by reason of the death of such survivor.

3. All interests of the beneficiary hereunder shall be inalienable and free from anticipation, assignment, attachment, pledge
or control by creditors or a present or former spouse of such beneficiary in any proceedings at law or in equity.

4. We reserve unto ourselves the power and right at any time during our lifetime to amend or revoke in whole or in part the
trust hereby created without the necessity of obtaining the consent of the beneficiary and without giving notice to the
beneficiary. The sale or other disposition by us of the whole or any part of the trust property held hereunder shall constitute as to
such whole or part a revocation of this trust.

5. The death during our lifetime, or in a common accident or disaster with us, of the beneficiary designated hereunder shall
revoke such designation, and in the former event, we reserve the right to designate a new beneficiary. Should we for any reason
fail to designate such new beneficiary, this trust shall terminate upon the death of the survivor of us and the trust property shall
revert to the estate of such survivor.

6. In the event of the physical or mental incapacity or death of one of us, the survivor shall continue as sole Trustee. In the
event of the physical or mental incapacity or death of the survivor of us, or if we both shall die in a common accident, we hereby
nominate and appoint as Successor Trustee hereunder whosoever shall at that time be beneficiary hereunder, unless such
beneficiary shall not have attained the age of 21 years or is otherwise legally incapacitated, in which event we hereby nominate
and appoint

(Name) __Henry P. Adams__ __Milton__ __Connecticut__ __06605__
City State Zip

(Address) __125__ __Barnum Street__
Number Street

to be Successor Trustee.

7. This Declaration of Trust shall extend to and be binding upon the heirs, executors, administrators and assigns of the
undersigned and upon the Successors to the Trustees.

8. We as Trustees and our Successor Trustee shall serve without bond.

9. This Declaration of Trust shall be construed and enforced in accordance with the laws of the State of
__Connecticut__.

Declaration of Trust

WHEREAS, WE, _____ and _____ ,

of the City/Town of _____ , County of _____ , State of _____ ,

are the owners of the contents of a rented house or apartment located at (and known as)

_____ in the said City/Town of _____ ,

(Apartment Number)   *(Street Number)*

State of _____ ;

NOW, THEREFORE, KNOW ALL MEN BY THESE PRESENTS, that we do hereby acknowledge and declare that we hold and will hold said contents and all our right, title and interest in and to said contents IN TRUST

1. For the use and benefit of:

(Name) _____ , of

(Address) _____

| Number | Street | City | State | Zip |

If because of the physical or mental incapacity of both of us certified in writing by a physician, the Successor Trustee hereinafter named shall assume active administration of this trust during our lifetime, such Successor Trustee shall be fully authorized, if the need arises, to dispose of all or any part of such contents and to pay to us or disburse on our behalf from the proceeds such sums from income or principal as appear necessary or desirable for our comfort or welfare. Upon the death of the survivor of us, unless the beneficiary shall predecease us or unless we all shall die as a result of a common accident, our Successor Trustee is hereby directed forthwith to transfer said contents and all our right, title and interest in and to said contents unto the beneficiary absolutely and thereby terminate this trust; provided, however, that if the beneficiary hereunder shall not have attained the age of 21 years, the Successor Trustee shall hold the trust assets in continuing trust until such beneficiary shall have attained the age of 21 years. During such period of continuing trust the Successor Trustee, in his absolute discretion, may retain the trust property herein described if he believes it to be in the best interests of the beneficiary so to do, or he may dispose of it, investing and reinvesting the proceeds as he may deem appropriate. Prior to the date upon which such beneficiary attains the age of 21 years, the Successor Trustee may apply or expend any or all of the income or principal directly for the maintenance, education and support of the beneficiary without the intervention of any guardian and without application to any court. Such payments of income or principal may be made to the parents of such beneficiary or to the person with whom the beneficiary is living without any liability upon the Successor Trustee to see to the application thereof. If such beneficiary survives us but dies before attaining the age of 21 years, at his or her death the Successor Trustee shall transfer, pay over and deliver the trust property to such beneficiary's personal representative, absolutely.

If among the contents of the house or apartment held hereunder there be any asset identifiable as having been covered by a separate declaration of trust in connection with which beneficiaries other than those named in this trust have been designated, the Successor Trustee of this trust shall assert no claim to such asset but shall promptly deliver up the same to the individual named as Successor Trustee of such other trust.

2. The beneficiary hereunder shall be liable for his proportionate share of any taxes levied upon the total taxable estate of the survivor of us by reason of the death of such survivor.

3. All interests of the beneficiary hereunder shall be inalienable and free from anticipation, assignment, attachment, pledge or control by creditors or a present or former spouse of such beneficiary in any proceedings at law or in equity.

4. We reserve unto ourselves the power and right at any time during our lifetime to amend or revoke in whole or in part the trust hereby created without the necessity of obtaining the consent of the beneficiary and without giving notice to the beneficiary. The sale or other disposition by us of the whole or any part of the trust property held hereunder shall constitute as to such whole or part a revocation of this trust.

5. The death during our lifetime, or in a common accident or disaster with us, of the beneficiary designated hereunder shall revoke such designation, and in the former event, we reserve the right to designate a new beneficiary. Should we for any reason fail to designate such new beneficiary, this trust shall terminate upon the death of the survivor of us and the trust property shall revert to the estate of such survivor.

6. In the event of the physical or mental incapacity or death of one of us, the survivor shall continue as sole Trustee. In the event of the physical or mental incapacity or death of the survivor of us, or if we both shall die in a common accident, we hereby nominate and appoint as Successor Trustee hereunder whosoever shall at that time be beneficiary hereunder, unless such beneficiary shall not have attained the age of 21 years or is otherwise legally incapacitated, in which event we hereby nominate and appoint

(Name) _____ , of

(Address) _____

| Number | Street | City | State | Zip |

to be Successor Trustee.

7. This Declaration of Trust shall extend to and be binding upon the heirs, executors, administrators and assigns of the undersigned and upon the Successors to the Trustees.

8. We as Trustees and our Successor Trustee shall serve without bond.

9. This Declaration of Trust shall be construed and enforced in accordance with the laws of the State of _____.

IN WITNESS WHEREOF, we have hereunto set our hands and seals this _____

day of _____, 19_____

            (First Settlor sign here) _____ L.S.

          (Second Settlor sign here) _____ L.S.

I, the undersigned legal spouse of one of the above Settlors, hereby waive all community property rights which I may have in the hereinabove-described trust property and give my assent to the provisions of the trust and to the inclusion in it of the said property.

            (Spouse sign here) _____ L.S.

Witness: (1) _____   Witness: (2) _____

STATE OF _____⎫ City

                            ⎬ or

COUNTY OF _____⎭ Town _____

On the _____ day of _____, 19_____, personally appeared

_____ and _____

known to me to be the individuals who executed the foregoing instrument, and acknowledged the same to be their free act and deed, before me.

(Notary Seal)

                                      _____

                                       Notary Public

CHAPTER 19

DECLARATION OF TRUST
For Naming
ONE PRIMARY BENEFICIARY
And
ONE CONTINGENT BENEFICIARY
To Receive
THE CONTENTS OF A RENTED HOUSE
OR APARTMENT HELD IN JOINT NAMES

INSTRUCTIONS:

On the following pages will be found a declaration of trust (DT-150-J) suitable for use in connection with the establishment of an inter vivos trust covering the contents of a rented house or apartment held in joint names, where it is desired to name some *one* person as primary beneficiary with some *one* other person as contingent beneficiary to receive such contents upon the death of the survivor of the two joint owners.

Enter the names of the two co-owners on the first line.

Cross out *"city"* or *"town,"* leaving the appropriate designation of your community. Next, give the exact location (apartment number and street number) of the premises the contents of which you are placing in trust.

Enter the names of the beneficiaries in the appropriate place in Paragraph 1.

Note that Paragraph 6 designates as Successor Trustee *"whosoever shall at that time be beneficiary hereunder,"* which means that in most cases you don't need to fill anything in there. However, if there is any possibility of a beneficiary who has not attained the age of 21 years receiving the property, make certain that you name an adult in this paragraph who can act as trustee for such beneficiary. Avoid naming as trustee a person not likely to survive until the beneficiary has attained age 21.

When completed in the manner shown on the reverse side hereof, make several photocopies for reference purposes and to give to the beneficiaries. Hold the original in safekeeping.

Important: Read carefully Note B on page 38, which applies to this declaration of trust.

DT-150-J

Declaration of Trust

WHEREAS, WE, **John J. Brown** and **Elizabeth A. Brown**, State of **Connecticut**, County of **Fairfax**,

of the City/Town of **Milton**

are the owners of the contents of a rented house or apartment located at (and known as) in the said City/Town of **Milton**

6A **525 Main Street**
(Apartment Number) (Street Number)

State of **Connecticut**

NOW, THEREFORE, KNOW ALL MEN BY THESE PRESENTS, that we do hereby acknowledge and declare that we hold and will hold said contents and all our right, title and interest in and to said contents IN TRUST

1. For the use and benefit of:

(Name) **Diane R. Brown - our daughter**

(Address) **525** **Main Street** **Milton** **Connecticut** **06605**
Number Street City State Zip

or, if such beneficiary be not surviving, for the use and benefit of:

(Name) **Jill A. Lynn - our niece**

(Address) **566** **Midland Street** **Portland** **Wisconsin** **53123**
Number Street City State Zip

If because of the physical or mental incapacity of both of us certified in writing by a physician, the Successor Trustee hereinafter named shall assume active administration of this trust during our lifetime, such Successor Trustee shall be fully authorized, if the need arises, to dispose of all or any part of such contents and to pay to us or disburse on our behalf from the proceeds such sums from income or principal as appear necessary or desirable for our comfort or welfare. Upon the death of the survivor of us, unless the beneficiaries shall predecease us or unless we all shall die as a result of a common accident, our Successor Trustee is hereby directed forthwith to transfer said contents and all our right, title and interest in and to said contents unto the beneficiary absolutely and thereby terminate this trust; provided, however, that if the beneficiary survives us but dies before attaining the age of 21 years, at his or her death the Successor Trustee shall transfer, pay over and deliver the trust property to such beneficiary's personal representative, absolutely.

If among the contents of the house or apartment held hereunder there be any asset identifiable as having been covered by a separate declaration of trust in connection with which a beneficiary other than the one named in this trust has been designated, the Successor Trustee of this trust shall assert no claim to such asset but shall promptly deliver up the same to the individual named as Successor Trustee of such other trust.

2. Any beneficiary hereunder shall be liable for his proportionate share of any taxes levied upon the total taxable estate of the survivor of us by reason of the death of such survivor.

3. The interests of any beneficiary hereunder shall be inalienable and free from anticipation, assignment, attachment, pledge or control by creditors or a present or former spouse of such beneficiary in any proceedings at law or in equity.

4. We reserve unto ourselves the power and right at any time during our lifetime to amend or revoke in whole or in part the trust hereby created without the necessity of obtaining the consent of the beneficiaries and without giving notice to the beneficiaries. The sale or other disposition by us of the whole or any part of the trust property held hereunder shall constitute as to such whole or part a revocation of this trust.

5. The death during our lifetime, or in a common accident with us, of both of the beneficiaries designated hereunder shall revoke such designation, and in the former event, we reserve the right to designate a new beneficiary. Should we for any reason fail to designate such new beneficiary, this trust shall terminate upon the death of the survivor of us and the trust property shall revert to the estate of such survivor.

6. In the event of the physical or mental incapacity or death of one of us, the survivor shall continue as sole Trustee. In the event of the physical or mental incapacity or death of the survivor of us, or if we both shall die in a common accident, we hereby nominate and appoint as Successor Trustee hereunder whosoever shall at that time be beneficiary hereunder, unless such beneficiary shall not have attained the age of 21 years or is otherwise legally incapacitated, in which event we hereby nominate

(Name) **Henry P. Adams**

(Address) **125** **Barnum Street** **Milton** **Connecticut** **06605**
Number Street City State Zip

to be Successor Trustee.

7. This Declaration of Trust shall extend to and be binding upon the heirs, executors, administrators and assigns of the undersigned and upon the Successors to the Trustees.

8. We as Trustees and our Successor Trustee shall serve without bond.

9. This Declaration of Trust shall be construed and enforced in accordance with the laws of the State of **Connecticut**

Declaration of Trust

WHEREAS, WE, _____ and _____,

of the City/Town of _____, County of _____, State of _____,

are the owners of the contents of a rented house or apartment located at (and known as)

_____ in the said City/Town of _____,

(Apartment Number)   *(Street Number)*

State of _____;

NOW, THEREFORE, KNOW ALL MEN BY THESE PRESENTS, that we do hereby acknowledge and declare that we hold and will hold said contents and all our right, title and interest in and to said contents IN TRUST

1. For the use and benefit of:

(Name) _____, of

(Address) _____

    Number   *Street*   *City*   *State*   *Zip*

or, if such beneficiary be not surviving, for the use and benefit of:

(Name) _____, of

(Address) _____

    Number   *Street*   *City*   *State*   *Zip*

If because of the physical or mental incapacity of both of us certified in writing by a physician, the Successor Trustee hereinafter named shall assume active administration of this trust during our lifetime, such Successor Trustee shall be fully authorized, if the need arises, to dispose of all or any part of such contents and to pay to us or disburse on our behalf from the proceeds such sums from income or principal as appear necessary or desirable for our comfort or welfare. Upon the death of the survivor of us, unless the beneficiaries shall predecease us or unless we all shall die as a result of a common accident, our Successor Trustee is hereby directed forthwith to transfer said contents and all our right, title and interest in and to said contents unto the beneficiary absolutely and thereby terminate this trust; provided, however, that if the beneficiary hereunder shall not have attained the age of 21 years, the Successor Trustee shall hold the trust assets in continuing trust until such beneficiary shall have attained the age of 21 years. During such period of continuing trust the Successor Trustee, in his absolute discretion, may retain the trust property herein described if he believes it to be in the best interests of the beneficiary so to do, or he may dispose of it, investing and reinvesting the proceeds as he may deem appropriate. Prior to the date upon which such beneficiary attains the age of 21 years, the Successor Trustee may apply or expend any or all income or principal directly for the maintenance, education, and support of the beneficiary without the intervention of any guardian and without application to any court. Such payments of income or principal may be made to the parents of such beneficiary or to the person with whom the beneficiary is living without any liability upon the Successor Trustee to see to the application thereof. If any such beneficiary survives us but dies before attaining the age of 21 years, at his or her death the Successor Trustee shall transfer, pay over and deliver the trust property to such beneficiary's personal representative, absolutely.

If among the contents of the house or apartment held hereunder there be any asset identifiable as having been covered by a separate declaration of trust in connection with which beneficiaries other than those named in this trust have been designated, the Successor Trustee of this trust shall assert no claim to such asset but shall promptly deliver up the same to the individual named as Successor Trustee of such other trust.

2. Any beneficiary hereunder shall be liable for his proportionate share of any taxes levied upon the total taxable estate of the survivor of us by reason of the death of such survivor.

3. The interests of any beneficiary hereunder shall be inalienable and free from anticipation, assignment, attachment, pledge or control by creditors or a present or former spouse of such beneficiary in any proceedings at law or in equity.

4. We reserve unto ourselves the power and right at any time during our lifetime to amend or revoke in whole or in part the trust hereby created without the necessity of obtaining the consent of the beneficiaries and without giving notice to the beneficiaries. The sale or other disposition by us of the whole or any part of the trust property held hereunder shall constitute as to such whole or part a revocation of this trust.

5. The death during our lifetime, or in a common accident with us, of both of the beneficiaries designated hereunder shall revoke such designation, and in the former event, we reserve the right to designate a new beneficiary. Should we for any reason fail to designate such new beneficiary, this trust shall terminate upon the death of the survivor of us and the trust property shall revert to the estate of such survivor.

6. In the event of the physical or mental incapacity or death of one of us, the survivor shall continue as sole Trustee. In the event of the physical or mental incapacity or death of the survivor of us, or if we both shall die in a common accident, we hereby nominate and appoint as Successor Trustee hereunder whosoever shall at that time be beneficiary hereunder, unless such beneficiary shall not have attained the age of 21 years, or is otherwise legally incapacitated, in which event we hereby nominate and appoint

(Name) _____ , of

(Address) _____
     Number   *Street*   *City*   *State*   *Zip*

to be Successor Trustee.

    7. This Declaration of Trust shall extend to and be binding upon the heirs, executors, administrators and assigns of the undersigned and upon the Successors to the Trustees.

    8. We as Trustees and our Successor Trustee shall serve without bond.

    9. This Declaration of Trust shall be construed and enforced in accordance with the laws of the State of

_____ .

    IN WITNESS WHEREOF, we have hereunto set our hands and seals this _____

day of _____ , 19_____ .

          (First Settlor sign here) _____ L.S.

          (Second Settlor sign here) _____ L.S.

I, the undersigned legal spouse of one of the above Settlors, hereby waive all community property rights which I may have in the hereinabove-described trust property and give my assent to the provisions of the trust and to the inclusion in it of the said property.

          (Spouse sign here) _____ L.S.

Witness: (1) _____   Witness: (2) _____

STATE OF _____   City

COUNTY OF _____   or
                                  Town _____

    On the _____ day of_____ , 19 _____ , personally appeared

_____ and _____

known to me to be the individuals who executed the foregoing instrument, and acknowledged the same to be their free act and deed, before me.

(Notary Seal)   _____

                                    Notary Public

CHAPTER 19

DECLARATION OF TRUST

For Naming

TWO OR MORE BENEFICIARIES, SHARING EQUALLY,

To Receive

THE CONTENTS OF A RENTED HOUSE

OR APARTMENT HELD IN JOINT NAMES

INSTRUCTIONS:

On the following pages will be found a declaration of trust (DT-151-J) suitable for use in connection with the establishment of an inter vivos trust covering the contents of a rented house or apartment held in joint names where it is desired to name two or more persons, sharing equally, to receive such contents upon the death of the survivor of the two owners.

Enter the names of the two co-owners on the first line.

Cross out *"city"* or *"town,"* leaving the appropriate designation of your community. Next, give the exact location (apartment number and street number) of the premises the contents of which you are placing in trust.

In Paragraph 1, indicate the *number of persons* you are naming (to discourage unauthorized additions to the list) and then insert their names. The one whose name appears *first* will be the Successor Trustee responsible for seeing to the distribution of the trust property.

Note that the instrument specifies that the named beneficiaries are to receive *"in equal shares, or the survivor of them/per stirpes."* Now, think carefully: If you have named three persons with the intention that if one of them predeceases you, *his* children will take *his* share, cross out *"or the survivor of them"* and *initial it.* If that is *not* what you want—if, for example, you prefer that the share of the deceased person be divided between the two surviving persons, cross out *"per stirpes"* and *initial it.* Remember, you <u>must</u> cross out either *"or the survivor of them"* or *"per stirpes"*—one or the other.

Note that Paragraph 6 designates as Successor Trustee *"the beneficiary named first above."* Whenever there is a possibility of a beneficiary who has not attained the age of 21 years receiving a share of the trust property, make certain that you name an adult in this paragraph who can act as trustee for such beneficiary. Avoid naming as trustee a person not likely to survive until the beneficiary has attained age 21.

When completed in the manner shown on the reverse side hereof, make several photocopies for reference purposes and to give to the beneficiaries. Hold the original in safekeeping.

Important: Read carefully Note B on page 38, which applies to this declaration of trust.

WHEREVER THE INSTRUCTION "INITIAL IT" APPEARS ABOVE,
IT MEANS THAT *BOTH* CO-OWNERS SHOULD INITIAL IT.

DT-151-J

Declaration of Trust

WHEREAS, WE. ___John J. Brown___ and ___Elizabeth A. Brown___, State of ___Connecticut___

of the City/Town of ___Milton___, County of ___Fairfax___

are the owners of the contents of a rented house or apartment located at (and known as) ___ in the said City/Town of ___Milton___

6A 525 ___Main Street___
(Apartment Number) (Street Number)

State of ___Connecticut___

NOW, THEREFORE, KNOW ALL MEN BY THESE PRESENTS, that we do hereby acknowledge and declare that we hold and will hold said contents and all our right, title and interest in and to said contents IN TRUST *JJB CAB* the survivor of them/per

1. For the use and benefit of the following ___three (3)___ persons, in equal shares, or the survivor of them/per stirpes:

> Diane R. Brown - our daughter
> Jill A. Brown - our daughter
> Dorothy Lynn - our niece

If because of the physical or mental incapacity of both of us certified in writing by a physician, the Successor Trustee hereinafter named shall assume active administration of this trust during our lifetime, such Successor Trustee shall be fully authorized, if the need arises, to dispose of all or any part of such contents and to pay to us or disburse on our behalf from the proceeds such sums as appear necessary or desirable for our comfort or welfare. Upon the death of the survivor of us, unless all the beneficiaries shall predecease us or unless we all shall die as a result of a common accident, our Successor Trustee is hereby directed forthwith to transfer said contents and all our right, title and interest in and to said contents unto the beneficiaries absolutely and thereby terminate this trust; provided, however, that if any beneficiary hereunder shall not have attained the age of 21 years, the Successor Trustee shall hold such beneficiary's share of the trust assets in continuing trust until such beneficiary shall have attained the age of 21 years. During such period of continuing trust the Successor Trustee, in his absolute discretion, may retain the trust property herein described if he believes it to be in the best interests of the beneficiary so to do, or he may dispose of it, investing and reinvesting the proceeds as he may deem appropriate. Prior to the date upon which such beneficiary ...

survives us but dies before the age of 21 years, at his or her death the Successor Trustee shall transfer, pay over and deliver the trust property being held for such beneficiary to said beneficiary's personal representative, absolutely.

If among the contents of the house of apartment held hereunder there be any asset identifiable as having been designated, the Successor Trustee of this trust shall assert no claim to such asset but shall promptly deliver up the same to the individual named as Successor Trustee of such other trust.

2. Each beneficiary hereunder shall be liable for his proportionate share of any taxes levied upon the total taxable estate of the survivor of us by reason of the death of such survivor.

3. The interests of any beneficiary hereunder shall be inalienable and free from anticipation, assignment, attachment, pledge or control by creditors or a present or former spouse of such beneficiary in any proceedings at law or in equity.

4. We reserve unto ourselves the power and right at any time during our lifetime to amend or revoke in whole or in part the trust hereby created without the necessity of obtaining the consent of any beneficiary and without giving notice to any beneficiary. The sale or other disposition by us of the whole or any part of the trust property held hereunder shall constitute as to such whole or part a revocation of this trust.

5. The death during our lifetime, or in a common accident with us, of all of the beneficiaries designated hereunder shall revoke such designation, and in the former event, we reserve the right to designate new beneficiaries. Should we for any reason fail to designate such new beneficiaries, this trust shall terminate upon the death of the survivor of us and the trust property shall revert to the estate of such survivor.

6. In the event of the physical or mental incapacity or death of one of us, the survivor shall continue as sole Trustee. In the event of the physical or mental incapacity or death of the survivor of us, or if we both shall die in a common accident, we hereby nominate and appoint as Successor Trustee hereunder the beneficiary first named above, unless such beneficiary shall not have attained the age of 21 years, or is otherwise legally incapacitated, in which event we hereby nominate and appoint as Successor Trustee hereunder the beneficiary whose name appears second above. If such beneficiary named second above shall not have attained the age of 21 years, or is otherwise legally incapacitated, then we nominate and appoint

___Henry P. Adams___ ___Milton___ ___Connecticut___ ___06605___
City State Zip

(Name) ___

(Address) ___125___ ___Barnum Street___
Number Street

to be Successor Trustee.

7. This Declaration of Trust shall extend to and be binding upon the heirs, executors, administrators and assigns of the undersigned and upon the Successors to the Trustees.

8. We as Trustees and our Successor Trustee shall serve without bond.

9. This Declaration of Trust shall be construed and enforced in accordance with the laws of the State of

___Connecticut___

Declaration of Trust

WHEREAS, WE, _____ and _____,

of the City/Town of _____, County of _____, State of _____,

are the owners of the contents of a rented house or apartment located at (and known as)

_____ in the said City/Town of _____,

(Apartment Number)   *(Street Number)*

State of _____;

NOW, THEREFORE, KNOW ALL MEN BY THESE PRESENTS, that we do hereby acknowledge and declare that we hold and will hold said contents and all our right, title and interest in and to said contents IN TRUST

1. For the use and benefit of the following _____ persons, in equal shares or the survivor of them/per stirpes:

If because of the physical or mental incapacity of both of us certified in writing by a physician, the Successor Trustee hereinafter named shall assume active administration of this trust during our lifetime, such Successor Trustee shall be fully authorized, if the need arises, to dispose of all or any part of such contents and to pay to us or disburse on our behalf from the proceeds such sums as appear necessary or desirable for our comfort or welfare. Upon the death of the survivor of us, unless all the beneficiaries shall predecease us or unless we all shall die as a result of a common accident, our Successor Trustee is hereby directed forthwith to transfer said contents and all our right, title and interest in and to said contents unto the beneficiaries absolutely and thereby terminate this trust; provided, however, that if any beneficiary hereunder shall not have attained the age of 21 years, the Successor Trustee shall hold such beneficiary's share of the trust assets in continuing trust until such beneficiary shall have attained the age of 21 years. During such period of continuing trust the Successor Trustee, in his absolute discretion, may retain the trust property herein described if he believes it to be in the best interests of the beneficiary so to do, or he may dispose of it, investing and reinvesting the proceeds as he may deem appropriate. Prior to the date upon which such beneficiary attains the age of 21 years, the Successor Trustee may apply or expend any or all of the income or principal directly for the maintenance, education and support of the beneficiary without the intervention of any guardian and without application to any court. Such payments of income or principal may be made to the parents of such beneficiary or to the person with whom the beneficiary is living without any liability upon the Successor Trustee to see to the application thereof. If any such beneficiary survives us but dies before the age of 21 years, at his or her death the Successor Trustee shall transfer, pay over and deliver the trust property being held for such beneficiary to said beneficiary's personal representative, absolutely.

If among the contents of the rented house or apartment covered by this instrument there be any asset identifiable as having been covered by a separate declaration of trust in connection with which beneficiaries other than those named in this trust have been designated, the Successor Trustee of this trust shall assert no claim to such asset but shall promptly deliver up the same to the individual named as Successor Trustee of such other trust.

2. Each beneficiary hereunder shall be liable for his proportionate share of any taxes levied upon the total taxable estate of the survivor of us by reason of the death of such survivor.

3. The interests of any beneficiary hereunder shall be inalienable and free from anticipation, assignment, attachment, pledge or control by creditors or a present or former spouse of such beneficiary in any proceedings at law or in equity.

4. We reserve unto ourselves the power and right at any time during our lifetime to amend or revoke in whole or in part the trust hereby created without the necessity of obtaining the consent of any beneficiary and without giving notice to any beneficiary. The sale or other disposition by us of the whole or any part of the trust property held hereunder shall constitute as to such whole or part a revocation of this trust.

5. The death during our lifetime, or in a common accident with us, of all of the beneficiaries designated hereunder shall revoke such designation, and in the former event, we reserve the right to designate new beneficiaries. Should we for any reason fail to designate such new beneficiaries, this trust shall terminate upon the death of the survivor of us and the trust property shall revert to the estate of such survivor.

6. In the event of the physical or mental incapacity or death of one of us, the survivor shall continue as sole Trustee. In the event of the physical or mental incapacity or death of the survivor of us, or if we both shall die in a common accident, we hereby nominate and appoint as Successor Trustee hereunder the beneficiary named first above, unless such beneficiary shall not have attained the age of 21 years, or is otherwise legally incapacitated, in which event we hereby nominate and appoint as Successor Trustee hereunder the beneficiary whose name appears second above. If such beneficiary named second above shall not have attained the age of 21 years, or is otherwise legally incapacitated, then we nominate and appoint

(Name) _____ , of

(Address) _____

     Number   *Street*   *City*   *State*   *Zip*

to be Successor Trustee.

   7. This Declaration of Trust shall extend to and be binding upon the heirs, executors, administrators and assigns of the undersigned and upon the Successors to the Trustees.

   8. We as Trustees and our Successor Trustee shall serve without bond.

   9. This Declaration of Trust shall be construed and enforced in accordance with the laws of the State of

_____ .

   IN WITNESS WHEREOF, we have hereunto set our hands and seals this _____

day of _____ , 19_____ .

                  (First Settlor sign here) _____ L.S.

            (Second Settlor sign here) _____ L.S.

   I, the undersigned legal spouse of one of the above Settlors, hereby waive all community property rights which I may have in the hereinabove-described trust property and give my assent to the provisions of the trust and to the inclusion in it of the said property.

                 (Spouse sign here) _____ L.S.

Witness: (1) _____   Witness: (2) _____

STATE OF _____   City

                               or

COUNTY OF _____   Town _____

   On the _____ day of _____ , 19_____ , personally appeared

_____ and _____

known to me to be the individuals who executed the foregoing instrument, and acknowledged the same to be their free act and deed, before me.

(Notary Seal)   _____

                                              Notary Public

A Family Trust with One's Spouse as Trustee

Many of those whose estates are less than the $200,000 which most qualified bank trust departments regard as the minimum which is of interest to them, nevertheless would like to leave what they have in a trust. Among other reasons, it creates in the minds of heirs the psychological impression that the assets are protected by an estate plan with the orderly functioning of which the heirs should cooperate in their own interests.

Some of those whose estates *are* large enough to invite the interest of a bank have heard a few horror stories about the treatment of beneficiaries by the trust department of their local bank, with the result that a deep suspicion of corporate trustees has been planted in their minds. As a consequence, they may refuse to use such facilities even though their estates are large.

Oftentimes it is the spouse who has heard the horror stories from widowed friends, and when she objects strenuously to the establishment of a trust which she envisions as placing her in the position of having to ask the trust officer of the bank for money, her husband defers to her opposition and the trust is never established. This is unfortunate, because a properly drawn trust can provide important tax and other advantages, and these do not require that the trust be held by a bank.

The solution can be a "family trust" of which the wife herself is trustee and under the terms of which she is directed to pay the life income to herself, with additional sums from principal being available if needed. Upon her death, a Successor Trustee, possibly an adult child or other trusted relative, assumes the duties of administering the trust in accordance with the instructions contained in the trust instrument.

On the pages which follow will be found duplicate copies (one for the settlor and one for the trustee-spouse) of a deed of trust (DT-153) suitable for establishing such a trust. It provides for the division of assets into marital and nonmarital parts, and directs that the trustee-spouse is to receive a distribution equal to 6 percent per year of the current value of the trust. At the beginning of each year, the trustee-spouse computes the then-value of the trust's assets, and determines the amount which represents 6 percent of that value. Thereafter, from the assets, she pays herself one-twelfth of that amount on the first of each month. This provides her with an annuity-like income which permits her to budget her expenditures, thus making it unnecessary for her to wait until a dividend check comes in before learning how much she will have available to spend.

In addition to the income distribution, she has the right to make withdrawals of principal from the *marital* portion of the trust. However, she may not draw upon the principal of the *nonmarital* portion, for those funds have been left to the children or to others with the understanding that she is to have the life income from them. Since she does not control that part of the trust, it will not be taxed upon her death. If she were *not* serving as trustee, whoever *was* serving in that capacity would have the discretionary authority to invade the principal of the nonmarital share in order to make additional funds available to her. Of course, she would have no occasion to call upon the principal of that nonmarital part of the trust unless she had completely exhausted the principal of the marital part to which she had ready access. To provide for the possibility of an emergency situation which finds her in dire need of principal from the nonmarital share, Section 7 of the instrument permits her to resign as trustee, to be replaced by the Successor Trustee named by her husband in the instrument, and that Successor Trustee can then exercise his/her/its discretionary power to make funds available from the principal of the nonmarital portion of the trust.

The trustee-spouse should be cautioned against making extravagant or unreasonable demands upon the principal of either part of the trust because any reduction of principal must inevitably be reflected in a diminution of subsequent income, which in turn would necessitate a further withdrawal from principal to alleviate the income shortfall. In the end the trust assets could be totally depleted, leaving nothing for her later years or for the children when she is gone.

The trust instrument, in its early paragraphs, requires simply the insertion of the names and addresses of the principal parties. In Section 2(B)(6), however, you must identify the beneficiaries who are to receive the balance of your estate remaining *after the death of your spouse,* and specify their respective shares. Three different boxes offer as many different options.

Box One permits you to name some one person to

receive the entire remaining trust fund. This would be appropriate, for example, in the case of a couple with one child; that child's name would be entered in Box One.

Box Two may be used when you wish to divide the remaining trust fund between two or more beneficiaries in equal shares. Note that the instrument provides that the funds are to be paid to those named *"or the survivor of them/per stirpes."* Now, think carefully: If you have named your three children with the understanding that if one child predeceases you, *his* children will take *his* share, cross out *"or the survivor of them"* and *initial it.* If that is *not* what you want—if, for example, you prefer that the share of your deceased child be divided between your two surviving children, cross out *"per stirpes"* and *initial it.* Remember, you <u>must</u> cross out *"or the survivor of them"* or *"per stirpes"*—one or the other.

With a little thought, you can adapt the instrument to your needs. Suppose, for example, that one son has already predeceased you, leaving a child or children. You will probably wish to direct his share to his children. If he has one child, simply list that child as one of the beneficiaries. If there are two or more children, list them as *"The living issue collectively of the Settlor's son, William C. Jones, Jr."* In that circumstance, the two children will divide the share which would have gone to their father had he lived. If one of your son's children is adopted and you wish to include such child as a beneficiary, don't say *"living issue,"* say *"living children, natural or adopted, collectively of the Settlor's son, William C. Jones, Jr."*

Number the beneficiaries. The list should then read something like this:

1. *The Settlor's daughter, Mary L. Jones.*
2. *The Settlor's son, George M. Jones.*
3. *The living issue collectively of the Settlor's son, William C. Jones, Jr.*
4. *The Settlor's daughter, Nancy Jones Dixon.*

In contrast, *Box Three* permits a distribution of *unequal* amounts to two or more beneficiaries, such distribution to be made *per stirpes;* that is, if any such named beneficiary be not living, his issue will take his share. If he has died leaving no issue, his share will be divided among the remaining named beneficiaries in equal shares, per stirpes.

All beneficiaries need not necessarily be *persons;* you may name a church, hospital, or college endowment fund, or a charity.

I knew a man who bequeathed his church $50,000 of his million dollar estate. Alas, by the date of his death, the estate had dwindled to $75,000. The church got the $50,000 and his widow only the remaining $25,000. It's a good idea, then, to avoid making bequests in a specific number of dollars. Instead, give a *percentage* of the trust fund. That way any significant increase or decrease in the value of the trust will be shared proportionately by all beneficiaries.

Think of your estate plan as a wheel. The hub is the *Deed* of Trust executed by you and by the person whom you have named as Trustee. In it you spell out your wishes as to the distribution of your assets when you are gone. Leading to the hub are the spokes of the wheel, a series of *Declarations* of Trust, the purpose of which is to get each of your assets into the hands of the Trustee at your death without the necessity for its going through probate. As you acquire new assets, you slip new spokes into the wheel to cover them. Chapters 20, 21, 22, and 23 provide forms of *Deeds* of Trust which will serve as the hub of your estate plan. The earlier chapters of this book provide forms of *Declarations* of Trust which will serve as the spokes of that plan.

The next thing to consider is the age at which the beneficiaries other than your spouse are to receive their share of the trust. It is seldom a boon to a young person to be handed a large sum of money to do with as he chooses; indeed, it can sometimes do great harm. A youth 18 years of age may be old enough to drink, to vote, or to be drafted into the military service, but rarely does he have the experience and judgment required to manage and conserve an inheritance. My own experience of half a century of estate planning suggests that, so long as the trust instrument is flexible and allows the Successor Trustee the discretion to supplement income to the beneficiary with payments from principal when the need is seen to be justifiable, it is better to withhold delivery of the whole amount earmarked for a young beneficiary until he has attained the age of 25 years; many settlors specify ages 30 or 35. Whichever age you select, there are four places in which it should be entered in the paragraph immediately following the names of the beneficiaries.

Finally, in Section 8 you must name a Successor Trustee to take over upon the death or incapacity of the trustee, your spouse. This can be an adult child, for example, or some other relative or trusted friend—or even a trust company. You should also name a *successor* Successor Trustee who can assume the responsibilities should the named Successor Trustee be unable or unwilling to assume or carry on the duties. If your trustee-spouse predeceases you, it does not mean that the trust plan has to be scrapped. True, you'll lose the tax benefit of the substantial marital deduction which your estate would have enjoyed had your spouse survived you, but the remaining provisions for the disposition of your estate will continue in effect, with the Successor Trustee acting in your spouse's stead.

Trust form DT-153 is provided in duplicate, with a copy for the settlor and another for the Trustee. When both have been completed in identical fashion, they should be signed before two witnesses and the signatures notarized. Make a sufficient number of photocopies to provide one to each beneficiary so he'll know what he's entitled to.

You must arrange, of course, for the trustee to obtain promptly upon your death the assets which are to constitute the trust property. This is accomplished by covering each and every one of your assets with one of the declarations of trust provided in the earlier chapters of this book. Use the instrument designed for naming one beneficiary to receive the asset; in the case of Bill Jones who has executed DT-153 naming his wife, Helen, as trustee, for example, that named beneficiary should be indicated as *"Helen M. Jones, Trustee under deed of trust executed by William C. Jones and said Helen M. Jones under date of* (date you both sign the deed)."

Advise the companies issuing your life insurance policies that you wish the beneficiary designations on the policies changed to read: *"Helen M. Jones, Trustee under deed of trust executed by William C. Jones and said Helen M. Jones under date of* (date you execute the deed of trust)." They will supply beneficiary change forms for your signature. Some companies will ask to see a copy of the trust or an excerpt of those provisions relating to the life insurance.

Execute a new will (Will Form W-11 in Chapter 29 is suggested), leaving your house, furniture, automobile, jewelry, and other personal effects not otherwise covered by a declaration of trust to your spouse, but directing that all other property, including specifically any stocks, bonds, or cash, be added to the trust account set up under the deed of trust. As of this writing, this procedure (called "incorporation by reference") is not permitted in a few states. Check this point with the trust department of your local bank.

It is suggested that you appoint as executor under your will the same person named as trustee under your trust—that is, your spouse.

It is suggested that the family home be directed into the trust upon the death of the settlor if it is presently held in his name alone, or upon the death of the surviving co-owner if it is now held in joint tenancy. This can be accomplished by using DT-101 or DT-101-J in Chapter 7, in conjunction with the appropriate quit claim deed. The family trust instrument, DT-153, makes provision for this arrangement if it is elected.

At the end of trust instrument DT-153 is a page headed "Schedule A." List there the principal assets (home, stocks, bank accounts, etc.) you are directing into the trust at your death. Please understand that assets so listed are in no way "frozen" into the trust nor will the trust assets be limited to the items listed. You may have disposed of all such items by the date of your death and replaced them with others. The trust fund will consist of all those assets of any kind and wheresoever situated which you have left covered by one of the declarations of trust in this book, and in which you have designated the trustee of this trust to receive the asset upon your death.

A final note: If a spouse has not demonstrated an ability to handle and invest money prudently, instruct her to put the money into a good mutual fund of blue chip securities which has been in existence for at least ten years. In this way, the trust assets will be provided with professional management. Explain to her that a brokerage account is not a suitable substitute for professional investment management. Incidentally, most mutual funds offer a "systematic withdrawal plan" under which they will forward a regular monthly check which will total 6 percent per year, providing a convenient way to implement the payout instructions in the deed of trust.

In those cases where there are substantial assets in the wife's name, acquired through inheritance or earlier or current business or professional activities, what is called for is a trust arrangement which is just the opposite of the one described above—the wife is the settlor and the husband is the trustee. Everything is just as it has been described above except that their roles are reversed. The instrument which follows, DT-153, has been designed for use in either situation. All of the instructions given above should be carefully followed. To get the trust assets to the trustee upon the death of the settlor, the same declarations of trust for naming one beneficiary should be used, the beneficiary being *"William C. Jones, Trustee under Deed of Trust executed by Helen M. Jones and said William C. Jones under date of* (date you both sign the deed)."

Deed of Trust

THIS AGREEMENT entered into by and between _____,

of the City/Town of _____, County of _____

and State of _____(hereinafter referred to as the "Settlor"), and _____

also of the said City/Town of _____, County of _____

and State of _____(hereinafter referred to as the "Trustee").

W I T N E S S E T H :

WHEREAS the Settlor desires at death to leave certain property in trust, and

WHEREAS the Trustee is willing to accept and administer such funds as Trustee under the terms of these presents.

NOW THEREFORE intending to be legally bound hereby, the Settlor and the Trustee do hereby covenant and agree as follows:

1. Separately, the Settlor has executed one or more Declarations of Trust in which the Trustee is named as beneficiary to receive certain assets described in Schedule A attached hereto and made a part hereof, and reserves the right to make additional assets, including life insurance policies on the Settlor's life, so payable.

2. Upon the Settlor's death, the Trustee shall divide the trust fund into two parts. One of said parts, herein termed the "marital share," shall consist of property of a value equal to the lesser of (a) the maximum marital deduction allowable in determining the federal estate tax payable by the Settlor's estate, or (b) the minimum amount which, after taking into account all credits and deductions available to the Settlor's estate for federal estate tax purposes (other than the marital deduction), will result in no federal estate tax. The other part shall consist of the remainder of the trust fund. In apportioning to the marital and nonmarital trusts specific assets previously valued for estate tax purposes, the Trustee shall insure that the two trusts share proportionately in any subsequent appreciation or depreciation in the value of such assets. Assets which do not qualify for marital deduction status, or assets not includable in the Settlor's gross estate for federal tax purposes, shall not be included in the marital share of the trust.

   (A) With respect to the "marital share" so called, the Trustee shall hold, manage, invest and reinvest the same as a trust fund upon the following terms and conditions:

   (1) The Trustee shall pay to the Settlor's spouse _____, in convenient monthly installments during his/her lifetime, the actual income from the trust or a sum equal to six (6%) percent per year of the value of the trust computed at the time of the Settlor's death and thereafter recomputed annually at the beginning of each calendar year, whichever is the greater, together with such sums from principal as the Settlor's spouse shall request be paid from time to time.

   (2) Upon the death of the Settlor's spouse, the Successor Trustee hereinafter named shall pay the then trust fund as such spouse shall appoint by specific reference to this instrument in his/her Will, and the Settlor hereby confers upon the said spouse the sole and unrestricted right to appoint the same by his/her Will, outright or in further trust, in favor of his/her estate or in favor of others. To the extent that said power shall not be effectively exercised, the trust fund herein created shall be added to the remaining part and shall be disposed of as hereinafter provided.

   (3) If the Settlor and the Settlor's spouse shall die in such circumstances that there is not, in the judgment of the Successor Trustee, whose decision shall be conclusive, sufficient evidence to determine readily which of them survived the other, then for the purposes of this trust, the Settlor's spouse shall be deemed to have survived the Settlor.

   (B) With respect to the remaining, "nonmarital," part of the trust fund, the Trustee shall hold, manage, invest and reinvest the same as a trust fund upon the following terms and conditions:

   (1) If requested by the executor or administrator of the Settlor's estate, the Trustee shall pay or reimburse said executor or administrator for the amount of any ante mortem claim, funeral expense or expense of administration which shall be allowed in connection with the settlement of such estate or, in the absence of formal probate administration, which the Trustee shall determine to be due and payable.

   (2) The Trustee shall pay to the proper taxing authority or reimburse the executor or administrator of the Settlor's estate for the amount of any succession, estate, transfer or similar tax, whether state or federal, which shall be imposed lawfully upon the Settlor's taxable estate or upon any beneficiary thereof as a result of the Settlor's death. The proceeds of employee death benefits or employee life insurance policies on the Settlor's life shall not be used to pay death taxes or otherwise be paid to the executor of the Settlor's estate.

   (3) From the balance of the trust fund remaining in the Trustee's hands, the Trustee shall pay to the Settlor's

spouse, _____, in equal monthly installments during such spouse's lifetime a sum equal to six (6%) percent per year of the value of this nonmarital part of the trust fund as computed at the time of the Settlor's death and thereafter recomputed at the beginning of each calendar year.

   (4) If the Trustee, pursuant to the provisions of Section 7 hereinafter set forth, shall have resigned at any time after the Settlor's death, the Successor Trustee hereinafter named is authorized thereafter to pay to the Settlor spouse or expend on his/her behalf at any time or from time to time, in addition to the income distribution specified above, such sums from the principal of the nonmarital part of the trust as the Successor Trustee in his/her/its sole discretion shall deem necessary or desirable for the comfort or well-being of the Settlor's said spouse.

(5) Upon the death of the Settlor's spouse, the Successor Trustee shall, if requested by the executor or administrator of the spouse's estate, or in the absence of formal probate administration, in such Trustee's own discretion, pay or reimburse such estate for the amounts of any funeral expenses or expense of the last illness and/or any taxes, debts or other post mortem expenses of the said spouse.

(6) Thereafter, the Successor Trustee shall dispose of the trust fund as specified in

Cross off	Box One below
two of the three	Box Two below
and initial	Box Three below

BOX ONE	BOX TWO	BOX THREE
The Trustee shall pay the entire balance of the trust fund to the Settlor's _____ *(Daughter, nephew, friend, church, etc.)* _____ *(Name)*	The Trustee shall divide the balance of the trust fund into as many equal parts as there shall be beneficiaries named below and shall pay one such part to each of the following, in equal shares, or the survivor of them/per stirpes: _____ _____ _____ _____ _____ _____	The Trustee shall pay the balance of the trust fund to the following, per stirpes, in the proportions shown: *Name* *Proportion to be paid to such beneficiary* _____ ___% _____ ___% _____ ___% _____ ___% _____ ___% _____ ___% *The share of any beneficiary who dies leaving no surviving issue shall be divided equally among the remaining named beneficiaries who are natural persons, per stirpes.*
and shall thereupon terminate the trust.	and shall thereupon terminate the trust.	and shall thereupon terminate the trust.

Notwithstanding the foregoing, if any beneficiary hereunder shall not have attained the age of _____ years, the Trustee shall hold such beneficiary's share of the trust assets in continuing trust until such beneficiary shall have attained the age of _____ years. Prior to the date upon which such beneficiary attains the age of _____ years, the Trustee may apply or expend any or all of the income or principal directly for the maintenance, education and support of the beneficiary without the intervention of any guardian and without application to any court. Such payments of income or principal may, in the Trustee's sole discretion, be made to the beneficiary or to the beneficiary's parents or to the person with whom the beneficiary is living, without any liability upon the Trustee to see to the application thereof. If such beneficiary survives the Settlor but dies before attaining the age of _____ years, at his or her death the Trustee shall transfer, pay over and deliver the trust property being held for such beneficiary to such beneficiary's personal representative, absolutely.

(7) If any provision of this instrument shall be unclear or the subject of dispute among the parties to the trust, the Trustee (or the Successor Trustee, if the latter shall then be actively serving) shall be fully authorized to construe such provision, and any such determination by the Trustee shall be final and binding upon all such parties.

3. With respect to community property: (a) if the assets, or any part of them, deposited in this trust shall constitute community property, their status as such community property shall remain unchanged; (b) all distributions of income from the trust while both parties are living shall be considered to be community property; (c) either party shall have the right to withdraw his or her portion of the community property, either before or after the death of the Settlor; (d) if the trust is revoked, its assets shall revert to the community.

4. All interests of a beneficiary hereunder shall be inalienable and free from anticipation, assignment, attachment, pledge or control by creditors or a present or former spouse of such beneficiary in any proceedings at law or in equity.

5. This trust is created upon the understanding that the issuer, custodian or transfer agent of any securities held hereunder shall be under no liability whatsoever to see to the proper administration of the trust, and that upon the transfer of the right, title

and interest in and to said securities, said issuer, custodian or transfer agent shall conclusively treat the transferee as the sole owner of said trust property and shall be under no liability to see to the proper application of the proceeds of such transfer.

6. The Trustee and any Successor Trustee shall have the following powers in addition to those given them by law, to be exercised in their sole discretion:

To sell, exchange, assign, lease, mortgage, pledge or borrow upon and in any manner to deal with and dispose of all or any part of the trust property, including the power to sell in order to make distribution hereunder, and to invest the proceeds of any sale or other disposition, liquidation or withdrawal, as often as may be necessary in the discretion of the Trustee, without being required to make application for more specific authority to any court of law or equity. The Trustee is specifically authorized to make all investments and reinvestments of the trust assets (except a reasonable amount of uninvested cash and any real estate which may be added to the trust during the Settlor's lifetime or, subsequently, through the instrumentality of the Settlor's Will or an inter vivos trust, which real estate the Trustee may deem it in the best interest of the beneficiaries to retain) in property of any character, real or personal, foreign or domestic, including without limitation, bonds, notes, debentures, mortgages, certificates of deposit, common and preferred stocks, or shares or interests in investment companies, regardless of whether such investments are considered legal for trust funds.

7. The trust herein created may be amended or revoked at any time during the lifetime of the Settlor by written notice from the Settlor to the Trustee. The Trustee may resign at any time during the lifetime of the Settlor by written notice to the Settlor. The Trustee may resign after the death of the Settlor upon written notice to the designated Successor Trustee and upon proper delivery of the assets of the trust to such Successor Trustee.

8. In the event of the Trustee's physical or mental incapacity, death, resignation or removal for cause,

the Settlor hereby appoints _____ as Successor Trustee.

If the said _____ shall be unwilling or unable to carry out such duties,

the Settlor hereby appoints _____ as Successor Trustee hereunder.

9. The Trustee and any Successor Trustee are specifically instructed by the Settlor to maintain the privacy and confidentiality of this instrument and the trust created hereunder, and are in no circumstances to divulge its terms to any probate or other court or other public agency with the exception of a tax authority.

10. The Trustee and any Successor Trustee shall serve without bond.

11. This Deed of Trust shall be construed and enforced in accordance with the laws of the State of

_____.

IN WITNESS WHEREOF, the parties hereto have hereunder and to a duplicate hereof, set their hands and seals as

of the _____ day of _____, 19_____.

The Settlor:

_____   _____ L.S.

Witness

Accepted:

The Trustee:

_____   _____ L.S.

Witness

STATE OF _____   City

COUNTY OF _____   or Town _____

On the _____ day of _____, 19_____, personally appeared

_____ and _____

known to me to be the individuals who executed the foregoing instrument, and acknowledged the same to be their free act and deed, before me.

(Notary Seal)   *Notary Public*

SCHEDULE A

Deed of Trust

THIS AGREEMENT entered into by and between _____ ,

of the City/Town of _____ , County of _____

and State of _____ (hereinafter referred to as the "Settlor"), and _____ ,

also of the said City/Town of _____ , County of _____

and State of _____ (hereinafter referred to as the "Trustee").

W I T N E S S E T H :

WHEREAS the Settlor desires at death to leave certain property in trust, and

WHEREAS the Trustee is willing to accept and administer such funds as Trustee under the terms of these presents;

NOW, THEREFORE, intending to be legally bound hereby, the Settlor and the Trustee do hereby covenant and agree as follows:

1. Separately, the Settlor has executed one or more Declarations of Trust in which the Trustee is named as beneficiary to receive certain assets described in Schedule A attached hereto and made a part hereof, and reserves the right to make additional assets, including life insurance policies on the Settlor's life, so payable.

2. Upon the Settlor's death, the Trustee shall divide the trust fund into two parts. One of said parts, herein termed the "marital share," shall consist of property of a value equal to the lesser of (a) the maximum marital deduction allowable in determining the federal estate tax payable by the Settlor's estate, or (b) the minimum amount which, after taking into account all credits and deductions available to the Settlor's estate for federal estate tax purposes (other than the marital deduction), will result in no federal estate tax. The other part shall consist of the remainder of the trust fund. In apportioning to the marital and nonmarital trusts specific assets previously valued for estate tax purposes, the Trustee shall insure that the two trusts share proportionately in any subsequent appreciation or depreciation in the value of such assets. Assets which do not qualify for marital deduction status, or assets not includable in the Settlor's gross estate for federal tax purposes, shall not be included in the marital share of the trust.

(A) With respect to the "marital share" so called, the Trustee shall hold, manage, invest and reinvest the same as a trust fund upon the following terms and conditions:

(1) The Trustee shall pay to the Settlor's spouse _____ , in convenient monthly installments during his/her lifetime, the actual income from the trust or a sum equal to six (6%) percent per year of the value of the trust computed at the time of the Settlor's death and thereafter recomputed annually at the beginning of each calendar year, whichever is the greater, together with such sums from principal as the Settlor's spouse shall request be paid from time to time.

(2) Upon the death of the Settlor's spouse, the Successor Trustee hereinafter named shall pay the then trust fund as such spouse shall appoint by specific reference to this instrument in his/her Will, and the Settlor hereby confers upon the said spouse the sole and unrestricted right to appoint the same by his/her Will, outright or in further trust, in favor of his/her estate or in favor of others. To the extent that said power shall not be effectively exercised, the trust fund herein created shall be added to the remaining part and shall be disposed of as hereinafter provided.

(3) If the Settlor and the Settlor's spouse shall die in such circumstances that there is not, in the judgment of the Successor Trustee, whose decision shall be conclusive, sufficient evidence to determine readily which of them survived the other, then for the purposes of this trust, the Settlor's spouse shall be deemed to have survived the Settlor.

(B) With respect to the remaining, "nonmarital," part of the trust fund, the Trustee shall hold, manage, invest and reinvest the same as a trust fund upon the following terms and conditions:

(1) If requested by the executor or administrator of the Settlor's estate, the Trustee shall pay or reimburse said executor or administrator for the amount of any ante mortem claim, funeral expense or expense of administration which shall be allowed in connection with the settlement of such estate or, in the absence of formal probate administration, which the Trustee shall determine to be due and payable.

(2) The Trustee shall pay to the proper taxing authority or reimburse the executor or administrator of the Settlor's estate for the amount of any succession, estate, transfer or similar tax, whether state or federal, which shall be imposed lawfully upon the Settlor's taxable estate or upon any beneficiary thereof as a result of the Settlor's death. The proceeds of employee death benefits or employee life insurance policies on the Settlor's life shall not be used to pay death taxes or otherwise be paid to the executor of the Settlor's estate.

(3) From the balance of the trust fund remaining in the Trustee's hands, the Trustee shall pay to the Settlor's

spouse, _____ , in equal monthly installments during such spouse's lifetime a sum equal to six (6%) percent per year of the value of this nonmarital part of the trust fund as computed at the time of the Settlor's death and thereafter recomputed at the beginning of each calendar year.

(4) If the Trustee, pursuant to the provisions of Section 7 hereinafter set forth, shall have resigned at any time after the Settlor's death, the Successor Trustee hereinafter named is authorized thereafter to pay to the Settlor's spouse or expend on his/her behalf at any time or from time to time, in addition to the income distribution specified above, such sums from the principal of the nonmarital part of the trust as the Successor Trustee in his/her/its sole discretion shall deem necessary or desirable for the comfort or well-being of the Settlor's said spouse.

(5) Upon the death of the Settlor's spouse, the Successor Trustee shall, if requested by the executor or administrator of the spouse's estate, or in the absence of formal probate administration, in such Trustee's own discretion, pay or reimburse such estate for the amounts of any funeral expenses or expense of the last illness and/or any taxes, debts or other post mortem expenses of the said spouse.

(6) Thereafter, the Successor Trustee shall dispose of the trust fund as specified in

Cross off	Box One below
two of the three	Box Two below
and initial	Box Three below

BOX ONE

The Trustee shall pay the entire balance of the trust fund to the Settlor's

_____

(Daughter, nephew, friend, church, etc.)

_____

(Name)

and shall thereupon terminate the trust.

BOX TWO

The Trustee shall divide the balance of the trust fund into as many equal parts as there shall be beneficiaries named below and shall pay one such part to each of the following, in equal shares, or the survivor of them/per stirpes:

_____

_____

_____

_____

_____

_____

and shall thereupon terminate the trust.

BOX THREE

The Trustee shall pay the balance of the trust fund to the following, per stirpes, in the proportions shown:

Name *Proportion to be paid to such beneficiary*

_____ ___%

_____ ___%

_____ ___%

_____ ___%

_____ ___%

_____ ___%

{ *The share of any beneficiary who dies leaving no surviving issue shall be divided equally among the remaining named beneficiaries who are natural persons, per stirpes.* }

and shall thereupon terminate the trust.

Notwithstanding the foregoing, if any beneficiary hereunder shall not have attained the age of _____ years, the Trustee shall hold such beneficiary's share of the trust assets in continuing trust until such beneficiary shall have attained the age of _____ years. Prior to the date upon which such beneficiary attains the age of _____ years, the Trustee may apply or expend any or all of the income or principal directly for the maintenance, education and support of the beneficiary without the intervention of any guardian and without application to any court. Such payments of income or principal may, in the Trustee's sole discretion, be made to the beneficiary or to the beneficiary's parents or to the person with whom the beneficiary is living, without any liability upon the Trustee to see to the application thereof. If such beneficiary survives the Settlor but dies before attaining the age of _____ years, at his or her death the Trustee shall transfer, pay over and deliver the trust property being held for such beneficiary to such beneficiary's personal representative, absolutely.

(7) If any provision of this instrument shall be unclear or the subject of dispute among the parties to the trust, the Trustee (or the Successor Trustee, if the latter shall then be actively serving) shall be fully authorized to construe such provision, and any such determination by the Trustee shall be final and binding upon all such parties.

3. With respect to community property: (a) if the assets, or any part of them, deposited in this trust shall constitute community property, their status as such community property shall remain unchanged; (b) all distributions of income from the trust while both parties are living shall be considered to be community property; (c) either party shall have the right to withdraw his or her portion of the community property, either before or after the death of the Settlor; (d) if the trust is revoked, its assets shall revert to the community.

4. All interests of a beneficiary hereunder shall be inalienable and free from anticipation, assignment, attachment, pledge or control by creditors or a present or former spouse of such beneficiary in any proceedings at law or in equity.

5. This trust is created upon the understanding that the issuer, custodian or transfer agent of any securities held hereunder shall be under no liability whatsoever to see to the proper administration of the trust, and that upon the transfer of the right, title

and interest in and to said securities, said issuer, custodian or transfer agent shall conclusively treat the transferee as the sole owner of said trust property and shall be under no liability to see to the proper application of the proceeds of such transfer.

6. The Trustee and any Successor Trustee shall have the following powers in addition to those given them by law, to be exercised in their sole discretion:

To sell, exchange, assign, lease, mortgage, pledge or borrow upon and in any manner to deal with and dispose of all or any part of the trust property, including the power to sell in order to make distribution hereunder, and to invest the proceeds of any sale or other disposition, liquidation or withdrawal, as often as may be necessary in the discretion of the Trustee, without being required to make application for more specific authority to any court of law or equity. The Trustee is specifically authorized to make all investments and reinvestments of the trust assets (except a reasonable amount of uninvested cash and any real estate which may be added to the trust during the Settlor's lifetime or, subsequently, through the instrumentality of the Settlor's Will or an inter vivos trust, which real estate the Trustee may deem it in the best interest of the beneficiaries to retain) in property of any character, real or personal, foreign or domestic, including without limitation, bonds, notes, debentures, mortgages, certificates of deposit, common and preferred stocks, or shares or interests in investment companies, regardless of whether such investments are considered legal for trust funds.

7. The trust herein created may be amended or revoked at any time during the lifetime of the Settlor by written notice from the Settlor to the Trustee. The Trustee may resign at any time during the lifetime of the Settlor by written notice to the Settlor. The Trustee may resign after the death of the Settlor upon written notice to the designated Successor Trustee and upon proper delivery of the assets of the trust to such Successor Trustee.

8. In the event of the Trustee's physical or mental incapacity, death, resignation or removal for cause, the Settlor hereby appoints _____ as Successor Trustee.

If the said _____ shall be unwilling or unable to carry out such duties, the Settlor hereby appoints _____ as Successor Trustee hereunder.

9. The Trustee and any Successor Trustee are specifically instructed by the Settlor to maintain the privacy and confidentiality of this instrument and the trust created hereunder, and are in no circumstances to divulge its terms to any probate or other court or other public agency with the exception of a tax authority.

10. The Trustee and any Successor Trustee shall serve without bond.

11. This Deed of Trust shall be construed and enforced in accordance with the laws of the State of

_____.

IN WITNESS WHEREOF, the parties hereto have hereunder and to a duplicate hereof, set their hands and seals as of the _____ day of _____, 19____.

The Settlor:

_____   _____ L.S.
Witness

Accepted:

The Trustee:

_____   _____ L.S.
Witness

STATE OF _____   City
                                    or
COUNTY OF _____   Town _____

On the _____ day of_____, 19____, personally appeared

_____ and _____

known to me to be the individuals who executed the foregoing instrument, and acknowledged the same to be their free act and deed, before me.

_____
(Notary Seal)   *Notary Public*

SCHEDULE A

A Family Trust with an Individual Other than One's Spouse as Trustee

In the previous chapter we discussed the advantages of a family trust, as distinguished from a trust of which a bank is trustee, and we noted the suitability of its use by persons whose estates are not large enough to invite the interest of a qualified corporate trustee or who, for one reason or another, simply prefer not to place their estates in the care of a bank after they are gone. One solution, it was pointed out, was the establishment of a trust of which one's spouse is trustee.

But many men recognize that their wives are not qualified by training or temperament to carry out the duties of trustee, and are concerned lest assets be squandered or imprudently invested. Widows who re-marry can be swayed in their judgment by their new partner with the result that funds required for the education of the settlor's children are committed to unwise business ventures. Too, many a woman who is sharp and business-like in her decisions at age 55 or 60 may be simply unable to cope with changing conditions when she is 70 or 75. Her health may decline to the point where she is physically unable to attend to even routine record-keeping, a handicap which she might be loath to acknowledge.

In my files is a newspaper clipping reporting the suicide of a 65-year-old California woman whose second husband explained that her sad end was traceable to financial worries. But only eleven years earlier her first husband had died leaving her $15 million! Doubtless he thought that he was bequeathing her financial security. Alas, he simply left her a job, one which was beyond her capabilities. A thoughtful husband, considering these possibilities, might conclude, "I'd better not saddle Helen with the responsibility. I'll name our eldest son, Philip, as trustee, instead."

On the following pages will be found duplicate copies (one for the settlor and one for the trustee) of a deed of trust (DT-154) which will be suitable for use in establishing a family trust with an individual other than one's spouse as trustee. In the main, it follows the pattern of the trust form provided in the previous chapter. It provides for the division of the trust assets into marital and nonmarital parts, and directs that the wife is to receive a distribution equal to 6 percent per year of the current value of the trust. At the beginning of each year, the trustee computes the then value of the trust's assets, and determines the amount which represents 6 percent of that value. Thereafter, from the assets, the trustee pays her one-twelfth of that amount on the first of each month. This provides her with an annuity-like income which permits her to budget her expenditures, thus making it unnecessary for her to wait until a dividend check comes in before learning how much she will have available to spend.

In addition to the income distribution, she has the right to make withdrawals of principal from the marital portion of the trust whenever she wishes. Unlike the trust described in the previous chapter, however, in this one she can also draw upon the principal of the nonmarital portion with the approval of the trustee. Those funds have been left to the settlor's children or to other persons with the understanding that the settlor's spouse is to have the life income from them. Since she is not trustee and therefore does not control that part of the trust, it will not be taxed upon her death. To gain that benefit, she has to forego "control"—that is, she must have the trustee's "approval" before she draws upon the principal of that second, nonmarital, share of the trust. Of course, she would have no occasion to call upon the principal of that nonmarital part of the trust unless and until she had completely exhausted the marital part to which she has ready access.

The wife should be cautioned against making extravagant or unreasonable demands upon the principal of either part of the trust because any reduction of principal must inevitably be reflected in a diminution of subsequent income, which in turn would necessitate a further withdrawal from principal to alleviate the income shortfall. In the end the trust assets could be totally depleted, leaving nothing for her later years or for the children when she is gone.

The trust instrument, in its early paragraphs, requires simply the insertion of the names and addresses of the principal parties. In Section 2(B)(6), however, you must identify the beneficiaries who are to receive the balance of your estate remaining *after the death of your spouse,* and specify their respective shares. Three different boxes offer as many different options.

Box One permits you to name some one person to

receive the entire remaining trust fund. This would be appropriate, for example, in the case of a couple with one child; that child's name would be entered in Box One.

Box Two may be used when you wish to divide the remaining trust fund between two or more beneficiaries in equal shares. Note that the instrument provides that the funds are to be paid to those named *"or the survivor of them/per stirpes."* Now, think carefully: If you have named your three children with the understanding that if one child predeceases you, *his* children will take *his* share, cross out *"or the survivor of them"* and *initial it.* If that is *not* what you want—if, for example, you prefer that the share of your deceased child be divided between your two surviving children, cross out *"per stirpes"* and *initial it.* Remember, you <u>must</u> cross out *"or the survivor of them"* or *"per stirpes"*—one or the other.

With a little thought, you can adapt the instrument to your needs. Suppose, for example, that one son has already predeceased you, leaving a child or children. You will probably wish to direct his share to his children. If he has one child, simply list that child as one of the beneficiaries. If there are two or more children, list them as *"The living issue collectively of the Settlor's son, William C. Jones, Jr."* In that circumstance, the two children will divide the share which would have gone to their father had he lived. If one of your son's children is adopted and you wish to include such child as a beneficiary, don't say *"living issue,"* say *"living children, natural or adopted, collectively of the Settlor's son, William C. Jones, Jr."*

Number the beneficiaries. The list should then read something like this:

1. *The Settlor's daughter, Mary L. Jones.*
2. *The Settlor's son, Philip M. Jones.*
3. *The living issue collectively of the Settlor's son, William C. Jones, Jr.*
4. *The Settlor's daughter, Nancy Jones Dixon.*

In contrast, *Box Three* permits a distribution of *unequal* amounts to two or more beneficiaries, such distribution to be made *per stirpes;* that is, if any such named beneficiary be not living, his issue will take his share. If he has died leaving no issue, his share will be divided among the remaining named beneficiaries who are natural persons, in equal shares, per stirpes.

Beneficiaries need not necessarily be *persons;* you may name a church, hospital, or college endowment fund, or a charity.

Avoid making bequests in a specific number of dollars. Instead, give a percentage of the trust fund. That way, any significant increase or decrease in the value of the trust will be shared proportionately by all beneficiaries.

The next thing to consider is the age at which those beneficiaries other than your spouse are to receive their share of the trust. It is seldom a boon to a young person

to be handed a large sum of money to do with as he chooses; indeed, it can sometimes do great harm. A youth 18 years of age may be old enough to drink, to vote, or to be drafted into the military service, but rarely does he have the experience and judgment required to manage and conserve an inheritance. My own experience of half a century of estate planning suggests that, so long as the trust instrument is flexible and allows the trustee the discretion to supplement income to the beneficiary with payments from principal when the need is seen to be justifiable, it is better to withhold delivery of the whole amount earmarked for a young beneficiary until he has attained the age of 25 years; many settlors specify ages 30 or 35. Whichever age you select, there are four places in which it should be entered in the paragraph immediately following the names of the beneficiaries.

Finally, in Section 8 you must name a Successor Trustee to take over upon the death or incapacity of the Trustee. This can be an adult child, for example, or some other relative or trusted friend—or even a trust company. You should also name a *successor* Successor Trustee who can assume the responsibilities should the named Successor Trustee be unable or unwilling to assume or carry on the duties. If your spouse predeceases you, it does not mean that the trust plan has to be scrapped. True, you'll lose the tax benefit of the substantial marital deduction which your estate would have enjoyed had your spouse survived you, but the remaining provisions for the disposition of your estate will continue in effect.

When the deed of trust has been filled in correctly, both the settlor and trustee should sign it before two witnesses, and the signatures should be notarized. Make a sufficient number of photocopies to provide one to each beneficiary so that he'll know what he's entitled to.

You must arrange, of course, for the trustee to obtain promptly upon your death the assets which are to constitute the trust property. This is accomplished by covering each and every one of your assets with one of the declarations of trust provided in the earlier chapters of this book. Use the instrument designed for naming one beneficiary to receive the asset; in the case of Bill Jones who has executed DT-154 naming his eldest son, Philip, as trustee, for example, that named beneficiary should be indicated as *"Philip Jones, Trustee under deed of trust executed by William C. Jones and said Philip Jones under date of* (date you both sign the deed).*"*

Advise the companies issuing your life insurance policies that you wish the beneficiary designations on the policies changed to read: *"Philip Jones, Trustee under deed of trust executed by William C. Jones and said Philip Jones under date of* (date you execute the deed of trust).*"* They will supply beneficiary change forms for your signature. Some companies will ask to see a copy of the trust or an excerpt of those provisions relating to the life insurance.

Execute a new will (Will Form W-11 in Chapter 29 is

suggested), leaving your house, furniture, automobile, jewelry, and other personal effects not otherwise covered by a declaration of trust to your spouse, but directing that all other property, including specifically any stocks, bonds, or cash, be added to the trust account set up under the deed of trust. As of this writing, this procedure (called "incorporation by reference") is not permitted in a few states. Check this point with the trust department of your local bank.

It is suggested that you appoint as executor under your will the same individual whom you have named as trustee of your trust.

It is suggested, too, that the family home be directed into the trust upon the death of the settlor if it is presently held in his name alone, or upon the death of the surviving co-owner if it is now held in joint tenancy. This can be accomplished by using DT-101 or DT-101-J in Chapter 7, in conjunction with the appropriate quit claim deed. The family trust instrument, DT-154, makes provision for this arrangement if it is elected.

At the end of trust instrument DT-154 is a page headed "Schedule A." List there the principal assets (home, stocks, bank accounts, etc.) you are directing into the trust at your death. Please understand that assets so listed are in no way "frozen" into the trust nor will the trust assets be limited to the items listed. You may have disposed of all such items by the date of your death and replaced them with others. The trust fund will consist of all those assets of any kind and wheresoever situated which you have left covered by one of the declarations of trust in this book, and in which you have designated the trustee of this trust to receive the asset upon your death.

A final note: If the trustee has not demonstrated an ability to handle and invest money prudently, instruct him or her to put the money into a good mutual fund of blue chip securities which has been in existence for at least ten years. In this way, the trust assets will be provided with professional management. Explain that a brokerage account is not a suitable substitute for professional investment management. Incidentally, most mutual funds offer a "systematic withdrawal plan" under which they will forward a regular monthly check which will total 6 percent per year, providing a convenient way to implement the payout instructions in the deed of trust.

In those cases where there are substantial assets in the wife's name, acquired through inheritance or earlier or current business or professional activities, a different trust arrangement is called for, with the wife as settlor, the husband as first beneficiary and with another individual as trustee. The instrument which follows, DT-154, has been designed for use in either situation. All of the instructions given above should be carefully followed. To get the trust assets to the trustee upon the death of the settlor, the same declarations of trust for naming one beneficiary should be used, the beneficiary being *"Philip Jones, Trustee under deed of trust executed by Mary L. Jones and said Philip Jones under date of* (date you both sign the deed)."

Deed of Trust

THIS AGREEMENT entered into by and between _____

of the City/Town of _____, County of _____

and State of _____ (hereinafter referred to as the Settlor"), and _____

of the City/Town of _____, County of _____

and State of _____ (hereinafter referred to as the "Trustee").

WITNESSETH:

WHEREAS the Settlor desires at death to leave certain property in trust, and

WHEREAS the Trustee is willing to accept and administer such funds as Trustee under the terms of these presents.

NOW THEREFORE intending to be legally bound hereby, the Settlor and the Trustee do hereby covenant and agree as follows:

1. Separately, the Settlor has executed one or more Declarations of Trust in which the Trustee is named as beneficiary to receive certain assets described in Schedule A attached hereto and made a part hereof, and reserves the right to make additional assets, including life insurance policies on the Settlor's life, so payable.

2. Upon the Settlor's death, the Trustee shall divide the trust fund into two parts. One of said parts, herein termed the "marital share," shall consist of property of a value equal to the lesser of (a) the maximum marital deduction allowable in determining the federal estate tax payable by the Settlor's estate, or (b) the minimum amount which, after taking into account all credits and deductions available to the Settlor's estate for federal estate tax purposes (other than the marital deduction), will result in no federal estate tax. The other part shall consist of the remainder of the trust fund. In apportioning to the marital and nonmarital trusts specific assets previously valued for estate tax purposes, the Trustee shall insure that the two trusts share proportionately in any subsequent appreciation or depreciation in the value of such assets. Assets which do not qualify for marital deduction status, or assets not includable in the Settlor's gross estate for federal tax purposes, shall not be included in the marital share of the trust.

(A) With respect to the "marital share" so called, the Trustee shall hold, manage, invest and reinvest the same as a trust fund upon the following terms and conditions:

(1) The Trustee shall pay to the Settlor's spouse _____, in convenient monthly installments during his/her lifetime, the actual income from the trust or a sum equal to six (6%) percent per year of the value of the trust computed at the time of the Settlor's death and thereafter recomputed annually at the beginning of each calendar year, whichever is the greater, together with such sums from principal as the Settlor's spouse shall request be paid from time to time.

(2) Upon the death of the Settlor's spouse, the Trustee shall pay the then trust fund as such spouse shall appoint by specific reference to this instrument in his/her Will, and the Settlor hereby confers upon the said spouse the sole and unrestricted right to appoint the same by his/her Will, outright or in further trust, in favor of his/her estate or in favor of others. To the extent that said power shall not be effectively exercised, the trust fund herein created shall be added to the remaining part and shall be disposed of as hereinafter provided.

(3) If the Settlor and the Settlor's spouse shall die in such circumstances that there is not, in the judgment of the Trustee, whose decision shall be conclusive, sufficient evidence to determine readily which of them survived the other, then for the purposes of this trust, the Settlor's spouse shall be deemed to have survived the Settlor.

(B) With respect to the remaining, "nonmarital," part of the trust fund, the Trustee shall hold, manage, invest and reinvest the same as a trust fund upon the following terms and conditions:

(1) If requested by the executor or administrator of the Settlor's estate, the Trustee shall pay or reimburse said executor or administrator for the amount of any ante mortem claim, funeral expense or expense of administration which shall be allowed in connection with the settlement of such estate or, in the absence of formal probate administration, which the Trustee shall determine to be due and payable.

(2) The Trustee shall pay to the proper taxing authority or reimburse the executor or administrator of the Settlor's estate for the amount of any succession, estate, transfer or similar tax, whether state or federal, which shall be imposed lawfully upon the Settlor's taxable estate or upon any beneficiary thereof as a result of the Settlor's death. The proceeds of employee death benefits or employee life insurance policies on the Settlor's life shall not be used to pay death taxes or otherwise be paid to the executor of the Settlor's estate.

(3) From the balance of the trust fund remaining in the Trustee's hands, the Trustee shall pay to the Settlor's spouse, _____, in equal monthly installments during such spouse's lifetime a sum equal to six (6%) percent per year of the value of this nonmarital part of the trust fund as computed at the time of the Settlor's death and thereafter recomputed at the beginning of each calendar year. The Trustee is further authorized to pay to the Settlor's spouse or expend for such spouse's maintenance and support, or for the maintenance, support and education of any child of the Settlor, such sums out of principal as the Trustee shall deem proper from time to time for any such purpose.

(4) Upon the death of the Settlor's spouse, the Trustee shall, if requested by the executor or administrator of the spouse's estate, or in the absence of formal probate administration, in such Trustee's own discretion, pay or reimburse such estate for the amounts of any funeral expenses or expenses of the last illness and/or any taxes, debts or other post mortem expenses of the said spouse.

(5) Thereafter, the Trustee shall dispose of the trust fund as specified in

Cross off	Box One below
two of the three	Box Two below
and initial	Box Three below

BOX ONE	BOX TWO	BOX THREE
The Trustee shall pay the entire balance of the trust fund to the Settlor's _____ *(Daughter, nephew, friend, church, etc.)* _____ *(Name)*	The Trustee shall divide the balance of the trust fund into as many equal parts as there shall be beneficiaries named below and shall pay one such part to each of the following, in equal shares, or the survivor of them/per stirpes: _____ _____ _____ _____ _____ _____	The Trustee shall pay the balance of the trust fund to the following, per stirpes, in the proportions shown: *Name Proportion to be paid to such beneficiary* _____ —% _____ —% _____ —% _____ —% _____ —% _____ —% *The share of any beneficiary who dies leaving no surviving issue shall be divided equally among the remaining named beneficiaries who are natural persons, per stirpes.*
and shall thereupon terminate the trust.	and shall thereupon terminate the trust.	and shall thereupon terminate the trust.

Notwithstanding the foregoing, if any beneficiary hereunder shall not have attained the age of _____ years, the Trustee shall hold such beneficiary's share of the trust assets in continuing trust until such beneficiary shall have attained the age of _____ years. Prior to the date upon which such beneficiary attains the age of _____ years, the Trustee may apply or expend any or all of the income or principal directly for the maintenance, education and support of the beneficiary without the intervention of any guardian and without application to any court. Such payments of income or principal may, in the Trustee's sole discretion, be made to the beneficiary or to the beneficiary's parents or to the person with whom the beneficiary is living, without any liability upon the Trustee to see to the application thereof. If such beneficiary survives the Settlor but dies before attaining the age of _____ years, at his or her death the Trustee shall transfer, pay over and deliver the trust property being held for such beneficiary to such beneficiary's personal representative, absolutely.

(6) If any provision of this instrument shall be unclear or the subject of dispute among the parties to the trust, the Trustee shall be fully authorized to construe such provision, and any such determination by the Trustee shall be final and binding upon all such parties.

3. With respect to community property: (a) if the assets, or any part of them, deposited in this trust shall constitute community property, their status as such community property shall remain unchanged; (b) all distributions of income from the trust while both parties are living shall be considered to be community property; (c) either party shall have the right to withdraw his or her portion of the community property, either before or after the death of the Settlor; (d) if the trust is revoked, its assets shall revert to the community.

4. All interests of a beneficiary hereunder shall be inalienable and free from anticipation, assignment, attachment, pledge or control by creditors or a present or former spouse of such beneficiary in any proceedings at law or in equity.

5. This trust is created upon the understanding that the issuer, custodian or transfer agent of any securities held hereunder shall be under no liability whatsoever to see to the proper administration of the trust, and that upon the transfer of the right, title and interest in and to said securities, said issuer, custodian or transfer agent shall conclusively treat the transferee as the sole owner of said trust property and shall be under no liability to see to the proper application of the proceeds of such transfer.

6. The Trustee and any Successor Trustee shall have the following powers in addition to those given them by law, to be exercised in their sole discretion:

To sell, exchange, assign, lease, mortgage, pledge or borrow upon and in any manner to deal with and dispose of all or any part of the trust property, including the power to sell in order to make distribution hereunder, and to invest the proceeds of any sale or other disposition, liquidation or withdrawal, as often as may be necessary in the discretion of the Trustee, without being required to make application for more specific authority to any court of law or equity. The Trustee is specifically authorized to

make all investments and reinvestments of the trust assets (except a reasonable amount of uninvested cash and any real estate which may be added to the trust during the Settlor's lifetime or, subsequently, through the instrumentality of the Settlor's Will or an inter vivos trust, which real estate the Trustee may deem it in the best interest of the beneficiaries to retain) in property of any character, real or personal, foreign or domestic, including without limitation, bonds, notes, debentures, mortgages, certificates of deposit, common and preferred stocks, or shares or interests in investment companies, regardless of whether such investments are considered legal for trust funds.

7. The trust herein created may be amended or revoked at any time during the lifetime of the Settlor by written notice from the Settlor to the Trustee. The Trustee may resign at any time during the lifetime of the Settlor by written notice to the Settlor. The Trustee may resign after the death of the Settlor upon written notice to the designated Successor Trustee and upon proper delivery of the assets of the trust to such Successor Trustee.

8. In the event of the Trustee's physical or mental incapacity, death, resignation or removal for cause,

the Settlor hereby appoints _____ as Successor Trustee.

If the said _____ shall be unwilling or unable to carry out such duties,

the Settlor hereby appoints _____ as Successor Trustee hereunder.

9. The Trustee and any Successor Trustee are specifically instructed by the Settlor to maintain the privacy and confidentiality of this instrument and the trust created hereunder, and are in no circumstances to divulge its terms to any probate or other court or other public agency with the exception of a tax authority.

10. The Trustee and any Successor Trustee shall serve without bond.

11. This Deed of Trust shall be construed and enforced in accordance with the laws of the State of

_____.

IN WITNESS WHEREOF, the parties hereto have hereunder and to a duplicate hereof, set their hands and seals as

of the _____ day of _____, 19____.

Witnessed by: The Settlor:

_____

_____   _____ L.S.

STATE OF _____   City
                             or
COUNTY OF _____   Town _____

On the _____ day of _____, 19____, personally appeared

_____, known to me to be the individual who executed the foregoing

instrument as Settlor, and acknowledged the same to be his/her free act and deed before me.

(Notary Seal)   _____
                                       Notary Public

Accepted:

Witnessed by: The Trustee:

_____

_____   _____ L.S.

STATE OF _____   City
                             or
COUNTY OF _____   Town _____

On the _____ day of _____, 19____, personally appeared

_____, known to me to be the individual who executed the foregoing

instrument as Trustee, and acknowledged the same to be his/her free act and deed before me.

(Notary Seal)   _____
                                         Notary Public

SCHEDULE A

Deed of Trust

THIS AGREEMENT entered into by and between _____,

of the City/Town of _____, County of _____

and State of _____ (hereinafter referred to as the "Settlor"), and _____

of the City/Town of _____, County of _____

and State of _____ (hereinafter referred to as the "Trustee").

WITNESSETH:

WHEREAS the Settlor desires at death to leave certain property in trust, and

WHEREAS the Trustee is willing to accept and administer such funds as Trustee under the terms of these presents.

NOW THEREFORE intending to be legally bound hereby, the Settlor and the Trustee do hereby covenant and agree as follows:

1. Separately, the Settlor has executed one or more Declarations of Trust in which the Trustee is named as beneficiary to receive certain assets described in Schedule A attached hereto and made a part hereof, and reserves the right to make additional assets, including life insurance policies on the Settlor's life, so payable.

2. Upon the Settlor's death, the Trustee shall divide the trust fund into two parts. One of said parts, herein termed the "marital share," shall consist of property of a value equal to the lesser of (a) the maximum marital deduction allowable in determining the federal estate tax payable by the Settlor's estate, or (b) the minimum amount which, after taking into account all credits and deductions available to the Settlor's estate for federal estate tax purposes (other than the marital deduction), will result in no federal estate tax. The other part shall consist of the remainder of the trust fund. In apportioning to the marital and nonmarital trusts specific assets previously valued for estate tax purposes, the Trustee shall insure that the two trusts share proportionately in any subsequent appreciation or depreciation in the value of such assets. Assets which do not qualify for marital deduction status, or assets not includable in the Settlor's gross estate for federal tax purposes, shall not be included in the marital share of the trust.

(A) With respect to the "marital share" so called, the Trustee shall hold, manage, invest and reinvest the same as a trust fund upon the following terms and conditions:

(1) The Trustee shall pay to the Settlor's spouse _____, in convenient monthly installments during his/her lifetime, the actual income from the trust or a sum equal to six (6%) percent per year of the value of the trust computed at the time of the Settlor's death and thereafter recomputed annually at the beginning of each calendar year, whichever is the greater, together with such sums from principal as the Settlor's spouse shall request be paid from time to time.

(2) Upon the death of the Settlor's spouse, the Trustee shall pay the then trust fund as such spouse shall appoint by specific reference to this instrument in his/her Will, and the Settlor hereby confers upon the said spouse the sole and unrestricted right to appoint the same by his/her Will, outright or in further trust, in favor of his/her estate or in favor of others. To the extent that said power shall not be effectively exercised, the trust fund herein created shall be added to the remaining part and shall be disposed of as hereinafter provided.

(3) If the Settlor and the Settlor's spouse shall die in such circumstances that there is not, in the judgment of the Trustee, whose decision shall be conclusive, sufficient evidence to determine readily which of them survived the other, then for the purposes of this trust, the Settler's spouse shall be deemed to have survived the Settlor.

(B) With respect to the remaining, "nonmarital," part of the trust fund, the Trustee shall hold, manage, invest and reinvest the same as a trust fund upon the following terms and conditions:

(1) If requested by the executor or administrator of the Settlor's estate, the Trustee shall pay or reimburse said executor or administrator for the amount of any ante mortem claim, funeral expense or expense of administration which shall be allowed in connection with the settlement of such estate or, in the absence of formal probate administration, which the Trustee shall determine to be due and payable.

(2) The Trustee shall pay to the proper taxing authority or reimburse the executor or administrator of the Settlor's estate for the amount of any succession, estate, transfer or similar tax, whether state or federal, which shall be imposed lawfully upon the Settlor's taxable estate or upon any beneficiary thereof as a result of the Settlor's death. The proceeds of employee death benefits or employee life insurance policies on the Settlor's life shall not be used to pay death taxes or otherwise be paid to the executor of the Settlor's estate.

(3) From the balance of the trust fund remaining in the Trustee's hands, the Trustee shall pay to the Settlor's

spouse, _____, in equal monthly installments during such spouse's lifetime a sum equal to six (6%) percent per year of the value of this nonmarital part of the trust fund as computed at the time of the Settlor's death and thereafter recomputed at the beginning of each calendar year. The Trustee is further authorized to pay to the Settlor's spouse or expend for such spouse's maintenance and support, or for the maintenance, support and education of any child of the Settlor, such sums out of principal as the Trustee shall deem proper from time to time for any such purpose.

(4) Upon the death of the Settlor's spouse, the Trustee shall, if requested by the executor or administrator of the spouse's estate, or in the absence of formal probate administration, in such Trustee's own discretion, pay or reimburse such estate for the amounts of any funeral expenses or expense of the last illness and/or any taxes, debts or other post mortem expenses of the said spouse.

(5) Thereafter, the Trustee shall dispose of the trust fund as specified in

Cross off two of the three and initial	Box One below
	Box Two below
	Box Three below

BOX ONE

The Trustee shall pay the entire balance of the trust fund to the Settlor's

_____
(Daughter, nephew, friend, church, etc.)

_____
(Name)

and shall thereupon terminate the trust.

BOX TWO

The Trustee shall divide the balance of the trust fund into as many equal parts as there shall be beneficiaries named below and shall pay one such part to each of the following, in equal shares, or the survivor of them/per stirpes:

_____

_____

_____

_____

_____

_____

and shall thereupon terminate the trust.

BOX THREE

The Trustee shall pay the balance of the trust fund to the following, per stirpes, in the proportions shown:

Name   *Proportion to be paid to such beneficiary*

_____ __%

_____ __%

_____ __%

_____ __%

_____ __%

_____ __%

{ *The share of any beneficiary who dies leaving no surviving issue shall be divided equally among the remaining named beneficiaries who are natural persons, per stirpes.* }

and shall thereupon terminate the trust.

Notwithstanding the foregoing, if any beneficiary hereunder shall not have attained the age of _____ years, the Trustee shall hold such beneficiary's share of the trust assets in continuing trust until such beneficiary shall have attained the age of _____ years. Prior to the date upon which such beneficiary attains the age of _____ years, the Trustee may apply or expend any or all of the income or principal directly for the maintenance, education and support of the beneficiary without the intervention of any guardian and without application to any court. Such payments of income or principal may, in the Trustee's sole discretion, be made to the beneficiary or to the beneficiary's parents or to the person with whom the beneficiary is living, without any liability upon the Trustee to see to the application thereof. If such beneficiary survives the Settlor but dies before attaining the age of _____ years, at his or her death the Trustee shall transfer, pay over and deliver the trust property being held for such beneficiary to such beneficiary's personal representative, absolutely.

(6) If any provision of this instrument shall be unclear or the subject of dispute among the parties to the trust, the Trustee shall be fully authorized to construe such provision, and any such determination by the Trustee shall be final and binding upon all such parties.

3. With respect to community property: (a) if the assets, or any part of them, deposited in this trust shall constitute community property, their status as such community property shall remain unchanged; (b) all distributions of income from the trust while both parties are living shall be considered to be community property; (c) either party shall have the right to withdraw his or her portion of the community property, either before or after the death of the Settlor; (d) if the trust is revoked, its assets shall revert to the community.

4. All interests of a beneficiary hereunder shall be inalienable and free from anticipation, assignment, attachment, pledge or control by creditors or a present or former spouse of such beneficiary in any proceedings at law or in equity.

5. This trust is created upon the understanding that the issuer, custodian or transfer agent of any securities held hereunder shall be under no liability whatsoever to see to the proper administration of the trust, and that upon the transfer of the right, title and interest in and to said securities, said issuer, custodian or transfer agent shall conclusively treat the transferee as the sole owner of said trust property and shall be under no liability to see to the proper application of the proceeds of such transfer.

6. The Trustee and any Successor Trustee shall have the following powers in addition to those given them by law, to be exercised in their sole discretion:

To sell, exchange, assign, lease, mortgage, pledge or borrow upon and in any manner to deal with and dispose of all or any part of the trust property, including the power to sell in order to make distribution hereunder, and to invest the proceeds of any sale or other disposition, liquidation or withdrawal, as often as may be necessary in the discretion of the Trustee, without being required to make application for more specific authority to any court of law or equity. The Trustee is specifically authorized to make all investments and reinvestments of the trust assets (except a reasonable amount of uninvested cash and any real estate

which may be added to the trust during the Settlor's lifetime or, subsequently, through the instrumentality of the Settlor's Will or an inter vivos trust, which real estate the Trustee may deem it in the best interest of the beneficiaries to retain) in property of any character, real or personal, foreign or domestic, including without limitation, bonds, notes, debentures, mortgages, certificates of deposit, common and preferred stocks, or shares or interests in investment companies, regardless of whether such investments are considered legal for trust funds.

7. The trust herein created may be amended or revoked at any time during the lifetime of the Settlor by written notice from the Settlor to the Trustee. The Trustee may resign at any time during the lifetime of the Settlor by written notice to the Settlor. The Trustee may resign after the death of the Settlor upon written notice to the designated Successor Trustee and upon proper delivery of the assets of the trust to such Successor Trustee.

8. In the event of the Trustee's physical or mental incapacity, death, resignation or removal for cause,

the Settlor hereby appoints _____ as Successor Trustee.

If the said _____ shall be unwilling or unable to carry out such duties,

the Settlor hereby appoints _____ as Successor Trustee hereunder.

9. The Trustee and any Successor Trustee are specifically instructed by the Settlor to maintain the privacy and confidentiality of this instrument and the trust created hereunder, and are in no circumstances to divulge its terms to any probate or other court or other public agency with the exception of a tax authority.

10. The Trustee and any Successor Trustee shall serve without bond.

11. This Deed of Trust shall be construed and enforced in accordance with the laws of the State of _____.

IN WITNESS WHEREOF, the parties hereto have hereunder and to a duplicate hereof, set their hands and seals as of

the _____ day of _____, 19_____.

Witnessed by: The Settlor:

_____

_____   _____ L.S.

STATE OF _____ }   City
                                                   or
COUNTY OF _____   Town _____

On the _____ day of _____, 19_____, personally appeared

_____ known to me to be the individual who executed the foregoing

instrument as Settlor, and acknowledged the same to be his/her free act and deed before me.

(Notary Seal)   _____
                                                             Notary Public

==

Accepted:

Witnessed by: The Trustee:

_____

_____   _____ L.S.

STATE OF _____ }   City
                                                   or
COUNTY OF _____   Town _____

On the _____ day of _____, 19_____, personally appeared

_____ known to me to be the individual who executed the foregoing

instrument as Trustee, and acknowledged the same to be his/her free act and deed before me.

(Notary Seal)   _____
                                                             Notary Public

SCHEDULE A

A Family Trust with a Bank as Trustee, with Investment Management by the Bank

Long ago in England, it was not unusual for the gentry to suffer confiscation of their estates by a reigning monarch whom they had displeased or who simply coveted their property. Only the clergy was safe from this unhappy practice, so it became not uncommon for prudent men of property to turn title to their confiscable possessions over to a churchman with the quiet understanding that he was to hold the property "in trust" for the uneasy owner in accordance with conditions agreed upon between them. The owner showed his gratitude for the protection thus afforded him by a periodic gift to the clergyman. So that there would be no misunderstanding, the agreement was generally spelled out in a deed by which title was transferred.

Thus was born the institution of trusteeship, with property held for the use and benefit of another under the terms of a "deed of trust." As time went on, the sanctity of the trust came to be spelled out in law, and the obligation of a trustee to perform his duties honorably and with reasonable efficiency was codified and standards of trust practice were established.

Particularly in America the practice of trusteeship has flourished and grown. This is understandable—obviously, the wealthiest country in the world has more individuals whose estates need the benefits of trusteeship. Today, large estates are invariably passed on in trust.

Few people have the proper background and training essential for the administration of property, especially invested property. Investment may have been a relatively simple matter a generation or two ago. Today, however, it is an extremely complicated procedure calculated to tax the skill of the most expert. The enormous task of gathering and evaluating facts upon which to base an investment decision is no job for a single individual, no matter how well educated, trained, or experienced he may be. In making major decisions as to trends, or minor ones relating to the purchase or sale of individual securities, group judgment is essential if individual human error is to be avoided.

Many persons concerned with the safety and productivity of their funds have turned to bank trusteeship to provide a measure of professional supervision and relief from the bookkeeping chores attendant upon the ownership of a diversified portfolio of individual securities. In many respects, bank trusteeship has had an admirable record—since this country's first trust company was organized in Philadelphia in 1812, there is no recorded instance of a dollar of trust funds being lost because of banking failure or dishonesty. There have been instances of poor judgment, of course, or of neglect by banks who by reason of their good reputation had so many trust accounts thrust upon them that they couldn't watch them all often enough. But by and large, the record of bank trusteeship has been good and it has been chiefly responsible for the perpetuation of the large estates in this country.

On the pages which follow will be found duplicate copies of an instrument suitable for establishing a living trust with a bank as trustee and investment manager.

Although you establish it during your lifetime instead of through the instrumentality of your will, it is normally not activated until your death. Accordingly, you pay no trustee's fees during your lifetime, because the assets don't pass to the bank until you are gone.

It is essential, however, that you get the assets to the bank promptly *at that time* without going through probate. The way to accomplish that is by covering each asset with one of the forms provided earlier in the book, using a declaration of trust for naming one beneficiary—which will be the bank with which you are setting up the trust.

CHAPTER 22

DEED OF TRUST
For Use In Establishing
A TRUST
With
A BANK AS TRUSTEE
And
INVESTMENT MANAGEMENT BY THE BANK

INSTRUCTIONS:

On the following pages will be found duplicate copies of a deed of trust (DT-155) which will be suitable for use in establishing a family trust with a bank as trustee and with investment management by that bank.

Here are the steps to take:

1. Take the deed of trust to the bank of your choice and invite that institution to accept the trusteeship. The bank will wish to submit your deed to its counsel. Most banks make no charge for the opening of the account, nor do they ordinarily make any annual charge during your lifetime since they have no duties to perform. Some banks prefer to give the trust "active" status by making a nominal charge of $10 annually during the lifetime of the settlor. In most cases, though, the bank's fee begins at your death.

2. The securities which you purchase during your lifetime should be registered: "(your name), *Trustee under Declaration of Trust dated* _____," using one of the trust instruments provided in Chapter 9. Note that that declaration of trust is a separate instrument used only in connection with the registration of your securities. It should not be confused with the deed of trust (DT-155) mentioned above. The declaration of trust is intended to insure that the securities will pass into the bank trust at your death without going through probate. (It may help you differentiate between the functions of the *declaration* and the *deed* if we explain that a declaration involves just one person— he *declares* that he is holding something in trust. A deed ordinarily involves more than one person; it is an agreement between the creator of the trust and the trustee, and it spells out the duties and responsibilities of the trustee.)

Note that you should name as beneficiary and Successor Trustee under the declaration of trust the same bank you have named as trustee under the deed of trust. It should read something like: *"The National Bank of Smithville, Trustee under deed of trust executed by William C. Jones and said National Bank of Smithville under date of* _____." Each time you purchase additional securities, have them registered in the exact same form and under the same declaration of trust.

3. Advise the companies issuing your life insurance policies that you wish the beneficiary designations on the policies changed to read as shown above. They will supply beneficiary change forms for your signature. Some companies will ask to see a copy of the trust or an excerpt of those provisions in it relating to the insurance.

4. Execute a new will (Will Form W-11 in Chapter 29 is suggested), leaving your automobile, jewelry, and other personal effects to your spouse, but directing that all other property, including specifically any stocks, bonds, or cash, be added to the trust account set up under the deed of trust. As of this writing, this procedure (called "incorporation by reference") is not permitted in a few states. Check this point with the trust officer at your local bank.

It is suggested that you appoint as executor under your will the same bank named as trustee under the deed of trust.

At your death, the trustee bank will collect the proceeds of your life insurance and add them to the securities which you have accumulated during your lifetime and which have passed to the trustee automatically at your death. The bank will thereafter invest and reinvest the trust funds and collect and disburse the income (and such sums from principal as you have authorized) to your wife during her lifetime. At her death, the income can continue to your children until they are 21, 25, 35, or such other age as you wish the principal to be made available to them. Your family will enjoy the security of bank trusteeship and they'll have a place where wise counsel will be available to them on their personal business or financial problems.

The following explanatory notes in "layman's language" are keyed to the letters appearing in the margin of the deed of trust (DT-155) which follows immediately hereafter.

A *It is generally desirable to take advantage of the "marital deduction" allowed when at least half of one's estate is left to one's spouse. There may well be instances, however, where the Settlor's wife has substantial means of her own and it would be disadvantageous to increase her estate by taking advantage of the marital deduction. The taxes ultimately assessed against the combined estates upon her death might far exceed the benefits gained by taking the marital deduction.*

B *Note that while the Settlor's wife can withdraw the whole marital trust at will, the Trustee is also authorized to disburse portions of the principal on her behalf should she be hospitalized or incompetent and unable to request them herself.*

C *A trust may qualify for the marital deduction either by giving the Settlor's wife free access to the marital portion or by conferring upon her the right to name who is to receive it at her death. In this case, qualification is made doubly certain by including both provisions. This arrangement enables her to make such distribution of her marital portion of the estate as is appropriate to the family conditions existing at that time, and also permits her to make tax-reducing gifts to heirs while she still lives.*

D *While in most cases, the income from both the marital and the nonmarital portion of the trust will be paid to the Settlor's wife, note that the instrument permits the Trustee in its discretion to withhold the income from the nonmarital portion of the trust and add it to the principal. The objective here is to allow the Settlor's wife to draw the income from the marital portion plus sums from principal equal to the income from the nonmarital portion which is being accumulated instead of paid to her. This would gradually reduce the marital portion (which would be taxable at her death), and build up the nonmarital portion (upon which no further estate tax will have to be paid). That portion of the payments to her which represented a distribution of principal from the marital portion would be completely tax-free. The retained income from the nonmarital portion would be taxable to the trust, and it is likely that this splitting of the taxable income would provide a tax saving. Obviously, the Settlor's wife would not request the Trustee's*

approval of a withdrawal from the nonmarital portion of the trust until she had exhausted the marital portion from which withdrawals could be made without asking anyone's approval. The very circumstances which would lead her to request such approval, then, would also serve to indicate the need to impose a little restraint to preserve her remaining security.

E *While the age at which the Settlor's children are to receive the principal is optional with the Settlor, it is suggested that it be one at which the children will be mature enough to use the money properly. Most Settlors choose age 35.*

Note that the principal is not wholly withheld from the children until the specified age. In addition to tuition, the Trustee might properly be called upon to pay the cost of opening an office for the Settlor's son who is entering upon the practice of medicine, or assist the Settlor's newly married daughter with the down payment on a home. The purpose of the trust is not to keep the money from the children but only to encourage them to use it intelligently.

F *Given two daughters, one hopelessly invalided and the other married to a prosperous businessman in a high tax bracket, the Settlor would undoubtedly himself choose to apportion a larger share of the income to his less fortunate child. This clause which permits the Trustee to "sprinkle" the income among the surviving beneficiaries according to their needs serves a useful purpose.*

G *Increasing numbers of Americans are benefiting from pension, profit-sharing and other plans under which they have a vested interest in the proceeds. This clause permits the inclusion of such proceeds in the trust. Where the procedure is permissible under state law, it also allows the Settlor's wife (or any other person) to add to the trust by will.*

H *In this era of multiple plant corporations, executives are subject to frequent geographical shifts. The city in which a man resides at his death may not necessarily be "home" to his family. This provision makes it possible to shift the trust to another, more conveniently located bank if his wife decides to "go back home."*

Deed of Trust

Made by and between _____,

of the City/Town of _____, County of _____

and State of _____ (hereinafter referred to as the "Settlor"),

and _____

of the City/Town of _____, County of _____

and State of _____ (hereinafter referred to as the "Trustee").

W I T N E S S E T H:

By this agreement the Settlor desires to create a revocable voluntary living trust which may consist of policies of life insurance hereinafter described and/or of other property which he may add to such trust from time to time, and the Trustee has agreed to accept the same under this agreement.

Separately, the Settlor has executed one or more Declarations of Trust in which the Trustee is named as beneficiary to receive certain assets described in Schedule A attached hereto and made a part hereof, and reserves the right to make additional assets, including life insurance policies on the Settlor's life, so payable.

SECTION A:

With respect to any property except policies of life insurance which now or hereafter may be placed in trust hereunder, the Trustee shall hold, invest and reinvest the same as a trust fund upon the following terms and conditions:

1. During the Settlor's lifetime, pay the income to him in convenient installments or expend or reinvest the same upon his written direction.

2. Upon the Settlor's death, add the trust fund herein created to the trust of the insurance proceeds established by Section B of this agreement and dispose of the same as a part thereof in accordance with the provisions of Section B-1 and B-2.

SECTION B:

The Settlor has delivered to the Trustee certain insurance policies on his life described in Schedule A attached hereto and made a part hereof, in which policies the right to change the beneficiary without consent is specifically reserved to the Settlor during his lifetime; and has executed and delivered or will execute and deliver to the Trustee proper instruments to enable the Trustee to be made the beneficiary under said policies as Trustee under this agreement, which policies and the proceeds thereof as and when received by the Trustee shall be held in trust and disposed of by the Trustee as hereinafter provided. Upon receipt by the Trustee of notice of the death of the Settlor the Trustee shall prepare such proofs of death and other documents as are required to collect the amounts payable upon the death of the Settlor under the terms of the policies then held by it as Trustee and shall present such documents to the companies issuing said policies and for that purpose it shall have full power to execute and deliver such instruments and to institute any action in law or equity as in its judgment may be necessary and proper but the Trustee shall not be required to institute any such action until it shall have been indemnified to its satisfaction against all expenses and liabilities which might be incurred thereby.

The Trustee shall divide the insurance proceeds received by it, together with the then trust fund established by the provisions of Section A, and together with any other property which may be added to this trust before or after the Settlor's death, into two parts. One of said parts, herein termed the "marital share," shall consist of property of a value equal to the lesser of (a) the maximum marital deduction allowable in determining the federal estate tax payable by the Settlor's estate, or (b) the minimum amount which, after taking into account all credits and deductions available to the Settlor's estate for federal estate tax purposes (other than the marital deduction), will result in no federal estate tax. The other part shall consist of the remainder of the insurance proceeds and the remainder of the trust fund established by the provisions of Section A. In apportioning to the marital and nonmarital trusts specific assets previously valued for estate tax purposes, the Trustee shall insure that the two trusts share proportionately in any subsequent appreciation or depreciation in the value of such assets.

1. With respect to the "marital share" so called, the Trustee shall hold, manage, invest and reinvest the same as a trust fund upon the following terms and conditions:

(a) The Trustee shall pay the income (and any other payment authorized by Paragraph 12A) to or for the benefit of the

Settlor's wife, _____, in quarterly or if convenient more frequent payments during her lifetime, together with such sums out of principal as she may request the Trustee in writing to pay to her from time to time and together with such sums out of principal as the Trustee in its sole discretion shall deem necessary for her support or maintenance.

(b) Upon the death of the Settlor's wife, the Trustee shall pay the then trust fund as she shall appoint by specific reference to this instrument in her Will, and the Settlor hereby confers upon his said wife the sole and unrestricted power to appoint the same by her Will, outright or in further trust, in favor of her estate or in favor of others. To the extent that said power shall not be effectively exercised, the trust fund herein created shall be added to the remaining part and shall be disposed of as hereinafter provided.

(c) If the Settlor and his wife shall die under such circumstances that there is not, in the judgment of the executor of the Settlor's estate, whose decision shall be conclusive, sufficient evidence to determine readily which of them survived the other, then for the purposes of this trust, the Settlor's wife shall be deemed to have survived him.

2. With respect to the remaining part of the insurance proceeds and trust fund, the Trustee shall hold, invest and reinvest the same as a trust fund upon the following terms and conditions:

(a) If requested by the executor or administrator of the Settlor's estate, the Trustee shall pay or reimburse said executor or administrator for the amount of any ante mortem claim, funeral expense or expense of administration which shall be allowed in connection with the settlement of his estate and which shall be certified to the Trustee by such executor or administrator.

(b) The Trustee shall pay to the proper taxing authority or reimburse the executor or administrator of the Settlor's estate for the amount of any succession, estate, transfer or similar tax, whether state or federal, which shall be imposed lawfully upon the Settlor's taxable estate or upon any beneficiary thereof as the result of the death of the Settlor and which shall be certified to the Trustee by such executor or administrator.

(c) The Trustee shall pay the income (and any other payment authorized by Paragraph 12A) from the balance of the trust fund remaining in its hands to the Settlor's said wife during her lifetime in quarterly or if convenient more frequent payments or in its sole and absolute discretion withhold and accumulate all or such part of such income (or other payment) as it shall determine and add the same to principal. The Trustee is further authorized to pay to the Settlor's wife or in its discretion expend for her maintenance and support or for the maintenance, support and education of the Settlor's children such sums out of principal as it in its sole discretion may deem proper from time to time for any such purpose.

(d) Upon the death of the Settlor's wife or upon the Settlor's death if she shall not survive the Settlor, the Trustee shall:

(i) If requested by the executor or administrator of the wife's estate, pay or reimburse her estate for the amounts of her funeral expenses and the expenses of her last illness as certified to the Trustee by such executor or administrator.

(ii) Divide the balance of the trust fund into as many equal parts as there shall be children of the Settlor then living and children of the Settlor then deceased leaving issue then living and shall:

(1) Pay one of said parts to the living issue collectively of each such child then deceased in equal shares.

(2) Pay one of said parts to each child of the Settlor then living and who shall have become _____ years of age.

(3) Hold, manage, invest and reinvest the remaining parts as one trust fund for the benefit of the children of the Settlor then living and who shall not have become _____ years of age and pay or expend all or none or so much of the income and principal to or for the benefit of each of said children as the Trustee in its sole discretion shall deem proper for their suitable maintenance, support and education until each such child shall become _____ years of age, at which time an equal share of the then principal of the trust fund shall be paid over to such child after making adjustment for the amount by which earlier payments of principal to one child may have exceeded those made to another child. If any such child shall die before becoming _____ years of age, then upon such child's death an equal share of said trust fund after adjustment as aforesaid, shall be paid over to such child's children in equal shares, or the survivor of them; if there shall be no such children then living, such shares shall be added equally to the remaining shares, if any, and held, managed and disposed of as a part thereof; if no such shares remain, such share shall be paid over to the Settlor's issue then living, in equal shares.

(4) Notwithstanding any of the foregoing directions, the share of each living issue of any deceased child of the Settlor, though vested, shall be held in trust and so much of the income and principal as the Trustee shall deem proper shall be paid to or for the benefit of such issue until he or she shall become twenty-one years of age.

SECTION C: Administrative Provisions

1. Unless directed in accordance with the provisions of Section A-1 and provided with the means to do so, the Trustee shall be under no duty to pay any premiums or other charges required to continue the said policies of insurance in force or to procure renewals thereof or otherwise to ascertain that said policies are kept in force.

2. The provisions of Section B shall apply only to such proceeds of said policies as may be due and payable to the Trustee upon the death of the Settlor, and all payments, dividends, surrender values and benefits of any kind which may accrue on any of said policies during the lifetime of the Settlor shall be payable to the Settlor and shall not be collected or disposed of by the Trustee.

3. The Settlor reserves to himself without the consent of said Trustee or of any beneficiary hereunder or of any beneficiary now or hereafter named in any policy now or hereafter deposited hereunder, the right to pledge any of said policies or any other property now or hereafter placed in trust hereunder to secure any loan now existing or hereafter made by any persons, firm or corporation to the Settlor, and further reserves the right to exercise any and all options, elections, rights, and privileges, including the right to borrow on said policies, given to him under the terms of any of said policies, and upon the request of the Settlor the Trustee will execute and deliver such documents as are necessary and proper to permit the Settlor fully to exercise such rights.

4. The Settlor shall have the right at any time during his lifetime to place additional property and/or insurance policies under the terms of this agreement upon delivering such property and/or insurance policies to the Trustee together with a written request that the Trustee place said additional property and policies under this agreement. Upon the delivery of any such additional property and policies and such written request to the Trustee, the Trustee shall issue a receipt therefore to the Settlor. The Settlor shall also have the right to add to the trust fund by an appropriate provision in his Will or to designate the Trustee as beneficiary of any other inter vivos trust or of any profit-sharing, pension, incentive compensation or other fund in which he may have an interest, and under the terms of which he has the right to name a beneficiary. The Trustee is further authorized to accept additions to this trust from any other source, testamentary or otherwise.

5. The Settlor shall have the right at any time during his lifetime to withdraw from the operation of this agreement any or all property and policies upon his written request delivered to the Trustee and upon delivery to the Trustee of a receipt for the property and/or policies so withdrawn, and upon such withdrawal and thereafter if required, the Trustee shall execute and deliver to the Settlor such instruments as are necessary and proper to transfer the interest of the Trustee therein.

6. The Settlor shall have the right at any time during his lifetime to terminate this agreement upon giving to the Trustee written notice of such termination, and upon termination the Trustee shall deliver to the Settlor against his written receipt all

property and policies then held hereunder and shall execute and deliver to the Settlor such instruments as are necessary and proper to transfer the interest of the Trustee therein to the Settlor. The Trustee shall have the right to resign during the Settlor's lifetime.

After the Settlor's death, by mutual agreement between the Settlor's surviving spouse and the Trustee, the Trustee may resign to be replaced by a Successor Trustee nominated by the beneficiary, provided that such Successor Trustee shall be a bank or trust company authorized by law to exercise fiduciary powers which shall have its principal place of business and be actively engaged in the trust business in the state in which the beneficiary then legally resides. Such Successor Trustee having filed its written acceptance with the Trustee, the latter, after finally accounting to the beneficiary or beneficiaries, shall deliver all of the trust assets held hereunder to the Successor Trustee and shall thereafter have no further duties or liabilities with respect thereto.

Should the Settlor's wife, surviving the Settlor, move and establish her domicile in another state, she may request the Trustee to and the Trustee shall resign, provided that she shall by written instrument filed with the Trustee name as Successor Trustee a bank or trust company authorized by law to exercise fiduciary powers which shall have its principal place of business and be actively engaged in the trust business in the state in which she shall have established her domicile. If such nominee shall accept said trust and file its written acceptance with the Trustee, the latter, after finally accounting to the beneficiaries, shall deliver all of the funds held in trust hereunder to the Successor Trustee and shall thereafter have no further duties or liabilities with respect thereto. All powers and discretions herein conferred upon the Trustee are conferred upon any Successor Trustee.

7. This agreement may be altered or modified at any time during the lifetime of the Settlor, by consent of the Settlor and the Trustee without the consent of any other person.

8. The Trustee shall receive reasonable compensation for its services hereunder but such compensation shall not exceed the amount customarily charged by corporate fiduciaries in the area for similar services.

9. In each year during the Settlor's lifetime that there have been no receipts or disbursements from the trust, the Trustee shall not be required to furnish any statement with respect to the trust property to the Settlor. After the Settlor's death, however, the Trustee shall furnish such an annual statement to his said wife during her lifetime and after the death of both the Settlor and his wife the Trustee shall furnish a similar annual statement with respect to each of the trust funds thereafter administered by it to the respective beneficiaries thereof or to their guardians if they be minors.

10. All interests of a beneficiary hereunder shall be inalienable and free from anticipation, assignment, attachment, pledge or control by creditors or a present or former spouse of such beneficiary in any proceedings at law or in equity.

11. To the extent that the assets or any part of them deposited in this trust shall constitute community property: (a) their status as such community property shall remain unchanged; (b) all distributions of income from the trust while both parties are living shall be considered to be community property; (c) either party shall have the right to withdraw his or her portion of the community property, either before or after the death of the Settlor; (d) if the trust is revoked, its assets shall revert to the community.

12. A. The Trustee is specifically authorized to make all investments and reinvestments of the trust assets (except a reasonable amount of uninvested cash and any real estate which may be added to the trust during the Settlor's lifetime or, subsequently, by reference in his Will, which real estate the Trustee may deem it in the best interests of the beneficiaries to retain) in property of any character, real or personal, foreign or domestic, including, without limitation, bonds, notes, debentures, mortgages, certificates of deposit, common and preferred stocks, shares or interests in investment companies and participations in any common trust fund maintained by the Trustee, without regard to the proportion which such property may bear to the entire amount of the trust and regardless of whether such investments are considered legal for trust funds.

The term "income" in this instrument shall be deemed to mean that portion of the distributions made upon securities or other investments of the trust which has been designated as "ordinary income" as distinguished from "capital gains." Whenever such portion of said distribution as shall be designated "ordinary income" shall be less than 6 percent of the total principal market value of the trust, then the Trustee is authorized and instructed to add to such distribution from "ordinary income" such portion of any distribution which has been designated as "capital gains" as shall be necessary to cause the total payment to the then income beneficiary or beneficiaries to equal 6 percent of the total principal market value of the trust. If such distributions from "ordinary income" and "capital gains" shall not together be sufficient to provide the income beneficiary or beneficiaries collectively with a sum equal to 6 percent per annum of the then current principal market value of the trust, then the Trustee is authorized and instructed to pay said income beneficiary or beneficiaries such amount of the principal of the trust as shall be required to maintain the total annual distribution to such beneficiary or beneficiaries at a minimum of 6 percent of the then current total principal market value of the trust. Where used herein, "principal market value" shall be deemed to mean the principal market value of the trust shown by the latest regular annual report of the Trustee. Except as provided in the foregoing, "capital gains" distributions shall be considered as principal and added to the corpus of the trust.

B. The Trustee may (a) sell, mortgage, lease, convey and exchange the whole or any part of the trust funds, whether real or personal, without court order and upon such terms as it shall deem best, (b) make any required division or distribution of the trust funds in cash or in kind or in both and at such values as it may fix, (c) apportion Trustee's and attorney's fees between income and principal, (d) register securities in the name of a nominee, (e) compromise claims by or against the trusts and (f) borrow funds for any trust purpose and secure the payment of such loans by the pledge of the whole or any part of the trust funds. The Trustee may make loans to the executors or administrators of the Settlor's estate, whether secured or unsecured, and may purchase and hold any asset of his estate whether or not it shall be considered a prudent trust investment.

13. The Trustee and any Successor Trustee shall serve without bond.

14. This agreement shall be construed and enforced in accordance with the laws of the State of

IN WITNESS WHEREOF, the said _____ has hereunto and

to a duplicate hereof set his hand and seal as Settlor and said _____ has

(Trustee Bank)

caused this instrument to be accepted and executed in duplicate by its duly authorized officer(s) as of the _____

day of _____, 19_____.

Witnessed by: THE SETTLOR:

(1) _____

                                              _____ L.S.

(2) _____

                                      FOR THE TRUSTEE:

(1) _____

                                              _____ L.S.

(2) _____

STATE OF _____   City
                                        or

COUNTY OF _____   Town _____

   Personally appeared _____, signer

and sealer as Settlor of the foregoing instrument, who acknowledged the same to be his free act and deed, before me this

_____ day of _____, 19_____.

(Notary Seal)   _____
                                            Notary Public

STATE OF _____   City
                                          or

COUNTY OF _____   Town _____

   Personally appeared _____, signer

and sealer of the foregoing instrument, as an officer of the _____

(name of Trustee Bank)

and acknowledged the same to be his free act and deed as such officer, and the free act and deed

of said _____

(Trustee Bank)

before me, this _____ day of _____, 19_____.

(Notary Seal)   _____
                                            Notary Public

SCHEDULE A

Deed of Trust

Made by and between _____,

of the City/Town of _____, County of _____

and State of _____ (hereinafter referred to as the "Settlor"), and _____,

of the City/Town of _____, County of _____

and State of _____ (hereinafter referred to as the "Trustee").

WITNESSETH:

By this agreement the Settlor desires to create a revocable voluntary living trust which may consist of policies of life insurance hereinafter described and/or of other property which he may add to such trust from time to time, and the Trustee has agreed to accept the same under this agreement.

Separately, the Settlor has executed one or more Declarations of Trust in which the Trustee is named as beneficiary to receive certain assets described in Schedule A attached hereto and made a part hereof, and reserves the right to make additional assets, including life insurance policies on the Settlor's life, so payable.

SECTION A:

With respect to any property except policies of life insurance which now or hereafter may be placed in trust hereunder, the Trustee shall hold, invest and reinvest the same as a trust fund upon the following terms and conditions:

1. During the Settlor's lifetime, pay the income to him in convenient installments or expend or reinvest the same upon his written direction.

2. Upon the Settlor's death, add the trust fund herein created to the trust of the insurance proceeds established by Section B of this agreement and dispose of the same as a part thereof in accordance with the provisions of Section B-1 and B-2.

SECTION B:

The Settlor has delivered to the Trustee certain insurance policies on his life described in Schedule A attached hereto and made a part hereof, in which policies the right to change the beneficiary without consent is specifically reserved to the Settlor during his lifetime; and has executed and delivered or will execute and deliver to the Trustee proper instruments to enable the Trustee to be made the beneficiary under said policies as Trustee under this agreement, which policies and the proceeds thereof as and when received by the Trustee shall be held in trust and disposed of by the Trustee as hereinafter provided. Upon receipt by the Trustee of notice of the death of the Settlor the Trustee shall prepare such proofs of death and other documents as are required to collect the amounts payable upon the death of the Settlor under the terms of the policies then held by it as Trustee and shall present such documents to the companies issuing said policies and for that purpose it shall have full power to execute and deliver such instruments and to institute any action in law or equity as in its judgment may be necessary and proper but the Trustee shall not be required to institute any such action until it shall have been indemnified to its satisfaction against all expenses and liabilities which might be incurred thereby.

The Trustee shall divide the insurance proceeds received by it, together with the then trust fund established by the provisions of Section A, and together with any other property which may be added to this trust before or after the Settlor's death, into two parts. One of said parts, herein termed the "marital share," shall consist of property of a value equal to the lesser of (a) the maximum marital deduction allowable in determining the federal estate tax payable by the Settlor's estate, or (b) the minimum amount which, after taking into account all credits and deductions available to the Settlor's estate for federal estate tax purposes (other than the marital deduction), will result in no federal estate tax. The other part shall consist of the remainder of the insurance proceeds and the remainder of the trust fund established by the provisions of Section A. In apportioning to the marital and nonmarital trusts specific assets previously valued for estate tax purposes, the Trustee shall insure that the two trusts share proportionately in any subsequent appreciation or depreciation in the value of such assets.

1. With respect to the "marital share" so called, the Trustee shall hold, manage, invest and reinvest the same as a trust fund upon the following terms and conditions:

(a) The Trustee shall pay the income (and any other payment authorized by Paragraph 12A) to or for the benefit of the

Settlor's wife, _____, in quarterly or if convenient more frequent payments during her lifetime, together with such sums out of principal as she may request the Trustee in writing to pay her from time to time and together with such sums out of principal as the Trustee in its sole discretion shall deem necessary for her support or maintenance.

(b) Upon the death of the Settlor's wife, the Trustee shall pay the then trust fund as she shall appoint by specific reference to this instrument in her Will and the Settlor hereby confers upon his said wife the sole and unrestricted power to appoint the same by her Will, outright or in further trust, in favor of her estate or in favor of others. To the extent that said power shall not be effectively exercised, the trust fund herein created shall be added to the remaining part and shall be disposed of as hereinafter provided.

(c) If the Settlor and his wife shall die under such circumstances that there is not, in the judgment of the executor of the Settlor's estate, whose decision shall be conclusive, sufficient evidence to determine readily which of them survived the other, then for the purposes of this trust, the Settlor's wife shall be deemed to have survived him.

2. With respect to the remaining part of the insurance proceeds and trust fund, the Trustee shall hold, invest and reinvest the same as a trust fund upon the following terms and conditions:

(a) If requested by the executor or administrator of the Settlor's estate, the Trustee shall pay or reimburse said executor or administrator for the amount of any ante mortem claim, funeral expense or expense of administration which shall be allowed in connection with the settlement of his estate and which shall be certified to the Trustee by such executor or administrator.

(b) The Trustee shall pay to the proper taxing authority or reimburse the executor or administrator of the Settlor's estate for the amount of any succession, estate, transfer or similar tax, whether state or federal, which shall be imposed lawfully upon the Settlor's taxable estate or upon any beneficiary thereof as the result of the death of the Settlor and which shall be certified to the Trustee by such executor or administrator.

(c) The Trustee shall pay the income (and any other payment authorized by Paragraph 12A) from the balance of the trust fund remaining in its hands to the Settlor's said wife during her lifetime in quarterly or if convenient more frequent payments or in its sole and absolute discretion withhold and accumulate all or such part of such income (or other payment) as it shall determine and add the same to principal. The Trustee is further authorized to pay to the Settlor's wife or in its discretion expend for her maintenance and support or for the maintenance, support and education of the Settlor's children such sums out of principal as it in its sole discretion may deem proper from time to time for any such purpose.

(d) Upon the death of the Settlor's wife or upon the Settlor's death if she shall not survive the Settlor, the Trustee shall:

(i) If requested by the executor or administrator of the wife's estate, pay or reimburse her estate for the amounts of her funeral expenses and the expenses of her last illness as certified to the Trustee by such executor or administrator.

(ii) Divide the balance of the trust fund into as many equal parts as there shall be children of the Settlor then living and children of the Settlor then deceased leaving issue then living and shall:

(1) Pay one of said parts to the living issue collectively of each such child then deceased in equal shares.

(2) Pay one of said parts to each child of the Settlor then living and who shall have become _____ years of age.

(3) Hold, manage, invest and reinvest the remaining parts as one trust fund for the benefit of the children of the Settlor then living and who shall not have become _____ years of age and pay or expend all or none or so much of the income and principal to or for the benefit of each of said children as the Trustee in its sole discretion shall deem proper for their suitable maintenance, support and education until each such child shall become _____ years of age, at which time an equal share of the then principal of the trust fund shall be paid over to such child after making adjustment for the amount by which earlier payments of principal to one child may have exceeded those made to another child. If any such child shall die before becoming _____ years of age, then upon such child's death an equal share of said trust fund after adjustment as aforesaid, shall be paid over to such child's children in equal shares, or the survivor of them; if there shall be no such children then living, such shares shall be added equally to the remaining shares, if any, and held, managed and disposed of as a part thereof; if no such shares remain, such share shall be paid over to the Settlor's issue then living, in equal shares.

(4) Notwithstanding any of the foregoing directions, the share of each living issue of any deceased child of the Settlor, though vested, shall be held in trust and so much of the income and principal as the Trustee shall deem proper shall be paid to or for the benefit of such issue until he or she shall become twenty-one years of age.

SECTION C: Administrative Provisions

1. Unless directed in accordance with the provisions of Section A-1 and provided with the means to do so, the Trustee shall be under no duty to pay any premiums or other charges required to continue the said policies of insurance in force or to procure renewals thereof or otherwise to ascertain that said policies are kept in force.

2. The provisions of Section B shall apply only to such proceeds of said policies as may be due and payable to the Trustee upon the death of the Settlor, and all payments, dividends, surrender values and benefits of any kind which may accrue on any of said policies during the lifetime of the Settlor shall be payable to the Settlor and shall not be collected or disposed of by the Trustee.

3. The Settlor reserves to himself without the consent of said Trustee or of any beneficiary hereunder or of any beneficiary now or hereafter named in any policy now or hereafter deposited hereunder, the right to pledge any of said policies or any other property now or hereafter placed in trust hereunder to secure any loan now existing or hereafter made by any persons, firm or corporation to the Settlor, and further reserves the right to exercise any and all options, elections, rights, and privileges, including the right to borrow on said policies, given to him under the terms of any of said policies, and upon the request of the Settlor the Trustee will execute and deliver such documents as are necessary and proper to permit the Settlor fully to exercise such rights.

4. The Settlor shall have the right at any time during his lifetime to place additional property and/or insurance policies under the terms of this agreement upon delivering such property and/or insurance policies to the Trustee together with a written request that the Trustee place said additional property and policies under this agreement. Upon the delivery of any such additional property and policies and such written request to the Trustee, the Trustee shall issue a receipt therefore to the Settlor. The Settlor shall also have the right to add to the trust fund by an appropriate provision in his Will or to designate the Trustee as beneficiary of any profit-sharing, pension, incentive compensation or other fund in which he may have an interest, and under the terms of which he has the right to name a beneficiary. The Trustee is further authorized to accept additions to this trust from any other source, testamentary or otherwise.

5. The Settlor shall have the right at any time during his lifetime to withdraw from the operation of this agreement any or all property and policies upon his written request delivered to the Trustee and upon delivery to the Trustee of a receipt for the property and/or policies so withdrawn, and upon such withdrawal and thereafter if required, the Trustee shall execute and deliver to the Settlor such instruments as are necessary and proper to release the interest of the Trustee therein.

6. The Settlor shall have the right at any time during his lifetime to terminate this agreement upon giving to the Trustee written notice of such termination, and upon termination the Trustee shall deliver to the Settlor against his written receipt all

property and policies then held hereunder and shall execute and deliver to the Settlor such instruments as are necessary and proper to transfer the interest of the Trustee therein to the Settlor. The Trustee shall have the right to resign during the Settlor's lifetime.

After the Settlor's death, by mutual agreement between the Settlor's surviving spouse and the Trustee, the Trustee may resign to be replaced by a Successor Trustee nominated by the beneficiary, provided that such Successor Trustee shall be a bank or trust company authorized by law to exercise fiduciary powers which shall have its principal place of business and be actively engaged in the trust business in the state in which the beneficiary then legally resides. Such Successor Trustee having filed its written acceptance with the Trustee, the latter, after finally accounting to the beneficiary or beneficiaries, shall deliver all of the trust assets held hereunder to the Successor Trustee and shall thereafter have no further duties or liabilities with respect thereto.

Should the Settlor's wife, surviving the Settlor, move and establish her domicile in another state, she may request the Trustee to and the Trustee shall resign, provided that she shall by written instrument filed with the Trustee name as Successor Trustee a bank or trust company authorized by law to exercise fiduciary powers which shall have its principal place of business and be actively engaged in the trust business in the state in which she shall have established her domicile. If such nominee shall accept said trust and file its written acceptance with the Trustee, the latter, after finally accounting to the beneficiaries, shall deliver all of the funds held in trust hereunder to the Successor Trustee and shall thereafter have no further duties or liabilities with respect thereto. All powers and discretions herein conferred upon the Trustee are conferred upon any Successor Trustee.

7. This agreement may be altered or modified at any time during the lifetime of the Settlor, by consent of the Settlor and the Trustee without the consent of any other person.

8. The Trustee shall receive reasonable compensation for its services hereunder but such compensation shall not exceed the amount customarily charged by corporate fiduciaries in the area for similar services.

9. In each year during the Settlor's lifetime that there have been no receipts or disbursements from the trust, the Trustee shall not be required to furnish any statement with respect to the trust property to the Settlor. After the Settlor's death, however, the Trustee shall furnish such an annual statement to his said wife during her lifetime and after the death of both the Settlor and his wife the Trustee shall furnish a similar annual statement with respect to each of the trust funds thereafter administered by it to the respective beneficiaries thereof or to their guardians if they be minors.

10. All interests of a beneficiary hereunder shall be inalienable and free from anticipation, assignment, attachment, pledge or control by creditors or a present or former spouse of such beneficiary in any proceedings at law or in equity.

11. To the extent that the assets or any part of them deposited in this trust shall constitute community property: (a) their status as such community property shall remain unchanged; (b) all distributions of income from the trust while both parties are living shall be considered to be community property; (c) either party shall have the right to withdraw his or her portion of the community property, either before or after the death of the Settlor; (d) if the trust is revoked, its assets shall revert to the community.

12. A. The Trustee is specifically authorized to make all investments and reinvestments of the trust assets (except a reasonable amount of uninvested cash and any real estate which may be added to the trust during the Settlor's lifetime or, subsequently, by reference in his Will, which real estate the Trustee may deem it in the best interests of the beneficiaries to retain), in property of any character, real or personal, foreign or domestic, including, without limitation, bonds, notes, debentures, mortgages, certificates of deposit, common and preferred stocks, shares or interests in investment companies and participations in any common trust fund maintained by the Trustee, without regard to the proportion which such property may bear to the entire amount of the trust and regardless of whether such investments are considered legal for trust funds.

The term "income" in this instrument shall be deemed to mean that portion of the distributions made upon securities or other investments of the trust which has been designated as "ordinary income" as distinguished from "capital gains." Whenever such portion of said distribution as shall be designated "ordinary income" shall be less than 6 percent of the total principal market value of the trust, then the Trustee is authorized and instructed to add to such distribution from "ordinary income" such portion of any distribution which has been designated as "capital gains" as shall be necessary to cause the total payment to the then income beneficiary or beneficiaries to equal 6 percent of the total principal market value of the trust. If such distributions from "ordinary income" and "capital gains" shall not together be sufficient to provide the income beneficiary or beneficiaries collectively with a sum equal to 6 percent per annum of the then current principal market value of the trust, then the Trustee is authorized and instructed to pay said income beneficiary or beneficiaries such amount of the principal of the trust as shall be required to maintain the total annual distribution to such beneficiary or beneficiaries at a minimum of 6 percent of the then current total principal market value of the trust. Where used herein, "principal market value" shall be deemed to mean the principal market value of the trust shown by the latest regular annual report of the Trustee. Except as provided in the foregoing, "capital gains" distributions shall be considered as principal and added to the corpus of the trust.

B. The Trustee may (a) sell, mortgage, lease, convey and exchange the whole or any part of the trust funds, whether real or personal, without court order and upon such terms as it shall deem best, (b) make any required division or distribution of the trust funds in cash or in kind or in both and at such values as it may fix, (c) apportion Trustee's and attorney's fees between income and principal, (d) register securities in the name of a nominee, (e) compromise claims by or against the trusts, and (f) borrow funds for any trust purpose and secure the payment of such loans by the pledge of the whole or any part of the trust funds. The Trustee may make loans to the executors or administrators of the Settlor's estate, whether secured or unsecured, and may purchase and hold any asset of his estate whether or not it shall be considered a prudent trust investment.

13. The Trustee and any Successor Trustee shall serve without bond.

14. This agreement shall be construed and enforced in accordance with the laws of the State of

_____

IN WITNESS WHEREOF, the said _____ has hereunto and

to a duplicate hereof set his hand and seal and said _____ has

(Trustee Bank)

caused this instrument to be executed in duplicate by its duly authorized officer(s) as of the _____

day of _____, 19_____.

Witnessed by: THE SETTLOR:

(1) _____

(2) _____   _____ L.S.

                                                          FOR THE TRUSTEE:

(1) _____

(2) _____   _____ L.S.

STATE OF _____ }   City
                                                          or
COUNTY OF _____ }   Town _____

Personally appeared _____, signer

and sealer as Settlor of the foregoing instrument, who acknowledged the same to be his free act and deed, before me, this

_____ day of _____, 19_____.

(Notary Seal)   _____
                                                                    Notary Public

STATE OF _____ }   City
                                                          or
COUNTY OF _____ }   Town _____

Personally appeared _____, signer

and sealer of the foregoing instrument as an officer of the _____

(name of Trustee Bank)

and acknowledged the same to be his free act and deed as such officer, and the free act and deed

of said _____

(Trustee Bank)

before me, this _____ day of _____, 19_____.

(Notary Seal)   _____
                                                                    Notary Public

SCHEDULE A

A Family Trust with a Bank as Trustee, with Investment Management by a Mutual Fund

An interesting and practical development in recent years has been a form of trust which I designed to combine the services of a local bank as trustee and a mutual fund as investment manager in a plan which embraces one's entire estate, including the proceeds of one's life insurance.

Four assumptions contribute to the growing popularity of this device as an effective instrument in estate planning:

1. Bank trusteeship has had one drawback—the occasional instance of poor judgment by a bank lacking adequate trust facilities, or neglect by a large, competent but overbusy bank.

2. This drawback can be substantially reduced by combining the custodial services of the local trust company with the management facilities of completely independent professional investment managers who beyond any question of doubt have both the time and the skill to perform their work well.

3. Such independent management is now relatively easy to find, especially in view of the development of mutual funds with their pursuit of high standards of management performance.

4. In this modern era with its development of the "package" concept, the idea of a new "trust package" which neatly combines a man's entire estate—lifetime investment accumulation, life insurance proceeds, and residue of odds and ends of property of which he may die possessed—into a single, tidy, well-managed package obviously strikes a responsive chord in every man wrestling with the problem of how best to preserve his family's financial security after he is gone.

It provides that a local trust company shall have physical possession of the assets. Its duties include safekeeping for those assets and the bookkeeping and accounting incidental to the trust administration. It also maintains personal contact with beneficiaries and exercises discretion with regard to disbursements where authorized to do so.

It is a "dry trust" during the settlor's lifetime—other than providing safekeeping for the settlor's will, trust property, and life insurance policies, the bank performs no active service (unless called up to do so) and therefore receives no compensation during this period.

Investment supervision of the trust should rest with independent investment managers selected by the settlor. There are many investment counsel firms who can provide such investment supervision. Obviously, the more competent the firm, the more accounts it already has with whom your account must compete for the managers' attention. One should choose carefully, bearing in mind that the whole purpose of the search for independent management is to avoid a similar competition with other accounts in the trust department of the bank itself.

The growth of mutual funds in recent years suggests that this practical device for providing investment management service to everyone, regardless of the individual's means, has met a need and done its job well. As more and more of the top-notch investment brains of the country gravitate toward the great aggregations of wealth represented by the mutual funds, it has become easier for the layman to find competent investment management.

Ordinarily, the principal factors in the choice of a trustee bank are faith and hope. Since bank trust accounts are private and confidential, there is usually no means by which one can measure the skill which the trustee bank has demonstrated in performing similar services for others in the past. The record of an isolated, unidentified trust account is not satisfactory—accounts have varying objectives and there are bound to be a few whose objectives, as reflected in their investment policy, coincide with a current economic trend and which therefore look good. Such an account would hardly reflect a true cross section of the bank's accounts generally. By and large, bank investment management must be chosen on the basis of faith in the institution's reputation and hope that it will do a good job.

The use of a mutual fund as the medium of investment in a living trust permits of the selection of management on a much more knowledgeable basis. The comparative performance of all mutual funds is meticulously recorded in standard reference books available in most libraries and it is a simple matter to establish the relative ability of any fund management—to the extent that the record of past performance is indicative of continuing capability.

Mutual funds have a quality of consistency. Having stated their investment objectives, they may not depart from those objectives without formal notice to each individual participant—and such changes are rare. When you select a fund whose objectives coincide with your own, you can be reasonably sure that those objectives will never change. Obviously, neither a trust company nor a mutual fund can guarantee that its stated objectives will be achieved.

The living trust undoubtedly will constitute a major proportion of your assets while you live and, since the trust will include all of your life insurance, it probably will be your family's sole security after you are gone. Management should be selected with great care, then, with due consideration being given to the stated investment objectives of the mutual funds from among which you will make your choice. There is risk in all investment, and mutual funds offer no assurance against investment loss. They endeavor to reduce risk through three things—careful selection, wide diversification, and continuing professional supervision. The investment of one's entire estate must necessarily differ from the investment of extra dollars. The plan can be very flexible, though—you may choose to invest in a growth-type common stock mutual fund during your lifetime, with instructions to the trustee to switch to a more conservative fund at your death. Most mutual funds offer accumulation plans which provide a means of acquiring their shares on a regular periodic basis. This offers a practical means of effectively employing small, otherwise uninvestible sums from income.

William J. Casey, former Chairman of the Securities and Exchange Commission and of the Export-Import Bank, and a noted tax attorney, has written:

The Dacey trust offers a unique, practical method of concentrating in one package the investment skill and saving discipline of a mutual fund plan, the mortality protection afforded by a life insurance contract and the experience and discretion of a corporate trustee in making capital available to meet family needs. It offers a fascinating range of possibilities.

On the pages which follow will be found a deed of trust suitable for use in establishing the type of trust described above. Securities, including mutual fund holdings, should be registered under Declaration of Trust DT-109, naming the bank as beneficiary.

CHAPTER 23

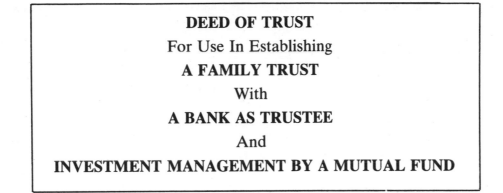

INSTRUCTIONS:

On the following pages will be found duplicate copies of a deed of trust (DT-156) which will be suitable for use in establishing a family trust under which a mutual fund management selected by you during your lifetime will, after your death, supply investment management of a trust account held by a local bank as trustee.

Here are the steps to take:

1. Take the deed of trust to the bank of your choice and invite that institution to accept the trusteeship. The bank will wish to submit your deed to its counsel. Most banks make no charge for the opening of the account, nor do they ordinarily make any annual charge during your lifetime since they have no duties to perform. Some banks prefer to give the trust "active" status by making a nominal charge of $10 annually during the lifetime of the settlor. In most cases, though, the bank's fee begins at your death, and it is a reduced charge (frequently 3 percent of ordinary income, or about $1.20 per year per $1,000 of trust assets) reflecting the vastly reduced bookkeeping involved in the holding of a single security, the mutual fund, paying four quarterly dividends, rather than a diversified portfolio with stock rights, stock dividends, splits, etc., and reflecting also the absence of any investment responsibility. If the local bank declines to serve at a reduced rate, seek another trustee. There is no point in paying for services not rendered.

Occasionally, a provincial trust company will assume the attitude that if it is good enough to be trustee, it is good enough to manage the money. I have observed that invariably these were banks whose investment management services I would hesitate to employ. I suggest that such an attitude forfeits the respect and goodwill of the community. A trust company exists to serve the fiduciary needs of the community—*all* of the fiduciary needs. If, during his lifetime, an individual has retained the services of a particular investment management, has come to have complete confidence in that management, and wishes to make certain that it will continue to serve his estate and his heirs when he has gone, he requires a specific fiduciary service which it is the obligation of the local trust company to provide. Like a small boy who petulantly removes himself and his baseball from a sandlot game because he is not allowed to pitch, the corporate trustee which won't "play" if it cannot manage the money deserves only scorn for a display of financial adolescence.

2. Purchase the mutual fund shares of your choice, registering them "*(your name), Trustee under Declaration of Trust dated _____,*" using DT-109 in Chapter 9. Note that this declaration of trust is a separate instrument used only in connection with the registration of the mutual fund shares. It should not be confused with the deed of trust mentioned in 1. above. The declaration of trust is intended to insure that the mutual fund shares will pass into the bank trust at your death without going through probate. (It may help you differentiate between the functions of the *declaration* and the *deed* if we explain that a declaration involves just one person—he *declares* that he is holding something in trust. A *deed* ordinarily involves more than one person; it is an agreement between the creator of the trust and the trustee, and it spells out the duties and responsibilities of the trustee.)

Note that you should name as beneficiary and Successor Trustee under the declaration of trust the same bank you have named as trustee under the deed of trust. Each time you purchase additional shares of the mutual fund, have them registered in the same manner and under the same declaration of trust.

3. Advise the companies issuing your life insurance policies that you wish to name the bank to receive the proceeds of the policies in its capacity as "Trustee under deed of trust executed by William C. Jones, and said ABC Trust Company under date of (date you executed the deed of trust)." They will

supply beneficiary forms for your signature. Some companies will ask to see a copy of the trust or an excerpt of those provisions in it relating to the life insurance.

4. Execute a new will (Will Form W-11 in Chapter 29 is suggested) leaving your automobile, jewelry, and other personal effects to your spouse, but directing that all other property, including specifically any stocks, bonds, or cash, be added to the trust account set up under the deed of trust. As of this writing, this procedure (called "incorporation by reference") is not permitted in a few states. Check this point with the trust officer at your local bank.

It is suggested that you appoint as executor under your will the same bank named as trustee under the deed of trust.

At your death, the trustee bank will collect the proceeds of your life insurance and add them to the mutual fund shares which you have accumulated during your lifetime and which have passed to the trustee automatically at your death via the DT-109. The bank will thereafter collect and disburse the income (and such sums from principal as you have authorized) to your wife during her lifetime. At her death, the income can continue to your children until they are 21, 25, 35, or such other age as you wish the principal to be made available to them—but during this entire period the investment of your combined trust account will be under the constant, watchful day-to-day supervision of the mutual fund management of your choice. Your family will enjoy the traditional safety and security of bank trusteeship with its splendid record going back more than a century and a half. They'll have the convenience of the local trusteeship, with wise counsel available to them on their personal business or financial problems. They won't have the local investment management, though, with its possible limitations.

The following explanatory notes in "layman's language" are keyed to the letters appearing in the margin of the deed of trust (DT-156) which follows immediately hereafter.

A *It is generally desirable to take advantage of the "marital deduction" allowed when at least half of one's estate is left to one's spouse. There may well be instances, however, where the Settlor's wife has substantial means of her own and it would be disadvantageous to increase her estate by taking advantage of the marital deduction. The taxes ultimately assessed against the combined estates upon her death might far exceed the benefits gained by taking the marital deduction.*

B *Note that while the Settlor's wife can withdraw the whole marital trust at will, the Trustee is also authorized to disburse portions of the principal on her behalf should she be hospitalized or incompetent and unable to request them herself.*

C *A trust may qualify for the marital deduction either by giving the Settlor's wife free access to the marital portion or by conferring upon her the right to name who is to receive it at her death. In this case, qualification is made doubly certain by including both provisions. This arrangement enables her to make such distribution of her marital portion of the estate as is appropriate to the family conditions existing at that time, and also permits her to make tax-reducing gifts to heirs while she still lives.*

D *While in most cases, the income from both the marital and the nonmarital portion of the trust will be paid to the Settlor's wife, note that the instrument permits the Trustee in its discretion to withhold the income from the nonmarital portion*

of the trust and add it to the principal. The objective here is to allow the Settlor's wife to draw the income from the marital portion plus sums from principal equal to the income from the nonmarital portion which is being accumulated instead of paid to her. This would gradually reduce the marital portion (which would be taxable at her death), and build up the nonmarital portion (upon which no further estate tax will have to be paid). That portion of the payments to her which represented a distribution of principal from the marital portion would be completely tax-free. The retained income from the nonmarital portion would be taxable to the trust, and it is likely that this splitting of the taxable income would provide a tax saving. Obviously, the Settlor's wife would not request the Trustee's approval of a withdrawal from the nonmarital portion of the trust until she had exhausted the marital portion from which withdrawals could be made without asking anyone's approval. The very circumstances which would lead her to request such approval, then, would also serve to indicate the need to impose a little restraint to preserve her remaining security.

E *While the age at which the Settlor's children are to receive the principal is optional with the Settlor, it is suggested that it be one at which the children will be mature enough to use the money properly. Most Settlors choose age 35.*

Note that the principal is not wholly withheld from the children until the specified age. In addition to tuition, the Trustee might properly be called upon to pay the cost of opening an office for the Settlor's son who is entering upon the practice of medicine, or assist the Settlor's newly married daughter with the down payment on a home. The purpose of the trust is not to keep the money from the children but only to encourage them to use it intelligently.

F Given two daughters, one hopelessly invalided and the other married to a prosperous business-man in a high tax bracket, the Settlor would undoubtedly himself choose to apportion a larger share of the income to his less fortunate child. This clause which permits the Trustee to "sprinkle" the income among the surviving beneficiaries according to their needs serves a useful purpose.

G Increasing numbers of Americans are benefiting from pension, profit-sharing, and other plans under which they have a vested interest in the proceeds. This clause permits the inclusion of such proceeds in the trust. Where the procedure is permissible under state law, it also allows the Settlor's wife (or any other person) to add to the trust by will.

H In this era of multiple plant corporations, executives are subject to frequent geographical shifts. The city in which a man resides at his death may not necessarily be "home" to his family. This provision makes it possible to shift the trust to another, more conveniently located bank if his wife decides to "go back home."

I In connection with the systematic distribution annually of 6 percent of the value of the trust, such payments would be accomplished, when ordinary income and capital gains distributions were together insufficient to provide such 6 percent payment, by liquidating enough of the underlying mutual fund shares to make up the deficit. The value of shares thus liquidated might be more or less than their cost; the trustee bank would in each case compute the gain or loss and advise the income beneficiaries. The Settlor should understand that the suggested 6 percent payment does not constitute a true "yield" or "income" from or "return" on the investments but rather is an annuity-like payment which may represent in part principal. Naturally, the Settlor should take into account that any invasions of principal necessitated by the inadequacy of the annual ordinary income and capital gains distributions could, if persisted in over a long period of time, ultimately substantially deplete or exhaust the principal, especially in a declining market.

Among other things, this type of income clause is regarded as an ideal hedge against a rising cost of living. In a period of inflated prices, when the beneficiaries' living cost may be assumed to have risen, the designated distribution of 6 percent of the then value of the trust property will represent a larger total number of dollars and therefore a larger purchasing power. From time to time, the value of the shares and the income they pay may, in the future as in the past, move in the opposite direction from the cost of living trend.

In carrying out the provisions of this section, it is common for the Trustee upon completion of the annual valuation of the trust property, to advise the beneficiary of the figure which constitutes 6 percent of such value. Thus, on a $100,000 trust, the Trustee would inform the beneficiary that it would pay out $6,000 during the coming year at the rate of $500 per month. This would provide the beneficiary with a regular monthly amount upon the basis of which she could budget her living expenses.

Deed of Trust

Made by and between _____,

of the City/Town of _____, County of _____

and State of _____ (hereinafter referred to as the "Settlor"), and _____,

located in the City/Town of _____, County of _____

and State of _____ (hereinafter referred to as the "Trustee").

WITNESSETH:

By this agreement the Settlor desires to create a revocable voluntary living trust which may consist of policies of life insurance hereinafter described and/or of other property which he may add to such trust from time to time, and the Trustee has agreed to accept the same under this agreement.

Separately, the Settlor has executed one or more Declarations of Trust in which the Trustee is named as beneficiary to receive certain assets described in Schedule A attached hereto and made a part hereof, and reserves the right to make additional assets, including life insurance policies on the Settlor's life, so payable.

SECTION A:

With respect to any property except policies of life insurance which now or hereafter may be placed in trust hereunder, the Trustee shall hold, invest and reinvest the same as a trust fund upon the following terms and conditions:

1. During the Settlor's lifetime, pay the income to him in convenient installments or expend or reinvest the same upon his written direction.

2. Upon the Settlor's death, add the trust fund herein created to the trust of the insurance proceeds established by Section B of this agreement and dispose of the same as a part thereof in accordance with the provisions of Section B-1 and B-2.

SECTION B:

The Settlor has delivered to the Trustee certain insurance policies on his life described in Schedule A attached hereto and made a part hereof, in which policies the right to change the beneficiary without consent is specifically reserved to the Settlor during his lifetime; and has executed and delivered or will execute and deliver to the Trustee proper instruments to enable the Trustee to be made the beneficiary under said policies as Trustee under this agreement, which policies and the proceeds thereof as and when received by the Trustee shall be held in trust and disposed of by the Trustee as hereinafter provided. Upon receipt by the Trustee of notice of the death of the Settlor the Trustee shall prepare such proofs of death and other documents as are required to collect the amounts payable upon the death of the Settlor under the terms of the policies then held by it as Trustee and shall present such documents to the companies issuing said policies and for that purpose it shall have full power to execute and deliver such instruments and to institute any action in law or equity as in its judgment may be necessary and proper but the Trustee shall not be required to institute any such action until it shall have been indemnified to its satisfaction against all expenses and liabilities which might be incurred thereby.

The Trustee shall divide the insurance proceeds received by it, together with the then trust fund established by the provisions of Section A, and together with any other property which may be added to this trust before or after the Settlor's death, into two parts. One of said parts, herein termed the "marital share," shall consist of property of a value equal to the lesser of (a) the maximum marital deduction allowable in determining the federal estate tax payable by the Settlor's estate, or (b) the minimum amount which, after taking into account all credits and deductions available to the Settlor's estate for federal estate tax purposes (other than the marital deduction), will result in no federal estate tax. The other part shall consist of the remainder of the insurance proceeds and the remainder of the trust fund established by the provisions of Section A. In apportioning to the marital and nonmarital trusts specific assets previously valued for estate tax purposes, the Trustee shall insure that the two trusts share proportionately in any subsequent appreciation or depreciation in the value of such assets.

1. With respect to the "marital share" so called, the Trustee shall hold, manage, invest and reinvest the same as a trust fund upon the following terms and conditions:

   (a) The Trustee shall pay the income (and any other payment authorized by Paragraph 12A) to or for the benefit of the

Settlor's wife, _____, in quarterly or if convenient more frequent payments during her lifetime, together with such sums out of principal as she may request the Trustee in writing to pay to her from time to time and together with such sums out of principal as the Trustee in its sole discretion shall deem necessary for her support or maintenance.

   (b) Upon the death of the Settlor's wife, the Trustee shall pay the then trust fund as she shall appoint by specific reference to this instrument in her Will and the Settlor hereby confers upon his said wife the sole and unrestricted power to appoint the same by her Will, outright or in further trust, in favor of her estate or in favor of others. To the extent that said power shall not be effectively exercised, the trust fund herein created shall be added to the remaining part and shall be disposed of as hereinafter provided.

   (c) If the Settlor and his wife shall die under such circumstances that there is not, in the judgment of the Executor of the Settlor's estate, whose decision shall be conclusive, sufficient evidence to determine readily which of them survived the other, then for the purposes of this trust, the Settlor's wife shall be deemed to have survived him.

2. With respect to the remaining part of the insurance proceeds and trust fund, the Trustee shall hold, invest and reinvest the same as a trust fund upon the following terms and conditions:

(a) If requested by the executor or administrator of the Settlor's estate, the Trustee shall pay or reimburse said executor or administrator for the amount of any ante mortem claim, funeral expense or expense of administration which shall be allowed in connection with the settlement of his estate and which shall be certified to the Trustee by such executor or administrator.

(b) The Trustee shall pay to the proper taxing authority or reimburse the executor or administrator of the Settlor's estate for the amount of any succession, estate, transfer or similar tax, whether state or federal, which shall be imposed lawfully upon the Settlor's taxable estate or upon any beneficiary thereof as the result of the death of the Settlor and which shall be certified to the Trustee by such executor or administrator.

(c) The Trustee shall pay the income (and any other payment authorized by Paragraph 12A) from the balance of the trust fund remaining in its hands to the Settlor's said wife during her lifetime in quarterly or if convenient more frequent payments or in its sole and absolute discretion withhold and accumulate all or such part of such income (or other payment) as it shall determine and add the same to principal. The Trustee is further authorized to pay to the Settlor's wife or in its discretion expend for her maintenance and support or for the maintenance, support and education of the Settlor's children such sums out of principal as it in its sole discretion may deem proper from time to time for any such purpose.

(d) Upon the death of the Settlor's wife or upon the Settlor's death if she shall not survive the Settlor, the Trustee shall:

(i) If requested by the executor or administrator of the wife's estate, pay or reimburse her estate for the amounts of her funeral expenses and the expenses of her last illness as certified to the Trustee by such executor or administrator.

(ii) Divide the balance of the trust fund into as many equal parts as there shall be children of the Settlor then living and children of the Settlor then deceased leaving issue then living and shall:

(1) Pay one of said parts to the living issue collectively of each such child then deceased in equal shares per stirpes.

(2) Pay one of said parts to each child of the Settlor then living and who shall have become _____ years of age.

(3) Hold, manage, invest and reinvest the remaining parts as one trust fund for the benefit of the children of the Settlor then living and who shall not have become _____ years of age and pay or expend all or none or so much of the income and principal to or for the benefit of each of said children as the Trustee in its sole discretion shall deem proper for their suitable maintenance, support and education until each such child shall become _____ years of age, at which time an equal share of the then principal of the trust fund shall be paid over to such child after making adjustment for the amount by which earlier payments of principal to one child may have exceeded those made to another child. If any such child shall die before becoming _____ years of age, then upon such child's death an equal share of said trust fund after adjustment as aforesaid, shall be paid over to such child's children in equal shares, or the survivor of them; if there shall be no such children then living, such shares shall be added equally to the remaining shares, if any, and held, managed and disposed of as a part thereof; if no such shares remain, such share shall be paid over to the Settlor's issue then living, in equal shares.

(4) Notwithstanding any of the foregoing directions, the share of each living issue of any deceased child of the Settlor, though vested, shall be held in trust and so much of the income and principal as the Trustee shall deem proper shall be paid to or for the benefit of such issue until he or she shall become twenty-one years of age.

SECTION C: Administrative Provisions

1. Unless directed in accordance with the provisions of Section A-1 and provided with the means to do so, the Trustee shall be under no duty to pay any premiums or other charges required to continue the said policies of insurance in force or to procure renewals thereof or otherwise to ascertain that said policies are kept in force.

2. The provisions of Section B shall apply only to such proceeds of said policies as may be due and payable to the Trustee upon the death of the Settlor, and all payments, dividends, surrender values and benefits of any kind which may accrue on any of said policies during the lifetime of the Settlor shall be payable to the Settlor and shall not be collected or disposed of by the Trustee.

3. The Settlor reserves to himself without the consent of said Trustee or of any beneficiary hereunder or of any beneficiary now or hereafter named in any policy now or hereafter deposited hereunder, the right to pledge any of said policies or any other property now or hereafter placed in trust hereunder to secure any loan now existing or hereafter made by any persons, firm or corporation to the Settlor, and further reserves the right to exercise any and all options, elections, rights, and privileges, including the right to borrow on said policies given to him under the terms of any of said policies, and upon the request of the Settlor the Trustee will execute and deliver such documents as are necessary and proper to permit the Settlor fully to exercise such rights.

4. The Settlor shall have the right at any time during his lifetime to place additional property and/or insurance policies under the terms of the agreement upon delivering such property and/or insurance policies to the Trustee together with a written request that the Trustee place said additional property and policies under this agreement. Upon the delivery of any such additional property and policies and such written request to the Trustee, the Trustee shall issue a receipt therefore to the Settlor. The Settlor shall also have the right to add to the trust fund by an appropriate provision in his Will or to designate the Trustee as beneficiary of any profit-sharing, pension, incentive compensation or other fund in which he may have an interest, and under the terms of which he has the right to name a beneficiary. The Trustee is further authorized to accept additions to this trust from any other source, testamentary or otherwise.

5. The Settlor shall have the right at any time during his lifetime to withdraw from the operation of this agreement any or all property and policies upon his written request delivered to the Trustee and upon delivery to the Trustee of a receipt for the property and/or policies so withdrawn, and upon such withdrawal and thereafter if required, the Trustee shall execute and deliver to the Settlor such instruments as are necessary and proper to release the interest of the Trustee therein.

6. The Settlor shall have the right at any time during his lifetime to terminate this agreement upon giving to the Trustee written notice of such termination, and upon termination the Trustee shall deliver to the Settlor against his written receipt all property and policies then held hereunder and shall execute and deliver to the Settlor such instruments as are necessary and

proper to transfer the interest of the Trustee therein to the Settlor. The Trustee shall have the right to resign during the Settlor's lifetime.

After the Settlor's death, by mutual agreement between the Settlor's surviving spouse and the Trustee, the Trustee may resign to be replaced by a successor trustee nominated by the beneficiary, provided that such successor trustee shall be a bank or trust company authorized by law to exercise fiduciary powers which shall have its principal place of business and be actively engaged in the trust business in the state in which the beneficiary then legally resides. Such successor trustee having filed its written acceptance with the Trustee, the latter, after finally accounting to the beneficiary or beneficiaries, shall deliver all of the trust assets held hereunder to the successor trustee and shall thereafter have no further duties or liabilities with respect thereto.

Should the Settlor's wife, surviving the Settlor, move and establish her domicile in another state, she may request the Trustee to and the Trustee shall resign, provided that she shall by written instrument filed with the Trustee name as successor trustee a bank or trust company authorized by law to exercise fiduciary powers which shall have its principal place of business and be actively engaged in the trust business in the state in which she shall have established her domicile. If such nominee shall accept said trust and file its written acceptance with the Trustee, the latter, after finally accounting to the beneficiaries, shall deliver all of the funds held in trust hereunder to the successor trustee and shall thereafter have no further duties or liabilities with respect thereto. All powers and discretions herein conferred upon the Trustee are conferred upon any successor trustee.

7. This agreement may be altered or modified at any time by consent of the Settlor and the Trustee without the consent of any other person.

8. The Trustee shall receive reasonable compensation for its services hereunder but such compensation shall not exceed the amount customarily charged by corporate fiduciaries in the area for similar services.

9. In each year during the Settlor's lifetime that there have been no receipts or disbursements from the trust, the Trustee shall not be required to furnish any statement with respect to the trust property to the Settlor. After the Settlor's death, however, the Trustee shall furnish such an annual statement to his said wife during her lifetime and after the death of both the Settlor and his wife the Trustee shall furnish a similar annual statement with respect to each of the trust funds thereafter administered by it to the respective beneficiaries thereof or to their guardians if they be minors.

10. All interests of a beneficiary hereunder shall be inalienable and free from anticipation, assignment, attachment, pledge or control by creditors or a present or former spouse of such beneficiary in any proceedings at law or in equity.

11. To the extent that the assets or any part of them deposited in this trust shall constitute community property: (a) their status as such community property shall remain unchanged; (b) all distributions of income from the trust while both parties are living shall be considered to be community property; (c) either party shall have the right to withdraw his or her portion of the community property, either before or after the death of the Settlor; (d) if the trust is revoked, its assets shall revert to the community.

12. **A.** The Trustee is specifically instructed to make all investments and reinvestments of the trust assets (except a reasonable amount of uninvested cash and any real estate which may be added to the trust during the Settlor's lifetime or, subsequently, by reference in his Will, which real estate the Trustee may deem it in the best interest of the beneficiaries to retain) in shares of _____, a registered mutual investment company. Should shares of the said Fund not be available for investment or reinvestment, or should there be a material change in the investment policies or professional standing of such Fund, then the Trustee may substitute for such Fund shares as may then be held or are thereafter to be purchased, the shares of another registered investment fund of good standing. When acting in accordance with the instructions contained herein, the Trustee shall be under no liability for the proper selection or supervision of the investments by the management of the Fund specified or such other fund as may be substituted. In the event that shares of the Fund or of a substitute meeting the requirements of this trust be not available, then the Trustee is authorized to invest, reinvest and otherwise manage the assets of the trust in its absolute discretion with due regard to the Settlor's desire to maintain at all times a balanced portfolio of investment securities.

The term "income" in this instrument shall be deemed to mean that portion of the distributions made upon securities or other investments of the trust which has been designated as "ordinary income" as distinguished from "capital gains." Whenever such portion of said distribution as shall be designated "ordinary income" shall be less than 6 percent of the total principal market value of the trust, then the Trustee is authorized and instructed to add to such distribution from "ordinary income" such portion of any distribution which has been designated as "capital gains" as shall be necessary to cause the total payment to the then income beneficiary or beneficiaries collectively to equal 6 percent of the total principal market value of the trust. If such distributions from "ordinary income" and "capital gains" shall not together be sufficient to provide the income beneficiary or beneficiaries with a sum equal to 6 percent per annum of the then current principal market value of the trust, then the Trustee is authorized and instructed to pay said income beneficiary or beneficiaries such amount of the principal of the trust as shall be required to maintain the total annual distribution to such beneficiary or beneficiaries at a minimum of 6 percent of the then current total principal market value of the trust. Where used herein, "principal market value" shall be deemed to mean the principal market value of the trust shown by the latest regular annual report of the Trustee. Except as provided in the foregoing, "capital gains" distributions shall be considered as principal and added to the corpus of the trust.

B. The Trustee may (a) sell, mortgage, lease, convey, and exchange the whole or any part of the trust funds, whether real or personal without court order and upon such terms as it shall deem best, (b) make any required division or distribution of the trust funds in cash or in kind or in both and at such values as it may fix, (c) apportion Trustee's and attorney's fees between income and principal, (d) register securities in the name of a nominee, (e) compromise claims by or against the trusts and (f) borrow funds for any trust purpose and secure the payment of such loans by the pledge of the whole or any part of the trust funds. The Trustee may make loans to the executors or administrators of the Settlor's estate, whether secured or unsecured, and may purchase and hold any asset of his estate whether or not it shall be considered a prudent trust investment.

13. The Trustee and any Successor Trustee shall serve without bond.

14. This agreement shall be construed and enforced in accordance with the laws of the State of

_____.

IN WITNESS WHEREOF, the said _____ has hereunto and

to a duplicate hereof set his hand and seal as Settlor and said _____ has
(Trustee Bank)

caused this instrument to be accepted and executed in duplicate by its duly authorized officer(s) as of the _____

_____ day of _____, 19_____.

Witnessed by: THE SETTLOR:

(1) _____

(2) _____   _____ L.S.

                                                      FOR THE TRUSTEE:

(1) _____

(2) _____   _____ L.S.

                                                      TITLE _____

STATE OF _____ ⎫ City
                                        ⎬ or
COUNTY OF _____ ⎭ Town _____

    Personally appeared _____, signer

and sealer as Settlor of the foregoing instrument, who acknowledged the same to be his free act and deed, before me, this

_____ day of _____, 19_____.

(Notary Seal)   _____
                                                      Notary Public

STATE OF _____ ⎫ City
                                        ⎬ or
COUNTY OF _____ ⎭ Town _____

    Personally appeared _____, signer

and sealer of the foregoing instrument as an officer of the_____
                                                      (name of Trustee Bank)

and acknowledged the same to be his free act and deed as such officer, and

the free act and deed of said _____
                                (Trustee Bank)

before me this _____ day of _____, 19_____.

(Notary Seal)   _____
                                                      Notary Public

SCHEDULE A

Deed of Trust

Made by and between _____ of the

City/Town of _____, County of _____

and State of _____ (hereinafter referred to as the "Settlor"), and _____,

located in the City/Town of _____, County of _____

and State of _____ (hereinafter referred to as the "Trustee").

WITNESSETH:

By this agreement the Settlor desires to create a revocable voluntary living trust which may consist of policies of life insurance hereinafter described and/or of other property which he may add to such trust from time to time, and the Trustee has agreed to accept the same under this agreement.

Separately, the Settlor has executed one or more Declarations of Trust in which the Trustee is named as beneficiary to receive certain assets described in Schedule A attached hereto and made a part hereof, and reserves the right to make additional assets, including life insurance policies on the Settlor's life, so payable.

SECTION A:

With respect to any property except policies of life insurance which now or hereafter may be placed in trust hereunder, the Trustee shall hold, invest and reinvest the same as a trust fund upon the following terms and conditions:

1. During the Settlor's lifetime, pay the income to him in convenient installments or expend or reinvest the same upon his written direction.

2. Upon the Settlor's death, add the trust fund herein created to the trust of the insurance proceeds established by Section B of this agreement and dispose of the same as a part thereof in accordance with the provisions of Section B-1 and B-2.

SECTION B:

The Settlor has delivered to the Trustee certain insurance policies on his life described in Schedule A attached hereto and made a part hereof, in which policies the right to change the beneficiary without consent is specifically reserved to the Settlor during his lifetime; and has executed and delivered or will execute and deliver to the Trustee proper instruments to enable the Trustee to be made the beneficiary under said policies as Trustee under this agreement, which policies and the proceeds thereof as and when received by the Trustee shall be held in trust and disposed of by the Trustee as hereinafter provided. Upon receipt by the Trustee of notice of the death of the Settlor the Trustee shall prepare such proofs of death and other documents as are required to collect the amounts payable upon the death of the Settlor under the terms of the policies then held by it as Trustee and shall present such documents to the companies issuing said policies and for that purpose it shall have full power to execute and deliver such instruments and to institute any action in law or equity as in its judgment may be necessary and proper but the Trustee shall not be required to institute any such action until it shall have been indemnified to its satisfaction against all expenses and liabilities which might be incurred thereby.

The Trustee shall divide the insurance proceeds received by it, together with the then trust fund established by the provisions of Section A, and together with any other property which may be added to this trust before or after the Settlor's death, into two parts. One of said parts, herein termed the "marital share," shall consist of property of a value equal to the lesser of (a) the maximum marital deduction allowable in determining the federal estate tax payable by the Settlor's estate, or (b) the minimum amount which, after taking into account all credits and deductions available to the Settlor's estate for federal estate tax purposes (other than the marital deduction), will result in no federal estate tax. The other part shall consist of the remainder of the insurance proceeds and the remainder of the trust fund established by the provisions of Section A. In apportioning to the marital and nonmarital trusts specific assets previously valued for estate tax purposes, the Trustee shall insure that the two trusts share proportionately in any subsequent appreciation or depreciation in the value of such assets.

1. With respect to the "marital share" so called, the Trustee shall hold, manage, invest and reinvest the same as a trust fund upon the following terms and conditions:

(a) The Trustee shall pay the income (and any other payment authorized by Paragraph 12A) to or for the benefit of the

Settlor's wife, _____, in quarterly or if convenient more frequent payments during her lifetime, together with such sums out of principal as she may request the Trustee in writing to pay to her from time to time and together with such sums out of principal as the Trustee in its sole discretion shall deem necessary for her support or maintenance.

(b) Upon the death of the Settlor's wife, the Trustee shall pay the then trust fund as she shall appoint specific reference to this instrument in her Will and the Settlor hereby confers upon his said wife the sole and unrestricted power to appoint the same by her Will, outright or in further trust, in favor of her estate or in favor of others. To the extent that said power shall not be effectively exercised, the trust fund herein created shall be added to the remaining part and shall be disposed of as hereinafter provided.

(c) If the Settlor and his wife shall die under such circumstances that there is not, in the judgment of the executor of the Settlor's estate, whose decision shall be conclusive, sufficient evidence to determine readily which of them survived the other, then for the purposes of this trust, the Settlor's wife shall be deemed to have survived him.

2. With respect to the remaining part of the insurance proceeds and trust fund, the Trustee shall hold, invest and reinvest the same as a trust fund upon the following terms and conditions:

(a) If requested by the executor or administrator of the Settlor's estate, the Trustee shall pay or reimburse said executor or administrator for the amount of any ante mortem claim, funeral expense or expense of administration which shall be allowed in connection with the settlement of his estate and which shall be certified to the Trustee by such executor or administrator.

(b) The Trustee shall pay to the proper taxing authority or reimburse the executor or administrator of the Settlor's estate for the amount of any succession, estate, transfer or similar tax, whether state or federal, which shall be imposed lawfully upon the Settlor's taxable estate or upon any beneficiary thereof as the result of the death of the Settlor and which shall be certified to the Trustee by such executor or administrator.

(c) The Trustee shall pay the income (and any other payment authorized by Paragraph 12A) from the balance of the trust fund remaining in its hands to the Settlor's said wife during her lifetime in quarterly or if convenient more frequent payments or in its sole and absolute discretion withhold and accumulate all or such part of such income (or other payment) as it shall determine and add the same to principal. The Trustee is further authorized to pay to the Settlor's wife or in its discretion expend for her maintenance and support or for the maintenance, support and education of the Settlor's children such sums out of principal as it in its sole discretion may deem proper from time to time for any such purpose.

(d) Upon the death of the Settlor's wife or upon the Settlor's death if she shall not survive the Settlor, the Trustee shall:

(i) If requested by the executor or administrator of the wife's estate, pay or reimburse her estate for the amounts of her funeral expenses and the expenses of her last illness as certified to the Trustee by such executor or administrator.

(ii) Divide the balance of the trust fund into as many equal parts as there shall be children of the Settlor then living and children of the Settlor then deceased leaving issue then living and shall:

(1) Pay one of said parts to the living issue collectively of each such child then deceased in equal shares per stirpes.

(2) Pay one of said parts to each child of the Settlor then living and who shall have become _____ years of age.

(3) Hold, manage, invest and reinvest the remaining parts as one trust fund for the benefit of the children of the Settlor then living and who shall not have become _____ years of age and pay or expend all or none or so much of the income and principal to or for the benefit of each of said children as the Trustee in its sole discretion shall deem proper for their suitable maintenance, support and education until each such child shall become _____ years of age, at which time an equal share of the then principal of the trust fund shall be paid over to such child after making adjustment for the amount by which earlier payments of principal to one child may have exceeded those made to another child. If any such child shall die before becoming _____ years of age, then upon such child's death an equal share of said trust fund after adjustment as aforesaid, shall be paid over to such child's children in equal shares, or the survivor of them; if there shall be no such children then living, such shares shall be added equally to the remaining shares, if any, and held, managed and disposed of as a part thereof; if no such shares remain, such share shall be paid over to the Settlor's issue then living, in equal shares.

(4) Notwithstanding any of the foregoing directions, the share of each living issue of any deceased child of the Settlor, though vested, shall be held in trust and so much of the income and principal as the Trustee shall deem proper shall be paid to or for the benefit of such issue until he or she shall become twenty-one years of age.

SECTION C: Administrative Provisions

1. Unless directed in accordance with the provisions of Section A-1 and provided with the means to do so, the Trustee shall be under no duty to pay any premiums or other charges required to continue the said policies of insurance in force or to procure renewals thereof or otherwise to ascertain that said policies are kept in force.

2. The provisions of Section B shall apply only to such proceeds of said policies as may be due and payable to the Trustee upon the death of the Settlor, and all payments, dividends, surrender values and benefits of any kind which may accrue on any of said policies during the lifetime of the Settlor shall be payable to the Settlor and shall not be collected or disposed of by the Trustee.

3. The Settlor reserves to himself without the consent of said Trustee or of any beneficiary hereunder or of any beneficiary now or hereafter named in any policy now or hereafter deposited hereunder, the right to pledge any of said policies or any other property now or hereafter placed in trust hereunder to secure any loan now existing or hereafter made by any persons, firm or corporation to the Settlor, and further reserves the right to exercise any and all options, elections, rights, and privileges, including the right to borrow on said policies, given to him under the terms of any of said policies, and upon the request of the Settlor the Trustee will execute and deliver such documents as are necessary and proper to permit the Settlor fully to exercise such rights.

4. The Settlor shall have the right at any time during his lifetime to place additional property and/or insurance policies under the terms of the agreement upon delivering such property and/or insurance policies to the Trustee together with a written request that the Trustee place said additional property and policies under this agreement. Upon the delivery of any such additional property and policies and such written request to the Trustee, the Trustee shall issue a receipt therefore to the Settlor. The Settlor shall also have the right to add to the trust fund by an appropriate provision in his Will or to designate the Trustee as beneficiary of any profit-sharing, pension, incentive compensation or other fund in which he may have an interest, and under the terms of which he has the right to name a beneficiary. The Trustee is further authorized to accept additions to this trust from any other source, testamentary or otherwise.

5. The Settlor shall have the right at any time during his lifetime to withdraw from the operation of this agreement any or all property and policies upon his written request delivered to the Trustee and upon delivery to the Trustee of a receipt for the property and/or policies so withdrawn, and upon such withdrawal and thereafter if required, the Trustee shall execute and deliver to the Settlor such instruments as are necessary and proper to release the interest of the Trustee therein.

6. The Settlor shall have the right at any time during his lifetime to terminate this agreement upon giving to the Trustee written notice of such termination, and upon termination the Trustee shall deliver to the Settlor against his written receipt all

property and policies then held hereunder and shall execute and deliver to the Settlor such instruments as are necessary and proper to transfer the interest of the Trustee therein to the Settlor. The Trustee shall have the right to resign during the Settlor's lifetime.

After the Settlor's death, by mutual agreement between the Settlor's surviving spouse and the Trustee, the Trustee may resign to be replaced by a successor trustee nominated by the beneficiary, provided that such successor trustee shall be a bank or trust company authorized by law to exercise fiduciary powers which shall have its principal place of business and be actively engaged in the trust business in the state in which the beneficiary then legally resides. Such successor trustee having filed its written acceptance with the Trustee, the latter, after finally accounting to the beneficiary or beneficiaries, shall deliver all of the trust assets held hereunder to the successor trustee and shall thereafter have no further duties or liabilities with respect thereto.

Should the Settlor's wife, surviving the Settlor, move and establish her domicile in another state, she may request the Trustee to and the Trustee shall resign, provided that she shall by written instrument filed with the Trustee name as successor trustee a bank or trust company authorized by law to exercise fiduciary powers which shall have its principal place of business and be actively engaged in the trust business in the state in which she shall have established her domicile. If such nominee shall accept said trust and file its written acceptance with the Trustee, the latter, after finally accounting to the beneficiaries, shall deliver all of the funds held in trust hereunder to the successor trustee and shall thereafter have no further duties or liabilities with respect thereto. All powers and discretions herein conferred upon the Trustee are conferred upon any successor trustee.

7. This agreement may be altered or modified at any time during the lifetime of the Settlor, by consent of the Settlor and the Trustee without the consent of any other person.

8. The Trustee shall receive reasonable compensation for its services hereunder but such compensation shall not exceed the amount customarily charged by corporate fiduciaries in the area for similar services.

9. In each year during the Settlor's lifetime that there have been no receipts or disbursements from the trust, the Trustee shall not be required to furnish any statement with respect to the trust property to the Settlor. After the Settlor's death, however, the Trustee shall furnish such an annual statement to his said wife during her lifetime and after the death of both the Settlor and his wife the Trustee shall furnish a similar annual statement with respect to each of the trust funds thereafter administered by it to the respective beneficiaries thereof or to their guardians if they be minors.

10. All interests of a beneficiary hereunder shall be inalienable and free from anticipation, assignment, attachment, pledge or control by creditors or a present or former spouse of such beneficiary in any proceedings at law or in equity.

11. To the extent that the assets or any part of them deposited in this trust shall constitute community property: (a) their status as such community property shall remain unchanged; (b) all distributions of income from the trust while both parties are living shall be considered to be community property; (c) either party shall have the right to withdraw his or her portion of the community property, either before or after the death of the Settlor; (d) if the trust is revoked, its assets shall revert to the community.

12. **A.** The Trustee is specifically instructed to make all investments and reinvestments of the trust assets (except a reasonable amount of uninvested cash and any real estate which may be added to the trust during the Settlor's lifetime or, subsequently, by reference in his Will, which real estate the Trustee may deem it in the best interests of the beneficiaries to retain) in shares of _____, a registered mutual investment company. Should shares of the said Fund not be available for investment or reinvestment, or should there be a material change in the investment policies or professional standing of such Fund, then the Trustee may substitute for such Fund shares as may then be held or are thereafter to be purchased, the shares of another registered investment fund of good standing. When acting in accordance with the instructions contained herein, the Trustee shall be under no liability for the proper selection or supervision of the investments by the management of the Fund specified or such other fund as may be substituted. In the event that shares of the Fund or of a substitute meeting the requirements of this trust be not available, then the Trustee is authorized to invest, reinvest and otherwise manage the assets of the trust in its absolute discretion with due regard to the Settlor's desire to maintain at all times a balanced portfolio of investment securities.

The term "income" in this instrument shall be deemed to mean that portion of the distributions made upon securities or other investments of the trust which has been designated as "ordinary income" as distinguished from "capital gains." Whenever such portion of said distribution as shall be designated "ordinary income" shall be less than 6 percent of the total principal market value of the trust, then the Trustee is authorized and instructed to add to such distribution from "ordinary income" such portion of any distribution which has been designated as "capital gains" as shall be necessary to cause the total payment to the then income beneficiary or beneficiaries collectively to equal 6 percent of the total principal market value of the trust. If such distributions from "ordinary income" and "capital gains" shall not together be sufficient to provide the income beneficiary or beneficiaries with a sum equal to 6 percent per annum of the then current principal market value of the trust, then the Trustee is authorized and instructed to pay said income beneficiary or beneficiaries such amount of the principal of the trust as shall be required to maintain the total annual distribution to such beneficiary or beneficiaries at a minimum of 6 percent of the then current total principal market value of the trust. Where used herein, "principal market value" shall be deemed to mean the principal market value of the trust shown by the latest regular annual report of the Trustee. Except as provided in the foregoing, "capital gains" distributions shall be considered as principal and added to the corpus of the trust.

B. The Trustee may (a) sell, mortgage, lease, convey, and exchange the whole or any part of the trust funds, whether real or personal without court order and upon such terms as it shall deem best, (b) make any required division or distribution of the trust funds in cash or in kind or in both and at such values as it may fix, (c) apportion Trustee's and attorney's fees between income and principal, (d) register securities in the name of a nominee, (e) compromise claims by or against the trusts and (f) borrow funds for any trust purpose and secure the payment of such loans by the pledge of the whole or any part of the trust funds. The Trustee may make loans to the executors or administrators of the Settlor's estate, whether secured or unsecured, and may purchase and hold any asset of his estate whether or not it shall be considered a prudent trust investment.

13. The Trustee and any Successor Trustee shall serve without bond.

14. This agreement shall be construed and enforced in accordance with the laws of the State of _____.

IN WITNESS WHEREOF, the said _____ has hereunto and

to a duplicate hereof set his hand and seal as Settlor and said _____ has

                                                  (Trustee Bank)

caused this instrument to be executed in duplicate by its duly authorized officer(s) as of the _____

_____ day of _____, 19_____.

Witnessed by:

(1) _____

(2) _____

THE SETTLOR:

_____ L.S.

(1) _____

(2) _____

FOR THE TRUSTEE:

_____ L.S.

TITLE _____

STATE OF _____ ⎫

COUNTY OF _____ ⎬ City or Town _____

Personally appeared _____, signer

and sealer as Settlor of the foregoing instrument, who acknowledged the same to be his free act and deed, before me, this

_____ day of _____, 19_____.

(Notary Seal)

_____

                                    Notary Public

STATE OF _____ ⎫

COUNTY OF _____ ⎬ City or Town _____

Personally appeared _____, signer

and sealer of the foregoing instrument, and acknowledged the same to be his free act and deed as such officer, and

the free act and deed of said _____

                                     (Trustee Bank)

before me, this _____ day of _____, 19_____.

(Notary Seal)

_____

                                    Notary Public

SCHEDULE A

CHAPTER 24

A Wife's Trust

The individual with a large amount of life insurance in force on his life may find it desirable to have the policies owned by his spouse, thus exempting the proceeds from federal estate tax at his death. The theory behind the arrangement is simple: Make the policy the property of your wife; they cannot tax your wife's property because you have died.

Obviously, this arrangement serves no useful purpose if your estate is modest and therefore not subject to federal estate tax. The practice of having insurance policies owned by one's spouse is most likely to be employed by persons with substantial estates seeking tax relief. It follows that these are quite likely to be the same individuals who, concerned with the preservation of their estates, will choose to set up a bank trust account.

Under the program described in detail in Chapters 22 and 23, the insured directs that his policies be payable to his trust account at the bank. If, however, those policies are owned by his wife, he has no authority to direct that the proceeds be paid into his trust account at his death. This does not mean that they cannot be gotten into his trust, though.

The procedure to accomplish this objective is as follows: The wife establishes her own inter vivos trust at the same bank where her husband has established his trust, her trust's assets consisting of the insurance policies on her husband's life owned by her. The trust instrument simply directs the trustee to collect the insurance proceeds at his death, add them to his trust account, and terminate her account. The husband's life insurance proceeds end up right where he wanted them, in one neat package in his trust account, but they have avoided completely the federal estate tax to which they would otherwise have been subject.

If the policies are presently owned by the husband, he can easily transfer such ownership to his wife to enable her to set up a "Wife's Trust," but if the policies currently have a cash value he should first borrow the full amount of that cash value or he will have made her a possible taxable gift. Invested in a certificate of deposit or a "money fund," it will probably earn nearly twice the interest (tax deductible) he pays the insurance company. Term insurance has no cash value, another reason why it is the best kind of insurance to own.

A suitable deed of trust (DT-157) for use in setting up a "wife's trust" will be found in the pages immediately following.

CHAPTER 24

DEED OF TRUST
For Establishing
A WIFE'S TRUST

INSTRUCTIONS:

On the following pages will be found duplicate copies of a deed of trust (DT-157) suitable for use to provide that the proceeds of life insurance policies owned by a spouse on the life of her husband shall pass into his bank-held trust upon his death.

At the top of the first page enter the name of the wife as settlor, and the bank's name as trustee. Cross off *"city"* or *"town,"* leaving the appropriate designation of your community.

In Paragraph 1, enter the name of the settlor's husband.

When completed, Paragraph 3 should read something like this: "Upon receipt of the proceeds of said insurance policies and the proceeds of any insurance policies on the life of the Settlor, and any additional amounts passing under the Settlor's will or otherwise, the Trustee shall deliver the entire amount to the ABC Trust Company of the City of Smithville, County of Fairfax and State of Michigan, as Trustee under the terms of a certain trust instrument executed by the Settlor's husband, William C. Jones, and said ABC Trust Company under date of (date of the husband's deed of trust), and the Settlor hereby directs and provides that after computation of all taxes due on the estate of the Settlor's said husband, the property received by virtue of this bequest shall be added to the marital share of the trust established by said husband and held by said Trustee to be administered and disposed of in accordance with the provisions of Section B thereof.

The settlor (the insured's wife) and the trustee bank should each retain one copy of the completed and executed agreement.

The insurance company issuing the policy on the husband's life should then be instructed by the wife in her capacity as owner of the policy to pay the proceeds at his death to the trustee bank with whom she has entered into this agreement.

Deed of Trust

Made by and between _____ ,

of the City/Town of _____ , County of _____

and State of _____ (hereinafter referred to as the "Settlor"),

and _____ ,

located in the City/Town of _____ , County of _____

and State of _____ (hereinafter referred to as the "Trustee").

W I T N E S S E T H :

By this agreement the Settlor desires to create a revocable voluntary living trust consisting of policies of life insurance hereinafter described and of other property which she may add to such trust from time to time, and the Trustee has agreed to accept the same under this agreement.

It is therefore agreed by and between the Settlor and the Trustee as follows:

1. The Settlor has delivered to the Trustee certain insurance policies (described in Schedule A attached

hereto and made a part hereof) on the life of her husband, _____ , of which policies the Settlor is the absolute owner and in which policies the right to change the beneficiary is specifically reserved to the Settlor during her lifetime. The Settlor has executed proper instruments to name the Trustee to receive the proceeds as beneficiary under such policies, said policies and proceeds to be held in trust and disposed of by the Trustee as hereinafter provided.

2. Upon receipt by the Trustee of notice of the death of the Settlor's said husband, the Trustee shall prepare such proofs of death and other documents as are required to collect the amounts payable upon the death of the Settlor's said husband under the terms of the policies then held by it as Trustee and shall present such documents to the companies issuing said policies and for that purpose it shall have full power to execute and deliver such instruments and to institute any action in law or equity as in its judgment may be necessary and proper but the Trustee shall not be required to institute any such action until it shall have been indemnified to its satisfaction against all expenses and liabilities which might be incurred thereby.

3. Upon receipt of the proceeds of said insurance policies and the proceeds of any insurance policies on the life of the Settlor, and any additional amounts passing under the terms of the Settlor's Will or otherwise, the Trustee shall deliver the entire amount

to _____

of the City/Town of _____ , County of _____ and State of _____ ,

as Trustee under the terms of a certain trust instrument executed by the Settlor's husband, _____

_____ , and said _____ under

date of _____ , and the Settlor hereby directs and provides that after computation of all taxes due on the estate of the Settlor's said husband, the property received by virtue of this bequest shall be added to the marital share of the trust established by said husband and held by said Trustee to be administered and disposed of by it in accordance with the provisions of Section B thereof.

Upon delivery of the property as above provided, this trust shall terminate forthwith.

4. With respect to insurance policies on the life of the Settlor or the Settlor's husband, the Trustee shall be under no duty to pay any premiums or other charges required to continue the said policies of insurance in force or to procure renewals thereof or otherwise to ascertain that said policies are kept in force.

With respect to insurance policies on the life of the Settlor's husband, the provisions of this trust shall apply only to such proceeds of said policies as may be due and payable to the Trustee upon the death of the Settlor's husband, and all payments, dividends, surrender values and benefits of any kind which may accrue on any of said policies during the lifetime of the Settlor's husband shall be payable to the Settlor and shall not be collected or disposed of by the Trustee.

The Settlor reserves to herself without the consent of said Trustee or of the beneficiary hereunder or of any beneficiary now or hereafter named in any policy now or hereafter deposited hereunder, the right to pledge any of said policies or any other property now or hereafter placed in trust hereunder to secure any loan now existing or hereafter made by any persons, firm or corporation to the Settlor, and further reserves the right to exercise any and all options, elections, rights and privileges, including the right to borrow on said policies, given to her under the terms of any of said policies, and upon the request of the Settlor the Trustee shall execute and deliver such documents as are necessary and proper to permit the Settlor to exercise such rights.

The Settlor shall have the right at any time during her lifetime to place additional insurance policies and/or other property under the terms of the agreement upon delivering such insurance policies and/or property to the Trustee together with a written request that the Trustee place said additional policies and/or property under this agreement. Upon the delivery of any such additional policies and/or property and such written request to the Trustee, the Trustee shall issue a receipt therefore to the Settlor. The Settlor shall also have the right to add to the trust fund by an appropriate provision in her Will.

The Settlor shall have the right at any time during her lifetime to withdraw from the operation of this agreement any or all policies and/or property upon her written request delivered to the Trustee and upon delivery to the Trustee of a receipt for the policies and/or property so withdrawn, and upon such withdrawal and thereafter if required, the Trustee shall execute and deliver to the Settlor such instruments as are necessary and proper to release the interest of the Trustee therein.

The Settlor shall have the right at any time during her lifetime to terminate this agreement upon giving to the Trustee written notice of such termination, and upon termination the Trustee shall deliver to the Settlor against her written receipt all policies and/or property then held hereunder and shall execute and deliver to the Settlor such instruments as are necessary and proper to transfer the interest of the Trustee therein to the Settlor. The death of the Settlor before her husband shall in no way affect the operation of this trust. Title to any insurance policies or other property held hereunder shall thereafter revert irrevocably to the Trustee who will continue to retain possession of them under the same terms and conditions which prevailed during the Settlor's lifetime. Upon the death of the Settlor's husband (the insured under the policies), the Trustee shall proceed in accordance with the provisions of Section 2 and 3 hereinbefore set forth. If at such time there shall be in existence no trust account thereinbefore established by the Settlor's husband, then the Trustee is authorized and instructed to pay the then trust fund to the Settlor's issue in equal shares, per stirpes. If the Settlor shall have died leaving no issue, then the Trustee is authorized and instructed to pay the then trust fund to the Settlor's heirs at law, in equal shares, per stirpes. The Trustee may resign at any time during the life of the Settlor.

5. This agreement may be altered or modified at any time by consent of the Settlor and the Trustee without the consent of any other person.

6. The Trustee shall receive reasonable compensation for its services hereunder but such compensation shall not exceed the amount customarily charged by corporate fiduciaries in the area for similar services.

7. The Trustee may (a) sell, mortgage, lease, convey, or exchange the whole or any part of the trust funds, whether real or personal, without court order and upon such terms as it shall deem best, (b) apportion Trustee's and attorney's fees between income and principal, (c) compromise claims by or against the trust, (d) borrow funds for any trust purpose and secure the payment of such loans by the pledge of the whole or any part of the trust funds, and (e) make loans to the executors or administrators of the Settlor's estate, whether secured or unsecured.

8. This agreement and its terms shall be construed and enforced in accordance with the laws of the State of

_____.

IN WITNESS WHEREOF, the said _____

has hereunto and to a duplicate hereof set her hand and seal as Settlor and said _____
(Trustee Bank)

has caused this instrument to be executed in duplicate by its duly authorized officer as of the _____

day of _____, 19_____.

Witnessed by:

THE SETTLOR:

(1) _____

(2) _____

_____ L.S.

FOR THE TRUSTEE:

(1) _____

(2) _____

_____ L.S.

TITLE _____

STATE OF _____ } City
or
COUNTY OF _____ } Town _____

Personally appeared _____, signer and

sealer of the foregoing instrument as Settlor, and acknowledged the same to be her free act and deed, before me, this

_____ day of _____, 19_____.

(Notary Seal)   _____
Notary Public

STATE OF _____ } City
or
COUNTY OF _____ } Town _____

Personally appeared _____, _____, of

(Title)

_____, signer and sealer of the

(Trustee Bank)

foregoing instrument, and acknowledged the same to be his free act and deed as such officer, and the free act and deed of

said _____

(Trustee Bank)

before me, this _____ day of _____, 19_____.

_____

(Notary Seal)   *Notary Public*

SCHEDULE A

Made by and between _____ ,

of the City/Town of_____ , County of _____

and State of _____ (hereinafter referred to as the "Settlor"),

and _____ ,

located in the City/Town of _____ , County of _____

and State of _____ (hereinafter referred to as the "Trustee").

WITNESSETH:

By this agreement the Settlor desires to create a revocable voluntary living trust consisting of policies of life insurance hereinafter described and of other property which she may add to such trust from time to time, and the Trustee has agreed to accept the same under this agreement.

It is therefore agreed by and between the Settlor and the Trustee as follows:

1. The Settlor has delivered to the Trustee certain insurance policies (described in Schedule A attached

hereunto and made a part hereof) on the life of her husband, _____ ,
of which policies the Settlor is the absolute owner and in which policies the right to change the beneficiary is specifically reserved to the Settlor during her lifetime. The Settlor has executed proper instruments to name the Trustee to receive the proceeds as beneficiary under such policies, said policies and proceeds to be held in trust and disposed of by the Trustee as hereinafter provided.

2. Upon receipt by the Trustee of notice of the death of the Settlor's said husband, the Trustee shall prepare such proofs of death and other documents as are required to collect the amounts payable upon the death of the Settlor's said husband under the terms of the policies then held by it as Trustee and shall present such documents to the companies issuing said policies and for that purpose it shall have full power to execute and deliver such instruments and to institute any action in law or equity as in its judgment may be necessary and proper but the Trustee shall not be required to institute any such action until it shall have been indemnified to its satisfaction against all expenses and liabilities which might be incurred thereby.

3. Upon receipt of the proceeds of said insurance policies and the proceeds of any insurance policies on the life of the Settlor, and any additional amounts passing under the terms of the Settlor's Will or otherwise, the Trustee shall deliver the entire amount

to _____

of the City/Town of _____ , County of _____ and State of _____ ,

as Trustee under the terms of a certain trust instrument executed by the Settlor's husband, _____

_____ , and said _____ under

date of _____ , and the Settlor hereby directs and provides that after computation of all taxes due on the estate of the Settlor's said husband, the property received by virtue of this bequest shall be added to the marital share of the trust established by said husband and held by said Trustee to be administered and disposed of by it in accordance with the provisions of Section B thereof.

Upon delivery of the property as above provided, this trust shall terminate forthwith.

4. With respect to insurance policies on the life of the Settlor or the Settlor's husband, the Trustee shall be under no duty to pay any premiums or other charges required to continue the said policies of insurance in force or to procure renewals thereof or otherwise to ascertain that said policies are kept in force.

With respect to insurance policies on the life of the Settlor's husband, the provisions of this trust shall apply only to such proceeds of said policies as may be due and payable to the Trustee upon the death of the Settlor's husband, and all payments, dividends, surrender values and benefits of any kind which may accrue on any of said policies during the lifetime of the Settlor's husband shall be payable to the Settlor and shall not be collected or disposed of by the Trustee.

The Settlor reserves to herself without the consent of said Trustee or of the beneficiary hereunder or of any beneficiary now or hereafter named in any policy now or hereafter deposited hereunder, the right to pledge any of said policies or any other property now or hereafter placed in trust hereunder to secure any loan now existing or hereafter made by any persons, firm or corporation to the Settlor, and further reserves the right to exercise any and all options, elections, rights and privileges, including the right to borrow on said policies, given to her under the terms of any of said policies, and upon the request of the Settlor the Trustee shall execute and deliver such documents as are necessary and proper to permit the Settlor to exercise such rights.

The Settlor shall have the right at any time during her lifetime to place additional insurance policies and/or other property under the terms of the agreement upon delivering such insurance policies and/or property to the Trustee together with a written request that the Trustee place said additional policies and/or property under this agreement. Upon the delivery of any such additional policies and/or property and such written request to the Trustee, the Trustee shall issue a receipt therefore to the Settlor. The Settlor shall also have the right to add to the trust fund by an appropriate provision in her Will.

The Settlor shall have the right at any time during her lifetime to withdraw from the operation of this agreement any or all policies and/or property upon her written request delivered to the Trustee and upon delivery to the Trustee of a receipt for the policies and/or property so withdrawn, and upon such withdrawal and thereafter if required, the Trustee shall execute and deliver to the Settlor such instruments as are necessary and proper to release the interest of the Trustee therein.

The Settlor shall have the right at any time during her lifetime to terminate this agreement upon giving to the Trustee written notice of such termination, and upon termination the Trustee shall deliver to the Settlor against her written receipt all policies and/or property then held hereunder and shall execute and deliver to the Settlor such instruments as are necessary and proper to

transfer the interest of the Trustee therein to the Settlor. The death of the Settlor before her husband shall in no way affect the operation of this trust. Title to any insurance policies or other property held hereunder shall thereafter revert irrevocably to the Trustee who will continue to retain possession of them under the same terms and conditions which prevailed during the Settlor's lifetime. Upon the death of the Settlor's husband (the insured under the policies), the Trustee shall proceed in accordance with the provisions of Section 2 and 3 hereinbefore set forth. If at such time there shall be in existence no trust account thereinbefore established by the Settlor's husband, then the Trustee is authorized and instructed to pay the then trust fund to the Settlor's issue in equal shares, per stirpes. If the Settlor shall have died leaving no issue, then the Trustee is authorized and instructed to pay the then trust fund to the Settlor's heirs at law, in equal shares, per stirpes. The Trustee may resign at any time during the life of the Settlor.

5. This agreement may be altered or modified at any time by consent of the Settlor and the Trustee without the consent of any other person.

6. The Trustee shall receive reasonable compensation for its services hereunder but such compensation shall not exceed the amount customarily charged by corporate fiduciaries in the area for similar services.

7. The Trustee may (a) sell, mortgage, lease, convey, or exchange the whole or any part of the trust funds, whether real or personal, without court order and upon such terms as it shall deem best, (b) apportion Trustee's and attorney's fees between income and principal, (c) compromise claims by or against the trust, (d) borrow funds for any trust purpose and secure the payment of such loans by the pledge of the whole or any part of the trust funds, and (e) make loans to the executors or administrators of the Settlor's estate, whether secured or unsecured.

8. This agreement and its terms shall be construed and enforced in accordance with the laws of the State of

_____.

IN WITNESS WHEREOF, the said _____

has hereunto and to a duplicate hereof set her hand and seal as Settlor and said _____

                                    (Trustee Bank)

has caused this instrument to be executed in duplicate by its duly authorized officer as of the _____

day of _____, 19_____.

Witnessed by: THE SETTLOR:

(1) _____

                    _____ L.S.

(2) _____

                    FOR THE TRUSTEE:

(1) _____

                    _____ L.S.

(2) _____

                    TITLE _____

STATE OF _____   City
                   or
COUNTY OF _____   Town _____

Personally appeared _____, signer and

sealer of the foregoing Agreement as Settlor who acknowledged the same to be her free act and deed, before me, this

_____ day of _____, 19_____.

(Notary Seal)   _____
                           Notary Public

STATE OF _____   City
                   or
COUNTY OF _____   Town _____

Personally appeared _____, _____
                            (Title)

of _____ signer
              (Trustee Bank)

and sealer of the foregoing instrument, and acknowledged the same to be his free act and deed, and the free act and deed of

the _____,
                  (Trustee Bank)

before me, this _____ day of _____, 19_____.

                  _____

(Notary Seal)   *Notary Public*

SCHEDULE A

CHAPTER 25

The "Pure Trust"

Granted that we live in an era which has spawned such tax reform plans as California's Proposition 13, it still does not seem possible that there are some among us who dream the impossible dream—living in these United States without paying a fair share of the cost of the governmental services from which we benefit.

There are people roaming this land, however, who are making a financial killing hawking a tax evasion scheme which promises to sharply reduce or even eliminate entirely all personal income and death taxes. This contrivance, variously labeled the "Pure-," "Equity-," "Educational-," "Apocalypse-," or "Family-Trust" (not to be confused with the "family trusts" described in this book), feeds upon the resentment so many feel toward a profligate government and its confiscatory taxes. But where would our country be if any significant number of its citizens simply stopped paying taxes, thereby increasing the burden upon those who *do* pay their taxes?

A trust is a very valuable—and valid—device for use in estate planning. Well-planned trusts can save a part of the taxes officially levied by state and federal government, and an inter vivos or "living" trust can eliminate all of the private "tax" levied by the legal profession on the probate estates of deceased persons. But the "Pure Trust" will prove to be nothing but a disaster for the unsophisticated individual who falls for the glib promises of its promoters that he will end up with a tax-free trust "just like Rockefeller's." The latest word I've had from the IRS: "We intend to continue vigorous enforcement action against taxpayers who use such sham devices."

Under the "Pure Trusts," an individual is advised to assign assets and income from current employment to a trust of which he and family members are trustees. Typical assets could include rental property, securities, and other income-producing property as well as such non-revenue-producing assets as the family residence and car. The promoters then advise that in exchange for such assignment, the creator of the trust may receive "compensation" as an officer, trustee, or director, as well as certain "fringe benefits," such as "pension rights," "tax-free use of a residence," and "educational endowments" for children.

According to the promoters, once the creator's income is shifted to the trust, the latter is supposedly taxed only on undistributed net income. The promoters misrepresent that substantially all living expenses of the grantor and his family may be deducted on the trust's income tax return on Form 1041 as business expenses, and that the balance may then be distributed among members of the creator's family or to a separate "nonprofit" educational trust, leaving little or no taxable income to be reported.

The "Pure Trust's" sponsors claim that the number of legitimate tax deductions is limited only by the imagination of the creator and his family. One promoter explains, for example, that "if you take your wife to dinner, that's a consultation between trustees—and you can deduct it."

All of one's assets become trust property, and since the trust never dies, the plan claims to offer 100 percent exemption from state or federal death taxes.

The IRS has repeatedly warned that the "Pure Trust" is a sham and it has brought trust after trust into the U.S. Tax Court, where it has yet to lose a case. It is an ironclad rule of tax law that "income must be taxed to him who earns it. Arrangements by which income is siphoned off and diverted to another individual or entity cannot be given effect for tax purposes" [*Horvat* v. *Commissioner,* 36 CCG Tax Ct. Mem. 476 (1977)].

IRS rulings do not have the force of law, and tax courts don't rule on the illegality of tax-avoidance schemes, only on the validity of the deductions claimed. The IRS is in the curious position of not being able to announce that the "Pure Trust" is "illegal." What it does do is go after the plan's users hammer and tongs. In each case, the taxpayer has been required to file a revised return and pay whatever tax he should have paid plus interest and a penalty. Aside from that there are the legal costs of a tax court fight, the drain on the taxpayer's time, the wear and tear on his peace of mind, and the undesirable publicity which invariably attends such actions.

A very considerable part of the cost is the commission which the creator pays to the promoters who sold him the bill of goods. Depending upon the size of the creator's income and the total value of his assets, this commission can run up to $50,000. One sponsor is credited with having taken in more than $10 million in fees during a two-year period! Avoid it.

CHAPTER 26

If You Change Your Mind . . .

Alas, permanence is not the hallmark of our modern society. Our homes, our automobiles, our refrigerators—seemingly all of the material things which make up our world—have a built-in obsolescence which dictates constant replacement.

Our financial planning is no exception to the rule. In the nervous age in which we live, in which the weekly visit to the psychoanalyst has become for many a status symbol, the best-laid financial schemes "gang aft agley," as Bobbie Burns put it.

Accordingly, having gotten you into this, I now must tell you how to get out of it in the event that you change your mind about any of the plans you've made.

On the pages which follow will be found several copies each of forms titled "Amendment to Declaration of Trust" and "Revocation of Trust."

AMENDMENTS

In most cases, the amendment you wish to make will involve changing either a beneficiary or the Successor Trustee whom you have named to act for a minor beneficiary. **Amendment Form A** is designed for use where it is desired to accomplish such changes in any of the following declarations of trust:

DT-101 DT-105 DT-109 DT-113 DT-117 DT-121 DT-125
DT-102 DT-106 DT-110 DT-114 DT-118 DT-122 DT-126
DT-103 DT-107 DT-111 DT-115 DT-119 DT-123 DT-127
DT-104 DT-108 DT-112 DT-116 DT-120 DT-124 DT-128

DT-129 DT-133 DT-137 DT-141 DT-145 DT-149
DT-130 DT-134 DT-138 DT-142 DT-146 DT-150
DT-131 DT-135 DT-139 DT-143 DT-147 DT-151
DT-132 DT-136 DT-140 DT-144 DT-148 DT-152

Amendment Form A-Joint is designed for use where it is desired to amend any of the following declarations of trust:

DT-101-J DT-105-J DT-109-J DT-113-J DT-117-J DT-121-J
DT-102-J DT-106-J DT-110-J DT-114-J DT-118-J DT-122-J
DT-103-J DT-107-J DT-111-J DT-115-J DT-119-J DT-123-J

DT-137-J DT-145-J DT-149-J
DT-138-J DT-146-J DT-150-J
DT-139-J DT-147-J DT-151-J

Note: Amendment Form A and **Amendment Form A-Joint** are similar except that the latter requires the signatures of the joint trustees.
Amendment Form B on pages 527 and 531 is intended for use with DT-153, DT-154, DT-155, DT-156, and DT-157.

GENERAL INSTRUCTIONS:

Amendment Forms A and A-Joint both include a place to identify the *existing beneficiary* as well as the *new one* whom you propose to substitute. Fill in both names. If you don't wish to change the beneficiary but simply wish to designate a different person as successor trustee for a minor beneficiary, insert the present beneficiary's name in the space provided for it, and in the space provided for naming a new beneficiary write "No change." Then drop down to the last paragraph of the amendment, check the *second* box and insert the name of the individual whom you wish to appoint as successor trustee for the minor in place of the one presently named.

Having first identified by date the declaration of trust you are now amending, you next identify the trust property involved in some such fashion as this:

"that certain piece of real estate located in the city (town) of Smithville and known as 500 Main Street"
"shares of common stock of the XYZ Company"
"the unincorporated business known as the Ajax Plumbing Supply"
"a certain trailer owned by me and located at the Smithtown Trailer Park"

If you change a beneficiary, across the original beneficiary's name in the declaration of trust write boldly in red "Amended (date)—see attached." If you change your designation of a successor trustee for a minor, enter the same notation in red across the name of the individual whom you are now relieving of that responsibility. (Remember, on all trusts the beneficiary is *also* the successor trustee; the "successor trustee" we are talking about replacing here is the one you have named to act if any beneficiary is a minor at the time of your death.) In a moment, we'll discuss what you do with the amendment when you have completed it and run off several photocopies.

Note: Whenever you amend a declaration of trust, always *cross out* boldly in red the provision which you are changing and write "Amended (date)." Make certain that any copies of the declaration you may have given to others are recovered or changed to reflect the amendment.

R E V O C A T I O N S

Revocation RE (Real Estate) may be used to revoke trusts established in *one* name under DT-101, DT-102, DT-103, or DT-104. **Revocation RE-J** may be used to revoke trusts established in *joint* names under DT-101-J, DT-102-J, or DT-103-J. These special forms to be used only with real estate have a quit claim deed on their reverse side to enable you to simultaneously transfer title to the real estate from yourself as trustee back to yourself as an individual.

Revocation Form A may be used to revoke trusts established in one name through the use of forms numbered from DT-105 up to and including DT-152. It does not apply to Deeds of Trust (DT-153 through DT-157), which are revoked by a letter to the Trustee.

Revocation Form A-J may be used to revoke trusts established in joint names through the use of forms numbered DT-105-J up to and including DT-151-J.

Note: Whenever you revoke a declaration of trust, either destroy that instrument or write boldly in red across its face "Revoked (date)." Make certain that you recover any copies of the declaration given to others.

Now, here's how to use the forms:

1. YOUR HOME

(a) *If you simply wish to change the beneficiary:*
Complete Amendment Form A if the account is in one name, or Amendment Form A-J if it is in joint names. After making several photocopies, file the original in the same land records office where you filed the original declaration of trust. When it is returned to you after microfilming, staple it to the original declaration of trust. Remember to write "Amended (date)— see attached" across the part of the original declaration of trust which you are changing.

(b) *If you wish to cancel the trust instrument entirely without naming a new beneficiary:*
Complete Revocation Form RE if the account is in one name, or Revocation Form RE-J if it is in joint names. By executing this form, you will have revoked the original declaration of trust by which you placed your real estate in trust. But you now hold that real estate in your capacity as trustee, so the next thing that

you must do is transfer title from *yourself as trustee* back to *yourself as an individual*. On the reverse side of the revocation form will be found a form of quit claim deed which you may use for this purpose. Complete it by inserting the same description of the property which appeared in the original quit claim deed which you executed when you created the trust, indicating the date of that deed and the volume and page number where it was filed in the land records. After completing and signing *both sides* of this document, and making some photocopies, file the original in the same office where you earlier filed the forms by which you placed the property in trust.

If you amend or revoke the trust, make certain that you recover and destroy any copies of the original forms which you may have given to beneficiaries or other persons to hold, the idea being to make sure that such copies do not become the basis for any claim after you are gone.

2. YOUR CHECKING OR SAVINGS ACCOUNT

(a) *If you simply wish to change the beneficiary:*
Complete Amendment Form A if the trusteed account is in one name, or Amendment Form A-J if it is in

joint names. After making several photocopies, staple the original to the original of the declaration of trust, and after crossing off the provision in that document which you have amended, return them to safekeeping. Deliver one of the photocopies to the bank where the account was established and ask that it be attached to the copy of the declaration of trust which you filed with that bank when the account was opened.

(b) *If you wish to cancel the trust arrangement entirely without naming a new beneficiary:*

No revocation form is necessary. Simply go to the bank, close the account, draw out the money, and ask for the return of the declaration of trust in their files. Deposit the money in a new account in your name alone.

3. YOUR MUTUAL FUND SHARES

(a) *If you simply wish to change the beneficiary:*
Complete Amendment Form A if the trusteed shares are in one name, or Amendment A-J if they are in joint names, and make several photocopies. If you hold a certificate for the shares and you have followed the instructions in Chapter 9, the original of the declaration of trust is attached to that certificate. Staple the original signed copy of the amendment to the declaration of trust. If the fund accepted a copy of the declaration of trust for filing when you registered the shares, write them a letter saying:

The undersigned is the registered owner of shares of XYZ Fund registered in the name of "(your name), Trustee u/d/t dated (date of trust)." In connection with such holdings, I have executed and filed with you a declaration of trust naming certain beneficiaries and a Successor Trustee. I have now executed an amendment to such declaration, copy of which I enclose. Kindly file this with the original declaration of trust and confirm to me that this has been done.

If the fund shares which you own were not actually issued to you in certificate form but are being held by the fund in an "accumulation account," probably with all dividends and distributions being automatically reinvested, write to the fund saying:

The undersigned is the registered owner of shares of XYZ Fund held in Account No. _____. In connection with such holdings, I have executed and filed with you a declaration of trust naming certain beneficiaries and a Successor Trustee. I have now executed an amendment to such declaration, copy of which I enclose. Kindly file this with the original

declaration of trust and confirm to me that this has been done.

If the original declaration of trust was *not* filed with the fund, it is unnecessary to communicate with the fund regarding the amendment.

(b) *If you wish to cancel the trust arrangement entirely without naming a new beneficiary:*
If you hold a share certificate, sign the back of it, have your signature guaranteed by a commercial bank, and send it by registered mail to the fund's custodian bank with a letter saying:

Enclosed is Certificate No._____ for_____ shares of XYZ Fund registered in the name of "(your name), Trustee u/d/t dated (date of trust)." I direct you to reregister the certificate, and any shares which you may be holding in an accumulation account, as follows: "(your name and address)." Please return to me the trust document now in your files.

If all your shares are on deposit with the fund, write the custodian bank saying:

The undersigned is the registered owner of shares of XYZ Fund held in accumulation account No. _____. Please reregister such shares and account as follows: "(your name and address)." Please return the trust document now in your files.

If no certificate has been issued to you, you obviously cannot sign the back of it. In that case, ask the broker who sold you the shares or the collateral loan department of a commercial bank for a "stock power," sign it and have your signature guaranteed by a commercial bank, and send it along with your letter to the fund.

4. YOUR SECURITIES

I know of no issuers or transfer agents who will accept a declaration of trust for permanent filing, so if you followed the instructions given in Chapter 9, the original signed declaration of trust is stapled to your stock certificates or bonds, or a photocopy of the original is attached to each of the individual securities.

(a) *If you simply wish to change the beneficiary:*
Execute Amendment Form A if the registration is in one name only, or Amendment Form A-J if it is in joint

names. After making an appropriate number of photocopies, staple a photocopy of the amendment to each photocopy of the original declaration of trust which is attached to a stock certificate or bond. Be sure to cross out in red the provision in the declaration which you have amended. No letter to transfer agents is required because you didn't file the original declaration of trust with them and it is therefore not necessary to put them on notice about the amendment.

(b) *If you wish to cancel the trust arrangement entirely without naming a new beneficiary:*

No revocation form is necessary. Simply sign the back of each certificate, have your signature guaranteed by a commercial bank, and mail it to the issuer or transfer agent with a letter asking that the securities be reregistered in your own name alone.

5. YOUR BROKERAGE ACCOUNT

(a) *If you simply wish to change the beneficiary:*

Execute Amendment Form A if the account is in one name, or Amendment Form A-J if it is in joint names. Make several photocopies and deliver one to the broker where the account is maintained. Ask him to file it with the copy of the declaration of trust which you filed with him earlier when you opened the trusteed account. Staple the original of the amendment to the original of the declaration of trust and place them in safekeeping.

(b) *If you wish to cancel the trust arrangement entirely without naming a new beneficiary:*

No revocation form is necessary. Instruct the broker that you wish to cancel the trustee registration of your brokerage account and hereafter just carry the account in your name. Be sure to recover the declaration of trust he is holding.

6. YOUR SAFE DEPOSIT BOX

(a) *If you simply wish to change the beneficiary:*

Execute Amendment Form A if the box is in one name, or Amendment Form A-J if it is in joint names. Make several photocopies, deliver one to the bank where the box is maintained and ask them to attach it to the copy of the declaration of trust which you filed with them earlier when you made the box subject to a trust.

(b) *If you wish to cancel the trust arrangement entirely without naming a new beneficiary:*

No revocation form is necessary. Simply instruct the bank to change the name on your box and register it in your name alone. Then ask for the return of your declaration of trust.

7. YOUR MORTGAGE, FIRST TRUST DEED, OR REAL ESTATE SALES CONTRACT

(a) *If you simply wish to change the beneficiary:*

Execute Amendment Form A if the asset is held in one name only, or Amendment Form A-J if it is in joint names. After making several photocopies, file the original in the land records office where the declaration of trust was filed earlier. When it is returned after microfilming, staple it to the original declaration of trust. Don't forget to cross off in the declaration the provision which you have now amended.

(b) *If you wish to cancel the trust arrangement entirely without naming a new beneficiary:*

Execute Revocation Form A (or Revocation Form A-J in the case of a joint trust) which appears in the following pages (note that it differs from the Assignment of Mortgage which you executed and filed when you established the trust). This document accomplishes the transfer of title in the mortgage, first trust deed, or real estate sales contract from yourself as trustee back to yourself as an individual. After making several photocopies, file the original in the land records office where you filed the declaration of trust. Finally, notify the person from whom you have been receiving payments in your capacity as trustee that the trust has been terminated and that in future all such payments are to be made to you as an individual.

8. A CONTRACT COVERING A COPYRIGHTED PROPERTY OR PATENT RIGHTS

(a) *If you simply wish to change the beneficiary:*

Execute Amendment Form A if the trust is in one name only, or Amendment Form A-J if it is in joint names. After making several photocopies, staple the original to the declaration of trust being amended. Send a copy to any individual or company with whom you earlier filed the declaration of trust and ask that it be filed with the declaration.

(b) *If you wish to cancel the trust arrangement entirely without naming a new beneficiary:*

Destroy or clearly mark the declaration of trust to indicate its revocation. Next, notify each individual or company with whom you had earlier filed copies of it that you have terminated the trust and that henceforth they should recognize that you hold the property as an individual owner and free of trust. Request the return of the document they are holding.

9. A PARTNERSHIP INTEREST

(a) *If you simply wish to change the beneficiary:*

Execute Amendment Form A. After making photocopies, staple the original to the declaration of trust being amended. Furnish the partnership with a copy, requesting that it be filed with the copy of the declaration filed with the partnership earlier.

(b) *If you wish to cancel the trust arrangement entirely without naming a new beneficiary:*
Notify the partnership that you have terminated the trust, that henceforth they should recognize that you hold the partnership interest as an individual and not as a trustee, and ask that they return to you the copy of the declaration of trust filed with them earlier. Be sure that you either destroy the original and all copies of the declaration, or that you clearly mark them "Revoked (date)."

10. A MOTOR VEHICLE OR TRAILER

(a) *If you simply wish to change the beneficiary:*
Execute Amendment Form A and staple it to the declaration of trust executed earlier when you put the vehicle in trust.

(b) *If you wish to cancel the trust arrangement entirely without naming a new beneficiary:*
Reregister the vehicle in your name alone.

11. AN UNINCORPORATED BUSINESS

(a) *If you simply wish to change the beneficiary:*
Execute Amendment Form A if the trust is in your name alone, or Amendment Form A-J if it is in joint names, and make several photocopies. If you earlier filed the declaration of trust in a local records office where documents such as powers of attorney are filed, file the amendment there, as well. When it is returned to you, attach it to the original declaration of trust and return both to safekeeping.

(b) *If you wish to cancel the trust arrangement entirely without naming a new beneficiary:*
If you earlier filed a declaration of trust in a local records office, you must now execute and file a Revocation Form A. Write "Revoked (date)" across the original declaration of trust. When the Revocation Form A is returned to you after filing, staple it to the revoked declaration of trust and put both in safekeeping.

12. PERSONAL EFFECTS OR CONTENTS OF A RENTED HOUSE OR APARTMENT

(a) *If you simply wish to change the beneficiary:*
You may either destroy the old declaration of trust and replace it with a new one reflecting your changed wishes as to the beneficiary designation, or you may execute Amendment Form A and staple it to the declaration of trust. Make certain that you don't leave any unamended copies of the declaration in the hands of ex-beneficiaries.

(b) *If you wish to cancel the trust arrangement entirely without naming a new beneficiary:*
Destroy the declaration of trust, making certain that no copies remain in the hands of persons who might make them the basis for a claim after you are gone.

13. A FAMILY TRUST WITH ONE'S SPOUSE AS TRUSTEE (DT-153)
A FAMILY TRUST WITH AN INDIVIDUAL OTHER THAN ONE'S SPOUSE AS TRUSTEE (DT-154)

Amendment Form B provides a means of altering the terms of any provision of the trust. Simply identify the section you wish to amend and then type the rewritten version of it in the space provided. If there isn't space enough for the changes you desire, you may make a typed copy of the entire form with space enough for your needs. Execute two copies of Amendment Form B so that settlor and trustee may each have a signed instrument.

If you cancel the trust entirely, make certain that you execute amendments or new declarations of trust covering any assets that you have directed into the trust you are canceling.

14. A FAMILY TRUST WITH A BANK AS TRUSTEE (Investment management by the bank) (DT-155)
A FAMILY TRUST WITH A BANK AS TRUSTEE (Investment management by a mutual fund) (DT-156)

Amendment Form B provides a means of altering the terms of any provision of the trust. In cooperation with the trustee bank, identify the section you wish to amend and type the rewritten version of it in the space provided. If there isn't space enough for the changes you desire, you may make a typed copy of the entire form with space enough for your needs. Execute two copies of Amendment Form B so that settlor and trustee may each have a signed instrument.

Amendment to Declaration of Trust

Executed this _____ second _____ day of _____ April _____, 19 80

WHEREAS, by Declaration of Trust dated _____ June 13, _____, 19 68,

I created in writing a Revocable Trust as a result of which a beneficial interest in

a savings account at the First National Bank, Milton _____ accrued to:

(Describe the trust asset)

Check One
- **x** the following individual
- ___ the following individuals as primary and contingent beneficiary(ies) respectively
- ___ the following individuals, to share equally
- ___ the following individual as primary beneficiary with my children, sharing equally, as contingent

beneficiaries

Insert name(s) of original beneficiary or beneficiaries

Donald Jordan

WHEREAS, by the terms of the said Declaration of Trust, I reserved full power to revoke or amend said Trust at any time without the consent of or notice to any beneficiary of said Trust created by me;

NOW, THEREFORE, pursuant to such power and right to revoke or amend, I do hereby revoke the aforesaid beneficiary designation and declare that henceforth under the terms of the said Declaration of Trust the aforesaid beneficial interest in the trust shall accrue to:

Check One
- **x** the following individual
- ___ the following individuals as primary and contingent beneficiary respectively
- ___ the following individuals, to share equally
- ___ the following individual as primary beneficiary with my children, sharing equally, as contingent

beneficiaries

Insert name(s) of new beneficiary or beneficiaries

Diane R. Brown, 525 Main Street, Milton, CT 06605

In the said Declaration of Trust, I designated an individual to serve as Successor Trustee if the beneficiary had not attained the age of 21 years at that time. With respect to that designation:

Check One
- **x** I affirm that it remains unchanged
- ___ I hereby revoke such designation, and in place of such individual I now designate _____, of

_____ _____ _____ _____
(Name)   City   State   Zip

_____ _____ _____
(Address)   Number   Street

as Successor Trustee.

_____ L.S.
John J. Brown
Settlor John J. Brown

(1) _____ *Anne Johnson* _____
Witness

(2) _____ *Josephine Ousley* _____
Witness

Amendment to Declaration of Trust

Executed this _____ day of _____ , 19 _____ ;

WHEREAS, by Declaration of Trust dated _____ , 19 _____ ,

I created in writing a Revocable Trust as a result of which a beneficial interest in

_____

(Describe the trust asset)

_____ accrued to:

Check

One

_____ the following individual

_____ the following individuals as primary and contingent beneficiary(ies) respectively

_____ the following individuals, to share equally

_____ the following individual as primary beneficiary, with my children, sharing equally, as contingent beneficiaries

Insert name(s)

of original

beneficiary or

beneficiaries

_____

_____

_____

_____ ; and

WHEREAS, by the terms of the said Declaration of Trust, I reserved full power to revoke or amend said Trust at any time without the consent of or notice to any beneficiary of said Trust created by me;

NOW, THEREFORE, pursuant to such power and right to revoke or amend, I do hereby revoke the aforesaid beneficiary designation and declare that henceforth under the terms of the said Declaration of Trust the aforesaid beneficial interest in the trust shall accrue to:

Check

One

_____ the following individual

_____ the following individuals as primary and contingent beneficiary respectively

_____ the following individuals, to share equally

_____ the following individual as primary beneficiary, with my children, sharing equally, as contingent beneficiaries

Insert name(s)

of new

beneficiary or

beneficiaries

_____

_____

_____

_____

In the said Declaration of Trust, I designated an individual to serve as Successor Trustee if the beneficiary had not attained the age of 21 years at that time. With respect to that designation:

Check

One

_____ I affirm that it remains unchanged

_____ I hereby revoke such designation, and in place of such individual I now designate

(Name) _____ , of

(Address) _____

            Number   *Street*   *City*   *State*   *Zip*

as Successor Trustee. _____ L.S.

                                                      Settlor

(1) _____ (2) _____

             Witness   *Witness*

Amendment to Declaration of Trust

Executed this _____ day of _____ , 19_____ ;

WHEREAS, by Declaration of Trust dated _____ , 19_____ ,

I created in writing a Revocable Trust as a result of which a beneficial interest in

_____

(Describe the trust asset)

_____ accrued to:

Check One
> _____ the following individual
>
> _____ the following individuals as primary and contingent beneficiary(ies) respectively
>
> _____ the following individuals, to share equally
>
> _____ the following individual as primary beneficiary, with my children, sharing equally, as contingent beneficiaries

Insert name(s)
of original
beneficiary or
beneficiaries
> _____
>
> _____
>
> _____
>
> _____ ; and

WHEREAS, by the terms of the said Declaration of Trust, I reserved full power to revoke or amend said Trust at any time without the consent of or notice to any beneficiary of said Trust created by me;

NOW, THEREFORE, pursuant to such power and right to revoke or amend, I do hereby revoke the aforesaid beneficiary designation and declare that henceforth under the terms of the said Declaration of Trust the aforesaid beneficial interest in the trust shall accrue to:

Check One
> _____ the following individual
>
> _____ the following individuals as primary and contingent beneficiary respectively
>
> _____ the following individuals, to share equally
>
> _____ the following individual as primary beneficiary, with my children, sharing equally, as contingent beneficiaries

Insert name(s)
of new
beneficiary or
beneficiaries
> _____
>
> _____
>
> _____
>
> _____

In the said Declaration of Trust, I designated an individual to serve as Successor Trustee if the beneficiary had not attained the age of 21 years at that time. With respect to that designation:

Check One
> _____ I affirm that it remains unchanged
>
> _____ I hereby revoke such designation, and in place of such individual I now designate

(Name) _____ , of

(Address) _____

Number	Street	City	State	Zip

as Successor Trustee.

_____ L.S.

Settlor

(1) _____   (2) _____

Witness   *Witness*

Amendment to Declaration of Trust

Executed this _____ day of _____ , 19_____ ;

WHEREAS, by Declaration of Trust dated _____ , 19_____ ,

we created in writing a Revocable Trust as a result of which a beneficial interest in

_____

(Describe the trust asset)

_____ accrued to:

Check One
- _____ the following individual
- _____ the following individuals as primary and contingent beneficiary respectively
- _____ the following individuals, to share equally

Insert name(s)
of original
beneficiary or
beneficiaries

_____

_____

_____

_____ ; and

WHEREAS, by the terms of the said Declaration of Trust, we reserved the power to revoke or amend said Trust at any time without the consent of or notice to any beneficiary of said Trust created by us;

NOW, THEREFORE, pursuant to such power and right to revoke or amend, we do hereby revoke the aforesaid beneficiary designation and declare that henceforth under the terms of the said Declaration of Trust the aforesaid beneficial interest in the trust shall accrue to:

Check One
- _____ the following individual
- _____ the following individuals as primary and contingent beneficiary respectively
- _____ the following individuals, to share equally

Insert name(s)
of new
beneficiary or
beneficiaries

_____

_____

_____

_____

In the said Declaration of Trust, we designated an individual to serve as Successor Trustee if the beneficiary had not attained the age of 21 years at that time. With respect to that designation:

Check One
- _____ We affirm that it remains unchanged
- _____ We hereby revoke such designation, and in place of such individual we now designate

(Name) _____ , of

(Address) _____

| Number | Street | City | State | Zip |

as Successor Trustee.

_____ L.S.
Signature of First Settlor

_____ L.S.
Signature of Second Settlor

(1) _____   (2) _____
    Witness   *Witness*

Amendment to Declaration of Trust

Executed this _____ day of _____, 19_____;

WHEREAS, by Declaration of Trust dated _____, 19_____,

we created in writing a Revocable Trust as a result of which a beneficial interest in

_____

(Describe the trust asset)

_____ accrued to:

Check One
- _____ the following individual
- _____ the following individuals as primary and contingent beneficiary respectively
- _____ the following individuals, to share equally

Insert name(s) of original beneficiary or beneficiaries
- _____
- _____
- _____
- _____; and

WHEREAS, by the terms of the said Declaration of Trust, we reserved the power to revoke or amend said Trust at any time without the consent of or notice to any beneficiary of said Trust created by us;

NOW, THEREFORE, pursuant to such power and right to revoke or amend, we do hereby revoke the aforesaid beneficiary designation and declare that henceforth under the terms of the said Declaration of Trust the aforesaid beneficial interest in the trust shall accrue to:

Check One
- _____ the following individual
- _____ the following individuals as primary and contingent beneficiary respectively
- _____ the following individuals, to share equally

Insert name(s) of new beneficiary or beneficiaries
- _____
- _____
- _____
- _____

In the said Declaration of Trust, we designated an individual to serve as Successor Trustee if the beneficiary had not attained the age of 21 years at that time. With respect to that designation:

Check One
- _____ We affirm that it remains unchanged
- _____ We hereby revoke any such designation, and in place of such individual we now designate

(Name) _____, of

(Address) _____

Number   Street   City   State   Zip

as Successor Trustee.

_____ L.S.
Signature of First Settlor

_____ L.S.
Signature of Second Settlor

(1) _____   (2) _____

Witness   *Witness*

Amendment to Deed of Trust

WHEREAS, under date of _____ , an agreement was entered into

between _____ ,

of the City/Town of _____ , County of _____ ,

State of _____ (hereinafter referred to as the "Settlor"),

and _____

of the City/Town of _____ , County of _____

and State of _____ (hereinafter referred to as the "Trustee"); and

WHEREAS, Paragraph 7 of the said agreement provides that it may be amended at any time by the Settlor;

NOW, THEREFORE, it is agreed by the Settlor and the Trustee that Paragraph _____ of said agreement shall cease to be effective as of the date of this Amendment and that the following shall be substituted therefor and shall hereafter be

known as Paragraphs _____ of the agreement entered into by the parties on _____ :

IN WITNESS WHEREOF, the Settlor and the Trustee have hereunto and to a duplicate hereof put their hands and seals as of the _____ day of _____, 19 _____.

THE SETTLOR:

_____   _____ L.S.
                    Witness

STATE OF _____ ⎫   City
                                                                        or
COUNTY OF _____ ⎭   Town _____

Personally appeared _____, signer and sealer as Settlor under the foregoing Amendment to Deed of Trust, who acknowledged the same to be his/her free act and

deed, before me this _____ day of _____, 19_____.

(Notary Seal)   _____
                                                                                    Notary Public

---

If the Trustee is an individual:

THE TRUSTEE:

_____   _____ L.S.
                    Witness

STATE OF _____ ⎫   City
                                                                        or
COUNTY OF _____ ⎭   Town _____

Personally appeared _____, signer and sealer as Trustee under the foregoing Amendment to Deed of Trust, who acknowledged the same to be his/her free act

and deed before me this _____ day of _____, 19 _____.

(Notary Seal)   _____
                                                                                    Notary Public

---

If the Trustee is a bank:

For THE TRUSTEE:

_____   _____ L.S.
                    Witness

                                                                    TITLE _____

STATE OF _____ ⎫   City
                                                                        or
COUNTY OF _____ ⎭   Town _____

Personally appeared_____ , signer and sealer on behalf of the Trustee under the foregoing Amendment to Deed of Trust, who acknowledged the same to be

his/her free act and deed, and the free act and deed of the _____
                                                                                                            (Trustee Bank)

before me this _____ day of _____, 19 _____.

(Notary Seal)   _____
                                                                                    Notary Public

2

Amendment to Deed of Trust

WHEREAS, under date of _____, an agreement was entered into

between _____,

of the City/Town of _____, County of _____,

State of _____ (hereinafter referred to as the "Settlor"),

and _____

of the City/Town of _____, County of _____

and State of _____ (hereinafter referred to as the "Trustee"); and

WHEREAS, Paragraph 7 of the said agreement provides that it may be amended at any time by the Settlor;

NOW, THEREFORE, it is agreed by the Settlor and the Trustee that Paragraph _____ of said agreement shall cease to be effective as of the date of this Amendment and that the following shall be substituted therefor and shall hereafter be

known as Paragraphs _____ of the agreement entered into by the parties on _____:

IN WITNESS WHEREOF, the Settlor and the Trustee have hereunto and to a duplicate hereof put their hands and seals as of the _____ day of _____, 19 _____.

THE SETTLOR:

_____   _____ L.S.
              Witness

STATE OF _____   City
                                            or
COUNTY OF _____   Town _____

Personally appeared _____, signer and sealer as Settlor under the foregoing Amendment to Deed of Trust, who acknowledged the same to be his/her free act and

deed, before me this _____ day of _____, 19_____.

(Notary Seal)   _____
                                                    Notary Public

---

If the Trustee is an individual:

THE TRUSTEE:

_____   _____ L.S.
              Witness

STATE OF _____ ⎫   City
                                    ⎬   or
COUNTY OF _____ ⎭   Town _____

Personally appeared _____ , signer and sealer as Trustee under the foregoing Amendment to Deed of Trust, who acknowledged the same to be his/her free act

and deed before me this _____ day of _____, 19 _____.

(Notary Seal)   _____
                                                    Notary Public

---

If the Trustee is a bank:

For THE TRUSTEE:

_____   _____ L.S.
              Witness

                                            TITLE _____

STATE OF _____ ⎫   City
                                    ⎬   or
COUNTY OF _____ ⎭   Town _____

Personally appeared_____ , signer and sealer on behalf of the Trustee under the foregoing Amendment to Deed of Trust, who acknowledged the same to be

his/her free act and deed, and the free act and deed of the _____
                                                                    (Trustee Bank)

before me this _____ day of _____, 19 _____.

(Notary Seal)   _____
                                                    Notary Public

Amendment to Deed of Trust

WHEREAS, under date of _____, an agreement was entered into

between _____,

of the City/Town of _____, County of _____,

State of _____ (hereinafter referred to as the "Settlor"),

and _____

of the City/Town of _____, County of _____

and State of _____ (hereinafter referred to as the "Trustee"); and

WHEREAS, Paragraph 7 of the said agreement provides that it may be amended at any time by the Settlor;

NOW, THEREFORE, it is agreed by the Settlor and the Trustee that Paragraph _____ of said agreement shall cease to be effective as of the date of this Amendment and that the following shall be substituted therefor and shall hereafter be

known as Paragraphs _____ of the agreement entered into by the parties on _____:

IN WITNESS WHEREOF, the Settlor and the Trustee have hereunto and to a duplicate hereof put their hands and seals as

of the _____ day of _____, 19 _____.

THE SETTLOR:

_____   _____ L.S.
Witness

STATE OF _____   City
                                          or
COUNTY OF _____   Town _____

Personally appeared _____, signer
and sealer as Settlor under the foregoing Amendment to Deed of Trust, who acknowledged the same to be his/her free act and

deed, before me this _____ day of _____, 19_____.

(Notary Seal)   _____
                                                     Notary Public

---

If the Trustee is an individual:

THE TRUSTEE:

_____   _____ L.S.
Witness

STATE OF _____   City
                                            or
COUNTY OF _____   Town _____

Personally appeared _____, signer
and sealer as Trustee under the foregoing Amendment to Deed of Trust, who acknowledged the same to be his/her free act

and deed before me this _____ day of _____, 19 _____.

(Notary Seal)   _____
                                                       Notary Public

---

If the Trustee is a bank:

For THE TRUSTEE:

_____   _____ L.S.
Witness

                                           TITLE _____

STATE OF _____   City
                                            or
COUNTY OF _____   Town _____

Personally appeared _____, signer
and sealer on behalf of the Trustee under the foregoing Amendment to Deed of Trust, who acknowledged the same to be

his/her free act and deed, and the free act and deed of the _____
(Trustee Bank)

before me this _____ day of _____, 19 _____.

(Notary Seal)   _____
                                                      Notary Public

Amendment to Deed of Trust

WHEREAS, under date of _____, an agreement was entered into

between _____,

of the City/Town of _____, County of _____,

State of _____ (hereinafter referred to as the "Settlor"),

and _____,

of the City/Town of _____, County of _____

and State of _____ (hereinafter referred to as the "Trustee"); and

WHEREAS, Paragraph 7 of the said agreement provides that it may be amended at any time by the Settlor;

NOW, THEREFORE, it is agreed by the Settlor and the Trustee that Paragraph _____ of said agreement shall cease to be effective as of the date of this Amendment and that the following shall be substituted therefor and shall hereafter be

known as Paragraphs _____ of the agreement entered into by the parties on _____:

1

IN WITNESS WHEREOF, the Settlor and the Trustee have hereunto and to a duplicate hereof put their hands and seals as of the _____ day of _____, 19 ____.

THE SETTLOR:

_____   _____ L.S.
           Witness

STATE OF _____   ⎫ City

COUNTY OF _____   ⎬ or
                                      ⎭ Town _____

Personally appeared _____, signer and sealer as Settlor under the foregoing Amendment to Deed of Trust, who acknowledged the same to be his/her free act and

deed, before me this _____ day of _____, 19 ____.

_____
(Notary Seal)   *Notary Public*

If the Trustee is an individual:

THE TRUSTEE:

_____   _____ L.S.
           Witness

STATE OF _____   ⎫ City

COUNTY OF _____   ⎬ or
                                        ⎭ Town _____

Personally appeared _____ , signer and sealer as Trustee under the foregoing Amendment to Deed of Trust, who acknowledged the same to be his/her free act

and deed before me this _____ day of _____, 19 ____.

_____
(Notary Seal)   *Notary Public*

If the Trustee is a bank:

For THE TRUSTEE:

_____   _____ L.S.
           Witness

TITLE _____

STATE OF _____   ⎫ City

COUNTY OF _____   ⎬ or
                                        ⎭ Town _____

Personally appeared_____ , signer and sealer on behalf of the Trustee under the foregoing Amendment to Deed of Trust, who acknowledged the same to be

his/her free act and deed, and the free act and deed of the _____
                                                        (Trustee Bank)

before me this _____ day of _____, 19 ____.

_____
(Notary Seal)   *Notary Public*

DACEY TRUST

Revocation of Trust

This instrument of revocation made this _____ day of _____, 19_____,

by _____;

WHEREAS, by Declaration of Trust dated _____, 19_____,
I created in writing a Revocable Trust as a result of which a beneficial interest in:

_____

(Describe the trust asset)

_____ accrued to:

Check

One

⎱ ⎰ _____ the following individual

_____ the following individuals as primary and contingent beneficiary respectively

_____ the following individuals, to share equally

_____ the following individual as primary beneficiary, with my children, sharing equally, as contingent beneficiaries

_____

_____

_____ ; and

WHEREAS, by the terms of the said Declaration of Trust, I reserve the full power and right to revoke said Trust at any time without the consent of or notice to any beneficiary of said Trust created by me;

NOW, THEREFORE, pursuant to the power and right of revocation aforesaid, I do hereby revoke in its entirety the Trust created by me by the aforesaid Declaration of Trust, to the end that as of the date of this instrument of revocation, I hold the former trust property free and discharged of all the Trust's terms and provisions in said Declaration of Trust contained.

_____   _____ L.S.
Witness   *Signature of Settlor*

_____
Witness

STATE OF _____ ⎱ City
                                          or
COUNTY OF _____ ⎰ Town _____

On the _____ day of _____, 19_____, personally appeared

_____

known to me to be the individual(s) who executed the foregoing instrument, and acknowledged the same to be _____ free act and deed, before me.

(Notary Seal)   _____
                                          Notary Public

To All People To Whom These Presents Shall Come, Greetings;

KNOW YE, THAT I,

(Name) _____, Trustee under Declaration of Trust

dated _____, do by these presents release and forever Quit-Claim to myself as an individual all right, title, interest, claim and demand which I as such Trustee have or ought to have in or to the property described as follows:

The consideration for this transfer is less than One Dollar.

Being the same premises earlier conveyed to the Releasor by an instrument dated _____, 19_____,

and recorded in Vol. _____, Page _____, of the _____ Land Records.

To Have and to Hold forever the premises with all the appurtenances, as an individual and free of trust, and agree that neither I as Trustee nor my successors as Trustees shall have or make any claim or demand upon such property.

IN WITNESS WHEREOF, I have hereunto set my hand and seal this _____ day of _____, 19_____.

(Signed) _____

Trustee under Declaration of Trust dated_____

Witness: (1) _____   Witness: (2) _____

STATE OF _____   City

or

COUNTY OF _____   Town _____

On the _____ day of _____, 19_____, personally appeared

_____, known to me to be the individual

who executed the foregoing instrument, and acknowledged the same to be _____ free act and deed, before me.

(Notary Seal)   Notary Public

Received for record _____ at _____. Attest: _____
                            Date   Time   Clerk

Revocation of Trust

This instrument of revocation made this _____ day of _____, 19_____,

by _____ and _____;

WHEREAS, by Declaration of Trust dated _____, 19_____,
we created in writing a Revocable Trust as a result of which a beneficial interest in

_____

(Describe the trust asset)

_____ accrued to:

Check

One

{ _____ the following individual

_____ the following individuals as primary and contingent beneficiary respectively

_____ the following individuals, to share equally

_____

_____

_____; and

WHEREAS, by the terms of the said Declaration of Trust, we reserve the full power and right to revoke said Trust at any time without the consent of or notice to any beneficiary of said Trust created by us;

NOW, THEREFORE, pursuant to the power and right of revocation aforesaid, we do hereby revoke in its entirety the Trust created by us by the aforesaid Declaration of Trust, to the end that as of the date of this instrument of revocation, we hold the former trust property free and discharged of all the Trust's terms and provisions in said Declaration of Trust contained.

_____ _____ L.S.
Witness *Signature of First Settlor*

_____ _____ L.S.
Witness *Signature of Second Settlor*

STATE OF _____ } City
or
COUNTY OF _____   Town _____

On the _____ day of _____, 19_____, personally appeared

_____ and _____

known to me to be the individuals who executed the foregoing instrument, and acknowledged the same to be their free act and deed, before me.

(Notary Seal) _____
Notary Public

To All People To Whom These Presents Shall Come, Greetings;

KNOW YE, THAT WE,

_____ and _____, Trustees

under Declaration of Trust dated _____, do by these presents release and forever Quit-Claim to ourselves as individuals all right, title, interest, claim and demand which we as such Trustees have or ought to have in or to the property described as follows:

> The consideration for this transfer is less than One Dollar.

Being the same premises earlier conveyed to the Releasors by an instrument dated _____, 19_____,

and recorded in Vol. _____, Page _____ of the _____ Land Records.

To Have and to Hold forever the premises with all the appurtenances, as individuals and free of trust, and agree that neither we as Trustees nor our successors as Trustees shall have or make any claim or demand upon such property.

IN WITNESS WHEREOF, we have hereunto set our hands and seals this _____

day of _____, 19_____.

_____
First Releasor

_____
Second Releasor

} *Trustees*

Under Declaration of Trust dated _____, 19_____.

Witness: (1) _____   Witness: (2) _____

STATE OF _____

COUNTY OF _____

City or Town _____

On the _____ day of _____, 19_____, personally appeared

_____ and _____ known to me to be the individuals who executed the foregoing instrument, and acknowledged the same to be their free act and deed, before me.

(Notary Seal)

_____
Notary Public

Received for record _____ at _____. Attest: _____

Date   Time   Clerk

Revocation of Trust

This instrument of revocation made this _____ day of _____, 19____,

by _____;

WHEREAS, by Declaration of Trust dated _____, 19____,
I created in writing a Revocable Trust as a result of which a beneficial interest in:

_____

(Describe the trust asset)

_____ accrued to:

Check

One

     _____ the following individual

     _____ the following individuals as primary and contingent beneficiary respectively

     _____ the following individuals, to share equally

     _____ the following individual as primary beneficiary, with my children, sharing equally, as contingent beneficiaries

_____

_____

_____; and

WHEREAS, by the terms of the said Declaration of Trust, I reserve the full power and right to revoke said Trust at any time without the consent of or notice to any beneficiary of said Trust created by me;

NOW, THEREFORE, pursuant to the power and right of revocation aforesaid, I do hereby revoke in its entirety the Trust created by me by the aforesaid Declaration of Trust, to the end that as of the date of this instrument of revocation, I hold the former trust property free and discharged of all the Trust's terms and provisions in said Declaration of Trust contained.

_____   _____ L.S.
       Witness   *Signature of First Settlor*

_____
       Witness

STATE OF _____   City
                              or

COUNTY OF _____   Town _____

On the _____ day of _____, 19____, personally appeared

_____

known to me to be the individual(s) who executed the foregoing instrument, and acknowledged the same to be _____ free act and deed, before me.

_____

(Notary Seal)   *Notary Public*

Revocation of Trust

This instrument of revocation made this _____ day of _____, 19_____,

by _____ and _____ ;

WHEREAS, by Declaration of Trust dated _____, 19_____,
we created in writing a Revocable Trust as a result of which a beneficial interest in:

_____

(Describe the trust asset)

_____ accrued to:

Check   _____ the following individual

        _____ the following individuals as primary and contingent beneficiary respectively

One   _____ the following individuals, to share equally

_____

_____

_____ ; and

WHEREAS, by the terms of the said Declaration of Trust, we reserve the full power and right to revoke said Trust at any time without the consent of or notice to any beneficiary of said Trust created by us;

NOW, THEREFORE, pursuant to the power and right of revocation aforesaid, we do hereby revoke in its entirety the Trust created by us by the aforesaid Declaration of Trust, to the end that as of the date of this instrument of revocation, we hold the former trust property free and discharged of all the Trust's terms and provisions in said Declaration of Trust contained.

_____   _____ L.S.
              Witness   *Signature of First Settlor*

_____   _____ L.S.
              Witness   *Signature of Second Settlor*

STATE OF _____ ⎱   City
                                                                  or
COUNTY OF _____ ⎰   Town _____

On the _____ day of _____, 19_____, personally appeared

_____ and _____
known to me to be the individuals who executed the foregoing instrument, and acknowledged the same to be their free act and deed, before me.

_____

(Notary Seal)   *Notary Public*

CHAPTER 27

What Action Should Your Successor Trustee Take?

1. IF THE TRUST ASSET IS REAL ESTATE HELD IN ONE NAME:

(A) **If you are the Successor Trustee/beneficiary named in a Declaration of Trust DT-101 or DT-102,** use the "Successor Trustee's Quit Claim Deed" (ST-QCD) which will be found on page 547, and

1. In the space provided on line one of the quit claim deed, enter your name;
2. In the space provided on line two, enter the name of the individual who established the trust;
3. In the space provided on line three, enter the date the declaration of trust was executed;
4. In the space provided on line four, enter your own name again;
5. In the space provided at line five, enter the description of the real estate as it appeared in the declaration of trust;
6. In the space provided on line six, *sign* your name *on* the line, before two witnesses, and *print* your name clearly just *below* the line;
7. In the space provided on line seven, enter again the name of the person who created the trust.
8. On line eight, enter again the date of the original declaration of trust of which you are serving as Successor Trustee.
9. File the quit claim deed, together with a copy of the declaration of trust and a certified copy of the Settlor's death certificate, in the same land records office where the declaration of trust was filed originally.

(B) **If as Successor Trustee you are one of the beneficiaries named in a Declaration of Trust DT-103,** you and the other beneficiaries must first decide whether you wish to retain the real estate or sell it.

1. If you and the other beneficiaries decide to *retain* the real estate, complete the Successor Trustee's Quit Claim Deed (ST-QCD) exactly as specified in (A) above, *except* that, in the space provided on line four, list all of the beneficiaries named in the declaration of trust

of which you are serving as Successor Trustee. Then, file the completed quit claim deed, together with a copy of the declaration of trust and a certified copy of the Settlor's death certificate, in the same land records office where the declaration of trust was filed originally.

2. If you and the other beneficiaries have decided to *sell* the real estate, you may do so in your capacity as Successor Trustee, giving the buyer a warranty deed signed "(your name), Successor Trustee under Declaration of Trust executed by (name of Settlor) under date of (date of the declaration of trust under which you were appointed)."

(C) **If, as Successor Trustee for minor beneficiaries under DT-101, DT-102, or DT-103,** you are assuming administration of a trust established by one Settlor, execute the "Successor Trustee's Notice," which appears on page 551, and file it, together with a copy of the declaration of trust by which the trust was established and a certified copy of the Settlor's death certificate, in the same land records office where the declaration of trust was filed originally.

(D) **If you are the Successor Trustee/First Beneficiary named in a declaration of trust DT-104,** use ST-QCD following the instructions in (A) above. If you are Successor Trustee but *not* a beneficiary named in the DT-104:

1. If the beneficiaries are *over* age 21, proceed as in (B) 1 or (B) 2 above, depending upon the decision of the beneficiaries as to the disposition of the real estate.
2. If the beneficiaries are *under* age 21, complete the "Successor Trustee's Notice" and file it, together with a copy of the declaration of trust under which this trust was established and a certified copy of the Settlor's death certificate, in the same land records office where the declaration of trust was filed originally.

2. IF THE TRUST ASSET IS REAL ESTATE HELD IN JOINT NAMES:

(E) **If you are the Successor Trustee/beneficiary named in a Declaration of Trust DT-101-J, or DT-102-J,** use the "Successor Trustee's Quit Claim Deed–Joint" (ST-QCD-J) which will be found on page 549, and

1. In the space provided on line one of the quit claim deed, enter your name;
2. In the spaces provided on line two, enter the names of the two Settlors who established the joint trust;
3. In the space provided on line three, enter the date the declaration of trust was executed;
4. In the space provided on line four, enter your own name again;
5. In the space provided on line five, enter the description of the real estate as it appeared in the declaration of trust;
6. In the space provided on line six, *sign* your name *on* the line before two witnesses and *print* your name clearly just *below* the line;
7. In the space provided on line seven, enter again the names of the two persons who established the joint trust.
8. In the space provided on line eight, enter again the date on which the original joint declaration of trust was issued.
9. File the quit claim deed, together with a copy of the declaration of trust under which you were appointed, and certified copies of the death certificates of the two Settlors, in the same land records office where the declaration of trust was filed originally.

(F) **If as Successor Trustee you are one of the beneficiaries named in a Declaration of Trust DT-103-J,** you and the other beneficiaries must first decide whether you wish to retain the real estate or sell it.

1. If you and the other beneficiaries decide to *retain* the real estate, complete the "Successor Trustee's Quit Claim Deed–Joint" (ST-QCD-J) exactly as specified in (E) above, *except* that in the space provided on line four, list the names of all of the beneficiaries named in the declaration of trust of which you are serving as Successor Trustee, including your own name. Then, file the completed quit claim deed, together with a copy of the declaration of trust and certified copies of the death certificates of the two Settlors, in the same land records office where the declaration of trust was filed originally.
2. If you and the other beneficiaries have decided to *sell* the real estate, you may do so in your capacity as Successor Trustee, giving the buyer a warranty deed signed "(your name), Successor Trustee under Declaration of Trust executed by (name of first Settlor) and (name of second Settlor) under date of (date of the declaration of trust under which you were appointed)."

(G) **If as Successor Trustee for minor beneficiaries under DT-101-J, DT-102-J, or DT-103-J** you are assuming administration of a trust established by two persons as joint trustees, execute the "Successor Trustee's Notice" on page 551, and file it, together with a copy of the declaration of trust and certified copies of the death certificates of the two Settlors, in the same land records office where the declaration of trust was filed originally.

NOTE:

If you, as the beneficiary who is receiving the real estate, wish to create a *new* trust naming one or more beneficiaries to receive the property at *your* death, a suitable declaration of trust in Chapter 7 should be selected and executed. Then complete the Successor Trustee's quit claim deed, entering on line four "(your name), Trustee under Declaration of Trust dated (date you sign the new declaration)." File both in the land records office, along with a copy of the old declaration of trust and death certificate as explained above.

---

3. IF THE TRUST ASSET IS A CHECKING OR SAVINGS ACCOUNT:

Display to the bank the declaration of trust under which you are named as Successor Trustee and the death certificate of the Settlor (both death certificates if there were two Settlors holding a joint trust) and instruct the bank to reregister the account as you direct, or to close it and deliver to you a check for the proceeds.

4. IF THE TRUST ASSET IS A STOCK, A BOND, OR A MUTUAL FUND:

Write to the issuer or transfer agent (or custodian bank, in the case of a mutual fund) saying:

Gentlemen:

Enclosed find certificate no. _____ for _____ shares of XYZ common registered in the name of (the deceased), Trustee u/d/t dated _____.

Such registered owner is now deceased, a death certificate being enclosed. Also enclosed is a copy of the trust instrument under which the shares were held, which instrument appoints the undersigned as Successor Trustee. Enclosed, too, is a signed stock power with signature guaranteed.

Kindly reregister the shares as follows:

Mary Smith
500 Main Street
Smithville, Mich.

Very truly yours,

_____

Mary Smith, Successor Trustee under Declaration of Trust executed by John Smith under date of _____.

A stock power is a piece of paper on which is printed the same thing that appears on the back of every stock certificate. It must be completed whenever securities are sold or transferred to another person. You can obtain a stock power from the broker through whom the securities were purchased or from the collateral loan department of a commercial bank. The signature must be "guaranteed" by either a commercial bank (not a savings bank) or a member firm of the New York Stock Exchange. Don't fill it in; just sign it as you have signed the letter above.

If the trust assets are mutual fund shares held in an accumulation account with the fund's custodian bank, alter your letter to simply refer to the account number and ask that the account be reregistered in your name.

5. OTHER TYPES OF ASSETS:

Type of asset	Who to be in touch with	What to tell them
Brokerage account	The brokerage firm where the account is maintained	Display the declaration of trust and a death certificate and direct them to transfer title to the account to you.
Safe deposit box	The bank where the box is maintained	Display the declaration of trust and a death certificate and direct them to make the box available to you.
Mortgage, first trust deed, or real estate sales contract	Land records office and the other party to the contract	Type a document similar to the Successor Trustee's Notice except delete the words "real property" and substitute *"mortgage," "first trust deed,"* or *"real estate sales contract,"* as the case may be, and file it in the land records office together with a copy of the declaration of trust and a death certificate.
Royalties on literary work or musical composition	The other party to the royalty contract	Display the declaration of trust and a death certificate and ask them to change their records to reflect that you are now the owner of the rights.
Royalties on patent rights	Company to whom the patent has been licensed	Display the declaration of trust and a death certificate and ask them to change their records to reflect that you are now the owner of the patent and the one entitled to the royalties.
Partnership interest	The partnership	Display the declaration of trust and negotiate an agreement with them on the partnership interest.
Motor vehicle	Motor Vehicle Department	Display the declaration of trust and the death certificate and request the transfer of the registration.
Trailer	Governmental agency or department registering or licensing the trailer	Display the declaration of trust and a death certificate and request transfer of the registration.

| Unincorporated business | The bank where the business's account is maintained | Display the declaration of trust and a death certificate, and state that you wish to execute a new signature card in connection with the account. |

To All People To Whom These Presents Shall Come, Greetings;

KNOW YE, THAT I, _____ as

Successor Trustee under Declaration of Trust executed by _____

under date of _____, and pursuant to the instructions
contained in said Declaration of Trust, do by these presents hereby release and forever Quit-Claim

unto _____

_____,

as beneficiary(ies) under said Declaration, all right, title and demand whatsoever which I as Successor Trustee under such instrument and as Releasor hereunder have or ought to have in or to the property located at:

To Have and to Hold the premises, with all the appurtenances, forever; and I declare and agree that as Successor Trustee, I shall have or make no claim or demand upon such property.

IN WITNESS WHEREOF, I have hereunto set my hand and seal this _____ day of _____, 19_____.

Signed, sealed and delivered in presence of

(Sign your name) _____ L.S.

(Print your name)_____

_____

Witness (1)

Successor Trustee under Declaration of Trust executed

by _____

_____

Witness (2)

under date of _____.

STATE OF _____

COUNTY OF _____

City
or
Town _____

Personally appeared before me this _____ day of _____, 19_____,

_____ known to me to be the signer and sealer

of the foregoing instrument, and acknowledged the same to be his/her free act and deed.

(Notary Seal)

_____
Notary Public

Received for record _____ at _____. Attest:_____

Date   Time   Clerk

SUCCESSOR TRUSTEE'S
QUIT CLAIM DEED—JOINT

To All People To Whom These Presents Shall Come, Greetings;

KNOW YE, THAT I, _____ as

Successor Trustee under Declaration of Trust executed by _____ and _____

under date of _____, pursuant to the instructions
contained in said Declaration of Trust, do by these presents hereby release and forever Quit-Claim

unto _____

_____

as beneficiary(ies) under said Declaration, all right, title and demand whatsoever which I as Successor Trustee under such
instrument and as Releasor hereunder have or ought to have in or to the property located at:

To Have and to Hold the premises, with all the appurtenances, forever; and I declare and agree that as Successor Trustee, I
shall have or make no claim or demand upon such property.

IN WITNESS WHEREOF, I have hereunto set my hand and seal this _____ day of _____, 19_____.

Signed, sealed and delivered in presence of   (Sign) _____ L.S.

_____   (Printed) _____

Witness (1)

_____

Witness (2)

Successor Trustee under Declaration of Trust executed by

_____ and _____

under date of _____, 19_____.

STATE OF _____   City
or
COUNTY OF _____   Town _____

Personally appeared before me this _____ day of _____, 19_____,

_____ known to me to be the signer and sealer

of the foregoing instrument, and acknowledged the same to be his/her free act and deed.

(Notary Seal)   *Notary Public*

Received for record _____ at _____. Attest:_____
          Date   *Time*   *Clerk*

Successor Trustee's Notice

TO WHOM IT MAY CONCERN:

The undersigned Successor Trustee under Declaration of Trust (see copy appended) executed by

_____ and _____
(Name of Settlor)   *(Name of second Settlor, if a joint trust)*

under date of _____, hereby gives notice that the Settlor (or both Settlors, if a joint trust) being now incapacitated within the meaning of Paragraph 1 of said Declaration of Trust, or deceased (see death certificate[s] appended), he has assumed the duties of Successor Trustee as specified in Paragraph 7 of the said Declaration of Trust.

WHEREFORE, he hereby serves notice that in his capacity as such Successor Trustee he has this day assumed title to the real property and/or other assets covered by said Declaration of Trust, and will hereafter administer the same in accordance with the instructions set forth in the said Declaration of Trust.

This instrument dated _____ , 19_____.

Witness (1) _____   (Signed) _____ L.S.

                                                     Successor Trustee under Declaration of Trust

Witness (2) _____   executed by_____
                                                         (Name of Settlor)

                                                         and by _____
                                                         (Name of second Settlor, if a joint trust)

                                                         under date of _____, 19 _____.

STATE OF _____   City
                                                         or
COUNTY OF _____   Town _____

On the _____ day of _____, 19_____, personally

appeared _____, known to me to be the individual who

executed the foregoing instrument, and acknowledged the same to be his/her free act and deed, before me.

(Notary Seal)

_____
Notary Public

CHAPTER 28

Taxes on Your Living Trust

The Internal Revenue Service has finally discovered the one-party revocable inter vivos trust and is rewriting its regulations relating to such trusts. Until now, the Department has been guided by regulations written during a previous generation when such a trust was relatively unknown.

Those regulations lumped all trusts into one category and specified that every trustee must apply for an "employer identification number" and file a tax return annually on a Form 1041 instead of the Form 1040 universally used by individuals. Don't ask me what an "employer identification number" has to do with a trust which is not an employer and has no employees—I've asked the IRS in Washington and they simply shrugged and explained that, actually, nobody there knew why it was so designated.

Until now, one was supposed to apply for the separate "employer identification number" for *each* individual trust established—one for *each* bank account, *each* stock or bond, *each* piece of real estate, and so on. One client of mine set up ninety-six separate trusts. In theory, the regulations called for him to apply for the issuance of ninety-six tax numbers and file ninety-six separate tax returns. If he had done so, each time he sold one stock and bought another, one existing number would become obsolete and he'd have to apply for a new one covering the new purchase. He wouldn't bother reporting the discards, of course, and in time the IRS computer would be showing an accumulation of dead numbers which it would assume were on active status. After two or three years, the computer would crank up and begin sending out letters asking why he'd stopped filing returns.

Well, he didn't do any of these things, of course. Instead, he simply meticulously reported the income from all of the trusts on his personal income tax return, Form 1040, just as if he had never set up the trusts. Actually, he did Uncle Sam a favor by not putting him through all the paper-shuffling involved in issuing and canceling a lot of tax numbers.

Considering that it is estimated that more than ten million such trusts have been established, with most settlors following my advice and simply providing their Social Security number instead of the "employer's identification number," the government should be grateful for the paper-shuffling saved them. The IRS has now advised me that it is rewriting the regulations to provide that in the case of a one-party inter vivos trust *in which the Settlor is his own trustee* and faithfully reports the income as his own income, it will henceforth waive the requirement that a separate tax number be applied for, and that the income can be reported on Form 1040. The taxpayer should show his appreciation for the Treasury's cooperative attitude by reporting the income meticulously on his Form 1040 along with his other income. It's a different story, of course, if after the death of the Settlor the assets are held in continuing trust for a minor beneficiary. The Successor Trustee *will* be required to apply for a separate tax number since the income collected is not his own.

As to death taxes: Below is a table showing the taxes payable on the estates of a man and his wife where he leaves everything to her at his death and comparing these with the total of the taxes payable on the same two estates where he has set up a trust under Form DT-153, DT-154, DT-155, or DT-156 provided in this book. The tax benefits of the trust will be immediately apparent.

	Total tax, estates of husband and wife, assuming that first spouse to die owns all property and . . .		
Value of property subject to tax	entire estate is left to survivor outright	. . . half of estate is left to survivor in a tax-saving trust	TAXES SAVED BY USE OF TRUST
$178,290	$ —	$ —	$ —
180,000	520	—	520
200,000	6,600	—	6,600
220,000	12,520	—	12,520
250,000	21,400	—	21,400
300,000	37,200	—	37,200
350,000	52,600	—	52,600
400,000	68,000	13,200	54,800
450,000	87,967	28,000	59,967
500,000	113,609	42,800	70,809
550,000	134,931	58,600	76,331
600,000	156,724	74,400	82,324
650,000	178,383	89,800	88,583
700,000	200,042	105,200	94,842
750,000	221,701	120,600	101,101
800,000	243,104	136,000	107,104
850,000	264,911	151,400	113,511
900,000	287,077	166,800	120,277
950,000	309,244	182,200	127,044
1,000,000	331,401	197,600	133,801

COMPARATIVE COSTS
OF SIX ESTATE TRANSFER METHODS

In this illustration we will assume the situation of one man with a total estate of $300,000 and another with an estate of $500,000. We will show how the net value of those estates to the heirs can vary greatly, depending upon which of six methods are selected for their distribution and management. In calculating transfer costs, we include federal estate taxes plus (a) state inheritance taxes and (b) *minimum* general and administrative expenses which prevail in Connecticut. The variation for residents of other states will not significantly alter the basic picture presented here. Our man is married and has two adult children, except that in the first transfer method we assume that his wife predeceases him. His wife has no separate estate. Transfer costs include those which apply on the transfer of property upon the death of the husband and his wife, thus showing the total shrinkage in passing the property to the next generation.

The first transfer method deals with the estate of an unmarried person who first wants to benefit a sister and/or parent and then, upon that individual's death, to have the estate go to nieces and nephews.

Method A

The man wills his estate outright to his sister and/or parent, who then, in turn, wills it outright to nieces and nephews.

or, alternatively

The same man wills his estate in trust for his sister and/or parent and upon the sister or parent's death, the trust terminates and the assets pass to the nieces and nephews.

Method B

The man's estate is willed to his wife outright, who in turn bequeaths it outright to their children.

Method C

The man's estate is willed to a trust, with income to his wife for life and the property to their children at her death.

Method D

The man wills to his wife outright an amount which permits his estate to qualify for the maximum marital allowance. The balance is left in trust for his wife. Upon her death, her marital allowance share plus the balance in trust passes outright to the children.

Method E (The Dacey "Family Trust," plus individual Declarations of Trust)

The man creates a "Family Trust" and then covers each of his assets with a declaration of trust, causing the asset

to pass to the family trust at his death. Thereafter, the income from the trust goes to his wife during her lifetime. Upon her death, her marital allowance share plus the balance in trust passes outright to the children. If he prefers, under Method E he can transfer all his assets to the family trust during his lifetime. Thereafter, he can observe the trustee's administration of those assets and thus watch his plan in operation, affording him an opportunity to change the plan if he is dissatisfied with its operation. This method accomplishes maximum savings in taxes and administration costs for his estate.

% of Estate Lost in Taxes and
Administration Fees

$300,000 Estate $500,000 Estate

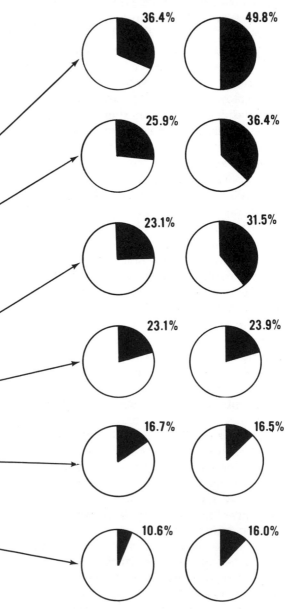

You'll Still Need a Will!

If you have read the foregoing chapters thoughtfully, careful selection and execution of one or more of the instruments provided should make it possible for you to eliminate completely the necessity for probating your estate. That doesn't mean, however, that you shouldn't have a will. It is not possible to anticipate and thus to exempt from probate every last asset with which you may be endowed at the time of your death.

For example, let's suppose that you have carefully inventoried every scrap of property you own and have covered each with an inter vivos trust arrangement excluding it from the jurisdiction of the probate court. On the way downtown tomorrow morning, your car is struck by a skidding truck, causing you fatal injuries. Your estate sues and collects a large financial settlement from the owner of the truck.

What is to become of that settlement? Who is to get it if you have left no will? You will have died "intestate" and the laws of the state in which you live will determine which of your relatives are entitled to share the wealth which your untimely passing has created. The persons whom the law designates as beneficiaries are not necessarily the same ones you might designate. It is important, then, that you have a will just in case there are some loose ends to your estate which you have not anticipated. If everything goes as you planned, and everything you leave is covered by an inter vivos trust, there'll be nothing to probate and your family can simply forget the will. It will be there, however, if it is needed.

Minor children are another important reason for having a will. If one parent dies, it is accepted without argument that the children continue in the custody of the surviving parent. If both parents die in a common accident or disaster, however, or if the surviving parent dies while any child is still legally a minor, the probate court will be called upon to act. By naming successor trustees for minor beneficiaries in any living trusts that you establish, you make it unneccessary for the court to appoint a special guardian of the *property* of your child. But there must also be a guardian of the child's *person*. Guardianship is a matter of state law, and there may be variances among the states. However, an underlying rule which appears to be universal is that an orphaned child is basically a ward of the court. In a will, a parent may name a guardian of a child's property receivable under the will, though not of his other property. Curiously, a parent has no *absolute* right to name a guardian of the child's person; the nomination amounts to little more than a request, with the court reserving the right to exercise its own judgment. At least, though, the will in which you name a guardian of your child's person will serve to indicate your wishes to the court.

Some wills are simple, brief, and to the point. Others, like the Mississippi, roll on and on, incorporating a heritage of three centuries or more of ponderous phrases and legalistic mumbo jumbo. This has come to be accepted practice and I suspect that if the average man were to be offered a will written in simple, straightforward modern-day English, without the usual complement of "whereas's," "now, therefore's" and "know all men by these presents," he'd feel cheated.

To supplement the selection of trust instruments which you have already examined, I have prepared a series of concise will forms which appear on the pages which follow. From among them, most readers can select an instrument which fits their particular situation and meets their particular needs. I've sprinkled a few "whereas's" and "now, therefore's" here and there to give them that traditional look, so you won't feel cheated. The instruments, numbered from 1 to 14, are first summarized in a series of explanatory notes which include precise instructions on filling out the form.

If there is something minor in a will which is not correct, you may cross it out and/or write in a few words to make it correct. Be sure to initial the change. If the alterations are other than minor, don't use the printed will; have it retyped correctly.

You must sign the will in the presence of three witnesses and a notary public. Yes, I know, some states require only two witnesses but the law may change or you may move, so humor me and make sure your will is ironclad. The three witnesses must be adults. They must be "disinterested" persons—that is, they must not benefit in any way from the terms and provisions of your will. They must be together and they must actually *see* you sign the will. The notary is there not to notarize *your* signature but the witnesses' signatures on the affidavit which is appended to the will. Actually, I know of no state that requires that the witnesses' signatures be notarized, but if there were no such affidavit, the witnesses would be called upon to appear in court when your will was being offered for probate to testify orally to the facts included in the affidavit. Against the possibility of their having died or being otherwise unavailable, the sworn affidavit makes their personal appearance unnecessary.

The execution of a will is an extremely serious business. There is an established procedure which must be strictly observed. This is no place for original ideas or shortcuts. Immediately following this section is a "script" covering the signing of a will. Follow it exactly.

Do everything slowly, methodically. Make sure you have it right. When you have filled out the form, before signing it make a photocopy. You, the witnesses, and the notary sign the *original* only. Nobody *signs* the copy; *print in* the names of all those who have signed the original, which should be put away in a safe place where it will be found by the people you want to have find it. If your only heirs at law are your two sisters, and you've left everything to one of them, the other one can get half of your estate after your death by getting to your will first and burning it. Many an unscrupulous relative has shared in an estate illegally by the simple process of finding and destroying a will which cut him off. Make sure your will is safe.

WILL FORM W-1	HUSBAND'S WILL LEAVING EVERYTHING TO WIFE, OR TO SOME <u>ONE</u> OTHER PERSON IF HIS WIFE DOES NOT SURVIVE HIM

Example:
John Smith and his wife Mary are childless. Mr. Smith wishes to leave his estate to his wife at his death. If Mrs. Smith does not survive him, though, he wishes his estate to go to his sister.

Procedure:
Using Will Form W-1, Mr. Smith:

1. Enters his name and place of residence at the top;

2. Enters his wife's name ("Mary Smith," not "Mrs. John Smith") in Paragraph "Second";

3. Enters his sister's name and address in Paragraph "Third";

4. Enters his wife's name as Executrix in the first sentence of Paragraph "Fourth." In the second sentence of Paragraph "Fourth" he enters the name of an adult to serve as Executor or Executrix if his wife does not survive him. This could be the contingent beneficiary (his sister) if she is not a minor;

5. Signs the document in the presence of three adult, disinterested witnesses and a notary public.

WILL FORM W-2	WIFE'S WILL LEAVING EVERYTHING TO HUSBAND, OR TO SOME <u>ONE</u> OTHER PERSON IF HER HUSBAND DOES NOT SURVIVE HER

Example:
John Smith and his wife Mary are childless. Mrs. Smith wishes to leave her estate to her husband at her death. If Mr. Smith does not survive her, though, she wishes her estate to go to her nephew.

Procedure:
Using Will Form W-2, Mrs. Smith:

1. Enters her name and place of residence at the top;

2. Enters her husband's name in Paragraph "Second";

3. Enters her nephew's name and address in Paragraph "Third";

4. Enters her husband's name as Executor in the first sentence of Paragraph "Fourth." In the second sentence of Paragraph "Fourth" she enters the name of an adult to serve as Executor or Executrix if her husband does not survive her. This could be the contingent beneficiary (her nephew) if he is not a minor;

5. Signs the document in the presence of three adult, disinterested witnesses and a notary public.

<table>
<tr><td>WILL FORM
W-3</td><td>HUSBAND'S WILL LEAVING EVERYTHING TO WIFE OR, IF SHE DOES NOT SURVIVE HIM, TO TWO OR MORE OTHER PERSONS WHOSE CHILDREN WILL TAKE THEIR SHARE IF THEY ARE NOT LIVING</td></tr>
</table>

Example:

John Smith and his wife Mary are childless. Mr. Smith wishes to leave his estate to his wife at his death. If Mrs. Smith does not survive him, though, he wishes his estate to be divided among his three sisters. The share of any sister not then living is to go to that sister's children in equal shares. If the deceased sister has left no children, Mr. Smith wants her share to be divided equally between his two surviving sisters.

Procedure:

Using Will Form W-3, Mr. Smith:

1. Enters his name and place of residence at the top;

2. Enters his wife's name in Paragraph "Second";

3. Enters in Paragraph "Third" the *number* of sisters to share his estate if his wife does not survive him, and their names;

4. Enters his wife's name as Executrix in the first sentence of Paragraph "Fourth." In the second sentence of Paragraph "Fourth" he enters the name of the person whom he wishes to have serve as Executor or Executrix if his wife does not survive him;

5. Signs the document in the presence of three adult, disinterested witnesses and a notary public.

<table>
<tr><td>WILL FORM
W-4</td><td>WIFE'S WILL LEAVING EVERYTHING TO HUSBAND OR, IF HE DOES NOT SURVIVE HER, TO TWO OR MORE OTHER PERSONS WHOSE CHILDREN WILL TAKE THEIR SHARE IF THEY ARE NOT LIVING</td></tr>
</table>

Example:

John and Mary Smith are childless. Mrs. Smith wishes to leave her estate to her husband at her death. If Mr. Smith does not survive her, though, she wishes her estate to be divided among her three nephews. The share of any nephew not then living is to go to that nephew's children in equal shares. If the deceased nephew has left no children, Mrs. Smith wants his share to be divided equally between her two surviving nephews.

Procedure:

Using Will Form W-4, Mrs. Smith:

1. Enters her name and place of residence at the top;

2. Enters her husband's name in Paragraph "Second";

3. Enters in Paragraph "Third" the *number* of nephews to share her estate, and their names;

4. Enters her husband's name as Executor in the first sentence in Paragraph "Fourth." In the second sentence of Paragraph "Fourth" she enters the name of the person whom she wishes to have serve as Executor or Executrix if her husband does not survive her;

5. Signs the document in the presence of three adult, disinterested witnesses and a notary public.

WILL FORM
W-5

HUSBAND'S WILL LEAVING EVERYTHING TO WIFE OR, IF SHE DOES NOT SURVIVE HIM, TO TWO OR MORE OTHER PERSONS, SHARING EQUALLY; IF ONE OF SUCH PERSONS DIES, THE SURVIVING PERSONS WILL DIVIDE HIS SHARE

Example:
John Smith and his wife Mary are childless. Mr. Smith wishes to leave his estate to his wife at his death. If Mrs. Smith does not survive him, though, he wishes his estate to be divided among his three brothers. The share of any brother who does not survive Mr. Smith is to be divided equally between the surviving brothers.

Procedure:
Using Will Form W-5, Mr. Smith:

1. Enters his name and place of residence at the top;

2. Enters his wife's name in Paragraph "Second";

3. Enters in Paragraph "Third" the *number* of brothers to share his estate if his wife does not survive him, and their names;

4. Enters his wife's name as Executrix in the first sentence of Paragraph "Fourth." In the second sentence of Paragraph "Fourth" he enters the name of the person whom he wishes to have serve as Executor or Executrix if his wife does not survive him;

5. Signs the document in the presence of three adult, disinterested witnesses and a notary public.

WILL FORM
W-6

WIFE'S WILL LEAVING EVERYTHING TO HUSBAND OR, IF HE DOES NOT SURVIVE HER, TO TWO OR MORE OTHER PERSONS, SHARING EQUALLY; IF ONE OF SUCH PERSONS DIES, THE SURVIVING PERSONS WILL DIVIDE HIS SHARE

Example:
John Smith and his wife Mary are childless. Mrs. Smith wishes to leave her estate to her husband at her death. If Mr. Smith does not survive her, though, she wishes her estate to be divided among her three nieces. The share of any niece who does not survive Mrs. Smith is to be divided equally between the surviving nieces.

Procedure:
Using Will Form W-6, Mrs. Smith:

1. Enters her name and place of residence at the top;

2. Enters her husband's name in Paragraph "Second";

3. Enters in Paragraph "Third" the *number* of nieces to share her estate if her husband does not survive her, and names them;

4. Enters her husband's name as Executor in the first sentence of Paragraph "Fourth." In the second sentence of Paragraph "Fourth" she enters the name of the person whom she wishes to have serve as Executor or Executrix if her husband does not survive her;

5. Signs the document in the presence of three adult, disinterested witnesses and a notary public.

WILL FORM
W-7

WILL LEAVING EVERYTHING TO TWO OR MORE PERSONS TO SHARE EQUALLY; IF ONE OF SUCH PERSONS DIES, HIS CHILDREN WILL TAKE HIS SHARE

Example:

John Smith is unmarried. He wishes to leave his estate to his three sisters at his death. If any sister does not survive him, he wishes the share of that sister to go to her children, in equal shares. If the deceased sister left no children, he wishes her share to be divided equally by his two surviving sisters.

Procedure:

Using Will Form W-7, Mr. Smith:

1. Enters his name and place of residence at the top;

2. Enters in Paragraph "Second" the *number* of sisters to share his estate, and their names;

3. Enters in Paragraph "Third" the name of the person whom he wishes to appoint as Executor/Executrix of his estate;

4. Signs the document in the presence of three adult, disinterested witnesses and a notary public.

WILL FORM
W-8

WILL LEAVING EVERYTHING TO TWO OR MORE PERSONS TO SHARE EQUALLY; IF ONE OF SUCH PERSONS DIES, THE SURVIVING PERSONS WILL DIVIDE HIS SHARE

Example:

Mary Smith is unmarried. She wishes to leave her estate to three distant relatives at her death. If any such relative does not survive her, she wishes that relative's share to be divided equally between the surviving relatives.

Procedure:

Using Will Form W-8, Miss Smith:

1. Enters her name and place of residence at the top;

2. Enters in Paragraph "Second" the *number* of persons to share her estate, and their names *and addresses* (if they are distant relatives, she may be the only one who knows their addresses);

3. Enters in Paragraph "Third" the name of the person whom she wishes to appoint as Executor/Executrix of her estate;

4. Signs the document in the presence of three adult, disinterested witnesses and a notary public.

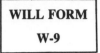

WILL FORM W-9   **WILL OF HUSBAND AND FATHER LEAVING EVERYTHING TO HIS WIFE, AND TO HIS CHILDREN IF HIS WIFE DOES NOT SURVIVE HIM**

Example:

John and Mary Smith have three children. Mr. Smith wishes to leave everything to his wife, and if she does not survive him, he wishes it to go to his children in equal shares. The share of any child who does not survive him is to go to that child's issue, in equal shares. If any child dies leaving no issue, that child's share is to be divided between the surviving children.

Procedure:

Using Will Form W-9, Mr. Smith:

1. Enters his name and place of residence at the top;

2. Enters the name of his wife in Paragraph "Second";

3. Enters in Paragraph "Fourth" the name of the person whom he wishes to have serve as guardian of his children if his wife does not survive him;

4. Enters the name of his wife as Executrix in the first sentence of Paragraph "Fifth." In the second sentence of Paragraph "Fifth" he enters the name of the person whom he wishes to have serve as Executor/Executrix if his wife does not survive him;

5. Signs the document in the presence of three adult, disinterested witnesses and a notary public.

WILL FORM W-10   **WILL OF WIFE AND MOTHER LEAVING EVERYTHING TO HER HUSBAND, AND TO HER CHILDREN IF HER HUSBAND DOES NOT SURVIVE HER**

Example:

John and Mary Smith have three children. Mrs. Smith wishes to leave everything to her husband, and if he does not survive her, she wishes it to go to her children in equal shares. The share of any child who does not survive her is to go to that child's issue in equal shares. If any child dies leaving no issue, that child's share is to be divided between the surviving children.

Procedure:

Using Will Form W-10, Mrs. Smith:

1. Enters her name and place of residence at the top;

2. Enters the name of her husband in Paragraph "Second";

3. Enters in Paragraph "Fourth" the name of the person whom she wishes to have serve as guardian of her children if her husband does not survive her;

4. Enters the name of her husband as Executor in the first sentence of Paragraph "Fifth." In the second sentence of Paragraph "Fifth" she enters the name of the person whom she wishes to have serve as Executor/Executrix if her husband does not survive her;

5. Signs the document in the presence of three adult, disinterested witnesses and a notary public.

WILL FORM	WILL FOR INDIVIDUAL WHO HAS ESTABLISHED A FAMILY TRUST;
W-11	**INCORPORATES THE BALANCE OF HIS ESTATE INTO THE TRUST**

Example:

John Smith has established a family trust. He wishes to leave his personal effects to Mrs. Smith but any stocks, bonds, cash, or real estate which he owns at the time of his death are to be added to his trust account.

Procedure:

Using Will Form W-11, Mr. Smith:

1. Enters his name and place of residence at the top;

2. Enters his wife's name in Paragraph "Second";

3. Enters in Paragraph "Third" the name and location of the person or bank with whom he has established the family trust, and the date of the trust instrument;

4. Enters in Paragraph "Fourth" the name of the person whom he wishes to appoint as guardian of his children (if they be minors) if his wife does not survive him;

5. Enters in Paragraph "Sixth" the name of the trustee of his trust to serve also as Executor;

6. Signs the document in the presence of three adult, disinterested witnesses and a notary public.

WILL FORM	WILL FOR WIFE OF INDIVIDUAL WHO HAS ESTABLISHED A FAMILY TRUST;
W-12	**LEAVES EVERYTHING TO HER HUSBAND IF HE SURVIVES HER; IF HE DOES NOT**
	SURVIVE HER, INCORPORATES HER ESTATE INTO HIS FAMILY TRUST

Example:

John and Mary Smith have three children. Mr. Smith has established a family trust. Mrs. Smith wishes to leave everything to her husband if he survives her. If he does not survive her, she wishes her personal effects to go to their children, but any stocks, bonds, cash, or real estate which she owns at her death are to be added to his family trust.

Procedure:

Using Will Form W-12, Mrs. Smith:

1. Enters her name and place of residence at the top;

2. Enters her husband's name in Paragraph "Second";

3. Enters in Paragraph "Third" the name of the trustee of the family trust which her husband has established, and the date of his agreement with that trustee;

4. Enters her husband's name as Executor in the first sentence of Paragraph "Fourth." In the second sentence of Paragraph "Fourth" she enters the name of her husband's trustee as Executor of her estate if her husband does not survive her;

5. Signs the document in the presence of three adult, disinterested witnesses and a notary public.

WILL FORM	**WILL OF PARENT LEAVING EVERYTHING TO HIS/HER CHILDREN TO SHARE**
W-13	**EQUALLY; IF ONE CHILD DIES, SUCH CHILD'S ISSUE WILL TAKE HIS SHARE**

Example:

John Smith, a widower, wishes to leave everything to his children. The share of any child who does not survive him is to go to that child's issue, in equal shares. If any such child dies leaving no issue, that child's share is to be divided between John Smith's surviving children.

Procedure:

Using Will Form W-13, Mr. Smith:

1. Enters his name and place of residence at the top;

2. Enters in Paragraph "Third" the name of the person whom he wishes to have serve as the guardian of his children if they be minors at the time of his death;

3. Enters in Paragraph "Fourth" the name of the person he wishes to appoint as Executor/Executrix of the will;

4. Signs the document in the presence of three adult, disinterested witnesses and a notary public.

WILL FORM	**WILL OF PARENT LEAVING EVERYTHING TO HIS/HER CHILDREN TO SHARE**
W-14	**EQUALLY; IF ONE CHILD DIES, THE SURVIVING CHILDREN WILL DIVIDE HIS**
	SHARE

Example:

Mary Smith, a widow, wishes to leave everything to her children. The share of any child who does not survive her is to be divided between her surviving children.

Procedure:

Using Will Form W-14, Mrs. Smith:

1. Enters her name and place of residence at the top;

2. Enters in Paragraph "Third" the name of the person whom she wishes to have serve as the guardian of her children if they be minors at the time of her death;

3. Enters in Paragraph "Fourth" the name of the person she wishes to appoint as Executor/Executrix of the will;

4. Signs the document in the presence of three adult, disinterested witnesses and a notary public.

The testator (the person making the will), the three witnesses, and the notary assemble. The testator signs the will. The three witnesses each sign the will in two places. The following is then said *aloud:*

NOTARY: "John Smith, do you identify this document as your Last Will and Testament, do you wish it to be so regarded, and have you signed it of your own free will?"

TESTATOR: "Yes."

NOTARY: "And have you requested that these persons witness your signature and make an affidavit concerning your execution of this will?"

TESTATOR: "I have."

NOTARY: "The witnesses will please raise their right hands. Do each of you individually declare under oath that Mr. Smith has identified this document as his Last Will and Testament and stated that he wished it to be so regarded?"

WITNESSES: (in unison) "He has."

NOTARY: "Has he signed it in your presence, saying that he was doing so of his own free will, and did he at that time appear to be of sound mind and legal age and free of undue influence?"

WITNESSES: (in unison) "Yes."

NOTARY: "Have you, in his presence and at his request, and in the presence of each other, affixed your signatures to this document as witnesses, and have you made this affidavit at his request?"

WITNESSES: (in unison) "We have."

NOTARY: "You may put your hands down."

The witnesses' affidavit at the end of the will is then notarized.

Last Will and Testament

KNOW ALL MEN BY THESE PRESENTS: That I, _____,

of the City/Town of _____, County of _____

and State of _____, being of sound and disposing mind and memory, do make, publish and

declare the following to be my LAST WILL AND TESTAMENT, hereby revoking all Wills by me at any time heretofore made.

FIRST: I direct my Executrix, hereinafter named, to pay all my funeral expenses, administration expenses of my estate, including inheritance and succession taxes, state or federal, which may be occasioned by the passage of or succession to any interest in my estate under the terms of either this instrument or a separate inter vivos trust instrument, and all my just debts, excepting mortgage notes secured by mortgages upon real estate.

SECOND: All the rest, residue and remainder of my estate, both real and personal, of whatsoever kind or character, and wheresoever situated, I give, devise and bequeath to my beloved wife:

_____, to be hers absolutely and forever.

THIRD: If my said wife does not survive me, then I give, devise and bequeath such rest, residue and remainder of my estate to:

(Name) _____, of

(Address) _____

     Number   *Street*   *City*   *State*   *Zip*

to be his/hers absolutely and forever.

FOURTH: I hereby appoint my wife _____ as Executrix of this my

LAST WILL AND TESTAMENT. If she does not survive me, then I appoint _____

as Executor/Executrix. I direct that no Exccutor/Executrix serving hereunder shall be required to post bond.

IN WITNESS WHEREOF, I have hereunto set my hand and seal at _____,

this _____ day of _____, 19_____.

       (sign here)_____ L.S.

Signed, sealed, published and declared to be his LAST WILL AND TESTAMENT by the within named Testator in the presence of us, who in his presence and at his request, and in the presence of each other, have hereunto subscribed our names as witnesses:

(1) _____ of _____

                                  City   *State*

(2) _____ of _____

                                  City   *State*

(3) _____ of _____

                                  City   *State*

AFFIDAVIT

STATE OF _____ } City
                                        or
COUNTY OF _____ } Town _____

    Personally appeared (1) _____

(2) _____ and (3) _____

who being duly sworn, depose and say that they attested the said Will and they subscribed the same at the request and in the presence of the said Testator and in the presence of each other, and the said Testator signed said Will in their presence and acknowledged that he had signed said Will and declared the same to be his LAST WILL AND TESTAMENT, and deponents further state that at the time of the execution of said Will the said Testator appeared to be of lawful age and sound mind and memory and there was no evidence of undue influence. The deponents make this affidavit at the request of the Testator.

                        (1) _____

                        (2) _____

                        (3) _____

Subscribed and sworn to before me this _____ day of _____, 19_____.

                               _____

(Notary Seal)   *Notary Public*

Last Will and Testament

KNOW ALL MEN BY THESE PRESENTS: That I, _____,

of the City/Town of _____, County of _____

and State of _____, being of sound and disposing mind and memory, do make, publish and

declare the following to be my LAST WILL AND TESTAMENT, hereby revoking all Wills by me at any time heretofore made.

FIRST: I direct my Executor, hereinafter named, to pay all my funeral expenses, administration expenses of my estate, including inheritance and succession taxes, state or federal, which may be occasioned by the passage of or succession to any interest in my estate under the terms of either this instrument or a separate inter vivos trust instrument, and all my just debts, excepting mortgage notes secured by mortgages upon real estate.

SECOND: All the rest, residue and remainder of my estate, both real and personal, of whatsoever kind or character, and wheresoever situated, I give, devise and bequeath to my beloved husband:

_____, to be his absolutely and forever.

THIRD: If my said husband does not survive me, then I give, devise and bequeath such rest, residue and remainder of my estate to:

(Name) _____, of

(Address) _____
       Number   *Street*   *City*   *State*   *Zip*

to be his/hers absolutely and forever.

FOURTH: I hereby appoint my husband_____as Executor of this my

LAST WILL AND TESTAMENT. If he does not survive me, then I appoint _____

as Executor/Executrix. I direct that no Executor/Executrix serving hereunder shall be required to post bond.

IN WITNESS WHEREOF, I have hereunto set my hand and seal at _____,

this _____ day of _____, 19_____.

       (sign here) _____ L.S.

Signed, sealed, published and declared to be her LAST WILL AND TESTAMENT by the within named Testatrix in the presence of us, who in her presence and at her request, and in the presence of each other, have hereunto subscribed our names as witnesses:

(1) _____ of _____
                               City   *State*

(2) _____ of _____
                               City   *State*

(3) _____ of _____
                               City   *State*

AFFIDAVIT

STATE OF _____ ⎤   City
                                                        ⎥   or
COUNTY OF _____ ⎦   Town _____

Personally appeared (1) _____

(2) _____ and (3) _____

who being duly sworn, depose and say that they attested the said Will and they subscribed the same at the request and in the presence of the said Testatrix and in the presence of each other, and the said Testatrix signed said Will in their presence and acknowledged that she had signed said Will and declared the same to be her LAST WILL AND TESTAMENT, and deponents further state that at the time of the execution of said Will the said Testatrix appeared to be of lawful age and sound mind and memory and there was no evidence of undue influence. The deponents make this affidavit at the request of the Testatrix.

(1) _____

(2) _____

(3) _____

Subscribed and sworn to before me this _____ day of _____, 19_____.

_____

(Notary Seal)   *Notary Public*

Last Will and Testament

KNOW ALL MEN BY THESE PRESENTS: That I, _____,

of the City/Town of _____, County of _____

and State of _____, being of sound and disposing mind and memory, do make, publish and

declare the following to be my LAST WILL AND TESTAMENT, hereby revoking all Wills by me at any time heretofore made.

FIRST: I direct my Executrix, hereinafter named, to pay all of my funeral expenses, administration expenses of my estate, including inheritance and succession taxes, state or federal, which may be occasioned by the passage of or succession to any interest in my estate under the terms of either this instrument or a separate inter vivos trust instrument, and all my just debts, excepting mortgage notes secured by mortages upon real estate.

SECOND: All the rest, residue and remainder of my estate, both real and personal, of whatsoever kind or character, and wheresoever situated, I give, devise and bequeath to my beloved wife:

_____, to be hers absolutely and forever.

THIRD: If my beloved wife does not survive me, I direct that the rest, residue and remainder of my estate shall be

divided into _____ equal parts, and I give, devise and bequeath one of such parts to each of the

following _____ persons, to be his/hers absolutely and forever:

The share of any person above named who shall not survive me shall be paid to such person's issue in equal shares, per stirpes; if such person has died leaving no issue, the part designated above as being for such person shall be divided among the other beneficiaries named above, in equal shares, per stirpes.

FOURTH: I hereby appoint my wife, _____, as Executrix of this my

LAST WILL AND TESTAMENT, if she be living. If she be not living, I appoint _____

as Executor/Executrix. I direct that no Executor or Executrix serving hereunder shall be required to post bond.

IN WITNESS WHEREOF, I have hereunto set my hand and seal at _____,

this _____ day of _____, 19_____.

(sign here) _____ L.S.

Signed, sealed, published and declared to be his LAST WILL AND TESTAMENT by the within named Testator in the presence of us, who in his presence and at his request, and in the presence of each other, have hereunto subscribed our names as witnesses:

(1) _____ of _____

                                                                   City   *State*

(2) _____ of _____

                                                                   City   *State*

(3) _____ of _____

                                                                   City   *State*

AFFIDAVIT

STATE OF _____ } City
                                          } or
COUNTY OF _____ } Town _____

    Personally appeared (1) _____

(2) _____ and (3) _____

who being duly sworn, depose and say that they attested the said Will and they subscribed the same at the request and in the presence of the said Testator and in the presence of each other, and the said Testator signed said Will in their presence and acknowledged that he had signed said Will and declared the same to be his LAST WILL AND TESTAMENT, and deponents further state that at the time of the execution of said Will the said Testator appeared to be of lawful age and sound mind and memory and there was no evidence of undue influence. The deponents make this affidavit at the request of the Testator.

        (1) _____

        (2) _____

        (3) _____

Subscribed and sworn to before me this _____ day of _____, 19_____.

                        _____

(Notary Seal)   *Notary Public*

Last Will and Testament

KNOW ALL MEN BY THESE PRESENTS: That I, _____,

of the City/Town of _____, County of _____

and State of _____, being of sound and disposing mind and memory, do make, publish and

declare the following to be my LAST WILL AND TESTAMENT, hereby revoking all Wills by me at any time heretofore made.

FIRST: I direct my Executor, hereinafter named, to pay all of my funeral expenses, administration expenses of my estate, including inheritance and succession taxes, state or federal, which may be occasioned by the passage of or succession to any interest in my estate under the terms of either this instrument or a separate inter vivos trust instrument, and all my just debts, excepting mortgage notes secured by mortgages upon real estate.

SECOND: All the rest, residue and remainder of my estate, both real and personal, of whatsoever kind or character, and wheresoever situated, I give, devise and bequeath to my beloved husband:

_____, to be his absolutely and forever.

THIRD: If my beloved husband does not survive me, I direct that the rest, residue and remainder of my estate shall

be divided into _____ equal parts, and I give, devise and bequeath one of such parts to each

of the following _____ persons, to be his/hers absolutely and forever:

The share of any person above named who shall not survive me shall be paid to such person's issue in equal shares, per stirpes; if such person has died leaving no issue, the part designated above as being for such person shall be divided among the other beneficiaries named above, in equal shares, per stirpes.

FOURTH: I hereby appoint my husband, _____, as Executor of this my

LAST WILL AND TESTAMENT, if he be living. If he be not living, I appoint _____

as Executor/Executrix. I direct that no Executor or Executrix serving hereunder shall be required to post bond.

IN WITNESS WHEREOF, I have hereunto set my hand and seal at _____,

this _____ day of _____, 19____.

(sign here) _____ L.S.

Signed, sealed, published and declared to be her LAST WILL AND TESTAMENT by the within named Testatrix in the presence of us, who in her presence and at her request, and in the presence of each other, have hereunto subscribed our names as witnesses:

(1) _____ of _____

        City   *State*

(2) _____ of _____

        City   *State*

(3) _____ of _____

        City   *State*

AFFIDAVIT

STATE OF ______________________________ } City or Town ______________________________

COUNTY OF ______________________________ }

Personally appeared (1) ______________________________

(2) ______________________________ and (3) ______________________________

who being duly sworn, depose and say that they attested the said Will and they subscribed the same at the request and in the presence of the said Testatrix and in the presence of each other, and the said Testatrix signed said Will in their presence and acknowledged that she had signed said Will and declared the same to be her LAST WILL AND TESTAMENT, and deponents further state that at the time of the execution of said Will the said Testatrix appeared to be of lawful age and sound mind and memory and there was no evidence of undue influence. The deponents make this affidavit at the request of the Testatrix.

(1) ______________________________

(2) ______________________________

(3) ______________________________

Subscribed and sworn to before me this ____________________ day of ____________________, 19_____.

(Notary Seal)

____

Notary Public

Last Will and Testament

KNOW ALL MEN BY THESE PRESENTS: That I, _____,

of the City/Town of _____, County of _____

and State of _____, being of sound and disposing mind and memory, do make, publish and

declare the following to be my LAST WILL AND TESTAMENT, hereby revoking all Wills by me at any time heretofore made.

FIRST: I direct my Executrix, hereinafter named, to pay all of my funeral expenses, administration expenses of my estate, including inheritance and succession taxes, state or federal, which may be occasioned by the passage of or succession to any interest in my estate under the terms of either this instrument or a separate inter vivos trust instrument, and all my just debts, excepting mortgage notes secured by mortgages upon real estate.

SECOND: All the rest, residue and remainder of my estate, both real and personal, of whatsoever kind or character, and wheresoever situated, I give, devise and bequeath to my beloved wife:

_____, to be hers absolutely and forever.

THIRD: If my beloved wife does not survive me, I direct that the rest, residue and remainder of my estate shall be

divided into _____ equal parts, and I give, devise and bequeath one of such parts to each of the

following _____ persons, to be his/hers absolutely and forever:

The share of any person above named who shall not survive me shall be divided among the other beneficiaries named above, in equal shares.

FOURTH: I hereby appoint my wife, _____, as Executrix of this my

LAST WILL AND TESTAMENT, if she be living. If she be not living, I appoint _____

as Executor/Executrix. I direct that no Executor or Executrix serving hereunder shall be required to post bond.

IN WITNESS WHEREOF, I have hereunto set my hand and seal at _____,

this _____ day of _____, 19_____.

(sign here) _____ L.S.

Signed, sealed, published and declared to be his LAST WILL AND TESTAMENT by the within named Testator in the presence of us, who in his presence and at his request, and in the presence of each other, have hereunto subscribed our names as witnesses:

(1) _____ of _____
                                              City   State

(2) _____ of _____
                                              City   State

(3) _____ of _____
                                              City   State

A F F I D A V I T

STATE OF _____ ⎫ City
                                            ⎬ or
COUNTY OF _____ ⎭ Town _____

   Personally appeared (1) _____

(2) _____ and (3) _____

who being duly sworn, depose and say that they attested the said Will and they subscribed the same at the request and in the presence of the said Testator and in the presence of each other, and the said Testator signed said Will in their presence and acknowledged that he had signed said Will and declared the same to be his LAST WILL AND TESTAMENT, and deponents further state that at the time of the execution of said Will the said Testator appeared to be of lawful age and sound mind and memory and there was no evidence of undue influence. The deponents make this affidavit at the request of the Testator.

                                        (1) _____

                                        (2) _____

                                        (3) _____

Subscribed and sworn to before me this _____ day of _____, 19_____.

                                        _____
(Notary Seal)   *Notary Public*

Last Will and Testament

KNOW ALL MEN BY THESE PRESENTS: That I, _____,

of the City/Town of _____, County of _____

and State of _____, being of sound and disposing mind and memory, do make, publish and

declare the following to be my LAST WILL AND TESTAMENT, hereby revoking all Wills by me at any time heretofore made.

FIRST: I direct my Executor, hereinafter named, to pay all of my funeral expenses, administration expenses of my estate, including inheritance and succession taxes, state or federal, which may be occasioned by the passage of or succession to any interest in my estate under the terms of either this instrument or a separate inter vivos trust instrument, and all my just debts, excepting mortgage notes secured by mortgages upon real estate.

SECOND: All the rest, residue and remainder of my estate, both real and personal, of whatsoever kind or character, and wheresoever situated, I give, devise and bequeath to my beloved husband:

_____, to be his absolutely and forever.

THIRD: If my beloved husband does not survive me, I direct that the rest, residue and remainder of my estate shall be divided

into _____ equal parts, and I give, devise and bequeath one of such parts to each

of the following _____ persons, to be his/hers absolutely and forever:

The share of any person above named who shall not survive me shall be divided among the other beneficiaries named above, in equal shares.

FOURTH: I hereby appoint my husband, _____, as Executor of this my

LAST WILL AND TESTAMENT, if he be living. If he be not living, I appoint _____

as Executor/Executrix. I direct that no Executor or Executrix serving hereunder shall be required to post bond.

IN WITNESS WHEREOF, I have hereunto set my hand and seal at _____,

this _____ day of _____, 19_____.

(sign here) _____ L.S.

Signed, sealed, published and declared to be her LAST WILL AND TESTAMENT by the within named Testatrix in the presence of us, who in her presence and at her request, and in the presence of each other, have hereunto subscribed our names as witnesses:

(1) _____ of _____
                                                              City   *State*

(2) _____ of _____
                                                               City   *State*

(3) _____ of _____
                                                               City   *State*

AFFIDAVIT

STATE OF _____ ⎫ City
                                                        ⎬ or
COUNTY OF _____ ⎭ Town _____

    Personally appeared (1) _____

(2) _____ and (3) _____

who being duly sworn, depose and say that they attested the said Will and they subscribed the same at the request and in the presence of the said Testatrix and in the presence of each other, and the said Testatrix signed said Will in their presence and acknowledged that she had signed said Will and declared the same to be her LAST WILL AND TESTAMENT, and deponents further state that at the time of the execution of said Will the said Testatrix appeared to be of lawful age and sound mind and memory and there was no evidence of undue influence. The deponents make this affidavit at the request of the Testatrix.

(1) _____

(2) _____

(3) _____

Subscribed and sworn to before me this _____ day of _____, 19____.

                                            _____

(Notary Seal)   *Notary Public*

Last Will and Testament

KNOW ALL MEN BY THESE PRESENTS: That I, _____,

of the City/Town of _____, County of _____

and State of _____, being of sound and disposing mind and memory, do make, publish and

declare the following to be my LAST WILL AND TESTAMENT, hereby revoking all Wills by me at any time heretofore made.

FIRST: I direct my Executor/Executrix, hereinafter named, to pay all my funeral expenses, administration expenses of my estate, including inheritance and succession taxes, state or federal, which may be occasioned by the passage of or succession to any interest in my estate under the terms of either this instrument or a separate inter vivos trust instrument, and all my just debts, excepting mortgage notes secured by mortgages upon real estate.

SECOND: All the rest, residue and remainder of my estate, both real and personal, of whatsoever kind or character

and wheresoever situated, shall be divided into _____ equal parts, and I give, devise and

bequeath one such part to each of the following _____ persons, to be his/hers absolutely and forever:

The share of any person above named who shall not survive me shall be paid to such person's issue in equal shares, per stirpes; if such person has died leaving no issue, the part designated above as being for such person shall be divided among the other beneficiaries named above, in equal shares, per stirpes.

THIRD: I hereby appoint _____ as Executor/Executrix of this my

LAST WILL AND TESTAMENT and I direct that such person shall serve without bond.

IN WITNESS WHEREOF, I have hereunto set my hand and seal at _____,

this _____ day of _____, 19_____.

(sign here) _____ L.S.

Signed, sealed, published and declared to be his/her LAST WILL AND TESTAMENT by the within named Testator/Testatrix in the presence of us, who in his/her presence and at his/her request, and in the presence of each other, have hereunto subscribed our names as witnesses:

(1) _____ of _____
                                           City   State

(2) _____ of _____
                                           City   State

(3) _____ of _____
                                           City   State

AFFIDAVIT

STATE OF _____

COUNTY OF _____

City
or
Town _____

Personally appeared (1) _____

(2) _____ and (3) _____

who being duly sworn, depose and say that they attested the said Will and they subscribed the same at the request and in the presence of the said Testator and in the presence of each other, and the said Testator signed said Will in their presence and acknowledged that he/she had signed said Will and declared the same to be his/her LAST WILL AND TESTAMENT, and deponents further state that at the time of the execution of said Will the said Testator appeared to be of lawful age and sound mind and memory and there was no evidence of undue influence. The deponents make this affidavit at the request of the Testator.

(1) _____

(2) _____

(3) _____

Subscribed and sworn to before me this _____ day of _____, 19_____.

_____

(Notary Seal)   *Notary Public*

Last Will and Testament

KNOW ALL MEN BY THESE PRESENTS: That I, _____,

of the City/Town of _____, County of _____

and State of _____, being of sound and disposing mind and memory, do make, publish and declare the following to be my LAST WILL AND TESTAMENT, hereby revoking all Wills by me at any time heretofore made.

FIRST: I direct my Executor/Executrix, hereinafter named, to pay all my funeral expenses, administration expenses of my estate, including inheritance and succession taxes, state or federal, which may be occasioned by the passage of or succession to any interest in my estate under the terms of either this instrument or a separate inter vivos trust instrument, and all my just debts, excepting mortgage notes secured by mortgages upon real estate.

SECOND: All the rest, residue and remainder of my estate, both real and personal, of whatsoever kind or character, and wheresoever situated, shall be divided into _____ equal parts, and I give, devise and bequeath one such part to each of the following _____ persons, to be his/hers absolutely and forever:

The share of any person above named who shall not survive me shall be divided among the other beneficiaries named above, in equal shares.

THIRD: I hereby appoint _____ as Executor/Executrix of this my LAST WILL AND TESTAMENT and I direct that such person shall serve without bond.

IN WITNESS WHEREOF, I have hereunto set my hand and seal at _____,

this _____ day of _____, 19____.

(sign here) _____ L.S.

Signed, sealed, published and declared to be his/her LAST WILL AND TESTAMENT by the within named Testator/Testatrix in the presence of us, who in his/her presence and at his/her request, and in the presence of each other, have hereunto subscribed our names as witnesses:

(1) _____ of _____
                                                         City   *State*

(2) _____ of _____
                                                         City   *State*

(3) _____ of _____
                                                         City   *State*

AFFIDAVIT

STATE OF _____ ⎫ City

COUNTY OF _____ ⎬ or

                                         ⎭ Town _____

    Personally appeared (1) _____

(2) _____ and (3) _____

who being duly sworn, depose and say that they attested the said Will and they subscribed the same at the request and in the presence of the said Testator and in the presence of each other, and the said Testator signed said Will in their presence and acknowledged that he/she had signed said Will and declared the same to be his/her LAST WILL AND TESTAMENT, and deponents further state that at the time of the execution of said Will the said Testator appeared to be of lawful age and sound mind and memory and there was no evidence of undue influence. The deponents make this affidavit at the request of the Testator.

                                        (1) _____

                                        (2) _____

                                        (3) _____

Subscribed and sworn to before me this _____ day of _____, 19_____.

_____

(*Notary Seal*)

                                                        Notary Public

Last Will and Testament

KNOW ALL MEN BY THESE PRESENTS: That I, _____,

of the City/Town of _____, County of _____

and State of _____, being of sound and disposing mind and memory, do make, publish and

declare the following to be my LAST WILL AND TESTAMENT, hereby revoking all Wills by me at any time heretofore made.

FIRST: I direct my Executrix, hereinafter named, to pay all my funeral expenses, administration expenses of my estate, including inheritance and succession taxes, state or federal, which may be occasioned by the passage of or succession to any interest in my estate under the terms of either this instrument or a separate inter vivos trust instrument, and all my just debts, excepting mortgage notes secured by mortgages upon real estate.

SECOND: All the rest, residue and remainder of my estate, both real and personal, of whatsoever kind or character, and

wheresoever situated, I give, devise and bequeath to my beloved wife: _____,
to be hers absolutely and forever.

THIRD: If my said wife does not survive me, then I give, devise and bequeath such rest, residue and remainder of my estate to my beloved children, natural or adopted, in equal shares, per stirpes, to be theirs absolutely and forever; *provided,* that the share of any child of mine who has died leaving no issue shall be divided among my surviving children in equal shares, per stirpes.

FOURTH: If my beloved wife does not survive me, I hereby appoint

(Name) _____, of

(Address) _____
   Number   Street   City   State   Zip

as guardian of such of my children as shall then be minors.

FIFTH: I hereby appoint my wife, _____, as Executrix of this my

LAST WILL AND TESTAMENT. If she does not survive me, then I appoint

(Name) _____, of

(Address) _____
   Number   Street   City   State   Zip

as Executor/Executrix of my estate. I direct that no Executor/Executrix serving hereunder shall be required to post bond.

IN WITNESS WHEREOF, I have hereunto set my hand and seal at _____,

this _____ day of _____, 19_____.

(sign here) _____ L.S.

Signed, sealed, published and declared to be his LAST WILL AND TESTAMENT by the within named Testator in the presence of us, who in his presence and at his request, and in the presence of each other, have hereunto subscribed our names as witnesses:

(1) _____ of _____
                  City   State

(2) _____ of _____
                  City   State

(3) _____ of _____
                  City   State

AFFIDAVIT

STATE OF _____ ⎫ City
                                                             ⎪ or
COUNTY OF _____ ⎭ Town _____

Personally appeared (1) _____

(2) _____ and (3) _____

who being duly sworn, depose and say that they attested the said Will and they subscribed the same at the request and in the presence of the said Testator and in the presence of each other, and the said Testator signed said Will in their presence and acknowledged that he had signed said Will and declared the same to be his LAST WILL AND TESTAMENT, and deponents further state that at the time of the execution of said Will the said Testator appeared to be of lawful age and sound mind and memory and there was no evidence of undue influence. The deponents make this affidavit at the request of the Testator.

(1) _____

(2) _____

(3) _____

Subscribed and sworn to before me this _____ day of _____, 19_____.

_____
(Notary Seal)   Notary Public

Last Will and Testament

KNOW ALL MEN BY THESE PRESENTS: That I, _____,

of the City/Town of _____, County of _____

and State of _____, being of sound and disposing mind and memory, do make, publish and

declare the following to be my LAST WILL AND TESTAMENT, hereby revoking all Wills by me at any time heretofore made.

FIRST: I direct my Executor, hereinafter named, to pay all my funeral expenses, administration expenses of my estate, including inheritance and succession taxes, state or federal, which may be occasioned by the passage of or succession to any interest in my estate under the terms of either this instrument or a separate inter vivos trust instrument, and all my just debts, excepting mortgage notes secured by mortgages upon real estate.

SECOND: All the rest, residue and remainder of my estate, both real and personal, of whatsoever kind or character, and

wheresoever situated, I give, devise and bequeath to my beloved husband: _____,
to be his absolutely and forever.

THIRD: If my said husband does not survive me, then I give, devise and bequeath such rest, residue and remainder of my estate to my beloved children, natural or adopted, in equal shares, per stirpes, to be theirs absolutely and forever; *provided,* that the share of any child of mine who has died leaving no issue shall be divided among my surviving children in equal shares, per stirpes.

FOURTH: If my beloved husband does not survive me, I hereby appoint

(Name) _____, of

(Address) _____
         Number   *Street*   *City*   *State*   *Zip*

as guardian of such of my children as shall then be minors.

FIFTH: I hereby appoint my husband, _____, as Executor of this my

LAST WILL AND TESTAMENT. If he does not survive me, then I appoint

(Name) _____, of

(Address) _____
         Number   *Street*   *City*   *State*   *Zip*

as Executor/Executrix of my estate. I direct that no Executor/Executrix serving hereunder shall be required to post bond.

IN WITNESS WHEREOF, I have hereunto set my hand and seal at _____,

this _____ day of _____, 19_____.

(sign here) _____ L.S.

Signed, sealed, published and declared to be her LAST WILL AND TESTAMENT by the within named Testatrix in the presence of us, who in her presence and at her request, and in the presence of each other, have hereunto subscribed our names as witnesses:

(1) _____ of _____
                                         City   *State*

(2) _____ of _____
                                         City   *State*

(3) _____ of _____
                                         City   *State*

AFFIDAVIT

STATE OF _____ } City

COUNTY OF _____ } or Town _____

   Personally appeared (1) _____

(2) _____ and (3) _____

who being duly sworn, depose and say that they attested the said Will and they subscribed the same at the request and in the presence of the said Testatrix and in the presence of each other, and the said Testatrix signed said Will in their presence and acknowledged that she had signed said Will and declared the same to be her LAST WILL AND TESTAMENT, and deponents further state that at the time of the execution of said Will the said Testatrix appeared to be of lawful age and sound mind and memory and there was no evidence of undue influence. The deponents make this affidavit at the request of the Testatrix.

(1) _____

(2) _____

(3) _____

Subscribed and sworn to before me this _____ day of _____, 19_____.

(Notary Seal)

_____
                                    Notary Public

Last Will and Testament

KNOW ALL MEN BY THESE PRESENTS: That I, _____,

of the City/Town of _____, County of _____

and State of _____, being of sound and disposing mind and memory, do make, publish and

declare the following to be my LAST WILL AND TESTAMENT, hereby revoking all Wills by me at any time heretofore made.

FIRST: I direct my Executor, hereinafter named, to pay all my funeral expenses, administration expenses of my estate, including inheritance and succession taxes, state or federal, which may be occasioned by the passage of or succession to any interest in my estate under the terms of either this instrument or a separate inter vivos trust instrument, and all my just debts, excepting mortgage notes secured by mortgages upon real estate.

SECOND: I give, devise and bequeath to my beloved wife, _____,

to be hers absolutely and forever, all my personal effects, such as jewelry, mementos, clothing, furniture, automobiles and similar items of a like nature, excluding, however, any stocks, bonds, cash or real estate.

THIRD: All the rest, residue and remainder of my estate, both real and personal, of whatsoever kind or

character and wheresoever situated, I give, devise and bequeath to _____

of the City/Town of _____ and State of _____, as Trustee,

under the terms of a certain trust executed by me and by said _____

as of _____ 19_____, and already in existence, and I specifically direct and provide that the property received by virtue of this bequest shall be held by said Trustee, to be administered in accordance with the provisions thereof, as an addition to the trust fund, and said Trustee shall dispose of said property as a part of said trust in accordance with the provisions thereof.

FOURTH: In the event that my wife does not survive me, I request that

(Name) _____, of

(Address) _____
     Number   *Street*   *City*   *State*   *Zip*

be appointed guardian of such of my children as shall then be minors.

FIFTH: This Will shall continue in full force and effect whether or not another child or children shall be born to me and my wife.

SIXTH: I make, constitute and appoint _____ as Executor of this my

LAST WILL AND TESTAMENT, to serve without bond.

IN WITNESS WHEREOF, I have hereunto set my hand and seal at _____,

this _____ day of _____, 19_____.

(sign here) _____ L.S.

Signed, sealed, published and declared to be his LAST WILL AND TESTAMENT by the within named Testator in the presence of us, who in his presence and at his request, and in the presence of each other, have hereunto subscribed our names as witnesses:

(1) _____ of _____
                                       City   *State*

(2) _____ of _____
                                       City   *State*

(3) _____ of _____
                                       City   *State*

AFFIDAVIT

STATE OF _____

COUNTY OF _____

City
or
Town _____

Personally appeared (1) _____

(2) _____ and (3) _____

who being duly sworn, depose and say that they attested the said Will and they subscribed the same at the request and in the presence of the said Testator and in the presence of each other, and the said Testator signed said Will in their presence and acknowledged that he had signed said Will and declared the same to be his LAST WILL AND TESTAMENT, and deponents further state that at the time of the execution of said Will the said Testator appeared to be of lawful age and sound mind and memory and there was no evidence of undue influence. The deponents make this affidavit at the request of the Testator.

(1) _____

(2) _____

(3) _____

Subscribed and sworn to before me this _____ day of _____, 19_____.

_____

(Notary Seal)

Notary Public

Last Will and Testament

KNOW ALL MEN BY THESE PRESENTS: That I, _____,

of the City/Town of _____, County of _____

and State of _____, being of sound and disposing mind and memory, do make, publish and

declare the following to be my LAST WILL AND TESTAMENT, hereby revoking all Wills by me at any time heretofore made.

FIRST: I direct my Executor, hereinafter named, to pay all my funeral expenses, administration expenses of my estate, including inheritance and succession taxes, state or federal, which may be occasioned by the passage of or succession to any interest in my estate under the terms of either this instrument or a separate inter vivos trust instrument, and all my just debts, excepting mortgage notes secured by mortgages upon real estate.

SECOND: All of the rest, residue and remainder of my estate, both real and personal, of whatsoever kind or character, and wheresoever situated, I give, devise and bequeath to my beloved husband: _____, to be his absolutely and forever.

THIRD: In the event that my said husband shall predecease me, I give, devise and bequeath to my beloved children all of my personal effects, such as jewelry, mementos, clothing, furniture, automobiles and items of a like nature, excluding, however, any stocks, bonds, cash or real estate. All of the rest, residue and remainder of my estate, both real and personal, of whatsoever kind or character and wheresoever situated, I give, devise and bequeath to

_____ of the City/Town of _____

and State of _____, as Trustee, under the terms of a certain deed of trust executed

by _____ and by the said _____

as of _____, 19____, and already in existence, and I specifically direct and provide that the property

received by virtue of this bequest shall be held by said _____, as such

Trustee, to be administered by it in accordance with the provisions thereof, as an addition to the trust fund, and said Trustee shall dispose of said property as a part of said trust in accordance with the provisions thereof.

FOURTH: I make, constitute and appoint my husband, _____,

as Executor of this my LAST WILL AND TESTAMENT, and if he shall not have survived me, then I make,

constitute and appoint _____ of

_____, as Executor. The Executor shall serve

without bond.

IN WITNESS WHEREOF, I have hereunto subscribed my name and affixed my seal this _____

day of _____, 19____.

(sign here) _____ L.S.

Signed, sealed, published and declared to be her LAST WILL AND TESTAMENT by the within named Testatrix in the presence of us, who in her presence and at her request, and in the presence of each other, have hereunto subscribed our names as witnesses:

(1) _____ of _____
                                          City   State

(2) _____ of _____
                                          City   State

(3) _____ of _____
                                          City   State

A F F I D A V I T

STATE OF _____ ⎫ City

COUNTY OF _____ ⎬ or

                                                         ⎭ Town _____

    Personally appeared (1) _____

(2) _____ and (3) _____

who being duly sworn, depose and say that they attested the said Will and they subscribed the same at the request and in the presence of the said Testatrix and in the presence of each other, and the said Testatrix signed said Will in their presence and acknowledged that she had signed said Will and declared the same to be her LAST WILL AND TESTAMENT, and deponents further state that at the time of the execution of said Will the said Testatrix appeared to be of lawful age and sound mind and memory and there was no evidence of undue influence. The deponents make this affidavit at the request of the Testatrix.

                                             (1) _____

                                             (2) _____

                                             (3) _____

Subscribed and sworn to before me this _____ day of _____, 19_____.

                                                  _____

(Notary Seal)   *Notary Public*

Last Will and Testament

KNOW ALL MEN BY THESE PRESENTS: That I, _____,

of the City/Town of _____, County of _____

and State of _____, being of sound and disposing mind and memory, do make, publish and

declare the following to be my LAST WILL AND TESTAMENT, hereby revoking all former Wills by me at any time heretofore made.

FIRST: I direct my Executor/Executrix, hereinafter named, to pay all my funeral expenses, administration expenses of my estate, including inheritance and succession taxes, state or federal, which may be occasioned by the passage of or succession to any interest in my estate under the terms of either this instrument or a separate inter vivos trust instrument, and all my just debts, excepting mortgage notes secured by mortgages upon real estate.

SECOND: All the rest, residue and remainder of my estate, both real and personal, of whatsoever kind or character and wheresoever situated, I give, devise and bequeath to my children, natural or adopted, in equal shares, per stirpes.

THIRD: I request that

(Name) _____, of

(Address) _____
          Number   *Street*   *City*   *State*   *Zip*

be appointed guardian of such of my children as shall then be minors.

FOURTH: I make, constitute and appoint _____

as Executor/Executrix of this my LAST WILL AND TESTAMENT, to serve without bond.

IN WITNESS WHEREOF, I have hereunto set my hand and seal at _____,

this _____ day of _____, 19_____.

          (sign here) _____ L.S.

Signed, sealed, published and declared to be his/her LAST WILL AND TESTAMENT by the within named Testator/Testatrix in the presence of us, who in his/her presence and at his/her request, and in the presence of each other, have hereunto subscribed our names as witnesses:

(1) _____ of _____
                                      City   *State*

(2) _____ of _____
                                      City   *State*

(3) _____ of _____
                                      City   *State*

AFFIDAVIT

STATE OF _____ } City

COUNTY OF _____ } or Town _____

Personally appeared (1) _____

(2) _____ and (3) _____

who being duly sworn, depose and say that they attested the said Will and they subscribed the same at the request and in the presence of the said Testator/Testatrix and in the presence of each other, and the said Testator/Testatrix signed said Will in their presence and acknowledged that he/she had signed said Will and declared the same to be his/her LAST WILL AND TESTAMENT, and deponents further state that at the time of the execution of said Will the said Testator/Testatrix appeared to be of lawful age and sound mind and memory and there was no evidence of undue influence. The deponents make this affidavit at the request of the Testator/Testatrix.

(1) _____

(2) _____

(3) _____

Subscribed and sworn to before me this _____ day of _____, 19_____.

_____

(Notary Seal)

Notary Public

Last Will and Testament

KNOW ALL MEN BY THESE PRESENTS: That I, _____,

of the City/Town of _____, County of _____

and State of _____, being of sound and disposing mind and memory, do make, publish and declare the following to be my LAST WILL AND TESTAMENT, hereby revoking all former Wills by me at any time heretofore made.

FIRST: I direct my Executor/Executrix, hereinafter named, to pay all my funeral expenses, administration expenses of my estate, including inheritance and succession taxes, state or federal, which may be occasioned by the passage of or succession to any interest in my estate under the terms of either this instrument or a separate inter vivos trust instrument, and all my just debts, excepting mortgage notes secured by mortgages upon real estate.

SECOND: All the rest, residue and remainder of my estate, both real and personal, of whatsoever kind or character and wheresoever situated, I give, devise and bequeath to my children, natural or adopted, in equal shares, or the survivor of them.

THIRD: I request that

(Name) _____, of

(Address) _____
   Number   *Street*   *City*   *State*   *Zip*

be appointed guardian of such of my children as shall then be minors.

FOURTH: I make, constitute and appoint _____

as Executor/Executrix of this my LAST WILL AND TESTAMENT, to serve without bond.

IN WITNESS WHEREOF, I have hereunto set my hand and seal at _____,

this _____ day of _____, 19____.

   (sign here) _____ L.S.

Signed, sealed, published and declared to be his/her LAST WILL AND TESTAMENT by the within named Testator/Testatrix in the presence of us, who in his/her presence and at his/her request, and in the presence of each other, have hereunto subscribed our names as witnesses:

(1) _____ of _____
             City   *State*

(2) _____ of _____
             City   *State*

(3) _____ of _____
             City   *State*

A F F I D A V I T

STATE OF _____ ⎫ City

COUNTY OF _____ ⎬ or

⎭ Town _____

Personally appeared (1) _____

(2) _____ and (3) _____

who being duly sworn, depose and say that they attested the said Will and they subscribed the same at the request and in the presence of the said Testator/Testatrix and in the presence of each other, and the said Testator/Testatrix signed said Will in their presence and acknowledged that he/she had signed said Will and declared the same to be his/her LAST WILL AND TESTAMENT, and deponents further state that at the time of the execution of said Will the said Testator/Testatrix appeared to be of lawful age and sound mind and memory and there was no evidence of undue influence. The deponents make this affidavit at the request of the Testator/Testatrix.

(1) _____

(2) _____

(3) _____

Subscribed and sworn to before me this _____ day of _____, 19_____.

_____

(Notary Seal)   Notary Public

Glossary of Legal Terms Used in Financial Planning

To assist the reader who may be unfamiliar with the usage of certain terms in trusts, estates, and taxation, this glossary attempts a nontechnical definition of such terms.

1. Disposition of Property at Death

A WILL is a document with which a person may dispose of his property at his death. A CODICIL is a document which amends or changes a will. An INVALID WILL is a document which, as a matter of law, is not effective to dispose of the property of a dead person (a DECEDENT). The EXECUTION of a will is the signing of a will (not to be confused with the duties of an Executor; see below) with the formalities required by law. The PROBATE of a will is the process of filing a will in a court and proving to the court that the will was signed by the decedent with all the formalities required by law, that the decedent signed of his own free will and understood what he was doing. A TESTAMENT or a LAST WILL AND TESTAMENT is a will. A TESTA-MENTARY DISPOSITION is a disposition of property by will. A TESTAMENTARY TRUST is a trust set up in a will. A TESTATOR (female-TESTATRIX) is a person who made a will. A decedent who made a will is said to have died TESTATE.

LETTERS TESTAMENTARY: a document issued by a court naming the person who is to carry out the terms of a will. An EXECUTOR (female-EXECUTRIX) is the person named in a will to carry out its provisions. An ADMINISTRATOR WITH WILL ANNEXED (female-ADMINISTRATRIX) is the person designated by a court to carry out the terms of a will where the will fails to name an executor, or the executor named is unable to act as such. REPRESENTATIVE, LEGAL REPRESENTATIVE, or PERSONAL REPRESEN-TATIVE are general terms referring to an executor or administrator. An ESTATE is the property left by a decedent. (An additional meaning is given in section 4.)

A LEGACY or BEQUEST is a gift made by will. A DEVISE is a gift of real property (land, buildings, etc.) made by will. To BEQUEATH or DEVISE is to make a gift by will. A LEGATEE or DEVISEE is a person named in a will to receive a legacy, bequest, or devise. A RESIDUARY LEGATEE is one who is given the balance of an estate after payment of claims, expenses, taxes, and all specified legacies.

INTESTACY refers to a decedent who left no will; he is said to have died INTESTATE. INTESTATE SUC-CESSION is the disposition of the property of a decedent who left no will in accordance with the LAWS OF INTESTACY (also called LAWS OF DESCENT AND DISTRIBUTION) to persons who bear certain relationships to the decedent and who are variously referred to as HEIRS, HEIRS-AT-LAW, LEGAL HEIRS, NEXT-OF-KIN, and DISTRIBUTEES. An ADMINISTRATOR (female-ADMINISTRATRIX) is a person appointed by a court to take charge of the estate of an intestate decedent. LETTERS OF AD-MINISTRATION: a document issued by a court which designates the person to act as administrator.

EXPENSES OF ADMINISTRATION are the expenses incurred by an executor or administrator in carrying out the terms of a will or in administering an estate in accordance with provisions of law. These include the fees of a probate or surrogate's court and of the executors or administrators, attorneys' fees, accoun-tants' fees, and appraisers' fees.

2. Lifetime Disposition of Property

A DONOR is a person who makes a gift. A DONEE is a person who receives a gift. An INCOMPLETE gift is no gift at all because the donor did not complete the gift by delivery of the property or a document of transfer to the donee. An INTER VIVOS gift is one made by the donor during his lifetime. A TESTAMENTARY gift is one made by will. A gift IN CONTEMPLATION OF DEATH is a gift made by the donor shortly before his death (a period of three years before death, for tax purposes) because he believes he will die shortly. A gift IN TRUST is a gift of property to a trustee to hold for the benefit of someone else. A GIFT TAX is a tax imposed on the making of gifts.

3. Transfers of Property in Trust

A TRUST is a relationship of confidence or trust in which one person assumes an obligation to hold and manage property for the benefit of another person. If the parties express their intention to create a trust, usually in writing, it is called an EXPRESS trust. A TRUST AGREEMENT or TRUST INDENTURE is the document which expresses the terms of the trust; it is an agreement between the person who is transferring property, called the SETTLOR (sometimes DONOR or GRANTOR), and the person receiving and agreeing to manage the property, called the TRUSTEE, for the benefit of another person, called the BENEFICIARY. If the settlor names himself as trustee, the trust document is called a DECLARATION OF TRUST.

If the interest of a beneficiary does not begin unless some event (such as surviving someone else) occurs, he is a CONTINGENT beneficiary; if his interest is limited to income earned, he is an INCOME beneficiary; if his interest is solely in distributions of principal, he is a PRINCIPAL beneficiary; a beneficiary who is to receive distributions as long as he lives is said to have a LIFE INTEREST (sometimes incorrectly referred to as a LIFE ESTATE) and is referred to as a LIFE BENE-FICIARY; the beneficiary who is to receive the property upon the termination of the trust is loosely referred to as a REMAINDERMAN, and his interest is generally called a REMAINDER. The property transferred in trust is variously called the RES, CORPUS, or PRINCIPAL.

VARIOUS TYPES OF TRUSTS

If the trust is set up to operate during the lifetime of the settlor, it is called an INTER VIVOS, LIVING, or LIFETIME trust; if it is set up in his will, it is called a TESTAMENTARY TRUST.

Special names are sometimes used to identify trusts which contain special features: If the settlor retains the power to revoke a trust, the trust is called REVOCA-BLE; if he does not retain power to revoke a trust, the trust is called IRREVOCABLE; if the trustee has the power to terminate the trust, it is called TERMINA-BLE; if the trust property is to be returned to the settlor upon termination, it is called REVERSIONARY; trusts, which for income tax reasons are set up for a fixed number of years, are referred to as SHORT-TERM TRUSTS—such as a TEN-YEAR TRUST—(sometimes referred to as a REVERSIONARY TRUST); if the trust property is to be given to a charity upon the termination of the trust, it is loosely called a CHARITABLE REMAINDER TRUST; a trust which prohibits a beneficiary from selling his interest or pledging it to secure a loan and prevents his creditors from seizing his interest is called a SPENDTHRIFT TRUST; a trust which gives the trustee the power, in his discretion, to distribute or to withhold distribution or to determine the distributive shares of various beneficiaries is called a DISCRETIONARY TRUST; SPRINKLE TRUSTS give the trustee discretion to determine the amounts of income or principal to be distributed to various beneficiaries; an ACCUMULATION TRUST requires the trustee to accumulate the income earned over a period for some future distribution or other purpose; a POUR-OVER TRUST is a living trust which receives or is to receive a legacy under the terms of a will, as distinguished from a TESTAMENTARY TRUST which is set up in the will.

A POWER OF APPOINTMENT is a power given to a beneficiary to designate persons to receive certain distributions from a trust. A LIMITED or SPECIAL POWER OF APPOINTMENT limits the persons who may be chosen to receive distributions. A GENERAL POWER OF APPOINTMENT does not limit the persons who may be chosen to receive distributions. A POWER OF INVASION is a power given to either a beneficiary or the trustee to make distributions from principal if the income distributions are for some reason inadequate.

A CUSTODIAN FOR A MINOR is akin to a trustee whose duties and powers are set forth in a state statute which provides for gifts of securities or money to minors by registration of the securities or the deposit account in the name of the CUSTODIAN.

LEGALS or INVESTMENTS LEGAL FOR TRUST-EES are the investments which a trustee is permitted to make by state law where the trust agreement fails to set forth the trustees' investment powers. In some states, a LEGAL LIST is provided, that is, a statutory list of securities legal for trustees to invest in. In some states, however, where the trust agreement fails to set forth the trustees' investment powers, the trustee may invest under the PRUDENT MAN RULE, that is to say, in any security, such as a mutual fund, in which a prudent man considering the permanent disposition of his funds would invest with due regard to the income as well as the probable safety of the capital to be invested.

4. Property Terms

An ESTATE is an interest in property. (An additional meaning is given in section 1.) A TENANT is a person who holds an interest in property. A LIFE ESTATE or LEGAL LIFE ESTATE is an interest in the use of, or income from, property for someone's life. The holder of such interest is called a LIFE TENANT. A RE-MAINDER is an interest in property which is to be enjoyed after the expiration of a LIFE ESTATE. The holder of such interest is called a REMAINDERMAN. A REVERSION is the right to the return of property after a life estate or a fixed number of years. A FUTURE INTEREST is loosely used to mean any interest which cannot be enjoyed until some future time.

A TENANCY IN COMMON is the holding of frac-tional undivided interests by several persons in the same property. A JOINT TENANCY WITH RIGHT OF SURVIVORSHIP is the holding of fractional undivided interests of two persons, each of whom has the right to the entire property if and when he survives the other. A JOINT TENANCY is loosely used to mean a joint tenancy with right of survivorship but in most states its legal meaning is a tenancy in common. A TENANCY BY THE ENTIRETY describes a joint tenancy with right of survivorship for a husband and wife.

COMMUNITY PROPERTY (as used in eight states with a French or Spanish law tradition) refers to a partnership interest of a husband and wife in the property of both accumulated during the marriage by the efforts of either of them.

5. Corporate Terms

A CORPORATION is a business organization created in accordance with statute (STOCK CORPORATION LAW or BUSINESS CORPORATION LAW) to permit its owners to limit their liability for its debts to their investment in the corporation. Ownership of a corporation is referred to as ownership of its STOCK or SHARES of stock which are represented by CERTIFICATES of ownership of shares of stock, also called STOCK CERTIFICATES; the owners of the corporation are therefore referred to as STOCKHOLDERS or SHAREHOLDERS. When an investor makes an investment in a corporation, it is said to ISSUE its stock to him; the stock is REGISTERED in his name on the books of the corporation and certificates representing the shares of stock purchased are delivered to him.

The stock of a corporation may be divided into COMMON stock and PREFERRED stock, which has special rights, such as a prior right to dividends.

When an investor lends money to a corporation, it is said to issue a DEBT SECURITY to him. The debt securities of a corporation may be issued in many forms; thus BONDS, which are usually secured by mortgages, DEBENTURES, which are usually unsecured, NOTES, which are commercial paper usually used in borrowing from banks or for evidencing trade debts, and CONVERTIBLE BONDS or DEBENTURES, which give the holder the right to surrender the security in exchange for stock.

AUTHORIZED stock refers to the amount of stock which a corporation is authorized by law to issue. OUTSTANDING stock refers to the amount of stock in the hands of the stockholders. TREASURY stock refers to previously issued stock reacquired by the corporation from its stockholders and held for future disposition. STOCK RIGHTS or WARRANTS are rights of stockholders to purchase more stock of a corporation; sometimes referred to as a right to SUBSCRIBE to more stock.

The stockholders elect a BOARD OF DIRECTORS who set corporate policy and appoint the executive officers (PRESIDENT, VICE-PRESIDENT, TREASURER, and SECRETARY) to execute the board policies in operating the corporation.

A DIVIDEND is a distribution of money or property or stock made by a corporation to its stockholders; if the dividend is a return of part of the stockholders' investment, it is called a CAPITAL dividend and sometimes a LIQUIDATING dividend; if it is paid out of the earnings of a corporation, it is called an ORDINARY INCOME dividend; if it is paid by a registered open-end investment company (a mutual fund) out of the profits from the sale of securities, it is called a CAPITAL GAIN or SECURITY PROFITS distribution; if the dividend is paid in the stock of the corporation paying the dividend, it is called a STOCK dividend; and if the stockholder has the option to take a cash or a stock dividend, it is called an OPTIONAL dividend or an OPTIONAL STOCK dividend.

6. Federal Income Tax Terms

The dictionary defines INCOME as the gain or benefit from labor, business, or property. In general, it means the same thing in law, but, specifically, whether or not any given item is treated as income may vary under the many tax and related statutes.

GROSS INCOME, for an individual, is the aggregate of his incomes from all sources without deduction for the expenses of producing such incomes. GROSS RECEIPTS are the receipts of a business without any deductions whatsoever. NET INCOME is basically an accounting term which means the business revenues minus the business expenses. ADJUSTED GROSS INCOME is a tax term which, for an individual, means the sum of his salary, his interest income, his dividend income, his net income from a business or profession, his net income from rents, etc. TAXABLE INCOME is the amount on which the tax is computed; it is the result of subtracting from adjusted gross income all allowable DEDUCTIONS and EXEMPTIONS.

The allowable deductions may be the STANDARD DEDUCTION ($3,400 in the case of husband and wife filing a joint return, $1,700 in the case of a married person filing a separate return, or $2,300 in the case of a single person), or the ITEMIZED DEDUCTIONS, that is, deductions for charitable contributions, medical and dental expenses, interest, casualty losses, etc. TAX CREDITS are amounts which the taxpayer may deduct from the tax itself.

TAX-FREE or TAX-EXEMPT income is income which for statutory or constitutional law reasons is not subject to income taxation. In reporting dividend income, the taxpayer may deduct from his gross income $100 for an individual, $200 for husband and wife filing a joint return of dividends received from certain U.S. business corporations. This deduction is called the DIVIDEND EXCLUSION.

A CAPITAL ASSET is basically an investment; it may be a share of stock, a bond, an interest in real estate or a mine, etc. A CAPITAL GAIN OR LOSS is a gain or loss from the sale of an investment. A LONG-TERM capital gain or loss is a gain or loss on the sale of an investment which had been owned for more than one year prior to the sale. A SHORT-TERM capital gain or loss is a gain or loss on the sale of an investment which had been owned for one year or less prior to the sale. Security profits (capital gain) distributions from mutual funds are considered long-term gains no matter how long the fund shares have been owned prior to the distribution.

7. Federal Estate Tax Terms

The term ESTATE TAX, in general, refers to a tax on the property and interests in property left by a decedent or on the transfer of such property as a result of death; it is also referred to as an INHERITANCE tax, or a DEATH tax.

THE GROSS ESTATE of a decedent is the aggregate of the property and interests in property which he leaves, property which he gave away within three years of his death IN CONTEMPLATION OF DEATH, the face amount of insurance on his life owned by him, property which he had the power to give away even though not owned by him, property which he had transferred to trusts which he could revoke during his lifetime or over which he retained certain kinds of controls or which were really substitutes for a will. THE TAXABLE ESTATE, the amount on which the tax is computed, is the result of subtracting from the value of the gross estate certain allowable DEDUCTIONS (such as debts, taxes, losses, and charitable bequests) and EXEMPTIONS. The GROSS ESTATE TAX is the amount of tax computed on the taxable estate. From the gross estate tax may be subtracted certain CREDITS to arrive at the NET ESTATE TAX against which there may be deducted a UNIFIED TAX CREDIT ($42,500 in 1980, $47,000 thereafter).

Where there is no provision in a will for the source of the funds from which the estate taxes are to be paid, state law generally provides for the APPORTIONMENT of the tax among the legatees.

Each estate is permitted a MARITAL DEDUCTION, that is, a deduction of the value of property left to a spouse. The maximum marital deduction is 50 percent of the ADJUSTED GROSS ESTATE (the gross estate minus expenses, debts, certain taxes, and certain losses) or $250,000, whichever is greater. No marital deduction is allowed for the value of property left to the spouse for a limited period or until the occurrence or nonoccurrence of some event. Such interests are called TERMINABLE.

8. Federal Gift Tax Terms

A GIFT TAX is a tax on the gift of property by the DONOR to the DONEE. Each donor is allowed to make gifts worth up to $3,000 to each donee each year free of gift tax. This $3,000 allowance is called the ANNUAL EXCLUSION. By filing a joint GIFT TAX RETURN with his spouse, the donor can increase the annual exclusion to $6,000 for each donee. This is spoken of as GIFT SPLITTING because for tax purposes the gift is treated as having been given half by the husband and half by the wife. Gifts in excess of the annual exclusion, requiring the filing of gift tax returns, will be totaled at the time of death and charged against the Unified Tax Credit. Gifts to a spouse qualify for MARITAL DEDUCTION. A 100 percent deduction is allowable for the first $100,000 in gifts between spouses, no deduction for the next $100,000, and 50 percent after gifts reach the $200,000 level. No marital deduction is allowed for TERMINABLE INTERESTS (interests for a limited period).

ORDER FORM

The National Estate Planning Council
180 Church Street
Naugatuck, CT. 06770

Gentlemen:

Enclosed find check or money order for $_____. Please send me the instruments checked below. It is my understanding that each form with instruction sheet is $2.00, with the exception of DT-153, DT-154, DT-155, DT-156 and DT-157, and Amendment Form B, which are provided in duplicate at $4.00 per set.

REAL ESTATE:
_____DT-101
_____DT-102
_____DT-103
_____DT-104
_____QCD

_____DT-101-J
_____DT-102-J
_____DT-103-J
_____QCD-J
_____QCD-SPEC.

BANK ACCOUNT:
_____DT-105
_____DT-106
_____DT-107
_____DT-108

_____DT-105-J
_____DT-106-J
_____DT-107-J

SECURITIES:
_____DT-109
_____DT-110
_____DT-111
_____DT-112

_____DT-109-J
_____DT-110-J
_____DT-111-J

BROKERAGE ACCOUNT:
_____DT-113
_____DT-114
_____DT-115
_____DT-116

_____DT-113-J
_____DT-114-J
_____DT-115-J

SAFE DEPOSIT BOX:
_____DT-117
_____DT-118
_____DT-119
_____DT-120

_____DT-117-J
_____DT-118-J
_____DT-119-J

MORTGAGE, ETC.:
_____DT-121
_____DT-122
_____DT-123
_____DT-124
_____AM

_____DT-121-J
_____DT-122-J
_____DT-123-J
_____AM-J
_____AM-SPEC.

COPYRIGHT:
_____DT-125
_____DT-126
_____DT-127
_____DT-128

PATENT:
_____DT-129
_____DT-130
_____DT-131
_____DT-132

PARTNERSHIP:
_____DT-133
_____DT-134
_____DT-135
_____DT-136

MOTOR VEHICLE:
_____DT-137
_____DT-138
_____DT-139
_____DT-140

_____DT-137-J
_____DT-138-J
_____DT-139-J

PERSONAL EFFECTS:
_____DT-141
_____DT-142
_____DT-143
_____DT-144

UNINCORPORATED BUSINESS:
_____DT-145
_____DT-146
_____DT-147
_____DT-148

_____DT-145-J
_____DT-146-J
_____DT-147-J

RENTED HOUSE, APT.:
_____DT-149
_____DT-150
_____DT-151
_____DT-152

_____DT-149-J
_____DT-150-J
_____DT-151-J

FAMILY TRUST
SPOUSE TRUSTEE:
_____DT-153

FAMILY TRUST
NON-SPOUSE TRUSTEE:
_____DT-154

FAMILY TRUST
BANK MGNT.:
_____DT-155

FAMILY TRUST
BANK & MUTUAL FUND:
_____DT-156

WIFE'S TRUST:
_____DT-157

AMENDMENT FORMS
_____Amendment Form A
_____Amendment Form A-Joint
_____Amendment Form B

REVOCATION FORMS
_____Revocation Form RE
_____Revocation Form RE-Joint
_____Revocation Form A
_____Revocation Form A-Joint

SUCCESSOR TRUSTEE FORMS
_____ST-QCD
_____ST-QCD-J
_____Successor Trustee's Notice

WILL FORMS
_____W-1
_____W-2
_____W-3
_____W-4
_____W-5
_____W-6
_____W-7
_____W-8
_____W-9
_____W-10
_____W-11
_____W-12
_____W-13
_____W-14

Although not included in this book for lack of space, trust forms to cover a gift to minor, a reversionary trust, gas, oil or mining ventures, real estate limited partnerships (syndications), promissory notes, stamp or coin collections, antiques or works of art, or private libraries, and Power of Attorney forms are available on special request.

BOOKS BY NORMAN F. DACEY

Please send me _____ additional copies of *How to Avoid Probate—Updated!* at $14.95 in paperback, $19.95 in hardback.

Please send me _____ copies of *What's Wrong with Your Life Insurance* (paperback) at $3.95 per copy.

Please send me _____ copies of *Dacey on Mutual Funds* at $4.95 paperbound.

Please send me _____ COLLECTOR'S SETS of all three volumes at $20.95 each. Save almost 15%!

(Name) _____

(Street) _____ (City) _____ (State) _____ (Zip) _____

GIFT ORDER

Send the book(s) noted above to the following person(s) with a note indicating that it is a gift from me.

Name _____

Street _____

City _____ State _____

Zip _____

Name _____

Street _____

City _____ State _____

Zip _____

☐ Check or money order enclosed, or please charge my order to my account with:

☐ Master Charge**   ☐ American Express

Account Number _____

Expiration Date _____

**If using Master Charge, show 4 numbers above your name

_____

Signature _____

ALL ORDERS SUBJECT TO ACCEPTANCE BY CREDIT CARD ISSUER.